GLOBAL REPORT ON CRIME AND JUSTICE

Graeme Newman
Editor

Published for the United Nations
Office for Drug Control and Crime Prevention
Centre for International Crime Prevention

New York   Oxford
Oxford University Press
1999

Oxford University Press

Oxford New York
Athens Aukland Bangkok Bogotá Buenos Airies
Calcutta Cape Town Chennai Dar es Salaam Delhi Florence
Hong Kong Istanbul Karachi Kuala Lumpur Madrid Melbourne
Mexico City Mumbai Nairobi Paris São Paulo Singapore
Taipei Tokyo Toronto Warsaw

and associated companies in

Berlin Ibadan

Copyright © 1999 by the United Nations

Published by Oxford University Press, Inc..
198 Madison Avenue, New York, New York, 10016
http://www.oup-usa.org
1-800-334-4249

Library of Congress-in-Publication Data

Global report on crime and justice / Greame Newman.
     p. cm.
    Includes bibliographical references.
    ISBN 0-19-53316-1 (cloth). -- ISBN 0-19-513317-X (pbk.)
    1. Crime prevention. 2. Criminal justice, Administration of.
  3. Narcotics, Control. 4. Drug abuse—Prevention. 5. Criminal
statistics. I. Newman, Graeme R. II. Centre for International
Crime Prevention (United Nations)
HV7431.G445 1999
364—dc21
                                         99-19573
                                            CIP

9 8 7 6 5 4 3 2 1
Printed in the United States of America on acid-free paper.

Foreword
by the Executive Director of the Office for Drug Control and Crime Prevention

The work of the United Nations in fighting crime and promoting criminal justice has evolved through the years, in response to the changing needs of the organization's member states. Crime and justice are no longer simply local or national issues. They are global concerns which require careful study and concerted international action.

Much has been said about the new age in which we live and the coming century. The speeds today at which we communicate, travel and interact across borders are stunning. National boundaries have lost their traditional meaning. The advance of human technology has also brought complex new challenges to societies in the fields of crime and justice. Transnational organized crime has seized upon new technologies. Today it poses a fundamental threat to the security of societies. The United Nations programme on crime prevention and criminal justice needs to respond effectively to the changing situations faced by its members. Its priorities must be redefined and its efforts reoriented accordingly.

Specific steps are being taken. The reform measures proposed by Secretary-General Kofi Annan and approved by the General Assembly provide a valuable foundation in this direction. A new Office for Drug Control and Crime Prevention has been recently created in Vienna. The United Nations International Drug Control Programme and the Centre for International Crime Prevention are the two important arms of that Office. The Commission on Crime Prevention and Criminal Justice will continue to define the priorities and the new orientation of the Centre.

Our central focus will be operational activities dealing with organized crime, money laundering, the trafficking in human beings and corruption. The Office's work will be effectively supported by action-oriented research and analysis. Reliable data collection, sound analysis and effective communication are pivotal to policy formulation and programme development. Efforts to tackle priority concerns will be reinforced by on-going measures for effective judicial systems and integrated crime prevention strategies. The establishment and implementation of standards remain important.

Given the current situation of change, we present this *Global Report on Crime and Justice* as the synthesis of research and data gathered by the programme. The globalization of crime demands a comprehensive overview of the crime and justice field. This report addresses the nature of crime, the operations of national criminal justice systems, and the state of crime prevention from a cross-national perspective. It presents crime trends and operations of criminal justice systems on a comparative basis. Drawing on numerous sources from within the United Nations and beyond, it examines emerging developments in crime and justice around the world. The *Report* reveals a great diversity of experiences. Special emphasis was placed on comparing both the different ways countries approach crime and on the shared perspectives that exist between countries and regions.

The contributing authors to the *Global Report* have produced a global study of crime and justice, providing critical analyses and useful raw data in an easily understandable format. I am grateful to them for their fine work. I thank Professor Graeme Newman for lending his expertise to the project as Editor-in-Chief.

The *Global Report on Crime and Justice* is a joint production of several entities. Its concept originated with the United Nations Interregional Crime and Justice Research Institute. Two organizations deserve special gratitude: the Division of International Criminology of the American Society of Criminology, for facilitating the development of the project; and the Asia Crime Prevention Foundation, for its financial contribution. I wish to thank all involved for their support.

The audience of the *Report* extends beyond academia to include criminal justice decision-makers, legislators, parliamentarians, members of the law enforcement community, and court and prison personnel. Its comprehensive content is of value to the United Nations community, representatives of governments attending United Nations conferences, and journalists who cover international and domestic crime and justice issues. It is an instrument for mobilizing concerted international and national action against crime in all its guises.

The value derived from the data presented in this *Report* will help establish more fair, efficient, and humane criminal justice systems for offenders and victims of crime. Its publication sets the stage for the urgent task of combating organized crime and other emerging challenges in the field of crime prevention and criminal justice.

PINO ARLACCHI
Executive Director
Office for Drug Control and Crime Prevention

Acknowledgments

The following persons and organizations provided advice and assistance in obtaining information for the Global Report:

Mariano Ciafardini, Marino Esteban, Gervasio Landivar, *Argentine Ministry of Justice*
Rick Beattie, *Canadian Centre for Justice Statistics*
Vyatcheslav Knyazev, *Research Institute, Ministry of Interior, Russian Federation*
Luis Lackner, ILANUD
Msamba Sita, UNAFRI
Toichi Fujiwara, *Director,* UNAFEI
Adam Graycar, *Director, Australian Institute of Criminology*
Carol Kalish, *United States Bureau of Justice Statistics*
Jeremy Travis, *Director, United States National Institute of Justice*
Helen Burnham
Soros Foundation, *Center on Crime, Communities and Culture*
Phyllis Schultze, Director, Rutgers-NCCD Criminal Justice Library

Many persons wrote papers specially for the Global Report. These authors and the titles of their papers are listed at the end of the references section, and at the bottom of the boxes representing their contributions.

The Editor-in-Chief would like to thank especially Matti Joutsen and Uglješa Zvekic for their careful and painstaking review of the book.

The preparation of the Global Report on Crime and Justice was assisted by the financial contribution provided by the Asia Crime Prevention Foundation, in special consultative status with the Economic and Social Council.

ABBREVIATIONS

AIC	Australian Institute of Criminology
CICP	United Nations Centre for International Crime Prevention
CIS	Commonwealth of Independent States
HDI	Human Development Index
HEUNI	European Institute for Crime Prevention and Control, affiliated with the United Nations
ICCLR	International Centre for Criminal Law Reform and Criminal Justice Policy
ICPC	The International Centre for the Prevention of Crime (Montreal)
ICVS	International Crime (Victim) Survey
ILANUD	United Nations Latin American Institute for Crime Prevention and Treatment of Offenders
INTERPOL	International Police Organization
INCB	International Narcotics Control Board
ISISC	International Institute of Higher Studies in Criminal Sciences
ISPAC	International Scientific and Professional Advisory Council
LDCs	Least Developed Countries
NAASS	Naif Arab Academy for Security Sciences
OECD	Organisation for Economic Co-operation and Development
UNAFEI	Asia and Far East Institute for the Prevention of Crime and the Treatment of Offenders
UNAFRI	United Nations African Institute for the Prevention of Crime and the Treatment of Offenders
UNICEF	United Nations Childrens Fund
UNIDROIT	International Institute for Unification of Private Law
UNIFEM	United Nations Development Fund for Women
UNCJS	United Nations Survey of Crime Trends and Operation of Criminal Justice Systems
UNCJIN	United Nations Crime and Justice Information Network
UNDCP	United Nations Drug Control Programme
UNDP	United Nations Development Programme
UNESCO	United Nations Educational, Scientific and Cultural Organization
UNFRS	United Nations International Study of Regulation of Firearms
UNICRI	United Nations Interregional Crime and Justice Research Institute
WHO	World Health Organization

Contents

BOXES

FIGURES

TABLES

**GLOBAL
SNAPSHOTS**

Overview

A word of caution

The following observations regarding crime, criminal justice and crime prevention around the world provide an overview of the present situation. The observations are, of course, generalizations. The body of the report provides more detailed information as well as information on the sources of the data. **Because the quality of information varies considerably according to its source, caution should be exercised in interpreting the data provided in the report.** The reader is strongly urged, therefore, to read carefully the Introduction to the report where the validity and reliability of the data are examined, and the pitfalls in making inferences, especially those of a comparative nature, are exposed. *Making comparisons between two or more specific countries on particular items can be especially misleading, and should not be attempted without consulting the list of exceptions in Appendix 2.*

Sources of data

This report brings together, for the first time, enormous amounts of data that have been collected by the United Nations and ancillary bodies concerning crime, criminal justice and crime prevention over the past 25 years. The results of the five United Nations Surveys of Crime Trends and Operation of Criminal Justice Systems (UNCJS) form the backbone of this enterprise. The data are amply supplemented by other efforts: the International Crime Victims Survey (ICVS) conducted in some 60 countries across the globe and overseen by an international working group composed of the Ministry of Justice of the Netherlands, the Home Office of the United Kingdom and the United Nations Interregional Crime and Justice Research Institute; United Nations International Study on the Regulation of Firearms; many resolutions and papers produced by various United Nations bodies during the course of their particular programmes; and special contributions by many scholars, researchers, policy makers and administrators with specific expertise and knowledge.

Crime and its reporting

Crime is everywhere. Even though countries define crime differently in their criminal codes, no country is without crime.

An increasing number of countries now reports statistics concerning traditional crimes (murder, robbery, rape, theft, burglary, fraud and assault) to the United Nations surveys.

Crimes rates computed from surveys of victims are universally higher than those of official records.

While there are many known shortcomings of official crime statistics collected at the international level, the use of UNCJS data, for the purpose of making general inferences about groups of countries and trends over time, is reasonably reliable. Problems arise only when making comparisons between individual countries.

Personal experience of crime and justice

There is remarkable agreement around the world concerning the comparative seriousness of crimes.

No matter what part of the world, *over a five year period, two out of three inhabitants of big cities are victimized by crime at least once.*

The risks of being victimized are highest in Latin America and sub-Saharan Africa.

Violence against women is most prevalent in Latin America, Africa, North America, Australia and New Zealand.

Where women are more emancipated, the rates of violence against women are lower. *Less than one in three female victims of violence report their victimization to the police.* Reporting is particularly low in the countries of Latin America.

Two-thirds of victims of serious crimes who had reported their victimization to the police indicated an unmet need for help. Levels of demand for help among victims were highest in Central and Eastern Europe, Asia, Africa and Latin America.

Globally, *less than half of the victims who reported their cases to the police were satisfied with the response.* Levels of satisfaction with the police are the lowest among victims in Latin America, Central and Eastern Europe and Africa.

On average, *crime reported to the police continued to rise in the 1990s, as it had in the 1980s.* The most common crime reported was theft, followed by burglary. Violent crime (homicide, assaults, robbery) was a minority (around 10-15 percent) of all reported crime.

Crime recorded by the police

Theft rates were higher for industrial countries than non-industrial countries. Arab states generally reported very low rates for nearly all types of crime.

Cities around the world showed similar patterns for homicide and for robbery rates. However, high homicide rates were reported for several of the Latin American cities, New York and some northern European cities. (The UN Surveys requested data only nationally and in the largest city in the responding country.)

Civil law (including variations of it) is the most common basis of legal systems throughout the world. Customary justice systems are found in parts of sub-Saharan Africa. Other types of legal systems are Islamic, common law and socialist. However, *regardless of their legal systems, all countries have the three primary parts of the modern criminal justice system: police, courts and prisons.*

The justice process

The police are the front end of the criminal justice system. In some countries, however, the processing of suspects through the criminal justice system appears to be initiated by the prosecutor.

In all countries, *most people who come in contact with the criminal justice system as suspects of crime are males.* However, within these general findings, the distribution by age and gender of offenders involved with the criminal justice system varies among countries.

There were far fewer women and girls suspected of committing crimes in countries with low income than in those with high income.

In most countries *about half the suspects or those prosecuted are found guilty and convicted of an offence.*

For those convicted of serious crimes, prison is the universal sanction, applied more than any other punishment, and regardless of the type of legal system or level of development of a country.

Punishment

There are wide variations in the prison rates of various countries, and these do not appear to be dependent on the amount of crime in a country.

There is no overall world trend towards increase in prison population. Some countries showed enormous increases in prison populations, and others showed decreases. More countries reported increases than decreases. Countries in transition especially reported increases in prison populations and admissions.

Parole is not widely used throughout the world. It is used mostly by developed Western countries. There have been large increases in use of parole by some east European countries.

A small number of countries report statistics that suggest prison populations exceeding their prison capacity. There is no economic or development feature that distinguishes this group of countries.

Developing countries tend to have more prisoners awaiting trial than do developed countries.

The movement towards restriction and abolition of the death penalty is not unidirectional. Abolitionist countries are predominantly in Europe (both west and east) and Latin America.

The fine is the most frequently used non-custodial sanction for those convicted of less serious crimes, regardless of level of development of the country.

Non-custodial sanctions are used less in the regions of Africa, Latin America and Asia. The informal justice systems of many developing countries apply non-custodial sanctions without their being recorded by the criminal justice system. However, in industrial countries, warnings, cautions, fines and other non-custodial programs (such as restitution) are increasingly applied by police and prosecutors as a means of diverting such offenders away from the formal criminal justice system and finding of guilt.

Availability and use of non-custodial sanctions are policy choices, not directly tied to a country's level of development.

As a general pattern, greater use of non-custodial sanctions does not lead to less use of prison, or vice-versa.

In developing countries and countries in transition the public displays a marked preference for prison as a punishment.

Resources in criminal justice

In all countries, *police make up the majority of criminal justice personnel.*

The number of police per 100,000 population is increasing in the 1990s.

The number of police is unrelated to the amount of property crime, but may be related to the level of murder.

In all countries, men make up the majority of the criminal justice work force. However, there is a clear trend in recent years to employ more women in the criminal justice work force.

Industrial countries have a higher proportion of women in the criminal justice work force in all four occupations of police, prosecution, adjudication and corrections.

The ratio of adult convicted prisoners to adult prison beds varies hardly at all among countries. The ratio of prisoners to staff varies considerably. The developing country ratio of prisoners to staff is two to four times greater than that of developed (industrial) countries. Corrections staff per 100,000 population has risen 3.5 percent from 1990 to 1994.

Prisons are a resource that is universally employed. The growth of prisons applies to both industrial and non-industrial countries.

The range of expenditures on prisons and their operations is vast, from a low of $69 per prisoner to a high of $157,000 per prisoner.

The number of judges per 100,000 population is increasing in most countries. Common law countries have more judges per 100,000 population than do countries with other legal systems. Non governmental participation in criminal justice spans the globe, and is a way for countries to take advantage of their human and cultural resources.

Firearms and their control

In general, *countries that have higher firearm ownership rates also have higher firearm related death rates, including homicide rates,* though there are some exceptions.

Firearms are commonly used in domestic disputes where fatalities occur. In contrast, firearms are hardly used in the commission of sexual assault.

There is broad international concern for the control and regulation of firearms. Countries differ widely in how they translate concern about firearm ownership into public policy and legislation.

Most countries prohibit the ownership of firearms for civilians with a criminal record or a record of domestic violence.

Most countries use some form of registry in order to trace lost or stolen firearms.

The rate of firearm ownership around the world varies from less than one percent of households owning a firearm to as many as 50 percent of all households.

The majority of countries regulate the manufacture of firearms and their components.

Countries in post-conflict situations often become the source of large numbers of illicit weapons, and become a centre of illegal smuggling of weapons to criminals in neighbouring countries

The most common reason for owning a handgun is for protection against crime although there was considerable variation between countries and regions in this respect.

Drugs and drug control

In any one year, slightly over one in a thousand persons illicitly use heroin or other opiates, and two in a thousand illicitly use cocaine. It should be noted, though, that only a small fraction of the world's population uses drugs illicitly.

The number of types of illicit drugs has increased and their nature diversified in recent years.

Drug-related crimes have increased disproportionately in the last two decades when compared to other crime-related phenomena. World wide, types of crime committed by drug addicts are primarily acquisitive.

There are relatively few countries that keep centralized and internationally comparable records of illicit drug consumption.

The price of heroin and cocaine has fallen dramatically in recent years. This is primarily because, despite increased law enforcement interception efforts, the supply of drugs to consumers has greatly increased as a result of increased illicit production.

The economic incentives of the illicit drug trade serve to make organized trafficking extremely durable.

The available data suggest that the offenders in two thirds of the drug crime cases are given a non-custodial sentence.

Crime prevention

*Contrary to popular opinion, crime prevention **does** work.* There are now many well documented cases of crime prevention programmes successfully reducing and/or preventing crime.

Two basic features that all crime prevention programmes must address are: *social development* – reducing the social factors that pre-dispose young persons to become persistent offenders – often focusing on potential offenders; and *opportunity reduction* – making crime more difficult, more risky, or less rewarding to potential offenders – often focusing on potential victims.

Success of crime prevention programmes depends on the mobilization of local communities, local leadership, expertise, and commitment by government to crime prevention as a top priority.

Preliminary studies suggest that *prevention of crime is far more cost effective than paying for the processing of offenders through the criminal justice system.* Unfortunately, in spite of the promised cost savings, government commitment to crime prevention as a top priority often appears to be more rhetoric than action.

Only a small number of governments have established specialized crime prevention secretariats.

However, some governments (e.g., the Netherlands) have adopted extensive social and economic programmes that are designed specifically to foster crime reduction and prevention. This is possible in countries with centralized systems of government, but difficult in countries without a centralized system.

Areas in which crime prevention has worked include reduction and prevention of burglary, assault, violence against women, theft and vandalism.

Emerging issues: transnational crime

Transnational crime has emerged as a leading issue of the 1990s. This general category includes illicit trafficking in arms, drugs, children, women, immigrants, body organs, cultural artifacts, flora and fauna, nuclear materials and automobiles; terrorism; bribery, corruption and fraud; and money laundering.

Transnational crimes are very complex crimes, composed of many smaller crimes. They are thus extremely difficult to count. No systematic method of accounting for these crimes yet exists at the international level. Few countries record these crimes separately in their official statistics. There is an urgent need for the development of reliable and uniform data collection.

Illicit markets exist because there is a demand for illicit goods and services, and criminal organizations willing to meet that demand.

Organized crime now operates on a vast, global level. For example, the theft of cars, which was once a traditional crime of concern only to a particular country, is now a transnational crime because cars are stolen with a view for sale on the international illicit market.

The direction of illicit marketing is usually from the developing world to the developed world where demand is highest. The exception is luxury cars which, for example, are stolen in Western Europe and shipped to Eastern Europe and the Russian Federation.

Very often illicit trade is mixed in with licit trade, producing significant grey areas where it is difficult to identify illicit activities.

The overall impression from the information presented in this report is that crime and justice have a greater degree of independence from levels of economic development than has previously been considered. For example:

- All countries have prisons, and the prison rates are not generally related to either crime rates or levels of economic development.

- It is no longer clear that developing countries have higher violent crime rates than developed countries. In recent years, the levels have become pretty much the same.

- Victimization surveys have cast doubt on the assumption that developed countries have higher theft rates than developing countries (usually assumed to be so because developed countries have more movable property). It is now apparent that much theft in developing countries may not be reported to police.

These general findings are supported by the World Bank Report (1997) *thesis that sustainable economic development cannot occur without the basic guarantees of security provided by the rule of law.* An accountable criminal justice system is necessary in order to provide the building blocks for economic and human development. Without the guarantees of order and individual security provided by a criminal justice system that is accountable and open, development will stall, or take on distorted forms. While economic resources are no doubt helpful in establishing the actual day to day operations of criminal justice, they do not guarantee an adequate or effective system. *An accountable criminal justice system does not require money: only government commitment.* It is true that some expertise is needed in order to develop fully accountable and open criminal justice systems, but this expertise is available through many international channels, particularly through the United Nations, mostly for the asking.

The rule of law cannot be said to prevail in the international arena. The problem of crimes that transcend the borders of individual countries provides the greatest challenge to the international community. *Transnational crime, as these crimes have become known, defies the rule of law by operating beyond and across the borders of countries.* The result is that the ability of countries, at the international level, to coordinate their criminal justice systems is severely hampered by differing practices and laws. The establishment of a rule of law to govern transnational crime depends on the establishment of systematic data and information concerning these crimes, and cooperation of governments in producing these data. While this book is full of data for traditional crimes that occur within countries, few reliable statistics are available for transnational crimes. *A systematic method of accounting for transnational crime at the international level is urgently needed.*

The establishment of effective crime prevention strategies to prevent transnational crime from occurring is heavily dependent on countries working together to develop ways to (1) reduce demand for the illicit goods and services that are the bread and butter of organized criminal groups, and (2) to work with each other in combating the powerful international criminal organizations. *Strong and binding agreements among countries are needed.* While some small headway has been made concerning the international control of illegal drugs, in other areas of transnational crime, there has been little progress.

Page left blank

Introduction: Data sources and their use

Contributing authors: Graeme Newman and Gregory J. Howard

This book contains a wealth of information collected at the international level about many countries of the world. How this information was collected, how reliable it is, and where it came from are the subjects of this introduction. Also provided is a brief overview of the political history from which the criminal justice process of today has emerged. Without an understanding of this context at the international level, it is difficult to appreciate the richness of the information contained in this book, as well as the many difficulties one faces in drawing conclusions from the data and making comparisons among countries.

Crime, the justice process and the nation state

In the late twentieth century, the countries, provinces, states, regions and principalities of the world are overwhelmed by two seemingly opposing forces – the push towards diversity in parallel to the incessant globalization of culture, commerce and politics. Countries, while claiming their individual sovereignty, at the same time embrace the common trappings of post-industrial society – the free markets, the globalized media and communications, the consumer culture. The demand for diversity in many regions of the world has led to the fragmentation of once unified countries, and the process of globalization seems to lead to the leveling of cultures and the identification of common values in consumer products and their logos. There are few countries untouched by this "unifying" process.

It may come as a surprise to some when it is observed that one of the unifying or common features of all countries examined in this book is crime and the response to it. It is a surprise because it is well-known that countries, depending on their history, have quite different legal traditions, or some would say legal systems, so that what is defined as crime and how countries respond to it must vary according to their legal systems. However, Newman and Bouloukos (1996) have argued that the criminal justice system as it is known today grew out of the same historical period from which the modern nation state arose – the seventeenth century and later with nations as "world powers" organized for military and commercial conquest. The nation state developed many important bureaucratic structures to cope with commerce and economic change within and across its borders. Police and prisons appeared in response to the demands for social order required by the nation state in order to pursue its military and commercial goals. The police and prisons, together with courts, are now called *the criminal justice system*, an expression which was only invented in the second half of the twentieth century.

The last two decades of the twentieth century have seen a rush of states proclaiming themselves new and independent nations, and a major insignia of nation status is to boast a criminal justice system. Indeed, the success of establishing nationhood rests heavily today, as it did two centuries ago, on the "rule of law." As the President of the World Bank notes, "[A state's] ...ability to enforce the rule of law to underpin market transactions... will be essential to making the state contribute more effectively to development" (World Bank, 1997, p.iii). And so the rapid expansion of the "criminal justice model" (police-courts-prison system) continues. Not only was it exported and expanded during the eighteenth and nineteenth centuries by the colonialism of the major world powers, but it continues to be exported today because of the rapid changes in communications and transportation occurring in

...countries that have been unsuccessful in their transition to nationhood have failed to establish a modern police force and an accountable criminal justice system.

BOX 0.1

A short history of the collection of UN crime and justice statistics at the international level

The earliest known occasion that the collection of statistics on crime at the international level was considered was at the General Statistical Congress held in Brussels in 1853. The next known major effort was made at the International Congress on the Prevention and Repression of Crime, held in London in 1872. At these meetings a factor emerged which until relatively recently continued to remain in the foreground through all subsequent efforts, namely, the problem of comparability of definitions. Also, the rationale for attempting the collection of such statistics at the international level and of making cross-national comparisons with those statistics was a source of difficulty, although much less emphasized.

The issue of definitions still featured centrally in the conclusions of the International Penal and Penitentiary Foundation in 1946. Soon after that, the IPPF handed over most of its functions to the newly-formed United Nations Organization. In the early years of the organization, the United Nations paid attention intermittently to the possibility of developing the collection of criminal statistics at the international level. There are relevant Resolutions of the Economic and Social Council from 1948 and 1951, but, with the exception of one limited cross national crime survey conducted over the period 1937-1946, little seems actually to have been done until the early 1970s, when the present series of surveys was initiated by a Resolution at the General Assembly.

The Surveys, as the different sweeps were known, were started in 1977, covering five-yearly intervals from 1970. These were, as now, years of increasingly limited resources for the UN, and it would not have been possible in the 1980s to develop and improve the questionnaire without the help of a succession of institutions in the USA, which hosted expert group meetings to consider the results of one sweep and plan an improved version of the next. The hosts were: the School of Criminal Justice, Rutgers University, New Jersey, 1981; the Criminal Justice Center, Sam Houston State University, Texas, 1983; and the Bureau of Justice Statistics, US Department of Justice, Washington DC, 1986. In the early 1990s, smaller parallel meetings were held at the United Nations Interregional Crime and Justice Research Institute (UNICRI). The most recent was hosted by the government of Argentina in Buenos Aires in 1997.

Other inter-governmental organizations, such as the International Police Organization (INTERPOL), the Council of Europe, and the Organization of Economic Development have made attempts to collect similar statistics, but have concentrated on statistics of recorded crime, rather than of the criminal justice system as a whole.

The development of the present data base. The administration of justice has traditionally been seen primarily as an extension of the criminal law, in effect its implementation in practice. The discipline which therefore dominated both the making of the law and the administration of justice was jurisprudence; and the legal profession has always, and quite properly, paid great attention to definitions, but equally has tended to be unfamiliar with and sceptical, perhaps even apprehensive, of quantitative approaches. Legal specialists in international meetings have tended to take the position that each legal system has its own very specific set of definitions of what constitutes criminal acts and that comparison between them is of limited value. A number of these and related issues are reviewed in Chapter 3 of this volume.

The early rationale for collecting and comparing statistics at higher than the national level was originally, and continued to be until relatively recently, a part of criminological etiology, the search for the "causes" of crime. Such an origin is understandable as a product of the positivist optimism of using quantitative methods to establish explanations in the late nineteenth century. The Second Survey, developed at the Rutgers expert meeting, was the first sweep that reflected an explicit change in rationale. The focus of the surveys shifted away from the causes of crime to the operations of criminal justice systems. This focus was more in keeping with the overall mission of the United Nations – one of assisting governments in the management of criminal justice and, indeed, calling upon governments to provide an official accounting to the international community of their criminal justice operations. However, another problem arose as a result of this new-found rationale: the survey became highly detailed, requesting data concerning every level and aspect of the criminal justice system. In the second and third sweeps the survey questionnaire became excessively large, requesting too much detail, with the result that it became a burden on officials of member countries whose job it was to fill them in. It also became apparent that often no single national government department existed which had access to the variety of information requested. As noted in several boxes in this chapter, a number of governments have since developed whole governmental departments whose mission is to compile justice statistics. As a result, the Fourth and Fifth Surveys have been reduced somewhat in scope, and it is expected that subsequent surveys will be substantially shortened, administered more often (every two years instead of every five years), with special topic surveys[1] added to the core survey every five years.

Figures for recorded crime, are, of course, indicators of social behaviour, but in this context are most importantly seen as an indicator of the work load with which the agencies of the criminal justice system are faced. The remainder of the statistics are a record of how the system responds to that work load. Cross-national comparisons of different patterns of case-processing may generate a limited, but useful, picture of criminal justice in action. That may in turn prove to be a valid rationale for collecting statistics on crime and criminal justice at the international level.

Source: Burnham (Original paper, 1997)

the latter part of this century.

Thus, while it is obvious that all countries vary according to culture and legal system, there are strong forces at work to cut across this diversity. At the close of the twentieth century, all countries of the world are inextricably tied together by commerce, past colonization and historical circumstance. The rapidity of transportation and communications around the world has brought all countries, like it or not, much closer together than ever before. A murder trial in one country may affect another halfway around the world because it may be shown on television, reported on radio, or written about in magazines and newspapers. The rise of multi-national corporations in the latter half of the twentieth century has also forced economic and legal ties among countries of strikingly different politics and culture.

As will be seen throughout this book, crime remains ubiquitous in this period of great transition. The traditional crimes – murder, rape, robbery and theft – continue to pose a serious social and human problem with which all countries must deal. And the twentieth century response all over the world to such crime has been the growth, sometimes sudden but mostly incremental, of large and complex bureaucracies to deal with these crimes. This complex of bureaucracies is now called, in the twentieth century, *the criminal justice system.*

Legal systems and criminal justice systems

It is important to recognize that *legal systems* and *criminal justice systems* are not identical. Legal systems address mainly the ways in which cases and laws are defined and processed. They are the product in most cases of many centuries of social, cultural and legal history. These legal traditions are usually identified roughly as civil, common, Islamic, customary and socialist (see Chapter 3). But legal systems are silent on the actual organizational structure of the agencies that deal with crime. There is nothing in any of the legal systems reviewed in Chapter 3, for example, that says that prisons must or even can be used as a sanction. Prisons are relatively recent criminal sanctions (i.e., approximately 250-300 years old). The same may be said of the modern public police force, although of course the policing function is possibly as old as society itself. The legal systems reviewed in Chapter 3, with the exception of the socialist, are much older than the institutions of prison or policing. The only organizational structure that seems to be directly addressed by the legal traditions is the court, an institution that has a very long history. In general, though, it is reasonable to say that the police, prosecution and prison systems in the form that they are found today are of relatively recent origin.

Some countries, depending on their wealth and history, have developed larger and more complex criminal justice bureaucracies than others, and the development of these complex bureaucracies has resulted in greater availability of statistical and other data on crime and justice. At the same time, because of the differing legal traditions of countries, the kinds of data on crime and justice, particularly those on the processing

of offenders throughout the criminal justice system, may vary considerably (see Chapter 3 particularly). These distinguishing and unifying features of countries naturally affect the success and capability of the United Nations to collect information on crime and justice at the international level. In the face of this challenge, however, the United Nations has collected crime and justice statistics from member countries since 1977.

The United Nations Surveys of Crime Trends and Operation of Criminal Justice Systems (UNCJS)

The main aim of this report is to bring to the reader a synopsis of the statistical and descriptive information that has been collected through the vehicle of the UNCJS. This survey has been conducted by the United Nations Centre for International Crime Prevention (CICP) every five years since 1977 (see Box 0.1). The essential features of the UNCJS as a source of statistical information concerning crime and justice in member countries are as follows.

1. It is a survey of official statistics

The most important function of the UNCJS is that it collects statistics of a most official kind. The survey's main purpose is not to measure the exact amount of crime that exists in the world, but rather to provide an accounting of crime and the governmental response to it. As noted below, assessing the exact amount of crime in either the national or international context is beyond the capacity of current measurement techniques and probably always will be, given the inherently secretive nature of crime. Rather, the UNCJS challenges countries to develop national crime and justice recording systems that are systematic, coherent and predictable. That is, once a crime and justice system of reporting is established, information should be recorded and published on a regular basis. A model system of compiling crime and justice statistics may be seen in Box 0.2. A number of countries have developed sophisticated national statistical reporting systems over recent years. Examples of these systems are featured throughout this chapter (see Boxes 0.3, 0.4 and 0.5). Of course, the establishment of national reporting systems is a challenge in itself for many countries,

The survey's main purpose is not to measure the exact amount of crime that exists in the world, but rather to provide an accounting of crime and the governmental response to it.

Good practice in collecting and analyzing recorded crime data

System used. The most cost-effective way of collecting crime statistics is to do so as a by-product of an administrative system. In this way staff collecting the data see this job as serving a local operational purpose, and the data are likely to be better.

Use of computers. In countries where the constitutional arrangements permit and where resources are available, this administrative system can involve a common computer system for all areas. Other countries have regular summary data sent from police forces/units to a central point.

National standards and methodology. A common set of counting rules is usual for serious crimes, to ensure that all decisions about crime incidents are made in the same way. Only then can statistics based on these codes be added together to make a sensible national figure.

Scope of crime code list. Most countries collect data on only a small number of different crime types, with some incidents, such as minor road traffic and other petty and administrative offences not regarded as serious crimes for this purpose. The crime code list varies for each country, but the list in the UNCJS questionnaire is generally regarded as a minimum.

Analysis of crime data. All countries calculate crime rates per 100,000 population for comparative purposes, and this book, with some exceptions, follows the same rule. However, countries differ in the efficiency of their census estimates and more so in the accuracy of their inter-census estimates. Commentary on trends in crime figures is also important, so that the figures can be related to other phenomena such as changes in country boundaries and political events.

Dissemination arrangements. Countries vary in their arrangements for publishing the data and making them available to the UN. In most countries the police themselves make the data available. However, sometimes other agencies are in the lead, including the ministries of the interior or of justice. In some countries the central statistical agency is the source of the figures. The UN collecting agency is not always best placed to know which agency is responsible. The absence of some figures for some countries may reflect the fact that the wrong agency has been approached while variations in figures between surveys may also be caused by different agencies completing successive questionnaires. However, in some cases, the lack of information for a country reflects the lack of an organization with the responsibility to produce the figures. This is either because there are greater priorities or because the country places no importance on the release of such data.

Source: Lewis (Original paper, 1997)

or Australia) so that national police and justice statistics may be difficult to collate. The regular publication by countries of their national crime and justice statistics also provides a source that may be checked against the statistics that national correspondents report to the UNCJS. For planning purposes alone it is essential to collect quantitative data on all activities of the criminal justice agencies. For example, how many and how quickly are cases processed through a justice system? What is the ratio of staff to clients? How do police agencies respond to reported crime? To what agency do they report their statistics and activities? How many offenders are given what sentences and for what crimes? How many resources, both in terms of personnel and budgetary allocations, are expended on each area of criminal justice? These are just a few of the crucial questions that should be answered by all countries and for which statistics should be made available in the international arena.

2. Standard classification of crime and justice categories

Early attempts were made by the United Nations to codify the legal elements of criminal laws in member countries and to develop a kind of world criminal code. This mission of course failed because each country rightly insisted that its own legal definitions of crime categories and concepts were unique to that country since each possesses its own culture and law which are largely independent and separate from other countries (Newman and Vetere, 1977; Redo, 1986). However, beginning with the first survey conducted in 1977, a standard classification of crime definitions and justice categories (e.g., definition of "police") was developed with a view to statistical reporting at the international level, and this has been gradually refined and extended over the life of the surveys up to the present day. Over the past 20 years, more and more countries have adapted their own crime and criminal justice statistical definitions and procedures to the standard United Nations categories. One can see evidence of this in the extent to which countries have responded to each of the crime surveys.

especially those that do not have centralized criminal justice systems, where regions or provinces within the country have partial independence (for example, the USA, Canada

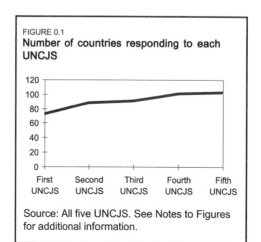

FIGURE 0.1
Number of countries responding to each UNCJS

Source: All five UNCJS. See Notes to Figures for additional information.

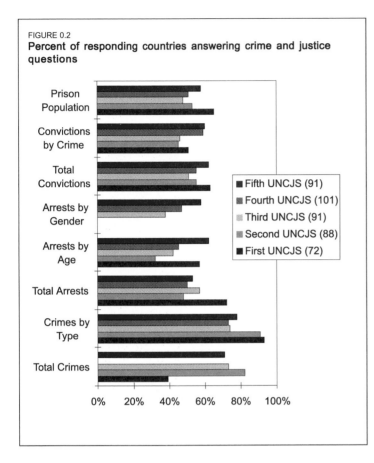

FIGURE 0.2
Percent of responding countries answering crime and justice questions

Legend:
- Fifth UNCJS (91)
- Fourth UNCJS (101)
- Third UNCJS (91)
- Second UNCJS (88)
- First UNCJS (72)

Categories (top to bottom): Prison Population, Convictions by Crime, Total Convictions, Arrests by Gender, Arrests by Age, Total Arrests, Crimes by Type, Total Crimes

X-axis: 0%, 20%, 40%, 60%, 80%, 100%

3. Ongoing and regular participation of member countries

As Figure 0.1 shows, the number of nations responding to the survey has grown with each data collection effort. Thus, when the UNCJS was first conducted, only 72 nations responded to it. Today, with the Fifth UNCJS, the number of responding countries stands at 103, although 12 of these responses were received too late to be included in the analyses reported in this volume. Thus, from the First to the Fifth UNCJS, the number of responding countries has increased by some 43 percent.

Of course, that a nation responds to the UNCJS does not mean that it provides data for all questions contained in the survey instrument. Figure 0.2 examines the responsiveness of reporting nations to a variety of data requests concerning crime and the criminal justice process across the five UNCJS. The first thing that can be noted about Figure 0.2 is that greater responsiveness is achieved for data requests regarding police records of criminal events. For most of the surveys, over 70 percent of the reporting nations were able to provide data

about the total number of crimes reported to the police, and the vast majority of these countries were able to provide some data about the specific types of crime reported to the police as well. It is important to note, however, that data for some categories of crime are more likely to be provided than others (see Box 0.6). The second observation that can be made from Figure 0.2 is that the responsiveness of the reporting nations drops when the data requests turn to information concerning offenders. Thus, from the total number of individuals arrested or brought into formal contact with the criminal justice system through the number of convicted offenders housed in prisons, typically less than 60 percent of the reporting nations are able to provide some data, and the proportion reporting can be as low as 30 or 40 percent for certain of the requests. Figure 0.3 also shows that the proportion of countries providing some data concerning the number of criminal justice personnel such as police and judges hovers at around 50 percent, although about 60 percent of the reporting countries are able to provide information about the number of prison personnel. From these observations, one can conclude that countries are best prepared to provide information about criminal events and are somewhat less prepared to provide information about offenders and criminal justice personnel.

A further general pattern emerges from Figure 0.2. The responsiveness of the countries tends to start out high with the First UNCJS, reaches a nadir with the Sec-

From the First to the Fifth UNCJS, the number of responding countries has increased by some 43 percent.

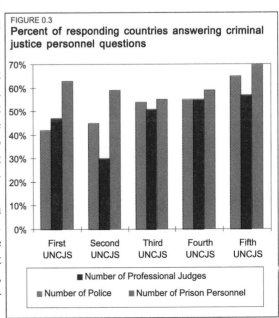

FIGURE 0.3
Percent of responding countries answering criminal justice personnel questions

Y-axis: 0% to 70%

X-axis categories: First UNCJS, Second UNCJS, Third UNCJS, Fourth UNCJS, Fifth UNCJS

Legend:
- Number of Professional Judges
- Number of Police
- Number of Prison Personnel

BOX 0.3

A national justice statistics initiative in Canada

In Canada, the lead responsibility for the collection of national statistics is centralized at Statistics Canada. The responsibility for the administration of Canada's justice system, however, is shared between two federal and more than 20 provincial and territorial government departments. In recognition of these facts, it was agreed in the late 1970s that the collection of statistics and information on justice in Canada should be a collaborative effort. Therefore, the federal, provincial and territorial departments with justice responsibilities, along with Statistics Canada, formed a unique partnership called the "National Justice Statistics Initiative" in which all jurisdictions share authority and responsibility for developing and maintaining a national justice statistics program. The operating arm of this Initiative is the Canadian Centre for Justice Statistics (CCJS), at Statistics Canada.

The National Justice Statistics Initiative. The mandate of the National Justice Statistics Initiative is to provide information to the justice community and the public on the nature and extent of crime and the administration of civil and criminal justice in Canada. Working through the CCJS, the energies of the Initiative are directed towards the production of useful information to support the legislative, policy, management and research agendas of the partners, and to inform the public.

The fundamental principle upon which the National Justice Statistics Initiative is based is partnership. Statistical needs and priorities are established by the departments and agencies responsible for the administration of justice. This process is accomplished through a number of committees.

The Justice Information Council consists of all Deputy Ministers with justice responsibility across Canada, together with the Chief Statistician of Canada. Its main responsibility is to provide strategic direction to the Initiative, and to review programmes, priorities and progress. With the assistance of representatives from each justice department, and a network of sector-specific advisory committees in the areas of police, courts and corrections, the Justice Information Council directs the national justice statistics program undertaken by the Canadian Centre for Justice Statistics.

The Canadian Centre for Justice Statistics (CCJS). The Canadian Centre for Justice Statistics was established in 1981. The CCJS develops and implements statistical surveys, and provides information, products and services to the partners in the initiative and the public. A wide range of statistical products and services is available from the CCJS including publications and reports, customized data tables, pre-packaged data sets and applications, and special studies on priority topics. To ensure the continued relevance and usefulness of its products, the Centre relies upon its federal-provincial-territorial committee structure to identify emerging information and data needs.

There are four basic types of information available from the CCJS:
- *caseload data,* which quantify the volume of activity (i.e., work load) in each sector of the justice system;
- *case characteristics data,* which describe the nature of the cases and clients dealt with;
- *revenues, expenditures and personnel data,* which quantify the costs of administering the justice system; and,
- *qualitative information,* which describes the structure, legislative authority and programmes of each sector.

Translating information needs into data products. Information needs are identified and defined through a consultation process with initiative partners. Committees oversee and approve each step in the development of survey strategy and design, and the statements of national data requirements in each of the justice sectors. To ensure that information requirements have been accurately translated in operational terms, data collection, processing and reporting systems are reviewed and evaluated following survey implementation.

Data collection and reporting strategies. The CCJS has adopted a microdata survey strategy which uses data collected as a by-product of the automated administrative and operational systems. This strategy was selected recognizing that the highest quality data available are those which are being used in the field for operational and administrative purposes. Rigorous data verification processes are also in place which require survey respondents to validate the data and information reported to the CCJS prior to its publication.

The role of technology. Computerized systems have been implemented in most sectors of the justice system in Canada. The CCJS provides technical advice and financial assistance to encourage the development and use of automated applications for the collection, storage and sharing of information. The transfer of technology, systems designs and data models is also a key strategy for improving the availability of data and information used in the administration of justice. This strategy has been instrumental in advancing the implementation of systems in Canada which have the capacity to provide data consistent with national survey information requirements.

CCJS products and services. Through a consultation process with the supporting network of justice agency committees and key data suppliers and users, the CCJS prepares an annual Operational Plan which defines the products and services which will be produced over the course of the coming year. On average, the CCJS produces about 40 products a year in the form of annual statistical reports, topical information bulletins called *Juristat,* reference documents and directories, data sets, and special study reports in priority policy areas. Many of these products are available in electronic format. All CCJS publications are announced through the Statistics Canada Daily which is available on the Internet at www.statcan.ca.

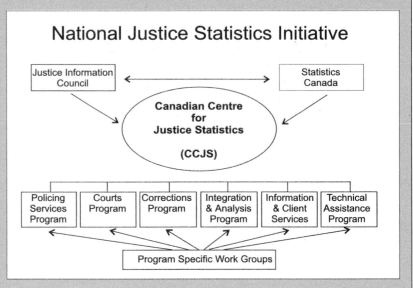

National Justice Statistics Initiative

Source: Beattie and Mihorean (Original paper, 1997)

BOX 0.4

The computerized information system of the Supreme Public Prosecutor's Office of South Korea

The Bureau of Computer System Management (BCSM) of the Supreme Public Prosecutor's Office (SPPO) of the Republic of Korea (ROK) was established in June, 1984. This bureau is responsible for the computerization of office work, construction of an information infrastructure, and coordinating and implementing information policy. The personnel of this bureau numbers 41 including the Director of the BCSM. The BCSM introduced a mainframe in 1984 and constructed the Case Administration Data Base (CADD) in 1986. The Fine Collection & Tracking Data Base was made available in October 1990. A second IBM mainframe system was installed in 1994.

The functions of BCSM are: implementation of the information initiatives of the Supreme Public Prosecutor's Office (SPPO); computerization and automation of the prosecutorial process; operation and maintenance of computer networks and computing equipment; provision of technological support; provision of various education and training programmes; and provision of on/off-line information services.

The structure of BCSM includes a Chief Information Officer, Secretariat division (five staff), programme development and management division (13 staff), database management division (six staff), system operation division (nine staff), and a network management division (six staff).

Jurisdiction. In the Republic of Korea, the central government has jurisdiction over all criminal cases so the system is rather simple and transparent. This simplicity is quite conducive to the development of database systems. The full administrative responsibility for law enforcement is assumed by the SPPO.

Administration of the database system. BCSM has computerized and maintained six major database systems: case administration; payroll administration; fine collection and tracking; drug enforcement administration; violent crime administration; and image information administration. All the data, except documents, are computerized.

The defining feature of the SPPO Information Infrastructure is CADD (case administration database). This system is capable of accommodating the overwhelming majority of needs of the users. BCSM has gathered data about 40 million cases. It is highly reliable and easily accessible.

A secure and reliable database is the cornerstone of efficient and effective law enforcement. Reliability, interoperability, ease of use, and security are the top concerns for the manager of these database systems.

The one remaining problem is that CADD is a hierarchical database and therefore less efficient. For this reason a pilot project was launched to convert CADD into a relational database. The key objective in this project is to provide a secure and reliable service that its users can trust.

Image Database Project. The SPPO has launched a massive project to preserve and make accessible the contents of about two million pages of court decisions and image information concerning violent crime, such as graphic cards, tables of the lineage of crime rings, etc. All of the archived court decisions and image data will be scanned and electronically stored.

This project is carried out by a contractor, KIA Information, Inc. This company has extensive experience and proprietary knowledge in this field. The second phase, launched in 1997 and scheduled for completion by December 1997, is estimated to cost a total amount of 220,000 US dollars. The goal of the first phase was the development of the Image Database Management Program and that of the second phase implementation and operation of this programme in the front

line prosecutors' offices. Court decisions and image data of violent crimes will be provided to all the personnel working in the prosecutorial system by the year 2000.

Bibliographic database and archive management system. The SPPO is committed to finding ways to make law enforcement more efficient and more transparent, to streamline the work flow, and to eliminate the redundant efforts which all law enforcement agencies experience. The personnel who are in charge of criminal investigation invest the majority of their time in making depositions. This chore is redundant because all of the criminal justice players, such as detectives, prosecutors and court clerks are doing the same thing all from scratch. The urgent, vital agenda is to dramatically reduce the effort and time for paper work. Accordingly, the BCSM has consulted with management information specialists extensively and concluded that it is necessary to categorize and classify all of the papers, and to construct a large library (i.e., database) system according to this categorization. Only by sharing the documents archived by others can the work load of the personnel be lessened.

This is why BSCM is trying to develop the CRITIS (Criminal Total Information System). In this CRITIS project, documents, instead of administrative data, are the key components of the database. Every document, including information, depositions, decisions not to prosecute, briefs, reports and manuscripts will be stored in the database and everyone will be able to search and retrieve the most relevant kind of documents. By doing this, the time to draft a document will be significantly curtailed. These databases will be linked to the CADD of the mainframe, and case administrative data will be readily available to the personnel who are doing paper work.

National network. Today, networks are the life blood of most organizations that rely on computing resources. For the SPPO, which is the principal law enforcement agency in the ROK, sharing of law enforcement information is vital. The future of law enforcement depends upon a modern, seamless, nation wide telecommunications network and upon the computers and information appliances that connect to it. This is why BCSM is going to connect every personal computer in the prosecutorial system by the year 2000. Personal computers will be a window through which everyone interacts with the whole prosecutorial system. *It also will be a window open to every one in the world.*

Integration of the law enforcement system. To avoid inefficiencies and duplication, the electronic system of all governmental law enforcement agencies, and the electronic network of each organization, should be integrated. To realize this ambitious goal of making a fully integrated network system, law enforcement organizations are initiating NCJN (National Criminal Justice System). An interagency team has met in order to monitor progress and update strategies as new problems unfold. The National Computerization Agency, which itself is funded by the Ministry of Information and Communication, has financed this project through 1997. Sufficient resources should be committed to allow rapid and effective policy implementation. In this project, SPPO will work with other law enforcement organizations such as police, the Supreme Court, the Immigration Bureau and the Correction Bureau of the Justice Ministry to ensure that the integration of the information systems is smoothly implemented and that the sharing of all the data concerning crime prevention and criminal justice is implemented appropriately in the on-line environment. SPPO is located in the center of the NCJN. In order to realize the enormous potential of the NCJN, the single most important thing is that every organization should give up an isolationist policy and adopt a policy of cooperation. Secondly, all organizations and agencies participating in this project will need to focus on pragmatic solutions based upon the principles of data sharing.

Source: Heechul Hwang (Original paper, 1997)

ond or Third UNCJS, and then moves upward through the Fourth and Fifth UNCJS. The proportion of nations providing some data about arrested offenders by age is illustrative of this general trend. In the First UNCJS, 57 percent of the reporting nations were able to submit data of this variety, but the proportion dropped to only 32 percent in the Second UNCJS. By the Fifth UNCJS, however, the proportion of reporting nations furnishing data on arrested offenders by age grew to 62 percent. One possible explanation for this trend is that the nations which responded to the inaugural United Nations Survey on Crime Trends and Criminal Justice Systems were those with the most sophisticated and complex data collection and reporting systems. As more countries responded to the UNCJS in the second and third rounds of data collection, the number of reporting countries with nascent data collection and reporting systems increased, leading to an overall decline in the responsiveness of the sample of nations to specific data requests. However, with each successive UNCJS, the responsiveness of the reporting countries has increased for almost every type of data request shown in Figures 0.2 and 0.3, suggesting that the UNCJS has succeeded in its primary goal of challenging nations to develop national crime and justice recording systems that are systematic, coherent and predictable.

4. Methodology of the UNCJS

The UNCJS statistics are probably the most official statistics on international crime and justice that are published anywhere.

The data from the UNCJS are compiled from a standard questionnaire sent to national officials via the United Nations Statistical Office. The official respondents then adapt their national level statistics to fit the categories of crime and justice defined by the UN Crime and Justice Survey questionnaire. These United Nations definitions and categories are found throughout this book in the relevant boxes in each chapter and in the various notes to chapters. It should be noted, however, that because the different agencies of criminal justice are often not part of one organization, and may indeed be operated almost independently of each other (e.g., the prison system and the policing organization), the ways in which such data are obtained and collated may be very different within each country. The often fragmented

way in which the questionnaire may be filled in by different officials from different bureaucracies sometimes introduces inconsistencies and contradictions in the statistics reported within a particular country's survey questionnaire. Therefore, *before drawing conclusions from these data, a careful examination of the sources for the statistics of the individual countries should be made.* This is why special effort has been made to include in the notes to tables and figures as much detail as possible on exceptions to the statistics reported.

5. The UNCJS statistics are political statements

There are many difficulties, for researchers and policy makers alike, in using and interpreting the UNCJS statistics. These statistics are, first and foremost, official statistics of member countries. *They are, in fact, probably the most official statistics of international crime and justice that are published anywhere.* One need only observe the ways in which countries behave internationally as entities – the ritual and care with which they make statements in the international arena – to realize that a country's open announcement in the international arena of the extent of its crime problem and its processing of offenders through the justice system is a major political event. Countries do not reveal such information to other countries (and often to their own citizens) unless this information has been rigorously checked, not only for its "validity" but also for the impression it creates. Nowhere has this fact been so clear in recent history as in the generation of crime statistics in the USSR and the refusal of that country to make known its crime and justice statistics to the international community. (Plans to establish a statistical reporting system in Russia are currently under consideration, as shown in Box 0.4.) Thus, the crime and justice statistics that a county makes available to the international community have an essential political element, with all the ramifications that this may entail. There have even been occasions in the past where member nations have made criminal justice data available to the UN Crime and Justice Survey but have not made them available to their own citizens.

Countries may also choose to report

BOX 0.5

The generation of crime statistics in the Russian Federation

In the Russian Federation, crimes against the state are investigated by the Federal Counterintelligence Service; military crimes are investigated by the Ministry of Defense; and all other crimes, about 95 percent of all cases, are investigated by the Ministry of the Interior.[1] In 1961, a statistical accounting system was put into place by Communist officials which held the Ministry of the Interior responsible for the generation of crime data. Today, criminal statistics in the Russian Federation are collected through the use of this data registration system, accomplished via a four-tiered format.

Local policing agencies assemble information on each crime investigated. The investigator in a case fills out five different statistical cards, each containing relevant information about the crime, the suspect, and the progress of the investigation (Lezhikov, 1995). These statistical records are then sent to regional computer information centers, where data from the approximately 70 regional police departments are also collected. All of this information is then aggregated further with the "zone-level integrated data banks." Finally, this information is fed to the upper level, or the Chief Information Center of the Ministry of the Interior.[2] In 1994, the Center processed 12 million documents and had a total of 50 million in their databases.

In 1994, President Yeltsin approved the "Federal Program of the Russian Federation on Strengthening Crime Control." Among the many goals outlined in this program, including cooperation between agencies of different Commonwealth of Independent States and improvement of law enforcement services, were proposals to improve the statistical collection system. A uniform criminal recording system was suggested for all agencies, as was a move toward paperless technology through the use of computers (Lezhikov, 1995).

Direct and immediate access to criminal records is vital, to both local agencies and federal legislators alike, if officials wish to keep in check the changing nature of crime in a changing Russian Federation. Up-to-date information allows Interior agents to monitor illegal activities of organized crime throughout such a vast country, look for criminal hot spots which demand increased budget allocations, and track trends in the structure of criminality over time. This database also becomes a tool for needed inter-agency cooperation, providing the empirical justification for financial and technical support (Lezhikov, 1995).

The Chief Information Centre (CIC) of the Ministry of the Interior consists of seven administrative subdivisions: the Criminal Information Centre; the Statistical Information Centre; the Computing Centre; the Centre for Computerization of Interior Agencies; the Industrio-economic Information Center; the Centre for Rehabilitation of Victims of Political Repression and Archival Information; and the Section of Science and Technical Information. The CIC is a multi-functional information agency staffed by a wide variety of attorneys, engineers, systems technicians, and specialists in, among other things, fingerprinting and telecommunications.

Among its many state-assigned tasks, the CIC carries out the collection and processing of criminal statistics, as well as the archiving of this information and its provision it to various government bodies and the public. It maintains centralized, automated data banks from which it provides authorized agencies information on events, subjects and persons. It also maintains similar databases on national and international scientific and technological materials and information. It also serves as a clearinghouse for software and database management systems for use in its agencies and subdivisions. Given this vast array of information, it assists local internal affairs agencies and institutions in their day-to-day operations, organizing informational research and technical operations.

The CIC works to implement presidential decrees relating to pardoned convicts and the restoration of justice for victims of political repression. The CIC also considers requests and investigates applications from organizations and individual citizens concerning these issues. In a similar vein, the CIC introduces and implements changes and amendments to the current operating procedures of local Interior agencies.

Today, the Ministry of the Interior is responsible for the collection of criminal statistics, using the same general accounting mechanism that was created in 1961. Its Chief Information Centre is a multifaceted information agency with several subdivisions. Statistical information on criminal acts, offenders and investigations are passed from the local to national level in a four stage aggregating process. In turn, the Centre not only collects and processes this information, handling over 10 million documents per year, but makes it available to interested agencies and the public. The Centre also acts as a depository for not only criminal, but national and international technological and scientific information as well.

Source: Pridemore (Original paper, 1997)

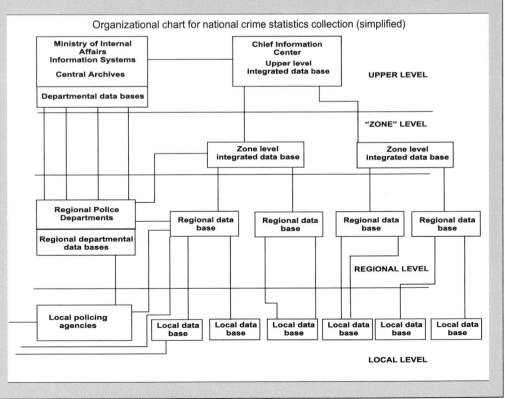

Organizational chart for national crime statistics collection (simplified)

BOX 0.6

Rape: the most reported crime by countries in the UNCJS

It may come as a surprise to readers that rape was the most reported crime by countries in the Fifth United Nations Survey of Crime Trends and Criminal Justice Systems since it is widely believed that rape is one of the most under-reported crimes. That is, victims tend, more than for any other crime, not to report their victimization to the police. But we have found that countries are more likely to report statistics on rape to the United Nations Survey of Crime Trends and Criminal Justice Systems than any other crime.

We can see in the figure accompanying this box that, of those countries that returned the questionnaire (91) the number of rapes recorded by the police was provided more often than were statistics for any of the other major crimes of homicide, assault, robbery, theft or drug crimes. This finding holds for every stage of the criminal justice system: police records, arrests, prosecutions and convictions (see Notes to Boxes for raw data). In fact, the proportion of countries providing statistics for rape convictions (60 percent) was quite a bit higher than for other crimes: 56 percent for robbery down to a low of 41 percent for homicide. While these statistics do not in any way indicate differential processing of offenders for rape, they do suggest that, at least at the international level of crime reporting, there is a much stronger sensitivity to reporting rape than other crimes. Perhaps an even more surprising finding is that the crime of homicide (completed intentional homicide in this case) was reported by countries less often than any other crime and at every level of the criminal justice process. It is likely that this result is a product of the very specific definitions prevailing in some countries of intentional homicide which may make it difficult for them to fit intentional homicide into the standard UN definition used in the survey.

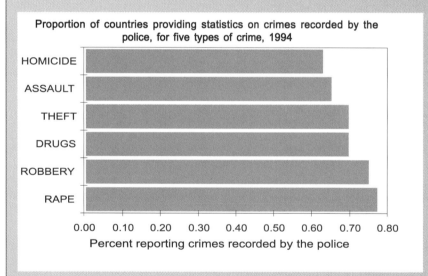

Proportion of countries providing statistics on crimes recorded by the police, for five types of crime, 1994

Percent reporting crimes recorded by the police

Source: Howard and Newman (Original paper, 1997). Rape statistics were reported more often for arrests, prosecutions and convictions. See Notes to Boxes for additional information.

crime statistics according to what may be "expected" of them. Box 0.6 shows, for example, that rape is the crime most reported by countries to the UNCJS. This is in stark contrast to the known very low reporting of rape by individuals to the police (see Chapter 1). This reporting pattern suggests that countries recognize the standards set by the United Nations and try to follow them.

In fact, from the United Nations' point of view, the publication of crime and justice data by member nations is a form of national accounting for what a country does to those who break the law and the extent to which its citizens suffer the costs and damage of crime. Such an accounting can only promote good government.

The above features would suggest that the crime statistics published by the UN Crime and Justice Survey do not measure crime as much as they reflect only the activities of the agencies that record the crimes. Even at the national level, this is a criticism that has been made against official crime statistics almost since the first day they were published. Many would argue that official statistics do not measure crime at all, or if they do, they measure only a tiny portion of it. Are the statistics provided by member nations to the UNCJS just diplomatic statements or are they true representations of the crime situation in each country? This question can be answered, though not easily, when one has a better understanding of what it means to measure crime at the international level, and indeed, what it means to measure crime at all.

The measurement of crime at the international level

Official statistics

For a long time now, criminologists have argued that the statistics officially recorded by police, or any other agent of the criminal justice system for that matter, are not an accurate measure of crime. Much research has been conducted this century in an effort to demonstrate that officially recorded statistics of crime under-report the amount of crime in society. For a long time, criminologists have widely believed that the true amount of crime is largely unknown. The unknown amount of crime in any given society is known as the "dark figure" of crime.

One might add that the legal purists would claim (as was the case until the late 1960s) that a crime cannot be said to have been committed until an individual is formally found guilty of the offence (i.e., convicted). While legally correct, this extreme approach no longer holds water. Most countries now use as their primary official measure of crime those crimes that are recorded by the police, whether or not they are subsequently processed further through the criminal justice system. The reason for this change in measurement is that the police are the closest official source to the larger "dark figure" of crime. Victimization surveys (discussed below) have spurred this change because they have unequivocally shown that many crimes are not even reported to the police for a variety of reasons.

The police have no hope of recording all crime that is committed or even reported, although improvements in technology certainly make this more of a possibility these days (see Box 2.6). Not all events that are recorded as crimes by the police are processed further through the criminal justice system, but this does not mean that the events were not in fact crimes. Case attrition begins when the police caution an offender and do nothing else (see Box 3.1). The different roles of police in different countries may also affect what events they record and how they do it (see also Boxes 2.2, 2.3 and 8.4). Thus, in some countries, the police may in fact have a highly developed and specific charge to record a great deal of information about citizens, some of it basic census information, and in fact much of it not directly related to the recording of crime at all (see Box 2.5). Further into the criminal justice process, the prosecutor may decide that there is not enough evidence to win a case. In some systems a prosecutor may find it easier to win a case if the offender is charged with a crime that is different from the one in fact committed. As a result of decisions made at successive stages of the criminal justice system by criminal justice functionaries, more and more cases drop out and the distribution of crime shifts.

When official statistics are used cross-nationally, there is also the special problem that many countries do not have a centralized or unified criminal justice system, so that the collection of crime and justice statistics on the national level may be an enormous challenge and for some an impossibility. In the United States, for example, there are a multiplicity of criminal justice systems – at a minimum 51 (one in each state and one at the federal level). Because of the highly decentralized system of government, however, there are many layers of criminal justice within each state. While the US Federal Bureau of Investigation (FBI) has traditionally collected statistics on crime

through a long-standing and still evolving uniform crime reporting system in which America's local police agencies provide data to the FBI, these data as measures of national crime trends are not without their critics. Moreover, other parts of the criminal justice system, such as courts, are also highly diversified. Indeed, the ability of the US to provide statistics, say, on the number of judges in the criminal justice system throughout the country is a major challenge. In order to do so, the country must develop an entire organization that is devoted to the collection of statistics on the national level. The United States, and a number of other countries, have developed such organizations (see Boxes 0.3, 0.4 and 0.5).

That there are seemingly insurmountable difficulties in the collection of valid and reliable crime data does not mean that official crime statistics at the international level are totally useless as a measure of crime itself. Although official crime statistics are driven primarily by the preparedness of the victim or witness to report crime to the police and by the recording practices of the police agency, it is known that some types of crime are more likely to be reported and recorded than others. For example, as is noted elsewhere, it is widely held that homicide is a highly reported and recorded crime, whereas it is also widely believed (and supported by victimization surveys) that rape is poorly reported by victims and often not recorded by the police.

For crimes that are well reported and recorded, one can make a check to see how the United Nations statistics compare to other official statistics for the same crimes. Homicide is a good choice for such an exercise. There are two other sources of official statistics on homicide available at the international level – those collected by the International Criminal Police Organization (INTERPOL) and those collected by the World Health Organization (WHO). The INTERPOL statistic on homicide is published annually along with a variety of other crimes and characteristics of offenders. These data are reported to INTERPOL by the police in INTERPOL affiliated countries. Since these data derive from police agencies, one would expect them to bear a close resemblance to the homicide figures recorded by the police in the UNCJS. The

At the international level, rape is the crime most reported by countries.

BOX 0.7

The reliability of the UNCJS: the case of homicide

Do the figures and statistics issuing from the United Nations Crime and Justice Survey provide a picture of crime and criminal justice that is similar to that offered by other official data sources? There are two other official sources of data on crime available for the same years as the United Nations data with which this question can be answered – the crime data published by the International Police Organization (INTERPOL) and the mortality statistics provided by the World Health Organization (WHO). Each of these data sources offers a measure of homicide. The purpose of this box is to assess the comparability of the UNCJS to these two other official data sources for the crime of homicide.

Other criminologists have provided answers to this question using data from the UNCJS. Huang and Welford (1989) reported comparisons between the homicide rates obtained from the First and Second UNCJS, INTERPOL and WHO for 1970 and 1980. They found that the correlation between the United Nations homicide rate and the INTERPOL rate for 1970 was moderate and significant while it was strong and significant for 1980. The United Nations and WHO rates were also significantly related in both years, although the correlation was stronger in 1970 than 1980. Bennett and Lynch (1990) reported on the equivalence of the three data sources using the First UNCJS. They found that the average homicide rate for individual nations over the years 1975 to 1980 tended to differ from data source to data source, with a difference on average of some 25 percent between the United Nations and INTERPOL data and an average difference of slightly more than 50 percent between the United Nations and WHO data. However, they also found that the figures were moderately and significantly correlated. Importantly, Bennett and Lynch found that when the nations' rates were aggregated, there was virtually no difference across the data sources. They concluded that the reliability of the homicide figures is questionable when the purpose of an analysis is to compare national homicide rates, but that the quality of the data is sufficient for assessing world crime characteristics. Huang's (1993) comparison of the number of murders reported for 1980 in the Second UNCJS, INTERPOL and WHO databases showed that the WHO numbers were almost always lower than those

provided by the United Nations and INTERPOL. This is to be expected since the WHO data refer only to completed acts of homicides while the United Nations and INTERPOL data refer to attempted homicides as well. When Huang subtracted the number of attempted homicides reported in the United Nations and INTERPOL databases from the total number of homicides, he found that the resulting numbers were in very close correspondence to those provided by the WHO database. Huang also found that the United Nations and INTERPOL numbers were nearly identical for all but five of the 26 countries that he examined and that the homicide rates created from these numbers were strongly and significantly correlated. Overall, these three studies support the conclusion that the United Nations data are reliable indicators of homicide, particularly when the data are used to assess rates of homicide worldwide.

The accompanying Figure shows a comparison of the median homicide rates derived from the UNCJS, INTERPOL and WHO for 1974, 1978, 1984, 1988 and 1993, a period which covers all five United Nations surveys. Importantly, the Figure only permits comparisons across data sources within each year since the complement of countries making up the median homicide rates varies from year to year (see methodological notes for further details about the construction of these homicide rates).

Examining the median homicide rates displayed in the Figure, it is apparent that the rates from the WHO data are consistently lower than both the United Nations and INTERPOL rates. This is to be expected because of the inclusion of attempts in the latter two measures of homicide. When attempts are removed from the United Nations and INTERPOL homicide rates, the median homicide rates for both of these data sources are virtually the same as the WHO rates (see raw data in the appendix for the specific numbers). The Figure also shows that the median homicide rates provided by the United Nations data tend to be higher than those derived from the INTERPOL data, except for 1984 when the INTERPOL rates are higher. While the United Nations figures tend to be higher, they are quite similar to the INTERPOL rates in 1974, 1978 and 1993. In 1984 and 1988, however, there is a wide mar-

CONTINUED NEXT PAGE

WHO provides a measure of homicide which is based on the classification of causes of death worldwide. This statistic, however, issues from a completely different official source – medical practitioners who make an assessment of the cause of death and classify it as a homicide or not. Because the WHO homicide statistic derives from a recording system operated by medical personnel and not police, one would expect, therefore, that the relationship between such a measure of homicide and the INTERPOL or the United Nations statistics will be weaker. This expected divergence in the two types of homicide measures will be exacerbated since the United Nations and

INTERPOL statistics also include attempts in their measure of homicide. Obviously, the WHO measure of homicide will not include attempts since it is a measure of the cause of death (i.e., completed homicides only). Because of this key difference, the WHO rates therefore should be lower than those from INTERPOL and the United Nations. Box 0.7 shows that these expectations are mostly supported by a comparison of these three sources of homicide data for years in each of the five UNCJS. Therefore, it is reasonable to conclude that, at least in the case of homicide, the United Nations crime statistics probably do in fact measure the amount of that crime and are not merely

BOX 0.7 CONTINUED

The reliability of the UNCJS: the case of homicide

gin between the rates issuing from these two official data sources. An examination of the data suggests that this problem might be explained by inconsistencies with respect to the inclusion of attempts in the total intentional homicide figure (see raw data in the Notes to Boxes).

The rates reflected in the Figure are aggregated over all countries with available data for each data source in each year. Another means of assessing the reliability of the United Nations data with respect to the two other data sources is to examine the homicide rates for individual nations. Such an examination reveals that there are often marked differences in the homicide rates obtained from one data source or another (see the raw data in the appendix for the specific homicide rates). For instance, for Chile in 1974, the United Nations data return a homicide rate of 14.26 per 100,000 population while the INTERPOL and WHO data provide rates of 7.17 and 2.25, respectively. Similarly, the United Nations data report that the homicide rate per 100,000 population in Bulgaria

Median homicide rates per 100,000 across time and data series

for 1993 is 10.80 while the INTERPOL data yield a rate that is nearly twice that (20.79) and the WHO data less than half (4.93). Of course, these are extreme cases, and the differences between the data sources are mitigated when attempts are removed from the United Nations and INTERPOL figures. Thus, when one looks at the correlation between these rates for the individual nations in each of the five years, one finds that the different data sources are moderately to strongly related to one another and generally statistically significant, although these measures of association suffer in 1984 and 1988. Again, when attempts are excluded from the United Nations and INTERPOL figures, the association between the data sources is much more robust (see the raw data in the notes to boxes for the specific correlation figures).

In sum, this analysis and previous research permit the general conclusion that, at least for the case of homicide, the data from the UNCJS are reliable indicators of crime and criminal justice when compared to other official sources of data. It is important to note, however, that the reliability of the United Nations data is lower when individual nations are examined. That is, the homicide rate for any given nation may vary considerably from data source to data source. But when the data for the individual nations are aggregated, the reliability of the United Nations data improves markedly.

Source: Howard, Freilich and Newman (Original paper, 1997). See Notes to Boxes for additional statistical information, including tables and other data concerning the Figure.

products of the political or bureaucratic activity of the police or the country reporting the statistic.

One final note is necessary before moving on to examine other ways of measuring crime that do not depend on official statistics: those published by the mass media. These may at times include or use officially reported crime statistics, which are those released to the press, sometimes with fanfare, by governmental spokespersons. However, other statistics can be generated by counting the number of crimes reported in the mass media, such as newspapers. These crimes may or may not find their way into the officially recorded statistics of the crimi-

nal justice system. They are statistics which are usually resorted to when there are no statistics of any kind available, whether official or "unofficial." Such statistics, often used in the case of transnational and other complex crimes, may provide quite a different picture of crime than those offered by official statistics (Box 0.8).

Comparing individual countries

As noted in Box 0.7, the UNCJS data are reasonably reliable when comparing countries that are grouped together according to some criteria (e.g., level of development). However, comparisons between individual

BOX 0.8

Official crime statistics and the media

The government of Argentina, in order to better understand the dynamic of crime within Argentina, funded a group of studies under the direction of the Politica Criminal of the Ministry of Justice. This series of studies, published in *Hacia un Plan Nacional de Politica Criminal*, served as an exploratory examination of Argentine crime and violence, but also as a means of establishing a state of analysis, reflection and debate on the prevention and containment of crime and violence for the criminological and penal community of Argentina (Secretaria de Justicia, 1996). While the majority of the studies were primarily examinations of the characteristics of specific crimes, victims, offenders, locations and times of occurrence, the studies did offer some interesting side issues. Going beyond the normal range of crime related questions, the Argentine government experimented with a limited and exploratory, but potentially important, examination of the prevalence of coverage of crime in the media. The following statistics were provided by the Politica Criminal of the Ministry of Justice of the Republic of Argentina.

The original study took place over the summer of 1991 and examined the reporting trends of eight different daily publications or newspapers. The primary variables included type of crime, specific newspaper, number of crime related articles, date of publication, location of crime, time period between occurrence of crime and article publication, and length of articles (in centimeters). Follow-up investigations were repeated in the summer of 1993 and the summer of 1994. The follow-up investigations examined four of the original eight newspapers, and provided initial results enabling comparisons between crime rates and media reporting trends. The preliminary results provided by the Ministry of Justice are those which relate the number of articles published, the amount of space taken by the articles in the daily publications and the crime rate during the three reporting periods (Secretaria de Justicia, 1996).

The initial study in the summer of 1991 covered a 47 day period during which the eight newspapers with the greatest circulation within Capital Federal (Buenos Aires) were tracked. Results revealed that over that time period 1866 total articles on crime appeared within the eight newspapers, resulting in a daily mean of 4.96 articles on crime per newspaper (Secretaria de Justicia, 1996). The two follow-up studies examined the four newspapers with the greatest circula-

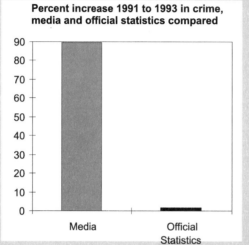

Percent increase 1991 to 1993 in crime, media and official statistics compared

tion located within the city of Buenos Aires: *Clarin*, *La Nacion*, *Pagina 12* and *Cronica*. Another study in the summer of 1993 tracked four newspapers for 31 days during which time a total of 1167 articles on crime were printed, yielding an average of 9.41 crime related articles per newspaper per day (Secretaria de Justicia, 1996). In the summer of 1994 a follow-up study of the same four newspapers over 31 days revealed a total of 1307 crime related articles, showing an increase to an average of 10.54 crime related articles per newspaper per day (Secretaria de Justicia, 1996). The Ministry of Justice in examining these numbers noted an increase of about 90 percent over the two year period from 1991 to 1993, and an increase of about 12 percent from 1993 to 1994, for an overall increase of about 112 percent over a four year period in mean number of crime related articles per newspaper per day. When compared with official national crime statistics, these reports yield different conclusions. Examination of official national crime statistics for total crime does not indicate a similar increase, as can be seen in the accompanying Figure.

The Argentine government, in order to understand the process driving these differences, further examined the role of individual newspapers in driving daily journal coverage of crime. The average amount of space per column devoted by each newspaper to crime related stories was examined to allow comparisons between four of the newspapers studied (Secretaria de Justicia, 1996). In terms of length of article, two newspapers devoted over 20 cm per column to crime related stories: *Cronica* — 23.9 cm and *Clarin* — 21.9 cm. These numbers showed that 39 percent and 36 percent, respectively, of each newspaper is devoted to crime related stories (Secretaria de Justicia, 1996). Meanwhile, *Pagina 12* averages 9.6 cm per column to crime related stories, or 16 percent of the total newspaper. *La Nacion* averaged even less, 5.9 cm per column, representing 10 percent of the total newspaper (Secretaria de Justicia, 1996). Of the crimes reported by the four newspapers studied, 40 percent of the articles covered crimes against the person (Secretaria de Justicia, 1996). Crimes against the person were the type of offence most often cited in articles; the next most cited type of offence, crime against property, covered only 19 percent of the total articles on crime (Secretaria de Justicia, 1996). These findings roughly conform to similar studies conducted in the United States and elsewhere (Graber, 1980; Chermak, 1995), which have shown that violent crime is grossly over-reported by the media. Official statistics in most countries mostly show that violent crime is relatively rare when compared to property crime. The media, however, provides the opposite picture.

Source: Chavez (Original paper, 1997)

countries are full of difficulties. The main reason for this is that the definitions used in the survey questionnaire are of necessity general, since, as noted earlier, legal definitions and recording practices in countries vary considerably. This means that there will be instances in which the data reported by a respondent country will not accurately reflect the exact situation in that country. If one tries to compare that country to another

that also has difficulties in adapting its internal statistics to the categories provided in the UNCJS questionnaire, misleading conclusions may result. The reader is therefore cautioned that, when comparing individual countries — or even when interpreting rankings of countries, of which there are many in this report — the list of exceptions in Appendix 2 should be carefully con-

BOX 0.9

The International Crime Victim Survey (ICVS): another count of crime

How crimes are counted. The International Crime Victim Surveys (ICVS) ask representative samples of individuals about selected offences they have experienced over a given time. They are interested in incidents whether or not reported to the police and, indeed, in the reasons why people do or do not choose to notify the police. Thus they provide a count of how many people are affected by crime, quite a different count from that offered by crimes recorded by criminal justice agencies in the course of their operations. The ICVS counts crimes against clearly identifiable individuals, excluding children. For the crimes it covers, the ICVS asks about incidents which by and large accord with legal definitions of offences, though in essence it accepts respondents' accounts of what happened – or at least the accounts they are prepared to give to interviewers. In this respect, the ICVS applies a broader definition of crime than the police who, if incidents are reported to them, are likely to filter out those which may not be felt to merit the attention of the criminal justice system.

The ICVS asks respondents about 11 main forms of victimization, two of which allow for further subdivision (see below). Household crimes are those which can be seen as affecting the household at large, and respondents report on all incidents known to them. For personal crimes, they report on what happened to them personally.

Household property crimes	*Personal crime*
theft of car	theft of personal property
theft from cars	pickpocketing
vandalism to cars	non-contact personal thefts
theft of motorcycles	sexual incidents
theft of bicycles	sexual assaults
burglary with entry	offensive behaviour
attempted burglary	assaults/threats
robbery	assaults with force
assaults without force	

In the surveys in developing countries and countries in transition, consumer fraud and corruption have also been covered. Consumer fraud was asked about in industrialized countries in 1992 and 1996, and corruption in 1996.

Respondents are asked first about their experience of crime over the last five years. Those who mention an incident of any particular type are asked when it occurred, and, if in the last year, how many times. All victims reporting incidents over the past five years are asked some additional questions about what happened.

History and management of ICVS. In 1987 plans for a fully standardized survey were aired at a meeting in Barcelona of the Council of Europe and these plans led to the International Crime Victim Survey project.

There have so far been three rounds of the ICVS. The first was developed by a Working Group set up in 1987, leading to fieldwork early in 1989.[1] Oversight of the surveys has been managed by the Working Groups, but a coordinator in each country has been responsible for the conduct of fieldwork and, where necessary, for ensuring a sound translation of the questionnaire. The technical management of most of the surveys in industrialized countries has been carried out by InterView, a Dutch survey company. InterView subcontracted fieldwork to survey companies in the participating countries, maintaining responsibility for the questionnaire, sample selection, and interview procedures. UNICRI was responsible for the face-to-face questionnaire and the monitoring of the ICVS in developing countries and countries in transition.[2]

Participation of countries. Fifteen countries took part in the first (1989) ICVS, including the cities of Warsaw (Poland) and Surabaya (Indonesia). The second (1992/94) round of the ICVS covered 11 industrialized countries. It also expanded to include standardized surveys in 13 developing countries, and six countries in transition mainly at the city level. These were taken forward largely by UNICRI which was keen to sensitize governments of developing countries and countries in transition on the dimensions and extent of crime in their urban areas – especially as police data on crime were often poor.

Full details of the 1989 and 1992 surveys in industrialized countries are reported in van Dijk *et al.*, (1990) and in van Dijk and Mayhew (1992). Further information and reports on the 1992 ICVS are presented in Alvazzi del Frate *et al.* (1993). Results from the developing world are reported in Zvekic and Alvazzi del Frate (1995).

The Third ICVS initiated at the beginning of 1996. Eleven industrialized countries took part. Thirty-four further surveys were conducted in developing countries and countries in transition under UNICRI's direction, mainly in 1996, but some in 1997 as well. Results of the 1996/97 round for 11 industrialized countries are reported in Mayhew and Van Dijk (1997).

All in all more than 130,000 people were interviewed around the world in 40 languages. Please consult the notes to this box for complete details of dates the surveys were conducted, countries involved, sample sizes, method of interview, language used and other methodological issues.[3]

Source: van Dijk (Original paper, 1997). See Notes to Boxes for information on country participation and other details.

---

sulted. There, countries have listed the adaptations they have had to make in order to provide statistics for the UNCJS categories.

Alternative measures: "Unofficial" statistics

The criticisms of and dissatisfaction with official records as an accurate measure of the amount and distribution of crime have naturally led criminologists to construct alternative measures of crime. The two major efforts in this regard are victimization surveys and self-report surveys. These techniques use questionnaires or interviews with samples of individuals who answer questions concerning whether they have been victimized by crime (victimization surveys: Box 0.9) or whether they have performed certain criminal acts (self-report surveys). The biggest advantages of victimization and self-report surveys are that they get closer to the "dark figure" of crime and that they

Delinquent behaviour among young people in the western world

Twelve countries — Finland, England and Wales, Northern Ireland, the Netherlands, Belgium, Germany, Switzerland, Portugal, Spain, Italy, Greece and New Zealand — and one American state (Nebraska), participated in a comparative self-report survey among young people — both males and females — aged 14-21. Data collection took place in 1992.

A common core instrument was developed covering the following fields:
* prevalence and frequency of delinquent behaviour, measured in several ways;
* circumstances of the act: where, alone or with others, what victims;
* reactions of the third parties, including the police;
* social and demographic variables; and
* some theoretical variables, related to social control theory.

Both face-to-face interviews and self-administered questionnaires were used. While a number of participants used a mixed approach, letting respondents complete themselves the more sensitive questions, response rates were satisfactory and ranged from 60 percent to about 90 percent.

Some preliminary results. A striking result was that overall delinquency prevalence rates were fairly similar among participating countries, whatever the sample used (national or city sample). The "ever" rates ("did you *ever* commit...") for total crime ranged roughly between 80 percent and 90 percent, while the "last year" rates ("did you commit....*last year*") ranged between 50 percent and 80 percent, with some exceptions.

The following rough outcomes show prevalence rates for property, violent and drug offences in five random national samples and seven random city samples.

Percent of respondents reporting that they had committed any of three categories of delinquent behaviour — last 12 months

	Property	Violence	Drugs
Netherlands	29.5	29.3	15.3
England and Wales	16.0	15.8	25.9
Portugal	21.4	29.5	11.3
Switzerland	33.5	29.1	20.9
Spain	20.1	34.5	15.4
Mannheim	20.7	21.7	7.0
Belfast	25.5	23.8	19.9
Liege	27.3	29.9	8.2
Athens	34.9	51.8	9.1
Omaha (Nebraska)	36.9	34.9	17.3
3 Italian cities	16.7	14.0	6.2
Helsinki	38.6	34.7	13.2

The rates for property offences are not that different, with the exception of England and Italy, which show lower rates and Omaha, Athens and Switzerland, which show higher rates. The rates for violence are relatively high because they cover violence against objects as well as against persons. In addition group fights occur more often than beating someone up. The following table shows that violence against objects has higher prevalence than against persons in five countries.

Percent reporting four violent acts in last 12 months

	Vandalism	Carrying weapon	Group fights, rioting	Beating up non-family
Netherlands	12.6	15.4	10.1	2.5
England and Wales	3.5	9.4	6.3	1.4
Portugal	16.1	10.8	11.1	2.5
Switzerland	17.0	11.2	8.8	0.9
Spain	16.3	8.4	17.2	2.3

It should be noted that violence rates in England and Wales differ quite substantially from the other countries. This could be due to the fact that the English participants introduced some changes in the common core instrument.

Source: Edited and abridged by Josine Junger-Tas, from Junger-Tas, Terlouw and Klein (1994). See also Box 2.10 for additional results of the international self-report survey.

---

are able to transcend the different definitions of crime in each country since the questionnaires construct their own crime categories which are the same in every country surveyed. Other advantages of victimization surveys are discussed in Chapter 1.

Of course, victimization and self-report surveys are dramatically different measures of crime compared to official measures because they rely on ordinary citizens to remember and report to an interviewer their experiences of crime. Official statistics, in contrast, are the result of an elaborate bureaucratic process, beginning usually (though not entirely) with the citizen reporting an event to the police who subsequently decide whether or not to record this event as a crime (see Chapters 2 and 3). Clearly, victimization and self-report surveys provide data on the amount of crime from a quite different perspective — an unofficial perspective which provides an alternative measure that is not contaminated by the official practices of police agencies or other statistical reporting bodies.

Non-official measures of crime in the international arena are relatively recent. As noted earlier in Box 0.1, the United Nations has collected official statistics on crime for some 25 years as an official part of its programme. However, the United Nations has never formally collected information from victimization surveys or self-report studies. These efforts have been conducted by researchers and administrators as a part of particular national efforts by a few countries (see Chapter 1). Although UNICRI has been closely involved in these studies, the ICVS are not a part of the regular United Nations programme. Three international victimization surveys have now been conducted, and these are discussed at greater length in Chapter 1. An exploratory international self-report study has only recently been conducted, a summary of which is presented in Box 0.10 and is also described in Box 2.8.

These alternative measures of crime do, however, bring with them their own special problems, especially when conducted at the international level. These may be summarized as follows.
* They are expensive to administer because they rely on sophisticated public opinion survey methodology.

- Because they often use interviews, they are subject to the well-known problems of interviewer bias and cultural differences in the ways respondents answer questions to interviewers ("respondent compliance").
- Cultural variations in sensitivity to certain types of crime, such as violence, may strongly affect the extent to which respondents report certain types of crime (e.g., domestic abuse; see Box 1.3).
- Interviewers, because of the ways in which questions are structured, must unavoidably suggest crimes to the respondents who may tend to over-report crime.
- There is an artificial quality to the crime reports because they depend on respondent memory, perception and reconstruction of the "crime."
- The responses to questions are difficult to relate to formal categories of crime since these categories are never used in the interviews.
- They may produce unpredictable results and countries may be embarrassed. That is to say, because they are "unofficial," the government has no control over how or when the results are published. Thus, a government may be caught off guard if such results are published in the mass media.

Official statistics and victim surveys: which are better?

Since self-report studies are still in a nascent stage of development, the primary question facing the user of international criminal statistics today is whether official statistics are preferable to victimization surveys. The relationship between official statistics and victimization statistics is a complex one, and it is considered further in Chapter 1. In anticipation of that discussion it is worth noting that the research and writing of countless criminologists and researchers this century makes it abundantly clear that the controversy of what is the "best measure" of crime, or what is the true make-up of the "dark figure" of crime, will likely not be settled for some time, if it can be at all. The reason for this is that the two approaches – the official records vs. the survey/interview methods – look at "crime" through very different lenses, which are linked in very differ-

FIGURE 0.4

Comparison between police data of UN Crime and Justice Survey (UNCJS) and victim survey data (ICVS), percent change in reported crime 1988-1995

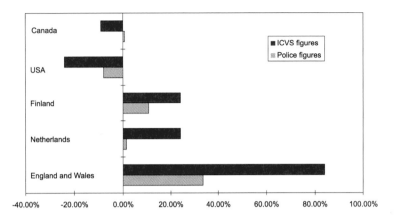

Source: Lewis (Original paper, 1997). See Notes to Figures for tabular data.

ent ways to the act of the original offender through the person or persons who report the crime, whether to the police or to a research interviewer. These two conditions of reporting a crime are vastly different. One is contrived (the interview) while the other is full of action and drama (the official report to the police).

Still, the two measures ought to be linked at some level, and some analysis of the data from the International Crime Victim Survey (ICVS) and the UNCJS suggests that this is indeed so. Data which allow a comparison of police recorded crime figures with victim survey figures only exist for a few countries and for a few years. Figure 0.4 shows this comparison for five Western countries over the period 1988-1995. The figure shows a tendency for the police figures to change less, in either direction, than the victimization figures. One would expect this to be the case since police figures are the result of bureaucratic activity which establishes standard procedures for recording events. These would not be expected to fluctuate drastically from year to year. In three countries, England and Wales, Netherlands and Finland, police figures during the period rose less than victimization figures. In the USA both figures dropped, but the police figures less than the victimization figures. In Canada, police figures stayed the same, but victimization figures dropped by nine percent. One may note that, while the general amounts of change vary consider-

..the utilization of the UNCJS statistics when the countries are grouped together is reasonably reliable.

ably between the two measures, the direction of change generally does not. The difference between the two measures is rather one of amount. As noted earlier, for methodological reasons one would expect that victimization surveys would report more crime than official records of crime. This expectation is born out by the data in Figure 0.4. Because of this rough coincidence in expected amount and direction of trends, it is likely that these two measures are related, even though they are measuring quite different responses. It cannot truly be said, however, that one is a more accurate measure of crime than the other. Official data view the "dark figure" from the window of the police while victimization surveys view the "dark figure" from the window of the victim.

Grouping countries together

As was noted above and demonstrated in Box 0.7, because individual countries must adapt their national statistics to fit the standard classification and definitions provided by the UNCJS, comparing individual countries according to those statistics is not recommended. However, as shown in Box 0.7, the utilization of the UNCJS statistics when the countries are grouped together is reasonably reliable, so that the international statistics when used with countries aggregated together into, say, regions or levels of development, may be useful for comparisons.

Of course, one needs sufficient numbers to make up a group, and there is also the question of what is represented when the countries are grouped together. There is much controversy as to how countries should be grouped together in order to make comparisons. One of the reasons for this is that many, if not most, of the social indicators that are commonly used to group countries (such as gross domestic product, the Human Development Index, level of development, etc.) are highly inter-correlated.

There are additional conceptual and methodological difficulties in grouping countries together. Regional groupings are often made in United Nations reports, and these are usually constructed on the basis of official United Nations geographic regions. However, without a clear policy or concept of what ties these regions together in addi-

tion to geographical proximity, it is difficult to make inferences from such groupings. Furthermore, different countries in these regions may exert greater statistical weight. For example, Canadians may not be pleased to have inferences drawn concerning crime rates of North America, when the weight of the crime rate in the United States will drastically affect any such North American crime rate.

The United Nations also has established more or less official groupings of countries in terms of levels of development, variously described as economic development, social development, and more recently human development – depending on the particular branch of the United Nations that is constructing the classification. These classifications emerge after considerable political exchange in the United Nations among member nations. Classification as a "least developed" country may signify that a particular country is more deserving of aid than a country not so classified.

The use of standard indicators such as gross domestic product, literacy level, population density, income levels, and many others, all have their supporters. While most of these indicators are related to the classifications developed by the United Nations mentioned above, the correlations are not perfect. There may be a few countries with high gross domestic product that are classified as developing countries.

Finally, because there are so few countries in the world (statistically speaking only some 200 entities), classifications that require too many categories result in few countries in some categories. While 91 countries are represented in the UNCJS, these are heavily weighted towards developed or industrialized countries and towards regions of the Western tradition. Therefore, any grouping of countries is bound to fall short in some categories, especially in regard to countries that are less developed.

Therefore a particular grouping has not been used consistently throughout the book. Contributing authors have used groupings of countries according to what appeared most relevant to the particular task at hand. The rationales for these groupings are always explained in the notes to the respective tables or figures. In many cases, however, the groupings have been determined

BOX 0.11

Complex crimes and street crimes: the case of BCCI

The dark figure of serious economic crimes is arguably much larger than that of street crimes. This is partly because sophisticated white-collar offenders are better able to slip through the cracks of a fragmented and out-of-date control system. Even when some cases appear to be solved, the reality is so complex that it defies efforts at classification.

A case illustrating these problems is that of BCCI, the Bank of Credit and Commerce International. BCCI cannot be categorized as "one case"; it is rather a mirror of global evils reflecting international networks of corruption and misconduct that are quite possibly continuing their operations to this day. They do not limit their activities to one kind of crime, but they mix various crimes with many legal and legitimate activities (Kerry, 1992; Passas, 1993, 1994, 1995, 1996; Truell and Gurwin, 1992).

The BCCI Case. BCCI was founded in 1972 by Agha Hasan Abedi, a Pakistani banker. At the beginning, capital was provided by Abu Dhabi authorities and the Bank of America. A very complex organizational structure developed over the years, encompassing a holding company in Luxembourg, and banks incorporated in Luxembourg and the Cayman Islands, as well as banks, subsidiaries, branches, agencies, offices, charitable organizations and oil and insurance companies in 72 countries. Although the bank was essentially insolvent from the middle 1970s, BCCI appeared to be operating with profit for many years. It grew very fast and covered many areas of the Third World that were shunned by other institutions. This was consistent with BCCI's official philosophy that it was a bank seeking to help the South in gaining a degree of self-dependence and autonomy.

During those years of apparent success, Abedi was travelling around the globe and associating with country leaders and other influential people — such as former US President Jimmy Carter, former UK Prime Minister James Callaghan, former German Chancellor Willy Brandt, and former UN Secretary Perez de Cuellar, among many others. BCCI clearly enjoyed the support of very powerful individuals and organizations from the West.

However, some serious problems started to emerge in the 1980s. In 1989, BCCI pleaded guilty to money laundering in the USA, while some of its managers were found guilty of similar charges after a trial in Tampa, Florida. In July 1991, BCCI was closed down in a global regulatory action coordinated by the Bank of England. The closure of the bank opened a Pandora's box, as reports about a long list of offences, frauds and deceptions made headlines in the press. As it turned out, BCCI illegally and secretly controlled several US financial institutions. Through a London affiliate, Capcom, BCCI had been losing hundreds of millions of dollars. Loans to a group of shipping companies were not being repaid and cost BCCI over $1 billion. To hide these huge problems and the fact that the bank was left with no capital, top managers devoted most of their time to falsifying accounts, keeping deposits off the records, and generating fake profits. In the end, depositors' money was used to cover some of the gaps in BCCI's books.

In addition to BCCI managers' misconduct, many clients and users of BCCI had been involved in offences ranging from money laundering and tax evasion to illegal arms trafficking, drug trafficking, coffee smuggling, politically-motivated violence, illegal transfer of technology, capital flight/currency violations, corruption, illegal covert intelligence operations, etc. Not all of these crimes were committed with the knowledge or collusion of BCCI managers. Yet, this case illustrates quite dramatically how vital banks are in the business of crime and how hard it is to distinguish white-collar and government/state crime from organized crime.

The structure of the BCCI group of entities and affiliates made regulatory supervision virtually impossible. London, where BCCI was headquartered, is not known for aggressive bank regulation. Luxembourg and the Cayman Islands, the main loci of incorporation for BCCI's banks, are no regulatory tigers either. Indeed, they are among a host of secrecy jurisdictions, which do not readily cooperate with control agencies and which effectively constitute a "black box" of international misconduct.

The control of transnational banking groups such as BCCI was fragmented with no central bank or supervisor having an overall view of what was happening within that group. Given this fragmentation of control, each country with some role or responsibility in supervising BCCI activities would apply its own rules and regulations. Some of these domestic laws are incompatible with each other. Moreover, the priorities and general traditions in different countries or among various control agencies are often at loggerheads. Thus, the fragmentation of control gives rise to conflicts of law or conflicts of interests and agendas of different organizations. Parochial controllers cannot contain effectively cosmopolitan criminals.

The role of professionals. The non-application of US and other laws owes much to the acts of respected Western professionals. Experienced and well-known European bankers were members of BCCI's board of directors, but they did not do much to prevent the problems that eventually destroyed the bank. In addition, BCCI recruited a high-powered team of lawyers to represent its interests. This legal team included former Federal Reserve (the US Central Bank) officials, former federal prosecutors and Clark Clifford, former counsel to presidents from Truman to Carter. In this way, regulators and law enforcers dealing with BCCI were sometimes dealing with former superiors.

Politicians who received information from BCCI lobbyists gave public speeches defending BCCI's character and record. Some politicians were recipients of campaign contributions from BCCI or BCCI front-men, while others openly socialized with the BCCI managers or shareholders.

Intelligence agencies from several countries used BCCI for the payment of their operatives in different countries or for the transfer of funds needed for covert operations — some of which were illegal. BCCI also served as a "listening post" for secret services keen to know about the activities of criminal enterprises and corrupt people around the world. In this light, there was little incentive for intelligence agencies to "blow the whistle" on BCCI.

Finally, the most reputable and well-paid accounting firms were unable to uncover frauds and warn the public of the coming disaster. (This is the most benign scenario; in ongoing legal actions, the argument is made that auditors were negligent or, in some cases, knowledgeable of inside and non-performing loans, illegal control of US banks, and manipulations of accounts.)

Conclusion. How is one to count the BCCI case? How can it be categorized for statistical purposes? What does it tell us about the dark figure of economic crime? BCCI is out of business and many of its crimes are cleared. Yet, we have not been able to address the evils of international crime. We have only smashed one of its mirrors. Despite the many investigations and legal actions, we still know less than 50 percent of the unlawful activities that went on through BCCI. Only some Pakistanis went to jail, raising the question of why some important Western participants appear to be "unavailable for prosecution." Some people thought that this case showed that the system can work against complex frauds. The evidence, however, points to the contrary conclusion. The BCCI case demonstrates that the system is not working. This case confirms that the best "organized crimes" are the crimes that we do not know about, the crimes that do not make the crime statistics.

Source: Passas (Original paper, 1997). See also Chapter 9 for additional information on complex crimes.

Role of criminal law in protection of the environment in China

China amended its criminal law in March 1997. For the first time, certain conducts degrading the environment, which cause death or injury to any person or such risk of significant magnitude, or damage the public or another person's property, are criminalized in the revised criminal law. Under the chapter of crimes against the order of social admin- istration, one special section deals with environmental crimes. The crimes described in each section include:

serious pollution (of soil, air and water);
importing waste materials;
endangering wild life;
destroying resources of land;
destroying resources of mines;
deforestation;
destroying biological diversity.

The penalty for these crimes may be a fine, criminal detention and imprisonment up to 15 years. If any corporation, enterprise, administrative unit or non-governmental organi- zation commits the above crime, the unit will be fined and its head will also be punished.

In addition to this section on environmental crimes, there is another section in the same chapter, which deals with crimes against the protection of cultural heritage. The crimes include: vandalization of cultural heritage; smuggling and trafficking in cultural relics; and illegally excavating ancient cultural ruins, cemeteries or fossils of historical, artistic and scientific value. The punishments for these crimes range from fine, criminal detention and imprisonment to the death penalty.

Source: Guo Jianan (Original paper, 1997)

by the availability of sufficient countries to make up the group.

Beyond traditional crime

The UNCJS does not attempt to measure crimes that go beyond what are usually called "traditional crimes." The crimes of murder, rape, robbery, assault and theft are the primary targets of statistical analysis throughout Chapters 2, 3 and 4. While the UNCJS does request information concern- ing fraud, bribery and drug crimes, responses to these questions are haphazard and diffi- cult to interpret. This is because the defini- tions of these crimes in the UNCJS is nec- essarily very general because these crimes are mostly very complex crimes that may in fact be composed of many smaller crimes. In addition the definitions in the criminal codes of responding countries may pertain to a variety of crimes, each of which may be partially related to the crime of, say, "fraud." For example, the crimes of embezzlement, theft by trickery, illegal gambling, false ad- vertising, pyramid schemes, blackmail, and many more could be subsumed under the general heading of "fraud." Furthermore, some countries may not even define some

of the acts (e.g., bribery) as criminal at all. Thus, while these crimes are considered briefly in Chapter 2, not a great deal of at- tention is given them in regard to the UNCJS data. The same mostly applies to the ICVS. Victims are asked questions in regard to per- sonal property and violence against the per- son. But it is particularly difficult to come up with questions that will tap into the web of actions and events that may produce vic- tims of fraud. Indeed, many such victims many not even know that they are or have been victims.

There are many criminologists who would insist that crimes that go beyond the traditional crimes are far more serious in the damage they do to individuals and society than the traditional crimes. Massive frauds may cause billions of dollars in loss (Box 0.11). Unfortunately, because of their com- plexity, these types of crimes are poorly re- corded statistically, and in fact cannot be re- corded as discrete crimes. Nor should they be because they may vary enormously in scope. One fraud on its own would seem insignificant in comparison to a crime such as the BCCI fraud. The social and economic impact of the latter case on its victims is equal to that of many thousands of tradi- tional thefts. Another problem also arises: who shall record such non-traditional crimes? They do not easily fit into the realm of the traditional police officer who records crimes reported by victims or witnesses. These are almost always confined to tradi- tional crimes. In fact, many of the exten- sive, complex non-traditional crimes are un- covered by other agencies of the government that may be far removed from the criminal justice system. The variety of agencies that deal with, for example, protection of the en- vironment may vary from local police to government departments that have special- ized personnel to evaluate pollution. Some countries may have passed laws that pro- vide criminal penalties for environmental pollution (Box 0.12), but others may not.

Finally, it is apparent that the more mas- sive the fraud or non-traditional crime, the more certain it will be international in scope. And this leads us to the most difficult prob- lem of all in recording these crimes: many may be what are now called "transnational crimes," so that the responsibility for record- ing such crimes may fall to many countries (Box 0.13).

Gauging transnational criminality: a new challenge for the United Nations Survey of Crime Trends and Criminal Justice Systems

One of the boldest experiments in the short history of international crime statistics was the UN Secretariat's effort to assess the prevalence and extent of transnational crime, as part of Fourth United Nations Survey of Crime Trends and Operations of Criminal Justice Systems (A/CONF. 169/15/Add.1, 4 April, 1995). Transnational crime was defined as "offences whose inception, proportion and/or direct or indirect effects involved more than one country" (para.9). The Secretariat, from the very outset, was aware of the difficulty of any such effort. The penal codes of nations and states do not categorize "transnational crimes," and consequently no official statistics are available. Yet globalization in general and with regard to crime in particular, necessitated the effort to gauge the extent of transnational crime, which increasingly affects the lives, the security, and the sense of safety of everyone on earth.

On the basis of experience — dating back to the Fifth UN Congress on the Prevention of Crime and the Treatment of Offenders (Geneva, 1975) — and in replies to the Secretariat's questionnaire as part of the Fourth UNCJS submitted by governments, inter-governmental and non-governmental organizations, the Secretariat identified 18 categories of transnational crime. All of them, as it turned out, are forms of organized crime (though it is theoretically possible that a single perpetrator may commit a transnational crime). All 18 categories are criminological concepts with the merest relation to penal code definitions:

Money-laundering	Terrorist activities
Theft of art and cultural objects	Theft of intellectual property
Illicit traffic in arms	Aircraft hijacking
Sea piracy	Land hijacking
Insurance fraud	Computer crime
Environmental crime	Trafficking in persons
Trade in human body parts	Illicit drug trafficking
Fraudulent bankruptcy	Infiltration of legal business

Corruption and bribery of public officials as defined in national legislation and of party officials and elected representatives as defined in national legislation.

Other offences committed by organized criminal groups. (As it turns out this "catch-all" group currently consists mainly of a lively trade in stolen motor vehicles, from west to east and north to south.)

Governments could hardly be expected to supply hard data on any of the categories. This makes it that much more important to obtain information from other sources. Thus, as to category three (theft of art and cultural objects), the fine arts trade groups have fairly reliable information on the amount of stolen art on the international market (45,000 items, with an increase of 2,000 per month). As to category four (theft of intellectual property), the US Software Publishers Association reports a loss of $7.5 billion annually. With respect to insurance fraud (a transnational crime by definition due to the international linkage, through reinsurance of the industry), the US losses to the industry and economy amount to $100 billion, annually.

Though governments could supply few statistics, their experience give us an indication of trends in transnational crime, thus confirming a criminological model which has emerged over the years

1. Local crimes, as customarily measured by crime statistics, victimization reports, or self-report studies, have remained local only in a formal sense. Rather, globalization has impacted many if not most "local criminality," thus making it more impervious to control by purely local efforts.

2. Foreign-impacted local crime, through organization, became truly transnational criminality. That type of criminality requires transnational response mechanisms which are in place only in rudimentary form; thus,

3. necessitating the creation of more formal and universal response mechanisms, at the enforcement (police) level and ultimately the elevation of (at least some) transnational crimes to the level of international crimes which can be tried in domestic as well as, ultimately, international tribunals. At that third stage the criminologically defined transnational crimes become modified in juridical terms — and thus more easily measurable; this has already happened with various forms of terrorism and narcotic criminality. Other transnational criminality will follow suit, despite the isolationism in some countries which currently retards this.

Meanwhile, how can we do a better job in gauging transnational crime which, like the Internet, keeps expanding uncontrolled?

(a) Progress has been made in assessing the value, amount and impact of the global drug trade (see Chapter 7).

(b) More reliance must be placed on data provided by affected industries as regards many of the economic transnational crimes.

(c) Intergovernmental organizations have the facility of assessing the transnational character of yet other forms of criminality. Thus, Interpol has made great progress in gauging the magnitude of the international trade in stolen automobiles (and their theft patterns in the first place).

(d) With respect to most other forms of criminality, it is necessary to develop sampling techniques in which transnational elements of "ordinary" criminality will reveal the transnational character.

(e) Ultimately, the newly constituted United Nations Centre for International Crime Prevention (Vienna), formerly the Crime Prevention and Criminal Justice Division, with its new focus on transnational organized crime, terrorism, and narcotic drug criminality, must renew its efforts to gauge transnational criminality, as part of the UNCJS.

Source: Mueller and Adler (Original paper, 1997)

For these reasons, one must acknowledge that the UNCJS is limited in its capacity to reflect both the breadth and depth of the crime problem throughout the world, especially if one views crime from a broader perspective than that of traditional crime. This is why boxes and a complete chapter concerning non-traditional crimes have been included. Those materials draw on a variety of information, both official and unofficial, along with media reports and research, in order to convey a picture of crime that lies beyond the scope of the UNCJS and victimization surveys. Chapter 7 on drug control and Chapter 9 on transnational crime, draw on a variety of sources and rely heavily on descriptive information, although statistical data are provided where possible.

Organization of the report

The first four chapters of the report follow the traditional process of the criminal justice system, beginning with the victims of crime (using ICVS data), and continuing through to the final disposition of the offender (using UNCJS data). The next three chapters deal with increasingly broader concerns, including the resources of criminal justice (using UNCJS data), firearm abuse and regulation using data of the UN International Study on the Regulation of Firearms (UNFRS), and drugs and their control. These are followed by a chapter on crime prevention using mostly research data, and finally a chapter that addresses emerging issues related to transnational crime and its control.

Chapter 1. *The Experience of Crime*. This chapter reviews the work of the International Crime Victimization Surveys (ICVS), providing a look at crime as it is first experienced by victims, and developing estimates of crime rates based on their reports to interviewers. While the crime rates are the major focus of the chapter, attention is also given to the useful information provided by respondents to the survey concerning their experiences and perceptions of the criminal justice system, with which they may or may not have come into contact as a result of their victimization.

Chapter 2. *Police Records of Crime*. This chapter moves to the next stage of the criminal justice process — the recording of an event as a crime by the police. The rules that police use to record and classify crimes immediately become important. The United Nations Survey of Crime Trends and Operation of Criminal Justice Systems (UNCJS) data are used as the basis for this chapter.

Chapter 3. *Bringing to Justice*. This chapter analyzes the data of the UNCJS concerning offenders and their processing, whether by police, prosecutors or judges. These are records of *offenders*, in contrast to those of the previous chapter which were police records of *events*. In addition, as is pointed out in the chapter, the processing, from arrest (or its equivalent) to charging and trial to conviction, is of offenders and not *cases*. It should be noted that each event may in fact have more than one offender. Furthermore, each case may have more than

one crime attached to it and may involve multiple offenders as well. Importantly, the filtering of offenders through the criminal justice system depends on how their cases are constructed and what avenues for processing are available in the particular country's justice system. This chapter provides a fascinating comparative picture of the filtering that occurs during the justice process.

Chapter 4. *Punishment*. The final stage in the processing of crime by the criminal justice system is punishment, sometimes called the "disposition" stage. This chapter utilizes data primarily from the UNCJS but also draws on other sources where necessary, such as the ICVS and Amnesty International. The data here are also concerned with offenders, most of whom have been convicted of a crime. The types and severity of punishments around the world are examined along with the extent to which punishment either strays or confines itself to acceptable conditions as defined by the United Nations Standard Minimum Rules for Treatment of Offenders.

Chapter 5. *Resources in Criminal Justice*. Drawing on data once again collected by the UNCJS, this chapter assesses the extent to which countries around the world provide resources to run their criminal justice systems. These resources are defined in terms of criminal justice personnel, budgets for operating and capital costs, and the quality of personnel, such as their level of education and their qualifications to perform criminal justice duties. The amount spent by governments on prisoners and prisons is of particular interest, as is the extent to which prisons may or may not be overcrowded in various countries.

Chapter 6. *Firearm Abuse and Regulation*. This chapter examines a problem that is both very old and very new in criminal justice. It is very old because guns have figured prominently in crime in many countries of the world for many years. It is very new because the concern about gun regulation has been precipitated in recent years by a number of tragic events involving firearms in particular countries as well as their link to international trafficking. Trafficking in firearms is also a key aspect of the new focus on transnational crime that is part of the perception of crime at the international level in the 1990s. Drawing on data from a recent United Nations survey of firearms use and regulation, as well as on data from the UNCJS, this chapter examines the use, abuse and regulation of firearms around the world and assesses their relationship to crimes of violence.

Chapter 7. *Drugs and Drug Control.* This chapter examines another crime that is both old and new. Abuse of drugs is probably as old as humankind. Its involvement with criminal activity is also not a new phenomenon. However, the international trafficking of drugs has reached, in the last decade, a level of sophistication unheard of in previous times. The globalization of commerce has no doubt contributed to this new sophistication, which of course involves highly skilled members of organized crime. This chapter reviews what is known at the global level of the extent of drug use and trafficking. The international attempts to control drug trafficking and some national solutions to drug crime are described. The complex relationship of drug use and trafficking to traditional crime and its processing through the justice system is of special interest.

Chapter 8. *International trends in crime prevention: cost-effective ways to reduce victimization.* Lest the picture painted by all chapters so far presented appear too bleak, this chapter provides much reason for optimism. Drawing on information and research from an enormous variety of published sources, this chapter highlights the major studies that have demonstrated success in reducing and/or preventing crime. A wide variety of crime prevention programmes are identified, and the work of international and national organizations in promoting knowledge and know-how in crime prevention is described. Not only are there many instances of successful crime prevention in many different countries, but it is also abundantly clear that, as the cliché goes, "prevention is better than a cure." The chapter demonstrates that a dollar spent on prevention can mean an enormous savings compared to the expense of processing an offender through the criminal justice system.

Chapter 9. *Emerging issues: trans--national crime and its control.* This topic defies the collection of simple statistical data on each transnational crime because these crimes are intrinsically highly complex and often composed of many separate crimes. Thus, the UNCJS and the ICVS are unable to provide much information on this. Instead, this chapter draws upon a wide variety of published research and reports concerning the major types of transnational crime. It first tries to define transnational crime and then proceeds to catalog the types of transnational crime that exist. It concludes by making reasonable estimates concerning the amount and extent of this new and threatening crime problem.

Page left blank

CHAPTER 1

The experience of crime and justice

Contributing author: Jan J. M. van Dijk

Introduction

Over the past 30 years a growing number of countries have conducted crime or victimization surveys to assess national or local crime problems. Such surveys ask representative samples of the general public about selected offences they might have experienced over a given time. It is then possible to construct rates of crime based on victim reports which offer an alternative measure of crime to that generated by official statistics. Throughout this book, the emphasis is mostly on official records of crime, since these are the main published crime data of most countries. They are also a more direct source of statistics concerning the operations of criminal justice systems of which victimization surveys can give only a partial picture. The victimization surveys may, however, offer an important picture of how the public views the criminal justice system as well as a number of other perceptions in regard to crime.

As we have seen in the Introduction, there are a number of methodological problems relating to the measurement of crime using official records, just as there are also difficulties in using victimization reports as a measure of crime. A special problem with victimization surveys is that, while they seem to overcome the thorny problem of the different legal definitions of crimes in different legal systems, they depend nevertheless on the cultural perception of crime that may affect the respondents. For example, respondents in one country may have a different "threshold" concerning what they perceive as an act of violence depending on the role and experience of violence in that country (see Box 1.3). This issue is ad-

dressed later in the chapter. For the moment, it is important to recognize that each measure of crime, whether victim survey or official record, is useful in its own right. Neither offers a complete picture of crime and criminal justice problems in any given country.

The International Crime Victim Survey (ICVS hereafter), which was initiated in 1987 (see Box 0.9), has been implemented so far in 55 different countries under the supervision of an international working group.[1] In total more than 133,821 citizens have been interviewed within the framework of the ICVS.[2] Details of the ICVS can be found in van Dijk *et al.* (1990), Alvazzi del Frate *et al.* (1993), Zvekic and Alvazzi del Frate (1995), and Mayhew and van Dijk (1997). Samples sizes varied between 1,000 in developing countries and 2,000 in most other countries. In developing countries and most countries in transition the interviews were carried out through face-to-face interviewing. In most developing nations and some nations in transition the survey was carried out among the inhabitants of the largest city (city surveys). Elsewhere well-spread samples were drawn from the national population. For a discussion of methodological issues the reader should refer to the publications just mentioned (see also Block, 1993; Lynch, 1993; and Stangeland, 1995) and as well consult the notes to tables and figures for this chapter.[3] It should be added that, until recently, these surveys have focused on individuals as victims of crime. There are, of course, victims who are not individuals but organizations, such as businesses. In some countries attempts are now being made to survey commercial victimization (Box 1.2).

Victimization surveys may offer an important picture of how the public views the criminal justice system.

Urban victimization rates across the world

The key findings of the survey are the percentages of the public victimized by crime over the past five years from the day respondents are interviewed. To ensure comparability of the rates from national surveys and city surveys, five year rates per country were calculated for respondents living in cities with more than 100,000 inhabitants (urban country rates). Data from countries where the survey was carried out twice or more were averaged. If, for example, a country participated in both 1989 and 1996 the two victimization rates were averaged. The victimization rates presented here give comparable information on the experiences of the public with crime over the course of five years in the period 1989-1996.

To be made more presentable, the data were also aggregated into rates for six global regions: the New World (USA, Canada, Australia, New Zealand), Western Europe (15 countries), Central and Eastern Europe (20 countries), Asia (China, Japan, India, Indonesia and Philippines), Latin America

Perhaps the most striking finding is that more than half of urban respondents report being victimized by crime, no matter what part of the world.

(Argentina, Bolivia, Brazil, Colombia, Costa Rica and Paraguay) and Africa (Egypt, South Africa, Tanzania, Tunisia, Uganda and Zimbabwe). Each country was given an equal statistical weight for the calculation of overall rates.

Perhaps the most striking finding revealed by Figure 1.1 is that more than half of urban respondents report being victimized by crime, no matter what part of the world they inhabit. It also shows that the overall five year victimization rates are highest in Latin America and Africa, where three of every four citizens living in urban areas were victimized at least once. The overall victimization rates are the lowest in Asian cities.

Table 1.1 presents the urban five year victimization rates for four different types of crime (additional crime categories are excluded) for the six global regions.[4] The distribution of car related crimes (car theft, theft from cars and car vandalism) stands out from other crimes: the highest rates are in the New World countries and Western Europe. The level of the latter crimes is determined by the availability of suitable targets.[5] It is of interest that property crimes are higher in Africa, which runs against the popular assumption that where there is more property (i.e., in developed industrialized nations) there is more to steal. Rather, the relatively high rates in Africa may reflect lack of security in dwellings and other aspects of social life.

Contact crimes (sexual harassment/sexual violence, assaults/threats and robbery) are highest in Latin America and Africa. The level of contact crimes here is about twice as high as elsewhere. The level of contact crimes is fairly high in the New World countries (Canada, USA, Australia and New Zealand). It is the lowest in Asia and Western Europe.

Special rates were calculated for violence against men and women.[6] The first rate includes assaults where force was actually used (excluding threats).[7] The second rate, for violence against women, includes both non-sexual assaults and sexual assaults (rape, attempted rape and other assaults with sexual connotations), excluding less serious sexual incidents. These results are displayed in Figure 1.2.

Violence against women shows a differ-

FIGURE 1.1
Percentage of the public victimized by *any* crime in urban areas, by region, 1989-1996*

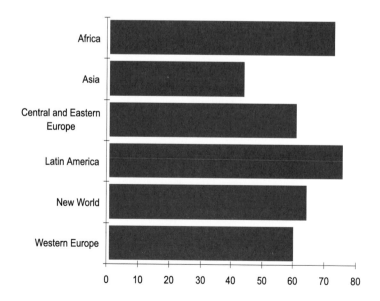

Source: van Dijk (1997b). See Notes to Figures for individual country rates, national rates and method of computation. Note that this Figure includes all crimes listed in Table 1.1, including violent crimes against women.

TABLE 1.1
Percentage of the public victimized by selected crimes: car crimes, burglary, other theft, and contact crimes over five years in urban areas of six global regions; results of the International Crime (Victim) Surveys, 1989-1996

	all	Africa	Asia	Central and Eastern Europe	Latin America	New World	Western Europe
number of countries	55	6	4	20	6	4	15
number of cases	67364	8108	10490	21972	8015	5951	12828
car crimes	29	22	8	28	30	45	37
burglary + attempt	20	35	11	18	32	23	14
other thefts	32	42	30	32	42	27	27
contact crimes	20	32	13	17	36	20	16

Source: van Dijk (1997b). See Notes to Tables for complete details of data sources and construction.

Domestic violence is a major social problem in Latin America, Africa and the New World countries.

ent pattern than violence against men. The results show that in the Western countries (Europe and the New World) men are as often assaulted as women. The level of violence is fairly high in the New World countries for both men and women. In the rest of the world there is a considerable gender difference: the risk of being assaulted is much higher for women than for men. The risk of being assaulted for men in Latin America or Africa is roughly equal to that in the New World countries. But the risk for women is 50 percent higher. In Asian cities women are also more at risk than men. These findings indicate that the violence problems of many developing countries specifically take the form of violence against women. Compared to European cities, Asian cities are safer for men, but this is not necessarily true for women.

As is known from previous analyses of the ICVS data (Alvazzi del Frate, 1995), assaults on women are more likely to be domestic in nature than assaults on men. In more than a quarter of these cases, the offender was known by name to the victim. In almost half the cases, the crime was committed in or near the victim's own home. Domestic violence, then, is a major social problem in Latin America, Africa and the New World countries in particular.

From these key findings the conclusion can be drawn that the notion of high crime rates as unique features of some unfortunate nations is not supported. The experience of being criminally victimized has become a statistically normal feature of urban life all over the world, though the type of victimization varies.

According to ICVS results the rates of property crimes have gone down in many of the most industrialized countries (Mayhew and van Dijk, 1997). One possible explanation is that improved security has reduced the opportunities for crimes like burglary and car theft. In the rest of the world, the level of protection against crime is considerably lower. In these countries no decline in crime trends is yet in evidence. If present trends in protection against crime continue, the gap in levels of safety between developed countries and developing coun-

FIGURE 1.2
Percentage of men and women victimized by violent crimes over five years in urban areas of six global regions; results of the International Crime (Victim) Surveys, 1989-1996

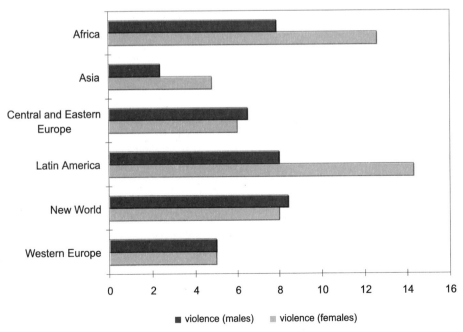

Source: van Dijk (1997b). See Notes to Figures for additional information.

tries will become even wider.

Other sources of data also indicate that certain groups in particular countries may be more victimized than others, particularly in regard to minority groups and the young (Box 1.1), and commercial establishments, whose losses may be especially high (Box 1.2)

The 1996 sweep of the ICVS included a question on the solicitation of bribes by government officials during the last year. The results show that this type of corruption is most diffused in Latin America (21.3 percent), Africa (18.8 percent) and Asia (14.6 percent). The rate was moderately high in Central and Eastern Europe (10.7 percent) and lowest in Western Europe (0.7 percent) and the New World countries (1 percent). The high prevalence of street level corruption in developing countries and countries in transition adds to the burden of conventional crime in these parts of the world (Zvekic and Alvazzi, 1993).

Crime as a universal concept

As noted in the introductory chapter, there are difficulties in using statistics of crimes recorded by the police for comparative purposes because of differences in legal definitions and recording practices. By bypassing the state agencies and interviewing individuals directly, survey researchers can overcome some of these obstacles. The credibility of the ICVS, however, hinges on whether citizens in different corners of the world share a set of basic norms defining criminal acts such as violence and theft. In the current philosophical climate of post-modernism, the assumption of shared norms cannot be taken for granted. It is most questionable concerning forms of (domestic) violence against women since the definitions of such offences may be even more culture-bound than definitions of other crimes (see Box 1.3).

Since the ICVS project originates from Western countries, cultural biases might have been introduced into its questionnaire and other instruments. To minimize such bias researchers from various regions, including those from developing countries, took part in evaluation sessions of the instruments

used. Although some questions were less relevant in some national settings than others — for example, questions concerning either cars or bicycles — respondents nowhere had serious difficulty in understanding the core questions on victimizations by crime. This result by itself lends some support to the assumption that certain basic concepts concerning conventional crimes are common, at least among the inhabitants of urban areas.

In the last two sweeps of the survey, victims were asked to assess the seriousness of the incidents they reported to the interviewer. The assessments were made on a simple three point scale, indicating very serious (3), somewhat serious (2) and not very serious (1). For each of the 17 subtypes of crime, the mean seriousness scores were calculated per country. The mean scores can vary between 1.00 and 3.00. If for instance half of the victims in a country said their experience of having been robbed was very serious and the other half said somewhat serious, the mean score for robbery in that country is 2.50.

On the basis of the mean scores, the crime types were subsequently rank ordered for all countries together and per region and country. Crime types which were rated as the most serious were given the highest rank.

The results show how victims in various regions and countries rank different types of crime in terms of seriousness. Table 1.2 presents the rank order of the different types of crime of the six global regions.[8]

The results show that the ranking of offences in seriousness terms shows a striking similarity across the regions. The degree of similarity between the rankings of the 17 crime types by the victims of the six regions can be expressed in correlations. All correlations are strong and statistically significant (p<0.001). The correlation between the African ranking and the overall ranking is .79. The other five correlations are .90 or more. Correlations between the ranking per country and the overall ranking are, with one exception, also very high and statistically significant (p=<0.05).[9]

The almost perfect correlations between the ranking of crime types by victims from six different regions indicates a high degree of consensus about the import of conven-

TABLE 1.2

Ranking of 17 types of crime in terms of seriousness by victims, per world region and overall

	all	Africa	Asia	Central and Eastern Europe	Latin America	New World	Western Europe
number of countries	52	6	4	20	6	4	12
car theft	1	1	1	1	1	4	2
joy riding	2	2	2	2	3	5	4
robbery with a weapon	3	4	5	5	6	2	1
violence against women	4	5	6	3	4	3	3
sexual harassment	5	3	7	4	5	1	6
motorcycle thefts	6	8	3	6	2	8	8
burglary	7	7	9	7	7	7	5
assault	8	9	4	8	8	6	7
robbery without a weapon	9	12	10	9	10	9	9
threats	10	17	12	12	9	11	11
pickpocketing	11	10	13	11	13	10	10
sexual violence	12	15	8	14	11	14	12
attempted burglary	13	16	14	16	15	12	13
other personal theft	14	13	16	13	14	15	14
bicycle theft	15	11	17	10	12	13	15
theft from car	16	6	11	15	16	16	16
car vandalism	17	14	15	17	17	17	17

Source: van Dijk (1997b). See Notes to Tables for complete tabular and correlational data.

tional crimes against individuals across the world. Victims consistently hold violence against women, robbery with a weapon, motorcycle theft and sexual harassment as the most serious types of crime. Moderately serious were considered burglary, theft from car, pickpocketing, car vandalism and threats. The least serious are considered car theft, joyriding, robbery without a weapon and other personal theft. There are very few deviations from this overall pattern.

The consensus on the seriousness of various types of conventional crimes must be based on a common understanding of the behavioural elements which make up these crimes and of their impact upon victims. It also implies that victims across the world apply similar standards for judging the seri-

---

BOX 1.2

Commercial victimization surveys

Commercial victimization surveys ask both retail and manufacturing premises directly about the crimes they have experienced in a particular period of time. The value of this particular approach is that:

- not all crimes are reported to the police by victims;

- police statistics do not separately identify the type of victim or gather much detail about the nature of the crime against commercial premises;

- although surveys of head offices are useful for gathering information kept centrally (e.g., by a national retail consortium), individual premises may not report all crimes to head office;

- surveys can measure the extent of repeat victimization of the same premises and identify the factors that put some premises at greater risk than others.

However, there are some disadvantages of this approach:

- such a survey is relatively costly;

- only crimes of which the victim was aware can be covered by such a survey;

- some offences, such as some types of theft and all types of fraud, are more difficult to detect and are therefore likely to be undercounted.

Results from such surveys confirm the large amount of crime actually suffered by commercial premises. For examples, results from the 1993 survey of commercial premises in England and Wales gave the following key points:

- eight out of ten retailers and two-thirds of manufacturing premises experienced one or more of the crimes covered by the survey in 1993;

- some premises suffered a disproportionate amount of crime: three percent of retailers experienced 59 percent of the crime counted by the survey and eight percent of manufacturers experienced two-thirds of the crime.

Risks for both retailers and manufacturers were higher than the risks for householders, and average financial losses were higher as well. Larger premises were at greatest risk of crime.

Source: Edited and abridged from Mirrlees-Black and Ross (1995)

The threshold of violence: a comparative study of USA and Japan

It is generally accepted that the US has the highest rate of violence in the industrial western world and Japan one of the lowest. This observation is generally supported by the data presented throughout this volume. The US homicide rate is roughly 20 times higher than Japan's. America is a broadly heterogeneous society with major economic and racial disparity and Japan is homogeneous with less economic disparity. Guns are notoriously easily available in the US and strictly prohibited in Japan (see Chapter 6).

While violent crime rates restrict the definition of violence to such behaviours as murder, assault and robbery, violence as a phenomenon is a progression from self-assertion to aggression (Goldstein, 1986), with behaviours on one end of the continuum considered emotional and psychological abuse, and those on the other end, such as physical assaults, defined by law as crimes. Being violent is not, therefore, restricted to criminal behaviour; it is the willingness to intentionally engage in acts that threaten, or inflict physical harm on another (Reiss and Roth, 1993).

This research is concerned with one's willingness to engage in behaviours that would be defined as violent. That is, at what point, or under what conditions, are people willing to change their behavioural response to a threat or challenge from defensive or passive to behavior that is designed to harm or inflict pain. We define this as the threshold of violence. Collectively, therefore, a lower threshold of violence should be reflected in a higher rate of violence.

Research design. As part of a larger project investigating the social and cultural differences in violence in Japan and the United States, the researchers investigated the threshold of violence by having respondents react to a mailed questionnaire. Random samples were drawn from city records in sub-communities in Tokyo, Mito, Japan, and Charlotte, North Carolina. The size of the American sample was 442 and 908 for Japan.

The questionnaire included a scenario which escalated the violent threat and asked the respondent to indicate his/her response. The threshold of violence was examined by looking at the proportion of respondents who changed their responses from scene to scene to increasingly more active/offensive interaction with the perpetrator.

In Scene 1, where the threat is verbal from the outside, there is no significant difference between the countries. Of the Americans, 91.8 percent would simply call the police, while 80 percent of the Japanese would do the same thing.

Scene 2 escalates the threat by having a drunk break down the door and wreck the house while looking for the daughter. The average American response is to confront the individual and verbally try to get him to stop; the primary Japanese response remains to call the police. The distribution changes when the person breaks into the house. While the median and modal responses in both countries remain to call the police, Americans begin to indicate that they would threaten the person with a weapon (11.7 percent), hit the person (6.7 percent) and use a weapon (18.8 percent). Only 2.2 percent of the Japanese indicate that they would use a weapon at this point.

In Scene 3 the perpetrator finds the daughter and threatens with a knife anyone who tries to stop him. At this point, 41.5 percent of the Americans say they would use a weapon, while 11.3 percent of the Japanese say they would use a weapon and 9.2 percent would try to leave the situation. Only 2.1 percent of the Americans say they would leave their home or ask their daughter to leave.

In the final scene the perpetrator actually grabs the daughter and begins to hit her and tear off her clothes. In this situation, the responses are somewhat parallel with the primary difference being the proportion who would use a weapon. More than half of Americans (58.5 percent) say they would use a weapon and another 22 percent would hit the person. The mean response is "hit," and both the median and mode are "use a weapon." The Japanese appear to have reached a threshold at this point as well, with 35.5 percent saying that they would use a weapon and 19.8 percent saying that they would hit the offender. The mean response for the Japanese, however, is somewhere between "yell at the person" and "threaten him." The median response is "hit the person" and the modal response is the same as the Americans: "use a weapon." For Americans, the threshold of violence appears to be the point of household entry; however, it is not strong until Scene 3 when the intruder threatens with a knife.

Conclusion. When feeling threatened, Americans are more likely than the Japanese to indicate that they would make some type of active, physical response. One turning point for Americans appears to be when someone enters their home or physically touches them.

Source: Friday, Yamagami and Dussich (Original paper, 1997). See Notes to Boxes for additional data.

ousness of these incidents.

The results lend support to the underlying assumption of the ICVS that definitions, perceptions and normative judgements about conventional crimes are fairly universal.

This conclusion has important methodological and theoretical implications for comparative victimological research. Although the legal definitions of conventional crimes differ, the meaning of basic concepts like street robbery, burglary or rape seem to be understood by the public in roughly the same way everywhere (Newman, 1976). There seems to be no *a priori* reason to refrain from comparative studies in this field. This finding also strengthens the case for the advancement of international standards for the treatment of victims.

The determinants of crime

The level of crime in different regions and countries calls for a criminological interpretation. Statistical analyses of the social correlates of national victimization risks can improve understanding of the social characteristics related to high levels of crime.

One major theoretical perspective currently used to understand levels of crime explains the extent of offending as broadly determined by factors which 1) increase the motivation to offend, or 2) present criminal opportunities (e.g., Felson, 1994; van Dijk, 1994). Motivational pressures have been interpreted as emanating from socio-economic "strain." Indicators of such strain are unemployment, income inequality or dissatisfaction with income. Motivations to offend have also been linked to the process of modernization, which is seen to weaken informal community control and impose modern norms of individualism and consumerism (e.g., Shelley, 1981). The importance of criminal opportunities stems from the notion that more people will be tempted to commit crimes if suitable opportunities for illegal profits abound.

Previous analyses confirmed that the levels of contact crimes and thefts are higher in nations where high proportions of people feel economically deprived (van Dijk, 1994b; Stangeland, 1995). In contrast, car related crimes are more common in more affluent nations where more households

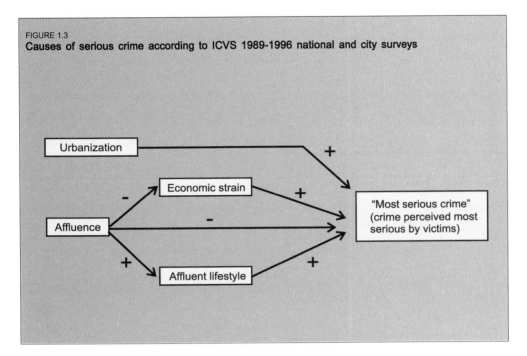

FIGURE 1.3
Causes of serious crime according to ICVS 1989-1996 national and city surveys

...57 percent of victimization rates in 49 countries can be explained by urbanization, economic strain and lifestyle.

own one or more cars. The data given in Table 1.1 confirm this. Crimes like bicycle theft are similarly opportunity-driven: more bicycles are stolen where ownership rates of bicycles are high. The highest rates for bicycle theft are for example found in the Netherlands, China, Japan, Sweden and Switzerland.

From a victimological perspective the most serious types of victimizations are particularly relevant. The analysis of the results for the 50 countries was therefore focused on three broad measures of the most serious forms of crime. The first draws together the crimes which are rated as the most serious by victims (e.g., burglary, thefts of and from cars), and the three most serious categories of contact crimes (robbery with weapon, violence against women and sexual harassment). This combined measure we call from hereon "more serious crime." The second measure is the subset of "contact crimes" itself (robbery, sexual assault and assault). Thirdly and finally we will look at the correlates of violence against women in particular.

A number of known risk-related variables, identified largely through analysis of earlier ICVS results, were examined with conventional covariate and multivariate techniques to assess their relative importance. In this analysis the data were used from all national and city surveys carried

out between 1989 and 1996. If several surveys were carried out in one country, the results from the most recent survey were used.

For more serious crime, the strongest factor explaining risks across different countries was urbanization (see Figure 1.3). Victimization by more serious crime is strongly correlated with increases in the proportion of the population living in larger cities (r=.69; p< 0.000; n=48).

Next, lower affluence was significantly associated with higher risk of victimization by more serious crime (r=-.45; p<0.001; n=48). This result provides a challenge to "modernization theory," which holds that less developed countries are characterized by lower levels of property crimes. Previous studies using police figures of recorded crimes as their measure of crime provide support for that perspective: the rates of police recorded crimes are lower in less developed countries (Bennett, 1991; Neapolitan, 1995). These conflicting findings might be explained by lower reporting rates and/or the fact that recording systems of the police are less well-developed in developing countries and the countries in transition.

The analysis showed furthermore that the relationship between affluence and serious crime is mediated by our measure of "socioeconomic strain": the proportion of young males who were dissatisfied with their

The results lend support to the assumption that definitions, perceptions and normative judgements about conventional crimes are fairly universal.

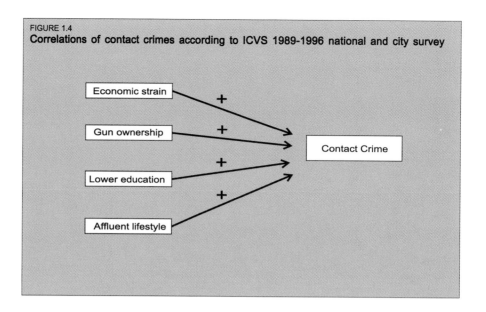

FIGURE 1.4
Correlations of contact crimes according to ICVS 1989-1996 national and city survey

Economic strain

Gun ownership

Lower education

Affluent lifestyle

Contact Crime

In countries where more young males – and others – suffer from resource deprivation, more violence against women is committed.

household income. In developing countries and the countries in transition there are more young males who feel economically deprived. This factor is strongly related to a high level of serious crime (r=.52; p<0.000; n=49). This relationship also appears in multivariate analyses.

The inverse relationship between affluence and serious crime is weakened, however, by an intervening factor: our measure for an outgoing life-style. In more affluent countries people go out more often in the evening for recreational purposes. In a multivariate analysis this factor is positively related to high crime risks (beta=.29; p<0.01; n=49).[10]

The factors urbanization, economic strain and life-style accounted for 57 percent of the variance in victimization rates of 49 countries (multiple R=.75).[11]

With regard to contact crimes (see Figure 1.4), economic strain was the strongest factor explaining risks (r=.62). A second factor of importance explaining the level of contact crime per country was the rate of handgun ownership (r=0.32; p>.05; n=53).[12] In countries where more households possess one or more handguns the risk of contact crime is higher. Gun ownership is significantly related to both the level of robberies (r=.37; p<.007; n=52) and the level of sexual incidents (r=.31; p=.02; n=53).[13] It is not statistically significantly related to non-sexual threats/assaults. However, the relationship between gun ownership and threats/assaults with a gun is very strong (r=.58; p<0.001;

n=37).[14] These findings are largely supported in Chapter 6 of this volume.

Statistically significant relationships were also found with life-style and level of education: risk of contact crimes are higher in countries where more people go out in the evening for recreational purposes and in countries where the average level of education is lower.

Together these four factors (strain, gun ownership, education and life-style) explain 68 percent of the variance in the country rates for contact crimes (multi R=.83).[15]

Previous analyses of ICVS data have shown that national homicide rates are clearly related to the level of gun ownership (Killias, 1993). The results of the analyses show that high levels of gun ownership such as in the USA, the former Yugoslavia, South Africa and several Latin American countries are strongly related to higher levels of violence in general.

Finally, it is widely regarded that certain groups in society are more victimized than others for a variety of reasons (Box 1.1). One of these groups is women, so that we looked at the correlates at macro level of violence against women. With regard to these risks economic strain was again the strongest predictor (r=.54). In countries where more young males – and others – suffer from resource deprivation, more violence against women is committed. Other macro-analytic studies have also found a relationship between resource deprivation and different forms of violence, including violence against women (Hsieh, Pugh, 1993).

Economic strain or resource deprivation is related to violence against women. Some economically deprived males seem to ventilate their stress and frustrations by assaulting women in their social environment.

In previous analyses a negative correlation was found between victimization by sexual violence and several indicators related to the advancement or status of women: in the developing world less sexual violence was measured in countries where women are better educated, marry at a higher age and take contraception measures more often (Alvazzi del Frate, Patrignani, 1995). In the present analysis violence against women was negatively related to the level of education of women (r=-.22). In accordance with feminist perspectives, violence against women is more prevalent in countries where women possess low status (Lenton, 1995).

The third factor which was found to be independently related to high risks of violence against women was the proportion of divorced women (r=.19). Further analyses showed that this relationship is only found among the developed countries. Countries with the highest rates of violence against women in the Western world are the USA, New Zealand, Finland, England and Wales, and Sweden. In these countries the divorce rate is fairly high. There is no obvious causal interpretation of the statistical relationship between high divorce rates and violence against women in the more affluent countries. It can also be argued, though, that at the micro level serious violence against women is strongly related to separation and divorce in the sense that women attempting to leave men are frequent homicide victims (Wilson and Daly, 1993). The hypothesis that at the macro level a causal relationship exists between high rates of separation and divorce and serious violence seems to merit further scrutiny. The three main factors together explain 44 percent of the variance in national rates of violence against women (multiple R=.66).[16]

The role of affluence is a complex one. It is positively related to most serious crimes only through the measure of life-style. The level of crime is determined by opportunity structures, such as an outgoing life-style and the ownership of cars or guns. Some of those

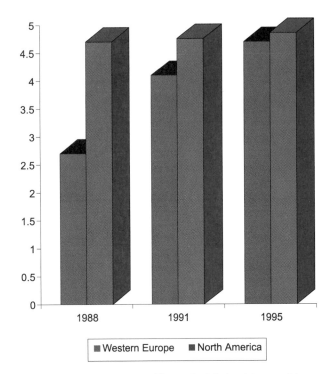

GLOBAL SNAPSHOT
Percent of respondents reporting victimization by assault or threats

Over a seven year period, victimization by violence has increased in Western Europe but remained stable in North America

■ Western Europe   ■ North America

Source: van Dijk (1997b). See Notes to Figures for tabular data, countries surveyed.

opportunity structures are more common in more affluent countries. Others, like gun ownership, are unrelated to levels of affluence (r=.11). The level of gun ownership is determined by cultural and legal traditions (see Chapter 6).

Taken together these results support the idea that in more affluent nations there is less economic strain, which reduces the propensity to seek profit by committing serious crime and/or violent crime. At the same time, though, a more outgoing life-style related to affluence may increase the supply of opportunities for certain forms of crime. Affluence, then, acts both as a brake on crime and a catalyst of it (see Figure 1.3). The dual impact of affluence on serious crime explains why risks of crime are high in almost all urban areas of the world, regardless of the level of affluence. These results challenge the conventional notion that the problems of crime are automatically solved by economic growth. To increase urban safety, special policies and measures

Affluence acts both as a brake on crime and a catalyst of it.

United Nations Declaration of the Basic Principles of Justice for Victims of Crime and Abuse of Power, 1985

Access to justice and fair treatment

4. Victims are entitled to access to the mechanisms of justice and to prompt redress, as provided for by national legislation, for the harm that they have suffered.

5. Judicial and administrative mechanisms should be established and strengthened where necessary to enable victims to obtain redress through formal or informal procedures that are expeditious, fair, inexpensive and accessible.

6. The responsiveness of judicial and administrative processes to the needs of victims should be facilitated by:

(a) Informing victims of their role and the scope, timing and progress of the proceedings and of the disposition of their cases, especially where serious crimes are involved and where they have requested such information;

(b) Allowing the views and concerns of victims to be presented and considered at appropriate stages of the proceedings where their personal interests are affected, without prejudice to the accused and consistent with the relevant national criminal justice system;

(c) Providing proper assistance to victims throughout the legal process;

(d) Taking measures to minimize inconvenience to victims, protect their privacy, when necessary, and ensure their safety, as well as that of their families and witnesses on their behalf, from intimidation and retaliation;

(e) Avoiding unnecessary delay in the disposition of cases and the execution of orders or decrees granting awards to victims.

7. Informal mechanisms for the resolution of disputes, including mediation, arbitration and customary justice or indigenous practices, should be utilized where appropriate to facilitate conciliation and redress for victims.

Restitution

8. Offenders or third parties responsible for their behaviour should, where appropriate, make fair restitution to victims, their families or dependents. Such restitution should include the return of property or payment for the harm or loss suffered, reimbursement of expenses incurred as a result of the victimization, the provision of services and the restoration of rights.

9. Governments should review their practices, regulations and laws to consider resolution as an available sentencing option in criminal cases, in addition to other criminal sanctions.

10. In cases of substantial harm to the environment, restitution, if ordered, should include, as far as possible, restoration of environment, reconstruction of the infrastructure, replacement of community facilities and reimbursement of the expenses of relocation, whenever such harm results in the dislocation of a community.

11. Where public officials or other agents acting in an official or quasi-official capacity have violated national criminal laws, the victims should receive restitution from the State whose officials or agents were responsible for the harm inflicted.

Compensation

12. When compensation is not fully available from the offender or other sources, States should endeavour to provide financial compensation to:

(a) Victims who have sustained significant bodily injury or impairment of physical or mental health as a result of serious crimes;

(b) The family, in particular dependents of persons who have died or become physically or mentally incapacitated as a result of such victimization.

13. The establishment, strengthening and expansion of national funds for compensation to victims should be encouraged.

Assistance

14. Victims should receive the necessary material, medical, psychological and social assistance through governmental, voluntary, community-based and indigenous means.

15. Victims should be informed of the availability of health and social services and other relevant assistance and be readily afforded access to them.

16. Police, justice, health, social service and other personnel concerned should receive training to sensitize them to the needs of victims, and guidelines to ensure proper and prompt aid.

17. In providing services and assistance to victims, attention should be given to those who have special needs because of the nature of the harm inflicted or because of factors such as those mentioned in paragraph 3 above.

Source: Edited and abridged from General Assembly Resolution 40/34 of 29 November, 1985

such as more stringent control of gun ownership are called for.

Some of the moderately affluent countries like South Africa, Argentina and Brazil seem, criminologically speaking, to be in double jeopardy. In their main cities fairly large groups of economically deprived adolescents converge with well-to-do members of middle classes, providing ample opportunities for crime. In addition, the level of gun ownership is high. Similar criminogenic situations arise in Western countries and countries in transition where income disparities are growing under the influence of global market forces and guns are becoming more widely available.

Victim empowerment

Modern criminal justice systems have traditionally been exclusively focused on the investigation of criminal cases and the prosecution, sentencing and punishment of offenders. In recent times criminal justice agencies in more and more countries have set themselves the task of rendering direct services to crime victims as an independent goal (Box 1.5). Many other governmental and voluntary organizations have also improved their provision of services to crime victims (Maguire and Pointing, 1988). International standards for this were formulated in the United Nations Declaration on the Basic Principles of Justice for Victims of Crime and Abuse of Power of 1985 (Box 1.4). By satisfactorily addressing the needs of victims that arise from their victimization, state agencies can help to empower them. Such victim empowerment has been shown to be of great psychological and practical importance for victims. The acknowledgment and practical and emotional support given by criminal justice personnel helps them to cope better with the consequences of their victimization and to regain their confidence in the state and the community at large.

For most crime victims the police is the single most important agency representing the criminal justice system. In the ICVS several questions deal with the interactions of the victims with the police.

Role of the victim in the criminal justice process

Sixteen out of the 30 nations (53 percent) supplying information to the *International Factbook of Criminal Justice Systems* stated that the victim does have a role beyond serving as a witness or providing evidence. The role is often of the nature of assisting at the trial, or formally appealing the prosecutor's decision not to prosecute or to dismiss the case. For example, in Hungary the victim can initiate the asking of questions at trial. In several countries, however, the prosecutor will not carry through with proceedings (in cases involving particular crimes) unless the victim initiates action. Also, in nations such as China and Hungary, there are certain circumstances where a case may be prosecuted privately, and in Venezuela, there are certain situations when a case *must* be prosecuted in this manner. This is not the same as a civil trial, and still involves criminal charges (rape is one of the crimes which is prosecuted in this manner in Venezuela).

For the most part, in countries where the victim has a role in some part of the criminal justice system, it is usually in the preparatory proceedings or during the trial itself. The victim usually has no part in the sentencing phase of the process, where such a separate stage exists in the legal system in question. There are some exceptions, however. For example, in the Republic of Ireland the victim is allowed to make a victim impact statement, and in Republic of Korea it is constitutionally prescribed that a victim may present his or her opinion during the sentencing phase (similar to a victim impact statement).

Finally, there does not seem to be a trend in terms of the "type" of nation which gives the victim a role in the criminal justice process. For example, there are both developed (e.g., Republic of Ireland) and developing (e.g., Costa Rica) countries that allow such a role, and there are also examples of both types of nations which do not allow the victim to play a part (e.g., Denmark and Sri Lanka, respectively). Also, nations with political systems ranging from communist to democratic can be found among those in which the victim does have a role. Conversely, there are a wide range of governing styles represented among nations which do not allow victim participation in the process.

Focus on England. There are specific helping agencies, such as Rape Crisis Centres, as well as a national umbrella organization known as the National Association of Victim Support Schemes. It provides a national voice to the victim movement, and also gives help on a case-by-case basis to victims referred by the police. Also, there is a Criminal Injuries Compensation Board which oversees a program for compensating victims of violent crime. This compensation occurs regardless of whether or not the offender is identified. Although the victim has no direct role in criminal prosecution, the United Kingdom has published a Victim's Charter which sets standards in order to guide criminal justice agencies in their interaction with victims.

Focus on Cuba. Cuba has organizations called Committees for the Defense of the Revolution (CDRs). These are neighborhood associations organized at the block level, and offer services such as medical care, social welfare assistance and counseling services to crime victims. These polyclinics are organized into a nationwide system. Even though it is evident that there is concern for giving assistance to victims, Cuba has no specific victims' rights legislation. Also, there are no special roles for victims in the criminal justice process, other than the standard functions of providing evidence and testimony at trial.

Does the victim have a role at any stage of the criminal justice process?

China	
Costa Rica	
Finland	
Germany	
Hungary	Australia
Italy	Bulgaria
Micronesia	Cuba
Netherlands	Denmark
Poland	England
Rep. of Ireland	Ghana
Romania	Israel
Russian Fed.	Kenya
Slovak Rep.	New Zealand
Slovenia	Papua N.G.
Republic of Korea	South Africa
Spain	Sri Lanka
Venezuela	Sweden
YES	NO

Is there any victim rights legislation?

Australia	
Bulgaria	
China	
Costa Rica	
Denmark	
England	
Germany	
India	
Israel	
Italy	
Japan	
Netherlands	
New Zealand	
Papua N. G.	Cuba
Rep. of Ireland	Micronesia
Russian Fed.	Kenya
Scotland	Romania
Slovak Republic	Slovenia
Republic of Korea	South Africa
Sweden	Sri Lanka
YES	NO

Source: Riviera (Original paper, 1997) adapted from the *International Factbook of Criminal Justice Systems*

Reporting to the police

Victims of crime were asked whether they or anybody else had reported the incident to the police. For all crimes together, the reporting rates are the highest in the New World countries (54 percent) and Western Europe (52 percent). Reporting rates are moderately high in Africa (40 percent) and in Central and Eastern Europe (35 percent). Reporting of crimes to the police is less common in Asia (31 percent) and Latin America (27 percent). In the latter region the reporting rates vary a lot across countries. It is low in Bolivia and Brazil but moderately high in Argentina (42 percent).

In general reporting percentages are higher for serious property offences such as car or motorcycle theft and burglary than for other types of crime.

Figure 1.5 shows that reporting of burglaries and violence against women is highest in New World nations and Western Europe. The reporting rates are much lower in

FIGURE 1.5
Percentages of offences victims who say they reported crime to the police in six global regions; results of the International Crime Victim Survey, 1989-1996, burglaries and violence against women

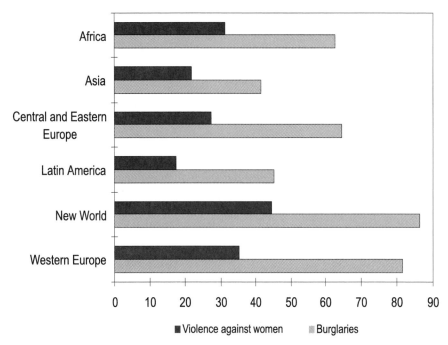

■ Violence against women   ▨ Burglaries

Source: van Dijk (1997b). See Notes to Figures for complete tabular information.

The "dark numbers" of property crimes are especially large in these countries. The prevailing modernist notion in comparative criminology that property crime rates are higher in the developed countries because of special opportunities for crime is untenable in the light of our findings. Previous empirical support for that notion has been largely based on a distorted picture of crime levels in developing countries given by police figures.

The reporting rates for contact crimes, and for violence against women in particular, are much lower in all six regions than those for property crimes. Globally, 39 percent of assaults on men are reported. The reporting rate of violence against women is even lower. Less than one in three instances of violence against women (non-sexual assaults and sexual assaults combined) are brought to the attention of the police (30 percent).

Police figures of various types of serious contact crimes reflect the small number of actual crimes ever reported to the police. Globally, the prevalence rate of serious violence against women, for example, is at least three times higher than indicated by police figures. Of the more serious types of crime, violence against women probably has the largest "dark numbers" (see also Box 2.7).

Asia, Central and Eastern Europe, Africa and Latin America. The difference is greatest for property crimes. The differences in reporting confirm the hypothesis that police figures in developing countries and countries in transition seriously underestimate the real level of crime.

Reasons for reporting and for non-reporting

An analysis at the level of individual victims showed that income level is the most important factor related to reporting of crimes.[17] The second most important factor is the perceived seriousness of the offence. Other relevant factors are age, level of education and gender. Older, better educated and male victims are somewhat more likely to report crimes to the police. In sum, victimizations which are more serious and concern socially established victims are most likely to be reported. Cases of assault are more likely to be reported if they are more seri-

TABLE 1.3
Reasons for not reporting crimes to the police in six global regions, five crimes combined (theft from cars, burglary with entry, robbery, sexual incidents and assaults/threats); International Crime Victim Survey, 1989-1996.

reasons no report	all	Africa	Asia	Central and Eastern Europe	Latin America	New World	Western Europe
number of countries	55	6	4	20	6	4	15
number of cases	35484	3494	2089	10101	4514	4917	10369
not serious	31	19	21	30	23	44	43
solved it	11	13	13	11	12	11	8
inappropriate	11	11	10	11	13	11	7
other authority	3	5	7	1	1	4	2
family	4	5	6	5	4	1	1
no insurance	2	1	2	3	4	1	2
could do nothing	21	21	24	29	23	12	18
will not do anything	16	11	13	19	37	6	9
fear/dislike	5	2	9	5	13	2	1
did not dare	5	7	4	4	4	8	2
other	9	6	7	6	4	18	14
do not know	2	1	.4	2	2	5	28

Source: van Dijk (1997b)

TABLE 1.4

Reasons for reporting burglaries and contact crimes to the police: International Crime Victim Survey 1996

Reasons for reporting	all	Africa	Asia	Central and Eastern Europe	Latin America	New World	Western Europe
number of countries	43	3	3	19	6	2	10
number of cases	3521	394	56	1463	461	253	895
Burglaries							
recover property	55	76	83	59	52	29	29
insurance	20	9	2	11	31	26	40
civic duty	36	25	45	35	21	44	45
offender caught	45	59	60	49	43	29	32
to stop it	30	21	61	25	35	21	17
to get help	15	23	26	12	11	10	9
other	5	1	0	2	4	14	11
do not know	0	0	0	2	0	0	0
Contact crimes							
recover property	22	2	40	20	31	7	9
insurance	10	4	5	4	36	4	6
should be	35	34	45	34	22	38	35
offender caught	48	56	67	48	48	39	33
to stop it	42	36	68	40	38	41	31
to get help	23	23	29	24	18	22	20
other	9	2	1	4	4	23	19
do not know	1	0	0	4	0	.0	0

Source: van Dijk (1997b)

ous in terms of injury and/or perceived seriousness and if the crime was committed by a known person. Statistically significant but less important factors are age, affluence and gender.[18]

Victims whose victimizations were not reported to the police were asked about their reasons for non-reporting to the police. The main reasons for non-reporting were that the incident was not serious enough or that the police could do nothing. The reasons for non-reporting are given in Table 1.3.

Victims in developing countries and countries in transition are less likely to say that their victimization was not serious enough for reporting to the police. This result is consistent with the higher seriousness scores given by crime victims in these countries. They more often say that the police could do nothing. A somewhat higher percentage of victims in Latin America said they feared or did not like the police and/or did not dare to report.

In the 1996 survey, those who had reported to the police were asked about their reasons. Previous analyses showed that sexual incidents and assaults/threats are re-

ported for different reasons than property offences. Table 1.4 shows the results for six regions for burglary and contact crimes.[19]

Victims of burglary quite often seek assistance of the police in recovering property. This is most notably the case in developing countries and countries in transition. Many victims wanted the offender to be caught and punished. Such retributive reasons were most evident in Asia and Africa. Many victims also referred to the moral obligation to report, especially in the Western countries and Asia. Insurance is a major reason for reporting in the more affluent countries. In the countries in transition this reason is often given by victims in Hungary (39 percent) and the Czech Republic (50 percent) where insurance is relatively common. In Latin America this reason is most often given in Argentina (42 percent) and Costa Rica (33 percent), where insurance is fairly common as well. In most African and many Asian and Latin American countries only between 10 and 20 percent of the respondents are insured against household burglary. In most industrialized countries the insurance rate is at least 70 percent. These differences go some way in explaining the lower

Globally, less than half of the victims who reported their cases to the police in 1996 were satisfied with the response.

reporting rate in the developing countries and countries in transition. In the latter countries victims report not to back up insurance claims but in the hope that their property will be reclaimed from the offender by the police. Financial considerations seem to play an important role in the expectations by victims of property crimes *vis a vis* the police.

As said, victims of contact crimes report to the police for different reasons. Victims of contact crimes were especially concerned with stopping what happened. Many also wanted help. Retributive reasons are also frequently mentioned. The moral obligation is again more in evidence in Asia than in Latin America.

The results concerning female victims of violence are similar. Globally, 50 percent want to stop what happened and 28 percent want to get help. There is little variation in this across regions.

Victims have a variety of reasons for reporting to the police, with moral, legal, financial and practical considerations all playing a role. Victims of violence often seek help from the police in a crisis situation. As noted earlier the lower levels of reporting of property crimes in Asia and Latin America and also in Africa and Central and Eastern Europe are related to a lower extent

of insurance cover. Lack of confidence in the police seems another determining factor behind non-reporting of crimes. The latter seems of significance for victims of violent crimes in particular. In some countries, notably in Latin America, fear or dislike of the police is also a factor. This issue is taken up again in the next section on victims' satisfaction.

Satisfaction with the police

All respondents who had reported a crime to the police over the last five years were asked whether they were satisfied with the way the police had dealt with their last report. The answers give an important performance indicator concerning the victim empowerment policies of the police. Globally, less than half of the victims who reported their cases to the police in 1996 were satisfied with the response.

Police forces around the world clearly have a long way to go to adequately empower crime victims. Satisfaction with the police was markedly higher in the Western countries. Even here, more than a quarter were dissatisfied though.

Since victims of property crimes report for different reasons than victims of violence, the levels of satisfaction may be different as well. Results for the six regions are given in Figure 1.6 for victims of burglary and victims of contact crimes.

Figure 1.6 shows that in the Western countries victims of contact crimes are less satisfied with the police response than victims of burglaries. One in three victims of contact crimes are dissatisfied. In the other regions the picture is reversed: more victims of contact crimes are satisfied than burglary victims. As a consequence the levels of satisfaction are less dissimilar across regions in the case of violent crimes than of property crimes. With regard to victims of violence the police in Western Europe are not performing much better than their counterparts in Asia.

Findings on the opinions of victims of assaults/threats and violence against women show a similar pattern. The relatively high level of satisfaction, however, must be seen against the background of relatively low reporting of such crimes.

Those who were dissatisfied were asked

FIGURE 1.6
Percentage of victims satisfied with the police after reporting burglaries and contact crimes respectively, in six global regions, results of the International Crime Victim Survey, 1996

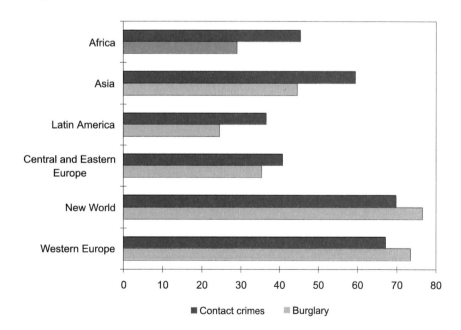

Source: van Dijk (1997b). See Notes to Figures for additional tabular information.

why they felt so. Table 1.5 shows that the most common reason for dissatisfaction was that the police "did not do enough" or "did not recover the goods." Roughly one in five victims were unhappy that the police did not keep them sufficiently informed. Some other main reasons given for dissatisfaction show interesting differences. In Asia, Latin America, Central and Eastern Europe and Africa, where satisfaction was relatively low, victims were more likely to be unhappy that the police did not recover their property or apprehend the offender. The reasons for dissatisfaction of Asian, African, Latin American and East European victims confirm that for them reporting is often motivated by the wish to reclaim stolen property. In more affluent nations, this financial consideration seems less pertinent because more victims are covered by insurance. This factor might well be one reason for the higher level of satisfaction with the police in Western countries. Victims whose losses are covered by insurance are less concerned about the outcome of the investigation. Such victims primarily want to be treated efficiently and with respect. Against this background the relatively high levels of satisfaction of burglary victims in the West are somewhat less impressive.

Around 13 percent of the dissatisfied victims said the police had been impolite or incorrect. Those in Asia were most likely to be dissatisfied for that reason. The latter finding suggests that in many Asian countries relationships between the victims and the police are particularly strained. As was previously stated, relatively many victims in these countries refrain from reporting because of fear or dislike of the police. Those that do report are indeed more likely to be dissatisfied with the treatment given because of impolite or incorrect behaviour on the part of the officers.

The reasons given for dissatisfaction by victims of contact crimes are fairly similar. The percentage of victims who felt the police did not do enough is high in all regions.

TABLE 1.5

Reasons for dissatisfaction with the police response, of victims of burglary and victims of contact crimes respectively, results of the 1996 International Crime Victim Survey

Reasons not satisfied	all	Africa	Asia	Central and Eastern Europe	Latin America	New World	Western Europe
number of countries	43	3	3	19	6	2	10
number of cases	1857	274	38	922	336	58	228
Burglary							
did not do enough	50	54	50	37	54	60	44
were not interested	29	21	18	32	37	37	33
did not find offender	37	33	55	44	35	28	26
did not recover goods	37	42	49	48	35	30	20
gave no information	20	16	9	13	23	30	27
incorrect/impolite	13	7	20	6	19	15	8
slow to arrive	15	26	16	9	8	18	14
other	9	6	2	5	4	19	21
do not know	1	0	0	1	1	5	0
Contact crime							
did not do enough	40	46	50	34	47	32	34
were not interested	29	22	34	29	43	18	30
did not find offender	25	30	35	29	31	12	16
did not recover goods	19	20	27	27	20	12	10
gave no information	16	16	27	10	17	10	14
incorrect/impolite	14	16	25	10	17	8	10
slow to arrive	9	11	16	7	8	7	7
other	9	11	0	45	2	18	15
do not know	0	0	0	2	0	0	.4

Source: van Dijk (1997b)

The complaint that the police had been impolite was also mentioned by about 15 percent of the victims, although this reason was given less often in Europe and the New World. Interestingly, this reason was most often mentioned by women who were victims of violence. Globally, one in five women who were dissatisfied mentioned this reason. In Latin America it was mentioned by one in three.

The findings indicate that the police in most countries fail to satisfy the demands of a large part of reporting victims. Dissatisfaction is the highest among victims of burglaries and other property crimes in less affluent countries where victims are dependent on the police for recovering their property or claiming compensation. In all regions, dissatisfaction is also high among victims of contact crimes. Victims of violence report crimes to stop what was happening and/or to get help. Obviously the police fail to satisfy these demands in many cases.

The findings indicate that the police in most countries fail to satisfy the demands of a large part of reporting victims.

In countries where levels of satisfaction of reporting burglary victims are lower, reporting rates are lower too.

Need for victim support

In the 1996 survey victims of more serious crimes who had reported to the police were specifically asked whether they had received support from a specialized agency. Figure 1.7 shows the results.

In most countries few victims had received such help. Of those who reported burglaries to the police four percent had received help. The level of support was the highest in the Western European countries. The level of support in these countries is generally a good deal higher than in previous sweeps of the ICVS. The United Kingdom stands out with a help rate of one in five (21 percent).

Of all victims of contact crimes[20] who reported to the police seven percent had been given such help. The highest help rates were in the New World countries and Western Europe. In this part of the world, levels of support for victims of violence have gone up over the past years. In all other countries lower percentages of such victims had been clients of victim support schemes.

Globally, ten percent of female victims of violence who had reported to the police had received specialized support. In the New World countries this percentage was 29 and

---

BOX 1.6

Rights of victims of crime in China

In the Chinese criminal procedure law, crimes are categorized as publicly prosecuted cases and privately prosecuted cases. Privately prosecuted cases are for some minor offences such as insult, defamation, abuse of family members, interference with force with the freedom of marriage and other minor offences against which the victim has conclusive evidence. Victims have different rights in these two categories of cases.

In the privately prosecuted cases, no public prosecutor finds an indictment before the court. The victim of crime brings a prosecution directly to court against his or her victimizer. The judge hears the case much as is done in civil procedure. As one of the contesting parties, the victim has the following rights:

to withdraw prosecution from court against the victimizer;

to bring a civil suit in the court on the damages for compensation by the victimizer;

to authorize somebody to represent him or her in the court;

to require the judge to call new witnesses;

to ask withdrawal of a judge or identifier;

to question the defendant, witness and identifier; and

to lodge an appeal against a sentence or decision.

The privately prosecuted cases represent a small part of crimes prosecuted in the court. The majority of crimes are prosecuted by public prosecutors. Before 1996, the publicly prosecuted cases were seen as the state's cases against the accused. In these cases, the victim was not one of the parties of the ongoing criminal lawsuit between the state and the accused, but seen as one of the participants in the proceedings and had fewer rights than he or she did in the cases prosecuted by the victim. In April 1996, China revised its criminal procedure law. In the revised law, the victim in the cases prosecuted by public prosecutors is taken as one of the parties except that the public prosecutor and his or her rights have increased.

Right to prosecute the accused. Traditionally, the state monopolizes the right to accuse an individual who commits a crime, especially a felony, since crimes are considered as threats to the social order and hostile attacks to the state which represents all the people. The revised criminal procedure law, however, breaches this tradition. It provides that the victim of crime may prosecute directly in court his or her victimizer "if he or she has enough evidence to prove the defendant should bear criminal responsibility for his/her act that violates the victim's rights of person or property and that the police or the prosecutor's office has decided not to investigate the defendant's responsibility" (Article 170).

Right to ask withdrawal of judge, prosecutor or identifier. If the responsible judge, prosecutor, police officer, court clerk, court translator or identifier has any relationship which may impose negative impact on fair judgment, the victim may ask any of them to withdraw from the positions they are holding in the court (Articles 28-29).

Right to make statement on the facts of crime and question defendant, witnesses and identifier in the court. As the revised criminal procedure law provides, the victim may make a statement on the facts of the crime, the impact the crime has imposed on him or her and the punishment he or she hopes to be applied to the defendant. The victim may question the defendant, witnesses and identifier before the court if he or she wishes to do so during the court investigation of the facts of crime.

Right to ask prosecutor to contest a judgment. If the victim disagrees with the sentence or decision made by the court, he or she may ask the prosecutor to contest it, although the victim cannot appeal to a higher court. The prosecutor's office must make a decision on whether it will contest the judgment or decision within five days after it receives the request of the victim. A higher court will try the case as a case of second instance and make a new judgment or decision which may overturn the judgment or decision made by a lower court.

Restitution over fine. In March, 1997, China revised its criminal law one year after its criminal procedure law was amended. The revised criminal law provides that, if a defendant is ordered to make restitution to the victim and a fine has been imposed, and his or her property is not enough to pay both, he or she should pay restitution to the victim first (Article 36).

Limitation of prosecution not working after reporting to criminal justice systems by victim. The revised criminal law provides that the offender will not be prosecuted beyond the prescribed limitation of prosecution. However, if the victim reports the crime to the police, but the prosecutor's office or court does not put it on record for investigation, the limitation of prosecution does not apply. Under such circumstances, the offender may be prosecuted beyond the limitation of prosecution set for his or her crime.

Source: Guo Jianan (Original paper, 1997)

in Western Europe 22. Elsewhere it was much lower.

Globally, much lower percentages of male victims of assaults received specialized help (4 percent).

Victims who had not received help from a specialized agency were asked whether they would have appreciated help in getting information, and practical or emotional support. Most victims of burglary and contact crimes reported that they would have welcomed specialized help.[21]

Two-thirds of victims of serious crimes who had reported to the police indicated an unmet need for help. Levels of demand were highest in Central and Eastern Europe, Asia, Africa and Latin America. There is obviously a huge gap between the need for such help and its actual provision.

These findings show that the standards for victim empowerment of the UN Declaration of Basic Principles of Justice for Victims of Crime and Abuse of Power are not sufficiently implemented. In relation to this, many victims are reluctant to report crimes to the police. This lack of confidence in the police implies that crime victims have often no authority to turn to and feel alienated (Box 1.5). Low reporting rates are also an impediment for effective crime prevention and control. The chances of arresting the offender and getting a conviction are largely dependent on the information supplied by the victim. If many victims are doubtful whether reporting to the police will do them any good, as is clearly the case in most developing nations, the effectiveness of the police is severely undermined. For more effective criminal investigations the cooperation of the victims is essential. This is another reason why the proportion of satisfied victims ought to be used as a performance measure for criminal investigation agencies.

FIGURE 1.7

Percentages of victims of burglaries, contact crimes and violence against women who received help from a specialized agency; results of the International Crime Victim Surveys, 1996

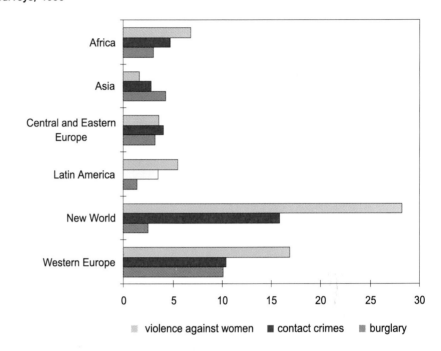

Source: van Dijk (1997b). See Notes to Figures for complete tabular information.

SUMMARY

THINGS IN COMMON	THINGS DIVERSE
• There is remarkable agreement around the world concerning the comparative seriousness of crimes. • All major and minor types of crime: burglary, robbery, assault, car theft, are recognized all over the world, no matter what region. • No matter what part of the world, over a five year period, two out of three of the inhabitants of big cities are victimized by crime at least once. • The chances globally to be victimised by serious contact crimes (robbery, sexual crimes or assault) are one in five. • The prevalence of both property crime and violent crimes is related to problems of economic hardship among the young no matter what region. • Violence against women is, like most serious crime, related to economic hardship. It is inversely related to the social status of women. • Globally, two in three victims of burglaries report their victimization to the police. Less than one in three female victims of violence do so. • Globally, victims feel alienated with no authority to turn to for help. Two-thirds of victims of serious crimes who had reported to the police indicated an unmet need of help. • Globally, less than half of the victims who reported their cases to the police were satisfied with the response	• Risks of being victimized are highest in Latin America and (sub-Saharan) Africa • The New World countries stand out with the highest rates of assaults on men. Violence against women is the most prevalent in Latin America, Africa and in the New World countries. • Where more people are economically deprived, crime rates are higher • The level of some property crimes such as vehicle crimes is related to ownership rates. Where more people drive around in cars and/or bicycles, more of those vehicles are stolen. • Where women are more emancipated, the rates of violence against women are lower. • Reporting is particularly low in the countries of Asia and Latin America. Only one in five of serious cases of violence are ever brought to the attention of the police. • Levels of demand for help among victims were highest in Central and Eastern Europe, Asia, Africa and Latin America. • Levels of satisfaction with the police are the lowest among victims in Latin America, Central and Eastern Europe and Africa.

CHAPTER 2

Police records of crime

Contributing author: Chris Lewis

Introduction

Chapter 1 concentrated on measures of crime obtained from victimization surveys. Useful though such surveys are, most countries find them very expensive to undertake and tend to use the more traditional measure of crime, that of **offences recorded by the police.** In the five UNCJS the traditional police measure of crime has been included each time. This chapter concentrates on this measure.

Problems in interpreting figures on recorded crime

As described in the Introduction to this report, despite attempts by the United Nations Survey of Crime Trends and Criminal Justice Systems to ensure that all countries follow the same definitions of crime, the legal and administrative systems of each country often constrain the statistics that are available. And although countries were asked to explain variations from standard definitions, to give all possible caveats about comparisons would make this chapter unreadable. The inquiring reader is urged to consult the original data bases freely available on the World Wide Web (http://www.ifs.univie.at/~uncjin/stats.html), the additional data in the notes to this volume, and the additional caveats outlined in the Introduction to this report.

Because of these problems, comments are restricted to those data which seem nevertheless to be most rigorous: less attention is given to detailed crime rates in favour of broad crime levels and small differences between countries are overlooked in favour of broad trends in crime rates.

BOX 2.1

Difficulties in interpreting recorded crime statistics

Despite all care, because the figures on which this chapter are based have been taken from a large scale collection system, involving many different people using several different languages, there will be occasional errors. At times, differences in the figures may represent differences in the circumstances of the countries reporting the figures rather than differences in the amount of crime.

The following caveats should be held in mind when reading this report.

Police recorded figures are not the same as the total amount of crime in a country:
- Many crimes are not reported to the police.
- Many events reported as crimes are not actually crimes and the police may not record them.
- The police may, for various other reasons, decide not to record the event as a crime.
- They may have already recorded it when reported by someone else.
- Local counting rules may mean they have already recorded an associated more serious offence.
- To improve their records, they may decide not to record some crimes unless they can also record they have solved them.
- In some circumstances police may wish to show their area to be safer than it is.

Comparisons across countries are not always valid:
- The structure and number of police personnel varies in different countries.
- The number of private security guards varies, for example, and crimes reported to them may not be recorded centrally.
- The amount of central control (e.g., in the definition of the figures) varies.
- Some countries count crimes when the police get to know about them, and some when the police choose to pass details on to prosecuting authorities.

The legal definition of a crime can vary from one country to another:
- Counting crime is a complex business; there is no international set of standards in defining crime.
- Types of crime which seem to be comparable are often not (e.g., comparisons of homicide are confounded by how deaths from drunken driving are recorded).

Differences in countries' social environment will also affect the crime figure comparison:
- Countries where telephones are more common will tend to report a higher proportion of crime.
- Countries where household insurance is more developed will also report a higher proportion.
- This is modified in some developed countries where household insurance premiums have been lowered for "no claims," leading to falls in crime reporting.
- Countries where police forces use more advanced technology tend to capture a higher proportion of actual crime.
- Comparisons of serious violent crime can be dependent on the availability of medical facilities (e.g., incidents which would be homicide in some countries can sometimes be avoided if medical care is available).

Comparisons across time may also be invalid due to changes in legal definitions, country boundaries and recording practices.

Source: Lewis (Original paper, 1997)

Definitions of recorded crime used in the Fifth UN Survey of Crime Trends and Operation of Criminal Justice Systems (UNCJS)

Intentional homicide refers to death deliberately inflicted on a person by another person, including infanticide. Countries were asked to indicate whether certain categories were charged or prosecuted as "aggravated assault."

Non-intentional homicide refers to death not deliberately inflicted on a person by another person. This includes the crime of manslaughter, but excludes traffic accidents that result in the death of persons.

Assault refers to physical attack against the body of another person, including battery but excluding indecent assault. Some criminal or penal codes distinguish between aggravated and simple assault depending on the degree of resulting injury. Countries were asked to provide the major criterion for this distinction if it applied in their country.

Rape refers to sexual intercourse without valid consent. Countries were asked to indicate whether statutory rape was included in the figures provided.

Theft refers to the removal of property without the property owner's consent. Theft excludes burglary or housebreaking. It includes the theft of a motor vehicle. Shoplifting and other minor offences (e.g., pilfering and petty theft) may or may not be included as thefts. Countries were asked to provide details.

Robbery refers to the theft of property from a person, overcoming resistance by force or threat of force.

Burglary refers to unlawful entry into someone else's property with an intention to commit a crime.

Fraud refers to the acquisition of the property of another by deception. Countries were asked to give details of whether the fraudulent obtaining of financial property was included.

Embezzlement refers to the wrongful appropriation of property of another which is already in one's possession.

Drug-related crimes refers to intentional acts that may involve cultivation, production, manufacture, extraction, preparation, offering for sale, distribution, purchase, sale, delivery on any terms whatsoever, brokerage, dispatch in transit, transport, importation and exportation of drugs and isotropic substances. Separate statistics on possession and traffic were requested.

Bribery and corruption refers to requesting and/or accepting material or personal benefit, or promise thereof, in connection with the performance of a public function or an action that may or may not be a violation of law and/or promising as well as giving material or personal benefit to a public officer in exchange for a requested favour.

Other refers to serious types of crime completely different from those listed above and regarded as serious and frequent enough to require a separate category in the criminal statistics of a particular country. Countries were asked to provide details.

Crimes recorded by the police refers to the number of penal code offences or their equivalent (i.e., various special law offences) but excluding minor road traffic and other petty offences, brought to the attention of the police or other law enforcement agencies and recorded by one of those agencies.

Source: United Nations Office at Vienna, Crime Prevention and Criminal Justice Division. Questionnaire of the Fifth UNCJS (1990-1994)

Definitions of recorded crime in the police figures

Figures on police recorded crime were collected by a questionnaire completed at the national level. The figures for the five years collected in each survey are generally comparable, but slight changes to the questionnaire between surveys or in the interpretation of the questionnaire can mean that comparisons between surveys are not so accurate. For this reason most of the comments in this chapter have been made on the Fifth UN Survey, covering the years 1990-1994.

The survey asked for data on the total recorded offences for each calendar year for homicides (total, intentional and non-intentional), frauds, assaults, embezzlements, rapes, drug-related crime, thefts, bribery and corruption, robberies, other types of serious crime, burglaries, and total recorded crime. The full definitions of these crime types can be found in Box 2.2.

Definition of police used in the UNCJS

Police or the law enforcement sector refers to public agencies whose principal functions are the prevention, detection and investigation of crime and the apprehension of alleged offenders. Countries differ in whether a prosecutor is a member of a separate agency or a member of the police or judiciary, and this can change in an individual country from time to time (e.g., in England and Wales a separate prosecuting agency was set up in 1986 to replace prosecuting authorities which had previously been associated with the police).

Many countries have several police systems, and the interpretation of the police numbers given in the survey is difficult. Countries with a federal structure often have provincial police; others may have police whose jurisdiction only extends to particular areas of the country (e.g., the capital city, royal parks, safari parks) and other police may have jurisdiction over certain types of offences (e.g., fraud, illegal trafficking in antiques, environmental crimes). In some countries there is no clear distinction between some police forces and some military units. The typical duties, even of regular police, may vary considerably from country to country. In fact, the day to day activities of the police officer may affect how and what is recorded as a crime, and even the level or rank of a police officer also contributes to what events are recorded as crimes. Examples of typical day to day activities of police in Thailand (Box 2.4), Japan (Box 8.4) and particularly China (Box 2.5), where police have extensive crime and other recording responsibilities, demonstrate how crimes may or may not end up as recorded statistics. Also to be noted is how police recording practices vary enormously from country to country, depending on the perceived and actual function of the police.

In more recent years, more and more policing functions have been taken over by private security employees (e.g., in shops, apartment buildings, hospitals, schools, etc.). Such guards typically do not have the right of arrest or investigation but are often the recipients of reports about crime. More detail can be found in Chapter 5 concerning private police. There are many countries without national crime reporting systems that nevertheless utilize local police recording of crime as their source of crime statistics. Other issues in regard to reporting and recording crime at the national and international levels are also discussed in the Introduction to this volume.

Public confidence in justice and crime reporting

"Modern methods of countering crime require public confidence in all crime prevention agencies and government departments responsible for eliminating long term causes of crime — and not just the police. The media's role is especially important. Without this, progress is impossible" (Lee and Klipin, 1997). This quotation relates to the present day situation in South Africa, but applies to all countries at all times.

The amount of crime the public reports to the police is directly proportional to the confidence the public has in the police, especially in whether the police are likely to be able to solve the crime experienced (Box 2.3 and see Chapter 1).

The reporting rate will also depend on whether the victim has any other means at his or her disposal (such as by taking action against the offender or reporting the incident to someone other than the police). For example, another member of the family or group, a private security guard, or some person in authority such as the headmaster of a school, the manager of a shop or a religious leader may be in a better position to address the crime than the police.

In many countries, especially the emerging market economies, the private security industry is very important, and very large numbers of such people are employed, often by the government (see Box 5.2).

BOX 2.3

Public confidence and crime prevention

The public, in various forms, participates in crime prevention in a number of ways. The now almost universally accepted model of successful crime prevention is based on:

- government accountability;
- investigation, detection and arrest of criminals;
- trials and sentencing;
- imprisonment and rehabilitation;
- partnership policing; and
- other partnership arrangements.

The public largely participates in this model by entering into individual and/or group cooperation with the police service and other elements of the justice system. However, in a democratic state, the accountability for crime prevention is ultimately in the hands of government as a whole. No other entity in a country can exercise this function — or should try to do so. The most important reason for this is that crime prevention and crime control will at some point involve the use of force and coercion — something which only the government can legitimately exercise in respect of its own citizens. The second reason is that many causes of crime can only be removed through government action.

This means that public involvement in crime prevention will always take the form of a partnership with the agencies of government. According to this model, public confidence in the process is critical. There are several ways of measuring public confidence in crime prevention measures. The most obvious is to ask the respondents how confident they are that crime prevention agencies are coping with crime. Another way is to ask people what can be done about crime. Yet another way of estimating public confidence is to ask people how safe they feel under the existing crime prevention systems. In terms of business perceptions, another indication of confidence is the decision to invest in the expansion of the businesses. *Finally, a key indicator of public confidence in the justice system is the willingness to report crime.*

Studies of all these types have been carried out recently in South Africa. In particular, a recent University of South Africa study confirmed results from many other countries that only 58 percent of victims reported to the police crimes committed against them. This varied from 94 percent for car theft to 3 percent for police corruption.

The media's role in all this is very important. By focusing on crimes that are committed, rather than on arrests and prosecutions, the public perception is that crime occurs without restraint. Also, this creates confidence in criminals who believe they can get away with murder because there is no evidence to the contrary. Finally, such media coverage creates demand for rapid action which may not be effective.

Source: Edited and abridged from Lee and Klipin (1997)

In many cases those in authority will choose not to take the case further, but rather will deal with it themselves without calling in the police. In such cases the authority will deal directly with the offender (i.e., by invoking disciplinary proceedings if the offender is an employee), or by employing informal criminal justice proceedings (i.e., in countries such as Nigeria; see Box 5.1). Such crimes are unlikely to be recorded by the official police, who would likely not regard them as part of their work load even if they knew about them.

This relationship between public confidence in crime prevention and the public preparedness to report crime is further discussed in Box 2.3.

A Thai police interrogation officer reports on his daily duties

After my graduation from the Royal Thai Police Academy in 1990, I was assigned to one of the police stations of the Metropolitan Police Bureau in Bangkok, Thailand. As a police officer, my primary responsibility was interrogation. I normally worked six hour shifts and rested 12 hours. The work schedule normally included four consecutive shifts followed by a day off. More specifically, I worked midnight shift (12 AM to 6 AM), morning shift (6 AM to 12 PM), afternoon shift (12 PM to 6 PM), and evening shift (6 PM to 12 AM) followed by a rest day. However, the schedules of detective, patrol and other officers are different from the interrogation officers.

Thai police interrogators must keep all records and evidence in a case from the beginning of each case until they have enough information and evidence to support the guilt of the accused. Then they collect all the records and pass them to the prosecutors. All crimes and complaints are recorded. That is the law. Further, anyone can ask the police to officially record their cases in the daily records, even if there is no crime involved. All records are maintained on a daily basis and can be presented as the evidence in court. The police make the decision whether or not to record an event. In principle, the law does not provide that kind of discretion, but in reality all police have to make the decision of which case will be recorded.

As an interrogation police officer, I worked with a wide variety of police professionals such as detectives, patrol officers, traffic officers, as well as the general population. My responsibility was to interrogate plaintiffs to determine if a criminal offence has actually occurred. The process would generally include identifying the charge, searching for evidence and witnesses, and interrogation to produce the case file. The file is then brought to prosecutors to be produced in the court. In sum, I work with a case from the moment a report is made until the time I produce evidence in the court on behalf of the state. Because of the variety of tasks an interrogation officer undertakes, the officers generally have considerable discretion.

Compared to detectives and patrol officers who basically arrest criminals and spend most of their time outside the station, an interrogation officer is assigned and expected to be at the station all the time except when he works on a case searching for evidence and witnesses. During the time that I worked, the afternoon shift and the evening shift were always busy. The midnight and the morning shifts were usually slow unless there was a big accident or a murder case. Apart from criminal cases, the interrogation officer is also responsible for determining fines for traffic violations.

I worked closely with detectives, patrol officers, as well as their supervisors. While patrol officers handed over to me criminal suspects, detectives received preliminary investigation reports from me to track the case. However, both detectives and patrol officers normally took the witness stand in each of the cases they worked. This meant that I had to interrogate the concerned officers about the case. Sometimes, it was difficult to get support from the other divisions within the same police station, particularly from detectives and patrol officers according to the chain of command. They are ranked lower than interrogation officers but they are under their own line-supervisors who are ranked the same as the interrogation officers. Generally, both of them have their own jobs to perform. If they are busy, the chance that I could get some support from them was less.

The police station in which I worked is located in the middle of Bangkok which is the old-town area. The town is congested with buildings, small streets, and many people. This area is generally referred to as Chinatown. The population consists of an equal distribution of the affluent, middle, working classes, and the poor. Though the majority are Chinese, other racial groups also live in this area. Because support within the police station is normally difficult to obtain, most interrogation officers normally get some help from the Chinese Foundation in some important cases such as homicide or those which involve a lot of people. The Foundation's workers, who normally work as a support group to interrogation officers, do not carry weapons. However, they tune into the police radio channel and keep abreast of various cases.

Source: Thakoon Nimsombun (Original paper, 1997), Police Lieutenant of the Royal Thai Police Department

Methodology for recorded crime figures

There is no one accepted methodology for defining, collecting, analyzing or publishing crime figures. There are elements of good practice as outlined in the Introduction to this volume. However, each country interprets this good practice in its own way. This interpretation is heavily dependent on the administrative system of each country, its state of development, and the amount of money it is able to spend on collecting and analyzing information about crime.

As a country's development progresses, its ability to cope with more sophisticated crime recording systems will grow also. Better systems come with growth in the availability of telephones to the general population, and progress in education, both among those collecting the data and those analyzing it. Also, the stability of a country's administrative system is very important for good crime figures. Countries which have undergone many recent changes in their form of government and administration are unlikely to have stabilized their crime data collections.

Developments in police technology are important: the easier it is to record crime, the more likely it is for crime to be recorded accurately and completely. This technology factor may contribute considerably to the body of data that is finally reported as a country's national statistics. Thus, in comparing crime rates between technologically developed and less developed countries, as will be attempted later in this chapter, the differential recording factor related to technology must always be considered. Box 2.6 gives an example of how police technology may affect crime recording. For a broader view of the different levels of police technology among countries, see Chapter 5.

Interpretation of police data based on the United Nations surveys

Global view of crime

All UN member states were asked to complete the UNCJS but recorded crime figures were received from at most 60 to 70 countries. This limits our ability to present information. Figures 2.1 and 2.2 show the gen-

BOX 2.5

A police officer's day and role in crime recording in China

The Peoples' Republic of China has two million police who are under the Ministry of Public Security. The Ministry has police agencies at the regional, provincial and municipal level, as well as police stations with Dispatch Posts in neighborhoods of the cities, towns and villages. The police maintain the peace, prevent crime, investigate criminal cases, protect the community and have a host of other duties (Lian, 1997). This box details a typical daily schedule of a Public Security officer. The Public Security officers comprise over 40 percent of the Public Security personnel, and their role involves contact with the ordinary citizens in their neighborhoods.

Huang Hai Wang. This Public Order officer serves in a Dispatch Post, a neighbourhood police unit, and satellite of the Chao Yang precinct station in Shenyang city, north central China. Mr. Wang is a 35 year old married man with one child and a high school education. He is typical of police persons holding the most common position in the Ministry of Public Security (police). The Public Order officer is at the lowest level of the national Ministry of Public Security hierarchy.

Mr. Wang works and lives in Chenyang, a crowded industrial city with over six million inhabitants who live very close together in large apartment buildings. Rapid development is at its peak here. Many buildings are going up to handle the large and growing population. People live in small apartments. Officer Wang lives in one such apartment in the area of the Post. His apartment is one of several provided to public servants by a local government factory. Fellow officers may live in similar apartment buildings constructed by the Ministry of Public Security for police and their families.

At 8 AM Public Order Officer Wang arrives by bicycle to the Dispatch Post where he works with 18 other police, some of whom are classified as Census Police and Criminal Police. Post officers are responsible for a small geographical area in which at least 20,000 people live. The Post is a substation to a district police station. The station or precinct is much like a central police station in the United States and other countries where a large number of police are involved in more complicated operations. The Dispatch Post could be compared to neighbourhood police boxes found in Korea and Japan (see Box 8.4).

Daily Routine. Officer Wang works seven days a week, eight hours a day. In addition, he is on duty once a week for 24 hours, and he remains overnight at the Post. With so much time spent at the Post, it is common for officers to spend off duty evenings at the Post talking and playing in the Post recreation room.

The police operate out of the Post in the neighbourhoods where citizens reside. They comprise over 40 percent of the Chinese police organization. They are not considered patrolmen in the western sense. Recently, China set up small police units called "Police patrolmen," but their duties are to walk the streets of business areas in the city and control crime. They have little contact with large numbers of citizens.

Officer Wang begins the work day scrutinizing or writing reports from the previous days and meeting with other officers of the Post. Census Officer units are part of the Post complement. Their duties include recording of births and deaths in the area. They keep track of who moves in and out of the area, grant permission for people to move out of the area, teach new mothers about child care, and even discuss with the parents a newborn's future. Crime Investigation Officers, a third police group at the Post, investigate crimes occurring in the Post precincts. Female police officers are most represented in this group.

Written records are kept at the Post on all citizens in the area, including citizen movements, population losses and gains, criminal records and other personal information. These records are kept updated. The intelligence gathered is to keep the government abreast of citizen behaviour. The files on citizens also determine food rations distribution, and the number of children entering school at all levels. The information is probably not seen as an oppressive measure by most citizens, but more as organized information which promotes the community and offers opportunities for life betterment for individuals.

Officer Wang spends part of the morning meeting citizens at the Post. People are making complaints, asking for permission to move away or telling of relatives who are coming into the area. Mr. Wang may make decisions about what to do with persons who are not following the local rules and policies set down by the central government. He and other officers will check public establishments, restaurants, dance halls, and meeting places. Some mornings each month he visits local schools to develop crime prevention programmes. Another two days a week he will teach the children about legal concepts and what are the characteristics of a good Chinese citizen.

Officer Wang spends the afternoon making contacts with the Public Security Committee operating in each neighborhood. The Public Security Committee office is manned by 20 volunteers. There are about 18 such offices in the territory of each Security Post. Each Committee office utilizes 20 to 30 lay people volunteers who are from that neighbourhood. They are retired teachers, military members and government officials who have free time and are elected by the citizens in the neighbourhood. Their role is to look for strangers and strange happenings, report problems among local citizens, and report law breaking to the Public Security Officer assigned to their neighbourhood. Each volunteer deals with 100 citizens.

Officer Wang gathers and exchanges information at the Public Security Committee office, completes forms, and writes about the situation of individual citizens in his/her neighbourhood. This information will be transferred to files at the Post and be the gist of written information passed on to the higher levels of the Public Security System.

The Public Security Committee members multiply the hands of the Public Security Officer, both as a source of social control and intelligence at the grass roots level. This intelligence/public service operation is much more involved than the police boxes of Japan (see Box 8.4). Interestingly, Officer Wang and his police counterparts minimize visiting citizens in their homes. Such home visits raise fear in those being visited. They meet in the Public Security Office which is a neutral area for both police and citizen.

Compilation of information on individual citizens in China is extensive. It seems that the public security officers at the local community level have the obligation to keep the records. Writing down information is the main vehicle of compiling intelligence. The officer writes down the information and sees that it is filed. In the Post there is one secretary who may use a typewriter. The information gathered is stored in files for each citizen. The Public Order Officer spends a lot of time with citizens. As in any bureaucracy, the Public Order Officer spends a great deal of time compiling and organizing records on the citizens and their activities. Police are not seen as servants of the people but as personnel representing the overriding presence of the government in keeping track of, and controlling the people. Behaviour control is high. Crime rates are low.

Source: Hoffman (Original paper, 1997)

FIGURE 2.1
World homicide rates, 1994 (per million population)

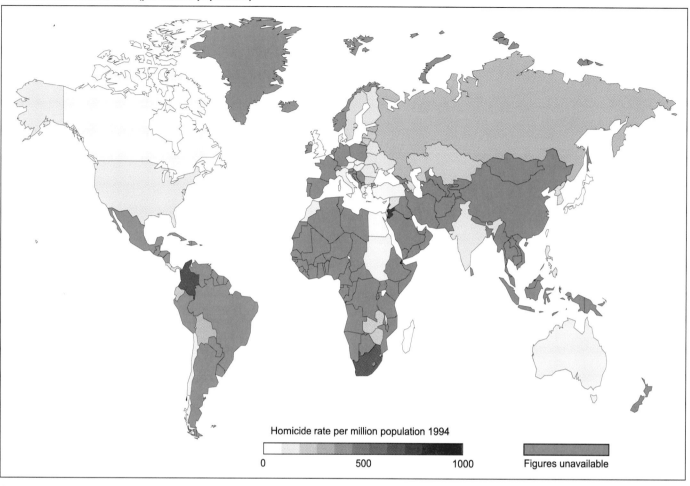

Homicide rate per million population 1994

0   500   1000   Figures unavailable

Source: Fifth UNCJS. See tables of raw data in Notes to Figures. Note: map is not to scale. The boundaries shown on this map do not imply official endorsement or acceptance by the UN.

BOX 2.6

Police technology and crime recording

Police in Derbyshire Constabulary in England and Wales have recently improved their technology for crime recording, which has greatly simplified the process.

Previously it took as long as 60 minutes to complete the process since a crime needs to be reported accurately. The officer on the beat would arrive at the scene of a crime and, after taking down all the details of the incident, would return to the police station to type up his notes for storage on the police computer system. As well as taking time, this reinforced public perception that the police were never around when wanted.

In collaboration with communications and software companies, Derbyshire police proposed a mobile voice and data so-

lution that involved giving officers palmtop computers and mobile phones. On arriving at the scene of the crime, all the details are entered on the digital notepad and, using the phone, the crime reports are then downloaded to the relevant police computer.

The palmtop computer has the ability to recognize handwriting which means that it is simple to enter scene of crime information. Once this is done, the only task is for the police officer to dial up the computer and transmit the data down the line.

Logging the data this way takes between ten and 15 minutes, compared with an hour before. The system is more accurate and subsequent retrieval is a great deal easier. Also police can interrogate the computer systems directly from their palmtop computer.

Edited and abridged from *Solving the Time Crime*, p. 23. Government Computing, Volume 11, No.6, London, 1997

eral patterns of crime rates throughout the world and the geographical pattern for homicide and theft rates. These are two offences for which reporting was quite high; however, figures are still unavailable for substantial areas of the world. As the figures show, the main areas for completeness of returns are Western and Eastern Europe.

Reports of crime are dominated by property crime, mainly theft and burglary (Figure 2.3). Theft comprises around half of all reported crime and burglary a further 20 percent. Personal crime constitutes a much smaller proportion, with assaults forming about seven percent and robberies a further six percent. Drug related crime made up about six percent.

This general pattern varies greatly throughout the world, however (Table 2.1). As a proportion of total reported crime, theft comprises as little as 20 percent in some countries but over 60 percent in others.

FIGURE 2.2
World theft rates, 1994 (per 10,000 population)

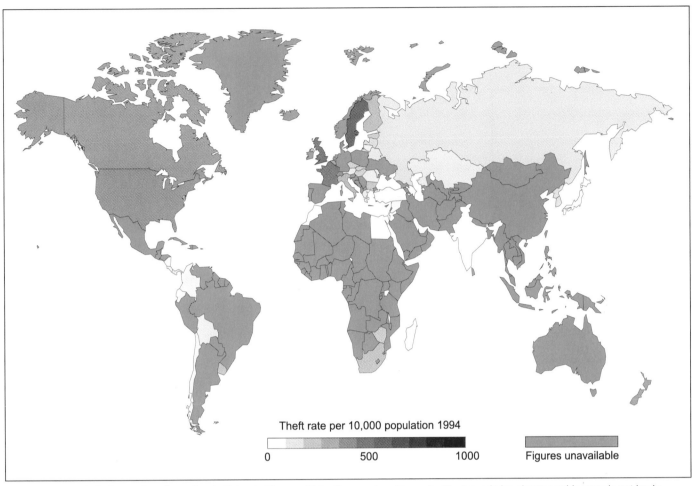

Theft rate per 10,000 population 1994

0   500   1000   Figures unavailable

Source: Fifth UNCJS. See tables of raw data in Notes to Figures. Note: the map is not to scale. The boundaries shown on this map do not imply official endorsement or acceptance by the UN.

Similarly, as a proportion of total reported crime, robbery comprises under one percent in most Western European countries but over ten percent in several Latin American countries.

Does reported crime change over time?

Reported crime changes considerably over time. Crime rates change at different rates for different offences and for different countries. Some of these changes, especially those between two different UN surveys, are almost certainly partly due to changes in definition of what is reported to the UN, or to boundary or legislative changes in the reporting country (see the Introduction to this volume). Where it is known that the changes are due to such factors they have been excluded from the analysis. Changes for the period 1990-1994 are more stable because the figures all come from the Fifth UNCJS.

However, changes over a longer period are likely to be more interesting, but are less easy to interpret because more than one UNCJS was involved.

Changes 1990-1994

For all types of offences, more countries reported an increase in crime over the period 1990 to 1994 than reported a stable situation or a decrease. The position is shown in Figure 2.4.

A large number of countries, however, showed a fall in crime over the period, with 17 out of 69 countries showing a fall in total crime and as many as 26 out of 60 countries showing a fall in robbery figures. In contrast, only seven countries reported that drug offences had fallen and only 12 countries reported that assaults had fallen. There were significant differences in the proportion of countries which showed a decrease

Theft comprises around half of all reported crime and burglary a further 20 percent.

Twenty years ago the homicide rate was much higher in developing countries. Today, it is much higher in industrialized countries

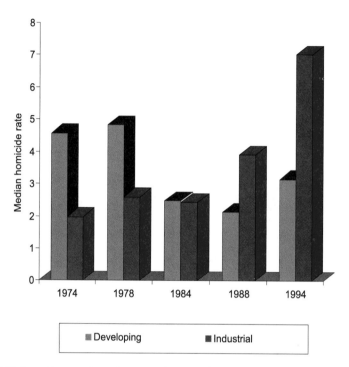

Source: UNCJS. Countries vary in each year and survey. See Notes to Snapshots for complete information, including individual country rates.

depending on the type of offence. Few countries showed stable crime rates over the period 1990-1994. The most stable offence type was rape, but even for rape only eight countries showed stability compared with 42 which showed a rise and 17 which showed a fall. For assaults, robbery and theft, only two countries reported that they had a stable crime rate during 1990 to 1994.

Changes 1986-1994

Changes between the mid 1980s and the mid 1990s are more difficult to interpret. Data have to be compared across two surveys, which restricts the number of countries. Moreover, during that period, a large number of political changes took place, especially in Eastern Europe, in several cases involving boundary changes (e.g., in Germany). Where comparisons are not possible,

FIGURE 2.3
Crime types reported to the UNCJS, 1994

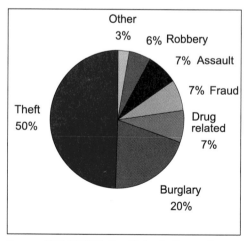

Source: Fifth UNCJS. See Notes to Figures for additional information.

GLOBAL REPORT ON CRIME AND JUSTICE

they have been excluded from this analysis. A rough summary of the changes reported by countries is presented in Figure 2.5. Nearly a quarter of countries reported falls in **homicide** of more than ten percent between 1986 and 1994. On the other hand a third of countries reported more than twice as many homicides during the period. Few countries showed a stable situation and there was very little pattern in the level of change shown.

There was more pattern in the reporting of **rape offences**, with about 40 percent of countries reporting a rise of between 10 and 50 percent. Thirteen more countries reported rises of more than 50 percent, and many of these will have done so because of police actions which show more sympathy to rape victims which, in most countries, has encouraged the reporting and recording of rape incidents to a greater extent than in the past (see Box 0.6 for further observations of rape as a "most reported crime"). On the other hand 12 countries either reported a fall in rape offences or a stable situation.

There was also great variation in the reported change in **thefts.** Forty percent of countries either reported a stable situation or a fall in the number of reported thefts. A further quarter of countries reported a rise of between 10 and 50 percent, which is comparable with the five percent year-on-year increase which some European countries such as England and Wales have reported for the whole of the twentieth century. Eight countries reported a more than doubling of the number of thefts, but some of these may have been due to changes in definitions.

Do crime rates vary around the world?

The reported rates from the UN survey for 1994 were analyzed for the following offences: rape, assault, theft, homicide, robbery, burglary, fraud, drug-related crime and embezzlement, since only these crimes had sufficient completeness of reporting for an analysis by country to be valid. Typically about 50 to 60 countries reported a figure for these crimes in 1994. These figures were converted to crime rates (see tables in notes to Figures 2.1 and 2.2) and then arranged according to the UN region in which the country was situated. The year 1994 was chosen as it is the latest date for which data

TABLE 2.1
Patterns in crime reporting, 1994

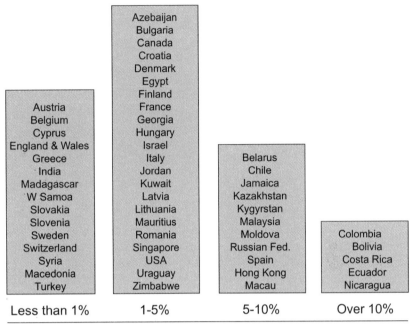

Robbery as a percentage of total crime

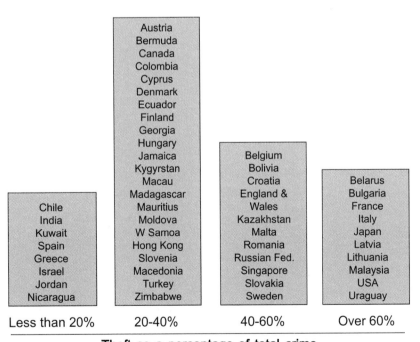

Theft as a percentage of total crime

Source: Fifth UNCJS. See Notes to Tables for additional information.

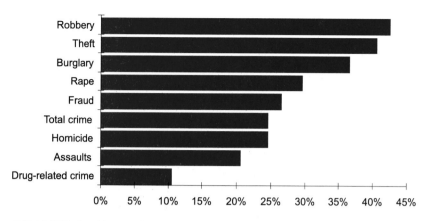

FIGURE 2.4
Percentage of countries reporting a fall in crime, 1990-1994

Source: Fifth UNCJS. See Notes to Figures for additional information.

are available. Examination of the figures showed that variation among regions was quite typical of all years.

There was considerable variation for every offence, both between regions and even within regions (see Box 2.7 for a discussion of crime trends within Western Europe). The patterns which emerged are noted below. However, not too much should be read into the differences shown, because the number of countries reporting from each region, for each offence, was very different. Any region with fewer than three countries reporting for a particular offence was excluded for that offence. There were always sufficient numbers reporting from the Western and Eastern European regions, from the Arab states and Latin America and (usually) from Africa. The extent of reporting from other regions was varied. Moreover the variation reported is not necessarily an indication that the actual occurrence of crime in those regions varies in the same way: we may simply be measuring a different propensity to report a particular crime in those regions or a regional variation in the way a crime is defined.

Even with these caveats, it is clear that Arab states reported a lower crime rate than other regions for all crimes except drugs-related crime. For property crimes such as burglaries and thefts, Western Europe and North America reported a far higher crime rate than other regions. For offences such as homicides and robberies, North America, Latin America and Africa reported high crime rates (Figures 2.6 and 2.7).

Rape offences

The number of rapes for 1994 was reported from 63 countries. Rates ranged from under ten to over 750 per million population, with well over half the countries reporting rates under 100 per million. The median reporting rate was 65 and three quarters of all countries reported a rate between 15 and 300 per million. The UN region with the highest median reporting rate was North

FIGURE 2.5
Countries reporting changes in homicides, thefts and rapes, 1986-1994

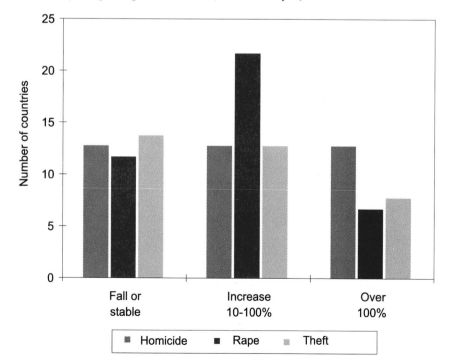

Source: 4th and 5th UNCJS. See Notes to Figures for additional tabular information.

America, and the lowest was the Arab states. Although the median reported rates in all other regions were much more moderate, there was considerable variation within all these regions

Assaults

The number of total assaults was reported from 52 countries. Rates for individual nations ranged from under 100 to over 10,000 per million population, with well over half of the countries reporting a rate of under 1,000. The median reporting rate was 780 per million, and three quarters of countries reported a rate between 140 and 4,200. High rates were reported in North America and sub-Saharan Africa. Low rates were reported from the Arab states and Eastern Europe. It is likely that problems of definition caused a good deal of this variation. Different countries record an assault in different ways, with some holding to a medical definition (e.g., days off work) and others holding to a legal definition. Moreover, it is likely that in countries where there is a good deal of experienced violence and homicide, less serious assaults will be less likely to be reported.

Homicide offences

Sixty-two countries reported homicide rates for 1994. Rates ranged from under five to over 800 per million. Three-quarters of countries reported rates between 18 and 230 per million population. There was quite a spread of rates reported in most regions. However, the lowest median reported rates were in Arab states and Western Europe, with highest rates reported in Latin America and sub-Saharan Africa. Rates in Eastern Europe and in North America were about the same. One reason for variation in homicide rates is the amount of firearms control in different countries and this could well account for the higher rates in North and Latin America, Africa and Eastern Europe. In these regions firearms regulations are not strong. Moreover, as a result of political change over recent times, the availability of illegal firearms is very high. Firearms regulations for different countries vary greatly. This topic is considered extensively in Chapter 6.

FIGURE 2.6
Median reported crime rates by region, 1994 (per million population)

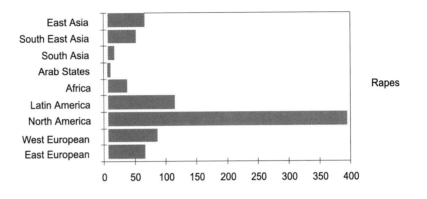

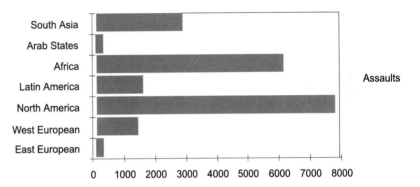

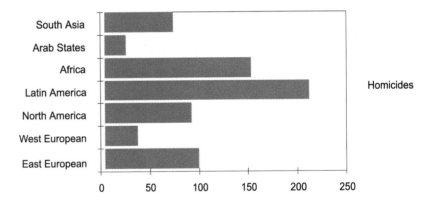

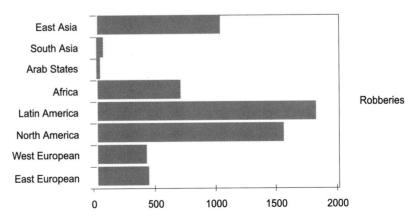

Source: Fifth UNCJS. See Notes to Figures for additional tabular data. Data on rape for North America may be inflated because of difficulties in interpreting Canadian data, since there is no legal definition of rape in Canada. See list of exceptions, Appendix 2.

BOX 2.7

The stabilization of crime trends in Western Europe: statistical artifact or reality?

During the postwar period, the amount of reported crime in Western European countries has increased considerably. This period of rapid increase has now apparently come to an end.

The accompanying graph presents the data on total crime recorded by the police in 15 Western European countries. Although a clear swing upwards can be noted in England and Wales and in Scotland beginning with 1988, and in Germany after the reunification, the dominant impression is one of stability. (The trends in individual offence categories varied, but confirm the same overall sense of stability.) An examination of the results of the international victimization surveys also supports the view that the steep increase in crime has flattened out.

It has become a commonplace to say that crime is increasing. This is what the public "knows," in part because it is the image that the media have portrayed for so long (up to the mid 1980s, by and large correctly). A simple and suitable explanation, the kind much favoured by the media, has been available for Western Europe: it has been regarded as self-evident that the integration brought on by the European Union, and the increasing crime rates in Central and Eastern Europe, have contributed to more and more crime in Western Europe. For example, the process of integration has raised the prospect of increased money-laundering, subsidy fraud and other types of economic crime within the European Union. The opening of European borders from east to west (and vice versa) makes possible an increase in the smuggling of cars, drugs, firearms, art, persons (as migrant workers, economic refugees and/or prostitutes) and dangerous substances.

And yet, the statistics on reported crime do not support such a view. Had the transformation in Central and Eastern Europe contributed to higher crime rates in Western Europe – for example because waves of foreigners would have come pouring over the borders in order to commit crimes – this should have been reflected in increases in crime in the countries most at risk such as Germany and Italy. The few countries with appreciable increases – England and Wales, and Scotland – are further away, and presumably the reason for increases in these countries would have to be sought somewhere else than in a "criminal contagion" from Central and Eastern Europe.

Data on recorded crime need not necessarily reflect the development in crime itself. Much crime remains unreported, and so the seeming stability may mask other changes, for example in the willingness of victims and bystanders to report offences.

A Council of Europe working group recently asked European governments to assess developments in crime that would be linked to the economic, political and social changes in Europe at the end of the 1980s and the beginning of the 1990s (Europe 1996). Both Western and Eastern European governments expressed concern over increases in, for example, organized crime in general, car thefts, economic crime, money laundering, arms trafficking, corruption, illegally exported refuse, immigration-related crime, visa and passport forgery, crime related to industrial legislation, in particular illegal recruitment of clandestine migrant workers, criminality linked with prostitution and other forms of sexual exploitation, and violence against foreigners.

We are thus faced with two opposing perceptions of crime trends in Europe. On one hand, the statistics on recorded crime and the available empirical data suggest that the growth in crime has flattened out. On the other hand, the authorities (and the public) have a strong sense that certain forms of serious crime have become more common and, in particular, that international organized crime has increased and strengthened.

Crime statistics that present aggregate amounts for traditional categories of crime cannot give an answer to this puzzle. The total of recorded crime may remain the same even if the structure of crime changes. For example, violence (such as assault and homicide) may become less common between intimates and more common between strangers, especially among socially dislocated young males living in decaying urban areas, or it may become more common as a means of conducting (illegal) business. Car thefts may become less common as "joy-riding" and more common in connection with organized trans-border smuggling. The amount of smuggling may remain the same, but the nature of the contraband may change from small quantities of alcohol and tobacco, to large quantities of stolen goods, firearms and even nuclear materials.

In addition, traditional crime statistics are poorly designed to convey a satisfactory image of the present prevalence and seriousness of such offences as environmental crime, the illegal smuggling of aliens, money laundering and economic crime. Much of this remains hidden to the authorities.

Even more refined statistics and the greater use of modern technology, however, cannot answer all questions. The randomness with which most forms of "modern" crime come to the attention of the police and the fact that each individual case tends to be unique make the plotting of any statistical trends well nigh a thankless task.

Thus, even improved statistics must be supplemented with research on the structure and amount of hidden crime in order to give us a better idea of what types of crime are being committed, by whom, against whom and with what effect.

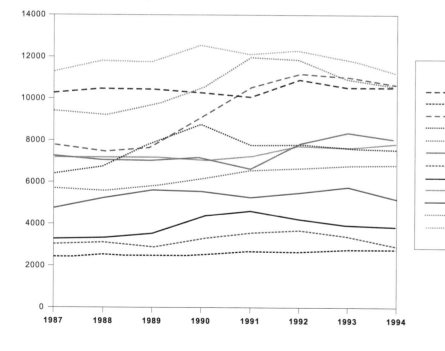

Crimes recorded by the police, 1987-1994, selected European countries (per 100,000 population)

Legend
- Denmark
- Eire
- England&W
- Finland
- France
- Germany
- Greece
- Italy
- Netherlands
- Norway
- Scotland
- Sweden

Source: Joutsen (1997a)

Robbery offences

Sixty-one countries reported their rates for robbery for 1994. These rates ranged from under ten per million population to over 5,000. The median rate was 524 per million population, and 90 percent of countries reported rates between 20 and 2,350, with three-quarters of all countries reporting a rate between 40 and 1,550. The region with the highest reported median rate for robbery was Latin America, closely followed by North America. East Asia and the African (sub-Saharan) regions reported rates around a half of American rates. Western and Eastern Europe reported much lower robbery rates, typically a quarter of those in America, and reported rates in the Arab states were extremely low.

Theft offences

The total number of thefts was reported from 59 countries. Rates ranged from under ten to over 2,600 per 10,000 population, with over 60 percent reporting a rate of under 100. The median reporting rate was 59, and 90 percent of countries reported a rate between three and 560 per 10,000. There were considerable variations in the median rates reported in the various UN regions. Theft rates were very much the lowest in the Arab states while moderate rates were reported in Sub-Saharan Africa, Eastern Europe and Latin America, and high rates were reported in Western Europe and North America.

Burglary offences

Only 53 countries reported burglary rates, with the median reported rate just under 2,000 per million population. However, the variation was very great, with Western Europe and North America reporting rates of over 10,000, and with some Western European countries reporting rates twice as high as this. In contrast the median rates in all other regions were at most 2,000.

Fraud offences

Sixty-two countries reported the number of fraud offences in 1994. The median rate was 450 per million population, with 90 percent of countries reporting rates between 34 and

FIGURE 2.7
Median reported crime rates by region, 1994 (per million population, except theft)

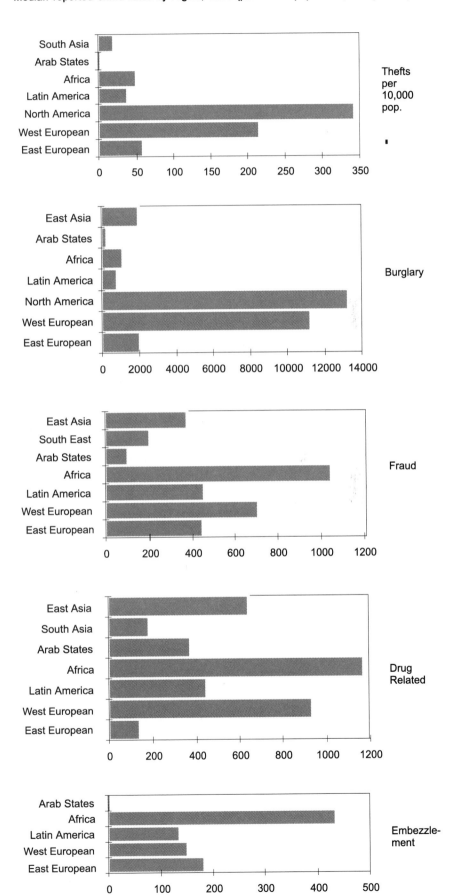

Source: Fifth UNCJS. See Notes to Figures for additional tabular data.

The lowest homicide and theft rates were reported by the Arab states.

4,293 per million. The variation was less than most other offences, with Arab states reporting the lowest rate at 105 and sub-Saharan African states reporting a rate of 1,049. Fraud in Western Europe was higher than the median, with reported fraud in East Asia and Latin America being around the median.

Drug-related crime

Fifty-seven countries reported drug-related crime numbers, and these showed the least variation throughout the world. The median reporting rate was 531 per million population, with Eastern Europe and Asia reporting a median rate of under 200 and African (sub-Saharan) states reporting a rate of over 1,100. Arab states reported a rate of 376, and Western Europe reported a high rate of 934 per million.

Embezzlement

Only 43 countries reported a rate for embezzlement, with many countries including the figure within other offences, such as theft or fraud. The median rate reported was 122 per million population, with Western and Eastern Europe and Latin America reporting only a little more than this. The rates reported in sub-Saharan Africa were very much higher. Arab states reported very low rates.

Urban life and crime

We saw in Chapter 1 that those who live in cities have a higher chance of being victimized by crime. The official records of crime also support this observation.

Crime in cities, 1994

The Fifth UNCJS asked countries to make a return to the UN of crime in their largest city, most often their capital. Not all countries were able to make such returns, but those cities for which data were received are listed in the Notes to Figures for Figure 2.8. The figures are for 1994 and hence show an incomplete picture for cities such as New York, where the number of homicides has been declining throughout the latter part of the 1990s.

High homicide rates were reported for several Latin American cities, New York and Northern European cities, with lower rates for other European cities, and very low rates for Hong Kong, Tokyo, Nicosia and Cairo.

More cities reported rates for robbery and although the pattern is less clear, there is much more variation than for homicide. It is not necessarily the same cities which are highest for both robbery and homicide. Indeed, Figure 2.8 shows that, although about three-quarters of the 35 cities show a reasonable relationship between homicide and robbery rates, about a quarter of cities do not follow any pattern.

A separate source of data also supports the notion that crime occurs at a much higher level in cities than in rural areas. These data were collected by the UN Statistics Division as a part of its effort in accumulating information on human settlements (Box 2.8). These data were collected using a similar method to that of the UNCJS, requesting national correspondents of member countries to provide statistics (crimes recorded by the police) for a standard set of crimes from their official records.

There are also many additional difficulties in comparing urban/rural crime rates. Police districts often do not coincide with urban/rural distinctions and what may be defined as rural in one country may not be so considered in another. Those in close-knit rural communities may be less inclined to report crimes to the police, or in the "anonymous city" bystanders may ignore crime around them. A number of these problems are outlined in Box 2.8. However, even taking into account all these difficulties, there seems to be a preponderance of evidence to support the claim that crime is, generally speaking, distributed more heavily into urban areas in most countries for which there are data.

Relation of homicide and theft rates to income and development of countries

Homicide and theft rates were examined to see whether they varied according to the income of the reporting country and the level of its development. There were some very clear patterns. When countries were arranged by their level of income, theft rates were seen to rise sharply as income rose,

BOX 2.8

Comparing crime in urban and rural areas: problems and an illustration

The measurement of urban and rural differences across countries presents special methodological problems. First, the designation of areas as urban and rural varies from country to country and thus the international comparability of urban-rural is seriously impaired. For example, urban in Ireland refers to cities and towns, including suburbs, of 1,500 or more inhabitants, while in Bulgaria, it refers to towns — that is, localities, legally established as urban, disregarding the number of inhabitants. Or, in Sweden, data on reported crimes in urban areas refer only to the Stockholm, Gothenburg and Malmo metropolitan areas and to the Uppsala community.

Another problem in the comparisons of urban and rural areas is the diversity of rural areas across countries, and very often even within one country. While urban areas tend to have common characteristics, such as urban centres, apartment buildings and main traffic arteries, rural areas cover everything from remote mountain villages and seaside resorts to high density settlements in relatively close proximity to urban agglomerations.

Yet another methodological issue concerns methods of recording crime. In most cases, crimes reported to the police are recorded on the basis of their place of occurrence. But police districts do not necessarily conform to the urban/rural subdivisions of the country. Jurisdiction of one police district may

spread to both urban and rural communities and it would be very difficult, if not impossible, to properly distinguish an urban/rural breakdown for statistics provided by such a district. In countries with more developed criminal justice statistics systems, though, these issues have been successfully resolved by introducing more complex coding procedures.

An illustration

Illustrative statistics on urban/rural differences in the level and structure of crime are presented in the *Compendium of Human Settlements Statistics 1995* (United Nations, 1995). These statistics were collected from national statistical offices and compiled by the United Nations Statistics Division. Due to the methodological complexities of providing data on crimes reported to the police by urban/rural breakdown, not many national statistical offices were able to comply with the request for data. Included here are the countries that provided such information.

Are city dwellers much more exposed to crime than is the case with rural populations? Indeed, these illustrative data indicate that crimes are reported more frequently in urban than rural areas. For example, in the Netherlands one crime is reported in urban areas every 37 seconds, whereas in rural areas the corresponding period is 117 seconds (almost two minutes). In urban areas of Cyprus, one crime

is reported every three hours, compared to over 11 hours in rural areas. In some countries this difference is even more significant: in Poland, in a four minute period there are over five reported crimes in urban areas and only one in rural areas. These data are comparable with information from other sources; for example, in the Federal District of Mexico City, which is a highly urbanized area, one crime is reported every two minutes (Reloj Delictivo, 1997).

Since the share of population living in urban and rural areas is not equal, it is necessary to provide crime rates in order to provide a balanced overview of the occurrence of crime. The crime rate reported here is a derived indicator showing the number of recorded crimes per 1,000 population in urban and rural areas, respectively.

The crime rates vary significantly from country to country, as shown in the Figure below. Still, a pattern of much higher crime rates in urban than in rural areas can be observed, with very few exceptions. In El Salvador, in Hungary, and in the Netherlands, for example, the urban crime rate was twice as high as in rural areas. In Poland, it was over three times as high.

Taking into account all the limitations of the data, statistics for these countries indicate that in both absolute (the total number of crimes) and relative terms (crime rates), crimes were much more frequent in urban than rural environments.

These illustrative data from the few countries supplying urban and rural data suggest the importance of urban/rural location in explaining the levels of crime.

How similar is the structure of reported crimes in urban and rural areas? Data show that by far the most frequently reported crime in both urban and rural areas were crimes against property. These crimes refer to all criminal offences against property, whether the victim is a person, household or institution. One half of all reported urban crimes in El Salvador were thefts and other crimes against property, while less than a third of all rural crimes fell in that category; in Finland, almost one third of all urban crimes were property crimes, compared to less than one fifth in rural communities. This was the case with all the countries for which data were available, with the exception of Ireland. Property crime rates are higher in urban than in rural areas, and in some cases they are twice as high, as in Hungary, or even higher, like in the Netherlands, Finland and Poland.[2]

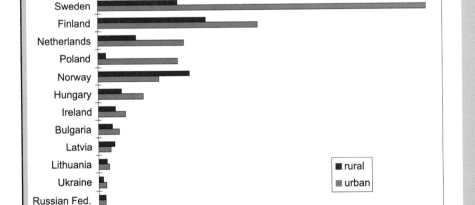

Crime rates per 1,000 population in urban and rural areas, around 1990[1]

Source: Srdjan Mrkic (Original paper, 1997). See Notes to Boxes for additional information.

with high income countries having a median theft rate of over 200 per 10,000 population, medium income countries having a rate of around 50 and low income countries having a rate of around two per 10,000. This mainly reflects the fact that there is a good deal more opportunity to steal in richer countries: however, it also reflects the likelihood that in countries with little wealth more possessions are held in common (Figure 2.9).

Homicide rates show a very different pattern, with higher rates in medium and low income countries compared to high income countries. The reasons for this are less easy to interpret; opportunities are the same in all countries, but better medical facilities and communications may save more lives in rich countries than in poor countries.

The pattern of crime when compared with the economic development status of countries is difficult to assess. This is because there were very few countries reporting crime which were classified as being least developed. The median rates in Figure 2.9 for least developed countries are thus likely to be unrepresentative.

Median theft rates for industrial countries were over 100 per 10,000 population compared with under 20 for developing countries, and this finding holds even when development is measured either by income or the UNDP development classification. However, the results for homicide by development are less clear. The median homicide rates for industrial countries and for developing countries were about the same in 1994 when measured by the UNDP development classification. However, when measured by income level, the medium income countries showed a rate of homicide much higher than the high income countries. It will also be noted that this finding does not conform with the Global Snapshot on page 50, where the homicide level is considerably higher for developed countries. Although there are several explanations for this difference, the main one is probably that the Global Snapshot included least developed countries within the developing country group.[1] In addition, it is difficult to ascertain how the various development indicators are related, and the extent to which

FIGURE 2.8
Homicide and robbery rates for 35 cities, 1994

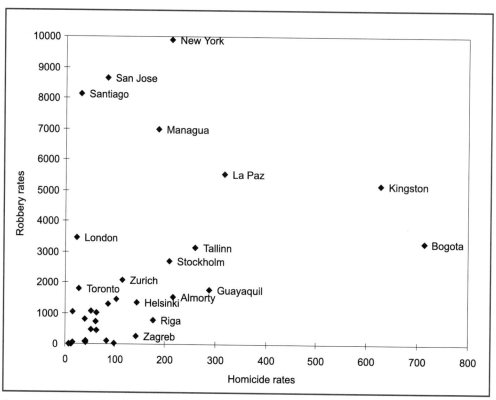

Source: Fifth UNCJS. See Notes to Figures for additional information.

they produce different groupings of countries. For example, the popular Human Development Index (a complex of various development indicators: see *UN Human Development Report*, 1994) produced no relationship with homicide rates and only a weak correlation with theft rates (see notes to Figure 2.9).

Unrecorded crime

So far, the crime reported in this chapter falls into the category of what criminologists call "traditional crime." We have focused mainly on those familiar crimes of homicide, assault, rape, robbery, theft and burglary, with a brief mention of fraud and embezzlement. These traditional, official categories of crime have become over the years of the UNCJS reasonably widely accepted international categories. However, there has been much recent concern about types of crime that, because of their nature and mode of committal, are unrepresented in the official police records of crime. In some cases, such crimes may in fact be reported and recorded by police, but do not find their way into official compilations of crime statistics. This is currently the problem with domestic violence (Box 2. 9; see also Box 6.1), although to some extent domestic violence may be measured more effectively by household victimization surveys.

However, police recorded crime figures and household victim surveys have increasingly become regarded in recent years as insufficient to give a full picture of the varied amount of crime, of different sorts, that occurs. In particular, there has been a need to produce measures of crime against sectors of the economy other than households and to look for methodologies that attempt to gather some figures for the whole area of organized, transnational and environmental crime.

Three methods of data collection can be mentioned here. First, there is the need to consider commercial victims, and this is covered by surveys of different types of commercial establishments. Box 1.2 in Chapter 1 considers some recent surveys which look at crime suffered by retailers and in manufacturing premises. Second, there has been considerable investment in surveys which ask offenders about their experience of of-

FIGURE 2.9
Homicide and theft rates by income and development, 1994

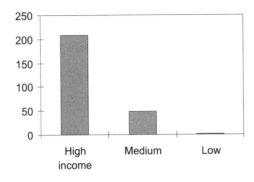

Thefts per 10,000 population, by income

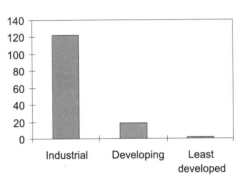

Thefts per 10,000 population, by development

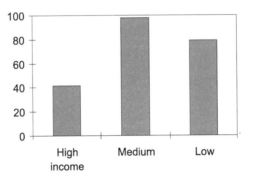

Homicides per million population, by income

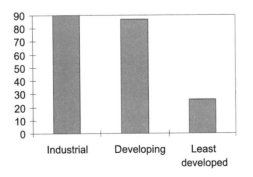

Homicides per million population, by development

Source: Fifth UNCJS and UN Human Development Report, 1996. See Notes to Figures for raw data and information on development and income classification criteria, including data on HDI.

fending. Such self-report studies give important insights into crime levels and, in particular, their relation to age of offending and to the socio-economic conditions of the offender. This is covered in Boxes 2.10 and 0.10. The final area of methodological development is the attempt to measure complex crimes such as organized crime, transnational crime and terrorism. The implications of these emerging problems are examined in detail in the next section and in Chapter 9.

Measuring complex crime

In this chapter we have been concerned with the challenges we face in measuring the amount and type of crime recorded by the police. As noted throughout this chapter, the UNCJS has confined its data collection to statistics on traditional crimes. There is good reason for this: these crimes, mostly, are relatively simple, discreet events. A homicide is a homicide; a burglary is a burglary. Even though there has been much discussion over the years concerning the definitions of these crimes internationally (Box 2.1), it has generally proved possible for most participating countries to adjust their official records of crime to fit these definitions. However, one can readily see that the definition of fraud, for example, is very broad and makes for much difficulty for national correspondents to provide statistics. This is because frauds of various kinds are not discreet events; rather, they may involve a long series of events all of which may be separate crimes in themselves (e.g., the BCCI case; see Box 0.11). Organized crime and transnational crime fit squarely into this category as well. They are complex events that defy quantitative measurement in the traditional way. This is why there is currently a search for new ways to measure them.

Organized crime. There has always been much controversy over attempts to define what is meant by organized crime. Different authors have used slightly different definitions over the years (Savona *et al.*, 1995; Fijnaut *et al.*, 1995), and this problem of definition has gotten in the way of attempts to collect information on organized crime. The same problems also apply to transnational crime, which is in many ways related to organized crime, and to environmental crime. Indeed, this problem of definition is compounded when many authors try to bring all of these together within the same typology.

The UN has sponsored a whole series of activities, conferences and resolutions in the area of organized crime. Documentation on this was most recently collated for the Ninth UN Congress in Egypt in 1995 (UN Action Against Organized Crime, 1995). In particular the papers for the World Ministerial Conference on Organized Transnational Crime in November 1994 (included in the Congress papers) are an excellent summary of the position.

Various attempts have been made by the UN to collect statistics on organized crime, but the most successful body for collecting data so far has been the European Union, which has been able to concentrate on a smaller geographical area. The typology used in recent years by the European Union, and which seems likely to be copied by other groups, is detailed in Box 2.11. This typology defined 11 characteristics which typify organized crime, of which six must be present for an incident or series of incidents to be defined as organized.

The latest published report of the European Union on organized crime concludes that present evidence clearly demonstrates the international dimension of organized crime. The foreign origin of suspects and criminal groups is the predominant characteristic of organized crime. Member states identify organized criminal activity as a world wide phenomenon operating across national boundaries which pose no significant obstacle to those involved (European Union, 1996).

Historical, cultural and geographic factors influence the distribution of organized criminal groups of foreign origin (e.g., the influence of countries of Eastern Europe on crime in Germany and Austria in the 1990s, and the longer-term influence of countries which were once colonies of countries such as the United Kingdom, Spain and Portu-

---

BOX 2.11

Measuring organized crime in Europe

Each year, the European Union (EU) produces a situation report on Organized Crime in the EU. This is based on data sent in by member states and by the EUROPOL Drugs Unit. The availability of data and the usefulness of the annual situation report have improved greatly over the 1990s, but a good deal still needs to be done in developing a workable methodology for measuring and describing the amount of organized crime which exists, either in one country or a region such as Western Europe. The present methodology of the EU consists of the following definitions. At least six of the following characteristics must be present, three of which must be those numbered 1, 5 and 11, for any crime or criminal group to be classified as organized crime.

1. Collaboration of more than two people;
2. Each with appointed tasks;
3. For a prolonged or indefinite period of time;
4. Using some form of discipline or control;
5. Suspected of the commission of serious criminal offences;
6. Operating on an international level;
7. Using violence or other means suitable for intimidation;
8. Using commercial or businesslike structure;
9. Engaged in money laundering;
10. Exerting influence on politics, the media, public administration, judicial authorities or economy;
11. Determined by the pursuit of profit and/or power.

Information on the following topics is required in country reports:
1. Characteristics of the suspects involved;
2. Criminal activities;
3. Places and regions of activity;
4. Resources involved;
5. Use of violence;
6. Use of "influence";
7. Money laundering.

Details on the following criminal activities are collected:
Narcotic drugs
Fraud
Counterfeiting/Forgery
Armed robberies
Kidnapping
Extortion
Vehicle theft
"Hit and run" burglaries
Thefts of artifacts and antiques/jewelry
Other forms of theft
Illegal firearms trading
Traffic in human beings
Prostitution
Child Pornography
Environmental crime
Illegal gambling schemes
Money laundering

Source: European Union, The Council. Situational report on organised crime in the EU, 1995.

---

gal). In contrast, in some small countries, such as Finland and Ireland, organized crime is almost entirely national in character.

Other features of organized crime covered in the European report include the following:

• in some countries commercial business type structures were used in three quarters of the cases;

• violence is often used both between and within groups and on victims;

• influence is used in only a minority of cases, typically 10 to 20 percent;

• well over half of the organized groups were involved in money laundering.

Wider reviews of organized crime have been undertaken by HEUNI (Savona et al., 1995; Liukkonen, 1997). The Italian Mafia (see Box 2.12) and other organized groups of Chinese, Russian and Columbian origin

BOX 2.12

Measuring organized crime in Italy

There are four main types of criminal organizations conducting illegal activities in a permanent and systematic way over portions of the Italian territory in at least four regions: the Sicilian Mafia, also called Cosa Nostra, the 'Ndrangheta in Calabria, the Camorra in Campania and the Sacra Corona Unita (of relatively recent origin) in Puglia. Each organization has a different history, cultural background and modus operandi, but some of their main illegal activities (such as extortion, drug trafficking and corruption) are similar.[1]

The Italian law has special prosecuting and sentencing provisions for organized crime activities, which were partly developed from the extensive experience in successfully fighting political terrorism (Marongiu and Biddau, 1996). For example, for criminal associations of the mafioso type (*associazione per delinquere di tipo mafioso*) severe penalties of up to 15 years in prison for involvement in the association alone are provided.

Defendants convicted of this crime also are allowed fewer privileges than other convicted criminals. However, the accused is entitled to a penalty reduction and other privileges if he or she decides to cooperate with the justice system by producing evidence that can be used to effectively fight organized crime (Official Gazette, August 7, 1992). An extensive witness protection programme for these *collaboratori di giustizia* and their families has been organized (Official Gazette, January 15, May 13, 1991; April 24, 1993; December 17, 1994).

The prosecution of organized crime, ransom kidnapping, drug trafficking and related crimes is conducted by the Anti-Mafia Public Prosecutor (*Procuratore Distrettuale Antimafia*).

The Ministry of the Interior has recently established a special agency of criminal investigation, called the DIA (*Direzione Investigativa Antimafia*) to be in charge of organized crime investigations. The DIA is directed by a high ranking Carabinieri, State Police or Chief Finance Guard Officer (*Direzione Nazionale Antimafia* or DNA; Marongiu and Biddau, 1996).

One of the most effective measures in organized crime investigation, repression and prevention is the computerized data processing system called SIDDA which contains all relevant information relative to Anti-Mafia investigations nationwide, and is also connected with a centralized data bank on bank deposits and money transfers. The Italian law also allows (Official Gazette, June 5, 1965) the seizure and confiscation of property and financial assets allegedly belonging to organized crime associates or anyhow deriving from their illegal activities.

In 1992, a total of 3,158 persons were charged with criminal association of Mafioso type (1,811 of them were arrested and incarcerated – 526 were allegedly affiliated to the Sicilian Mafia, 634 with the Neapolitan Camorra, 416 with the Calabrian 'Ndrangheta, and 235 with the Sacra Corona Unita or other Apulian criminal organizations). In the same year, 2,593 kilos of cocaine, 2,482 kilos of heroin and 43,953 kilos of cannabis sativa derivatives (hashish and marijuana) and other illegal drugs were confiscated. The total value of confiscated property (other than illegal drugs) and financial assets allegedly belonging to organized crime associates or anyhow deriving from their illegal activities was estimated at 238 billion Italian Lire (approx. 1 USD = 1700 Italian Lire).

In 1993, a total of 5,389 persons were charged with criminal association of Mafioso type. (1,727 of them were arrested and incarcerated – 508 were allegedly affiliated with the Sicilian Mafia, 548 with the Neapolitan Camorra, 514 to the Calabrian 'Ndrangheta, and 157 with

the Sacra Corona Unita or other Apulian criminal organizations). In the same year, 2,017 kilos of cocaine, 997 kilos of heroin and 23,166 kilos of cannabis sativa derivatives (hashish and marijuana) and other illegal drugs were confiscated. The total value of confiscated property (other than illegal drugs) and financial assets allegedly belonging to organized crime associates or anyhow deriving from their illegal activities has been estimated at 471 billion Italian Lire. The Finance Guard also confiscated other possessions (277 real estate units including villas, apartment buildings and land, plus 45 trading companies) whose value has not been determined.

In 1994, a total of 5,706 persons were charged with criminal association of Mafioso type (1,832 of them were arrested and incarcerated – 536 were allegedly affiliated with the Sicilian Mafia, 627 to the Neapolitan Camorra, 333 with the Calabrian 'Ndrangheta, and 336 to the Sacra Corona Unita or other Apulian criminal organizations). In the same year, 13,027 kilos of cocaine, 1,612 kilos of heroin and 52,504 kilos of cannabis sativa derivatives (hashish and marijuana) and other illegal drugs were confiscated. The total value of confiscated property (other than illegal drugs) and financial assets allegedly belonging to organized crime associates or anyhow deriving from their illegal activities has been estimated at 442 billion Italian Lire. The Finance Guard also confiscated other possessions (1,230 real estate units including villas, apartment buildings and land, plus 144 trading companies) whose value has not been determined.

In 1995, a total of 4,645 persons were charged with criminal association of Mafioso type (1,167 of them were arrested and incarcerated – 370 were allegedly affiliated with the Sicilian Mafia, 472 with the Neapolitan Camorra, 124 with the Calabrian 'Ndrangheta, and 201 with the Sacra Corona Unita or other Apulian criminal organizations). In the same year, 5,282 kilos of cocaine, 1,713 kilos of heroin and 31,432 kilos of cannabis sativa derivatives (hashish and marijuana) and other illegal drugs were confiscated. The total value of confiscated property (other than illegal drugs) and financial assets allegedly belonging to organized crime associates or anyhow deriving from their illegal activities has been estimated at 400 billion Italian Lire. The Finance Guard also confiscated other possessions (585 real estate units including villas, apartment buildings and land, plus 111 trading companies) whose value has not been determined. In 1995, the witness protection programme was in charge of 1119 *collaboratori di giustizia* and their families, for a total of 6017 persons under protection.

In 1996 a total of 6,122 persons were charged with criminal association of Mafioso type (3,025 of them were arrested and incarcerated – 1,221 were allegedly affiliated with the Sicilian Mafia, 839 with the Neapolitan Camorra, 597 with the Calabrian 'Ndrangheta, and 440 with the Sacra Corona Unita or other Apulian criminal organizations). In the same year, 3,904 kilos of cocaine, 2,216 kilos of heroin and 24,242 kilos of cannabis sativa derivatives (hashish and marijuana) and other illegal drugs were confiscated. The total value of confiscated property (other than illegal drugs) and financial assets allegedly belonging to organized crime associates or anyhow deriving from their illegal activities has been estimated at 1,596 billion Italian Lire. The Finance Guard also confiscated other possessions (1,265 real estate units including villas, apartment buildings and land, plus 72 trading companies) whose value has not been determined. In 1995, the witness protection programme was in charge of 1,273 *collaboratori di giustizia* and their families, for a total of 7,020 persons under protection.

Sources: Marongiu and Norfo (1997). From the official reports of the three main Italian state police corps (Polizia, Carabinieri and Guardia di Finanza). See Notes to Boxes for additional information and sources.[2]

have been identified. Chapter 9 examines this phenomenon as a problem of transnational crime.

An important general feature of organized crime is that the offences committed under this heading are typically prosecuted under the normal criminal code, in the same way as for other offences such as homicide, robbery or assault, etc., which are not "organized." In most statistical data collections such crimes are not identified separately. This problem, as we noted earlier, also applies to other types of crime, such as domestic violence. However, there are many examples where different countries have attempted to analyze crimes which can be attributed to a particular phenomenon, whether organized crime or political violence.

For example, the Japanese have published statistics to isolate separately specific crimes alleged to have been committed by one religious cult (Box 2.13). In South Africa Louw and Sekhonyane (1997) have shown how the number of murders due to political violence in the South African province of KwaZulu-Natal have decreased considerably since the national election in April 1994 (Figure 2.10). In common with a growing number of countries, South Africa also produces a quarterly report on the extent of organized crime in the context of their regular publication of recorded crime statistics (SAPS, 1/97). In most cases, the statistics in those reports have been derived from the reports of specialized police units set up in the countries involved in order to combat organized crime. Thus, the statistics are not consistent from one country to another, and there is likely to be a good deal of double counting with other traditional police statistics.

FIGURE 2.10
Monthly deaths caused by political violence: KwaZulu-Natal South Africa

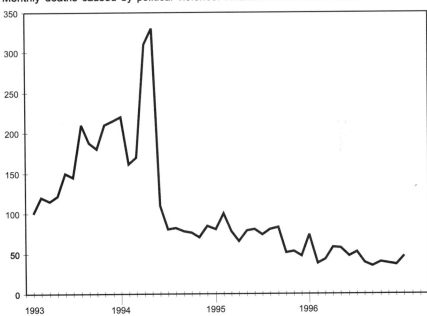

Source: Louw (1997). See Notes to Figures for tabular data.

SUMMARY

THINGS IN COMMON	THINGS DIVERSE
• Crime is universal. There is no country without crime.	• Reported crime rates for every offence varied greatly by country. Arab states generally reported very low rates for nearly all types of crime.
• On average, crime continued to rise in the 1990s, as it had in the 1980s.	• Many countries showed a fall in crime in the 1990s.
• The most common crime reported was theft, followed by burglary.	• Theft rates were higher for industrial countries than non-industrial countries.
• Violent crime (homicide, assaults, robbery) was a minority (around 10-15%) of all reported crime.	• Some countries reported a much higher proportion of violent crime than others.
• Most cities show similar patterns for homicide and for robbery rates.	• High homicide rates were reported for several Latin American cities, New York, New York, and Northern European cities.
• All countries reporting crime statistics to the United Nations Survey of Crime Trends and Operation of Criminal Justice Systems have been able to adapt their definitions of traditional crime categories to fit the United Nations definitions.	• There is no one accepted methodology for collecting crime figures recorded by the police. Figures for a particular country depend on that country's state of development, the role of the police and the extent to which police use technology.
• In all countries police recorded crime figures are acknowledged to give an incomplete picture of crime experienced by the population.	• A growing number of countries is developing new methods of measuring unrecorded crime, using victim surveys of various types, self-report surveys and complex measures of organized and transnational crimes.
• All countries found it very difficult to define and measure complex crime such as organized crime.	• Some country groupings, (e.g. the European Union) have made considerable progress collecting data on organized crime.

CHAPTER 3

Bringing to justice

Contributing authors: Satyanshu Mukherjee and Philip Reichel

Introduction: legal systems and justice statistics

If we are to make cross national comparisons of official crime rates and justice statistics, an understanding of the respective legal traditions of countries is essential. Legal traditions offer guidance in designing and establishing structures, both organizational and personnel, for criminal justice systems. Difficulties emerge the moment one tries to compare executive and administrative aspects of criminal justice systems, stages and steps in the systems, roles and responsibilities of agencies, procedures for dealing with events and actors, reliance on statistical data and research, etc. The situation could be further complicated by the system of government, the degree of autonomy granted to various geographic units within the country, the relationship between the judiciary, the executive and the legislature, and the role of the military in the day to day running of the country. In what follows, we provide a brief overview of the major legal traditions of the world, followed by a discussion of how these traditions affect criminal justice processing.

The world's legal systems

There are as many legal systems in the world as there are countries. In fact, upon recognizing the occasional state and province variations within some nations, there are considerably more legal systems than countries. The term *legal system* refers to attitudes, values and norms regarding the nature and role of law, including rules and practices for processing and functioning. The values and norms that underlie a legal system are sometimes referred to as the legal tradition. It is a broad concept that implies a deeply rooted and historically based heritage.

Comparative legal scholars do not agree on how many legal systems, or families, exist today. To paraphrase G.K. Chesterton, depicting legal families, as with art, consists of drawing a line somewhere. There is an arbitrary aspect to the delineation, but the resulting picture should make enough sense to people that it is reasonable if not precise. Some scholars suggest three legal families: civil law, common law and socialist (e.g., Merryman, 1985). Others, like David and Brierley (1985), identify four categories: civil law, common law, socialist law and religious/philosophical. The more recent prevailing strategy (e.g., Fairchild, 1993; Reichel, 1994) uses the David and Brierley grouping but substitutes Islamic law for the more general religious/philosophical category.

Even after deciding upon the number of categories to use, application to individual countries is often problematic. For example, colonization by sixteenth century powers meant that English, Spanish, French and other European legal systems were imposed on peoples on the other continents (cf., Newman and Bouloukos, 1996). Sometimes both the "tradition" and the "system" were successfully imposed; but other times the colonized people informally held to their indigenous tradition (e.g., Nigeria's customary courts; see Box 3.1 and Box 5.1) while formally incorporating the colonial power's legal system. Of course there were also situations where a country had already accepted one of the four basic legal traditions, only to find political, economic or religious reasons to include another tradition as well. For example, some Middle Eastern countries have found it beneficial to incorporate both Islamic and civil or common legal traditions

If we are to make cross national comparisons of official crime rates and justice statistics, an understanding of the respective legal traditions of countries is essential.

to accommodate international relations (civil or common law) while holding to cultural beliefs (Islamic law).

This section follows a categorization strategy that uses the four legal traditions of civil law, common law, socialist law, and Islamic families. However, to show the complexity of the issue, it also recognizes that some nations are best described as having a combination of traditions rather than being clearly linked to only one. Figure 3.1 shows the result of this classification strategy by depicting the 185 United Nations member states as falling into one of the four basic legal traditions, a combination of two basic traditions, or as being of some other category. Figure 3.2 portrays this classification scheme as it looks on a world map.

The following material offers a brief description of the four basic legal traditions. For more thorough information, see the works of Fairchild (1993) and Reichel (1994).

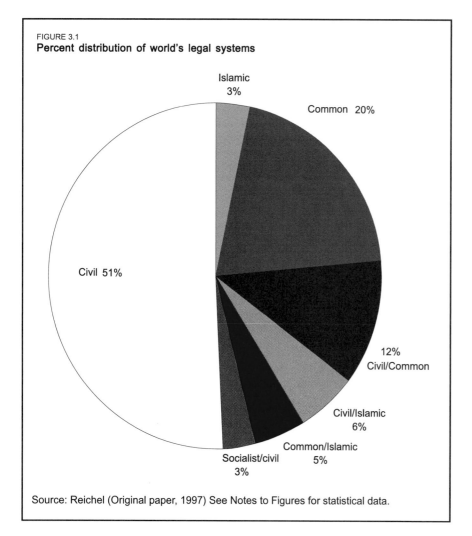

FIGURE 3.1
Percent distribution of world's legal systems

- Islamic 3%
- Common 20%
- Civil 51%
- 12% Civil/Common
- Civil/Islamic 6%
- Common/Islamic 5%
- Socialist/civil 3%

Source: Reichel (Original paper, 1997) See Notes to Figures for statistical data.

Civil law tradition

The oldest contemporary legal family is the civil law tradition. The primary source of law in this tradition is the written code as provided by rulers or legislators. This tradition originated in the written codes of Roman law and the written papal statements of the Roman Catholic church. While the Roman emperor used legal codes like the *Corpus Juris Civilis* (450 BC) to govern the secular world, the Roman Catholic church relied on papal decrees to provide order to the sacred realm. By the ninth century, both Roman law and canon law had experienced their heyday, and other parts of Europe began influencing the specifics of civil law. But the principle of the civil law tradition – laws must be written down in a systematically arranged manner – was well established by the time the Germans, French and others were having their say. It is codification that makes law binding because the written form means it was enacted by a recognized authority (for example, a monarch or a legislature) following formal procedures.

Contemporary countries identified as falling in the civil legal family were most likely inspired by the civil codes of France or Germany. The French *Code Napoléon* (1804) was especially influential in continental Europe and Latin America. It was developed to be an easily read and understood handbook that would allow citizens to figure out for themselves their legal rights and obligations. There was a desire for a simple, nontechnical and straightforward legal system that avoided the need for lawyers and their tendency toward technicality and complexity (Merryman, 1985).

Like their French contemporaries, nineteenth century Germans were intrigued with the idea of codification as a way to pull together a new nation. However, unlike the French, the Germans did not believe it was either desirable or possible to remove lawyers from the legal system. The German Civil Code of 1896 (effective in 1900) was a historically oriented, scientific and professional document that assumed lawyers would be needed to interpret and apply the law (Merryman, 1985).

It might seem that the resulting French and Germany civil codes were so dissimilar that it is inappropriate to place them in the same legal family. There are clear and important differences in the way the two codes identified and recorded legal principles, but there are overriding similarities that make each version of codification an example of the civil law tradition. Specifically, both the French and German codes incorporated a sharp separation of powers in which the legislator makes law and the judge does not. And that brings us back to the distinguishing feature of the civil law tradition – the source of law is codification by a political authority. The role of judges in this tradition is to apply, not make, law.

Common law tradition

In the common law tradition the customs of the people provide the original source of law. At some point these customs are put in written form, so a confusing aspect of the common law tradition is that it, like the civil law tradition, has written laws. But the distinction between the written laws of the common law tradition and codification in the civil law tradition is more than simple semantics. This becomes clear in a review of the history of common law's development.

In an attempt to return order to an increasingly disrupted kingdom, Henry II (1154-1189) issued the Constitutions of Clarendon (1164), which listed customs said to be the practice in England when the twelfth century had begun. The idea was that traditional, consistent and reasonable ways of deciding disputes – that is, custom – provided the appropriate source of law. Deciding whether something was "customary" fell to members of the community, who were sitting as a jury of peers. Judges were expected to follow legal custom by abiding by prior decisions in similar cases. In this manner, custom could be identified by reliance on the people and through reference to several cases. Importantly, however, the case was not considered the source of law; it merely provided proof that a legal principle (a custom) was once applied.

Eventually the practice of citing prior cases was done less to show custom and more as a way to reference authority. In this way common law developed a reliance on precedent or *stare decisis*, wherein courts are expected to abide by previously decided cases. Those cases were in written form, but they cannot be considered written law in the way the civil law tradition views "written." The prior cases reflected custom, albeit custom in writing, rather than reflecting specific decisions by rulers or legislators. The criminal statutes found in common law countries today must be considered in the same way. When common law legislatures prepare written penal statutes or codes, they are not so much making written law (as do civil law legislators) as they are proposing law. That is because final determination regarding the validity of a statute lies with the courts which will evaluate the legislature's work. In other words, civil law legislation stands on it own since the legislature is the source of law; but common law legislation is not authoritatively established until it passes examination of the courts.

Socialist law tradition

The designation of socialist law as a separate legal tradition is the most controversial of the four legal families. Valid arguments present socialist law as simply a modification of the civil law tradition and not different enough from that tradition to warrant independent standing. However, there are equally valid arguments recognizing the similarities between socialist and civil law, but maintaining that cultural and philosophical differences between the two allow separate classification. For example, the source of law in the socialist law tradition is in the principles of the socialist revolution. Both civil and socialist traditions view law as stemming from written codes, but the civil codes (according to the socialists) are the work of special interest groups, while the socialist codes represent the ideals of the people's revolution.

The legal system of the Union of Soviet Socialist Republics provided the philosophical and technical base for a socialist legal tradition. The demise of the USSR did not result in the immediate demise of the socialist legal tradition any more than the fall of the Roman Empire destroyed the civil law tradition. So, to understand the socialist law tradition today, we must consider its initial application in the USSR.

One characteristic setting the socialist legal tradition apart from others is its view of law as subordinate to policy. Law, under this tradition, is used to achieve a desirable end rather than being an absolute value limiting both the leaders' and the people's behaviour. The policy to which law is subordinate places the rights of the collectivized economy and the socialist state above any rights the individual might have. Socialists see the subordination of law to policy as an improvement over the civil law and common law traditions because subordinated law can be used as a tool to achieve socialist economic and educational goals.

David and Brierley (1985) addressed the economic role played by socialist law when they contrasted it with civil and common law's role in capitalist economies. Law in a capitalist economy tells the citizens that a just and moral society, achieved through law as an absolute value, results in economic order. Under the socialist legal tradition, economic order, achieved through law as a tool, results in a just and moral society. The reversal of attitudes toward law's role in the economy gives the socialist legal tradition different ideas about law than those found in civil and common law traditions.

Law's educational role remains a key feature in today's socialist law countries. In the Peoples' Republic of China, and other countries following a socialist legal tradition, such as Cuba, law operates to educate people about the principles of socialism and to guide them toward the communist ideal. Socialist judges do not simply apply the law, as they do in civil law countries, nor do they make or validate the law, as they do in common law countries. Judges in the socialist legal tradition must help ensure the success of government policy by educating the people.

One must recognize, however, the rapid social, economic and legal changes that many socialist, or formerly socialist, countries are undergoing during the last decade of the twentieth century. New legislation in Russia enacted in direct response to the expanding demands of an emerging free market economy, and the constant enactment of new law in China in response to rapidly changing economic conditions mean that while remnants of socialist law remain, they are being rapidly overtaken by new law, especially in the realm of commerce, which tends to shape law more and more into the civil law tradition. In actual fact, law in many former and current socialist countries is in a state of flux. For this reason these countries have been identified in charts and maps as "socialist/civil."

The Islamic law tradition

Unlike the other three traditions, Islamic law is of divine origin. For Muslims, the law's authority is based on God's (Allah's) commands rather than on long-held traditions (as in common law), directives by state power (as in civil law), or philosophical standards (as in socialist law).

Islamic law is called the *Shari'a*, the path to follow. A unique feature of the *Shari'a* is its singularity of purpose. Islam recognizes no distinction between a legal system and other controls on a person's behaviour. The *Shari'a* is not simply used for one aspect of a Muslim's daily routine — it is the very essence of that routine. A citizen under a civil or common law tradition can probably find a time or place where an otherwise illegal behaviour is allowed. That would not be possible under the Islamic legal tradition because there are no situations where the *Shari'a* does not apply. In a sense, the *Shari'a* is more a "life-style" system than simply a legal system.

The primary ingredients of the *Shari'a* are the *Qur'an* (Islam's holy book) and the *Sunna* (the statements and deeds of the prophet Muhammad). Because only a few verses in the *Qur'an* contain actual rules, and since the *Sunna* is similarly sparse in its identification of norms, two other sources were used to provide a comprehensive code of law for Islam. But these secondary sources also led to different schools of thought within Islam. As a result, Islamic law is not uniformly applied throughout Islamic countries any more than civil, common or socialist law is consistent across nations following those traditions.

The first secondary source of the *Shari'a* is analogical reasoning (*qiyas*). In attempts to apply the *Qur'an* and *Sunna*, some Muslims took a strict interpretation and believed every rule of law must be derived from one of these two sources. Others believed human reason and personal opinion should be used to elaborate the law. In the ninth century, the jurist Shafi'a proposed a compromise wherein human reason could be used

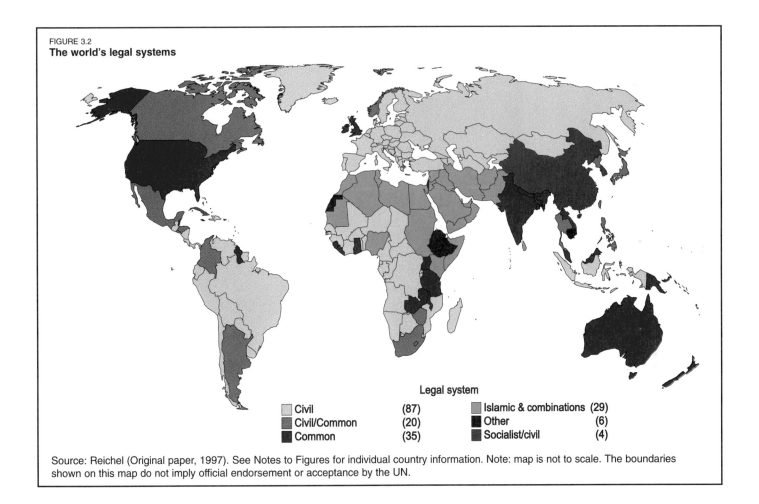

FIGURE 3.2
The world's legal systems

Legal system

Civil	(87)		Islamic & combinations	(29)
Civil/Common	(20)		Other	(6)
Common	(35)		Socialist/civil	(4)

Source: Reichel (Original paper, 1997). See Notes to Figures for individual country information. Note: map is not to scale. The boundaries shown on this map do not imply official endorsement or acceptance by the UN.

to fill gaps left by the *Qur'an* and *Sunna*. But that reasoning must have had divine law as its starting point. For example, judges could sentence persons committing sodomy (not mentioned in the *Qur'an* or *Sunna*) to the same penalty the *Qur'an* provides for adultery by reasoning that sodomy and adultery are similar offences (cf. Lippman *et al.*, 1988).

The other secondary source of Islamic law is consensus by legal scholars (*ijma*). Following Muhammad's death, the leaders of the Muslim community used consultants to interpret the *Qur'an* and *Sunna*. Some scholars became more prominent than others and eventually four schools of thought developed. Within each school, interpretations and solutions were produced when qualified jurists had unanimous agreement on a given point. By the end of the ninth century, the four schools had developed documents explaining how their school interpreted questions or solved unique cases. Since there was consensus among jurists within a particular school, an opinion by an

individual judge was transformed to a statement of divine law.

With the *Qur'an* and *Sunna* as primary sources, and *qiyas* and *ijma* as secondary, the *Shari'a* was complete. The law came from Allah, rather than a political authority, and where gaps remained they were filled only after showing a link to the divine. In this manner, the Islamic legal tradition presents yet another view of law's role in society.

Legal systems and criminal justice processing

How, why and when crimes are recorded and offenders identified and processed through the criminal justice system may depend in large part upon the processing strategy that attaches to the prevailing legal tradition in a country. These practices may or may not be related to the particular legal system. In general, the choice of processing strategies which may be linked to the country's legal tradition can be categorized as falling into the inquisitorial, adversarial or informal types. The following discussion is imprecise since there are many exceptions to the generalizations made. However, in the spirit of providing a brief and broad overview of procedures, this typology is offered as a reasonable portrayal of ways to process offenders.

The inquisitorial process

Herbert Packer (1968) suggested that approaches used to process people through a criminal justice system are ones that emphasize either the efficiency of action or the legitimacy of action. He called the former a *Crime Control Model* and the latter a *Due Process Model.* Although Packer did not suggest that these models could be used to distinguish among legal traditions, they offer a reasonable paradigm for such a distinction. Specifically, the civil law tradition and its inquisitorial process seem to have a particular link to the Crime Control Model. The common law tradition and its adversarial process follow the Due Process Model. Since the procedural aspects of socialist and Islamic law traditions seem to have much in common with the civil law tradition, it is possible to hold discussion to just two types of adjudication procedures. For simplicity, the present discussion concentrates on the civil and common families.

Before discussing the civil and common law traditions as exemplifying the inquisitorial and adversarial models, it is necessary to make clear the following: the values underlying both models are the same. This is an important point since there could be a tendency to believe the models express opposite values. Cole (1989) explains it by noting that the Crime Control Model assumes that freedom is so important that every effort must be made to repress crime. The Due Process Model, on the other hand, assumes freedom is so important that every effort must be made to ensure that criminal justice decisions are based on reliable information. In this way, both models seek to guarantee social freedom. One does so by emphasizing efficient processing of wrongdoers (the Crime Control Model), while the other emphasizes effective restrictions on government invasion in the citizen's life (the Due

Process Model). The greater threat to freedom, says the Crime Control Model, is the criminal trying to harm us or take our property. For the Due Process Model, the greater threat to freedom comes from government agents, like police officers and prosecutors, who are trying to restrict our freedom of movement. Of course social freedom requires law-abiding citizens to be free from unjustifiable intrusion by either criminals or by government agents. However, it seems that nation-states have a hard time achieving both goals simultaneously. One is emphasized at the expense of the other, but neither can be identified as qualitatively better. It is important to keep that in mind when suggesting that a particular legal tradition might emphasize one of the two models.

Under the Crime Control Model, the most important function served by the criminal justice system is to ensure human freedom by allowing citizens to be secure in person and property from the actions of criminals. To operate successfully, the model requires a high rate of apprehension and conviction following a process that emphasizes speed and finality. It is an administrative, almost managerial, model that mirrors the inquisitorial process found in most countries of the civil law tradition. Because the emphasis on speed and finality might mean that innocent people are rushed through the system without recourse, the inquisitorial process excludes, at an early stage, persons apprehended but not likely to be guilty. This model has confidence in the ability of police and prosecutors to identify and release the "probably innocent" suspects, while sustaining action against the "probably guilty" ones.

The civil law tradition follows the Crime Control Model in the sense that its inquisitorial process relies on screening techniques to weed out suspects who are likely innocent, while processing with speed and finality those who are likely guilty. This is seen in several aspects of the inquisitorial process. For example, Ingraham (1987) notes that pre-arrest and pretrial detention procedures in civil law countries often allow police to detain accused persons for 24 to 72 hours (with judicial authorization typically required for periods after 24 hours) while they investigate charges against the person. In several common law countries, on the other hand, even limited periods of investigative detention before arrest are not allowed. Instead, formal arrest must occur to detain the suspect.

Differences in pre-arrest and pretrial detention procedures are important when considering information like arrest statistics among countries. Using the United States as an example, Ingraham (1987) suggests that common law tradition jurisdictions are forced to initiate the arrest process very early. In civil law countries, like France, the inquisitorial process allows for limited periods of investigative detention before arrest. That means the French need not resort to formal arrest as early as do United States jurisdictions. Thus, if arrest statistics in France are compared with those in the United States this may result in a misunderstanding of any perceived differences if one is unaware of how soon police must resort to arrest in each country.

The adversarial process

In its emphasis on legitimacy of action over efficiency of action, the Due Process Model requires many checks on the use of official power. This model insists on a formal fact-finding process that results in a more deliberate movement through the criminal justice system. Like the Crime Control Model, the Due Process Model seeks the truth regarding the accused's involvement in the offence. The Crime Control Model uses the inquisitorial process to detect the truth by emphasizing the screening process and continuing to investigate the matter, even into the trial, until the truth is known. The Due Process Model believes truth is determined better by forcing the state to constantly show its actions toward the accused were appropriate. This makes the adversarial process more suitable to the Due Process Model since the search for truth is believed to arise from a free and open competition over who has the correct facts. The struggle is between the state and the defendant operating as adversaries. This contrasts with the inquisitorial process' view of the state and the defendant as equal parties seeking a similar truth.

Because the adversarial and inquisitorial processes differ in how they believe truth is best determined, the two procedures give

different authority to the legal actors. This is most clearly seen in the role of the judge. Under the inquisitorial process judges have considerable power and influence starting in the investigation stage and continuing through the trial. In this manner the inquisitorial judge is essentially an investigator out to make sure all the information necessary to make the correct decision in the case is available for consideration by the judge. The judge in an adversarial proceeding, however, shares power with the prosecution and the defense. As a result, the adversarial judge is less like an investigator and more like a referee.

When comparing things like prosecution and conviction statistics among countries, it is important to be aware of each country's adjudication style – inquisitorial or adversarial. Since the inquisitorial process, as often found in the civil legal tradition, has presumably screened out the "probably innocent" and is likely to accept into evidence any information that helps determine the defendant's role in the offence, one might expect a high percentage of convictions. Convictions under the adversarial system might be more difficult to accomplish since fewer suspects may be excluded before arrest and since some culpable evidence may have been excluded at trial. This suggests that cross-national comparisons of prosecution and conviction statistics are best interpreted with an understanding of whether the countries follow an inquisitorial or adversarial process.

Informal processing

Under the discussion of the inquisitorial process, we noted that differences in the use of investigatory detention might affect the arrest statistics reported by countries following the adversarial process compared with those using inquisitorial procedures. Discussion of the adversarial process noted that the two types of adjudication might also affect prosecution and conviction statistics. These points are made to simply warn us about the difficulty of country comparison based on statistics that may imply very different things than their titles suggest. That is, arrest, prosecution and conviction statistics do not necessarily measure the same things in all countries just because the countries use

Customary justice: a day in an informal court of justice in Nigeria

On the day of the trial, the parties to the case are seated by the village chief's servants, and other guests are seated too. Then the chief or the chief and his invited elders will come in and take their seats. The chief brings out "kola-nut" and "alligator pepper" — a traditional delicacy served to guests when they visit a man as a first thing before any discussion — and gives it to his oldest male relative to pass to the rightful person. Generally among the Ibos, the oldest person or the chief breaks the kola-nut and the servants pass it to the people in the court from the oldest to the youngest. In some Ibo towns, the youngest person breaks the kola-nut and serves it to the elders before the younger persons.

After the kola-nut and the alligator pepper are eaten, the chief calls the victim to present his case. After the victim has presented his case, and pointed out his witnesses, the accused is called upon to defend himself. If the accused has his own witness or witnesses, he must mention them. When the victim and the accused are presenting their cases or evidence, all witnesses must be out of earshot from the court. This court follows the inquisitorial approach in which the burden of proof is on the defendant.

The defendant's defenses include an alibi, self-defense, revenge (acceptable under customary law), and ignorance of the law (acceptable under customary law) (Anyebe, 1985).

After the village chief has heard all of the evidence, he orders the witness or witnesses for the victim to come into the court to tell the court what they know about the case. After that, the chief orders the witness or witnesses of the accused to enter the court and tell the court what they know about the case. Both parties are allowed to cross-examine each other and their witnesses.

After hearing all of the evidence, the parties in the case and their witnesses are ordered by the chief to leave the court and stay out of earshot from the court. The chief then asks his fellow elders what they think the judgment should be. After allowing his invited elders to air their views on the case, he tells them what his judgment will be. In most cases, his invited elders agree with him. After the chief has decided what the judgment will be, he orders the parties to be brought back into the court.

The chief then explains the customary law that applies to the case and announces his judgment. If any party in the case does not like the decision of the village chief, he could take his case to the formal customary criminal court or to a Magistrate's Court. And if a party found guilty refuses to carry out the penalty imposed upon him by the village chief, the village chief and the victim can take the case to either the formal customary criminal court or to a Magistrate's Court. This warning of an alternative outcome terrifies accused persons, and it makes them respond to the chief's court. In either case, the chief will bear witness against the accused. Unmistakably, in most cases, the formal customary criminal court or the Magistrate's Court sustains the prior decision of the village chief. Unlike the American, English or Nigerian English based criminal court of appeals, the appellate jurisdiction of the formal customary criminal court is to decide the case appealed, and it can impose a penalty more severe than the one imposed by the village chief's court.

Source: Edited and abridged from Ebbe (Original paper, 1997)

ing how a process works in actuality as well as studying how it is supposed to work. This "law in action" versus "law on the books" distinction is important in any attempt to understand how a country's justice system operates. Often the informal law in action part is only identified after lengthy periods of observation. Other times, however, the informal aspect of a country's social control system is more readily apparent. Because the open, if not official, informal processing of suspects and defendants can influence a country's crime and justice statistics, it is necessary to mention that process.

Since some countries have informal responses to even serious offences, some crimes never appear in the official statistics. The result may be a reduced violent crime rate for those countries compared to the violent crime rate in countries where similar acts are more regularly recorded. Consider, for example, Saudi Arabia's use of *diyya*.

The *Shari'a* allows, and even encourages, non-legalistic responses to misbehaviour — even to serious acts like murder. Souryal (1987) notes that criminal complaints are often resolved through arbitration even before a police record is made. That means those acts never appear in official crime statistics. While such informal responses may be found in many countries for less serious offences, Groves, Newman, and Corrado (1987) explain that even homicide statistics are probably higher in Saudi Arabia than official counts indicate. The deflated homicide (and other crimes against the person) statistics are partly explained as a result of the *Qur'an* tempering retaliation by encouraging forgiveness. When retaliation for a crime against the person is waived by the victim or the victim's family, *diyya* is applied instead. Al-Sagheer defines *diyya* as "money paid to a harmed person or his heir in compensation for a felony committed against him" (1994). Since the paying of *diyya* presumably deters the offender and compensates the victim or his heirs, there is no need for more formal action and the act is not officially tallied.

Besides unofficial, therefore unrecorded, responses to crime, it is also possible that countries might informally sanction convicted offenders. That strategy may result, for example, in a lower percentage of of-

the same titles on graphs reporting those statistics. That caution does not mean countries cannot be compared. Instead, it simply warns us that comparison of justice statistics must be undertaken with an understanding of, and appreciation for, the way things like the legal tradition and adjudication process can influence the statistics.

A similar problem is presented by another strategy used to process offenders through the justice system. All countries have ways of handling suspects and defendants that are not official or formal strategies. Sociologists and political scientists, especially, have noted the importance of study-

fenders on probation or in prison than is found in another country where sanctioning is more typically formal and official. Japan may be an example of a country where informal responses to offenders can affect the country's official statistics. Upham (1987) presents Japan's justice process as an example of bureaucratic informality where sanctions are often private, indirect, ambiguous and unrecorded. For persons familiar with the publications of Japan's justice bureaus, this perspective may seem contradictory since Japan keeps and publishes some of the most thorough crime and justice statistics in the world. However, because of the reliance on bureaucratic informality, some offences and offenders never make it to the record books.

Japan's Research and Training Institute (1990) reported that the 1988 crime clearance rate by Japan's police was higher than the clearance rates in the United States, the United Kingdom, West Germany or France. In the United States, for example, 70 percent of the homicides and 17.5 percent of the larcenies were cleared by police during 1988. In that same year Japanese police cleared 96.6 percent of Japan's homicides and 55.7 percent of the larcenies. To most accurately compare clearance rates in these two countries it is important to know some differences in terminology. The clearance rate for American police reflects a suspect being arrested, charged with committing an offence, and turned over to the court for prosecution. In Japan, however, a crime is reported as cleared when the police tell the prosecutor the crime has been solved. No arrest is necessary. Given these differences in what counts as "cleared," the variation in clearance rates between the United States and Japan seems less glaring.

Other crime and justice statistics in Japan are as impressive as the clearance rates. Over 99 percent of the offenders eventually coming before a judge in Japan are convicted and nearly 99 percent of those convicted receive a prison sentence. However, because of informal control mechanisms at each stage in the justice process, these statistics should be considered with additional knowledge. For example, the 99 percent conviction rate hides the fact that most of the cases are not contested by the defendant. Also, saying that 99 percent of those convicted receive a prison sentence seems impressive until we realize that over half those prison sentences are suspended — with the offenders usually not even being placed under supervision (see Reichel 1994).

Bringing attention to Japan's use of informal techniques for responding to offenders, and the resulting impact that nonofficial response might have on Japan's crime and justice statistics, is not meant to be a critical appraisal. It is quite likely that Japan would still have enviable clearance, crime and prosecution rates even if everyone was handled formally and officially recorded. Strong arguments can be made that informal social control strategies are more effective than are formal techniques. The point is not to criticize or unveil the Japanese process. Instead, the goal is to remind us that crime and justice statistics are appropriately compared only after understanding each country's legal system, adjudication process, and the specific operation of its criminal justice system.

The remainder of this chapter is concerned with presenting data provided by the United Nations Crime and Justice Surveys.

The generation of justice statistics

As was noted in the introductory chapter to this volume, criminal justice systems around the world present some similarities. Elements such as the police, courts and prisons are found in almost all countries, albeit their names may be different. The roles and functions of these elements may also be similar, but the methods used to fulfill these roles and functions may be different. While operating policies and procedures for the police, for example, may be similar, practices may differ. And as we have seen above, depending upon what legal systems the countries follow, the sequence or steps between the beginning and end of the criminal justice system may differ.

We have seen in the previous chapter that the police make up the front-end of the criminal justice system. A crime for which the victim wishes a response must be reported to the police. The police initiate the investigation, determine the status of the criminal incident, and make an arrest (see Box 3.2). In many countries, the police officer may also be the prosecutor; in others

Elements of criminal justice systems such as the police, courts and prisons are found in almost all countries, albeit their names may be different.

BOX 3.2

Making an arrest in England

The basic reason for arrest is to secure someone's temporary detention to make them available for judicial processing, typically for a criminal charge. Arrest will not necessarily entail pretrial detention. Police bail can be issued quickly, so that no more than a few hours may elapse before a person's liberty is regained. As an alternative to arrest, appearance at court may be secured by a summons.

The circumstances whereby a police officer or other citizen comes to make an arrest vary. For example, a court may issue an arrest warrant. In such cases, arrest by a police officer is a simple (but not necessarily an easy) matter. Even if the court lacks jurisdiction to issue the warrant, the officer is protected from any action. A second circumstance occurs when police arrests follow information from, and complaints by, victims and witnesses (Reiner 1985). This is the most common circumstance in which arrest occurs. In such cases, there can be a degree of reflection by the police about whether or how to effect an arrest.

A police officer in England or Wales is called to, or happens upon, a place where there is a problem. In some cases, he or she is expected to help, not to cast immediate blame. Sometimes there is no blame to cast: a storm has brought down a healthy tree, which is disrupting traffic. Sometimes, in addition to immediate help, actions must be taken to secure evidence for later use. For example, a truck has shed its load, which may have been insufficiently secured. Finally, the officer is implicitly required to take action against a person who is, putatively, to blame for something. The person blamed may or may not be present. If present, the officer must decide whether to arrest. An arrestable offence is (to simplify) one where the maximum penalty is not less than five years in prison. The law on arrest, set out in the Police and Criminal Evidence Act 1984 s24 applies to both police officers and other citizens:

"(4) Any person may arrest without a warrant –
anyone who is in the act of committing an arrestable offence;
anyone whom he has reasonable grounds for suspecting to be committing such an offence.
Where an arrestable offence has been committed, any person may arrest without a warrant –
anyone who is guilty of the offence;
anyone whom he has reasonable grounds for suspecting to be guilty of it.
Where a constable has reasonable grounds for suspecting that an arrestable offence has been committed, he may arrest without a warrant anyone whom he has reasonable grounds for suspecting to be guilty of the offence.
A constable may arrest without a warrant –
anyone who is about to commit an arrestable offence;
anyone whom he has reasonable grounds for suspecting to be about to commit an arrestable offence."

It will be noted that the difference between the powers of citizens and those of police officers is primarily one of permitted anticipation. Police officers may anticipate a crime in making an arrest (so long as they can satisfy due process rules afterwards). Other citizens may not.

As is usual, the wonderful coolness of the law books contrasts with the hurly-burly of street life. Police training in England and Wales directs attention to respect for the individual, even allowing arrested people to pay for their own taxi to the police station as an alternative to travelling in police transport.

What traps await officer or citizen in exercising the power to arrest? If powers of arrest are exceeded, a charge of the crime of false imprisonment may ensue. False imprisonment exists in "the unlawful and intentional or reckless restraint of a victim's freedom of movement from a particular place" (Smith 1996). An arrested person must be informed of the ground of his or her arrest at the time or as soon as is practicable thereafter. This has pitfalls. If the precise crime specified has not been committed, the arrest is not valid.

An arrester must have a valid ground for the arrest in mind *when he or she makes it*. This is not a trivial requirement in chaotic situations.

The difficulty with due process standards is their distance from policing reality. It is clear that a decision is made with subsequent attention to satisfying disinterested third parties about adherence to due process (Sanders 1993). To give the flavour of the discretion needed, two cases from the recent experience of the first author can be used. An elderly man paid the store checkout person for several bags of shopping but also took a bar of chocolate. He appeared to suffer from dementia. Instead of arrest, he received an instant caution at the scene (which he almost certainly never understood and immediately forgot). A more formal approach (which would protect the officer from allegations of neglect of duty) would be to arrest the man and at the police station have the designated custody officer deal with the matter by way of refused charge, or to send an advice file to the prosecuting authority (the Crown Prosecution Service) that to proceed with the case would not be in the public interest.

In the second case, a man lived with his elderly mother and reported her to the police as missing from home. He last saw her the previous day when they had argued about her relationship with a younger man. Her body was found in a stream at the rear of their home. The attendant circumstances are such that the son could have been arrested on suspicion of murder. Instead, he was "invited" to the police station to assist with the police enquiry. Had he refused to attend voluntarily, a decision to arrest may well have been made. In the event, the postmortem examination showed injuries to the mother consistent with a fall. The distinction between the invitation and arrest is important not least because the amount of time which may elapse after an arrest and before charge or release is tightly controlled.

Source: Henshaw and Pease (Original paper, 1997)

---

the work of prosecution is carried out by an agency different from the police.

It is the sequence of police, prosecution, courts and prisons that separates the United Nations survey questionnaire into its four respective parts. The police part covers up to the stage of arrest of a suspect, and countries that do not have a separate prosecution service sometimes use this arrest or charges laid statistic as their indicator of prosecution.

Statistics on offenders, including suspects, persons prosecuted and those convicted, are much more problematic than those on recorded crime. The United Nations survey does not seek information on the recorded crimes that are cleared or solved. Countries that publish statistics on the crimes cleared show that a large number of recorded crimes are never cleared or solved. The arrest/suspect data provided by the responding countries do not indicate whether the suspects were responsible for all the recorded crimes or only a portion of these. Furthermore, the arrest/suspect data could fall in any one of the following categories, and as such may not be comparable:

(i) the number of distinct persons arrested, (i.e., if a person is arrested on a number of occasions within a year he/she is counted only once);

(ii) the number of persons arrested may mean a person arrested several times for different incidents during the year and counted each time arrested;

(iii) the number of persons charged and brought before the courts;

(iv) the number of persons suspected of committing crimes – not necessarily arrested;

(v) the number of individuals named as suspects by the victim or complainant;

(vi) the number of persons warned, admonished or cautioned – not necessarily arrested.

Responses to the United Nations survey and communications with respondents from a number of countries highlight these and other differences. Similar issues emerge at the prosecution and trial levels – that is, whether the prosecution and court trial statistics relate to individual offenders, charges or arrests. It is this type of difficulty that poses problems in assessing filtering of offenders or case attrition in the criminal justice system, particularly in a federal system of government. Wherever possible an attempt will be made to highlight this filtering process from the United Nations survey data. Before this is done, here is an example of filtering.

Through Crime Victim Surveys or Crime and Safety Surveys (as we saw in Chapter 1), a number of countries now have a rough measure of the true extent of crime. But these surveys do not include questions on all crimes and for all places. They do not as a rule include drug offences, fraud or offences against business, offices, schools, etc. When these statistics are included along with official data of offender processing, considerable attrition occurs, as can be seen in Box 3.3.

BOX 3.3

Case attrition in New South Wales, Australia

Crime and safety surveys are becoming quite regular in Australia, and states have their own surveys. The State of New South Wales has been conducting these surveys annually since 1990. The example presented here relates to 1996 and only to four crimes: break and enter and attempted break and enter of households, motor vehicle theft, assault and robbery. Statistics from this survey and police and court records for 1996 show the following attrition pattern:

1. Incidents of victimizations	446,000	100.0%
2. Victimizations reported to police	239,700	53.7%
3. Crimes recorded by police	178,682	40.1%
4. Crimes cleared	33,113	7.4%
5. Suspects brought before courts for trial	33,457	7.5%
6. Offenders convicted	18,901	4.2%
7. Offenders given prison sentences	2,864	0.6%

NB These estimates are based on statistics produced by various agencies and relate only to the four offences stated above and offenders processed for these offences.

The statistics reveal that well over 92 percent of these four crimes that occurred in 1996 were never solved by the arrest or identification of suspects. Of all the suspects brought before courts charged with one of these crimes, a little over half were convicted, and only one in seven of those convicted received a prison sentence. Looking at the data from another angle, it appears that one offender was sentenced to a term of imprisonment for every 156 crimes of break and enter, motor vehicle theft, assault or robbery. This filtering/case attrition process is illustrated in the Figure below which displays the filtering of cases for breaking and entering, motor vehicle theft, robbery and assault..

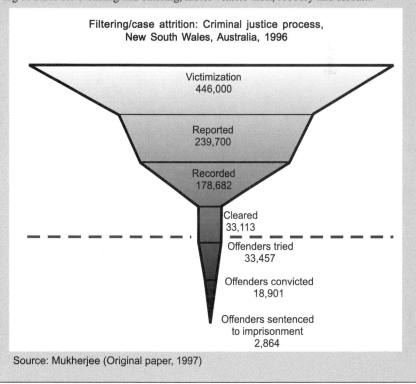

Filtering/case attrition: Criminal justice process, New South Wales, Australia, 1996

Victimization 446,000

Reported 239,700

Recorded 178,682

Cleared 33,113

Offenders tried 33,457

Offenders convicted 18,901

Offenders sentenced to imprisonment 2,864

Source: Mukherjee (Original paper, 1997)

The Fifth United Nations Survey

In this chapter we draw entirely upon the data collected by the Fifth United Nations Survey of Crime Trends and Operation of Criminal Justice Systems. The survey, which

TABLE 3.1
Crime filtering, 1994 (per 100,000 population)

	Total Suspects	Total Prosecutions	Total Convictions	Total Sentences
Belarus	638	56	516	363
Croatia	837	610	412	36
Cyprus	536	146	104	19
Denmark	2826	3166	528	50
Egypt	33	12406	7371	56
Estonia	621	621	485	173
Finland	4157	1744	1677	52
Hong Kong	821	557	423	178
Hungary	1165	1003	763	87
Italy	1302	1051	361	45
Japan	302	95	47	30
Latvia	524	457	443	271
"FYRM"*	1124	692	386	54
Rep Of Moldova	410	383	350	167
Slovakia	913	794	476	103
Slovenia	1637	480	377	28
Turkey	410	2700	1228	34

*"The Former Yugoslav Republic of Macedonia"

Source: Fifth UNCJS. The UNCJS asked two separate questions in regard to offender based statistics for each stage of the criminal justice processing, except sentencing. One question asked for data by offence type, which also included an "other" category. The other question asked for statistics by age and gender. The data above are based on the data by gender. This question was used because it appeared overall to provide the most consistent data. However, anomalies do exist in these data. The reader is cautioned to consult the list of exceptions in Appendix 2 before interpreting this table. Please see Notes to Tables for more information.

covers the five year period 1990-1994, requested data from each country on the number of suspects, number prosecuted, number convicted and the number sentenced to a term of imprisonment. Not all countries could provide statistical information on all the items; 17 countries did. The data from these countries have been included in Table 3.1. The data reflect at least two major types of differences in processing alleged offenders. First, the offender processing rate varies significantly across countries. For example, Chile's suspect rate in 1994 was 5,011 per 100,000 population and Japan's rate was only 302. Differences of even greater magnitude were obtained in the prosecution and conviction stages. Second, if convictions and sentences of imprisonment reflect punitiveness, the data show that some countries relative to others are more punitive. For example, in Chile, courts convict one in 20 suspects, and one in four of those convicted go to prison. However, these statistics can be misleading. For example, in Japan, one in three suspects is prosecuted, of those prosecuted one in two is convicted, and of those convicted two out of three are sent to prison. Although, on the surface, it may appear that Japan is highly punitive, Japan's suspect rate is 17 times smaller than that of Chile. The assessment of the com-

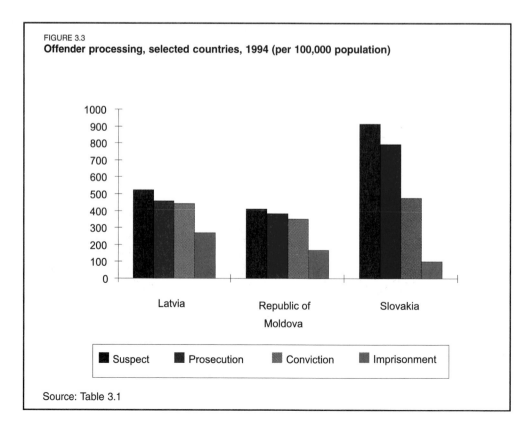

FIGURE 3.3
Offender processing, selected countries, 1994 (per 100,000 population)

Source: Table 3.1

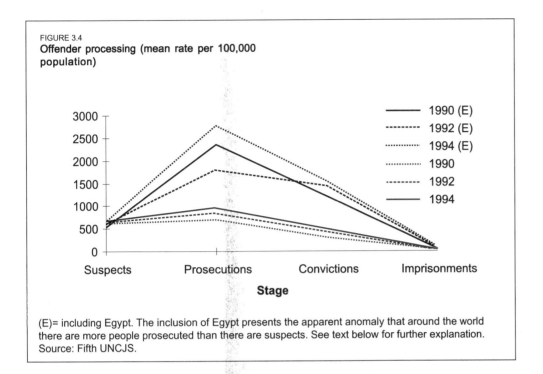

FIGURE 3.4
Offender processing (mean rate per 100,000 population)

Legend:
- 1990 (E)
- 1992 (E)
- 1994 (E)
- 1990
- 1992
- 1994

(E)= including Egypt. The inclusion of Egypt presents the apparent anomaly that around the world there are more people prosecuted than there are suspects. See text below for further explanation.
Source: Fifth UNCJS.

parative "punitiveness" of a country is a highly complex task, which is examined more closely in Chapter 4.

Another pattern emerges from data for Latvia, Republic of Moldovia and Slovakia. As shown in Figure 3.3, a relatively high proportion of suspects are prosecuted, convicted and sent to prison. While punitiveness may be one explanation for the high rate of imprisonment, it is also possible to speculate that these recently independent countries may not have had the time to design and implement suitable alternatives to imprisonment, partly because the priorities of the nation had to be on other aspects of society and partly because of constraints on resources. Future surveys may be able to throw more light on the matter. The differences between countries in the rates of processing offenders, therefore, could be for a number of reasons, including differences in the legal tradition and the criminal justice system.

The survey data clearly show that a case filtering process cannot properly be described by using both the number of suspects and the number of prosecutions. Also, although comparisons between countries are not planned for this chapter, it is often very difficult to avoid mentioning names of countries that influence the overall suspect, prosecution and conviction rates in a significant

GLOBAL SNAPSHOT
Known suspects reported in each of the five UNCJS (per 100,000 population)

With the exception of 1985, developing countries have arrested offenders at a lower rate than industrialized countries. Rates for industrialized countries have fluctuated considerably during the past 20 years.

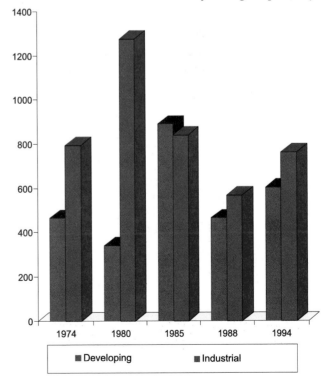

■ Developing   ■ Industrial

Source: Five UNCJS. Countries may vary in each year and survey. See Notes to Snapshots for complete information, including individual country rates.

TABLE 3.2
Number of suspects by gender and age and rate of all suspects, 1994 (per 100,000 population)

	Adult Male	Adult Female	Juvenile Male	Juvenile Female	Total	Rate
Austria	139417	34280	21128	3838	198663	2474
Azerbaijan	12932	891	803	11	14637	196
Bahamas	4156	246	418	33	4853	1771
Bermuda	1223	199	132	21	1575	2500
Bolivia	42951	21855	13603	5957	84366	1166
Bulgaria	63590	6515	10727	543	81375	964
Canada	390342	80198	101675	25524	597739	2044
Chile	618224	43295	33707	6065	701291	5011
Colombia	62095	3963	4263	272	70593	204
Croatia	50687	2602	2866	95	56250	1249
Cyprus	964	68	52	0	1084	148
Denmark	50366	11840	6625	1189	70020	1345
Ecuador	26437	2616	3205	230	32488	290
France	566647	99716	98934	10404	775701	1343
Georgia	6730	443	715	9	7897	145
Hong Kong	28415	5164	13568	2637	49784	821
Hungary	93836	11179	13331	1148	119494	1165
India	5871205	246767	15664	3155	6136791	668
Indonesia	122465	2245	3944	50	128704	67
Jamaica	22008	8661	2932	1468	35069	1405
Japan	144810	31887	105260	26008	307965	247
Kyrgyzstan	17087	2331	1344	98	20860	454
Latvia	10538	1084	1610	118	13350	524
Lithuania	16028	2226	2843	193	21290	572
Madagascar	5324	751	105	30	6210	43
Marshall Islands	1680	81	0	0	1761	3261
Morocco	176684	37648	4573	989	219894	827
Nicaragua	23840	2395	256	41	26532	603
Qatar	4543	213	344	6	5106	946
Rep of Korea	1138424	176513	102167	6514	1423618	3203
Rep of Moldova	14011	1485	2182	172	17850	410
Romania	142354	13799	14012	4600	174765	769
Russian Fed.	1068871	171743	184582	16372	1441568	974
Saint V.& Gren.	3655	491	125	17	4288	3863
Sao T.& Princ.	1044	230	127	38	1439	1151
Slovakia	35339	2826	4855	258	43278	809
Slovenia	21022	3006	7122	637	31787	1637
Sudan	287624	71115	38371	9975	407085	1406
Sweden	66556	13653	17621	4062	101892	1161
Syrian Arab Rep	40401	2894	4112	1204	48611	351
Ukraine	197310	39155	30202	2479	269146	518
USA	7844213	1823300	1660549	549126	11877188	4557
Western Samoa	91	1	2	0	94	57
Yugoslavia	85368	5864	5577	204	97013	923

Source: Fifth UNCJS

way. Just to illustrate this point, the reader is asked to examine the data in Table 3.1. The prosecution rate of Egypt was more than the aggregate of all the other countries included in the Table, except Turkey. The reasons for these differences in prosecution statistics may be many. The apparent anomaly that there are more prosecutions than suspects reported by some countries, such as Egypt, may be explained by recording practices. For example, prosecutions maybe recorded by the number of crimes for which a suspect is prosecuted, rather than according to the number of persons who are prosecuted for a single crime. Figure 3.4 displays these various patterns and also offers trends in processing rates. Data in the figure clearly show that either suspect status or prosecution should be treated as the first stage of bringing a person to justice for his/her crimes. The data also show that there has been a gradual increase in suspect and conviction rates between 1990 and 1994, but the rate of imprisonment has remained fairly stable. It is apparent that a large majority of offenders who are convicted by courts do not receive a custodial sentence. Indeed, for this group of countries, on an average, the imprisonment rate is only about six percent of the conviction rate, almost exactly the rate in New South Wales (Box 3.3).

Suspects by gender and age

A much larger group of countries, 44 in all, supplied data for suspects by gender and by age (juvenile or adult). But this information was available only for total suspects and not by offence. Nevertheless, the data shown in Table 3.2 include countries from most regions of the world and, with the notable exception of China, includes all the countries with large population. The data, therefore, produce a relatively representative sample of all the countries of the world. The suspect status is the first stage when the identity of an alleged offender is known and therefore represents the first point of contact with the criminal justice system. A suspect is not necessarily a person in custody but may be on bail pending charges and trial.

Table 3.2 presents data on the number of suspects in each country in 1994 by gender and age and rates of total suspects per

---

BOX 3.4

Age of criminal responsibility around the world

As we can see from the table below, the age of criminal responsibility varies widely around the world. For instance, the lowest minimum age is six (Sri Lanka) while the highest minimum age is under 21 (Indonesia). Similarly, the lowest adult age is 15 (Saint Vincent) while the highest adult age is 21 (Hong Kong).

Even within continents, there is much variation. For example, in Europe, England makes the minimum age ten and the adult age 18 while Finland has 15 as the minimum age and 21 as the adult age. In the same vein the Republic of Korea has 14 as the minimum age and 20 as the adult age while its fellow Asian country Singapore has seven as the minimum age and 17 as the adult age.

There is one common feature: the majority of countries attribute full adult criminal responsibility to age 18 or older.

Age of criminal responsibility

Country	Min.age Respons.	Age of full adult	Country	Min.age Respons.	Age of full adult
Albania	14	18	Kyrgystan	16 (14)	18
Armenia	16 (14)	18	Latvia.	16 (14)	18
Australia	7	16	Liechtenstein	14	19
Austria	14	20	Lithuania	16 (14)	18
Azerbaijan	16 (14)	18	"FYRM"*	14	18
Bahamas	7	18	Madagascar	under 18	18 +
Belarus	16 (14)	18	Malta	9 (14)	18
Belgium	18 (16)	18	Mauritius	under 18	18 +
Bermuda	under 16	16 +	Micronesia	under 16	16 +
Bolivia	15	21	Moldova	16 (14)	18
Bulgaria	14	18	Morocco	under 16	16 +
Canada	12	18	Netherlands	12	18
Chile	under 18	18+	New Zealand	10	18
China	under age 16	16+	Nicaragua	under 16	16 +
Colombia	under 18	18+	Nigeria	7	17
Costa Rica	12	18	Norway	15	18
Croatia	14	18	Papua N. G.	7	18
Cyprus	under 17	17 +	Peru	under 18	18 +
Czech Rep.	15	18	Poland	17 (16)	18
Denmark	15	18	Portugal	16	20
Ecuador	under 18	18 +	Qatar	under 18	18 +
Egypt	under 18	18 +	Rep. Korea.	14	20
Eng. & Wales	10	18	Romania	14	18
Estonia	13	18	Russia	16 (14)	18
Finland	15	21	Saint V.& Gren.	8	15
France	13	19	West. Samoa	under 18	18 +
Georgia	14	18	S. Tome & Princ.	16	18
Germany	14	18	Scotland	8 (16)	21
Ghana	under 18	18 +	Singapore	7	17
Greece	under 17	17 +	Slovakia	15	18
Hong Kong	7	21	Slovenia	14	18
Hungary	14	18	Spain	16	18
Iceland	15	18	Sri Lanka	6	17
India	under 16	16 +	Sudan	under 18	18 +
Indonesia	under 21	21 +	Sweden	15	21
Ireland	7 (14)	18	Switzerland	7 (15)	18
North. Ireland	under 17	17 +	Syria	under 18	18 +
Israel	12	18	Tajikistan	16 (14)	18
Italy	14	18	Turkey	11	18
Jamaica	12	18	Ukraine	16 (14)	18
Japan	14	20	USA	under 18	18 +
Jordan	under 18	18 +	Uruguay	under 18	18 +
Kazakhstan	16 (14)	18	Venezuela	under 18	18 +
Kenya	7	18	Yugoslavia	14	18
			Zambia	under 18	18 +

*"The Former Yugoslav Republic of Macedonia"

Sources: Freilich, 1997. There are many exceptions and qualifications to these data. See Notes to Boxes for a full description and detailed sources.

FIGURE 3.5
Number of adult male suspects per adult female suspects, 1994

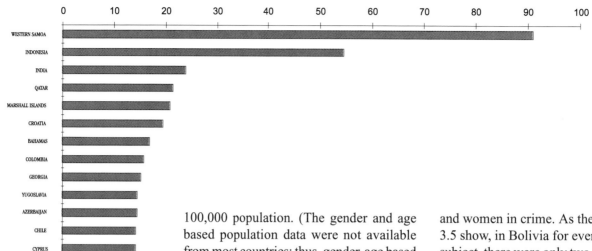

Source: Fifth UNCJS

100,000 population. (The gender and age based population data were not available from most countries; thus, gender-age based rates of suspects could not be calculated.) As is apparent from the table, suspect rates of countries vary enormously, from a low of 43 for Madagascar to a high of 5,011 per 100,000 population for Chile. That is to say, whereas one in over 2,300 people in Madagascar was a suspect in 1994, the corresponding figure for Chile was one in 20; for all the countries put together, one in about 80 people was a suspect.

Table 3.2 also shows that the largest group of suspects in each of the countries was adult males and the smallest was juvenile females. Because of a lack of population data, it is not possible to say much about the volume of suspects in each of the gender-age groups. Thus, while the largest number of suspects in a country are adult males, their rate per 100,000 relevant population may be much lower than the rate of juvenile males. Of course, the definition of juvenile varies from one country to another. But crime statistics from many countries show that young people are over represented in most crimes (Box 3.4), as does the processing and treatment of juvenile offenders (see Box 3.5). An intuitive analysis of the data in Table 3.2 also offers the same impression.

While the rate of participation of gender-age groups in crime cannot be assessed from the Fifth United Nations Survey, it is possible to examine the relative participation of males and females as adults and juveniles. Figures 3.5 and 3.6 explore the female to male ratio among adults and juveniles respectively. There appears substantial difference in the level of participation of men and women in crime. As the data in Figure 3.5 show, in Bolivia for every adult female subject, there were only two adult male suspects; in Western Samoa for each adult female, there were 91 adult male suspects; the average number of adult males per female suspect for all the countries is 12. There are some regional differences, but the data require a different type of analysis. For example, the female to male suspect ratio appears quite similar in the countries of Western Europe and North America; in these countries for every adult female there were between four and six adult male suspects. Economically developed countries of Asia and former Eastern Europe can also be categorized with the previous group. However, a proper analysis of the data requires collection of data on other aspects of a society, especially the "protective" attitude toward women and girls in various countries.

Figure 3.6 displays the number of juvenile male suspects per juvenile female suspects. In this case as well, Bolivia and Jamaica have the least number of boys per girl suspects in 1994. Very few girls are taken as suspects in Georgia, Indonesia, Azerbaijan and Qatar. The average number of boys per girl suspects for all the countries was 16, and the median number was ten. All the West European and North American countries in the sample have fewer boys per girl suspect than France (ten).

Convictions by gender and age

Not all countries that supplied suspect data were able to provide court statistics; indeed, less than half of these countries pro-

FIGURE 3.6
Number of juvenile male suspects per juvenile female suspects

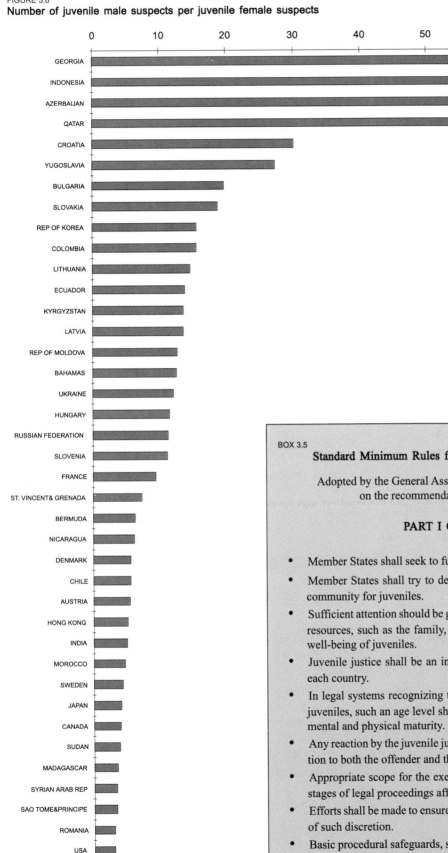

Source: Fifth WCS

BOX 3.5
Standard Minimum Rules for the Administration of Juvenile Justice

Adopted by the General Assembly, 29 November 1985 (resolution 40/33),
on the recommendation of the Seventh UN Congress

PART I GENERAL PRINCIPLES

- Member States shall seek to further the well-being of juveniles and their families.
- Member States shall try to develop conditions to ensure meaningful lives in the community for juveniles.
- Sufficient attention should be given to positive measures involving mobilization of resources, such as the family, volunteers and community groups, to promote the well-being of juveniles.
- Juvenile justice shall be an integral part of the national development process of each country.
- In legal systems recognizing the concept of an age of criminal responsibility for juveniles, such an age level shall not be fixed too low, bearing in mind emotional, mental and physical maturity.
- Any reaction by the juvenile justice system to juvenile offenders shall be in proportion to both the offender and the offence.
- Appropriate scope for the exercise of discretionary power shall be allowed at all stages of legal proceedings affecting juveniles.
- Efforts shall be made to ensure sufficient accountability at all stages in the exercise of such discretion.
- Basic procedural safeguards, such as the presumption of innocence, the right to be notified of charges, the right to remain silent, the right to counsel, the right to the presence of a parent or guardian, the right to confront and cross-examine witnesses and the right to appeal, shall be guaranteed at all stages of proceedings.
- The juvenile's right to privacy shall be respected at all stages.

Source: Abridged from UN document A/CONF.121/14

FIGURE 3.7
Ratio of adult male convictions per female convictions, 1994

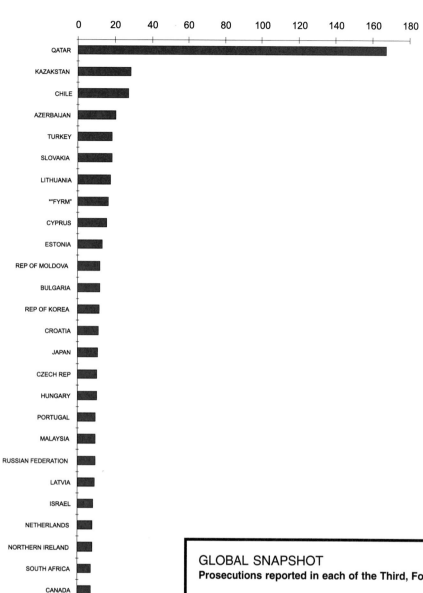

*"Former Yugoslav Republic of Macedonia"

Source: Fifth UNCJS

vided data on convictions by various courts. On the other hand, some countries which did not supply suspect data were able to submit court data. In all, 38 countries offered information on the number of convictions by gender and age. The overall conviction rate per 100,000 population was 510; this rate was the highest in Sweden (1,743) and lowest in Japan (47).

Because of the lack of gender-age specific population data, only a superficial analysis of the conviction data can be made. It appears that, compared to suspects, more adult males per adult females were convicted in the courts of law, suggesting attrition of cases involving females. The average conviction ratio for all the countries in the sample was 15 adult males per adult female; Austria convicted the least number of males (four) per female and Qatar convicted the most number of males (167) per female (see Figure 3.7).

On average, 17 boys for each girl were convicted of a crime by the courts. Data in Figure 3.8 show that the ratio in Finland and Italy was the lowest (i.e., fewer boys per girl were convicted). In Slovakia, on the other hand, for each girl more than 80 boys were convicted. The rate of conviction depends very much on the legal system, type of crime, quality of evidence, availability of legal aid and assistance, type of social

---

GLOBAL SNAPSHOT
Prosecutions reported in each of the Third, Fourth and Fifth UNCJS (per 100,000 population)

Data for prosecutions are especially difficult to obtain because of the wide variations in offender processing according to the prevailing type of legal tradition. With the exception of 1988, developing countries have formally prosecuted offenders at a lower rate than industrialized countries. Developing country rates have also been relatively more stable than those of industrial countries.

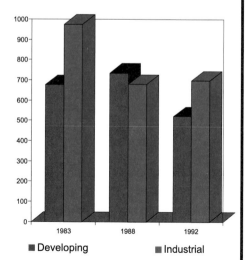

Source: Third, Fourth and Fifth UNCJS. Countries may vary in each year and survey. See Notes to Snapshots for complete information, including individual country rates.

FIGURE 3.8
Number of juvenile male convictions per juvenile female convictions, 1994

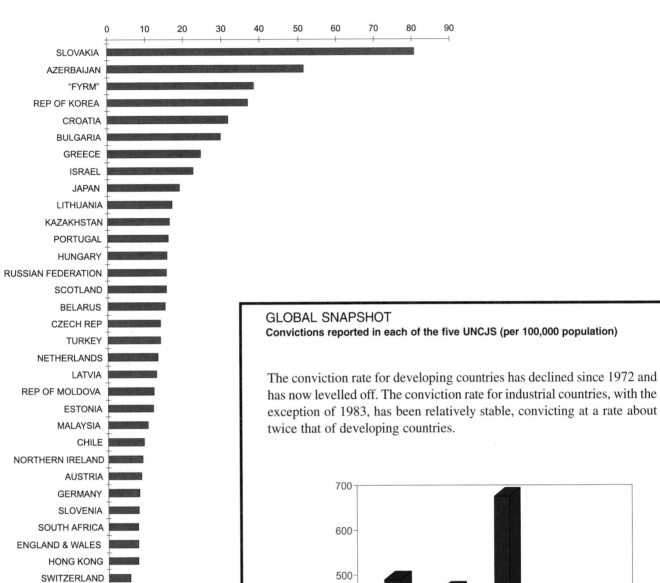

Source: Fifth UNCJS

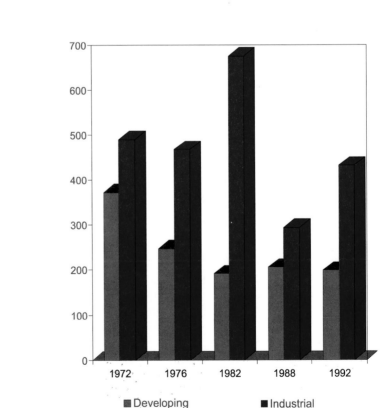

GLOBAL SNAPSHOT
Convictions reported in each of the five UNCJS (per 100,000 population)

The conviction rate for developing countries has declined since 1972 and has now levelled off. The conviction rate for industrial countries, with the exception of 1983, has been relatively stable, convicting at a rate about twice that of developing countries.

Source: Five UNCJS. Countries may vary in each year and survey. See Notes to Snapshots for complete information, including individual country rates.

services available, judicial attitude toward convicting young girls, etc. Indeed, some countries have specific programs for diverting juveniles, both boys and girls, away from the criminal justice system at various points of the process (see Box 3.6).

BOX 3.6

Diversion: keeping people out of the formal judicial process in Canada

Diversion attempts to keep persons accused of less serious offences from further involvement with the formal justice system, often by dealing with them at the community level. The United Nations *Convention on the Rights of the Child* (Article 40) states that measures other than judicial proceedings should be used to deal with children who have infringed the law, whenever appropriate (see also Box 3.5).

In Canada the diversion of youth aged 12 to 17 can occur at two points in the criminal justice process. As can be seen in the Figure below, at the point of initial contact with the youth, the police officer has four options: to take no action; to divert the person from the formal system with an informal warning or other such action; to recommend to the Crown that the person be considered for a pre-charge alternative measures program; or to charge the person. Once an individual has been charged, the Crown has two options: to refer the person to a post-charge alternative measures program; or to proceed with the case through the court process. Diversion, therefore, involves two fairly distinct responses:

- Police Discretion – decision by the police officer to deal with the incident informally rather than laying charges; and,
- Alternative Measures – decision by the Crown to deal with the incident through formal alternative measures programs, either at the pre- or post-charge stage.

Juvenile diversion began in the 1970s in some jurisdictions in Canada and was formally incorporated into the *Young Offenders Act* (*YOA*) in 1984. The *YOA* also gives provinces/territories the authority to develop alternative measures programs. Alternative measures programs divert individuals from criminal prosecution and court-imposed dispositions and deal with them in a less formal environment. The *YOA* also allows communities to become involved in alternative measures through the establishment of youth justice committees. These committees are based on the concept of community members assuming responsibility and becoming involved in addressing criminal justice problems within their own community. Until recently, formal alternative measures programs have only been sanctioned in law for youth. However, in 1996 similar legislative authority was proclaimed into law for adult alternative measures. The extent to which these measures are presently being used for adults is not yet known.

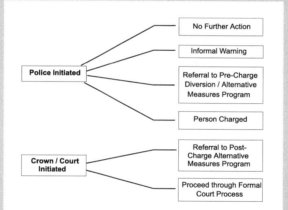

A complete national picture of the proportion and characteristics of youth cases diverted into alternative measures programs is currently not available. However, data available for some jurisdictions suggest that the number of youth referred to alternative measures ranges from approximately 15 percent to 33 percent (Moyer, 1996). A survey conducted by the Canadian Centre for Justice Statistics (CCJS, 1994) indicates that the majority of youth referred to alternative measures programs are first-time offenders suspected of committing property offences, especially theft under $1,000. The survey found that the majority of youth referred were males between the ages of 12 and 15 years. Even though females represent a smaller portion of the total number of offenders, they are more likely than their male counterparts to be referred to alternative measures.

The structure and content of alternative measures programs also vary. Most sanctions from alternative measures programs are short-term in nature, involving reparative sanctions more often than counselling. Typical sanctions from alternative measures agreements include community service work, charitable donations, attendance at educational sessions (e.g., anti-shoplifting programs), essays/posters or other assignments, restitution/compensation to the victim and victim apologies. According to a survey by CCJS (1994), the most frequent outcomes of the agreement were apologies to the victim and community service. Some programs provide support to the individual offender, while others focus on teaching certain skills, or attempting to change attitudes or behaviours. Counselling and victim-offender mediation or reconciliation do not appear to be common interventions. *More than 90 percent of young persons accepted into alternative measures programs successfully complete them.*

Certain alternative measures programs in Canada stand out in their focus and approach. The Dispute Resolution Centre for Ottawa-Carleton has, since 1987, offered the province of Ontario's only post-charge, pretrial criminal court mediation program which focuses on both adults and youth. The underlying philosophy of restorative justice (see also Box 4.11) guides the program's interventions that focus on victim-offender mediation, reconciliation and restitution. The youth are normally referred through joint referrals by the Crown Attorney and the Defence Counsel, and mediations are performed by trained volunteers under the supervision of Centre staff.

Kweskohte is another example of an alternative measures program in Saskatchewan that offers a pre-charge diversion option for Aboriginal youth. Kweskohte offers offenders, victims and their families a family conference approach that fosters their empowerment to reconcile and resolve the situations arising from criminal acts. Aboriginal elders are directly involved in the program and assist in providing counselling to the offender and the victim, in establishing initial client contact and in facilitating conferences. Referrals are made to the program directly by the police at the pre-charge stage.

The goals of the community-based hearings held by Kweskohte are to reconcile and restore peace and harmony to individuals, families and the community affected by the offences committed by young people. The agreements reached may see the youth agree to carry out specific activities and/or to participate in programs and services to address their individual needs. By completing the agreement, the youth will avoid criminal charges.

In Canada, there has been a significant increase in the number of Youth Justice Committees over the past few years. These Committees are sanctioned by the *YOA* and are made up of volunteers from the community who work in collaboration with officials from the criminal justice system and other community-based agencies. Although they may differ between communities in their role and functions, Youth Justice Committees do share some common principles. These guiding principles include:

- the entitlement of victims to be involved in the resolution process;
- the right of society to protection;
- the need for offenders to assume responsibility for their actions;
- that young persons and victims have rights and responsibilities;
- that citizens have a role to play in the resolution of offences and the rehabilitation of offenders; and,
- that the least intrusive alternative consistent with the protection of society should be utilized.

Source: Trevethan and MacKillop (Original paper, 1997)

Suspects and those convicted, by crime type

This section describes the rates of suspects and convictions for each of the four offences of homicide, assault, robbery and theft. Not all countries supplied data for all the four crimes and as such the number of countries listed for each of them differs. Tables 3.3 to 3.6 present data on suspect and conviction rates per 100,000 population.

Table 3.3 presents data on the rates of suspects and convictions for homicide. It is important to bear in mind that the definition of even this serious crime varies and offences that are included in this category may also vary. Thus, while some countries may include only intentional homicide in this category, others may add non-intentional homicide and even attempted homicide. In the five year period between 1990 and 1994, the rate of suspects for homicide has increased in a few countries and decreased in others. The data in Table 3.3 are unusual in some respects. In a number of countries the rate of conviction was higher than the rate of suspects. This can happen for a number of reasons, the important one being the time it takes to collect evidence and go to trial. The case of Egypt requires a special mention. As can be seen from Table 3.3, the conviction rate in Egypt is many times more than the suspect rate. This is partly because more alleged offenders are processed by prosecutors than by the police. But even considering this factor, the conviction rate is relatively high. Finally, it is clear from Table 3.3 that in Bulgaria, Estonia, Latvia and the Russian Federation, the increases in the homicide suspect rate have been very significant.

Table 3.4 displays the suspect and conviction rates for assault. While fluctuations in the rates of suspects and convictions are not as substantial as observed for homicide, there appears a great variation in the suspect rate of countries. For example, in Azerbaijan in 1994 there were only four suspects per 100,000 population, and in Finland and Austria there were 347 and 377 suspects, respectively, per 100,000 population. Some unusual differences between suspect and conviction rates are also apparent: in Chile only one in six suspects was convicted in 1994; in Belarus the conviction rate was higher than the suspect rate; and in Fin-

In Bulgaria, Estonia, Latvia and the Russian Federation, the increases in homicide suspect rate have been very significant.

TABLE 3.3
Homicide suspect and conviction rates (per 100,000 population)

	Suspects		Convictions	
	1990	1994	1990	1994
Austria	3.4	3.4	5.0	3.6
Azerbaijan	4.1	7.0	2.6	5.7
Belarus	6.1	8.2	4.8	6.8
Bulgaria	3.6	9.1	3.1	2.9
Chile	6.6	6.2	6.7	7.3
Croatia	7.5	8.2	5.4	5.6
Cyprus	2.2	1.9	1.0	0.5
Egypt	3.1	2.6	96.7	49.0
Estonia	7.0	19.8	4.2	10.5
Georgia	4.9	3.5	3.8	4.3
Greece	2.6	3.0	3.9	1.8
Hong Kong	3.2	1.6	1.2	0.9
Hungary	3.3	4.7	2.3	3.7
India	10.8	10.3	4.5	4.5
Italy	4.4	4.4	9.0	8.3
Jamaica	14.5	14.0	5.7	6.2
Japan	1.7	1.5	0.6	0.6
Jordan	4.8	6.1	0.7	1.5
Latvia	5.5	10.0	5.1	6.5
Lithuania	5.3	13.5	11.0	10.5
Rep. Korea	12.3	13.0	1.4	1.2
"FYRM"*	3.9	3.9	2.2	1.9
Rep. Moldova	5.3	7.2	4.1	6.3
Russian Fed.	9.7	17.8	8.0	14.4
Singapore	2.1	1.7	1.0	1.2
Slovenia	4.8	5.8	2.3	2.0
Sweden	5.6	4.6	3.0	2.0
USA	9.2	8.5	4.4	0.1

*"Former Yugoslav Republic of Macedonia"
Source: Fifth UNCJS

TABLE 3.4
Assault suspect and conviction rates (per 100,000 population)

	Suspects		Convictions	
	1990	1994	1990	1994
Austria	344.4	377.4	139.9	127.2
Azerbaijan	2.0	4.0	1.5	3.6
Belarus	16.3	19.7	17.7	22.4
Chile	216.5	258.3	29.5	30.7
Croatia	26.5	29.4	5.1	3.5
Cyprus	15.0	17.6	6.2	3.5
Estonia	11.0	15.0	8.6	13.0
Finland	363.5	347.2	183.3	158.4
Georgia	3.1	5.7	2.5	1.0
Hong Kong	86.1	90.2	38.2	34.1
Hungary	61.4	69.0	23.1	43.1
Italy	32.8	37.3	1.7	4.9
Japan	25.9	21.8	3.4	2.9
Kazakhstan	17.9	19.8	7.9	12.6
Latvia	14.0	19.3	15.2	16.0
Qatar	68.3	55.4	27.6	12.0
"FYRM"*	23.5	28.6	53.3	38.7
Rep.Moldova	7.4	9.7	0.5	0.4
Singapore	17.0	15.7	4.7	6.0
Slovakia	80.8	73.8	28.6	34.2
Slovenia	86.7	100.1	48.2	40.9
Sweden	119.8	141.9	82.3	100.1

*"Former Yugoslav Republic of Macedonia"
Source: Fifth UNCJS

TABLE 3.5
Robbery suspect and conviction rates (per 100,000 population)

	Suspects		Convictions	
	1990	1994	1990	1994
Austria	15.0	18.0	5.4	7.4
Azerbaijan	1.8	3.8	2.2	3.7
Belarus	29.1	51.2	22.2	39.8
Bulgaria	7.4	39.5	3.2	5.3
Chile	136.8	117.6	17.1	23.4
Croatia	4.9	6.0	2.5	3.4
Cyprus	2.2	3.5	0.9	1.0
Egypt	1.2	1.2	1.9	3.4
Estonia	30.6	74.8	6.6	15.2
Finland	36.3	29.8	13.4	9.9
Georgia	2.9	4.9	2.7	5.9
Greece	2.7	4.4	0.5	0.7
Hong Kong	39.4	36.8	18.7	18.6
Hungary	15.6	20.7	10.5	15.3
India	4.1	3.2	0.8	0.7
Italy	13.3	15.8	7.0	10.3
Jamaica	68.2	64.4	0.0	0.0
Japan	1.3	1.9	0.4	0.7
Kazakstan	19.9	28.7	50.0	70.0
Latvia	37.2	21.2	24.9	14.9
Rep. Korea	13.2	15.9	5.4	3.5
"FYRM"	3.3	7.6	1.2	1.6
Rep. Moldova	17.5	20.4	12.1	19.7
Russian Fed.	24.9	50.5	27.3	57.3
Singapore	18.2	12.9	5.6	3.3
Slovakia	25.9	20.7	9.0	10.6
Slovenia	7.7	18.1	2.2	3.8
Sweden	10.8	9.8	6.5	6.2

*"Former Yugoslav Republic of Macedonia"
Source: Fifth UNCJS

land and Austria less than half of the suspects were convicted on charges of assault.

Robbery is an offence which is defined as a violent offence in some countries and as a property offence in others. As the data in Table 3.5 show, countries such as Japan, Egypt, Azerbaijan, Georgia, India, Cyprus and Croatia have relatively low suspect rates compared to other countries. Chile recorded the highest suspect rate among the countries listed. As noted for homicide and assault, there are some exceptional situations. In a few countries the conviction rate is higher than suspect rate, and in Kazakstan, conviction rate is two and a half times higher than suspect rate.

Theft appears to be the offence for which the maximum number of individuals are taken as suspects. As can be seen in Table 3.6, some countries show very substantial increases in suspect rates between 1990 and 1994. Belarus, Bulgaria, Estonia, Kazakhstan, Lithuania and the Russian Federation show sharp increases in suspect rates

for theft. Conviction rates in some countries were higher than suspect rates and significantly lower than suspect rates in others.

Conclusion

This chapter is based on the responses to the Fifth Survey received by early 1997. The countries that responded by then did not adequately represent all the regions of the world. Only half a dozen countries each from Western and Southern Europe, the Arab states, Asia and the Pacific, and Latin America and Caribbean responded to the survey questions pertinent to this chapter; some 15 countries of Eastern Europe and the Commonwealth of Independent States also responded. Hence, regional comparison would not be a reasonable option.

The World Development Report 1997 examines income distribution and places countries in low income, lower middle income, upper middle income and high income categories. Looking at the countries that supplied data on the number of suspects (see Figure 3.9), it is quite clear that the sus-

TABLE 3.6
Theft suspect and conviction rates (per 100,000 population)

	Suspects		Convictions	
	1990	1994	1990	1994
Austria	282	258	187	153
Azerbaijan	20	44	15	41
Belarus	129	332	97	277
Bulgaria	98	567	43	55
Columbia	30	51	2	2
Croatia	192	206	86	63
Cyprus	138	105	27	20
Estonia	129	342	67	323
Georgia	29	48	16	52
Greece	67	81	29	23
Hong Kong	204	242	115	136
Hungary	282	254	92	121
India	26	21	7	7
Italy	183	193	36	56
Japan	127	118	10	11
Kazakhstan	119	242	301	425
Latvia	151	271	98	227
Lithuania	130	312	75	249
Qatar	59	77	65	76
"FYRM"*	211	312	78	83
Rep. Moldova	141	223	88	196
Russian Fed.	167	382	106	273
Singapore	214	240	96	76
Slovakia	129	226	50	223
Slovenia	470	413	171	98
Sweden	330	329	393	370

*"Former Yugoslav Republic of Macedonia"
Source: Fifth UNCJS

FIGURE 3.9
Suspect rates and GNP per capita, 1994 (US dollars, per 100,000 population)

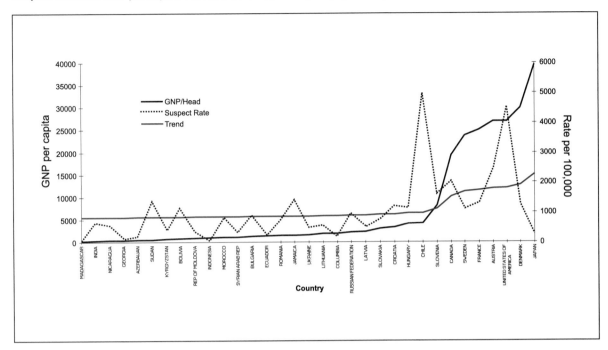

Source: Fifth UNCJS; UNDP (1995)

pect rate per 100,000 population was the highest among the high income countries. Also, with rare exception, the number of suspects per 100,000 population increases as the level of income increases. Thus for example, with very few exceptions, the suspect rate for low and lower middle income countries was well below 1,000 per 100,000 population. In upper middle and high income countries the rate of suspects at times exceeded 5,000 per 100,000 population. Suspects are detected or arrested by the police and therefore the rate could be influenced by the resources available to the police. Richer countries may be able to allocate more resources, personnel, technology and communication facilities, all of which can enhance the capacity of the police.

SUMMARY

THINGS IN COMMON	THINGS DIVERSE
• The legal systems of over half the countries of the world are the product of the civil law tradition.	• The common law tradition is the next most common basis of legal systems, followed by Islamic law, and various combinations of Islamic, civil and common law.
• Elements of criminal justice systems such as the police, courts, and prisons are found in all countries, albeit their names may be different.	
• The police are the front end of the criminal justice system.	
• In all countries, most people who come in contact with the criminal justice system are males.	• Differences among countries in the involvement with the criminal justice system vary by age and gender. The suspect rate varied between a low of 43 in Madagascar and a high of 5011 in Chile per 100,000 population.
• Adult males constitute the largest group of suspects in all countries.	• The ratio between adult male suspects and suspects of other age-gender group varies among countries. In Western Samoa there were 91 adult male suspects for each adult female suspect and in Bolivia there were only two adult male suspects for each adult female suspect, There were 79 juvenile males for each juvenile female suspect in Georgia and only two juvenile male per juvenile female suspect in Jamaica.
	• There were far fewer women and girls suspected of committing crimes in countries with low income than in those with high income.
• In most countries about half the suspects or those prosecuted are found guilty and convicted of an offence.	• The conviction rate varies across countries, with a low in Japan of 47 and a high in Egypt of 7371 per 100,000 population. The ratio of male to female conviction rate is higher in low income countries than in high income countries.

CHAPTER 4

Punishment

Contributing authors: Hiroyuki Shinkai and Uglješa Zvekic

Punishment is the state's response to criminal law breakers. It is the last phase of the criminal justice system, the end of a long and complicated process that began with the commission and detection of an offence. Although such a generic term as "punishment" certainly evokes other meanings, only the state-based legal context is considered in this chapter. Therefore, not considered are informal punishments such as those a parent or teacher may apply to a child, or punishments meted out as a result of the informal process of adjudication in customary justice (Boxes 5.4 and 3.1), even though they are frequently applied. Only those punishments that are officially recorded as part of the criminal justice process of conviction and sentencing are considered. Also not considered are the forms of institutional placement that might have similar outcomes to criminal punishment, and which occur as a result of a procedure that operates outside the criminal justice process (United Nations, 1992). Examples of these "parallel punishments" are the "incarceration" of individuals in mental hospitals or of youth in various types of welfare institutions.

The following sections provide an overview of the present situation of punishment in the world, based mainly on the results of the Fifth UNCJS and the International Crime Victim Surveys (ICVS). Where methodologically appropriate, reference is also made to previous UNCJS in order to provide an impression of change over time.

The variety of punishments used around the world

The Fifth UNCJS listed the following categories of official punishment: life imprisonment, corporal punishment, deprivation of liberty, control in freedom, warnings or admonition, fines, and community service orders. "Deprivation of liberty " is taken to be punishment by incarceration, and "control in freedom" as probation related punishment.[1]

At the outset, it is important to note that this section deals with the *types of punishments* reported by countries and not with the *amount of punishment* delivered. One cannot conclude that one country is more or less punitive than another based on the percentages of types of punishments reported because these percentages take into account only the spectrum of punishments available in a particular country. The question asks how many people were sentenced to a particular punishment. Of course, if one considered one punishment, (e.g., corporal punishment) to be far more punitive or harsh than another punishment, and a country preferred this clearly above all other punishments, then perhaps a judgment of comparative harshness could be made. This is, however, a value judgement about the comparative severity of punishments, regardless of to whom or how many such a punishment is applied.

Figure 4.1 displays the types of punishment imposed on adult offenders in countries and territories in 1994. Equivalent figures for juveniles are not available in the UN Crime and Justice Survey, so Figure 4.1 may reflect only a part of the whole spectrum of criminal punishment. Punishments that may well be under-represented are corporal punishment of juveniles, which is less commonly used on adults (Newman, 1995), and incarceration in a variety of juvenile institutions. Capital punishment, although not included in the Fifth Survey, is discussed in a separate section below.

It is clear from Figure 4.1 that the most popular sanction is prison. However, wide

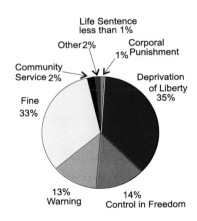

FIGURE 4.1
Types of punishments applied to adult convicted persons, 34 countries, 1994

Source: Fifth UNCJS. See Notes to Figures for additional tabular information.

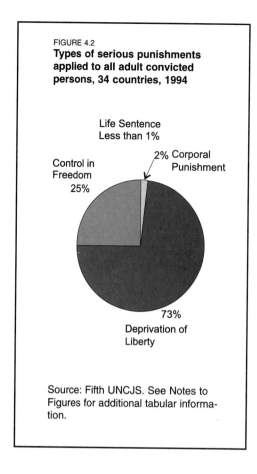

FIGURE 4.2

Types of serious punishments applied to all adult convicted persons, 34 countries, 1994

Life Sentence
Less than 1%

2% Corporal Punishment

Control in Freedom 25%

73% Deprivation of Liberty

Source: Fifth UNCJS. See Notes to Figures for additional tabular information.

tences imposed in Japan (95 percent), Myanmar (82 percent), England and Wales (79 percent), Germany (78 percent), Egypt (78 percent), Finland (73 percent) and Austria (71 percent).

However, this tendency was not the general rule. There are countries that rely heavily on custodial sanctions (more than 60 percent of the adjudicated cases). These are Colombia (100 percent), Greece (96 percent), Mexico (92 percent), Republic of Moldova (83 percent) and Italy (60 percent). A caution is in order here. It is possible that in these countries, statistics are available only on offences of a certain seriousness so that cases which would — as in many countries — merit, for example a fine, are not noted. The heavy reliance on custodial sanctions is more strikingly evident from Figure 4.2, which presents the breakdown of the use of various punishments excluding fines and warnings, since these sanctions can be considered to be imposed mostly for minor crimes and are, generally, considered to be less serious punishments. Thus one is able to gain an impression of the sentencing pattern for relatively serious crimes.[2]

The more complex pattern of punishments among countries is displayed in Table 4.1. This table represents the results of an exploratory analysis[3] which identified five possible groupings of the countries which have provided responses to the Fifth Survey. These can be characterized as follows: (1) countries that mainly use imprisonment; (2) countries that mainly use fines (possibly for minor offences); (3) countries that mainly rely on warnings; (4) countries that

variations among countries were apparent. For example, it might be expected that harsher sanctions, such as deprivation of liberty, would be less used if lesser penalties, such as warnings and fines, were available. The data available from some countries appeared to confirm this expectation. For instance, minor punishments such as warnings comprised more than 70 percent of the total sentences in Slovenia (74 percent). Fines comprise more than 70 percent of the sen-

TABLE 4.1

Typology of sentencing patterns

Pattern	Countries and Territories
Imprisonment	Colombia, Greece, Mexico, Republic of Moldova
Fines	Myanmar, Austria, Egypt, England and Wales, Finland, Germany, Japan
Warning	Slovenia
Combination of deprivation of liberty and control in freedom	Andorra, Azerbaijan, Costa Rica, The Czech Republic, Israel, Lithuania, Republic of Korea
Mixture of sentencing schemes, but primary reliance on deprivation of liberty	Belarus, Canada, Cyprus, Estonia, Georgia, Hong Kong, Italy, Kazakstan, Netherlands, Northern Ireland, Portugal, Scotland, Slovenia, South Africa, Turkey, Zambia.

Source: Fifth UNCJS

use control in freedom (probation) and imprisonment as major sentencing options but show a slight preference for control in freedom; (5) countries that use a variety of sentencing options but primarily favour deprivation of liberty.

We may conclude from the complex pattern of punishment preferences operating among the countries reporting their use of different types of punishment that there appears to be a dependent relationship between the punishments of deprivation of liberty and control in freedom.

What factors differentiate countries with the high use of such types of punishment as imprisonment from those with a high use of non-custodial sanctions, and vice versa?

The most obvious explanation is that high use of one type of penalty in one country might have some association with the country's crime situation. One can speculate that the more crime there is in one country, the more convictions there are and, furthermore, the tougher are the sentences. This was not, however, confirmed in the analysis of the Fifth UN Crime and Justice Survey. A simple bivariate correlation between volume of sentencing (measured by total sentencing rate per 100,000 general population) and crime rates (measured by total crime rate and violent crime rate[4] recorded by the police per 100,000 general population) did not show significant associations.[5] This holds true for each type of punishment.

It might also be reasonable to speculate that the diverse use of punishments might have some association with the developmental status of each country. After all, developing countries have less resources at their disposal. Building prisons, for example, is very expensive (see Chapter 5). And training of probation officers to supervise non-custodial sanctions requires an expensive and well developed educational structure.

The analysis of the indicators and sentencing practices presented above did not confirm any significant association among them with development level of a country using the standard UNDP classifications of development. Such results suggest that the use of punishment is independent of the country's developmental or economic situation or regional differences, but is more or less dependent on the availability and acceptability of the sentencing options.

So far, only the *types of punishment*

employed by member countries and territories have been examined. Let us move on to consider the *amount of punishment.*

The prison population

Since imprisonment or deprivation of liberty consists of confining an offender to an institution under close supervision for a certain period of time, it is frequently referred to as a "custodial sanction." In 1957, in order to ensure humane treatment of prisoners the United Nations promulgated the Standard Minimum Rules for the Treatment of Prisoners (see Box 4.4). Similarly, the Council of Europe (1987) established European Prison Rules.

Table 4.2 presents the imprisonment rates per 100,000 resident population in 1994 for total persons incarcerated. Total incarceration includes sentenced prisoners as well as prisoners awaiting trial. Those awaiting trial may include, depending on the recording practice, legal system and bureaucratic organization of the prison system, those not yet convicted and awaiting trial, as well as those who have been convicted but who have appealed their conviction and are awaiting the outcome of appeal. In some cases countries have been unable to break down the numbers of those awaiting trial from total incarcerated. Thus, as a rough and general measure of how many citizens are incarcerated by the criminal justice system, the total incarceration rate is probably the best measure.

It can be seen that in 1994 Belarus (478), Burnei Darussalam (313), Latvia (360), the Russian Federation (580) and the United States of America (554) incarcerated more than 300 persons per 100,000 general population.

The rate of convicted prisoners per 100,000 is presented in Table 4.3 and shows that countries which recorded higher total incarceration rates also had high rates of convicted persons incarcerated. Belarus (363), Burnei Darussalam (250), Kyrgyzstan (229), Latvia (271), the Russian Federation (411) and Ukraine (241) incarcerated more than 200 persons per 100,000 population. The United States did not provide data on convicted prisoners for the UN Crime and Justice Survey; however, according to the national official statistics, its equivalent rate is about 389 (Magurie and Pastore 1995).

Results suggest that the use of punishment is independent of the country's developmental or economic situation or regional differences.

TABLE 4.2
Total persons incarcerated, 1994 (per 100,000 population)

Russian Federation	580	Uruguay	102
USA	554	Bulgaria	99
Belarus	478	England & Wales	95
Latvia	360	Australia	94
Bermuda	359	Mexico	93
Ukraine	345	Austria	92
Brunei Darussalam	313	Italy	90
Kyrgyzstan	300	Macau	88
Zambia	294	Tonga	87
Estonia	294	Colombia	85
Lithuania	278	Peru	84
Singapore	255	Sao Tome&Principe	79
Panama	215	Kiribati	79
Rep. of Moldova	215	Turkey	74
Hong Kong	199	Nicaragua	74
Romania	195	Belgium	74
Cook Islands	195	Vanuatu	73
Israel	189	Sweden	70
Czech Rep	181	Sri Lanka	68
Thailand	177	Denmark	67
Guyana	175	a"FYRM"	63
Poland	160	Finland	62
Chile	156	Liechtenstein	58
Madagascar	151	Netherlands	57
Georgia	141	Malta	56
Western Samoa	141	Solomon Islands	56
Slovakia	139	Uganda	54
Rep. of Korea	138	Slovenia	52
New Zealand	126	Croatia	50
Hungary	124	Marshall Islands	43
Malaysia	123	Japan	37
Costa Rica	119	Bangladesh	34
Canada	118	Nepal	34
Northern Ireland	116	Albania	30
Fiji	110	Cambodia	26
Luxembourg	109	Philippines	26
El Salvador	109	Cyprus	25
Scotland	109	Sudan	24
China	107	Indonesia	23
Papua New Guinea	107	India	22
Portugal	102	Greece	16
		Kuwait	2

a"The Former Yugoslav Republic of Macedonia"
Source: Fifth UNCJS. See Notes to Tables for additional information.

Regional variations

There are quite large variations in imprisonment rates across the regions of the world. Figure 4.3 shows the total incarceration rate and convicted prisoners rate in each world region in 1994. The New World (Australia, Canada, New Zealand and the United States of America) showed the highest incarceration rate (255), mainly due to the high rate in the United States. It is followed by countries in transition (Eastern Europe, 214), and then by Africa, Latin America and Asia. Western European countries recorded a much lower incarceration rate (85). Also, in the case of the convicted prisoner rate, the New World exceeded the other regions (189), followed by the countries in transi-

tion (148). It is interesting to note the wide discrepancies between the convicted prisoners rate and total incarceration rate in Africa and Latin America.

Prison admissions

The nature of the prison population in one jurisdiction or even in one prison does not remain stable throughout a year. Some prisoners are admitted, others are released; some change their legal status from a remand prisoner to a convicted prisoner, and so on. The prison population changes every day and at every moment. The prison population discussed in the previous section refers to a static or "frozen" figure derived by selecting a given day in a year and providing a count for that day. The prison population level may also be kept artificially stable because of such factors as prison capacity, although it may be argued that this capacity has not limited intake into prisons in the past so that overcrowding has resulted. However, it has also become a practice in some countries to release prisoners before their term has expired in order to make space for new admissions. The question of overcrowding will be considered in more detail later in this chapter, and is also examined in Chapter 5. The prison population figure includes various types of prisoners: some stay for longer and others for shorter periods of time.

The admissions rate tells us how many prison admissions have occurred in a given country and in a given year. As such, prison admissions present an active picture of the turnover of prisoners. Caution is needed when interpreting these figures, however, since the same person can be sentenced to imprisonment more than once in a given year and therefore this should not necessarily be interpreted as the number of persons admitted to prison (Council of Europe, 1996). Nevertheless, admission rates are calculated according to number of admissions per 100,000 population to ease international comparison. The results for all admissions to prison are presented in Table 4.4.

It is striking to note that there are huge differences in the number of people who enter the prison system. The highest rate in 1994 was recorded in the Russian Federation: 1,542 persons per 100,000 population entered prison throughout the year. This is followed by Chile (930), Singapore (704),

TABLE 4.3

**Total convicted persons incarcerated 1994
(rate per 100,000 population)**

Russian Federation	411
United States of America	389
Belarus	363
Bermuda	300
Latvia	271
Brunei Darussalam	250
Ukraine	241
Kyrgyzstan	229
Singapore	223
Lithuania	198
Hong Kong	178
Estonia	173
Rep. of Moldova	167
Israel	161
Western Samoa	141
Guyana	118
Slovakia	103
Canada	97
Czech Rep.	96
Costa Rica	96
Northern Ireland	88
Hungary	87
Scotland	86
Australia	82
Malaysia	80
Luxembourg	76
Rep. of Korea	75
Zambia	71
England & Wales	68
Bulgaria	68
Portugal	65
Austria	60
Chile	59
Sweden	59
Egypt	56
a"FYRM"	54
Finland	52
Madagascar	51
Denmark	50
Macau	49
Mexico	48
Italy	45
Nicaragua	40
Malta	37
Belgium	37
Panama	36
Croatia	36
Turkey	34
Netherlands	32
Japan	30
Marshall Islands	28
Slovenia	28
Philippines	26
Colombia	24
Peru	23
El Salvador	21
Uganda	20
Cyprus	19
Sao Tome&Principe	16
Sudan	16
Indonesia	15
Uruguay	11
Georgia	9
Liechtenstein	6
Kuwait	1

a"The Former Yugoslav Republic of Macedonia"
Source: Fifth UNCJS. See notes to Tables for
additional information

Bermuda (633), Qatar (575) and Guyana (474). The rate was lowest in the Philippines (7), followed by the Marshall Islands (30), Croatia (31), Indonesia (32) and Japan (39)

It would be more comparable to look at prison admissions by convicted prisoners rather than total prison admissions since the latter might contain mixed types of prisoners such as non-convicted prisoners, convicted prisoners, prisoners for administrative punishment, etc. Also, certain categories may not apply to some countries, making comparison of total admissions very difficult. The prison admission rate of convicted offenders per 100,000 general population is presented in Table 4.5.

There are large differences in the convicted offender prison admission rates. The highest rate for 1994 was again recorded by the Russian Federation (582), followed by Kazakhstan (338), Bermuda (311) and Kyrgyzstan (303), while the lowest was recorded in Indonesia (15), followed by Sao Tome and Principe (17), Cyprus (21), Slovenia (28), the Marshall Islands (30) and El Salvador (30).

Changes over time

The question of changes in prison populations over time is a very complex one. A brief overview is provided in this section. In a later section the question of increasing prison populations is examined, since this has been an issue of serious concern for many years.

Out of 65 countries which provided data, 30 show a consecutive increase in the total incarceration rate from 1990 to 1994, while seven show a steady decrease in the period covered by the survey. The rest of the countries show somewhat more stable conditions. Belarus and the Czech Republic increased their total prisoner rates more than twofold between 1990 and 1994 (from 204 to 478 and from 79 to 181, respectively). Italy also experienced a 100 percent increase during this period (from 45 to 90). No substantial decrease in imprisonment rates is observed except for the Marshall Islands (from 80 to 43) and Macau (193 to 88).

Twenty-eight out of 64 countries and territories which provided data reported an increase in the convicted prisoner rate, while eight reported consecutive decreases. Among those countries which reported an

Belarus, Brunei Darussalam, Latvia, Russian Federation and the USA incarcerated more than 300 persons per 100,000 population in 1994.

increase, the Czech Republic and Italy more than doubled their rates between 1990 and 1994 (from 39 to 96 and from 19 to 45, respectively). Changes in prison populations over time is an important issue today, especially in regard to the concern about prison overcrowding. This issue will be considered in more detail below.

Prison admission rates are more meaningful for identifying changes over time than for identifying differences between countries. Because they measure the more dynamic process of movement of persons into prison, changes in admissions over time may reflect policy changes concerning the use of prisons and thus a country's sentencing practice. Changes in admissions may also reflect the criminalization or decriminalization of particular conduct (Kuhn, 1996) which results in a more active use of prison as a punishment. Figure 4.4 clearly shows the upward trend of prison admissions of convicted

tal incarceration rates. In fact, it may be an important finding that close to half the countries reported decreases in admissions of convicted offenders. The relationship between the levels of imprisonment of those who are not yet convicted and those already convicted are quite complex. This issue will be further considered later in this chapter.

Imprisonment, admissions and socio-economic status

Judging from the variations from one country to another in use of prisons, it would be very tempting to conclude that those countries with exceptionally high imprisonment or admission rates are more "punitive" than those with lower rates. However, the implications of such an inference depend largely on what is meant by a "punitive." The argument is somewhat circular. Are countries more punitive because they incarcerate more, or do they incarcerate more because they are punitive? From an international point of view, we prefer to take the position that changes and levels in prison use, whether measured by admissions or prison populations, are direct reflections of the policies and practices of the criminal justice systems of the respective countries. The fact is that in no countries do those who are incarcerated represent a cross section of the whole society of that country (Pease, 1994). Certain classes of individuals are usually found more often among the incarcerated population. Generally speaking, these tend to be those who are economically disadvantaged, ethnic minorities or both (see Box 4.1).

Could variations in the imprisonment rate be attributed to the socio-economic and/or regional status of a country? [7,8]

Statistical analysis for the total incarceration rate per 100,000 population produced no meaningful association with industrial development, human development, or GNP per capita of countries. Similar results were obtained from UNICRI analysis of the Fourth UN Crime and Justice Survey.

If the comparison is restricted to the sentenced (or convicted) prisoners, there are no significant associations with either the human development or income indexes. However, there is a moderately significant association in relation to the developmental

FIGURE 4.3
Incarceration rate by world regions, 1994 (per 100,000 population)

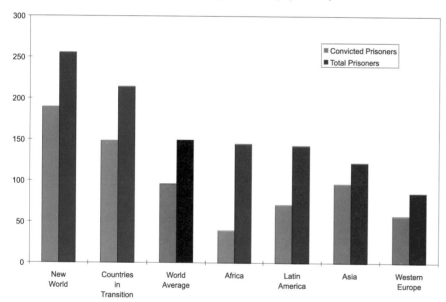

Source: Fifth UNCJS. See Notes to Figures for additional information.

prisoners in countries in transition compared to Western Europe. There were insufficient data to provide comparisons for other regions of the world.

It is also of interest that the most substantial changes from 1990 to 1994 reported by countries were those of total incarceration rates. Changes in admission rates were, on the whole, reported less often than those of prison rates, whether of convicted or to-

TABLE 4.4
Total prison admissions 1994 (per 100,000 population)

Russian Federation	1542
Chile	930
Singapore	704
Bermuda	633
Qatar	575
Guyana	474
South Africa	459
Canada	420
Zambia	419
Scotland	411
Brunei Darussalam	313
England & Wales	304
Estonia	302
Malaysia	298
Sudan	290
Denmark	290
Hong Kong	263
El Salvador	254
Kyrgyzstan	249
Costa Rica	244
Lithuania	244
Madagascar	235
Austria	217
United States of America	208
Belarus	207
Western Samoa	206
Panama	196
Israel	189
Hungary	178
Italy	176
Malta	174
Finland	171
Belgium	169
Latvia	163
Sweden	162
Czech Rep	160
Georgia	141
Rep. of Moldova	124
Uganda	112
Macau	108
Ukraine	107
Turkey	99
Nicaragua	97
Slovakia	96
Slovenia	91
Jamaica	89
Columbia	85
Northern Ireland	84
Peru	83
Portugal	80
[a]"FYRM"	78
Sao Tome&Principe	71
Egypt	68
Cyprus	66
Rep. of Korea	65
Bulgaria	55
Greece	47
Japan	39
Indonesia	32
Croatia	31
Marshall Islands	30
Philippines	7

[a]"The Former Yugoslav Republic of Macedonia"
Source: Fifth UNCJS. See Notes to Tables.

stage. Industrialized countries tend to incarcerate more sentenced prisoners than developing countries and least developed countries. Although the significance level is not very high (p<.07), it is the most significant value throughout the analysis.[9]

From these results, it may be concluded that, *from an international level,* the socioeconomic status of countries which are represented by the UNDP indices on industrial development, human development and GNP per capita have very little, if any, association with variations in total prison admissions and prison admission as a result of conviction. It should be recognized, however, that this conclusion refers to the international level of analysis, treating whole countries as the unit of analysis. It is entirely possible (and indeed probable; see Box 4.1) that *within* each country, economic and

TABLE 4.5
Prison admissions of convicted offenders, 1994 (per 100,000 population)

Russian Federation	582
Kazakhstan	338
Bermuda	311
Kyrgyzstan	303
Latvia	257
Singapore	234
Brunei Darussalam	221
Rep. of Moldova	215
Western Samoa	206
Lithuania	198
Costa Rica	193
Sudan	189
Estonia	173
Georgia	141
Guyana	118
Zambia	95
Scotland	88
Malaysia	84
Rep. of Korea	80
Luxembourg	76
England & Wales	68
Chile	63
[a]"FYRM"	52
Greece	38
Croatia	37
Belgium	32
El Salvador	30
Marshall Islands	30
Slovenia	28
Cyprus	21
Sao Tome&Principe	17
Indonesia	15
Mauritius	0

[a]"The Former Yugoslav Republic of Macedonia"
Source: Fifth UNCJS. See Notes to Tables for additional information. Due to an error in the wording of the UNCJS questionnaire, these data may be unreliable.

The lowest admissions rates to prison were reported by the Philippines, Marshall Islands, Croatia, Indonesia and Japan.

ethnic factors may play an important role. More data are needed, of course, to support this speculation.

Early release (parole)

Although prisoners in many countries are sentenced to definitive periods of incarceration, some can be released before their terms are completed by amnesty, earning "good time" or through parole. The early release system, be it parole or "good time," is one of the few means at the disposal of the authorities to control their prison population, and thus to control the "overcrowding problem" (discussed in a subsequent section). At the same time, such a system is sometimes criticized for creating a "revolving door" situation in which, as soon as one convicted prisoner is sent to the prison, another convicted prisoner will leave it. The UN Crime and Justice Survey requests the number of persons subjected to parole in a given year and in a given day. The fact that few countries provided data suggests that many countries do not possess such a system.

Parole can be measured in two ways: the number of parolees on a given day, and the number of offenders paroled in a year. The number paroled in a given year is a more dynamic measure than the static one of counting the number of parolees on a particular day. It also proved to be the most common measure, since there were too few responses to include the parolees on a given day in this report.

The United States paroled the largest number of prisoners in 1994 in terms of general population (158 per 100,000), followed by Finland (107), Kyrgyzstan (83), Turkey (77) and Lithuania (75). Belarus recorded a huge (more than six fold) increase in parole decisions between 1990 and 1994 (from 7 to 47). Estonia, Kyrgyzstan, Latvia and Lithuania experienced dramatic increases, whereas England and Wales saw a huge decrease in the parole decisions.

Is there any relationship between prison rates and parole rates? Table 4.6 shows the distribution of parole and prison use for those countries providing this information. The policy and practical implications of those distributions may be quite significant. What are the policy and practical implications of having a high imprisonment rate and low parole rate? Such a system leaves little room for adjustment of sentence after conviction, which is in effect what parole is. Countries falling into this category might be considered as having the most severe prison policies. In contrast, those countries with low prison use and high parole use may be considered as the most "flexible" or least severe in sentencing policy. Of course, each country would have to be examined separately in order to draw any definite conclusion. The problem with making any firm conclusions concerning severity of sentencing at this point in the analysis is that how long persons spend in prison is not known.

Prison overcrowding

It is often stated that prison overcrowding is a permanent problem in many countries. This leads to a deterioration of the living and working conditions of both inmates and corrections officers.

There are several explanations for overcrowding. Although imprisonment is a major element of the conventional punishment system, the correctional authorities cannot control the flow into prisons. On the other hand, police and prosecutors in some jurisdictions are often given great discretion in controlling the number of cases to be processed. Thus the agencies administering

Belarus and the Czech Republic increased their total prisoner rates more than twofold between 1990 and 1994.

FIGURE 4.4

Change in prison admission by convicted prisoners, Western and Eastern Europe.

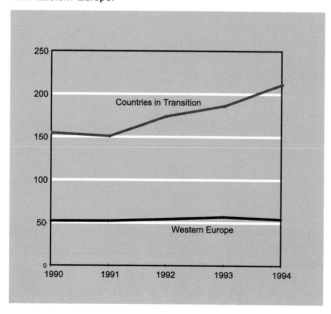

Source: Fifth UNCJS. See Notes to Figures for additional information.

GLOBAL REPORT ON CRIME AND JUSTICE

Allowing for changes in countries reporting for each period, developing country rates have remained roughly stable over 20 years. Prison rates have clearly increased among industrialized counties, with an overall rate in 1992 close to double that of 1972.

Source: First, Second, Third, Fourth and Fifth UNCJS. Countries may vary in each year and survey. See Notes to Snapshots for complete information, including individual country rates.

punishment, be it imprisonment or probation, may suffer from heavy overcrowding and increasing work loads over which they have no control.

There are vastly diverse ways to measure overcrowding. Here, the simplest method is used and involves comparing the state-set capacity of prisons (i.e., number of beds) and the actual number of prison inmates in a given day. If the latter exceeds the former (more than 100 percent), one could conclude that the prison system is generally overcrowded.

Table 4.7 presents the occupancy rate of 41 countries and territories. The highest rate, thus the most overcrowded nationally, recorded in 1994 was in Sudan (962 percent), followed by the Republic of Korea (479

percent), Belarus (165 percent), Madagascar (156 percent), and Portugal (123 percent). Other countries and territories in which the incarcerated prisoners exceeded the number of provided prison beds (i.e., with a rate over 100 percent) are Chile, Czech Republic, Hungary, Israel, Nicaragua and Singapore. Kuwait recorded the lowest rate (two percent), followed by Macau (39 percent), Greece (42 percent), Former Yugoslav Republic of Macedonia (53 percent), Mauritius (54 percent) and Slovenia (58 percent). It can be seen, however, that most countries report rates at or below 100 percent capacity.

Among these countries and territories, 21 recorded an increase in the prison occu-

There are vastly diverse ways to measure over-crowding.

BOX 4.1

Foreigners in Dutch correctional facilities

Ethnic composition of Netherlands incarcerated population, 1995 (by place of birth)

South America (Dutch Antilles) 19%

Other/unknown 1%

Asia 4%

Africa (Morocco) 14%

Europe (Netherlands, Germany, Turkey) 62%

Minorities make up approximately 9% of the total population (15.4 million) in the Netherlands. The following percentages give some indication of the distribution. Percentages are given for males in the population: Turkey (1.2%), Surinam (1.1%), Morocco (1.05%), and the Netherlands Antilles (0.4%) (Centraal Bureau voor de Statistiek, 1997; table 18; p. 49). While their numbers in the population are low, it must be kept in mind that ethnic minorities tend to concentrate in large cities where crime rates are high and social conditions are poor.

While Dutch citizens comprise half of the correctional facility population, approximately 30% of those incarcerated are from the following countries: Surinam (10%), Morocco (8%), the Netherlands Antilles (6%) and Turkey (5%). The percentage of incarcerated Moroccan males under the age of 25 is relatively high (13% of the incarcerated population). This figure far surpasses other ethnic groups (Surinam, 8%, Netherlands Antilles, 7% and Turkish citizens, 5%). The percentage of incarcerated males over the age of 30 is particularly high for those born in Surinam (accounting for a full 12% [30-39 years of age] to 13% [+40 years of age] of the population). The percentage of males ages 30-39 from the Netherlands Antilles and Morocco is much lower (7% for both groups) in the 30-39 age category and decreases radically in the +40 age category to (4% and 3% respectively) (Centraal Bureau voor de Stastiek; 1996; p. 42 and table 4.7, p. 46).[1]

The prison population in the Netherlands has increased over the past five years (1990-1995) from 6,892 in 1990 to 10,329 in 1995 and an important population shift has occurred. In 1990, Dutch citizens comprised 55% of the prison population. This figure decreased in 1995 to 50%. A concurrent 5% increase was witnessed in the percentage of Africans who were incarcerated in 1995, from 8% (1990) to 13%. The distribution of other foreigners in Dutch correctional facilities remained relatively stable over the five year period increasing or decreasing only 1%. This increase in the number of Africans being held in Dutch facilities is probably attributable to the number of illegal aliens awaiting deportation.[2]

The Department of Correctional Services divides the prison population, based on the country of birth, into the following categories: Netherlands, West Europe (Germany, Turkey and other), Africa (Morocco and other), Asia (Middle-East and other), South America (Surinam, Dutch Antilles and other), "other America" and unknown.

If one considers the offences for which foreigners are incarcerated, the following table displays a distinct pattern. Other crime types have been omitted from this table which is why the rows do not add to 100%.[3]

The offence with the most variance is the violation of the Opium Law (drug offence). Fifteen percent of all offenders are incarcerated for this offence. Those groups showing the highest rate of incarceration for this crime are Turkey, Germany and South America (in particular from Surinam, and the Netherlands Antilles).

Over a third (34%) of offenders are incarcerated for having perpetrated, or are awaiting trial for the commission of, violent crimes. Those groups showing the highest rate of incarceration for this crime are Dutch citizens, and those born in Surinam, Turkey and the Netherlands Antilles.

It is interesting to note that all ethnic minorities were incarcerated at a lower rate than their Dutch counterparts in relation to the perpetration of property offences. Only 10% of Turkish inmates are incarcerated for the perpetration of property offences.

One note of caution must be made here. For some ethnic minorities there is a large percentage of persons incarcerated for whom the offence category is "unknown" (18% of all Moroccans, 28% of all detainees from the Middle-East and 18% in the "other America" category). It is possible that were the offence category known, the above figures could be altered considerably.

The population of young Moroccan males incarcerated for criminal offences is significantly higher than for other ethnic groups. Moroccans incarcerated pending deportation (illegal alien status) also represent the second largest group of detained foreigners.

In conclusion, the findings concerning ethnic minorities in Dutch prisons (those convicted of criminal offences) mirrors the findings concerning ethnic, racial and religious minorities in many other countries as well. Ethnic minorities constitute a small proportion of the total population, a high percentage of those living in large cities afflicted by high unemployment and low educational levels and poor job skills. They also represent an above-average percentage of the prison population when compared to their actual numbers in the population.

Source: Aronowitz (Original paper, 1997). See Notes to Boxes for additional tables of data and other sources.

Percent of crime types for which ethnic groups are incarcerated, 1995

	% Violent offences	% Property offences	% Drug offences	% Unknown
Netherlands	37	37	10	6
Germany	30	28	26	8
Turkey	42	10	31	5
Africa	27	27	10	29
Morocco	33	33	10	18
Asia	28	23	14	25
Middle-East	25	27	11	28
South America	38	24	27	5
Surinam	38	26	23	5
Netherlands Antilles	43	23	25	4

pancy rate while 13 countries registered a decrease in this rate since 1990. It was not possible to make this comparison in seven countries due to the lack of data for 1990. Attention should be drawn to the dramatic (close to double) increase in the occupancy rates in Belarus, Czech Republic and Hungary. They are in line with the increase in their prison populations mentioned in the previous sections. A similar table is presented in Chapter 5 (Table 5.17), using convicted prisoners rather than total prisoners, and while there was some change in ranking of countries, the general findings were confirmed: most countries did not report prisons filled beyond capacity.

The figures presented here might be contrary to the common outcries of the ubiquitous "overcrowding problem" of prisons may be overcrowded while other wings or buildings in the same prison may not be so. (For relevant information on prison conditions, see below.)

Such an extensive analysis could only be possible if the national prison system were analyzed individually, which is beyond the scope of this chapter.

Increasing prison population

Inflation of the prison population poses a challenge to policy makers and governments in many parts of the world. Figure 4.5 shows the upward trend of the incarceration rate in several regions within the Fifth UNCJS period. The New World clearly displayed increasing prison populations whereas Asia, Latin America and

The United States paroled the largest number of prisoners in 1994, followed by Finland , Kyrgyzstan, Turkey and Lithuania.

TABLE 4.6
Distribution of parole and prison use, 1994.

	High prison use	Low prison use
High Parole use	USA, Kyrgyzstan, Lithuania, Slovakia, Hungary, Belarus, Latvia, Canada, Israel,	Finland, Turkey, Sweden, Denmark, Panama
Low Parole use	Czech. Rep., Bermuda, Russian Fed., Ukraine, Estonia, Scotland, Singapore, Guyana, Hong Kong, Costa Rica.	Sao Tome & P., Croatia, Austria, Rep. Korea, Chile, Portugal, "Former Yugoslav Republic of Macedonia", Japan, Belgium, Marshall Islands, England and Wales, Indonesia, Bulgaria.

Source: Fifth UNCJS. See Notes to Tables for information on method of classification.

worldwide. However, before such a conclusion is made, the difficulties in accurate measurement of prison overcrowding should be noted. The problem of "overcrowded prisons" may not be equal to the above-mentioned occupancy rate. First of all, in some jurisdictions, the capacity of prisons may be changed simply by providing extra beds in the same place although this does not meet the standard envisaged by the UN standard minimum rules (see Box 4.4). Therefore, a cell block may be quite congested but not "overcrowded." More importantly, the above-mentioned occupancy rate only considers the prisoner population and prison capacity of the whole country. One prison in a country may be overcrowded while others are not. Moreover, one wing or one building of a prison

Africa showed a somewhat stable situation. Western Europe remained at the lowest level but showed a steady increase.

The most notable changes were recorded in countries in transition. Some countries, such as Bulgaria, Czech Republic, Slovak Republic, Hungary, Poland and Romania, which experienced nearly "revolutionary" changes in regimes in 1989-1990, reduced prison populations dramatically by means of collective amnesty. They, however, later experienced sharp increases in prison populations. Other countries in the region which gained independence from the former Soviet Union (Estonia, Latvia, Lithuania, etc.) experienced less dramatic change (Box 4.3; see also Walmsley, 1996).

The increase of the prison population can be affected by several factors. Kuhn

BOX 4. 2

Reducing the prison population: the case of Finland

During the 1960s Finland's prisoner rate was unusually high when compared with the other Nordic countries, although the actual crime rates in Finland were in many cases lower than in these countries, with the exception of homicide and serious violence. On the other hand, the clearance rates were high and many of the convicted offenders were sentenced to imprisonment. In addition, prison sentences in Finland were longer than the Nordic average – this was particularly so with theft and other property offences. However, although the crime rates and the number of persons sentenced have increased since the 1960s the prison rate has decreased significantly.

The crime control experts in different institutions in the 1970s shared the view that the high prison rate was a disgrace and that the number and length of prison sentences should be reduced. Finland is a fairly expert-oriented country where crime control reforms are concerned. The government acted upon the experts' advice.

The reform ideology indicated that the aim of punishment should be to show the disapproval of the society of the act and to demonstrate the limits of acceptable behaviour. It was also noted that the immediate effect of a penalty is very limited. For this reason, the length of a prison sentence was a minor issue compared to the act of punishment itself. The ultimate question was: if the rehabilitative effects of prison sentences are negligible, if we reject the idea of determining the length of prison sentences on the basis of their incapacitation benefits, can our long prison sentences be defended on the basis of a cost-benefit assessment of their general prevention effect? The answer in Finland was "no."

During the 1970s, the major project on rewriting the entire legislation on criminal law was initiated based on the aforesaid thinking. Also, other reforms were launched which had an effect on prisoner rate.

There were two important decriminalizations during the last 35 years which indirectly affected the size of the prison population. The first was the crime of public drunkenness, which was abolished from the Criminal Code in 1968. Prior to that there had been a large number of persons fined for this offence who could not pay their fines. As a result, they had to serve a conversion sentence in prison. The other one concerned conscientious objectors belonging to the Jehovah's Witnesses. According to law, conscientious objectors who refuse to accept any form of military service were to be sentenced to a fixed term of imprisonment. The penalty was abolished for members of Jehovah's Witnesses in 1985.

A reform concerning theft offences also came into force in 1972 resulting in an increase in the use of fines and conditional prison sentences for theft offences since the 1970s. The reform on drunken driving entered into force in 1977 and it led to the use of unconditional imprisonment only in cases where the offender had a certain high blood alcohol percentage or where damage was caused. Although there was a massive increase in the number of drunken driving offences at the end of the 1980s and in the early 1990s, the number of unconditional prison sentences increased only slightly due to the use of fines and conditional sentences.

After the reform on conditional imprisonment in 1976, which enabled sentences of up to two years to be set conditionally, there has been a strong trend to increase the use of conditional prison sentences. The earlier strict conditions to the use of this sanction were also loosened and the combining of a conditional prison sentence with an unconditional fine was allowed. This meant in practice a real increase in the use of conditional imprisonment while the use of unconditional sentences decreased since 1976.

The use of shorter unconditional imprisonment can also largely explain the reduction in the prisoner rate. The aforesaid reforms concerning theft offences and drunken driving have significantly contributed to this reduction. Also, the reform of 1973 specifying that the time spent in pretrial detention must always be subtracted from the final sentence shortened the length of prison sentences.

The actual length of imprisonment can further be managed by pardoning and parole. Pardoning had not been used much for the purpose of reducing prisoner rates. The paroling rules were liberalized in 1976 by lowering the minimum serving time from six months to four months, and in 1988 the time was reduced to 14 days. These reforms have had an immediate impact on prisoner rates.

During the 1990s, there have been only small changes in prisoner rates. However, the structure of the prison population has changed: the number of prisoners serving short sentences has decreased as have the admission rates. Simultaneously, the number of long-term prisoners has grown and the respective lengths of imprisonment have increased.

Source: Kanguspunta (Original paper, 1997)

TABLE 4.7
Occupancy rate in prison; 1990, 94

	(%) 1990	(%) 1994
Sudan	1105	962
Rep. of Korea	475	479
Belarus	83	165
Madagascar	149	156
Portugal	117	123
Hong Kong	136	121
Singapore	--	118
Nicaragua	87	113
Czech Rep.	55	109
Chile	127	109
Hungary	64	107
Israel	101	105
England & Wales	101	100
Scotland	83	99
Costa Rica	83	96
Marshall Islands	154	96
Malta	72	96
Denmark	85	93
Bulgaria	119	90
Guyana	100	90
Austria	85	90
Russian Federation	--	89
Latvia	94	88
Northern Ireland	79	84
Finland	86	84
Slovakia	62	83
Liechtenstein	--	82
Rep. of Moldova	93	79
Lithuania	68	77
Western Samoa	67	77
Cyprus	91	77
Uganda	66	75
Japan	74	71
Kyrgyzstan	--	66
Bermuda	89	63
Croatia	40	60
Slovenia	58	58
Mauritius	52	54
*"FYRM"	38	53
Greece	43	42
Macau	--	39
Kuwait	--	2

*"Former Yugoslav Republic of Macedonia"
Source: Fifth UNCJS. See Notes to Tables for additional information.

(1996) noted that the prison population can be influenced by fluctuations in non-convicted (i.e., remand) prisoner admissions, convicted prisoner admissions, length of sentence, and availability and use of release mechanisms.

An examination of Kuhn's hypothesis can be made by comparing the ratio between remand prisoners and convicted prisoners. It may be that the remand prison population, and not the convicted prisoners, boosts the prison population and results in overcrowding, or vice versa. Such a definition of the problem is helpful in formulating effective strategies to tackle the problem. If

BOX 4.3

Fluctuations in prison rates in Central and Eastern Europe

Over a remarkably brief period, from 1989 to 1991, the countries in Central and Eastern Europe underwent a fundamental change in ideology. These countries moved from single-party government and a centrally planned economy to multi-party democracy and a free market.

The change in ideology had a clear impact on crime, on crime control and on the use of prisons. In the spirit of reform, many countries declared amnesties. (In the case of Czechoslovakia, a single amnesty at the beginning of 1990 led to the release of three-quarters of all convicted offenders, and over 40 percent of those held in pre-trial detention.) However, the increase in reported crime that accompanied the social, cultural and economic transition soon led, in many countries, to a call for more punitive measures, which filled up many of the recently emptied cells.

As noted by Walmsley (1996, p. 6) the pace of change and its impact varied from one country to the next. The impact on the prison population tended to be the greatest in those countries where the political changes amounted to a revolution (Albania, Bulgaria, the Czech and Slovak Republics, Hungary, Poland and Romania). In countries that gained independence after having been constituent republics of the former Soviet Union (Belarus, Estonia, Latvia, Lithuania, Moldova, the Russian Federation and Ukraine) and the former Yugoslavia (Croatia and Slovenia), the changes and their impact tended to be considerably less dramatic.

In some cases (for example in Albania, Croatia, Latvia, Poland, Romania and the Russian Federation) the disappointment of some prisoners in not being released under an amnesty, coupled with the uncertainty among the staff over how to interpret the new emphasis on human rights and liberal prison regimes, led to riots. More generally, the release of large numbers of prisoners caused unease among the public, whose concern was heightened by media accounts of an increase in crime.

As a result, the prisoner rates in many countries began to go back up. In the case of Belarus and Ukraine, the prison population per capita in 1995 was higher than in 1985, before the political changes. In the Czech Republic, Lithuania and Slovakia, the prison population has risen to somewhat less than the level during the 1980s. However, this increase in prisoner rates did not prove inevitable: in such countries as Bulgaria, Hungary, Moldova and Slovenia, the prison population has remained on much the same lower level it achieved in the aftermath of the changes.

If all of the prisoners in Central and Eastern Europe are added together, the overall prisoner rate in 1995 was 465 per 100,000 in population. This figure, however, is dominated by the large population and large number of prisoners in the Russian Federation; if this country is left out of the calculations, the prisoner rate for the remaining countries drops to 272 per 100,000. Even this, however, does not show the variety: three countries, Belarus, the Russian Federation and Ukraine, had over 500 prisoners per 100,000 population in 1995, while in five countries – Albania, Bosnia-Herzegovina, Croatia, The Former Yugoslav Republic of Macedonia ("FYRM") and Slovenia – the rate was reported to be on par with the general level in Western Europe, at or below 100 per 100,000 in population.

Many of those countries where the prison population has increased have had to face a variety of difficulties, ranging from physical crowding, shortage of personnel for supervision and shortage of work, to a shortage of beds, food and adequate health services, and a resulting increase in communicable disease, such as tuberculosis.

Crowding was so serious in some prison systems that they had more prisoners than places. The most severe difficulties of this kind were in Romania, where the prisons were reported to have an occupancy rate of 145 percent, or 45 percent over capacity. Prisons were also reported to be overcrowded in Belarus, the Czech Republic, Hungary, Poland, Romania, the Russian Federation and Ukraine. (At the other extreme, prisons in Bosnia-Herzegovina and Slovenia were reported to have an occupancy rate of only 40 percent.)

This drop and subsequent increase in the prison population in many Central and Eastern European countries shows once again that crime rates alone cannot explain fluctuations in prison populations. In many Central and Eastern European countries crime rates – including rates for the more serious crimes – have been stable or even decreasing for several years. Generally speaking, Central and Eastern European crime rates have remained stable since 1992/1993. Nonetheless, as noted, prison populations in most countries have continued to increase. This suggests that there has been a change in attitude towards the use of imprisonment, a growing belief that imprisonment is preferable to the alternatives.

Source: Joutsen (Original paper, 1997). See Notes to Boxes for additional sources.

Prison rates per 100,000 in countries of Central and Eastern Europe

	1985	1990	1995
Albania	**30	**90	*95
Belarus	**310	**140	505
Bosnia-Herzeg.	n.a.	n.a.	85
Bulgaria	**170	**125	110
Croatia	**75	**30	55
Czech Republic	270	80	190
Estonia	455	220	270
Hungary	220	120	120
Latvia	640	320	375
Lithuania	405	230	360
"FYRM"	n.a.	n.a.	*60
Moldova	*520	**275	275
Poland	270	120	170
Romania	260	110	200
Russian Fed.	n.a.	**470	690
Slovakia	225	70	150
Slovenia	70	40	30
Ukraine	**340	**185	600

Figures marked with an asterisk may be unreliable since they are inconsistent with information from other sources. Figures marked with two asterisks are taken from the country reports in Walmsley (1997), and are approximate figures. For Ukraine, the first figure is for 1986. Source: Walmsley (1997), pp. 5 and 7. See Notes to Boxes for complete table, including dates on which 1995 count was taken.

Eleven countries show occupancy rates above the 100 percent level.

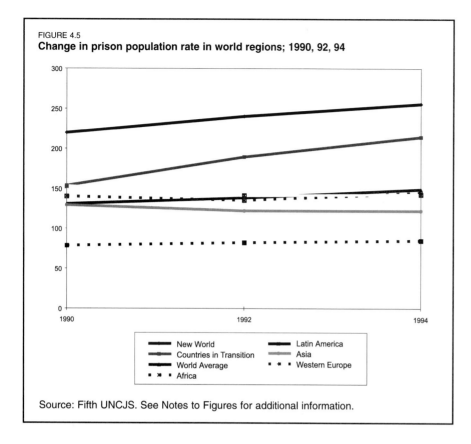

FIGURE 4.5
Change in prison population rate in world regions; 1990, 92, 94

Legend:
- New World
- Countries in Transition
- World Average
- Africa
- Latin America
- Asia
- Western Europe

Source: Fifth UNCJS. See Notes to Figures for additional information.

the remand prisoner is the factor which boosts the prison population, and therefore the main factor contributing to overcrowding, this calls for the introduction of speedy trials, bail systems and restructuring of pre-trial detention. The problem could also derive from an increase in crime, longer adjudicated sentences, relative unavailability of alternatives and unavailability of the early release system.

Figures 4.6 and 4.7 present the ratio of remand prisoners and sentenced prisoners in the total prison population[10] relative to geographic regions and to the UNDP classification of development. It can be seen that the more developed the countries are, the lower the proportion of remand prisoners kept in the prison system. This observation holds true with other established measures of development such as GNP and the UNDP Human Development Index. All provide essentially similar results (see notes to Figures 4.6 and 4.7).

Length of sentence can also be a contributing factor to prison overcrowding. If an adjudicated sentence is fairly long and an early release system (parole or "good time") does not exist, the prison population will easily rocket upwards if there is a regular flow of new admissions to prison. But

short term sentences can also lead to over-crowding with turnover rates. Unfortunately, it is not possible to identify the average effective sentence by crime type because too few countries provided this information. However, a few countries did provide this information, each of which can provide an illustrative example. It should be noted, however, that the selection is by no means representative; rather, it is based purely on availability of data. The data available are presented in Figure 4.8.

England and Wales showed a low but steady increase in the total prisoner rate. Total admissions to prison is far above the total prisoners. It is understandable that changes regarding the prisoner (intake and release) can occur more than once in a year. This also suggests that the pre-conviction detention period is quite short. Nevertheless, total incarceration steadily increased following the increase of total prison admission rate. The convicted prisoner rate remains stable notwithstanding the increased imprisonment adjudication of adults and the drastic decrease of parole, both of which would have increased convicted prisoners. Therefore, it may be explained by a decrease of the total sentencing length served or other factors that are not listed here, such as decrease of juvenile adjudication, introduction of other release mechanisms, etc.

A similar pattern of higher admission rate with a lower total prisoner rate was also found in **Finland** (see Box 4.2). This again suggests a shorter pre-conviction detention period and therefore more frequent turn-overs. The ratio between total prisoners and convicted prisoners remains relatively the same. However, the most notable difference is a relatively high sentencing rate of adults to deprivation of liberty and its drastic decrease between 1992 and 1994. The discrepancy between sentencing rate and actual prisoner rate may be explained by sentencing options, such as split sentences, and/or other means such as creating the prison waiting list. Tornudd (1994) attributed this to policy makers' commitment to reduce prison population.

The total prisoner rate in **Japan** remains low and has decreased steadily. The total admissions is closer to the total prisoners, which suggests a smaller turnover of prisoners and therefore possibly longer pre-conviction detention periods than in England

and Wales and Finland. The sentence lengths are considerably longer, but this may be compensated for by the less frequent occurrence of such sentences suggested by the low rate of adults sentenced to deprivation of liberty.

Latvia recorded some fluctuation but at the already high level of use of incarceration. The total admission rate to prisons is lower than the total prisoner rate: this suggests that there is a longer pre-conviction period than in Finland, England and Wales and even Japan. The length of the effective sentence remains stable, but within an average longer duration of stay in prison. Also, the use of imprisonment sentences is increasing. Increased use of parole may contribute to slowing down the upward trend of the convicted prisoner rate, but not necessarily the total prisoner rate. Therefore the increase in total prison population in Latvia may be caused by a combination of both longer sentences served and the increase of pre-conviction detention.

Belarus showed a strong increase in the total prisoner rate. The convicted prisoner rate is also increasing, but the gap between total prisoners and convicted prisoners is widening. This indicates that there is also an increase in remand prisoners. Although yearly admissions to prison increased, they are not more than the total prisoner rate in volume. This suggests that prisoners tend to stay longer in the institution. The parole rate also increased but not sufficiently to reduce the increased prison population.

Prison conditions[11]

The UN Crime and Justice Survey provided little information on actual conditions in prisons (Boxes 4.5 and 4.6).

In 1955, the First United Nations Congress on the Prevention of Crime and the Treatment of Offenders adopted the Standard Minimum Rules for the Treatment of Prisoners (see Box 4.4), that sought "to set out what is generally accepted as being good principle and practice in the treatment of offenders" (Rule 1). In promoting these rules, the Economic and Social Council adopted the Procedures for the Effective Implementation of the Standard Minimum Rules for the Treatment of Prisoners. Non-governmental organizations (NGOs) also made efforts to promote this spirit and to en-

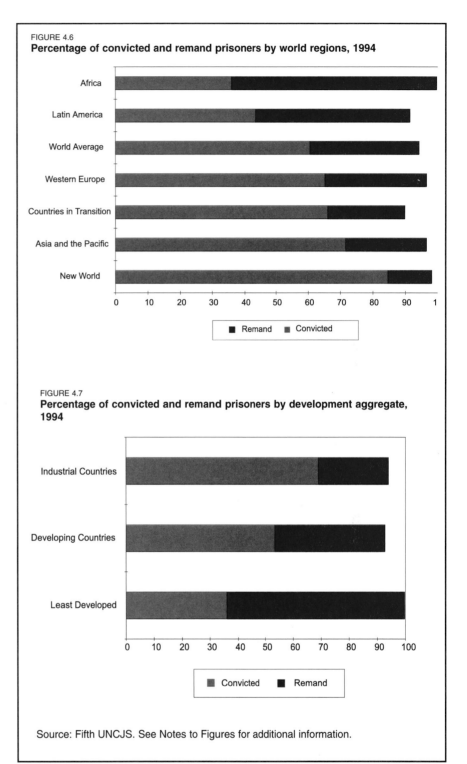

FIGURE 4.6
Percentage of convicted and remand prisoners by world regions, 1994

FIGURE 4.7
Percentage of convicted and remand prisoners by development aggregate, 1994

Source: Fifth UNCJS. See Notes to Figures for additional information.

sure its effective implementation.[12]

A recent United Nations study on the implementation of the Standard Minimum Rules (United Nations, 1996c) reveals somewhat more qualitative information. Rule 8 stipulates the separation of prisoners according to different categories, such as gender and legal status. Almost all the countries that responded to the survey (72) reported that male and female prisoners were

FIGURE 4.8

Variations in parole, total prisoners, convicted prisoners, total admissions, sentences to prison (per 100,000 population) and average time spent in prison (in weeks), 1990-1994: selected countries. (Key on page 105)

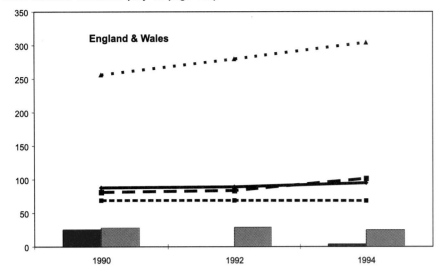

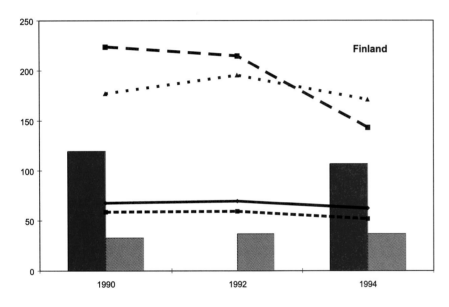

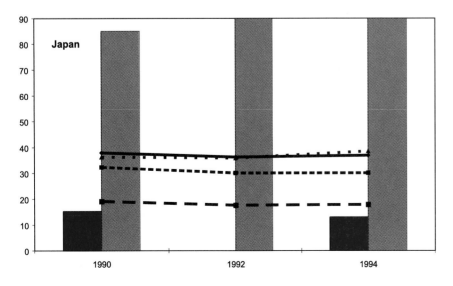

Source: Fifth UNCJS. See Notes to Figures for additional information and tables.

detained either in separate institutions, or in separate premises of an institution. However, the separation of untried (remand) prisoners and convicted prisoners is adopted by only just over half of the responding countries, mainly due to resource problems. (The question of criminal justice resources in relation to prisons is considered in the following chapter.)

Because of resource problems, only one-sixth of the countries are able to allow prisoners to permanently occupy individual cells or rooms at night (Rule 9). Rule 10 requires that accommodation, especially sleeping accommodation, meet all health requirements, with due regard being paid to climatic conditions and particularly to the cubic air content, minimum floor space, lighting, heating and ventilation. The responses concerning floor space and cubic air space are presented in Tables 4.8 and 4.9. More than one-quarter of the countries reported difficulties in constructing windows that would allow for the entry of fresh air.

Rule 13 requires that adequate bathing and shower installations be provided so that every prisoner may be enabled and required to have a bath or shower, at a temperature suitable to the climate, as frequently as necessary for general hygiene according to the season and geographical region, but at least once a week in a temperate climate. The responses are presented in Table 4.10. Three-quarters of the responding countries always provided prisoners with separate beds or bedding (Rule 19). However, in some countries this practice is exceptional or rare. The requirements for food to be of a nutritional value that is adequate for health and strength, of wholesome quality, well prepared and served by administration to all prisoners (Rule 20) is applied in all countries.

Less than one-third of the responding countries reported insufficient work to keep all prisoners actively employed (Rule 76). Another third reported that there was enough work for almost all prisoners. However, the wages received by the prisoners for their work vary considerably, ranging from wages that are almost equivalent to that of the lowest grade prison officers to three percent of such wages (see Box 4.5 and Box 4.6).

One-third of the responding countries was able to provide all prisoners with some form of education (Rule 77; see Box 4.4). When this is limited to all illiterate prison-

FIGURE 4.8 CONTINUED

ers, the positive response increased by 50 percent. The requirement for every prisoner who is not employed in outdoor work to have at least one hour, weather permitting, of suitable exercise in the open air was followed by three-quarters of the responding countries.

While some three-quarters of countries reported daily access to a qualified medical officer, this is still not the case in regard to a number of countries.

Privileges can be awarded in three-quarters of responding countries. This includes remission, parole, home leave, extra or longer visits including contact visits, better work conditions, etc. (Box 4.6). Almost all the responding countries reported that prisoners could only be punished in accordance with laws or regulations made known to them previously, and that they were given a proper opportunity to present their defense before the imposition of a disciplinary measure. The prohibition of the use of corporal punishment, punishment involving the placement of the prisoners in a dark cell, and all cruel, inhumane and degrading punishments for disciplinary purposes was complied with in four-fifths of the responding countries.

Five-sixths of the responding countries reported that prisoners have the opportunity to make requests or complaints to the director of the institution or the officer authorized to represent him or her, every day upon request or at least three times a week (Rule 36). Almost all countries have their penal institutions regularly inspected (Rule 55). However, less than half require the prison administration to follow the inspector's recommendations.

As far as contact with the outside world is concerned, Rule 37 stipulates that prisoners shall be allowed, under necessary supervision, to communicate with their family and reputable friends at regular intervals, both by correspondence and by receiving visits. There are great variations among the countries. Some allow visits no more than once a month while others allow them more than six times a month or upon request (see Box 4.6). Some countries set different standards for remand prisoners and convicted prisoners.

When compared with the previous UNCJS, which gathered information for 1985-1989[13], the following positive changes

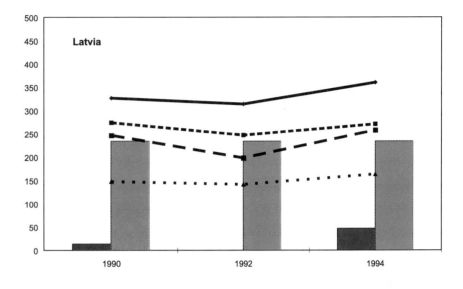

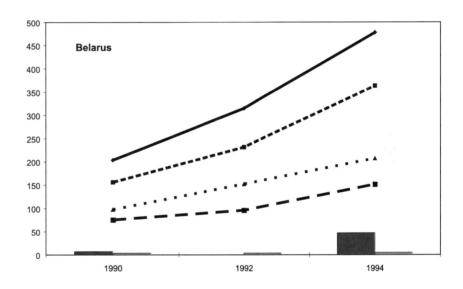

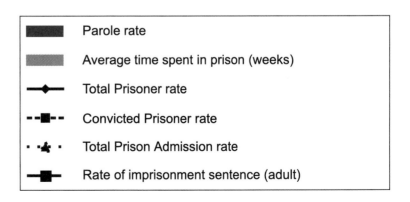

Source: Fifth UNCJS. See Notes to Figures for additional information and tables.

Standard Minimum Rules for the Treatment of Prisoners (Abridged)
Approved by the Economic and Social Council, 31 July 1957
(resolution 663 C I (XXIV)), on the recommendation of the First Congress

Men and women in detention are to be held in separate facilities; likewise, untried and convicted prisoners, those imprisoned for civil offences and criminal offenders, and youths and adults shall be housed separately.

Cells for individuals should not be used to accommodate two or more persons overnight; dormitory facilities are to be supervised at night.

Prisoners shall be provided with adequate water and toilet articles, and required to keep themselves clean.

Prisoners not allowed to wear their own clothing are to be provided with an adequate and suitable outfit, with provisions for laundry and changes of clothes.

Prisoners outside an institution for an authorized purpose are to be allowed to wear their own clothing.

Every prisoner shall be provided with a separate bed and clean, separate and sufficient bedding.

Wholesome, well-prepared food is to be provided prisoners at usual hours.

Drinking water shall be available whenever needed.

If not employed in outdoor work, every prisoner shall have at least one hour of exercise in the open air, weather permitting.

Young prisoners and others of suitable age and physique are to receive physical and recreational training.

A medical officer with some knowledge of psychiatry is to be available to every institution.

Prisoners requiring specialized treatment are to be transferred to a civil hospital or appropriate facility.

A qualified dental officer shall be available to every prisoner.

Prenatal and postnatal care and treatment are to be provided by women's institutions; where nursing infants are allowed to remain with their mothers, a nursery staffed by qualified persons is needed.

Every prisoner shall be examined by the medical officer shortly after admission; prisoners suspected of contagious diseases are to be segregated.

The medical officer shall see all sick prisoners daily, along with those who complain of illness or are referred to his attention.

The medical officer is to report to the director on prisoners whose health is jeopardized by continued imprisonment and on the quality of the food, hygiene, bedding, clothing and physical regimen of the prisoners.

Every institution shall maintain for the use of prisoners a library with recreational and instructional books.

Transport is to be at the expense of the prison administration, and equal conditions shall obtain for all prisoners.

The administration shall carefully select every grade of personnel and maintain in their minds and the public's the important social service they provide.

To these ends, pay, conditions and benefits shall be suitable to professional and exacting service.

Personnel are to be sufficiently educated, and to receive ongoing courses and training.

As far as possible, personnel should include psychiatric, social work and education professionals.

The director shall be a qualified administrator, retained on a full time basis and residing on the premises or in the immediate vicinity.

Staff personnel are to be able to speak the language of the greatest number of prisoners, and to retain the services of an interpreter when necessary.

In larger institutions, at least one medical officer should reside on the premises or in the immediate vicinity.

In others, a medical officer shall visit daily and reside near enough to be available for emergencies.

Prison officers are to receive physical training in the use of force.

Source: The full text of the Standard Minimum Rules, including Part 2 Special Categories, may be found in many United Nations documents, and also at the UNCJIN web site: http://www.ifs.univie.ac.at/~uncjin/uncjin/html. The original document issued from the first United Nations Congress on Prevention of Crime and Treatment of Offenders, 1955. A/CONF/6/C.1/L.1

---

are reported: more opportunity for baths and showers; increased availability of medical service; less disciplinary measures exercised on prisoners; less use of corporal punishment as a disciplinary measure; and improved access to information. Negative trends include: more difficulty in separat-

TABLE 4.8
Floor space per prisoner

Size of room (square meters)	Number of countries
Up to 3	23
3-5	15
6-10	13
11-15	4
More than 15	1

TABLE 4.9
Cubic air space per prisoner

Size of room (cubic meters)	Number of countries
Up to 10	25
11-30	23
31-50	3
More than 50	3

TABLE 4.10
Frequency of entitlement to bath or shower

Frequency	Hot water	Cold water
Less than once a week	1	-
At least once a week	17	1
At least twice a week	4	1
At least three times a week	4	10
At least daily/on request	18	11
Depends on prisoners' behaviour	-	2

Source: United Nations (1996c)

ing prisoners according to their categories (age, legal status and gender); greater use of dormitories; less availability of individual beds or bedding; less cleanliness; and fewer educational opportunities.[14]

Capital punishment

Capital punishment is the ultimate form of punishment, and involves the elimination of offenders from society. It should not be confused with *corporal punishment*, which involves the infliction of physical harm on offenders. Corporal punishment was reported in use by only four countries of the total that responded to the UN Crime and Justice Survey. Typical examples are the amputation of a hand and flogging. Even though there certainly are strong arguments against corporal punishment, it should not be confused with unrestricted torture because it is executed after careful consideration of evidence and fair consistency.[15] It is also argued that such punishment has a strong deterrent effect.[16]

In contrast, capital punishment is in wide use around the world, and it is probably the most controversial of all punishments. The effect of its specific deterrence is absolute because it permanently removes the offender from society. There is a heated debate about its deterrent effects on the general public — that is, the extent to which those who might commit a crime are deterred from doing so by the execution of a known criminal. Research findings produce conflicting results.[17]

Hood (1996) reported that, according to a recent United Nations report (United Nations, 1996b), 90 countries retain capital punishment on their statute books, 58 have completely abolished it, and 14 have abolished it for ordinary crimes. Out of the 90 countries which retain capital punishment, 30 are considered to be *de facto* abolitionist countries in that they have not executed anyone over the past ten years[18] (see Figure 4.9).

Compared to 1988 (Figure 4.10), there was a definite increase in the number of countries that have abolished the death penalty. However, this did not accompany a substantial decrease of retentionist countries. Moreover, there is evidence that countries regarded to be *de facto* abolitionist countries recommended execution and therefore returned to being retentionist countries. The movement towards the restriction and abolition of the death penalty is not unidirectional. Indeed, the history of the use of capital punishment during this century is one of constant change in some countries, particularly the United States (Box 4.7) and countries undergoing political change such as Russia (Box 4.8).

There is a strong need for accurate information on the death penalty. Hood (1996) termed the situation quite accurately: "Those countries which are known from other (than the UN) sources to make the greatest use of execution were precisely those who most of-

Notes on an Egyptian prison (house of reform)

Mansoura House of Reform or correctional facility (hereafter MHR) is located in the city of Mansoura, the capital city of the state Dakhalia. Mansoura is about 100 kilometers from Cairo and has a population of over 1,500,000. The MHR is more than 100 years old and is located in the heart of the city. The facility's neighbours include the university campus and a major sports stadium.

MHR has about 400 inmates on any given day. However, the daily figures fluctuate. This facility includes inmates convicted for less serious crimes as well as those awaiting trial. Those awaiting trial are segregated from convicted inmates. The facilities include women inmates who are housed in separate buildings within the MHR premises. It is not uncommon to find persons under trial living in the MHR for many years. Offenders convicted of serious (violent) offenses are sent to a prison in Abu Zabal.

Daily routine

Roll Call. The MHR resembles a typical high security prison. It has high walls and barbed wire with armed guards in observation towers. Prisoners are awakened at 6 AM every morning. After they wash up, they assemble for roll call at 6:30 AM. The inmates are expected to be presentable. Those who fail to observe the dress code are punished.

During roll call, all those in the facilities assemble in an open area. Inmates from each unit are identified by the specific unit guards or officers who stand in the front and behind each group. There are no boundaries between the groups of inmates. This is a major event of the day during which time inmates are assigned their daily chores. At this time, prisoners are informed about the day's major news stories, incoming officers, new social workers or visiting dignitaries, and officer retirements. The names of inmates who will be released on good behaviour as well as those inmates receiving sentence remissions are also announced. Further, all administrative matters, complaints and needs are addressed during daily roll call. Roll call may last between 30 minutes to an hour depending on the amount of administrative chores for the day.

After roll call inmates return to their respective units for breakfast. Each unit has its own kitchen and dining rooms. The menu, however, is common for all units. The food is balanced and nutritious. A typical breakfast consists of two eggs, cheese, beans, jam, flat bread, tea, coffee or milk, and yogurt.

After breakfast inmates adhere to the assigned chores. Inmates are generally assigned

chores based on their aptitude for specific work. Some inmates who opt to attend classes are offered the opportunity within the facilities. It is not uncommon to find some inmates preparing for high school and at times, college level courses.

Some inmates work in the laundry and in the kitchen facilities. Some are assigned to small scale industries within the facilities. These industries include furniture making, bread making, plumbing and metal and electrical work. The women's units have facilities for sewing uniforms and working with handicrafts. Those inmates engaged in production receive a small wage for their services. These activities help inmates to not only learn a trade, but also to stay busy during their time in the facility.

The prison products are generally sold in the open market. Proceeds from the sales are diverted back to the house of reform. These resources help improve physical infrastructure as well as other inmate needs such as new television sets, shoes and uniforms.

Lunch is served at 1 PM and generally includes meat or chicken, rice, soup, vegetables, salad, fruit of the day, and bread. After lunch inmates rest till 3 PM, at which time they return to work for two more hours. Sometimes inmates do not have work to keep them occupied the entire day. On such days they work out or play games such as soccer and volleyball. In addition, they have a recreation hour from 5 to 6 PM.

Dinner, consisting of fish or beans, yogurt, bread, cheese, jam and fruits, is served at 8 PM. Units are locked up depending on the daylight and season. However, inmates can move about in their respective units until 10 PM.

Families can visit inmates on a regular basis. Families can bring special food if the inmates choose.

Source: El-Kassas and Nalla (Original paper, 1997). This summary has been reconstructed from an interview with Mr. El-Kasses Madhy, a visiting scholar at Michigan State University. Mr. El-Kasses was assistant lecturer of Sociology in Mansoura University, Mansoura, Egypt. Mr. Kassas used to accompany students on observational visits to the prison (house of reform) as a part of their field work.

BOX 4.6

Notes on the prison system of Thailand

As of July 1996 there were 114,588 native born persons and 3,754 foreigners or "farangs" in prisons or correctional institutions in Thailand. About 9,500 of these were inmates appealing their sentences, with roughly 25,000 awaiting trial. These two groups are not generally segregated from inmates who have been sentenced by the courts.

Work is at the center of prison life in Thailand. Every convicted inmate is required to engage in what the Department of Corrections calls "useful" work in all prisons and correctional institutions, though those on remand are only responsible for cleaning their own cells and do not have to engage in the same work schedule as convicted prisoners. Prisoners receive 50 percent of the net profit that a prison industry produces, and 80 percent if the prisoner is working on a community service project outside the prison.

Prisoners are allowed regular visits from families and friends and, twice a year, the Department holds a "Family Day" for all qualified inmates in every prison all over the country. During this ten day period, relatives of inmates are able to have contact visits which, in the case of trusted prisoners, may involve conjugal relationships.

Though the food provided is basic, three meals a day are provided. Health services are generally inadequate, due to a shortage of full-time physicians, and serious medical or psychiatric cases requiring emergency treatment or intensive care are usually referred to hospitals in major cities close to the prison.

The Thai authorities provide voluntary religious programs for all inmates and arrangements are made to enable prisoners of non-Buddhism faiths to practice the religion they follow. Prisoners are allowed to write letters to friends and relatives, but officials heavily censor both outgoing and incoming mail.

Prisoners may be released prior to the end of a sentence by receiving one of two kinds of Royal Pardon. The first is the individual pardon, where each prisoner who believes he or she has a good case submits a petition to the Ministry of Interior. In the second situation particular classes or types of prisoners (for example, foreign drug dealers involved in relatively minor offences) may be pardoned by the King on special or important national events.

In 1996 Thailand's Ministry of Interior was seeking a royal pardon or clemency for 25,000 prisoners as part of the 50th anniversary celebrations of King Adulyadej's accession to the throne. Of this number it was expected that 20,000 would be freed and 5,000 would have their sentences significantly reduced.

Discipline is very strict in Thai prisons and privileges such as visits from relatives or writing letters are swiftly withdrawn if prison rules are broken. Instruments of restraint such as leg chains, handcuffs and leg irons are used often, though the Thai authorities say that they only use these devices in "special circumstances."

On three occasions this writer has visited prisons in the country, the last time being in July 1996, when permission was obtained to assess the condition of foreign inmates incarcerated in Klongprem Central, the main prison in the country. At Klongprem, I was given unrestricted access to prisoners and was able to converse with them in privacy, without them fearing repercussions. There are 100 nationalities represented in Thai prisons, with 77 percent from other Asian countries and 12 percent from Africa. The next highest categories are from Europe (7 percent), America (3 percent), and Australia and New Zealand (1 percent).

The male farangs sleep shoulder to shoulder, four or five to a cell. A light burns fiercely day and night and an open Thai style toilet dominates each room. Females are housed in a separate prison where community living is the norm, with anywhere between 40 and a 100 packed into tiny dormitories.

Most prisoners I talked to said there was little violence or rape in prison. "As long as we keep to ourselves, and as long as we obey the prison officers, they do not hassle us," one said. However, most prisoners told me that punishments for attempting to escape were severe and included leg and hand restraints as well as severe beatings.

What especially struck me about security in the prison was the lack of guns worn by the guards and the relatively small number of officers guarding the inmates. There were 156 guards in Klongprem to watch over 6000 prisoners.

Source: Wilson (Original paper, 1997)

---

ten failed to reply with the details requested by the United Nations."

The United Nations adopted Safeguards Guaranteeing Protection of the Rights of Those Facing the Death Penalty (United Nations, 1996b), calling for its restricted use and for protecting the human rights of persons facing capital punishment.

Non-custodial sanctions

Non-custodial sanctions avoid the placement of offenders in prisons and/or other institutions. Although there are several types of non-custodial sanctions, they all share one thing in common: they are often a "mirror image of prison." Or, to put it another way, they are prison-inspired contrasts to prisons. Joutsen and Zvekic (1994) suggested that this category of punishment be divided into two groups: (1) types of sanction which imply supervision and control, and (2) those sanctions that do not imply such control. These groups contain the types of non-custodial sanctions presented in Table 4.11.

In some systems, and increasingly so, provisions are made for a combination of custodial sanctions and non-custodial sanctions, and a combination of different non-custodial sanctions. Such combinations may give the sentence more weight and tailor it to the characteristics of offenders while meeting the expectations of the court and the community.

In general, such non-custodial punishment is considered less costly than traditional imprisonment and avoids the harmful effects associated with total incarceration. Also, it can be more conducive to social reintegration.

The UNCJS shows that many countries either do not have the categories of non-custodial sanctions requested by the survey or do not possess statistical data on their use. Four categories of non-custodial sanctions are referred to: control in freedom[19]; warning[20]; fine; and community service order.

In most of the countries responding to the UNCJS, the fine is the most frequently used non-custodial sanction. It ranges from 95 percent in Japan, through more than 70 percent in the Western European countries, to much lower percentages in the countries in transition and the developing world. Just over 50 percent of convicted adults received warnings and admonitions in a number of both Western and Central/Eastern European countries (with as many as 74 percent in Slovenia), compared to an almost negligible percentage in the developing world, with the exception of South Africa (23 percent). Control in freedom and community service orders appear to be less utilized sanctioning options across the board.

Probation, or control of freedom, is the imposition of a certain restriction on the freedom of offenders without strictly placing them in a prison. It may be associated with monitoring by the authority (probation officers). It is claimed that probation is less costly than imprisonment and is able to avoid the harmful effects associated with strict incarceration. There are several newer types of *intermediate sanctions,* which are intended to fill the continuum between probation and imprisonment, such as house arrest and intensive supervised probation, that are frequently associated with electronic monitoring (Box 4.10).

Probation is defined in the UN Crime and Justice Survey as "a procedure whereby an individual found guilty of a crime is released by the court without imprisonment to the supervision of an official." Because probation is often used for juvenile offenders, data are presented for both adults and juveniles in Table 4.12, which reports the number of adults and juveniles placed under probation per year.[21]

The results show considerable variations in the prevalence rate among the countries in 1994: from 0.8 per 100,000 population (Indonesia) to 536 (USA). Canada and England and Wales have the highest probation rates next only to the USA. Even though the lack of the total number of juveniles who received criminal convictions prevents us from carrying out a conclusive analysis, when the conventional wisdom (according to which juveniles represent smaller numbers in the criminal justice systems) is taken into account, this might well mean that juveniles are more likely to receive probation

The movement towards the restriction and abolition of the death penalty is not unidirectional.

FIGURE 4.9
Capital punishment around the world

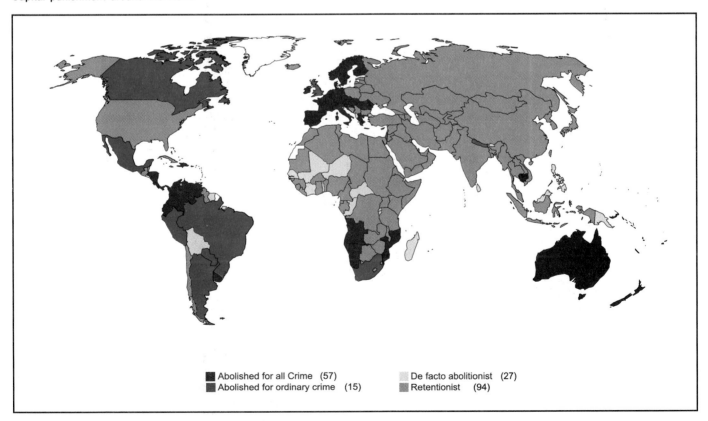

Abolished for all Crime (57)   De facto abolitionist (27)
Abolished for ordinary crime (15)   Retentionist (94)

Source: Amnesty International (1997). Note: map is not to scale. The boundaries shown on this map do not imply official endorsement or acceptance by the UN.

BOX 4.7

The death penalty: focus on the United States

Legal Developments. The modern era of capital punishment in the United States began a quarter-century ago, when the US Supreme Court issued its landmark ruling in *Furman v. Georgia* (1972). The *Furman* decision invalidated all state and federal death-penalty laws throughout the country. The laws then in effect gave juries unregulated discretion to decide whether offenders convicted of capital crimes should be sentenced to death. By a vote of 5-4, the Justices of the Supreme Court declared that such sentencing procedures violated the constitutional prohibition against cruel and unusual punishments. The laws were deficient *procedurally*: when juries were entrusted with unfettered discretion to decide whether convicted offenders should live or die, the risk that capital sentences would be imposed arbitrarily or would be tainted by racial or other invidious discrimination was constitutionally intolerable. The Justices did not go so far in *Furman* to rule that capital punishment was inherently unconstitutional.

State legislatures wasted little time in revising their death-penalty laws in response to the *Furman* decision. By 1976, 35 states had passed new capital sentencing statutes, and the Supreme Court was again asked to consider their constitutionality. In *Gregg v. Georgia* (1976) and its companion cases, the Supreme Court announced that the death penalty was a constitutionally acceptable form of punishment, which lawfully could be administered under the new "guided discretion" sentencing procedures adopted by a majority of the states.

Different forms of guided-discretion capital sentencing legislation were approved by the Supreme Court, which made it clear that the US Constitution does not require that all death-penalty laws conform to a single model as long as a few fundamental procedures are observed. It now appears that death-penalty laws are constitutionally sufficient if they satisfy the following requirements:

1. In capital trials evidence relevant to sentencing must be offered at a separate hearing following the guilt-innocence trial.

2. The legislature must narrow the class of offences punishable by death. This requirement means that the prosecution must prove the existence of one or more aggravating factors associated with a crime – for example, that the victim of a murder was a police officer.

3. An offender who is eligible for the death penalty cannot be restricted from presenting mitigation evidence at the penalty trial.

4. A death-sentenced offender must be given the right to appeal the sentence to a higher court.

5. A capital sentence cannot be grossly disproportional to the offender's crime. The Court has ruled that the US Constitution forbids the death penalty for the crimes of rape (of an adult) and kidnapping.

Death Penalty Facts and Figures. In 1997, 38 of the 50 states in the US had effective death penalty laws, and death-sentenced prisoners awaited execution in all but four of those states (see Figure above). Legislation enacted by the US Congress in 1994 made over 60 federal crimes punishable by death. Voters in the nation's capital recently rejected an initiative to enact the death penalty for crimes committed in Washington DC.

Over 3,150 prisoners were under sentence of death as of midyear 1996. Capital sentences were not distributed evenly throughout the country. Three states – California (444), Texas (394) and Florida (349) –

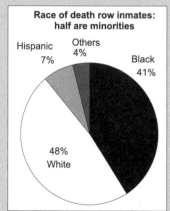

Race of death row inmates: half are minorities

Hispanic 7%
Others 4%
Black 41%
48% White

accounted for well over one-third of the country's death-sentenced population, and 11 states (including four with no offenders under sentence of death) and the federal government had ten or fewer prisoners awaiting execution. Death row prisoners overwhelmingly were men (98.4 percent). Nearly half (48 percent) of death-sentenced prisoners were white, while 41 percent were black, and 7 percent were Hispanic (see Figure below left).

The death-sentenced population has grown steadily by roughly 150 to 200 offenders for each of the past several years. Since 1977, when executions resumed in the post-*Furman* era, the average time lapse

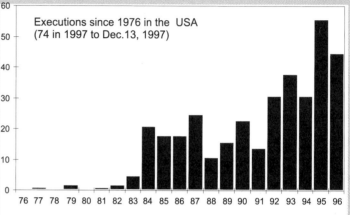

Executions since 1976 in the USA
(74 in 1997 to Dec.13, 1997)

between imposition of sentence and execution has been in excess of eight years, with some prisoners' executions postponed 17 years or longer. In an effort to accelerate the pace of executions, the US Congress enacted legislation in 1996 that put demanding new time limits (six or 12 months from the date an appeal becomes final, depending on other state laws) on death-sentenced prisoners to petition the federal courts for habeas corpus relief.

The decade of the 1930s produced the most executions in the United States over the past century. The peak year for executions was 1935, when 199 offenders were put to death. Executions have been far less regular in the modern era, although they have become increasingly common over the last 20 years, as can be seen in the accompanying Figure.

Administrative Issues. Several questions have been raised about the death penalty's application under the revised statutes. For example:

• Minors are punishable by death in a majority of the states that practice capital punishment. While 14 states and federal law restrict the death penalty to offenders who were at least 18 years old when they committed their crimes, in 24 states offenders as young as 16 or 17 can be executed. The Court has interpreted the federal Constitution to forbid the capital punishment of 15 year old offenders.

• Mentally retarded offenders remain punishable by death in 27 states.

• Researchers in several states have uncovered evidence that racial considerations influence charging and sentencing decisions in capital cases, thus undermining the evenhanded administration of the death penalty.

• At least 68 people have been convicted, sentenced to death, and spent time (often, several years) on death row under the authority of post-*Furman* capital punishment laws, only later to be exonerated of wrongdoing and released from prison.

• The American Bar Association has noted that the resources for, and the qualifications and performance of counsel who are appointed to represent accused capital offenders, are often woefully inadequate.

Source: Acker (Original paper, 1997). Source of Figures: Death Penalty Information Center (http://www.essential.org/dpic/dpicexec.html)

than adults. Japan shows an extreme tendency in this direction in that the number of juveniles who receive probation is ten times higher than adults.

The United States of America showed the highest prevalence rate of probation (536), followed by Canada (269), England and Wales (217), Scotland (117) and the Russian Federation (101).

From 1990 to 1994, 16 countries and territories increased their use of probation, while another 11 decreased their rates. A remarkable increase was recorded in Belarus (213 percent) and the Netherlands (79 percent). On the other hand, Germany recorded a dramatic decrease (52 percent), as did Lithuania (46 percent).

This overview shows that there are, in reality, quite limited alternative options. While, on the one hand, the search for ef-

FIGURE 4.10
Abolitionist and retentionist countries in 1988 and 1996

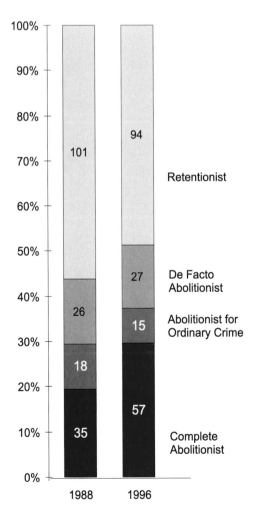

Source: Data are taken from Amnesty International

TABLE 4.11
Types of non-custodial sanctions

Sanctions that imply supervision and control:	Sanctions that do not require supervision or control:		
	Monetary payments	Withdrawal of rights	Other
• probation and suspended or conditional imprisonment with supervision • community service • home probation • open, ambulant or contract treatment	• fine • compensatory payment • reconciliation • personal reparation • confiscation	• suspension of licenses • prevention from assuming an electoral office	• suspended sentences without supervision • good behaviour bonds

fective and credible non-custodial sanctions continues, on the other, there are considerable variations in the proportion of the use of imprisonment and non-custodial sanctions. However, it does appear that certain regional patterns in the use of non-custodial sanctions exist. For instance, these are less used in Latin America, Africa and Asia (excluding Japan and the Republic of Korea), while the New World and Europe (both West and East) are more non-custodial oriented. Yet, this does not mean that the greater use of non-custodial sanctions results in a less systematic use of imprisonment. Rather, non-custodial sanctions are "probably more often a response to restrict prison use than a route to low prison use" (Pease, 1995) — an issue which will be addressed below.

As in the previous sections, one might consider the questions concerning the relationship between the prevalence of probation or the prevalence of overcrowding and the socio-economic status of the country. However, too few countries responded to these questions to allow such analysis.[22]

Public attitudes toward punishment

A number of instances have been identified where the official data were highly suggestive of particular public policies concerning the purposes and practices of criminal punishment. It has been seen, for example, that some countries imprison many more people than do others, and do not allow for early release as well. One assumes that these patterns do not occur randomly: rather, they issue from specific policies and legislation of particular countries.

Policy-makers may well respond that all they do is translate into practice what the public wants. In fact, it may be argued that

in order for punishment to be credible it is important that it is predictable (certain) and that it "conveys the message that punishment is implemented seriously both to the public and to the judiciary in order to ensure acceptance" (Albrecht, 1996).[23] Several countries have developed their own scheme for assessing such a view point.[24] In addition, it is clear that if traditional punishments such as prison are to work the close positive participation of the public is necessary in order to arrange the successful return of the inmate to the community (Box 4.9).

Within the framework of the ICVS (see Chapter 1), a joint endeavor by the Ministry of Justice of the Netherlands, the UK Home Office and UNICRI was carried out in 1989, 1992 and 1996/97. It involved some 60 countries all over the world, and more than 130,000 people were interviewed about their victimization experiences. The respondents were also asked about the preferred sentence to be given to a 21 year old burglary recidivist.[25] Despite the numerous problems encountered, and in particular problems of interpretation linked with the target of the theft, namely a colour TV set, the value of which and possibility of replacing vary across countries, certain patterns in punishment orientation did emerge (Figure 4.11).

Just over four in ten of all respondents chose imprisonment as the most appropriate sentence for a young recidivist burglar. On a regional level more than half in the New World and Latin America and even three-quarters in Asia and Africa opted for imprisonment. On the other hand, some 40 percent of the respondents from countries in transition and 28 percent from Western Europe favoured imprisonment.

Following imprisonment, the next most

Non-custodial sanctions are less costly and avoid the harmful effects of imprisonment.

preferred sentencing option was community service, which was favoured by almost one-third of the respondents. Community service was the preferred sentence in Western Europe by almost half of the respondents, followed by approximately one-third each

TABLE 4.12
Annual probation rate 1990, 94 (per 100,000 population) and persons on probation, 1994

	1990 Rate	1994 Rate	Adult	Juvenile
Belarus	16.1	50.3	5212	--
Belgium	35.3	47.9	4824	--
Bermuda	19.7	34.9	20	2
Bulgaria	8.1	10.1	825	28
Canada	248.6	268.9	78639	--
Chile	7.0	8.8	1226	--
Costa Rica	98.3	81.1	2490	--
Denmark	41.7	32.4	--	--
England & Wales	177.3	217.2	82908	28838
Germany	52.8	25.5	11384	9413
Hong Kong	53.5	55.1	869	2472
Indonesia	1.5	.8	1172	277
Jamaica	27.1	41.6	594	444
Japan	63.8	47.2	5054	53815
Latvia	30.4	--	--	--
Lithuania	17.0	9.6	356	0
Macau	60.2	83.3	88	261
Malta	2.0	13.7	31	19
Marshall Islands	13.0	14.8	8	0
Mexico	.3	1.0	938	--
Netherlands	44.3	79.1	--	--
Nicaragua	4.4	4.2	--	--
Northern Ireland	--	75.9	963	275
Qatar	--	1.9	--	10
Rep. of Korea	21.1	39.0	0	17237
Rep. of Moldova	14.4	10.0	370	65
Russian Fed.	--	100.8	--	--
Scotland	80.8	117.1	5978	32
Slovenia	49.0	35.8	691	4
Sweden	78.2	77.8	6634	201
USA	655.3	536.2	--	--
Western Samoa	22.0	--	--	--
Portugal	--	.50	--	--

Source: Fifth UN Crime and Justice Survey. See Notes to Tables for additional details.

in Latin America and in countries in transition. Only ten percent of the respondents from Asia and Africa opted for some sort of community service.

Regional variations regarding a fine as a favoured sentencing option for a young recidivist burglar were not pronounced and averaged nine percent. A suspended sentence was thought to be the most appropriate sentence by six percent of the respondents, ranging from two percent in Asia and Africa to eight percent in the countries in transition and Western Europe.

As regards imprisonment, the range of

BOX 4.9
Prison and community: the Uganda Discharged Prisoners' Aid Society

Researchers at the United Nations African Institute for the Prevention of Crime and Treatment of Offenders (UNAFRI) have demonstrated that inmates may be returned to their local communities without difficulty provided proper preparations and support are provided on behalf of the inmate and other social actors. This approach requires that all social actors involved with the inmate — social workers, family members, neighbours, the victim and his or her family, religious leaders, and the Uganda Discharged Prisoners' Aid Society (UDPAS) — be contacted some time before the inmate is released, and that the inmate work towards reconciliation with all parties involved. This requires, among other things, considerable input from volunteers and organizations in order to enable communication among all these social actors. One important voluntary organization is the Uganda Discharged Prisoners' Aid Society.

The Uganda Discharged Prisoners' Aid Society is one of the important social organs for the rehabilitation of ex-prisoners. It is a voluntary charitable organization run under the auspices of the Prisons Department. The society is open to people from all walks of life: people from various religious organizations, businessmen and women, civil servants, and professionals such as criminologists, sociologists, social workers, etc. The history of the Uganda Discharged Prisoners' Aid society is linked with the history and development of similar societies in Britain. From 1948 (after the 2nd World War) up to 1957 some forms of after care services to some discharged prisoners were undertaken by the Provincial Commissioners, and the Public Relations, Social Welfare and Probation Departments. This after care work, handled through the official government machinery, was mainly confined to contacting local authorities and relatives of the prisoners and ex-prisoners with the aim of resettling them. Some attempts were also made to obtain employment for a few ex-prisoners. Towards the end of 1957 the Luzira Discharged Prisoners' Aid Committee was formed. The Prisons Department and the Department of Probation and Social Welfare continued to provide some assistance to some prisoners and ex-prisoners in collaboration with the Luzira Discharged Prisoners' Aid Committee. This committee would eventually become the Uganda Discharged Prisoners' Aid Society.

It is of interest to note that the Luzira Discharged Prisoners' Aid Association was formed in 1957 when the Standard Minimum Rules for the Treatment of Prisoners were approved by the United Nations. The formation of the society was prompted by a circular letter, No. 688/7, dated 20th June, 1957, from the Home Secretary for Colonies, which directly followed the approval of the United Nations Standard Minimum Rules for the Treatment of Prisoners. At the instigation of the Commissioner of Prisons in 1974, a national organization of the Uganda Discharged Prisoners' Aid Society was formed with branches in the city and most of the major towns of Uganda. However, due to political instability in the 1970s and 1980s, most of the branches of the society in country towns have become dormant.

Aims and Objectives of the Society

- To educate the public to realize the need and importance of accepting and resettling ex-prisoners back into the society.
- To inculcate into the minds of ex-prisoners a desire to work with the rest of the citizens for the betterment of the nation.
- To cooperate with Discharged Prisoners' Aid Societies and similar organizations in Africa and elsewhere.
- To work in cooperation with other voluntary organizations in the country.
- To work in liaison with the appropriate government organs for furthering the aims and objectives of the society.

The local community approach to inmate release in Uganda has been promoted by UNAFRI and has been based upon several United Nations and related instruments such as the Tokyo Rules, the Beijing Rules, the Riyadh Guidelines, and the United Nations Rules for the Protection of Juveniles Deprived of their Liberty.

Source: Sita, Edanyu and Aliobe (Original paper, 1996)

variation in Western Europe goes from 57 percent in Northern Ireland (and 50 percent in England and Wales and Scotland) to three

A remarkable increase in probation was recorded in Belarus (213 percent) and the Netherlands (79 percent).

percent in Switzerland. Both in Canada and the USA imprisonment is the most favoured sentence. This supports the findings of the 1989 and 1992 ICVS, according to which Anglo-Saxon countries are more prison-centric than other industrialized countries. Other regions exhibit less variation as regards imprisonment as the sentencing option, although among the countries in transition only 19 percent of the respondents from Croatia, as compared with over 60 percent in Albania and Romania, favour imprisonment.

Similarly, there is some support for community service in non-Anglo-Saxon industrialized countries, in Latin American countries and among the countries in transition, in particular in Croatia, the Czech Republic, Hungary, Poland, Slovenia and Yugoslavia. Citizens from Albania, Mongolia, the Philippines, Uganda and Zimbabwe show little appreciation for this sentencing option.

When the data were arranged so as to compare industrialized against developing countries and countries in transition, there was a marked preference for imprisonment in developing countries and countries in transition. This may be explained by at least four factors (Figure 4.12). First, there are generally fewer non-custodial sentences available, as well as difficulties in implementation fol-

lowing conviction (Joutsen and Zvekic, 1994). Second, support for imprisonment appears to be higher in countries where crime is highest, particularly when no other available and practical solutions exist. Third, how the public feels about punishment is often formed by vicarious information, traditional belief systems and socio-legal heritage — for example, in the industrialized nations, the demand for imprisonment was higher among "anglophone" countries independently of personal victimization experiences or other crime-related factors.[26] Finally, one should consider that many of the countries classified as "developing" were in fact once colonies of industrialized countries. Industrialized countries have left their prison systems in these former colonies.

There is a certain level of correspondence in the regional patterns based on public attitudes to punishment, on the one hand, and the predominant actual use of non-custodial sanctions and imprisonment, on the other. This seems to indicate at least two things: first, a degree of independence in types of sentencing from the geopolitical and developmental position; second, that public attitudes do reflect, to a certain degree, the actual availability of sentencing options and their use in practice. In other

Anglo-Saxon countries are more prison-centric than other industrialized countries.

FIGURE 4.11
Favoured sentence by regions, ICVS, 1996

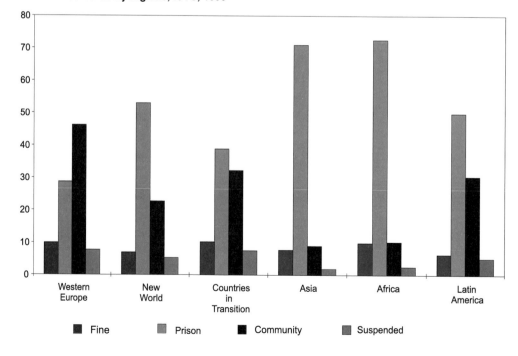

Source: ICVS. See Notes to Figures for further details.

words, it is just as possible that public attitudes are influenced by penal systems and penal practice, as that policy makers are influenced by public attitudes.

Do victims of crime prefer harsher sentences for offenders than do non-victims? The analysis of the 1989 ICVS results relating to industrialized countries found that there was no tangible difference between those who have and those who have not been victimized (Kuhn, 1992). The 1996 results confirm this and show no substantial differences in sentencing preferences between victims and non-victims. This holds true even after probing victims of specific crime types, such as burglary, contact crime or vehicle-related offences.

Therefore, the differences in sentencing preferences may be independent of the experience of victimization and could depend on historical traditions, real or perceived crime conditions of the residential area, and availability of information on sentencing options.

In sum, though the evidence is not complete, it is sufficiently strong to suggest that it is possible for policy makers to lead the way in making new sentencing options available.

Non-custodial sanctions: alternatives to prison?

While there is no clear trend in terms of one or another category of non-custodial sanctions taking the predominant place within the conventional punishment paradigm and sentencing practice, it is clear that prison is a strongly entrenched mode of punishment all over the world.

Progressive reformers in criminal punishment have always hoped that non-custodial sanctions would divert offenders who otherwise would have received imprisonment, and hence decrease the prison population. For example, restorative justice (Box 4.11) has become very popular among developed countries in recent years, though it has been well known in many African countries in the form of informal customary justice (Boxes 3.1 and 5.1). However, it is recognized that the introduction of community supervisory practices increases the percentage of the population under some form of criminal justice surveillance (see, for example, in the United States, Travis *et al.*, 1992). A study in France also showed that the increased use of alternative sanctions did not prevent a steady increase in imprisonment (Laffargue and Godefroy, 1989). Even attempts to divert (Box 3.6) offenders away from the criminal justice system before criminal trial do not appear to have affected the prison rates.

A strong reason for this may be that, "since imprisonment is characterized as a default option, the other sentences must represent themselves as like prison in pertinent ways, and will struggle to bring other criteria to bear on sentencing decisions" (Pease, 1995). Consequently, a trend has developed towards introducing more punitive components in the framework of the non-custodial sanctions even though in original concept the alternative might be intrinsically non-punitive. Furthermore, increased punitiveness has intruded into non-custodial sanctions through the use of sanctions that more clearly mimic prison, such as boot-camps, which are in fact short-term prisons, and electronic tagging, which deprives the offender of liberty without incarceration.[27]

It should be noted that, from an international perspective, the traditional punishment paradigm has always embraced the notion of respect for human rights. However, these human rights concerns were mostly, although not exclusively, restricted to the issues of criminal procedure and severe pun-

The way is open for policy-makers to lead the way in making new sentencing options available.

FIGURE 4.12
Favoured sentence by development status, ICVS, 1996

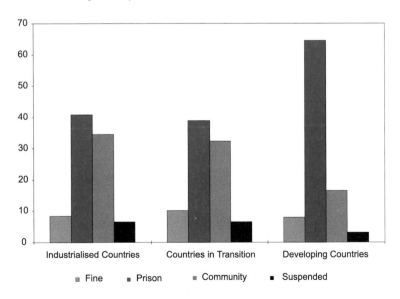

Source: ICVS. See Notes to Figures for further details.

Intermediate sanctions: electronic monitoring and house arrest

Some alternatives to imprisonment (e.g., fines and probation) have been available to policy makers for a long time. Since the 1970s, community service orders have become quite popular, and in the 1980s and 1990s intensive supervision for probationers has become common. Home detention, house arrest and home confinement have recently received serious consideration.

The requirements behind house arrest are not new. A number of programs, such as probation, intensive supervision, etc., used curfew conditions, meaning the offender had to reside at home during certain hours of the day. In a number of countries curfew conditions are used for juvenile offenders under a certain age. What is new is the introduction of electronic monitoring in conjunction with house arrest. Not all house arrests are backed up by electronic monitoring. Indeed, available statistics show only less than ten percent of house arrests are backed up by electronic monitoring.

Although the use of electronic monitoring began in the 1980s and grew sharply, experiments at Harvard University began 20 years earlier. The equipment and gadgets, such as anklets, bracelets, etc., used today are fairly sophisticated and sleek in appearance. Details from the United States and Australia, where evidence of its use is available, show the following uses of electronic monitoring:
1. It is used in conjunction with house arrest in pretrial detention in some jurisdictions.
2. Offenders receiving a prison sentence are placed on house arrest with electronic monitoring instead.
3. In some jurisdictions, early release prisoners are placed on house arrest with electronic monitoring.

The technology of electronic monitoring progressed during the mid 1980s. The electronic surveillance is described as (a) an active system or continuous signalling approach, (b) a passive system or a programmed contact approach, and (c) a combination of both or hybrid monitoring equipment. An active system consists of a small radio transmitter attached to the offender's ankle or wrist using an irremovable plastic strap and a field monitoring device to receive the transmitter's signal. A home monitor unit is connected to the main power and telephone line. If the signals do not reach the host device, it will report an offender's absence. The process may lead to a notice of suspected violation. This is the system used in the majority of instances.

A passive system does not use continuous radio signals. A central monitoring station sends a random call to an offender and records the offender's identity. The offender must respond to the call. The system either uses something like a keystone that the offender wears or it records some biologically unique feature, such as the offender's face or voice. This system, because of multiple daily calls, appears more intrusive than the active system.

The hybrid monitoring equipment uses a combination of both the above systems. It uses the ankle/wrist transmitter band, and when a signal is lost, it uses a secondary method such as voice recording or facial picture over a visual phone. This system introduces the considerable inconvenience of wearing an ankle/wrist band and answering frequent phone calls. The use of this system is becoming quite common.

By the late 1980s a "drive-by" system had been created. This system allows surveillance officers to determine from an automobile whether the offenders are in designated places.

House arrest using electronic monitoring now exists in all states of the United States, South Australia and the Northern Territory in Australia, Saskatchewan in Canada, and Singapore.

The use of electronic monitoring was experimented with in England and Wales in the late 1980s. An assessment of the pilot project was not a resounding success. However, the 1991 Criminal Justice Act (amended by Criminal Justice and Public Order Act of 1994) introduced a curfew order with electronic monitoring as a community based sentenced. Although introduced on a national basis, it was initiated on a trial basis in three pilot areas. Under the scheme, offenders sentenced to a curfew order may be required to remain at a place designated by the court for a minimum of two and a maximum of 12 hours per day for a period of six months. The trials began in July 1995, and the information currently available suggests that this community sentence could work. Although the running costs appear low, in order for the scheme to be expanded nationally the number of offenders placed under this scheme needs to be increased.

Source: Mukerjee (Original paper, 1997). See Notes to Boxes for sources used in preparation of this paper.

ishments (e.g., torture, the death penalty and imprisonment) or, in the post-communist societies, to repressive non-custodial supervision and enforced treatment. The introduction of human rights concerns in the field of non-custodial sanctions and the crime prevention area is of a more recent date. Based on the recommendation of the Eighth United Nations Congress on the Prevention of Crime and the Treatment of the Offenders, the United Nations adopted the Standard Minimum Rules for Non-Custodial Measures (General Assembly Resolution 45/110). The Rules provide basic principles for promoting the use of non-custodial measures and are intended to promote greater community involvement in the management of criminal justice. Also, the Council of Europe (1992) adopted European Rules on Community Sanctions and Measures.

In sum, it appears that many of the conventional, non-custodial sanctions are doomed to share the common destiny of imprisonment. Their *raison d'être*, their acceptability, expansion, reduction and change are intrinsically tied to the place and role of imprisonment within the prevailing punishment paradigm built around conventional crimes, conventional actors and conventional models of criminal justice.

New directions and alternatives

Faced with issues of globalization, the fall of autocratic ideologies, and concerns with the cost of managing social processes and order, there appears to be a revitalization of the vision of the post modern society (that is, largely countries now termed in the UNDP classification as "industrialized" though many are now "post industrial") as a "tension-management system" (Moore, 1974). While this change in orientation may be evident in developed countries, the increased globalization of criminal justice and crime (Box 0.13 and also Chapter 9) cannot but affect developing countries as well.

A number of authors, such as Albrecht (1996) and Garland (1997), to cite just two, tend to describe the criminal justice system as a risk management system with a focus shifted from the consequences of individual human behavior to risks attributed to social actors. This orientation of the criminal justice systems then takes place in the context of "high crime rates as a normal social fact" (Garland 1996) and the marginalization of moral and humane-centered arguments within punishment philosophy and practice. "Risk assessment and risk management are not new elements of penal practice, but they now have a centrality and a formality which they have never had before...To the extent that the penal system becomes increasingly rationalized, increasingly accountable, and increasingly cost-conscious, it becomes increasingly focused upon risks" (Garland, 1997). The organizational and professional concern with management and accounting/ auditing issues tend to replace substantive social goals with internal organizational goals, and even for policy-makers reduction of risk is seen as a central issue. Hence the more frequent recourse to incarceration and a call for punitiveness of non-custodial sanctions. The two are no longer seen as opposed to each other but rather as control mechanisms to reduce risks.[28]

The one major exception to this risk aversion approach in public policy in the world is the reconciliation program, as seen, for example, in South Africa. Here, policy makers have taken enormous risks to try to

It is clear that prison is a strongly entrenched mode of punishment all over the world.

BOX 4.11

Family group conferences and restorative justice in New Zealand

Introduction. This box describes the role family group conferences play in the youth justice system in New Zealand, drawing from research we conducted in 1990 and 1991 (for more information, see Maxwell and Morris [1993] and [1996]). The youth justice system in New Zealand deals primarily with 14 to 17 year olds who offend, but can, in certain situations, deal with offending by those aged 10 to 14.

The practice of youth justice in New Zealand. The intention underlying the Children, Young Persons and their Families Act 1989 is to encourage the police to adopt low key responses to juvenile offending wherever possible. The intention of the legislation is to allow families and victims to be involved in the process and to influence outcomes. The Youth Court cannot make a disposition unless a family group conference has been held, and it must take into account the recommendations put forward by the family group conference.

Family group conferences are held for those young people arrested (nine percent in 1993) and those not diverted or warned by the police (ten percent in 1993). Thus around 20 percent of all young offenders known to the police are dealt with in this way. That means around 5000 family group conferences are held each year. The family group conference is made up of the young person, his or her advocate if one has been arranged (usually only arrest/court cases), members of the family and whoever they invite, the victim(s) or their representative, the police, the social worker if one has been involved with the family, and the youth justice coordinator (the employee of the Department of Social Welfare responsible for managing the youth justice process).

Family group conferences can take place wherever the family wishes, provided (since 1994) the victim agrees. Most commonly they are held in rooms in the Department of Social Welfare or in community rooms, and occasionally they are held on marae (meeting houses) or in the family's home. The family group conference can only proceed where the young person has not denied the alleged offences or has already been found guilty at court. The main goal of the family group conference is to formulate a plan about how best to deal with the offending taking into account the views of the victims, the need to make the young person accountable for his or her offending, and any measure that may prevent future reoffending by enhancing the well-being of the offender or strengthening the family. The range of possibilities here are limitless (as long as they are agreed by the parties) but could include an apology, community work, reparation or involvement in some programme.

Family group conferences and victims. We found in our research that, for nearly half the family group conferences, at least one victim or victims' representative was present. Victims gave a range of reasons for taking part. Some stressed the value of expressing their feelings to the offender and of making sure that the offender learned from the experience; others wanted to contribute to the offender's rehabilitation or to show their support for the process or for offenders of their cultural group; and yet others emphasized their own interests: they wanted to get reparation. There will always be a minority of victims who choose not to participate in a restorative process but our research found that only six percent of victims, when asked, said that they did not wish to meet the offender.

Our research also showed that many of the victims found the family group conference to be a positive process. About 60 percent of the victims interviewed described the family group conference they attended as helpful, positive and rewarding. A smaller proportion of victims, about a quarter, said that they felt worse as a result of attending the family group conference. There were a variety of reasons for this. The most frequent and perhaps the most important was that the victim did not feel that the young person and/or his or her family were truly sorry.

About half the victims in our sample were satisfied with the outcomes. Some were dissatisfied because they saw the decision of the family group conference as too soft or too harsh. But, more frequently, victims were dissatisfied because the promised arrangements fell down afterwards.

Family group conferences and accountability. About 85 percent of the young people in our sample who took part in family group conferences agreed to carry out what we have called "active penalties," that is to say community work, reparation and the like. If we add "apologies" to this, the figure comes closer to 95 percent. Custodial or residential penalties are rarely recommended by family group conferences.

Family group conferences and reconvictions. We analyzed data on the reconvictions up to December 1994 of the original 1990-91 family group conference sample. A matching sample against which to compare these data is not available. However, our general conclusion after reviewing other local and overseas reconviction studies is that the proportion reconvicted in the first year following a family group conference (26 percent) is certainly no worse and is possibly better than samples dealt with in the criminal justice system. Regression analysis also suggested that those offenders who failed to apologize to victims were three times more likely to be reconvicted than those who had apologized.

Source: Morris and Maxwell (Original paper, 1997)

BOX 4.12

The South African Truth and Reconciliation Commission

In order to understand the nature and implications of the Truth and Reconciliation Commission in South Africa, it is important to see the Commission both in the national and the international contexts.

South Africa, oppressed and oppressors together, were imprisoned by the chains with which one group sought to bind the other for many generations. In 1910 when the first South African constitution was promulgated, it exemplified white hegemony and was fundamentally undemocratic, excluding as it did the vast majority of the population. This undemocratic and racist constitution was further entrenched when the National Party came into power in 1948. Under the National Party, through its policy of apartheid, a policy of domination was enforced which was not only a denial of basic political rights but a systematic piece of social engineering which embraced every area of life from birth to death. Thus, the system of apartheid determined state policies relating to land, housing, residence, schools and universities, transport, health services, sport, hotels, restaurants and even cemeteries. In other words, apartheid was a system of minority domination of statutorily defined color groups on a territorial, residential, political, social and economic basis.

Although the cards seemed to be stacked against South Africa achieving a relatively peaceful and relatively democratic election, the transition from oppression, exclusivity and resistance to a new negotiated, democratic order in 1994 has been realized.

But the miracle didn't drop out of the sky. It had to be worked for, argued over and costly decisions involving compromise on both sides had to be made, the most important of which was that neither side could win through force of arms or violence. The State could not suppress the resistance to its system of apartheid, nor could the liberation movements overthrow the State through force. It was only when the negotiations started and people from both sides stared, and sometimes glared, at each other across a table that it was made possible by agreement for the armed struggle of the liberation movements to be suspended. In other words, it was through negotiation rather than prior to negotiation that this decisive step was taken.

However, because of the social and economic legacy, there remains unfinished business which has to be tackled, otherwise it will be impossible to sustain the miracle, consolidate democracy and ensure a peaceful future for all South Africans. Part of this unfinished business is dealing with the legacy of the past. The appointment of the Truth and Reconciliation Commission is an attempt to assist this process.

The title of the founding Act speaks volumes for the fundamental intent of the Truth and Reconciliation Commission, i.e., The Promotion of National Unity and Reconciliation Act. The long title of the Act develops this essential theme. In part it requires the Commission to "establish the truth in relation to past events as well as the motives for and circumstances in which gross violations of human rights occurred, and to make the findings known in order to prevent a repetition of such acts in the future; the pursuit of national unity, the well-being of all South African citizens and peace require reconciliation between the people of South Africa and the reconstruction of society: in order to advance such reconciliation and reconstruction, amnesty shall be granted in respect of acts, omissions and offenses associated with political objectives committed in the course of the conflicts of the past."

The Commission is divided into three committees: the Human Rights Violations Committee, the Reparation and Rehabilitation Committee, and the Amnesty Committee. There is also a large Investigative Unit and a Witness Protection Program. The Commission was appointed not by presidential decree but by an Act of Parliament. More than 200 people were publicly interviewed after which 25 names were submitted to the President. He appointed the final 17 commissioners. The process therefore was democratic and open.

Part of the unique nature of the South African commission lies in its efforts to avoid an amnesty which would amount to impunity. As such, amnesty applications must be made on an individual basis and are dependent on accountability and disclosure. It was hoped that the combination of the judicial stick and the commission's carrot would emerge as a potent force in flushing out former operatives who had adopted a wait-and-see approach. Adding to the pressure to apply for amnesty by 10 May 1997 was the possibility of perpetrators being exposed by other witnesses or by the commission's 60 strong investigation team. If amnesty is not applied for and incriminating facts come to light, perpetrators may be tried in a court of law.

The Human Rights Violations Committee collects statements from victims and/or survivors right across the country and has been holding public hearings throughout South Africa which offer the victims/survivors a platform – for the first time ever – from which to tell their stories.

The Reparation and Rehabilitation Committee has to make recommendations to Parliament in terms of assisting victims both at an individual and a community level. Many victims have requested financial assistance for medical expenses or bursary funds, but the Committee is also looking at community reparations in the form of clinics, community centers, monuments and symbolic reburials.

Essentially the Truth and Reconciliation Commission is committed to the development of a human rights culture and respect for the rule of law in South Africa. In attempting to do this there is an irreducible minimum and that is a commitment to truth. As Roberto Canas of El Salvador puts it, "Unless a society exposes itself to the truth it can harbour no possibility of reconciliation, reunification and trust. For a peace settlement to be solid and durable it must be based on truth."

Source: Dr Alex Boraine, Vice Chairperson, South African Truth and Reconciliation Commission (Original paper, 1997)

---

outflank the normal punitiveness of society by undertaking a massive reconciliation program in order to avoid the endless chain of recrimination and resentment that would naturally have followed the application of harsh punishments to those who had committed crimes prior to the emergence of the new society and constitution of South Africa (Box 4.12). This has been a public policy of incredible courage. It is also a fascinating real life experiment with an alternative to *punishment* (as opposed to an alternative to *prison*).

The risk approach to criminal justice also holds organizations to be responsible actors, perhaps even more than individuals. White collar crime and organized crime are a central focus of concern (Chapters 2 and 9).

The importance of organizations as criminal actors also calls for the acknowledgment of corporate liability, and in some cases a mere organizational membership or leadership role gives rise to criminal responsibility. Moreover, such a process of criminal "responsibilitization" is becoming shared among public and private actors (Garland, 1996) and leads to a convergence between sanctions and sanction severity for both intentional and negligent behaviour (Albrecht, 1996).

Thus, the range of non-custodial sanctioning options has recently increased not so much as a consequence of efforts to avoid prison but rather as a combined result of changes in the criminal justice orientation ("the risk management"), increased opportunities to rely on and/or combine criminal with administrative sanctions, and as a response to challenges posed by new criminal actors and new criminal processes. Some of the older non-custodial sanctions found their way into this new punishment paradigm, such as the fine, confiscation, and temporary or permanent banishment from the exercise of a profession or the holding of an office. Others, such as forfeiture and seizure, preliminary injunction, sequestration, clean up and restoration orders, exclusion from government contracts (particularly in relation to drug trafficking, organized crime, economic crime, environmental crime, corruption and money laundering) were never meant to be the true alternatives to imprisonment. They are meant to deal with different actors and consequences of criminal actions for which neither imprisonment nor the old prison-inspired non-custodial sanctions alone, if at all, were ever deemed appropriate and potentially effective.[29] The "new" risk aversive non-custodial sanctions designed to reduce risk and respond to new types of criminality are listed below. It will be recognized that many if not all of them are punishments that have been traditionally used in response to "white-collar crime" (that is to say, crime committed by and within corporations and businesses and other organizations, including government bureaucracies). These punishments may include:

- Forfeiture and seizure
- Preliminary injunctions
- Closure of enterprises
- Sequestration, including disqualification of members of management for a given period
- Compensation and confiscation
- Clean-up and restoration orders
- Prohibition of specified activities
- Annulment or suspension of licenses
- Adverse publicity orders
- Exclusion from government contracts

As noted, there is a wide policy discretion in determining types of offences and punishments. Still, the punishment paradigm today may be summarized as corresponding to different targeted values and costs. The relationships may be illustrated as follows:

Type of Punishment	Punishment Values/ Costs
Death penalty	Life
Corporal punishment	Body integrity
Imprisonment	Freedom and Time
Non-custodial sanctions	Freedom, Duty and Reparation
Risk aversive non-custodial sanctions	Patrimony and Position

SUMMARY

THINGS IN COMMON	THINGS DIVERSE
• For serious crimes, prison is the universal sanction, applied more than any other punishment, and regardless of the legal system or level of development of a country.	• There are wide variations in the prison rates of various countries, and these do not appear to be dependent on the amount of crime in a country.
• There is no overall world trend towards increase in prison population.	• There are vast differences among countries. Some showed enormous increases in prison populations, and others showed decreases. More countries reported increases than decreases. Countries in transition especially reported increases in prison populations and admissions.
• Parole is not widely used throughout the world.	• Parole is used mostly by developed Western countries. There have been large increases in use of parole by some East European countries.
	• A small number of countries report statistics that suggest prison populations that exceed their prison capacity. There is no economic or development feature that distinguishes this group of countries.
	• Developing countries tend to have more prisoners awaiting trial than do developed countries.
• The movement towards restriction and abolition of the death penalty is not unidirectional.	• Abolitionist countries are predominantly in Europe (both West and East) and Latin America.
• The fine is the most frequently used non-custodial sanction regardless of level of development of the country.	• Non-custodial sanctions are used less in the regions of Africa, Latin America, and Asia. However, the informal justice systems of many developing countries apply non-custodial sanctions without their being recorded by the criminal justice system.
• Availability and use of non-custodial sanctions are policy choices.	• Greater use of non-custodial sanctions does not lead to less use of prison, or vice-versa.
• Public attitudes to punishment generally conform to the actual sentencing options available.	• In developing countries and countries in transition the public displays a marked preference for prison as a punishment.

CHAPTER 5

Resources in criminal justice

Contributing authors: Graeme Newman and Gregory J. Howard

What are the resources of a criminal justice system?

The resources available to a criminal justice system are crucial. No matter what the ideals of a particular criminal justice system are (for example, "due process of law"), if the resources are not available to implement these ideals, justice will not be done.

There are both tangible and intangible aspects to criminal justice resources. The tangible resources of a criminal justice system are:

- personnel
- financing
- capital equipment

The personnel of the criminal justice system are police of varying kinds, court personnel including prosecutors, magistrates and their assistants, and the staff of correctional services which may include custodial officers, prison wardens, probation officers, parole officers, teachers in prisons, therapists and so on.

Financing refers to the annual budget provided the criminal justice system to keep it operational. The majority of this money is typically spent on personnel, which are the most expensive budgetary item for the majority of countries, even those with low individual income levels. The annual budget of the criminal justice system may vary from year to year, depending most directly on political and policy concerns, for a national criminal justice system must compete for resources against other arms of government such as the military, welfare, health care, trade, foreign affairs, transportation and education.

Capital equipment refers to physical plant such as buildings, courtrooms, prisons, police stations, computers, transportation and communications equipment.

Though extremely important to the smooth functioning of modern criminal justice systems, there are many countries — particularly those agrarian and village-oriented (see Box 5.1) — that do not rely heavily on such physical equipment as police cars, computers or even courtrooms. It is apparent from the World Crime Surveys (UNCJS), however, that although the use of prisons varies widely among countries, all countries nevertheless have prisons, which represent an important and substantial investment in capital equipment.

The intangible resources of a criminal justice system both depend on and enhance the tangible resources. The intangible resources of criminal justice are:

- the educational quality of its personnel
- the sophistication of its organizational structure
- the political culture in which the criminal justice system is rooted

It is a reasonable and widely held belief that a better educated criminal justice work force will operate a better criminal justice system. That is, justice will likely be done when offenders are in the hands of an educated work force. One might expect, therefore, that in those countries with a less developed system of education the effective delivery of criminal justice may suffer. This view is probably reasonable with one notable caveat: in countries with a well developed informal system of criminal justice, education as it is thought of today — formal education in schools — may be less relevant. In this case, the level of education means something quite different: the intelligence and sensitivity that an individual derives from the oral traditions of his or her culture (see Box 5.1 for the example of Nigeria; see also Boxes 3.1 and 8.6). What-

FIGURE 5.1

Median distribution of personnel in the criminal justice work force (1994: 31 countries; 1986: 30 countries)

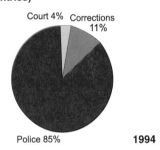

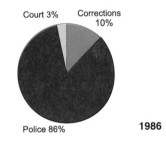

Source: Fourth and Fifth UNCJS. See Notes to Figures for further information.

"Due process of law" is impossible without the resources to implement it.

ever the local circumstances, it still remains true that an enlightened criminal justice system depends on the enlightened quality of its actors. Consequently, the likelihood that justice is done may not depend on how many or how few criminal justice personnel a country can boast, but rather on their quality as individuals.

Of course, criminal justice is a complex process which relies not only on the quality of individual actors, but also on the way in which they are able to work together. That is, the extent to which the criminal justice system is organized to achieve its stated goal.

The most important goal of criminal justice in any country is to deliver justice. The extent to which the various parts of the criminal justice system work together is important to achieving this goal. Unfortunately, as was noted in the Introduction, coordinated action is rarely if ever achieved in the criminal justice system, even in the most developed countries which spend a lot of money on personnel, equipment and education. In fact, this problem of coordination has affected considerably our efforts to collect information on criminal justice resources because in many countries the different parts of the criminal justice system operate independently and are financed separately. Finding the right department of an organization to obtain relevant resources information can prove very difficult.

A country's political culture is composed of the values and beliefs that are the stuff of a nation's pride and heritage. But a nation's heritage may be speckled with conflict as well as consensus. Out of this complex historical process, law emerges, and the bedrock of criminal justice is established. There may be countries in which the political culture appears to be highly congruent with the criminal justice system, such as Singapore, and this is generally borne out by the data presented in this report. Other countries sometimes appear as though their political culture conflicts with the criminal justice system, a view widely held of the criminal justice system in the United States. It is, however, particularly difficult to measure (let alone define) political culture. One hesitates to draw conclusions concerning this aspect of criminal justice resources. In fact, the data collected by the UNCJS limit us essentially to the basic and mostly tangible aspects of criminal justice resources.

The criminal justice work force

If the criminal justice system is considered as comprising the standard police, courts and corrections, one may examine the distribution of criminal justice personnel according to these stages in criminal justice. Figure 5.1 displays the proportions of the criminal justice work force devoted to each

---

BOX 5.1

Informal customary justice in Nigeria

The traditional system of criminal justice based on immemorial customs and traditional norms is what we refer to as informal customary criminal justice. This traditional system of justice is informal because it does not require written records of the procedures or written accounts of the testimonies of the parties and their witnesses. This informal system of justice has survived colonial intervention — the English-based criminal justice system and the formalized customary criminal justice system. The informal customary criminal justice system reflects the social order and social organization in pre-colonial Nigeria.

The informal customary court is where a village leader is the sole judge. He is the chief of his village. He may or may not be the oldest person in the village. He became the village leader either by inheritance or by a combination of very high intelligence, profound knowledge of the customs, norms and traditions, old age, and charismatic personality.[1] These judges (tribal, town and village chiefs) have no formal training in customary law. Expertise in informal customary law is based on acquisition of sound intelligence, mastery of the culture's oral history, and sound memory. A village chief or a town chief who is endowed with the above qualities will have a lot of cases brought to his court from villages and towns far away from his village. Informal customary law may vary from tribe to tribe and from town to town, yet, in principle, the same types of criminal offences are brought to the informal customary courts.

The informal customary court is held in the village leader's central hall called "Obi" by the Ibos. It is usually located in front of the village chief's main residential house. Bordering the "Obi" (the chief's court) on both sides are the houses of the village chief's wives, staff of servants, and his adult sons. The entire compound is usually surrounded by five to six foot walls.[2]

The criminal offences that are brought to the village chiefs are petty theft, grand larceny, simple battery, aggravated assault, fraud, rape, trespassing, conspiracy, contempt of community sanctions, molesting someone else's child, indecent exposure, desecrating a holy shrine or a holy place, etc. The informal customary criminal court cannot sentence a person found guilty to a term of imprisonment. Rather, the typical sentences in an informal customary criminal court are compensation, restitution, fine, community service, some days of farm work for the victim, and — in case of rape — marriage to the raped woman.[3]

The informal customary criminal courts are the foundations of the contemporary criminal justice system in Nigeria. The village chief is not paid by the Nigerian government. However, in a criminal case, in addition to the penalty imposed upon the person found guilty of the act, he/she will also pay the cost of the trial to the chief. It is called a "fine." If the presumed victim fails to prove his/her case, he/she alone will pay the cost as determined by the chief

Whatever happens, it is cheaper to settle a criminal case in the court of a village chief (informal customary criminal court) than at the formal customary criminal court or at the Magistrate's Court (see Box 3.1). In both formal and informal customary criminal courts, prosecution and defense attorneys are not required, but a defense attorney is required in a Magistrate's Court. The village chief's court is found in all ethnic groups or tribes of Nigeria. *The village chief-based informal customary criminal court system predominates all other justice systems in Nigeria.*

Source: Edited and abridged from Ebbe (Original paper, 1997)

---

section of the criminal justice system.

In all four previous United Nations Surveys of Crime Trends and Criminal Justice Systems it has been found that police or law enforcement personnel make up by far the largest portion of personnel in the criminal justice system. While the definitions of these occupations vary from one country to another, the United Nations has established standard definitions to which respondent countries attempt to conform in filling out their questionnaires (see Appendix 1). Because the percentage allocation of personnel to the three sectors of the criminal justice system has been constant for at least 15 years, it is likely that the variation in definitions of the occupations has not been a serious reporting problem. Of the countries providing information for 1994 (see Figure 5.2), only in Madagascar, Liechtenstein, Estonia, Finland, Republic of Moldova and Turkey did police make up less than 80 percent of the total criminal justice personnel. In the case of Madagascar, only 57 percent of criminal justice personnel were police, while eight percent were court personnel, and a very large 35 percent were corrections personnel. In contrast, the countries with the highest allocation of criminal justice personnel to policing were Costa Rica (99.6 percent) and Singapore (94 percent).

It is likely that the reason why the majority of criminal justice personnel are universally police is that the police must provide a much greater variety of services than other personnel in criminal justice whose jobs are much more narrowly defined. Judges have a very clearly defined role no matter in what legal system they serve. Corrections officers, mostly employed in prisons, also have a much more clearly defined job than do police. Police must, depending on the country, direct traffic, respond to emergency calls, attend to car accidents, patrol streets, collect local census information from residents, investigate crimes, conduct surveillance, arrest and sometimes prosecute offenders, attend to domestic disputes, and conduct border patrol, to name but a few of the many duties they must perform. In some countries, they even perform duties similar to the military.

Differences among countries in proportions of personnel in the three major stages of the criminal justice system may be due to a number of factors. Countries with a very high proportion of their personnel in policing may place more political or policy importance on a policing presence. This is borne out by the finding reported above that Singapore, a country proud of its record of strong societal control, has a very high proportion of its criminal justice personnel in policing. The variations in personnel allocations by different countries to the various levels of the criminal justice system may be seen in Figure 5.2.

While the distribution of criminal justice personnel in police, courts and corrections provides interesting insights into a country's resource allocation, so also do the criminal justice occupations themselves. As noted earlier, often the different levels of the criminal justice system operate indepen-

FIGURE 5.2
Proportions of personnel in police, courts and corrections functions, 1994

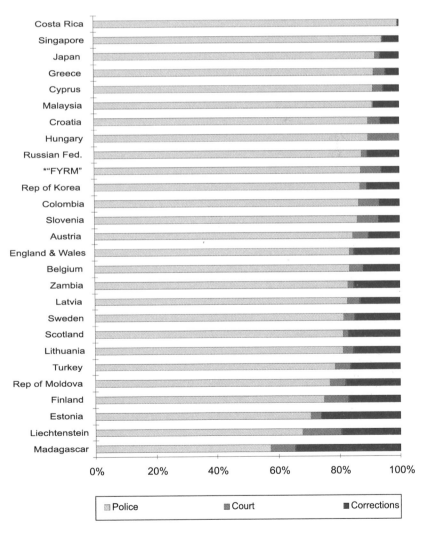

*"The Former Yugoslav Republic of Macedonia"
Source: Fifth UNCJS. See Notes to Figures for additional details.

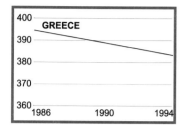

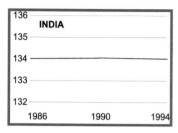

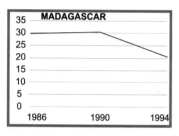

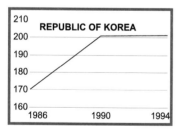

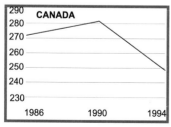

Source: Fourth and Fifth UNCJS

dently of each other, so that factors external to the criminal justice system (such as, for example, the amount of crime) may affect their operation. Let us examine each of these criminal justice work force occupations separately.

Police

We can see by comparing Table 5.1 to Figure 5.2 that the countries with high proportions of police personnel in the system also have high rates of police per 100,000 population. Singapore has the second highest rate, closely following the Russian Federation. And Madagascar has the second lowest policing rate. In general, there is no apparent difference according to the level of economic development of countries, though the rate for industrial countries is somewhat higher according to the Fifth UNCJS. The median for developing countries was 283 police per 100,000 population, compared to 346 for industrial countries. One is inclined to conclude from a perusal of Table 5.1 that if there is any substantial regional factor operating, it is that the Russian Federation and the former states of the USSR display unusually high policing rates. This could be a function of the confusion between military and non-military definitions and roles of policing in those countries, as well as the special problems of social order they face, resulting in a greater need for more police.

Trends in policing

There are also some startling statistics in Table 5.2, which shows how much police forces have increased or decreased from 1990 to 1994. While the overall rates of police per 100,000 have slightly increased since 1990 (1.7 percent), some countries have experienced a substantial increase, and others a substantial decrease. It is clear from Table 5.2 that those countries suffering social unrest and political disorder during the 1990s have considerably increased their police forces, with Slovakia, Ukraine and Mexico showing an increase of over 60 percent, and other states that have experienced turbulence showing increases of over 30 percent. In contrast, some countries have shown decreases. In fact the USA shows a decline in the policing rate of just over nine percent, and this

during a period in which the United States government campaigned to increase police forces throughout the country.

Regional variations are especially diffi-

TABLE 5.1
Number of police per 100,000 population, 1994

Russian Federation	1224.58
Singapore	1074.68
Uruguay	830.88
Bermuda	796.83
Kazakhstan	778.66
Bahamas	743.43
Croatia	669.60
Hong Kong	639.89
Saint V.& Grenadines	598.20
Lithuania	544.99
Cyprus	522.89
Northern Ireland	520.46
Malta	507.14
Jordan	468.81
Latvia	463.46
Estonia	436.22
Panama	432.75
Malaysia	429.65
Peru	429.33
Ukraine	418.61
Slovenia	412.05
Greece	383.02
Austria	367.00
Scotland	359.64
Slovakia	352.23
France	349.28
England & Wales	346.69
Belgium	344.37
*"FYRM"	317.79
Kiribati	312.99
United States of America	300.06
Hungary	292.77
Western Samoa	283.54
Sweden	281.99
Chile	275.62
Colombia	274.91
Australia	274.65
Marshall Islands	268.52
Canada	249.00
Rep of Moldova	241.20
Denmark	237.69
Finland	231.91
Romania	214.16
Japan	207.62
Rep of Korea	203.72
Liechtenstein	190.32
Turkey	189.89
Philippines	155.02
Nicaragua	145.15
India	134.12
Spain	128.70
Zambia	106.81
Morocco	100.38
Egypt	37.16
Costa Rica	36.34
Madagascar	21.31
Mexico	4.61

*"Former Yugoslav Republic of Macedonia"
Source: Fifth UNCJS

cult to determine because not enough countries from each region responded to the surveys (see Introduction). However, Figure 5.3 displays trends for selected countries from different geographic regions for which there were sufficient data from each of the Fourth and Fifth UNCJS. The Republic of Korea stands out as a country that has markedly increased its policing work force since 1986, a period that coincides with the rapid economic development of that country. In contrast, the level for India has remained relatively stable. It would be expected, if India follows the same pattern of economic development as Korea, that there will be an increase in policing personnel in the next five years. Canada, in line with the United States, is among those countries that show a decrease in policing rates from 1990, placing it in the company of the Philippines and Madagascar. It is of interest that Madagascar has reported very low levels of policing now in each of the last two UNCJS.

The extent to which the trends for each of these countries depart from the overall world trend is difficult to determine. However, if the sample of countries in Table 5.2 is taken as "representing" the world, it can be seen that the general world trend is towards increasing the size of the national police forces, relative to population.

Making comparisons

A number of possible reasons why some countries have higher rates of policing than others has already been indicated. However, at this point, it should be noted that one important factor producing different statistics reported by each country is that policing functions vary widely, not only across coun-

Taking all countries together, the level of economic development does not appear to be consistently related to the level of policing.

TABLE 5.2
Trends in policing rates by country, percent change, 1990-1994

Increase in policing		Decrease in policing	
Mexico	69	India	-1
Ukraine	65	Malta	-1
Slovakia	65	Japan	-1
Croatia	45	Egypt	-1
Romania	38	Hong Kong	-1
Rep of Moldova	30	Jordan	-2
Western Samoa	28	Malaysia	-2
Hungary	25	Australia	-2
Kazakhstan	22	Finland	-3
Turkey	22	Uruguay	-4
Russian Federation	21	Spain	-5
Slovenia	17	Denmark	-5
Colombia	17	Cyprus	-6
Costa Rica	11	Bahamas	-7
Kiribati	11	Canada	-8
Chile	10	United States of America	-9
Rep of Korea	9	Bermuda	-13
Lithuania	8	Marshall Islands	-20
Scotland	6	Philippines	-20
Saint V. & Grenadines	6	Zambia	-20
Belgium	5	Madagascar	-31
France	4	Latvia	-32
Greece	2		
Liechtenstein	2		
Panama	2		
Singapore	2		
Morocco	2		
Austria	2		
Peru	1		
England & Wales	1		
Sweden	1		
Northern Ireland	0		

Source: Fourth and Fifth UNCJS

tries but within countries as well. There are problems in some countries in distinguishing between policing and military personnel, with very substantial overlap in some cases. There are also problems of distinguishing regulatory personnel (e.g., those who investigate tax evaders) from "regular" police (Nalla and Newman, 1993). If one considers such acts as environmental pollution as falling within the realm of criminal justice (as is more and more common these days – see Box 0.12), then a valid comparison and assessment of policing should include those personnel who investigate and regulate environmental pollution. Although the UNCJS attempts to carefully define "police" (see Appendix 1), one nevertheless cannot be sure that the difficulties in categorizing police for statistical recording purposes have been overcome by the country respondents.

Private police: the dark figure of policing

Quite possibly the most serious omission of data on policing in the UNCJS is that respondent countries are asked only to report on government paid personnel. In many countries private agencies have arisen to take over the functions of some aspects of criminal justice, and this is especially true of policing. While private policing has a long history in industrial countries, it is also becoming a major growth industry in emerging market economies (see Box 5.2). It is important to take into account the substantial increases in private policing that have taken place throughout the world in recent years when making comparisons

among countries concerning their overall rate of policing. Unfortunately, the ratio of private to public police throughout the world is unknown. In the United States, it is estimated that there are at least twice (*The Economist*, 1997) and maybe three times (Box 5.2) the number of private police as public police, and that this gap will continue to widen. Because the bulk of private police is composed of security guards who are most often employed by large private corporations, one would expect the most substantial increases in private policing to occur in emerging market economies where corporate activity is also increasing rapidly. Unfortunately, there are few international data that would allow us to investigate this speculation (Box 5.2). The unknown numbers of private police truly make up a "dark figure" of policing.

Policing and crime rates

It is sometimes argued that the reason why a country has a high rate of policing is because there is more crime to police. An elementary way to examine this proposition is to match the rates of crime to the rates of policing. Figure 5.4 shows that there is a variable relationship between policing rates and crime rates depending on the country and whether the crime rate is measured by

A private policeman guards a local restaurant in Delhi. Source: Nalla (Original paper, 1997)

GLOBAL SNAPSHOT
Twenty years of policing world wide (per 100,000 population)

The rate of policing for developing countries has remained considerably lower than for industrialized countries ever since 1978. Policing rates for both developing and industrialized countries have increased over the period, with the greatest increase shown by industrialized countries.

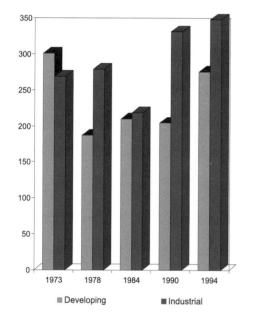

Source: first through fifth world crime surveys. Note that reporting countries may differ from period to period. See Notes to Snapshots for additional tabular information.

either the rate of theft or rate of murder per 100,000 population.

It may be argued, of course, that the reason why countries have a low crime rate is because they do in fact have a lot of police to keep the crime rate down. One could look to Singapore for support of this argument. Singapore has a very high policing rate (1,075 per 100,000), and its crime rates of both murder (1.71) and theft (919.56) are very low. However, the scatter plots (Figure 5.4) show that other countries do not reflect this relationship between policing and crime rates. For example, Sweden has a very high theft rate (nearly 6,000 per 100,000), but has an average level of policing (282 per 100,000). Colombia has a high murder rate of 78 per 100,000 but an average level of policing at a rate of 275. And the Russian Federation has a very high policing rate of 1,225 per 100,000, but a comparatively high murder rate of 20, and theft rate of 888.

An argument could be made that the policing rate may be related to the murder rate, if the outlier Colombia is removed. There is some evidence to support this contention, since the correlation coefficient between the policing rate and the murder rate is .09 with Colombia included, and .39 with Colombia excluded. Furthermore, the measure of murder is usually taken to be a more reliable and valid measure of crime cross nationally than is theft. But since there are only 51 countries responding (out of a possible total of more than 140 member countries of the United Nations), a definite conclusion cannot be drawn beyond that of strong suggestion. There are many countries left out, the USA for one.

It is likely that other factors beyond crime play a part in determining the levels of policing in a country. It is often suggested that one of those factors may be the level of economic development. This matter will be examined more closely shortly when government expenditures on criminal justice are reviewed. For the moment, let us turn to the next level of the criminal justice system, the level of the courts.

Judges

The rates of judges per 100,000 population in 1994 varied from a low of .38 (Table 5.3)

BOX 5.2

Private police in emerging markets: a quiet revolution

Emerging market countries[1] constitute about half the world's population. One of the features most emerging markets share is the potential for an expanded role for private police (the security guard industry). While some countries like China have traditionally relied on the state police to offer security functions to private enterprises, others such as Singapore and India have had *laissez faire* policies regarding the growth of the private security industry.

Security guard demographics. Data on the number of private police in all countries, regardless of economic development, are difficult to obtain. Confusion stems from definitions of private policing which include a wide variety of functions such as alarms, investigative services, safety, guards and electronic surveillance.

A small country such as Singapore (population: 2.6 million) has more than 200 security guard companies employing approximately 15,000 to 20,000 security guards (Nalla and Hoffman, 1996).

It is a more complex process to obtain data from countries such as India, with a population of nearly one billion. The larger security guard vendors employ as many as 12,000 people, and hundreds of smaller firms have as few as 20 employees. The telephone directory yellow pages in large metropolitan cities such as Bangalore, Bombay, Calcutta, Hyderabad, Madras and New Delhi indicate that the number of private security vendors ranges from 40 to over 70 per city. These vendors provide all varieties of security services including contract guards. Interviews with the listed security vendors suggest that for every listed provider there is at least one unlisted vendor.

Ratio of private to public police. In Singapore, there are two security guards for every police officer (Nalla, 1996). This ratio is similar to that found in other developed economies; the US has a police/security guard (or officer) ratio of 1:3. In 1991, the Indian police strength stood at 1,152,586 (Raghavan and Natarajan, 1996). Vendors estimate security guards number at least twice the police strength.

Characteristics of private police. Research on the private guard industry in Singapore (Nalla and Hoffman 1996) suggests that security guards are typically male, 40 years and above, with a secondary education and some law enforcement or military experience. Most security guards in India are male, retired from the military and over 50 years of age. In recent years, younger personnel have been recruited into guard services because of the prevailing labour market conditions.

Government contracting. In India, government industries such as Hindustan Petroleum and Bharat Heavy Plates and Vessels are mandated to employ a paramilitary force, the Central Industrial Security Force (CISF), to secure vital installations. Private companies can out-source their contract services to the CISF as well. Some states such as Maharastra[2] contract security guards for Government of India undertakings.

Training. In a study of security guards in Singapore (Nalla and Hoffman 1996), strong support was found for government-sponsored training as well as training in the areas of fire prevention, public relations, and the use of force. Guards believed that training would improve public attitudes toward security guards,[3] reduce employee turnover, and attract more qualified candidates to the job. The study also indicated an interest among the owners of security agencies in Singapore to work toward mandating training for all security guards. Private security guard training in India is similar to that of other countries. The duration of guard training found by the study ranged from eight weeks to as little as one day. Some of the guards interviewed indicated that they receive no training before being assigned to a job.

Source: Abridged from Nalla (Original paper, 1997). See Notes to Boxes for additional information.

---

in Malaysia, to a high of 27.19 in Germany. All countries with judicial rates above the median of 6.9 were from Europe, with only two exceptions. It is likely that the number of judges in particular countries depends primarily on the type of legal system and only secondarily on the level of economic development. This is evident in Table 5.3. Those countries with the highest judicial rates were

FIGURE 5.4
Policing rate by crime rate, 1994 (per 100,000 population)

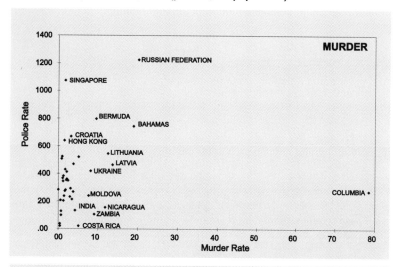

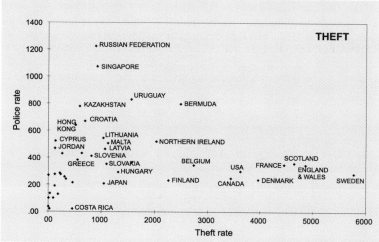

Source: Fifth UNCJS. See Notes to Figures for tabular data upon which this chart is based.

There is generally no consistent relationship between policing rates and crime rates.

cess. In some countries, particularly in Africa, there are systems of criminal justice that depend on direct participation of lay people at almost every stage of the criminal justice system. These systems may be formal or informal, as noted in Chapter 3 and those from non-common law countries. The countries with the low rates were those with common law traditions such as England and Wales, the United States and Hong Kong, or those with Islamic law traditions such as Sudan.

For countries reporting there has been a median increase of 4.5 percent in the number of judges per 100,000 population. However, as usual, there is considerable variation. Table 5.4 shows that while the majority of countries reported increases in judicial rates from 1990, a substantial minority also reported decreases.

Lay judges

Different legal systems and traditions also foster a variety of ways for the participation of ordinary citizens in the justice pro-

TABLE 5.3
Judges per 100,000 population and legal tradition, 1994

	Rate	Legal tradition
Germany	27	Civil
Luxembourg	27	Civil
Slovenia	26	Civil
Liechtenstein	26	Civil
Croatia	23	Civil
Hungary	21	Civil
Slovakia	21	Civil
Czech Rep	20	Civil
Austria	20	Civil
*"FYRM"	19	Civil
Finland	18	Civil
Uruguay	14	Civil
Greece	13	Civil
Portugal	13	Civil
Estonia	12	Civil
Belgium	12	Civil
Bulgaria	12	Civil
Costa Rica	11	Civil
Colombia	11	Civil
Cyprus	9	Civil/Common
Turkey	9	Civil
Russian Federation	9	Civil
Malta	8	Civil
Latvia	7	Civil
Qatar	7	Civil/Islamic
Lithuania	7	Civil
Kazakhstan	7	Civil
Belarus	7	Civil
Israel	6	Common
Rep of Moldova	6	Civil
Kyrgyzstan	5	Civil
Kiribati	5	NA
Georgia	5	Civil
Sweden	4	Civil
USA	4	Common
Macau	4	NA
Chile	4	Civil
Singapore	3	Common
Rep of Korea	3	Civil/Common
Northern Ireland	3	Common
Scotland	3	Civil/Common
Myanmar	3	NA
Hong Kong	2	Common
Sudan	2	Common/Islamic
Japan	2	Civil/Common
England & Wales	2	Common
Zambia	2	Common
Indonesia	2	Civil/Islamic
Jamaica	1	Common
Madagascar	1	Civil
Malaysia	<1	Common

*"Former Yugoslav Republic of Macedonia"
Source: Fifth UNCJS. See Notes to Tables for additional sources.

in Box 5.1. These unpaid — or very often nominally paid — personnel may reasonably be considered an important resource of any country's criminal justice system. Such persons may be involved in common law systems by serving on juries, or in civil systems by acting as lay judges. In fact, the point of the criminal justice process at which the participation of lay people is probably most common throughout the world, regardless of the legal tradition, is at the judicial level (see Box 5.3).

Because of the mostly unpaid nature of lay participation and the often informal role of these personnel, it is particularly difficult to obtain statistical information concerning their utilization in different countries. For example, the extensive use of an informal criminal justice system in Nigeria (Box 5.1) probably means that a large portion of everyday criminal justice in that country is not represented in the data collected by the UNCJS since national statistics depend almost entirely on established formal bureaucracies that keep written records of their activities. However, Table 5.5 shows that a number of countries were able to report

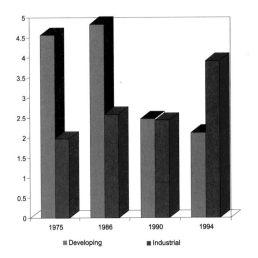

GLOBAL SNAPSHOT
Judicial personnel world wide over 20 years (median rates per 100,000 population)

Judicial personnel rates have fluctuated widely for developing countries over the 20 year period. Rates have increased dramatically in 1994 for industrialized countries after a 15 year period of stability.

Source: first through fifth world crime surveys. Note that reporting countries may differ from period to period. See Notes to Snapshots for additional tabular information.

some data on lay judges. From those countries responding, it would seem that lay judges are used more in civil law countries, four of which report lay judges at a rate

TABLE 5.4
Trends in rates of judges by country, percent change, 1990-1994

Increase	
Macau	166
Estonia	106
Cyprus	59
Bulgaria	51
Czech Rep	44
Belarus	36
Malaysia	30
Russian Federation	29
Qatar	27
Slovakia	26
Hungary	22
Lithuania	21
Germany	20
Singapore	19
Georgia	18
England & Wales	17
Latvia	16
Portugal	11
Rep of Korea	10
Costa Rica	9
Columbia	6
Malta	4
Slovenia	3
Belgium	3
Zambia	1
Jamaica	<1
Japan	<1

Decrease	
Chile	-1
Austria	-1
Israel	-1
Greece	-1
Uruguay	-2
United States of America	-2
Northern Ireland	-3
Hong Kong	-4
Indonesia	-6
Liechtenstein	-6
Turkey	-9
Finland	-10
Myanmar	-10
*"FYRM"	-12
Sudan	-12
Rep Of Moldova	-15

*"The Former Yugoslav Republic of Macedonia"

Source: Fifth UNCJS. See Appendix 1 for definitions of occupational categories.

Lay participation in criminal justice

Lay participation in legal decision-making has been around since antiquity. Medieval Europe gave birth to the jury which is utilized to this day in common-law countries, and to the Scabini or the Schoeffen courts which survived as mixed tribunals in civil-law countries.

Lay participants have long been considered cornerstones of the democratic administration of justice. In fact, most of the countries in the world do not leave solely to professional judges the responsibility of deciding about guilt and punishment in criminal cases.

Lay participants are persons who have neither education in legal issues nor training in legal decision-making. They are selected to decide criminal cases together with fellow lay participants and/or with professional judges. Professional judges, on the other hand, are typically law school graduates who have passed a bar exam and have been appointed or elected as judges. They may wear robes, wigs, or other symbols of their position. They represent the government and the state.

Some countries assign the responsibility of conducting the trials in serious criminal cases and deciding about the legal issues to professional judges, while lay participants have the responsibility of deciding the facts (the jury system, utilized in, e.g., the United States and the United Kingdom). Other countries assign all of these functions to tribunals which are composed of both professional judges and lay participants (the system of mixed tribunals, utilized in, e.g., Austria, Croatia, Germany,

Hungary, Poland and Sweden). However, even in the countries with very extensive systems of lay participation, there is a tendency to treat less serious cases differently in order to reduce the expenses associated with trials. This can be achieved by either assigning only the least serious cases to be tried by lay persons (the system of justices of the peace in the United States or magistrates in the United Kingdom) or by reducing the size of the judicial panel or replacing the panel with only one decision-maker, a professional judge (this system is used in Croatia, for example).

Types of lay participation in criminal justice include:

- the jury, most common in the United States;
- stipendiary and lay magistrates, including justices of the peace, most common in England and Wales;
- lay courts such as those in Cuba;
- mixed tribunals common in central, eastern, and northern Europe.

Some countries do not currently utilize any form of lay participation. Prominent examples of the few countries in which the decision-makers are exclusively professional judges are Korea, Saudi Arabia and Japan. Japan had a jury system in the mid 1920s; however, it was later abolished (Lempert, 1992).

For additional information concerning lay participation in legal decision making, please see Box 3.1.

Source: Abridged from Ifkovic (Original paper, 1997)

---

higher than 100 per 100,000. It also appears that those countries reporting few lay judges are primarily from the common law tradition. The ratio of lay to professional judges is also revealing. Among the highest users of lay judges, there are ten times more lay judges than professional judges. Among the low users of lay judges, the ratio is reversed, with the USA, for example, using many times more professional judges than lay judges. While this distinction may be due to the US common law system, it is to be noted that England and Wales displays a higher ratio of lay to professional judges. There are 13 countries reporting zero use of lay judges. While these countries make up

a diverse group, of interest is that the Russian Federation and two former Soviet states, Estonia and Lithuania, are included, which contrasts with the high use of lay judges by Slovenia, Hungary, Slovakia and the Czech Republic.

Finally, among the countries responding, there appears to be a strong indication of a decline in the numbers of lay judges. For the period 1990-1994, the number of lay judges declined by 5.8 percent, with 11 out of the 16 countries reporting a decrease.[1]

Prosecutors

The prosecutor is the most complex criminal justice occupation from a comparative perspective. The common law tradition, for example, is essentially based on a notion of private prosecution: offenders are pros-

TABLE 5.5
Lay and professional judges, 1994 (per 100,000 population)

	Lay Judges	Professional Judges
Slovenia	301	26
Kiribati	143	5
Croatia	140	23
Hungary	120	21
Slovakia	108	21
Sweden	91	4
Czech Rep	85	20
Scotland	83	3
Finland	80	18
England & Wales	58	2
Liechtenstein	32	26
Belgium	22	12
Sudan	12	2
Latvia	7	7
Uruguay	5	14
Malta	2	8
Jamaica	2	1
Cyprus	1	9
USA	<1	4
Hong Kong	<1	2
Zambia	<1	2
Belarus	0	7
Costa Rica	0	11
Estonia	0	12
Indonesia	0	2
Israel	0	6
Japan	0	2
Lithuania	0	7
Luxembourg	0	27
Portugal	0	13
Rep of Moldova	0	6
Russian Federation	0	9
Singapore	0	3
Turkey	0	9

Source: Fifth UNCJS

GLOBAL REPORT ON CRIME AND JUSTICE

ecuted on behalf of the victim or complainant, not the government. Thus, in England and Wales, a senior police officer is often the individual who instigates prosecution, either carrying out the prosecution himself and acting as the prosecutor at the trial, or hiring a solicitor to conduct the prosecution on his behalf – that is to say, in theory at least, on behalf of himself as a private citizen not the government (Kress, 1976; see Box 5.4).

In contrast, the prosecutor in the United States (also called the district attorney) acts on behalf of the citizens who elected him, even though the US system of law is based on the common law system. Some have argued that the US public prosecutor actually derives from the civil law system of France or other countries of Europe in which the prosecutor (often also a judge) acts clearly on behalf of the state to investigate and prosecute the case (Kress, 1976). However, the difference in the American prosecutor is that the district attorney is an elected official, who by dint of that election may or may not be independent of the state government, beholden to those who elected him (usually the county government level).

In sum, the comparison of the numbers of prosecutors in different countries may involve the counting of quite different persons who serve quite different functions.

If we examine Table 5.6 we see quite a striking finding: the countries with the highest rate of prosecutors per 100,000 are all countries in transition in Central and Eastern Europe. Perhaps a reason for this finding is that the role of the prosecutor in the socialist legal systems is to be more strongly representative of the state, and to play a very wide role in the processing of criminal cases. However, this cannot be the complete explanation, because the US prosecutor probably plays the key role in processing the majority of criminal cases. The difference is that he or she is not a career public servant but is an elected official (though in a large city such as New York City, the assistants to the DA may stay in public service for an extended period of time, and are not elected). In the socialist system, the prosecutor is a national career public service position. This means that such positions are more likely to be systematically counted in a bureaucracy, and thus statistics on prosecutors are prob-

ably more easily available than in non-socialist systems. This would explain, for example, why the US has never reported this statistic for the UNCJS.

It is apparent from Table 5.6 that those countries of Western Europe which have civil law based systems (e.g., Finland, Spain, Germany, Portugal) report rates of prosecutors that are generally higher than those of common law based systems such as England and Wales (although, as we have noted above, England and Wales employs senior police officers as prosecutors, who are probably not counted in their statistic).

There was also a difference between industrial and developing countries. The median rate for prosecutors in developing countries (19 countries) was 2.5 per 100,000 compared to 7.9 for industrial countries (28 countries).[2]

Corrections personnel

There are wide variations in the number of corrections staff per 100,000 population among the countries providing information. The rates range from a high of 314 corrections personnel per 100,000 for Bermuda, to a low of 1.44 for Egypt. The most obvious factor that should affect the number of correctional personnel in a country is the actual number of persons in prison. Figure 5.5 shows that there is generally a relationship between the number of convicted prisoners per 100,000 and the rate of corrections personnel: those countries with high convicted prisoner rates tend to have high rates of correctional workers as well.[3]

However, it is likely that economic development also affects the number of corrections officers in a given country. The bottom five countries in number of cor-

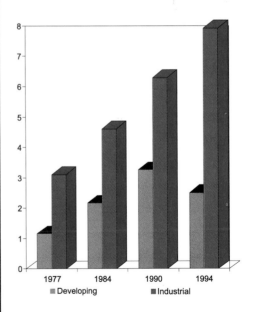

GLOBAL SNAPSHOT
Prosecutor personnel world wide since 1977 (median rates per 100,000 population)

The rate of prosecution personnel has increased steeply for industrialized countries. Developing countries have a rate of prosecutor personnel less than half that of industrialized countries, and there is no clear suggestion of increase in developing country rates.

■ Developing   ■ Industrial

Source: first through fifth world crime surveys. Note that reporting countries may differ from period to period. See Notes to Snapshots for additional tabular information.

BOX 5.4

The US District Attorney: a prosecutor of diverse legal, national and cultural origins

Possessing almost unlimited discretionary powers, the district attorney is the most important figure in America's system of criminal justice administration. These powers stem from the unique fact that the public prosecutor exists in a system which was initially premised on a common law concept of private prosecution. The discretion involved in charging and plea-bargaining decisions exemplifies the power granted a civil law official to administer a common law jurisprudence. How did such a figure arise?

Whereas Americans describe their legal system as based upon the English common law, the public prosecutor is a figure virtually unknown to the English system. This is important because of the pivotal role of the district attorney in America's criminal justice system. The prosecutor has been said to be "police, prosecutor, magistrate, grand jury, petit jury, and judge in one," possessing, as former US Attorney General and Supreme Court Justice Robert Jackson put it "more control over life, liberty, and reputation than any other person in America."

The English common law tradition. In common law, a crime was viewed not as an act against the state, but rather as a wrong inflicted upon the victim. The aggrieved victim, or an interested friend or relative, would personally arrest and prosecute the offender, after which the courts would adjudicate the matter much as they would a contract dispute or a tortious injury. Thus, there was no English common law analogue to the American district attorney until 1879, when the sharply limited office of director of public prosecutions was created. At least in theory, this common law system of private prosecution still exists in England today. Lord Patrick Devlin declared that when the police officer conducts prosecutions, he is legally "acting not by virtue of his office but as a private citizen interested in the maintenance of law and order"; the only differentiation from a private citizen being a slightly broader power of arrest, after which arrest the officer may hire a solicitor to prepare the case on his or her personal behalf against the defendant. However, in 1986 legislation separated somewhat the role of prosecutor from that of police.

The civil law tradition: the French *procureur*. Given the enormous power of the American public prosecutor, one may ask whether the American colonies somehow chose to adopt a civil law official, to administer a common law jurisprudence.

The most frequently claimed source of such a public prosecutor is France, but it is

well to note that the evidence for French influence is entirely circumstantial, based on the similarity of prosecutorial institutions rather than on any direct link; for example, the Louisiana Territory was not purchased from France until 1803, a century after the Connecticut legislature established a modern public prosecutor's office. The concept of public prosecution was, however, well established in France by the time of America's colonization. In modern France, the state-appointed *procureur public* receives complaints, supervises police behaviour, initiates investigations, prepares charges and controls the conduct of the trial and all other phases of a prosecution.

The Dutch *schout*. France is not the only claimed civil law ancestor of the public prosecutor. It is argued that the American district attorney is a direct descendant of Holland's *schout*, a public official who prosecuted all criminal cases under Dutch law. (Records do clearly indicate that *schouts* practiced in the New World, at least in New Amsterdam – later New York City.) The theory is premised on the fact that the Netherlands was the only power besides England which actually governed portions of areas which became the original 13 states: the colony of New Netherland claimed control of parts of what are today Connecticut, New York, New Jersey, Pennsylvania and Delaware. These, indeed, seem to be the states where the public prosecutor first made an appearance in the English colonies. By 1686, Pennsylvania appears to have had at least one prosecuting attorney on its public payroll and, by that same year, there was a public prosecutor in a New Jersey Quaker community. Further, district attorneys existed all over New Jersey by 1747 at the latest.

Intriguing as the Dutch hypothesis is, however, the Netherlands' claims beyond New Amsterdam seem exaggeratedly based on a small settler population. Further, Holland's period of political control was, in any event, quite brief, lasting only from 1653 until 1664.

This search for the source of US public prosecution has also seen a claim advanced for the Scottish system and even other major immigrant groups, such as the Germans or Poles, which formed significant minorities within the colonies. Indeed, it is probably this ethnic conglomerate of the colonies which has led some otherwise cautious historians to opt for a "spontaneous combustion theory" for the creation of the public prosecutor in America.

Source: Kress (Original paper, 1997)

TABLE 5.6

Prosecutors per 100,000 population, 1994

Russian Federation	19
Kazakstan	19
Azerbaijan	16
Lithuania	16
Latvia	16
Belarus	14
Kyrgyzstan	12
Hungary	11
Bermuda	11
Rep of Moldova	11
Colombia	11
Slovakia	10
Portugal	10
Liechtenstein	10
Cyprus	10
Western Samoa	9
Estonia	8
Sweden	8
Czech Rep	8
Belgium	8
Denmark	7
Slovenia	7
Georgia	7
Bulgaria	7
Croatia	7
Luxembourg	7
Germany	7
Finland	7
**"FYRM"	6
Qatar	5
Scotland	5
Sao Tome&Principe	5
Andorra	5
El Salvador	4
England & Wales	4
Turkey	4
Australia	4
Greece	4
Peru	4
Spain	3
Indonesia	3
Costa Rica	3
Austria	2
Madagascar	2
Philippines	2
Macau	2
Singapore	2
Rep of Korea	2
Japan	2
Panama	2
Egypt	1
Malaysia	1
Sudan	1
Zambia	1

*"Former Yugoslav Republic of Macedonia"

Source: Fifth UNCJS. See Appendix 1 for definitions of prosecutor.

rections staff per 100,000 population (Hungary, Egypt, El Salvador, Indonesia and Madagascar) are all representative of either least developed countries or emerging market economies. In fact the convicted prisoner to corrections staff ratio reveals that developing countries have a median of 2.6

prisoners to one staff, whereas industrial countries have a median of only 1.8 to one staff (Table 5.7).

The scatter plot of Figure 5.5 and the data in Table 5.7 demonstrate clearly that, while it is a reasonable general conclusion that both economic development and convicted prisoner rate are important determinants of corrections staff rates, there are nevertheless wide variations among the countries. Some have high prison populations and low staff rates, and others the reverse. Why this variation exists is a question well worth asking. Are these rates the result of planned inmate staff ratios on the part of the countries? Or have they simply arisen as a result of fortuitous circumstances?

Trends in correctional staffing

The overall trend for corrections staffing is a slight increase of 3.5 percent from 1990 to 1994 (37 countries). This observation must be seen as tentative. Taking into account the years 1986 to 1990, with only 16 countries reporting, a slight decrease is apparent. In addition, some countries with a known substantial increase in prison populations were not represented in that sample.[4] Figure 5.6 provides a glimpse of a selection of countries each from a different geographic region (as defined by the United Nations). Countries from Europe (west and east) show a slight decline from 1986 to 1990, and a slight increase since 1990. The developed Asian countries of Korea and Singapore increased their correctional officer rates from 1986 to 1990, in line with the observed increases they have shown in levels of policing. Japan, although increasing its rate slightly from 1986 to 1990, has decreased its rate in the years 1990 to 1994. Japan's rate still remains substantially lower, in general, than other developed nations.

One would expect the trends in staffing to closely follow trends in the prison population. In fact, while the median increase from 1990 to 1994 for correctional officers was 3.5 percent the median increase for convicted prisoners was 6.4 percent. Figure 5.7 shows that there is general coincidence between changes in prison staff and changes in prison populations for most countries. If there have been increases in prisoners there have been increases in staff, and vice versa.

TABLE 5.7
Ratio of convicted prisoners to correctional staff for industrial and developing countries, 1994

INDUSTRIAL COUNTRIES		DEVELOPING COUNTRIES	
Belarus	12.28	Egypt	38.68
Kyrgyzstan	5.96	El Salvador	4.88
Ukraine	5.64	Zambia	4.85
Georgia	3.95	Sudan	4.30
Russian Federation	3.79	Madagascar	3.93
Rep Of Moldova	3.73	Singapore	3.86
Latvia	3.40	Costa Rica	3.65
Australia	2.38	Guyana	3.13
*"FYRM"	2.24	Rep Of Korea	3.01
Japan	2.20	Hong Kong	2.68
Bulgaria	2.12	Brunei Darussalam	2.61
Greece	2.00	Panama	2.51
Lithuania	1.88	Malaysia	1.97
Marshall Islands	1.88	Colombia	1.90
Luxembourg	1.64	Mexico	1.53
Switzerland	1.62	Mauritius	1.48
Portugal	1.49	Chile	1.41
Austria	1.42	Indonesia	1.22
Hungary	1.38	Turkey	.85
Czech Rep	1.21	Cyprus	.66
Sweden	1.14	Sao Tome&Principe	.54
Estonia	1.06	Kuwait	.01
Scotland	.98		
Finland	.93		
England & Wales	.93		
Bermuda	.98		
Slovenia	.86		
Croatia	.80		
Belgium	.76		
Denmark	.66		
Macau	.64		
Northern Ireland	.48		

*"The Former Yugoslav Republic of Macedonia"
Source: Fifth UNCJS

Women in the criminal justice work force

The extent to which a country uses all its available human resources in its work force may be assessed by the extent to which women participate. Figure 5.8 reveals that the proportions of women in criminal justice occupations vary considerably according to the criminal justice function and to the extent of industrialization of the country. Though the number of countries reporting is small, in general, industrial countries have a higher participation of women in the criminal justice work force in all four occupations of policing, prosecution, judging and corrections. Of interest, when all countries are considered together regardless of level

DEVELOPING (22 COUNTRIES)
1 STAFF FOR EVERY 2.6 INMATES

INDUSTRIAL (26 COUNTRIES)
1 STAFF FOR EVERY 1.8 INMATES

of development, is the comparatively high level of women participating in the prosecution process (32 percent) and judicial levels (27 percent) of the criminal justice system. This possibly reflects on the traditional male role of policing in many countries, though there are some countries re-

FIGURE 5.5
Correctional staff and convicted prisoners, 1994 (per 100,000 population)

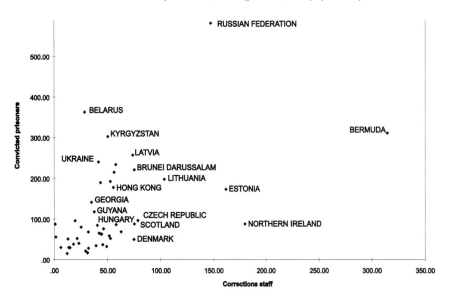

Source: Fifth UNCJS. See Notes to Figures for tabular data on which this chart is based.

FIGURE 5.7
Percent change in corrections staff and convicted prisoners, 1990-1994 (per 100,000 population)

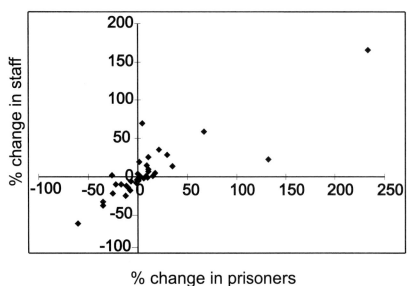

% change in prisoners

Source: Fifth UNCJS. See Notes to Figures for additional information.

FIGURE 5.6
Prison staff rates, selected countries, 1986-1994 (per 100,00 population)

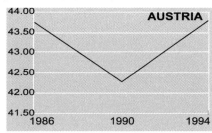

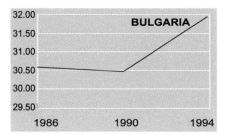

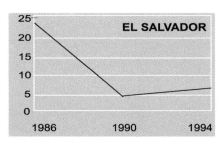

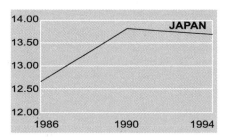

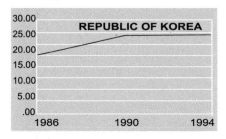

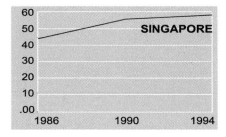

Source: Fourth and Fifth UNCJS. See Notes to Figures for additional information.

GLOBAL REPORT ON CRIME AND JUSTICE

porting relatively high participation of women in policing. These may be countries which have an established tradition of female participation in military activities such as countries of the former USSR: Latvia, the Russian Federation and Lithuania (and, if the former Yugoslavia is included as a "fringe" eastern bloc country, Slovenia; see Table 5.9). In fact, it has been found that with minor exceptions, countries that reported high rates of female participation in policing also reported higher rates in other criminal justice occupations, and vice versa for those reporting low participation in policing.

It is apparent that the increase in the par-

INCREASE

Russian Fed.
Colombia
Spain
Slovakia
Belgium
Cyprus
Mexico
Mauritius
Croatia
Greece
Chile
Ukraine
Rep.Moldova
Austria
Romania
Turkey
India
Malta
Hungary
Scotland
Marshall Islands
Kazakhstan
Morocco
Rep of Korea
North. Ireland
Malaysia
Kiribati
Canada
Hong Kong
Saint V.& Gren.
Egypt
Finland
Slovenia

DECREASE

Singapore
West. Samoa
Denmark
USA
Zambia
Philippines
France
Latvia

Source: Fifth UNCJS. See Notes to Tables for additional information.

GLOBAL SNAPSHOT
Prison personnel since 1970 (rates per 100,000 population)

The rates of prison personnel have increased steadily for industrialized countries, and are generally higher than those of developing countries. However, there have been periods in which developing countries displayed higher rates of prison personnel than industrialized countries. There is no clear trend for the rates of developing countries to increase during the reporting period.

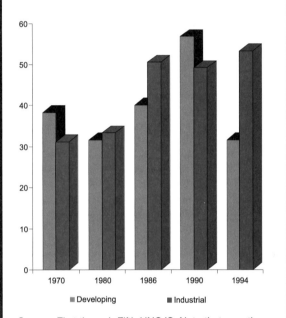

Source: First through Fifth UNCJS. Note that reporting countries may differ from period to period. See Notes to Snapshots for additional tabular information.

ticipation of women in the criminal justice work force is part of an overall trend. Since 1990, the percentage of women in policing has risen by 25 percent, for female prosecutors 35 percent, and female judges 45 percent. As Table 5.8 shows, the overwhelming majority of countries reported an increase of women in policing for the period 1990 to 1994.

Quality of the work force

As noted in the introduction to this chapter, the quality of personnel is also an important indicator of the depth of a country's human resources in criminal justice. The qualifications for judges are reasonably self explana-

..the participation of women in the criminal justice work force is part of a global trend.

FIGURE 5.8
Proportion of the criminal justice work force that were female, 1994

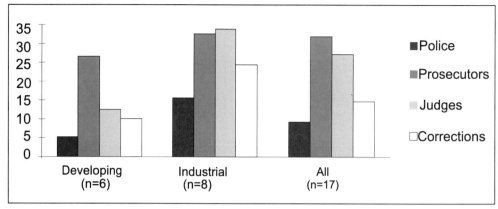

Source: Fifth UNCJS. See Notes to Figures for tabular data.

tory: judges must be legally trained (unless they are lay judges or part of an informal customary law system). However, the levels of training and educational qualifications for other criminal justice personnel such as police are less obvious. Should a line police officer be required to have a university degree, for example? Will such qualification guarantee that he or she will do a better job? We should like to know, then, what the general standards are around the world in regard to police officers.

The *International Factbook of Criminal Justice Systems* provides some elementary information concerning the training and qualifications of police officers for a small number of countries. It is, of course, espe-

cially difficult to make comparisons among countries concerning educational qualifications because the educational systems of countries differ considerably. Add to this the widely diverse structures of police organizations in different countries, and we have a very difficult problem in making direct comparisons between countries. Nevertheless, it is possible to make some basic observations about overall qualifications and police training which may perhaps serve to raise questions and stimulate further investigation into this area.

According to Weiss (1997) the *International Factbook of Criminal Justice Systems* reports three basic types of law enforcement training: "physical fitness," "classroom" and "field training." Physical fitness is described as specific physical pursuits, such as martial arts, running, jumping, climbing or sports; classroom practices are indicated by such specific course subject headings as law, law enforcement techniques, criminology, traffic situations, investigative techniques or interpersonal skills; field training is described as on-the-job training, an internship or a probationary period.

Table 5.10 reveals some remarkable information. This table reports length of training, on average, for new recruits and line officers. Countries often ranked among the highest in economic development (Canada and USA for example) are ranked within the shortest length of law enforcement training. Also surprising is Singapore, a big spender in criminal justice, which provides comparatively shorter training periods. Japan, famous for its effective community policing system, ranks only in the middle in

TABLE 5.9
Ranking of countries by percent of criminal justice work force who were female, 1994

Sweden	33
Russian Federation	23
Slovenia	22
Latvia	22
Scotland	21
Madagascar	16
Lithuania	14
Austria	14
Zambia	13
Rep of Moldova	9
*"FYRM"	8
Greece	7
Singapore	6
Cyprus	5
Liechtenstein	5
Turkey	3
Rep of Korea	1

*"The Former Yugoslav Republic of Macedonia"
Source: Fifth UNCJS

GLOBAL REPORT ON CRIME AND JUSTICE

training length. Dominant, however, is Western Europe, whose countries are all within the top group providing two or more years training.

It is clear from Table 5.11 that the overwhelming qualification for police recruitment is some high school education, with very few requiring some college education. However, comparisons and conclusions should be made with caution. Because of the complex structure of policing in many countries, the level of educational qualities may differ drastically within each country. For example, while the USA is listed as requiring "some college," it is quite clear and well known that in many isolated local jurisdictions in the United States, formal educational qualifications may not be necessary. Thus, before those countries not requiring any formal educational qualifications for admission to policing are dismissed as "backward," we should note that there may be jurisdictions within many countries in which few qualifications are required, and others in which many qualifications are required. There is also the possibility that in the case of some countries, possibly South Korea,

TABLE 5.11
Qualifications required for new recruits, ca. 1994

SOME HIGH SCHOOL	ELEMENTARY SCHOOL
Poland	
Australia	
Bulgaria	
China	
Costa Rica	
Germany	
Hungary	
India	
Israel	
Italy	
Kenya	
Malta	
Netherlands	
Nigeria	
Repub. of Ireland	Ghana
Romania	Slovenia
Russian Fed.	
Singapore	**NONE**
Slovakia	
South Africa	Micronesia
Spain	New Zealand
Sri Lanka	Rep. Korea
Sweden	
Venezuela	

SOME COLLEGE

Canada
Denmark
USA

Source: Weiss (Original paper, 1997), Newman *et al.* (1996). See Notes to Tables for further information.

TABLE 5.10
Length of police training, new recruits or line officers, ca. 1994

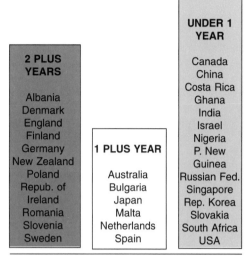

2 PLUS YEARS	1 PLUS YEAR	UNDER 1 YEAR
Albania	Australia	Canada
Denmark	Bulgaria	China
England	Japan	Costa Rica
Finland	Malta	Ghana
Germany	Netherlands	India
New Zealand	Spain	Israel
Poland		Nigeria
Repub. of Ireland		P. New Guinea
Romania		Russian Fed.
Slovenia		Singapore
Sweden		Rep. Korea
		Slovakia
		South Africa
		USA

Source: Weiss (Original paper, 1997), Newman *et al.* (1996). See Notes to Tables for further information.

formal education may be undertaken by the police training academy itself.

Of interest is the inclusion of Albania in the group of two plus years of police training. The time at which this information was collected (about 1993) was before the strife in Albania fully broke out. It is also possible that the length of training reported may have been for military related law enforcement. In fact, some countries have made an explicit link between military training and law enforcement training. Israel, for example has made it possible for national military service recruits (compulsory in Israel) to undergo law enforcement training (see Box 5.5).

Expenditure on criminal justice

In previous surveys, few countries have provided information concerning their annual expenditures on criminal justice. There are many reasons for this, the main one being that the criminal justice system is not a unitary system in any country. That is, prisons are typically administered by different organizations or departments of government than are courts or policing. While this is something of a problem in counting personnel, it is much more of a problem when it comes to expenditure since financing is often conducted in separate government de-

In contrast to North America, the countries of Western Europe consistently demand higher qualifications from their new recruits, and subject them to much longer law enforcement training.

Compulsory national service in the Israel National Police

In August 1995, after protracted debate in the Foreign Affairs and Security Committee of the Knesset, an amendment was passed to the Security Service Act permitting Israelis to do their compulsory military service in Israel National Police (INP) units other than the Border Guard Police (the INP's Border Guard has been part of the compulsory military service system for many years).

In Israel, every male and female citizen, with certain exceptions, must spend from two to three years in military service, beginning at age 18. The INP, however, can recruit, under the new amendment, only those draftees who express their specific, written consent to INP service. Moreover, the INP recruits are allowed six months probationary service, during which they may retract that consent and return to the regular military national service. So far, not more than a handful have done so: the hundreds of others have found, apparently, that police work suits them well.

Four hundred male and female recruits of the first intake have now completed basic military training in the Israel Defense Forces (IDF) and have transferred to INP units around the country. Another 700 will soon join them.

The INP officer directing the training of this new type of recruit claims that they have preferred the INP over army service in the hope of a more interesting job content. The women especially want to avoid the mere clerical chores often accorded them in the army. Many of both sexes see their period in the INP as a way to try out a possible career avenue.

The INP has designed a special training track for this intake. Both the methods and the pace of teaching and training have been redesigned for them. Socialization to police work and culture and the great difference between army and police service are particularly prominent topics. The training officers are well aware that, on the streets, the public will not distinguish between one type of policeman and another. The young national service recruits will have to perform every police role expected of them, taking full personal responsibility for their performance. Their commitment to their new role, therefore, cannot be less than solid.

The INP does not plan to treat this new intake as inferior to its regular recruits but, on the contrary, to give them serious and interesting work to do. It has been found that the more that is demanded from the trainees, the more pleased they are since, apparently, the pressure signals to them that they will be accorded a respectable role.

From the INP's point of view, this new intake brings a special benefit — social linkages. Sons and daughters from sections of society that hitherto had little to do with the police are now deeply involved in it. The INP sees them as very desirable ambassadors of its relationship with the wider community.

Source: Edited and abridged from Rogel (1996)

partments which may be unrelated to criminal justice itself. It is therefore much more difficult to obtain these data. This problem is particularly acute in sectors of the criminal justice system that may be heavily dependent on physical equipment (e.g., prisons that require building and maintenance, policing that requires expensive operational equipment). In addition, expenditures which include salaries of personnel may reflect the general salary levels of the country, and therefore comparison across nations should be made only with great caution. Comparisons of expenditures may reflect differential salary levels within countries and across levels of the criminal justice system. Finally, fluctuations in currency rates affect the interpretation of dollars based data, especially where hyperinflation has occurred during the period. This has been a particular problem in our data for the new independent states of the former Soviet Union. In addition, there have been some significant population changes from one year to the next because of the profound political changes that have occurred in Europe during the period reported. For these reasons, very few countries provided up to date information.

Combined expenditure on all sections of criminal justice produced only limited data since, for reasons noted above, not all countries responding were able to provide information for each level of the criminal justice system. However, for those that did, it can be seen in Figure 5.9 that in 1994 Switzerland was the biggest spender with $468 per head, followed by the Netherlands and Finland. The bottom spenders were Turkey, Hungary, Colombia and Madagascar (with only 12 cents per capita). Of interest once again is the comparatively low expenditure by Japan ($63.44) compared to other developed countries.

Criminal justice expenditure and economic development

The general explanation for variation in expenditure on criminal justice is that countries with more money will spend more on criminal justice. If the countries are grouped according to their economic development, this explanation receives some support.

Figure 5.10 suggests that the difference between the industrial and developing countries in expenditures per head of population is considerable, and this holds true for all sectors of criminal justice, although it looks as though there is less difference for corrections. But in Figure 5.13, where more countries could be listed since only prison expenditures are considered, there is a substantial difference between industrial and developing countries. The expenditures are generally several times higher for industrial as against developing countries. The range of expenditures across countries, however, is remarkable if police, courts and corrections are examined separately, thus allowing for a larger number of countries responding.

The expense per person on police ranges from a high of $575 in Northern Ireland, to 5 cents in Madagascar and 20 cents in India (see Figure 5.11 and notes to that figure for listing of all countries). Croatia, Guyana, Israel, Madagascar, Nicaragua and Philippines spend less than $1 per head of population on corrections, compared to Bermuda's high of $175, and Northern Ireland's $138 (see Figure 5.12 and notes to that figure for listing of countries). Court expenditures also range widely, from Madagascar (3 cents) and Cyprus (62 cents), to Finland ($37) and Northern Ireland ($34). In general, it was found that those countries that tended to spend less on one section of criminal justice also spent less on all other aspects of criminal justice.

Figure 5.11 also generally supports the contention that countries with more money spend more on criminal justice. This figure shows the distribution of expenditure on police according to the gross domestic product per capita of each country. (Too few countries provided complete data to construct a chart showing expenditure on all criminal justice levels.) It is strikingly clear from the scatter plot that the higher the GDP the higher the expenditure on policing. The one clear exception is Japan, with a very high GDP but a low expenditure on policing. This is surprising considering that Japan is well known for its community polic-

ing tradition, and its effectiveness in preventing crime (see Box 8.4). That it also apparently costs Japan less than other developed countries is quite remarkable, and deserves further study. As noted below, Japan also seems to spend less on police equipment than other countries of similar economic level.

Technology as a resource

We noted at the beginning of this chapter that the amount of expenditure on equipment and technology is also a measure of criminal justice resources. Unfortunately, there is very little comparative information concerning this topic. Where there is information available, it is in regard to policing which utilizes technology and other equipment more visibly than other parts of the criminal justice system. One may get a rough idea of levels of equipment in countries by examining the three main types of police equipment and technology: automobiles, electronic equipment and weaponry.

While it may appear obvious that the richer countries will have more to spend on technology and equipment and as a general rule this is borne out by the data, there are nevertheless interesting individual country variations. Table 5.12, which draws information from the *International Factbook of Criminal Justice Systems* (Newman *et al.*, 1996) concerning levels of automobile

The big spenders on criminal justice in 1994 were Northern Ireland, Hong Kong and Finland.

FIGURE 5.9
Expenditure per capita on all levels of criminal justice, 1994 (US dollars)

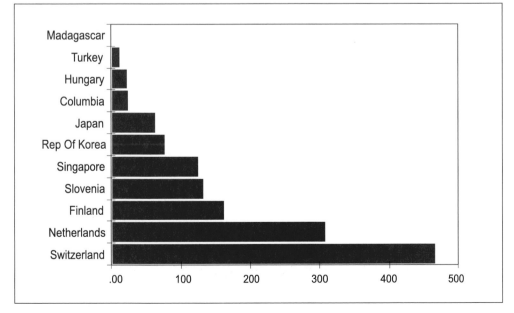

Source: Fifth UNCJS. See Notes to Figures for additional tabular information.

FIGURE 5.11
Police expenditure per capita by Gross Domestic Product, 1994

National policies and traditions play a larger role in determining the level of a criminal justice resource such as weaponry than does the level of economic development.

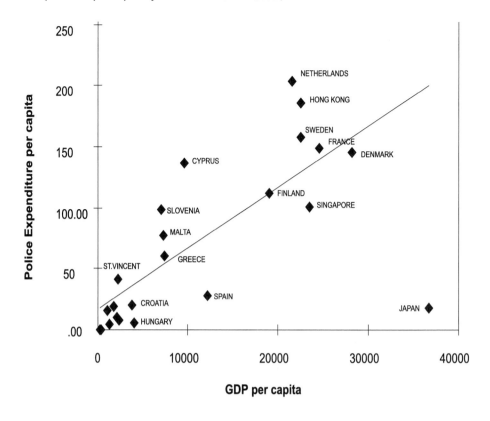

GDP per capita

Source: Fifth UNCJS and World Bank. See Notes to Figures for additional information.

equipment, shows that even with information available from so few countries, a difference between the developed countries (i.e., in this case Western Europe, North America and Australasia) and less developed countries is apparent. It is possible, however, that some countries appear lower in levels of police automobiles because of their much higher policing rate, so that the amount of technology in relation to the number of police may appear low.

For example, it was noted earlier in this chapter how South Korea had increased its police manpower drastically over the last ten years (see Figure 5.3). A small amount of information is available to throw some light on this trend. Table 5.13 reveals that the ratio of police to police vehicles varies considerably among the countries for which there was information. Basically, the same pattern emerges: those countries usually considered to be among the more developed nations also report very low police to vehicle ratios. South Korea bears out our previous speculation: it has a very high ratio of police to vehicles. Since South Korea is recently highly modernized, it is likely that the number of police has increased at a much more rapid rate than has the number of automobiles.

However, much of Korea's recent economic development has been in the area of

FIGURE 5.10
Expenditure per capita on criminal justice, 1994 (US dollars)

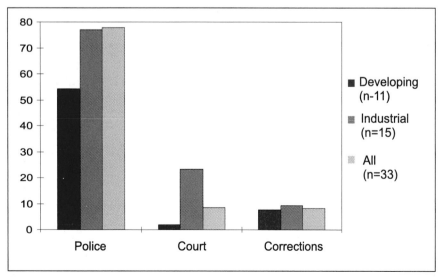

Source: Fifth UNCJS. See Notes to Figures for additional tabular information.

GLOBAL REPORT ON CRIME AND JUSTICE

high technology, so one might reasonably expect South Korea's rates to be higher, along with other developed countries, with respect to availability of electronic equipment. Table 5.14 supports this view. All countries (with the exception of Costa Rica) classified high in auto equipment also were classified high in electronic equipment. South Korea, however, has moved up into the high category for electronic equipment.

Weaponry is another measure of criminal justice resources, but one which is perhaps more controversial. Some countries, such as Japan, are averse to the availability of too much weaponry for law enforcement personnel. Other countries, such as the USA, see weaponry as essential for law enforcement to do its job. Yet in other countries in which there is civil strife, such as Albania, there may be an abundance of weaponry available, even though that country is not classified as a developed or industrial country.

Table 5.15 demonstrates this difference in national policies and conditions quite clearly. Australia, USA and New Zealand still remain among the top users of weaponry in law enforcement. However, they are joined by Sri Lanka and Bulgaria, countries not usually thought of as developed and industrialized. These are countries, however, in which there has been civil strife. For example Albania, though it was rated low in automobile equipment, is here classified medium in weaponry. Of further interest are those countries *not* classified in the top group: Denmark, the Netherlands and Sweden in the medium category, and Finland and Japan in the bottom group. These countries are usually ranked high in industrial development, yet they have reported low levels of weaponry for law enforcement. In fact, with the exception of Germany, all countries of Western Europe are not ranked in the high group. This is a clear case in which national policies and traditions play a larger role in determining the level of a criminal justice resource — in this case weaponry — than does the level of economic development. The variety in national policies and traditions in regard to guns for civilians is also reviewed in Chapter 6.

Prison expenditure

Prisons require a heavy investment in the capital equipment of usually large, specialized buildings. These are typically expensive to run and maintain. Not only must the salaries of guards be budgeted, but expenditures for the care of inmates, ranging from basic necessities (clothing and food) to health and other amenities are necessary too, assuming that the prison conditions are to measure up to the United Nations Standard Minimum Rules for the Treatment of Prisoners (see Box 5.6).

There are vast differences in expenditures on prisons for the countries providing such information. However, caution should be used in making any comparisons. There are salary and currency problems that plague interpretation of budgetary data such as these, and there is also the question of whether expenditures are *operating* expenditures only, or whether in some cases they also include capital expenditures (though the Fifth Survey questionnaire requested respondents to distinguish between these two types of expense). The building of a new prison could vastly inflate the expenditure on prisons if recorded as an expense all in the year it was built or for which it was contracted. This would not occur if the accounting practice was to capitalize the expense over several years. Thus, accounting practices could very seriously affect the final statistic that a country reports to the UNCJS. Salary bases are also obviously significant when making comparisons of expenditure

TABLE 5.12
Levels of automobile equipment, ca. 1994

HIGH	MEDIUM	LOW
Australia	Bulgaria	Albania
Canada	China	Micronesia
Costa Rica	Cuba	Poland
Denmark	Hungary	Romania
Germany	India	
Japan	Malta	
Netherlands	P. New Guinea	
New Zealand	Rep. Korea	
USA	Singapore	
	Slovakia	
	Slovenia	
	South Africa	
	Spain	
	Sri Lanka	
	Sweden	

Source: Weiss (Original paper, 1997), Newman *et al.* (1996). See Notes to Tables for further information.

TABLE 5.13
Number of police per police vehicle, ca. 1994

Albania	40
Spain	20
Rep. of Korea	12
Sweden	10
Hungary	9
China	8
Singapore	8
P. New Guinea	7
Slovenia	6
Germany	5
Slovakia	5
Sri Lanka	5
Australia	5
South Africa	5
Denmark	5
Malta	4
New Zealand	4
USA	2
Costa Rica	2
Netherlands	2
Japan	1

Source: Weiss (Original paper, 1997). See Notes to tables for additional data.

in human services cross nationally.

We can see from Figure 5.13 that the difference in expenditure on prisons between industrial and developing countries is as vast as the difference in expenditure on police and courts already presented in Figure 5.10. However, because of the reduced number of countries with data available on expenditures in all areas of criminal justice, the size of the difference cannot be clearly appreciated. Figure 5.13 makes the difference much clearer.

No evidence for a world wide prison overcrowding situation was found.

The scatter plot in Figure 5.12 also supports the contention that the richer the country, the more it will spend on prisoners. That figure presents the expenditure per capita on prisons in relation to gross domestic product per capita (GDP). There is a very clear relationship here, although there are the usual outliers. Japan, for example, with its very high GDP spends comparatively little on its prisons. This is in contrast to the countries in the middle of the plot, which are mainly those of Western Europe and Asia. These countries, with healthy economies, spend a middling amount on prisons — in most cases more than Japan. With the exception of the Netherlands, Hong Kong and Canada, however, they are spending below what their GDP per capita would suggest they could afford. Switzerland provides the best example: its prison expenditure is closely in line with its GDP. In fact Switzerland and Malta could be regarded as the trend setters in expenditure on prisons: Switzerland as an example for countries with a high

TABLE 5.14
Levels of electronic equipment, ca. 1994

HIGH	MEDIUM	LOW
Australia		Costa Rica
Canada		Cuba
China		Ghana
Denmark		India
England		Kenya
Germany	Albania	Slovakia
Hungary	Micronesia	Slovenia
Israel	Nigeria	Spain
Japan	Papua New	Sri Lanka
Malta	Guinea	
Netherlands	Poland	
New Zealand		
Rep. Korea		
Romania		
Singapore		
USA		

Source: Weiss (Original paper, 1997), Newman *et al.* (1996). See Notes to Tables for further information.

GDP, and Malta as the trend setter for countries with a low GDP.

It could be argued that the reason why some countries spend more or less on pris-

TABLE 5.16
Annual expenditure per convicted prisoner, 1994 (US dollars)

Northern Ireland	158197
Switzerland	112145
*Sweden	90806
*USA	73205
Denmark	64932
England & Wales	61721
Bermuda	56510
Japan	47873
Scotland	46235
Luxembourg	43885
Cyprus	39284
Slovenia	31786
Hong Kong	28341
Portugal	22442
Finland	18908
Austria	17980
Belgium	15767
Uruguay	10949
Rep of Korea	10122
Hungary	9788
Singapore	9593
Czech Rep	8903
*Brunei Darussalam	4253
Colombia	4028
Turkey	3384
Slovakia	2962
Panama	2871
Costa Rica	1923
Croatia	1231
Guyana	542
Madagascar	70

*1990 data
Source: Fifth UNCJS. See Notes to Tables for additional information.

TABLE 5.15
Levels of weaponry, ca. 1994

HIGH	MEDIUM	LOW
Australia	Albania	
Bulgaria	Cuba	
China	Denmark	
Costa Rica	Ghana	Micronesia
Germany	Malta	Finland
Hungary	Netherlands	Japan
India	Papua New	Kenya
Italy	Guinea	Poland
New Zealand	Rep. Korea	Republic of
Singapore	Slovakia	Ireland
Sri Lanka	Slovenia	Romania
USA	South Africa	Russian Fed.
	Spain	Venezuela
	Sweden	

Source: Weiss (1997), Newman *et al.* (1996). See Notes to Tables for further information.

FIGURE 5.12
Prison expenditure per capita by GDP per capita, 1994 (US dollars)

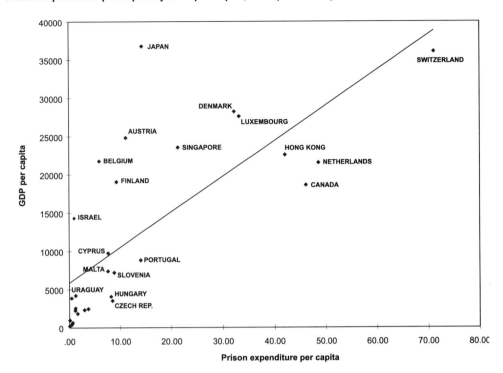

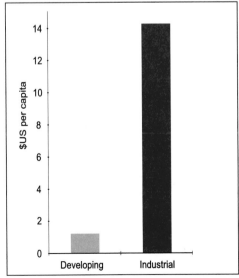

ons is because they have more or less prisoners. An examination of the expenditure per prisoner can answer this question.

Table 5.16 displays the range of expenditures per convicted prisoner reported by member countries. The annual dollar expenditure per prisoner ranges from an incredible high of $158,197 per prisoner in Northern Ireland, to a low of $70 per prisoner in Madagascar. This range in expenditure is truly astonishing.

We can see from this table that Japan, which appeared in the scatter plot of Figure 5.12 to spend quite a bit less per capita of the general population on prisoners compared to other industrialized nations, is among the very high spenders when measured according to expenditure per prisoner. Japan spends a much smaller amount per capita of the general population on prisons, yet at the same time spends a high amount per prisoner. Its relatively low incarceration rate of 30 per 100,000 no doubt makes this possible.

Shifting prison expenditure: private prisons

A growing trend around the world is to shift responsibility (and hopefully, some of the cost) on to private companies to establish correctional facilities which they will then manage for a fee on behalf of the government. Indeed, the growth over the last ten years is spectacular, as can be seen in Figure 5.14.

Private prisons were first established in the United States in 1986 and now over 63,500 prisoners are held in private facilities in that country (Thomas, 1996). How-

FIGURE 5.13
Per capita expenditure on prisons by industrial and developing countries, 1994 (US dollars)

Source: Fifth UNCJS. See Notes to Figures for further tabular information.

BOX 5.6

Private prisons in Australia

In Australia, the opportunity for the development of private prisons was created in Queensland when in 1988 a Commission of Inquiry (known as the Kennedy Review) recommended that one correctional facility should be managed by the private sector under contract to the Queensland Corrective Services Commission. Subsequently the management of the Borallon prison, which was designed and built by the government, was let to private contract in late 1989 and was officially opened in 1990. The following table (adapted from Harding, 1995) summarizes the current state of development of private prisons in Australia since that date.

Year	Company	Prison	Capacity	Cumulative Total	Cumulative Percentage
1990	CCA	Borallon, Qld	389*	389	2.9
1992	ACM	Arthur Gorrie, Qld	628**	1017	7.1
1993	ACM	Junee, NSW	600	1617	11.1
1995	Group 4	Mt Gambier, SA	110	1727	10.8
1996	CCA	Melton, Vic	125	1852	11.0
1997	ACM	Sale, Vic	600	2452	14.2
1997	Group 4	Laverton, Vic	600	3052	17.6

* Originally 240, or 1.8 percent of the national total at that time
** Originally 380, or 2.6 percent of the national total at that time

The above table shows that a total of seven private prisons have either been opened since 1990 or were under construction in 1997. They are located in four of the six states, and are run by three separate companies. All of the companies have significant foreign links: CCA (Corrections Corporation of Australia) and ACM (Australasian Correctional Management) with the United States, and Group 4 with the United Kingdom. By the end of 1997 they will house 3052 prisoners, or 17.6 percent of the Australian total. This is expected to increase to around 20 to 25 percent by the year 2000.

Most Australian private prisons have contracts which are summarized as DCFM (Design, Construct, Finance and Manage) but the early Queensland examples were for M only, that is, for a private company to run a prison which is owned by the government, and the contract for Junee was DCM.[1]

The development of private prisons has provoked considerable controversy. Some commentators, for example, have expressed the view that the punishment of offenders is a task which should only be undertaken by the government itself. It would be morally wrong, it is argued, for a private company to make a profit from the suffering of others. There are two responses that may be made to this argument. In the first place, if private prisons are morally wrong, how can private schools and private hospitals be morally acceptable? Do we care more for our offenders that we care for our health or the well-being of our children? Secondly, the distinction between the allocation of punishment (i.e., sentencing) and the administration of punishment (managing prisons, etc.) must be clearly understood. There is no suggestion that the quantum of punishment to be imposed will not continue to be determined by our judges and magistrates.

As far as comparative costs are concerned, the publicly available information is equivocal, but governments would hardly be likely to award contracts to private companies if they were not less expensive than the costs of public prisons. There is, however, one authoritative study from the United Kingdom which found that "on average, privately operated prisons offered an operational cost saving of 11 to 17 percent, depending on the cost measure used" (Dunmore, 1996). The financial details of the contracts for private prisons as yet have always been regarded as "commercial in confidence," but it is likely that there will be less secretiveness in the future as a result of freedom of information legislation and the possible listing of one or more of the companies on the stock exchange.

A vital consideration, probably the most vital consideration, is the extent to which private prisons maintain standards in relation to a wide range of issues. These include: security, safety (of both prisoners and staff), physical space, health services, nutrition, hygiene, hours out of cells, the provision of constructive work and education, training, treatment (especially drug and alcohol), recreational programs, appropriate arrangements for the resolution of grievances and disciplinary matters, and access for private and professional visitors. It is usual for the relevant government to appoint an experienced correctional administrator as a monitor to each private prison to ensure that standards in all of these areas (as set out in the contract) are maintained. Some contracts provide for financial penalties to be imposed for breaches such as escapes, riots, deaths, etc.

One recent study in Australia found that the numbers of deaths from all causes in private prisons was marginally lower than would have been expected when the numbers of deaths in public prisons were studied against the background of the numbers of prisoners in both systems (Biles, 1997). Most contracts today also require that testing for drugs be routinely conducted. For example, a contract for a 600 bed prison may require that at least 100 urine specimens be tested each month from a random selection of prisoners and that not more than five percent yield positive results. A penalty may be imposed if that limit is exceeded.

Even though private prisons are still fairly new anywhere in the world there is mounting evidence, as yet largely anecdotal, to suggest that one consequence has been for government prisons to improve their performance and also to reduce their costs. It seems that the competition between the two sectors has been beneficial.

Finally, the ultimate test of the desirability or otherwise of private prisons must be in terms of the impact that they make on recidivism or re-offending. Research into recidivism is always difficult and time-consuming, but Australia is now facing a situation where, uniquely in the world, it will soon be possible to start a longitudinal project which would compare the outcomes in terms of future criminal behaviour of public versus private prisons. The ideal site for such a project would be Victoria, where from the beginning of 1998 approximately half of all of the prisoners in the state will be in private prisons. Even though many prisoners would inevitably spend part of their sentences in both the public and private sectors, it would not be too difficult to devise a methodology for the project which took that into account, and eventually (it would take at least five and most likely up to ten years) would answer the question of which of the two systems produces the better results.

Source: Biles, (Original paper, 1997)

ever, this is minuscule when seen against the total of 1.6 million prisoners in that country. In the United Kingdom there are as of 1997 approximately 3,500 prisoners in private facilities, out of a total of 57,600 prisoners. The proportions of the total numbers of prisoners in these two countries are very much lower than the proportion in Australia where in mid 1997 there were 3,052 private prison places out of a total of approximately 17,300 prisoners in the nation. A comparison of the percentage of total prisoners held in private facilities in 1997 is striking:

United States 3.9
United Kingdom 6.1
Australia 17.6

At the end of 1995 there were 104 privately managed secure adult facilities in the United States. They were located in 17 states, with the highest numbers being in Texas, Florida, Tennessee and Arizona. These private prisons were run by 15 management firms, the largest of which are Corrections Corporation of America and Wackenhut Corrections Corporation. These two companies control over 75 percent of all private corrections facilities in the United States.

In the United Kingdom at the same time there were six private corrections facilities being run, or under construction, by four companies, the largest being Group 4 Prison and Court Services Ltd. The first private prison to be opened in England is HM Prison Wolds at Hull. It has a capacity of 335 and received its first prisoners in 1992. In the following year HM Prison Blackenhurst at Redditch received its first prisoners, and in 1994 new private prisons were also opened at Doncaster and Rochdale. Two other private facilities in South Wales and Liverpool were under construction at the end of 1995 and were due to receive their first prisoners in 1997.

Much controversy has arisen as a result of this shifting of responsibility for corrections away from what many see as essentially and unequivocally a government responsibility. Questions as to whether by resorting to private prisons costs can be reasonably reduced, security maintained, health and safety of inmates and staff assured, and

most importantly recidivism reduced are yet to be settled. In countries where the utilization of the private sector as a criminal justice resource is most developed there have been mixed results, and there are ongoing controversies (Box 5.6). It is clear, however, that this resort to the private sector for criminal justice resources will continue in the near future.

Of course, the question of maintaining proper prison conditions is not one that concerns only the private sector. It applies as much or more to government run facilities as well.

Resources and basic prison conditions

The UNCJS does not collect detailed information on the conditions of prisons throughout the world. It does, however, obtain a rough statistic on the number of prison beds available in a country's prison system. The UN Standard Minimum Rules for the Treatment of Prisoners (see Box 4.4) states that there should be no more than two persons per cell.[5] If one assumes two beds per cell, this means that the UN standard is one prisoner to one bed. The median prisoners to beds was superior to the UN standard. In fact the median number of prisoners to beds was .68. However, the range of prisoners to beds varies from a high of 3.8 prisoners to one bed for Brunei Darussalam, to a low of .10 for Uruguay (Table 5.17).

FIGURE 5.14

Rated growth capacity of private secure adult correctional facilities, 1987-1996

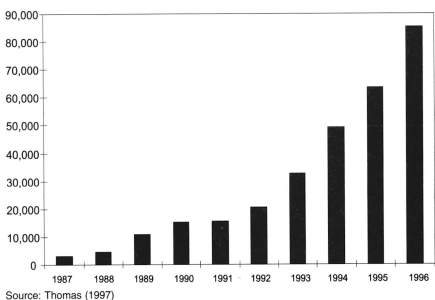

Source: Thomas (1997)

There are, of course, measurement problems. When the ratio of prisoners to beds is examined, one must also recognize that some countries may have recorded a high number of beds available, but they may be located in empty prisons. Some of the states in the USA for example, built new prisons in the early 1990s, only to find that there was insufficient money budgeted to staff them. Inmates were therefore crowded into

TABLE 5.17
Ratio of convicted prisoners to beds, 1994

Brunei Darussalam	3.84
Rep of Korea	2.79
Costa Rica	1.67
Australia	1.43
Belarus	1.29
Singapore	1.10
Hong Kong	1.07
Greece	1.01
Sweden	1.00
Western Samoa	.99
Russian Federation	.88
Kazakhstan	.88
Rep of Moldova	.80
Scotland	.80
Ukraine	.78
Portugal	.78
Hungary	.75
England & Wales	.73
Northern Ireland	.73
Switzerland	.72
Mauritius	.72
Finland	.69
Denmark	.69
Kyrgyzstan	.67
Bulgaria	.64
Slovakia	.63
Japan	.63
Belgium	.63
Marshall Islands	.63
Latvia	.62
Austria	.62
Guyana	.61
Bermuda	.60
Cyprus	.59
Czech Rep	.57
Lithuania	.55
Madagascar	.52
Mexico	.51
Colombia	.50
Chile	.49
El Salvador	.47
Croatia	.47
*"FYRM"	.43
Slovenia	.35
Sao Tome&Principe	.32
Peru	.31
Macau	.22
Uruguay	.10
Kuwait	<.1

*"The Former Yugoslav Republic of Macedonia"
Source: Fifth UNCJS

a smaller number of prisons. Thus the officially measured rate of prisoners to beds could provide a quite different picture of inmate living conditions than the actual conditions. However, which countries could be reporting their data under such conditions is not known.

A perusal of Table 5.17 suggests that the data are consistent for at least some countries. For example, Japan shows a very low prisoner to bed ratio — not surprising given the earlier findings that Japan is a very high and efficient spender on criminal justice. It is impressive that only eight out of 44 countries reported rates of more than one prisoner to a bed.

No difference between industrial and developing countries was found. The median prisoner to bed ratio was .7 for industrial countries, and .73 for developing countries. This is in contrast to the clear differences in expenditure on prisons already reported between industrial and developing countries. And it was seen earlier when reviewing the prisoner to staff ratios that there were marked differences between industrial and developing countries.

International resources of criminal justice

In addition to resources available within nations, there are a number of resources that can be called upon by countries in times of need or assistance. These resources are provided in basically three ways:

- Assistance by NGOs[6]
- Assistance from international organizations such as the United Nations
- Direct assistance of one country by another.

Developing countries and countries in economic transition adapt with difficulty to the challenge of crime as they often struggle with limited resources and inadequately trained staff. However, crime does not stop at the doorsteps of developing countries and countries in transition. As is noted throughout this report, crime has become increasingly global in nature, expanding beyond national borders. Experience shows that, lacking the necessary legal mechanisms and infrastructure, these countries risk becoming safe havens for criminal organizations.

Prison staff training: a resources problem addressed at the international level

The corrections system of each nation is charged with keeping citizens in conditions that deprive them of what would normally be their basic rights. That alone demands a highly trained and competent staff.

To help nations develop their own training programs, the International Scientific and Professional Advisory Council of the United Nations Crime Prevention and Criminal Justice Programme (ISPAC) developed a model training manual as a guide. It is divided into a series of individual sections and contains detailed lesson plans for individual subjects.

The draft manual is organized as follows:

Section I contains a list of the basic training every person who supervises prisoners or detainees should be given. The section provides a brief description of each section, an approximation of the minimum time necessary to teach it and any special notes about the activity.

Section II contains a list of the minimum on-going or annual training necessary for correctional personnel to maintain a minimum standard of proficiency.

Section III contains sample training modules and lesson plans on certain items that should be taught in a consistent manner in all correctional systems. These include certain staff safety and human rights subjects.

Section IV contains information on the training of trainers and on training techniques, including the use of experienced staff as on-the-job trainers and coaches.

Section V contains information on testing mechanisms and processes.

Section VI contains information on specific skills and traits necessary to be an effective correctional officer.

Section VII contains credits and index of sources and references for material used in the manual.

Section VIII contains information on the various UN and other international standards that impact on corrections.

The basic correctional officer training course designed by ISPAC was gathered by a review of more than 100 training programmes conducted in individual correctional institutions, training academies and educational institutions. Though most of the information comes from organizations located in North America and Europe, material from six continents was reviewed. In some cases, where no formal written material was available, ISPAC Resource Committee members interviewed individuals responsible for training or gleaned material from articles. The material in the ISPAC Manual is what was found to be an almost universally agreed upon set of minimum information people working in a correctional facility should have included in their initial training. The time suggested for the training of each course is a compilation of what was gathered from the material reviewed. After ISPAC developed the basic training programme, the material was presented to groups of correctional personnel and trainers at workshops/training sessions in several nations. Their input was used to modify the initial material.

Samples of various manuals are available on the ISPAC Web Site at http://www.ispac-italy.org. Another source of information about the training of prison staff and good prison practice is the work of Penal Reform International (1995).

Source: Hill, Original paper, 1997b.

As a consequence, international organizations such as the United Nations are strongly committed to assisting requesting countries in improving their capacity to cope with crime and to improve their criminal justice system.

The United Nations Development Programme (UNDP), for instance, has mounted a 36 million dollar effort to promote good governance in developing countries. The project is providing resources for free elections, efforts to strengthen the judiciary and the rule of law, parliamentary accountability, and free press. UNDP has set aside 35 percent of its current budget for good governance, up from 14 percent in 1994-1995, out of an annual budget which has averaged 900 million dollars.

The Centre for International Crime Prevention (CICP), the UN body expressly concerned with matters of crime prevention and criminal justice, has developed a number of technical cooperation activities with requesting governments and with the assistance of other agencies such as UNDP. A small staff of under 20 full-time staff and a modest annual operating budget of about 3.5 million dollars has forced the Centre to focus its operational activities. Technical cooperation activities consist mainly of needs assessment and fact-finding, training, development of curricula, workshops, seminars and expert

The anatomy of a technical assistance project: Report from a consultant in the field

The United Nations Crime Prevention and Criminal Justice Division was asked, in conjunction with other UN agencies, to help train corrections staff in Bosnia and Herzegozina and the Republic of Srpska. The prison systems of the Federation and the Republic of Srpska were once part of one united system which had 12 penal institutions located throughout Bosnia and Herzegovina. The young generally fight wars, so many staff were taken into the armies.

The basic approach to training adhered to four principles:

1. The training must be consistent with accepted United Nations and international standards and norms and, due to the provisions of accords reached by both parties to help end the fighting, in line with the Council of Europe Prison Rules.

2. The training must be consistent with the laws of the entities and with the established prison procedures.

3. The training must be practical and be easily incorporated into the ongoing operation of the system after the UN and other international agencies were no longer operating in the area.

4. Though new concepts and principles were to be incorporated, consistent with the changing system of government, those previous activities and programmes that were effective were to be maintained.

The design of the technical assistance was to follow a series of carefully planned steps.

Step 1. Ministers and political leaders (representatives of UN and other international agencies) were visited in order to review the purpose of the project and the proposed method of operation. Methods of recruitment and economic realities impacting the prison system were covered. Every type of facility was visited in all the geographical regions. Local neighbourhoods where inmates and staff were likely to come from were visited in order to better understand the social structure and cultural realities each would bring with them to the prison.

Step 2. Using as a model the *Basic Training Manual for Correctional Workers* (see Box 5.7), a draft training manual was prepared for the two entities. The manual contained 36 detailed lesson plans. The material in the manual incorporated the laws, prison procedures and techniques used in each entity and was modified to reflect the culture, social structure and customs of the geographical region.

Step 3. The second visit was used to meet with personnel at both a ministerial level and, again, with personnel from each of the individual prisons. A translated copy of the Table of Contents and two sample lesson plans were used to go over the initial draft of the manual to insure it was in line with their expectations and that it included what they wanted it to. The draft manual was then translated into the local languages and sent to Justice Department officials of each entity, individual prison personnel, and other UN and international agency personnel who had an interest in the prison system.

Step 4. The third visit included meetings with representatives of each entity to review the manual and to make needed changes. Each entity brought representatives of security, re-socialization programmes and general staff from each prison. Representatives of the ministry also attended. Working both in small groups and as a committee of the whole, the manual was critically evaluated and participants recommended more than 100 changes or additions.

Step 5. Within a month, individualized training aids were produced for each lesson plan. Copies of the final training manual were delivered to each entity. Both an instructor's manual and a student's manual/workbook were developed and they were provided both in hard copy and on computer disk.

Step 6. Consultants worked with the trainers to answer any questions they had on how to teach various subjects and to help them establish the needed documentation to record the training each trainee received.

Step 7. The final stage was to meet with ministry and other officials (including UN and other international agency personnel). The purpose was to handle any final questions and to provide a link between the entities and correctional professionals in other nations to help them keep current on changing techniques and methods. This also was the final step in moving the "expertise" away from the UN and its consultants and into the hands of the prison personnel in each entity.

Source: Edited and abridged from Hill (Original paper, 1997)

---

meetings, expert assistance and advisory services on substantive, legal and administrative issues, and the exchange and dissemination of information.

The CICP is involved with numerous technical cooperation, training and assistance projects which aim to strengthen the capacity of governments to cope with new and emerging criminal threats.

As crime prevention and criminal justice has been included as one of the eight priority areas of the UN for the coming years, it is likely that commensurate resources to address these complex matters will expand.

An example: training prison personnel

The most common type of UN assistance is that of training of personnel. The UN conducts many technical assistance projects which are an important international resource in criminal justice.

In almost any prison in the world, the prison staff, because of the heavy work commitment necessary, has little time for training, whether as initial training or during their careers. This is especially true in developing countries where the resources devoted to training are very small. The need to supply the delicate service in prisons hinders, in fact, in almost all prison administrations, the possibility of organizing the training course on a satisfactory basis.

From a human rights perspective, prison staff training must ultimately be standardized at an international level. It is possible, in fact, to predetermine the training based on international documents concerning the fundamental rights universally recognized in international agreements, on the standard minimum rules, and on the main UN codes of conduct. Of course it is certainly not possible to predetermine from the outside the training on the internal prison regulations and, in general, on all that which concerns the level of the internal legislation.

The analysis of the situation of the country's correctional structure will help considerably in the definition of the contents and methods of teaching. It is important to note that despite some basic homogeneity, the purposes of various correctional systems differ slightly (i.e., some may stress rehabilitation or reintegration back into society as a crime-free person, others might stress punishment for committing acts against society, while still other systems might have victim or state compensation as their major purpose), and that, consequently, a precise analysis of the main purpose of imprisonment must be made by each country prior to developing their training material. Boxes 5.7 and 5.8 outline two technical assistance projects and their impact.

With the many problems experienced by countries in transition, especially those of Eastern Europe, the UN has provide extensive technical assistance in the training of peace-keeping police. The handbook on *United Nations Standards for Peace-Keeping Police* was one outcome of this assistance. In fact, the CICP prepares and disseminates many handbooks and manuals on a variety of topics of concern to many countries, such as computerization in criminal justice, model crime statistics reporting, and many others. These manuals are often used as part of training programs conducted in particular countries as the need and demand arises (Box 5.8).

BOX 5.9

Training police as peacekeepers in Bosnia

Following the signing of the Dayton Accords in December 1995, the UN created the International Police Task Force (IPTF) as part of its civil development effort in Bosnia. The IPTF had two functions: monitoring and training. As monitors, police personnel from 34 countries, wearing distinctive dark blue uniforms with individual country patches on the sleeves and the UN's distinctive sky-blue berets, were deployed to observe Bosnian police operations. Ultimately about 1,200 officers were recruited. Unarmed and without the power to arrest, their function was to give advice, to report violations of the Dayton Accords as well as international human rights, and to assist local forces in assessing their own needs.

As trainers, the IPTF instigated and supervised the development of what was hoped to be an effective democratic police force. It did so by drafting seven principles of democratic policing which, when adopted by the contending factions of the Bosnia government in April 1996, established operational standards for measuring progress toward those principles, and began long-range efforts to develop a strategic plan for the reconstruction of the Bosnian police.

Reconstruction of the Bosnian police as a democratic force was a daunting task. Initially, the Bosnian police lacked everything except personnel. Its physical infrastructure had been destroyed during the bitter ethnic war. Police officers themselves were mostly untrained soldiers demobilized after the war. Indeed, the first task of the IPTF was to reduce a force from approximately 40,000 to a manageable cadre of 10,000.

Reconstruction had to take place in a country devastated by war, where approximately 80 percent of the non-agricultural population was unemployed, perhaps as much as 60 percent of the housing stock had been damaged or destroyed, and much of the civilian population had become refugees. Public transportation was nonexistent. Much of the country was still covered by land mines, most of them unmarked and unrecorded.

Because the Dayton Accords established a governmental system that was without historical precedent and because the three Bosnian factions — Muslims, Croats and Serbs — were committed to it only as a way to stop a cruel war, rather than as a blueprint for a constitutional future, every suggestion by the IPTF for reconstruction of the police system had political implications. This affected fundamental matters such as command centralization or decentralization, political accountability, and the location within the police structure of specialized functions such as border security, training and criminal record-keeping.

Decision-making was also complicated by the presence of multiple actors and interests in Bosnia. Peacemaking, involving the disarming and separation of the warring parties, was the responsibility of Implementation Force (IFOR), which meant NATO and Russia. Although its presence was crucial to the success of policing, it steadfastly refused to engage in policing, such as resettling refugees, capturing war criminals or enforcing law. The UN effort was multilateral, both in being responsible to the Security Council and having multiple contributors. Major donors expected their opinions to be influential, and their nationals, although seconded to the UN, were always sensitive to the national interests they necessarily represented. UN personnel often maintained close relations with their varied embassies in Sarajevo. It has been estimated that there were as many as 200 nongovernmental organizations working in Bosnia, including the Red Cross, the Council for Security and Cooperation in Europe, and numerous private foundations.

In addition to impaired logistics and complicated command, the international police effort in Bosnia was hampered by a lack of information about pre-war traditions, institutions and structures. Undoubtedly this was available in local languages, but it was not available in the major international languages, especially English. Consequently, suggestions were made that could not possibly succeed, that reinvented procedures and structures that already existed, or that simply ignored prior experience.

Until recently peacekeeping meant the insertion of military troops between combatants as a deterrent to further violence. Since the ending of the Cold War, however, peacekeeping has taken on a new character. It now includes policing, which means the maintenance of civil order after military conflict has stopped. Peacekeeping personnel are no longer exclusively military, but are police officers and other criminal justice practitioners sent from around the world to supervise and rebuild shattered criminal justice institutions. This has been the UN's peacekeeping role in Haiti, Bosnia, Kampuchea and Namibia. With the refocusing of international attention from interstate to intrastate conflict, it is clear that peacekeeping as policing will be a growing mission for the international community.

Source: Bayley (Original paper, 1997)

SUMMARY

THINGS IN COMMON	THINGS DIVERSE
• In all countries, police make up the majority of criminal justice personnel.	• Differences among countries in occupational distribution of criminal justice personnel are due to the different roles and definitions of criminal justice occupations, and the political structure of the country.
• The number of police per 100,000 population is increasing in the 1990s. • The number of police is unrelated to the amount of property crime, but may be related to the level of murder.	• Individual countries display great diversity in their levels of policing in relation to their levels of crime. Some countries with high crime rates may report low policing rates (Sweden); countries with low crime rates may report high policing rates (Singapore); countries with low crime rates may report low policing rates (Japan); and countries with high crime rates may report high policing rates (Colombia).
• In all countries, men make up the majority of the criminal justice work force. • There is a clear trend in recent years to employ more women in the criminal justice work force.	• However, a small number of countries has resisted increasing employment of women in the work force, even in those less traditionally male occupations, such as in the courts. • Industrial countries have a higher proportion of women in the criminal justice workforce in all four occupations of police, prosecution, adjudication and corrections.
• The ratio of adult convicted prisoners to adult prison beds varies hardly at all among countries. • Corrections staff per 100,000 pop. has risen 3.5% from 1990 to1994.	• The ratio of prisoners to staff varies considerably. The developing country (non-industrial) ratio of prisoners to staff is 2 to 4 times greater than that of developed (industrial) countries.
• Prisons are a resource that is universally employed. The growth of prisons applies to both industrial and non-industrial countries.	• The range of expenditures on prisons and their operations is vast, from a low of $69 per prisoner to a high of $157,000 per prisoner.
• The number of judges per 100,000 population is increasing in most countries.	• Common law countries have more judges per 100,000 population than do countries with other legal systems.
• Non governmental participation in criminal justice spans the globe, and is a way for countries to take advantage of their natural human and cultural resources.	• Non governmental participation in criminal justice takes on many forms: private security and private prisons, lay judges, common law juries, and customary justice in African nations. Lay participation in criminal justice, though a great tradition in non-industrial countries of Africa, is slowly declining in the West, with the possible exception of the United States.

CHAPTER 6

Firearm abuse and regulation

Contributing author: John Walker

The international community has lately been shocked by horrific incidents involving firearms abuse. Two incidents in Canada in recent years (1989 and 1996) resulted in 14 deaths and nine deaths respectively from firearm wounds. In Japan in November of 1994 a female college student working in a restaurant was shot in the head and killed in a robbery attempt — a violent incident rare in Japan. This was followed in March, 1995, when the Commissioner General of the National Police Agency of Japan was shot and seriously injured on his way to the office.

In spite of widespread international concern about increasing levels of firearm-related harm, prior to 1996 only limited data sources on levels of firearm-related crime and causes of death, including homicides and suicides, were available. Thus, in 1996 the United Nations International Study on Firearm Regulation (UNCICP, 1997) was conducted in response to the request of the Economic and Social Council (ECOSOC Resolution 1995/27, IV A, paragraphs 7 and 8), on the recommendation of the Commission on Crime Prevention and Criminal Justice at its fourth session (Vienna, 30 May-9 June, 1995). The study covers the following topics:

- criminal cases, accidents and suicides in which firearms are involved, including the number of such cases and the number of victims involved, and the status of firearms regulation by the law enforcement authorities;
- the situation with regard to transnational illicit trafficking in firearms;
- national legislation and regulations relevant to firearms regulation; and
- relevant initiatives for firearms regulation at the regional and interregional levels.

An initiative concerning firearm regulation was first discussed at the Ninth United

On March 13, 1996, 16 children and their teacher were killed by a gunman in Dunblane, Scotland. Soon after, on April 28, 1996, a man shot and killed 35 people in Hobart, Australia.

Nations Congress on the Prevention of Crime and the Treatment of Offenders (Cairo, Egypt, May 1995). A resolution was introduced by Japan, co-sponsored by 29 other countries, and then adopted unanimously by all member states.[1] The Congress expressed its concern over the high inci-

In several countries, horrific incidents involving guns may have been instrumental in bringing about stricter systems of firearms regulation.

FIGURE 6.1

Deaths caused by a fatal wound inflicted by a firearm (aggregate estimate comprised of firearm suicides, firearm accidents and firearm homicides; per 100,000 population)

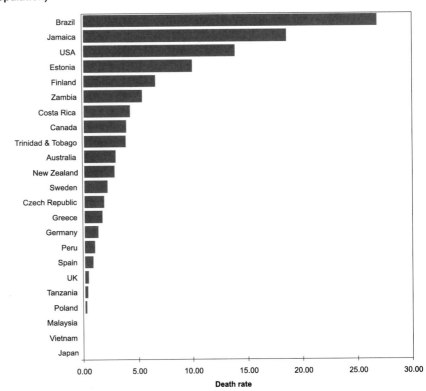

Source: UNFRS, 1997. See Notes to Figures for additional information.

FIGURE 6.2
Suicide deaths caused by firearm wounds (per 100,000 population)

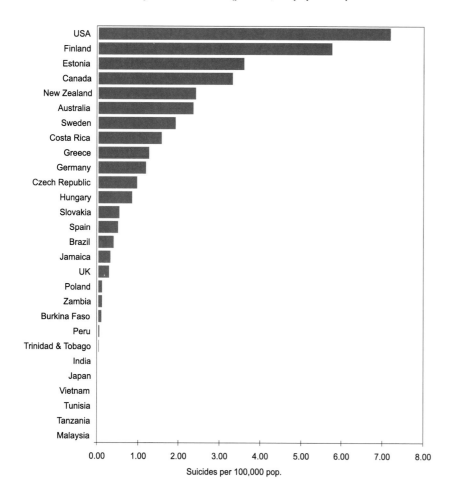

Suicides per 100,000 pop.

Source UNFRS, 1997. See Notes to Figures for additional information.

Europe: Austria, Belarus, Belgium, Czech Republic, Denmark, Estonia, Finland, Germany, Greece, Hungary, Luxembourg, Moldova, Poland, Romania, Russian Federation, Slovakia, Spain, Sweden, UK

Latin America/Caribbean: Argentina, Brazil, Costa Rica, Ecuador, Jamaica, Mexico, Peru, Trinidad & Tobago

North America: Canada, USA

Oceania: Australia, New Zealand, Papua New Guinea

Given the number of countries and the criteria that had been applied to the selection of countries, it should not be assumed that the results of this research study are globally representative. Nonetheless, the study sample can be viewed as a reasonable, international cross section of countries. The estimated total population of responding countries for the year 1995 is 3.7 billion people, which represents 65 percent of the estimated world population of 5.7 billion people. Of these countries, five are classified as least developed, 17 are developing, and 24 are industrial according to the UNDP classification used throughout this report.

Firearm-related death and accident statistics

Civilian owned firearms are identified as causes of death — both in homicides and suicides — in many countries around the world. Wherever firearms are used, accidents causing death and injury also occur. A number of different sources of data are available at the national and supra-national levels, either from police or health agencies, providing national level information on:

- total numbers of deaths caused by firearms;
- number of suicides overall and suicides caused by firearms;
- number of deaths caused by firearms accidents.

Deficiencies in data quality or response rates can essentially be attributed to the fact that, for many countries, detailed statistics on causes of death are either not maintained or not easily available, either by the police or by health authorities. The information presented here represents the most recent annual statistics reported, which differ by country. As in other chapters of this report,

dence of crimes, accidents and suicides involving the use of firearms in society, without appropriate regulation of their possession and storage or training in their use and, *inter alia*, was concerned that the persons most likely to use firearms for criminal activities have easy access to them. The Congress declared an urgent need for effective strategies to ensure the proper regulation of firearms at both the national and transnational levels. Approximately 50 countries were invited to participate in the survey. The project team focused on member states of the Commission on Crime Prevention and Criminal Justice, ensuring that there was an equitable geopolitical representation of countries.[2] A completed survey questionnaire was received from a total of 46 countries, namely:

Africa: Burkina Faso, Guinea, South Africa, Tanzania, Tunisia, Uganda, Zambia

Asia: China, India, Japan, Malaysia, Philippines, Singapore, Vietnam

relevant yearly figures are included in the explanatory tables in the Appendix. Because differences in record-keeping methodologies exist, for both public health and crime statistics, international comparisons must be made cautiously.[3] For example, some countries provide statistics that include deaths caused both by firearms and explosives, without separating the two.

In the 23 countries reporting statistics for the rate of firearm-related death — an aggregate count of suicides, homicides and accidents — figures range from a minimum of 0.07 (Japan) to a maximum of 26.97 (Brazil) per 100,000 (see Figure 6.1). Most countries report firearm-related death rates of five per 100,000 persons or less.

Firearm-related suicide. In the 28 countries reporting statistics for the rates of firearm-related suicide, figures range from a minimum of 0.005 (Malaysia) to 7.23 (United States) per 100,000 (see Figure 6.2). The percentage of suicides committed with firearms ranges from 0.22 (Japan) to 70 percent (Brazil). Firearm suicide is generally high in the Baltic countries and British Commonwealth countries (i.e., Australia, Canada, New Zealand). Firearm use in suicide appears to be extremely limited in a number of countries; Hungary, India, Japan, Malaysia, Poland, Slovakia, Tanzania, Trinidad & Tobago, and United Kingdom report a figure of less than five percent.

Firearm-related accidents. Generally, the firearm accident death rate is significantly lower than that of other firearm harms (i.e., suicide, homicide). In the 27 countries reporting statistics for the rate of firearm-related accidents, figures range from a minimum of 0.00 (Tunisia) to a maximum of 0.75 (Brazil) per 100,000. We can see from Figure 6.3 that three countries stand out clearly with very high firearm accident rates in comparison to other countries. These are Brazil, USA and Trinidad & Tobago.

Firearms and crime

Homicides caused by firearms, and firearm homicides caused by handguns. Thirty-three countries report statistics for the rate of firearm-related homicide; rates range from 0.00 (Singapore) to 26.63 (South Africa) per 100,000 (see Figure 6.4). The percentage of homicides committed with fire-

arms ranges from 0.00 (Singapore) to 88.39 percent (Brazil). Fourteen countries report statistics for the percentage of firearm homicides in which victims were killed by a handgun; figures range from 0.00 (Argentina, New Zealand) to 92 percent (United Kingdom). Nine countries report figures greater than or equal to 50 percent. Few countries could provide data to this degree of specificity.

Victims of firearm homicide killed under circumstances in which there was a domestic or family relationship between the offender and the victim. Twenty countries

FIGURE 6.3
Accident deaths caused by firearm wounds (per 100,000 population)

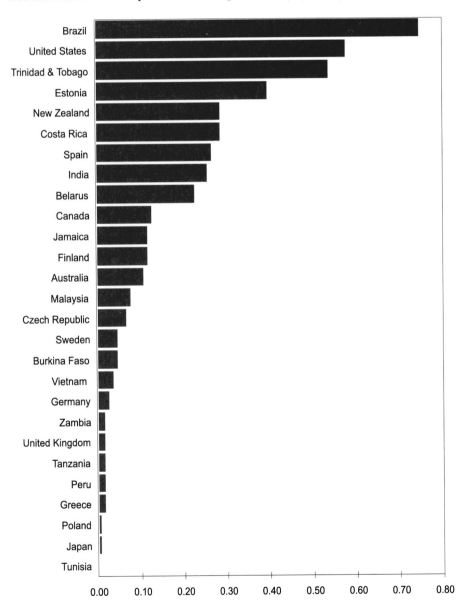

Source: UNFRS, 1997. See Notes to Figures for additional information.

reported statistics for the number of domestic/family homicides involving firearms. The rates of firearm-related homicide range from 0.00 (Burkina Faso, Singapore) to 10.33 (Jamaica) per 100,000. In 16 countries able to provide statistics, the mean percentage of homicides in which there was a domestic or family relation between the offender and victim committed with a firearm was 26.99, ranging from 0.00 (Singapore) to 80 percent (Peru).

Persons wounded by firearms in the course of a criminal act. The UN International Study on Firearm Regulation (UNFRS) reported that 18 countries provided statistics for the rate of firearm-related wounds occurring in the course of a criminal act. Rates range from a minimum of 0.00 (Tunisia) to a maximum of 247.15 (Brazil) per 100,000, with a median rate of 1.2.

Brazil's rate is extremely high in relation to other countries (Table 6.1).

Thefts/robberies involving the use of a firearm. Twenty-five countries reported statistics for the number of thefts/robberies involving a firearm. The rates of thefts/robberies and similar firearm-related thefts/robberies range from a minimum 0.00 (Burkina Faso) to 127.35 (Brazil) per 100,000. The mean percentage of thefts/robberies using firearms was 19.06, ranging from 0.00 (Burkina Faso) to 95 percent (Zambia). Caution is required in the interpretation of these figures, and accompanying notes should be read with care, as some countries reported only robberies (i.e., thefts involving violence or the threat of violence) and others included a broader range of types of theft.

Sexual assaults involving the use of a firearm. Twelve countries reported statistics for the rates of sexual assault involving firearms, ranging from a minimum of 0.00 (Burkina Faso, Estonia, Moldova, Singapore, Slovakia) to 11.67 (Jamaica) per 100,000. The mean percentage of sexual assaults in which a firearm is used was 4.1, ranging from 0.00 (Burkina Faso, Estonia, Moldova, Singapore) to 20 percent (Brazil).

FIGURE 6.4
Homicide victims killed by a firearm (per 100,000 population)

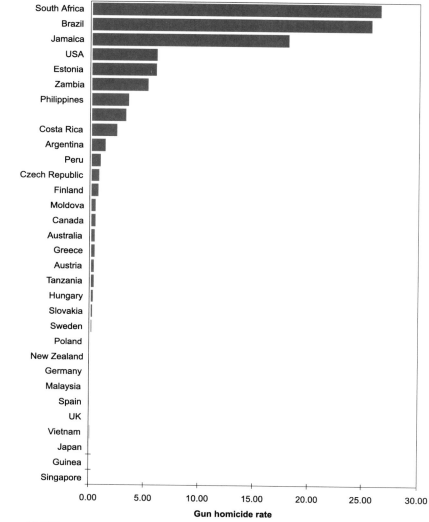

Source: UNFRS, 1997. See Notes to Figures for additional information.

TABLE 6.1
Number of firearm wounds due to criminal acts, 1995

Brazil	393,000
Jamaica	1,308
United Kingdom**	609
Peru*	545
Poland	493
Costa Rica	438
Trinidad & Tobago	196
Guinea	134
Burkina Faso	130
Zambia	116
Vietnam	74
Tanzania	57
Spain	39
Japan	33
Estonia	30
Moldova*	29
Singapore	2

*1996   **1994

Source: UNFRS, 1997. See Notes to Tables for additional tabular data.

GLOBAL REPORT ON CRIME AND JUSTICE

FIGURE 6.5
Percent of crime types in which firearms are used

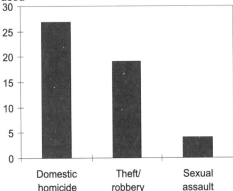

Source: UNFRS, 1997. See Notes to Figures for additional tabular information.

In sum, these data present persuasive evidence that the gun is generally less favoured in committing sexual assault, but is most prevalent in domestic violence and in commission of robbery/theft (Figure 6.5). The use of firearms in domestic violence adds to the already high level of international concern about the many types of domestic abuse prevalent around the world (Box 6.1).

Stolen firearms

The rate of lost and stolen firearms for countries providing such data are reported in Figure 6.6. The actual numbers ranged from one (Zambia) to 17,492 (South Africa). However, to gain a clearer understanding of the international situation, Figure 6.6 converts numbers into rates per 100,000 firearms owned by civilians. Eighteen countries provided statistics for both the number of firearms owned and the number of reports of lost/stolen firearms. We can see that the number of reports of lost and stolen firearms ranges from 2.44 (Japan) to 1,059.16 (Argentina) per 100,000 firearms owned. It is clear that there is considerable variance among responding countries in this regard.

The cross national comparison of firearm ownership is, however, a most complex matter. This is because countries vary widely in how they record firearm ownership, what types of firearms are required to be registered, the extent to which the registration of firearm ownership is required, and if required, how seriously it is enforced. The UNFRS did, however, attempt to measure firearm ownership.

BOX 6.1
Domestic violence around the world

Violence and the threat of violence are concerns for women around the world. This can take many forms, including assaults by spouses and other intimate partners, sexual assault, rape in war, child marriage, dowry-related murder, honor killings, female infanticide, trafficking of women and forced prostitution, and female genital mutilation.[1] These various forms of violence against women are increasingly recognized as important public health and human rights issues because of the grave emotional, physical, social and economic repercussions they have for victims and their children.

Governments in many developed and developing countries worldwide have begun to implement laws, policies and services to assist female victims of violence, to increase public education and awareness, and to reduce the occurrence of these behaviours. One important activity has been to respond to calls from researchers, policy makers, law makers and service providers for reliable data about the prevalence and nature of acts of male violence against women.

A broad range of research has proliferated, including qualitative ethnographic studies of victims, health outcome studies, and evaluations of service delivery, to name a few. Recognizing the limitations of data gathered through state agencies (such as police or health clinics) for acquiring complete and reliable information about acts of violence that are notoriously under-reported, there has emerged a strong preference for surveys using the random selection method of interviewing women in the population. This method reduces the biases inherent in interviewing only women who use certain services, contact certain agencies for help, or who differ from women in the general population in other ways.

Representative sample surveys on violence by men against their wives have recently been conducted in a variety of countries with good results. They include highly industrialized countries like Canada, the United States, Great Britain and Australia, but also developing countries like Nicaragua, Mexico and Cambodia.

Sophisticated techniques of computer-assisted interviewing, interviewer training and random selection have facilitated survey work on very sensitive topics in highly developed countries. Acquiring representative samples of women willing to be interviewed in countries with heightened machismo like Nicaragua and Mexico, or countries emerging from decades of war and pervasive violence such as Cambodia, present special challenges. Through ingenuity and community-building at the local level, and skill building at the international level, researchers in many developing countries have succeeded in documenting a problem that affects significant proportions of women in these countries each year.[2] Based on these surveys the percentage of women reporting sexual or physical violence by their spouse (various surveys and time periods) is as follows:

Papua New Guinea, 1996 .... 62%	Canada, 1993 .... 29%
Nicaragua, 1996 .... 52%	Chile, 1993 .... 26%
Malaysia, 1989 .... 39%	Australia, 1996 .... 23%
Korea, 1992 .... 37%	United States, 1996 .... 21%
Mexico, 1992 .... 33%	Cambodia, 1995 .... 16%
Colombia, 1990 .... 30%	England and Wales, 1996 .... 1%

As is the case with any international crime data, the results of these widely disparate surveys should be interpreted cautiously. There are important differences in methodology among these surveys, required in part by the resources available and in part by the local laws and culture in the countries of the women responding. Accurate interpretation of these statistics requires an understanding of the history, culture, and legal and social systems of each country.[3] In most cases, the definitions of violence are based on a series of behaviourally-specific questions rather than legal or emotional labels (such as "battering" or "rape"). Also, the figures cover violence at any time during a marital relationship, including common-law partners, but some refer only to current spouses, and some only to the one-year period preceding the interview.

Notwithstanding the difficulties in making comparisons cross-culturally, and despite significant cultural differences among these countries, the results of these surveys show that developed and developing countries alike harbour significant levels of male violence against women in the domestic realm. When details about the level of violence are reported in these studies, they indicate that the experience of spousal violence crosses socio-economic lines and is not easily predicted by one or two causal factors.

Source: Johnson (1997). See Notes to Boxes for the widely differing methodologies used. In several instances these figures are not comparable, particularly that of England and Wales.

FIGURE 6.6
Reported lost or stolen firearms, 1995 (per 100,000 firearms owned)

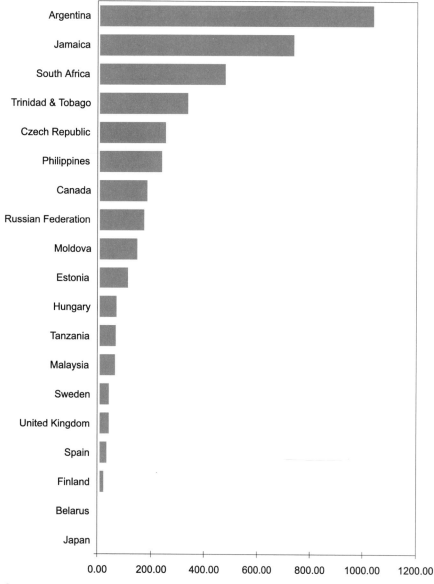

Source: UNFRS, 1997. See Notes to Figures for additional tabular information.

Levels of civilian firearm ownership

All responding countries maintain administrative information on both firearm owners and firearms owned. Most administrative databases on firearms and firearm owners are maintained at a national level, although some are maintained regionally and some even locally. The German and Japanese systems for registering owners are for long guns only (although as Japan totally prohibits the private ownership of handguns, this is to be expected). All others are concerned with owners of both long guns and handguns. In each country for which information was provided, the system contains information on each firearm owned. Many systems are com-

puterized. No country, however, allows public access to the database.

Rates of ownership and of licensing, however measured, vary enormously from country to country (Figure 6.7).

- Almost 14 million firearms licensees were covered in the UNFRS. National rates vary between 0.24 licensees per 1,000 persons (Singapore) and 215 licensees per 1,000 persons (Finland).
- Over 23 million firearm owners were covered, at national rates varying between 0.24 owners per 1000 persons (Singapore) and 122 per 1,000 (Germany).
- Almost 32 million firearms were covered, at national rates of between 0.14 per 1,000 persons (Uganda) and 411 per 1,000 (Finland).
- The percentage of households with at least one firearm varied between 0.007 percent (Malaysia) and 50 percent (Finland).

The rates of firearm ownership are also probably affected by the national regulatory systems operational in individual countries. The extent and effectiveness of these systems vary considerably.

National civilian firearm regulatory systems

There are six main issues involved in assessing national firearm regulation:

- the existence of regulations prohibiting/restricting the *ownership* of firearms by civilians;
- the existence of regulations prohibiting/restricting the *importing* of firearms for civilian use;
- the existence of regulations prohibiting/restricting the *exporting* of firearms for civilian use;
- the existence of regulations restricting the *movement* of firearms by civilians within the country;
- the existence of regulations prohibiting/restricting the *manufacturing* of firearms for civilian markets, and
- the distribution of *legislative authority* for regulation of firearms.

The UNFRS attempted to identify the general practice in each country, given that some countries have regional differences in regard to these six categories. It was found that legislative authority regarding ownership and possession, domestic sale, import and export, and manufacturing for the majority of countries ultimately resides at the national level. Import and export regulation is a national responsibility in all countries, while Australia, China, the Czech Republic, Finland and the United Kingdom share some other regulatory powers regionally. Note that the administration and enforcement of such legislation, however, is often the responsibility of regional governments.

The main findings of the UNFRS on prohibitions and restrictions on civilian ownership of firearms were (see Table 6.2):

- the majority of responding countries prohibit the ownership of certain firearms;
- the majority of responding countries restrict the ownership of all firearms;
- some countries prohibit the ownership of all firearms.

Nine countries have no prohibitions for either handguns or long guns. Poland, Papua New Guinea and Belgium have no prohibitions on handguns. Argentina and Ecuador prohibit the ownership of all long guns, while Belarus, Japan, the Russian Federation and Vietnam prohibit all handguns (with only some officially sanctioned exceptions — for example, the Japanese Olympic sports team). Luxembourg and Malaysia prohibit the ownership of both handguns and long guns.

The main findings on imports, exports and restrictions on movement are:

- the majority of responding countries prohibit the import of some firearms, and restrict the import of all others;
- the majority of responding countries prohibit the export of some firearms, and restrict the export of all others;
- the majority of responding countries restrict the movement of some or all firearms from one part of their country to another.

Only the Czech Republic and Romania indicated that they have neither prohibitions nor restrictions on the importation of firearms. Luxembourg and Malaysia, which maintain a total prohibition on gun ownership, also prohibit the import of all types of firearms, along with Vietnam, Trinidad & Tobago and Peru. Japan prohibits the import of all handguns but only some long guns, while Argentina prohibits the import of all long guns and has no prohibitions on handguns.

In most countries, similar levels of pro-

hibition or restriction are adopted in relation to both the export and import of firearms, although several countries which restrict all imports of firearms do not place the same degree of restriction on their exportation (e.g., Argentina, Brazil and Zambia).

Around two-thirds of responding coun-

FIGURE 6.7
Comparative rates of legal civilian firearm ownership

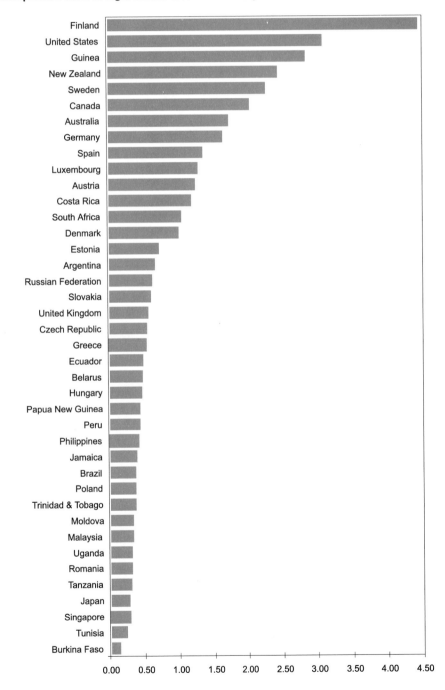

Source: UNFRS, 1997. Please see Notes to Figures for tabular data and an explanation of how this scale was constructed. The various measures of ownership rates presented in the supporting table have been averaged and combined into a single scale. The average ownership level is that of Denmark.

All responding countries except Brazil and Finland place some prohibitions or restrictions on firearm ownership by civilians with a criminal background.

tries restrict the movement of some or all firearms within the country; the remainder impose no restrictions on movement. Few countries differentiate between long guns and handguns in this respect.

The main findings on firearm manufacturing for civilian markets are:

- the majority of responding countries restrict the manufacture of firearms, firearm components and ammunition, and some totally prohibit their manufacture;
- nine responding countries totally prohibit the manufacture of both long guns and handguns: Greece, Luxembourg, Papua New Guinea, Peru, Singapore, Trinidad & Tobago, Tunisia, Uganda and Vietnam; only Moldova and Romania have no restrictions on manufacturing firearms.

Conditions imposed on civilian firearm ownership

The UNFRS also reviewed the procedures that have to be followed for a person to legally own a firearm, and then the nature of the administrative systems used to monitor registered owners and their firearms. The issues raised included:

- the purposes for which firearms ownership and use are permitted;
- the procedures which have to be followed in order to obtain a license to own and use a firearm; and
- the restrictions placed on ownership/use in terms of factors such as age, citizenship, criminal record and mental health.

The majority of responding countries require a license, permit or some other form of official documentation for the purchase of all firearms. No country is without regulatory requirements for the purchase of at least certain firearms.

Certain procedures are common to the purchasing process in a number of countries. The most common requirements for the purchasing process include the following: training certification, fee, background check and the provision of a photo. Also, this process varies by weapon type or class in the majority of responding countries.

For the most responding countries, few prohibitions or restrictions were based on the citizenship of purchaser. On the other hand, all responding countries prohibit the ownership of firearms for civilians on the basis of age, primarily to those under the age of 18, and occasionally for those under age 21 (for age of criminal responsibility, see Box 3.4).

All responding countries except Brazil and Finland place some prohibitions or restrictions on firearm ownership by civilians with a criminal background.

All responding countries except for Finland and Trinidad & Tobago place some prohibitions or restrictions on firearm ownership by civilians with a history of

TABLE 6.2
Countries prohibiting civilian ownership of certain types of firearms

	All Handguns Prohibited	Certain Handguns Prohibited	No Prohibitions on Handguns
All Long Guns Prohibited	Luxembourg Malaysia	Argentina Ecuador	
Certain Long Guns Prohibited	Belarus Japan Russian Federation Vietnam	Australia Austria Brazil Canada Czech Republic Costa Rica Estonia Guinea Hungary India Jamaica Mexico Moldova New Zealand Peru Philippines Singapore Slovakia South Africa Spain Tanzania Trinidad & Tobago United Kingdom USA	Belgium Papua New Guinea Poland
No Prohibitions on Long Guns			Burkina Faso Denmark Finland Germany Romania Sweden Tunisia Uganda Zambia

Source: UNFRS, 1997

mental illness. Most responding countries prohibit the ownership of firearms for civilians with a record of domestic violence.[4] A number of responding countries prohibit the ownership of firearms for civilians for various other reasons (e.g., the ownership of firearms is often prohibited for civilians with a dependency on narcotics or alcohol).

The majority of responding countries permit the possession of firearms for the purposes of hunting, target shooting, collection, protection and private security. The regulations of Vietnam are the most restrictive, allowing ownership only of shotguns for the purpose of hunting.

The majority of responding countries also allow for persons other than the owner to possess a firearm; such possession is usually only permitted if the non-owner is legally permitted ownership of firearms, though occasionally this requirement is waived if the user is under direct supervision of the owner. The majority of responding countries place restrictions on the storage of firearms and ammunition, and firearms must usually be stored in such a way as to preclude immediate use (i.e., unloaded or otherwise disabled; secured in a safe or locked cabinet). The majority of responding countries place restrictions on the transport of firearms (e.g., firearms must often be unloaded for transport). Lastly, the majority of responding countries restrict the carriage of firearms (e.g., often carrying firearms requires a special permit or similar official approval).

Because many countries restrict the sale, export, ownership and manufacture of firearms, the possibility for the infraction of these restrictions is of course created by these restrictions. Furthermore, because the restrictions on ownership and commerce in firearms varies so widely from country to country, smuggling and other illegal dealings in firearms is a problem of international significance.

Firearm smuggling and other illegal dealings

Most responding countries stated that there is some illegal importation of firearms and ammunition (see Table 6.3). A number of countries stated that it is a frequent occurrence. Illegal import of components was less common.

Twenty-five countries described actual incidents of illegal importation of firearms. They range from the simple means of carrying undeclared firearms through customs at airports, or concealing them in motor vehicles crossing land borders, to highly sophisticated and systematic methods involving falsification of documentation and concealment in other commodities. While these survey responses are not necessarily representative of the wider picture around the world, they come from every continent and are highly illustrative of the sophisticated nature of the illegal transport of firearms.

The most common themes in the responses appear to be the widespread availability of firearms either stolen from military sources or surpluses from regional military conflicts, and their illegal importation to support criminal activities of various kinds.

Currently existing known methods include: mail/telephone orders; courier service deliveries; visitors leaving their firearms behind with friends or using them to pay their hunting guides; visiting foreign gun shows and returning with undeclared firearms and parts; domestic manufacture/assembly of restricted and prohibited firearms from imported parts; association with other smuggled commodities such as tobacco, alcohol and drugs; transport in passenger cars, trucks or boats in caches; and hired fishing boats bringing firearms ashore in fishing ports in areas of low coastal surveillance.

Specific "commercial" methods for illegal smuggling identified were short-orders at the manufacturing stage, false documentation and reporting, concealment with other commodities, and diversion from military supplies.

Again, while it cannot be regarded as a representative sample, the survey response shows a wide range of firearms involved in illegal importation, as well as a wide range of manufacturing countries, shipment origins and purposes.

Types of firearms smuggled

The following types of firearms were reported in the UNFRS to be objects of smuggling operations: AK47, "revolvers or semi-automatic pistols of lower end quality," 9mm

Most responding countries prohibit the ownership of firearms for civilians with a record of domestic violence.

pistols, .22 rifles, ball-cartridge firearms, "firing pencils," pistols (TT), automatic guns (PPS), revolvers (Taurus), pistols (Glock), bazookas and hand grenades, illegal night vision equipment, pipe guns, Tokarev-type handguns, sport shotguns and silencers, Browning and Langer pistols and ammunition, 7.62 mm rounds, self-defense sprays (CS, CN, Pepper, etc.), stun guns (electric shock devices), Luger .22 pistols, 5.6 mm Arminus revolvers and ammunition, .35 Super P-35 pistols and ammunition, Para pistols and ammunition, Uzi submachine-guns with silencers, military pistols "models 54 and 59," plastic explosives, electronic detonators, bomb remote control panels, and multi-purpose wireless stations.

Countries reported as the location of manufacturers: Austria, Belgium, Brazil, Russian Federation, China, Czech Republic, France, Germany, Italy, Philippines, Poland and Spain.

Countries or regions reported as shipment origins of illegal imports: Africa, Angola, Argentina, Australia, Burundi, Canada, China, Czech Republic, EU member states, former Yugoslavia, France, Germany, Ghana, Latvia, Mali, Mozambique, Namibia, Nicaragua, Paraguay, Philippines, Poland, Russian Federation, Rwanda, South Indonesia, Thailand, the Baltic states, USA, Zaire and Zimbabwe (see Figure 6.8).

Smuggled firearms are apparently for use in a variety of mostly illegal activities, including terrorism, murder, armed robbery, organized crime, assault, drug offences, illegal re-export, tribal fights, "aiding of rebel elements," insurrection, personal protection, and "guarding farm buildings, crops and cattle." In addition refugees were reported to exchange firearms for food.

By contrast, most responding countries found no evidence to suggest that illegal manufacture of firearms, components or ammunition was common. Fourteen countries described cases of illegal manufacturing of firearms, including instances of illegal modifications of arms, almost all being on a very small scale and for local use rather than export.

Law enforcement officials believe that a high proportion of firearms illegally sold to civilians are sold to individuals who would be unlikely to obtain an approved firearms acquisition certificate. In some cases, firearms dealers themselves are implicated in the illegal sales, through the falsification of documentation. Many of the firearms are subsequently recovered from crimes, including murder, assault with intent to murder, home invasions, robberies and narcotics-related crime. Firearms are frequently stolen from private homes during burglaries in which other types of property are also targeted. For example, in the United Kingdom during 1994 the police recorded over 1,000 offences of burglary and theft in which firearms, other than air weapons, were reported to have been stolen. In a research study *The Theft of Firearms* (Corkery, 1994), it was reported that only 16 percent of stolen firearms were known to have been recovered. Among those, 18 percent were known to have been used in crime before recovery. In a further study by Morrison and O'Donnell (1995), most of a sample of convicted armed robbers said they obtained their firearms through informal criminal contacts.

In the United States between January 1996 and September 30 1996, approximately 2,500 firearms thefts were reported to the Bureau of Alcohol, Tobacco and Firearms (ATF) as having been committed against federal firearms license holders. These thefts involved approximately 12,000 firearms.

TABLE 6.3
Incidence of illegal firearm importation

Frequent	Some	Few	None
Brazil	Australia	Belarus	Luxembourg
Ecuador	Austria	Czech Republic	Moldova
Germany	Belgium	Finland	Singapore
Guinea	Burkina Faso	Greece	Tunisia
India	Canada	New Zealand	Vietnam
Jamaica	China	Peru	
P.N. Guinea	Costa Rica	Philippines	
South Africa	Estonia	Romania	
	Japan	Uganda	
	Malaysia	United States	
	Poland		
	Russian Fed.		
	Spain		
	Tanzania		
	Trinidad & Tobago		
	United Kingdom		
	Zambia		

Source: UNFRS, 1997. See Notes to Figures for additional information.

FIGURE 6.8
Known illegal flows of firearms

Note: These flows should not be interpreted as comprehensive nor even current.
They are indicative of the experiences of responding countries only.

Source: UNFRS, 1997. Note: map is not to scale. The boundaries shown on this map do not imply official endorsement or acceptance by the UN.

Recovering stolen firearms

The majority of countries train law enforcement personnel in the identification of firearms and in the use of firearms tracing technology (where tracing is defined as the systematic tracking of firearms and explosives from manufacturer to purchaser and/or possessor, for the purpose of aiding law enforcement officials in identifying suspects involved in criminal violations, establishing stolen status, and proving ownership). For example, the United States Bureau of Alcohol, Tobacco and Firearms stated that during 1996, there were over 140,000 firearms trace requests received by their National Tracing Center (UNFRS, 1997). Based on information obtained from the National Crime Information Center, law enforcement agencies recovered an estimated 225,000 firearms.

Virtually all countries use some form of firearms or owners registry to trace lost or stolen firearms; this database is usually computerized, either as part of police operations or a special-purpose agency. Several also refer to international agencies such as INTERPOL, or key regional influences such as the US Bureau of Alcohol, Firearms and Tobacco. Most describe weaknesses such as incompleteness of the records and difficulties in obtaining information from other agencies. Perhaps significantly, several of the less developed countries rely only on manufacturers assistance to trace recovered firearms.

The penalties for smuggling and other illegal firearms dealings

Smuggling and other illegal firearms dealings are treated very seriously in all respondent countries. Singapore, which may impose the death penalty, or life imprisonment and caning of not less than six strokes for trafficking in firearms, emerges as having the most severe penalties of the responding countries. Four others — India, Jamaica, Japan and Uganda — can impose life imprisonment for illegal import/export trading,

The status of firearms control in Europe

European countries appear to differ greatly in the extent to which firearms are owned. In several countries (in particular Switzerland and the Nordic countries), a large proportion of households — up to one third — own firearms, usually rifles and shotguns. In other countries, very few households report owning a firearm. Switzerland is a unique case in that the system of military service requires that a large number of citizens keep a government-issued firearm at home, with ammunition.

Europe is a unique region in that it has a system — indeed two systems — for the regional regulation of firearms: the European Convention on the control of the acquisition and possession of firearms by individuals, prepared by the Council of Europe, and the Directive on the control of the acquisition and possession of weapons, prepared by the European Union. Although there are considerable differences from country to country concerning the regulation schemes in force, the effect of these two schemes can be seen, primarily in Western Europe.

The more restrictive national schemes place tight controls on who can manufacture, sell, export and import firearms, and on who can acquire and possess firearms. In almost all countries for which information is available, the authorities have discretion in deciding on licenses; firearm ownership and possession is not a right in these countries.

Some elements appear to be common to almost all schemes of regulation in Europe. There are more or less standard conditions for receiving a license to own and possess a firearm: minimum age, absence of a criminal record, not suffering from a mental illness, and there is a presumption of safe use and lack of danger to the public; some national schemes cite problems with alcohol and drugs as a reason for refusing a license. Furthermore, a firearms license is usually issued for a certain period only and at the discretion of the authorities, and often the applicant must demonstrate a legitimate interest in obtaining the license; licenses are more readily obtainable for target shooting and hunting than for self-defense. Finally, a distinction is made between unlicensed weapons, weapons for which a declaration is sufficient, weapons for which a license is required, and prohibited weapons.

Some national schemes require that an applicant for a firearms license demonstrate that he or she has undergone training in the handling of firearm. Germany requires the passing of an examination.

Europe is, despite its regulatory schemes, a major source and arena for the illicit traffic in firearms. This is due to a number of factors, most notably the dissolution of the (former) USSR and (former) Yugoslavia, with the consequent erosion of government control. Illegal firearms are proliferating throughout Europe and are finding their way into the hands of ordinary offenders, organized criminal gangs, terrorists, quasi-militias and other elements.

Source: Edited from Joutsen (1996)

Bilateral and other international agreements with specific regard to firearms appear to be limited in number and in scope.

while Greece, Slovakia and South Africa may also impose prison sentences over 20 years in serious cases. In all responding countries, the most serious offences can attract a sentence of imprisonment, often of five years or more. Fourteen countries have maximum sentences for smuggling between five and ten years. In only four responding countries was the maximum term below five years. Several countries mentioned the possibility of additional fines and/or confiscation of assets in large scale smuggling cases.

Simple possession of an illegal firearm, or breaches of firearm licensing conditions, generally attracts a maximum penalty of five years imprisonment. For very serious cases (e.g., involving automatic weapons or machine guns) South Africa can impose up to 25 years imprisonment. For relatively minor offences, many countries mention that a proportional fine may be imposed instead of a prison term, at the court's discretion.

International agreements on firearm regulation

Bilateral and other international agreements with specific regard to firearms appear to be limited in number and in scope. The bilateral regulation of trade and movement of firearms appears mostly to fall under more general agreements on the prevention and reduction of crime (for comparison, see Box 9.11 on extradition). More common, however, is for the control of firearms to be included in broad-ranging trade and/or customs agreements, with the emphasis being on informal cooperation between governments rather than official treaties.

The narratives provided by the survey respondents included some examples of international agreements. For example, the response from Greece described bilateral agreements including cooperation in the matters of illegal trade in weapons, spare parts and ammunition, with Albania, Hungary, Russia, Cyprus, Romania, Bulgaria and China.

Poland has signed a number of bilateral agreements on crime prevention, including "offences against life, health, freedom and property, terrorism and international organized criminality, and illegal trafficking in firearm, ammunition, explosives and toxic substances." The general purpose of such agreements is to establish an exchange of information on rules and procedures in arms exports in order to avoid re-export of arms and military technology without knowledge of the country of origin. The countries involved include: Belarus, Bulgaria, Croatia, Cyprus, Czech Republic, Germany, Greece, Hungary, Latvia, Lithuania, Morocco, Romania, Russian Federation, Slovakia, Ukraine and the United States.

The multilateral Wassenaar Arrangement on export controls for conventional arms and dual-use goods and technologies, signed by 33 countries in 1996, is designed to contribute to regional and international security by promoting transparency and greater responsibility with regard to trans-

TABLE 6.4
Countries where significant regulatory changes and/or firearm incidents have occurred recently

Country	Changes regarding ownership	Changes regarding possession	Initiatives to prevent illegal dealings	Initiatives to increase coordination	Initiatives to promote awareness	Recent incidents	Proposals for legislative/ administrative change
Argentina	√					√	
Australia	√	√	√	√	√	√	√
Austria							√
Belarus			√				√
Belgium	√	√				√	
Brazil							√
Burkina Faso	√	√	√	√	√		√
Canada	√	√	√	√	√	√	√
China	√	√	√	√	√	√	√
Costa Rica	√		√	√			
Czech Rep.	√	√				√	
Ecuador						√	
Estonia	√	√	√	√	√	√	
Finland						√	√
Germany			√			√	√
Guinea	√	√	√	√		√	
Hungary	√		√			√	
India			√	√	√	√	√
Jamaica			√	√	√	√	√
Japan	√		√	√	√	√	√
Malaysia			√	√	√		
Mexico	√		√	√	√	√	√
Moldova			√		√	√	√
New Zealand	√	√	√		√	√	√
P.N.G.	√		√		√		
Peru	√		√		√		√
Philippines				√	√	√	√
Poland	√		√	√	√	√	√
Russian Fed.	√	√					
Slovakia		√					
South Africa	√	√	√	√	√	√	√
Spain	√		√	√	√	√	
Sweden	√			√			
Trinidad-Tob.	√		√	√	√	√	√
Uganda			√	√	√		
U.K.	√	√	√	√	√	√	√
U.S.A.	√	√	√	√	√	√	
Vietnam	√			√			
Zambia			√			√	√

Source: UNFRS, 1997

fers of conventional arms and dual use goods and technologies, preventing destabilizing accumulations. It seeks to ensure that transfers of these items do not contribute to the development or enhancement of military capabilities which undermine these goals, complementing existing control measures for weapons of mass destruction and their delivery systems. A secretariat has been created, based in Vienna, to facilitate the future work of the Arrangement, and a work program has been agreed to further its central purposes.

Among the most comprehensive and of-

Twenty-seven countries reported the occurrence of one or more incidents involving criminal use of firearms which have served to raise public concern and to focus the attention of government.

ten quoted multilateral agreements are those amongst the European Community countries, of which the earliest mentioned was the European Convention of Strasbourg of 28 July 1978, which established a European classification of weapons which must be integrated into national legislation. This convention is ratified by Austria, Denmark, Finland, Germany, Iceland, Italy, Luxembourg, the Netherlands, Portugal, Spain and Sweden. The Agreements of Schengen of 14 June 1985 require eventual harmonization of national legislations regulating weapons and ammunition. Belgium, France, Greece, Germany, Luxembourg, Italy, the Netherlands, Portugal and Spain are members of Schengen.

The European Directive of the European Community of 18 June 1991 foresees a classification of weapons, and a harmonization of national legislation and rules to regulate the movement by civilians of firearms from one country to another. The Schengen countries plus the United Kingdom are signatories to this Directive. In the United Kingdom, for example, this Directive was implemented by the passage of the Firearms Act (Amendment) Regulation 1992.

The Directive's provisions were designed to compensate for the abandonment of systematic border controls, in line with the Single Market. The compensatory measures prescribed are:

- partial harmonization to minimum standards of EC states' firearms law based on the classification of firearms into four categories;
- introduction of the European Firearms Pass (EFP) for individuals wishing to take firearms to other EC states, and of the Article 7 authority for those wishing to acquire a category B firearm in another EC state;
- a harmonized community licensing system for commercial and permanent firearms movements (i.e., import and export);
- a Weapons Information Exchange System (WIES) under which a state is to be notified of every commercial/permanent transfer of firearms to its territory from another EC state and the acquisition/possession of firearms by one of its residents in another EC state.

Signatory countries are free to implement tougher legislation, and both Germany and Spain indicated that they have done so (see

Virtually all countries use some form of firearms or owners registry to trace lost or stolen firearms.

Box 6.2).

In African countries, there is a general agreement involving countries in eastern and southern Africa, with the resolve to fight all forms of cross border crime, including control of firearm and ammunition movement within the states of the region. The intended objective of this agreement is to bring under control all firearm components and ammunition and create a peaceful region devoid of illegal firearm and ammunition activities.

On the question of information sharing, both the US Federal Bureau of Alcohol, Tobacco and Firearms and INTERPOL were mentioned by several countries as valuable sources of shared information.

Policy and public education initiatives

While most countries authorize their law enforcement agents to carry firearms (see Box 6.4 and Box 6.5), a number of countries have recently made changes in the legislation or administration regarding civilian ownership of firearms — the majority serving to increase the restrictive nature of the regulatory system (see Table 6.4). Changes included the introduction of various safety training or psychological tests, requiring more detailed information from candidates upon application for ownership, stricter penalties for firearms-related offences and introduction of a licensing requirement where none existed previously. Among certain European countries, legislative changes have been made to conform to the European Commission Weapons Directive.

Australia recently resolved that the ownership of firearms is "not a right but a conditional privilege," introducing the requirement that a genuine reason be provided by the applicant prior to the granting of ownership privileges (see Box 6.3). Canada has introduced comprehensive new legislation, mandating, among other things, the universal licensing of firearm owners, and the registration of all firearms. Papua New Guinea has imposed a total ban on the issuance of new firearms licenses to civilians and described recent changes that introduced heavier fines and longer terms of imprisonment for any breach of the provisions of the act, and introduced identification cards for license holders which was not the practice prior to 1993. The United States introduced a mandatory five day waiting period for purchasing handguns, enabling law enforcement officers to check the background of each purchaser prior to delivery.

Only three changes in legislation or administration were reported that may be classified as less restrictive: Estonia recently repealed a 1993-95 prohibition on foreign ownership and relaxed the storage requirements for single firearms, and in Britain the Firearms (Period of Certificate) Order 1994 extends the life of all firearm and shotgun certificates granted or renewed after 1 January 1995 from three years to five years. Both Estonia and the United Kingdom also reported other changes in legislation or administration of a restrictive nature.

Australia, Canada, Czech Republic, Estonia, South Africa and the United Kingdom have recently installed some form of prohibition on the ownership or possession of fully or semi-automatic (military/paramilitary) firearms and the parts and ammunition for such weapons. In 1992, New Zealand tightened legislative controls on semi-automatic firearms. A prohibition on the possession of short-barreled firearms (including shotguns and some handguns) and of high powered handguns was also reported by some countries. Burkina Faso limited handgun ownership to one per person, and established a maximum calibre of 7.65 mm for civilian use.

In Brazil, Denmark, Finland, India, Jamaica, Poland and South Africa, future comprehensive reform of civilian firearms legislation is pending or is currently being discussed. Of note, Brazil is drafting legislation making the illegal possession and use of firearms a criminal offence; it is not so at present.

Twenty-five countries reported significant recent initiatives to prevent illegal importing, exporting, smuggling or dealings; four countries reported specifically that no such initiatives exist. Initiatives included tightening border controls through tougher customs regulations, employment of technological innovations and trained personnel in the policing of borders and trade centers, and increased cooperation (e.g., bilateral agreements, memorandums of understanding) between governments of neighbouring countries and also with private industry (i.e., freight companies, airlines). In a large number of countries, the penalties for illegal

---

BOX 6.3

Firearms to prevent crime?

The perception that a firearm can be considered an effective crime prevention device is frequent in some countries and many people depend on a firearm for protection. The following table shows that the crime prevention reason for firearm ownership differs from country to country and that this particular reason for ownership does not always vary in correspondence to the rate of ownership in these regions.

Gun ownership (per 100 population) and percent reporting gun ownership for crime prevention purpose, by regions, 1996

	Western Europe	New World	Countries in transition	Africa	Asia	Latin America
gun ownership	17.8	36.5	11.7	6.6	4.1	15.9
c.p. purpose	8.6%	21.8%	28.7%	79.4%	34.6%	65.7%

In the United States 57 percent of the respondents said they owned a weapon for hunting, while another 39 percent said that the purpose of ownership was self-protection and prevention of crime. Although it was possible to provide multiple responses, this proportion of respondents believing in firearms for crime prevention is among the highest reported to the survey.

In countries such as Canada and Finland, the relatively high ownership rates were explained by the respondents with hunting purposes and sometimes the need to be ready to face wild animals which may attack isolated houses. In these countries ownership with the purpose of crime prevention was mentioned in less than one percent of the cases.

In Switzerland, 64 percent of the respondents declared that a firearm was in their household because they belong to the army. This is because the military system in Switzerland envisages that all male citizens remain enrolled in the army until they are 55 years old, thus participating in periodical retraining, and taking care of their own military weapon, which is normally kept in the household. The purpose of crime prevention was mentioned by seven percent of the owners only.

The Federal Republic of Yugoslavia represents a different situation. There is a tradition of ownership of firearms in this country and, furthermore, it has recently emerged from a period of disintegration of the former Yugoslavia. War was spreading all around and contributed to increased feelings of fear, on the one hand, and to more availability of weapons on the other. According to the Yugoslav survey coordinator, the ownership rate of 30 percent is an underestimate of the actual number of weapons existing in Belgrade. The main purpose for ownership reported was prevention of crime, followed by the statement that a weapon has always been in the respondent's family.

In Argentina the large majority of the firearm owners (65 percent) declared that they owned it to protect themselves from crime. This was the case with most of the firearm owners from Latin America, Asia and Africa, although actual rates of ownership varied, the lowest being in Asia and Africa.

The above examples show different patterns of ownership and use of weapons. While it appears that there is no correlation between burglary and firearm ownership as such, a strong correlation was found between both burglary and attempted burglary and ownership with a purpose of crime prevention (.962 and .926 respectively).

Finally, respondents who declared owning a weapon for crime prevention purposes also perceived high chances of burglary within the next 12 months (correlation =.73).

Source: Edited and abridged from Alvazzi del Frate (1997)

---

dealings have been increased.

Twenty-four countries reported the existence of initiatives taken by law enforcement agencies to improve the coordination or overall effectiveness of the enforcement of firearm regulations. Reported initiatives include: introduction or increased use of

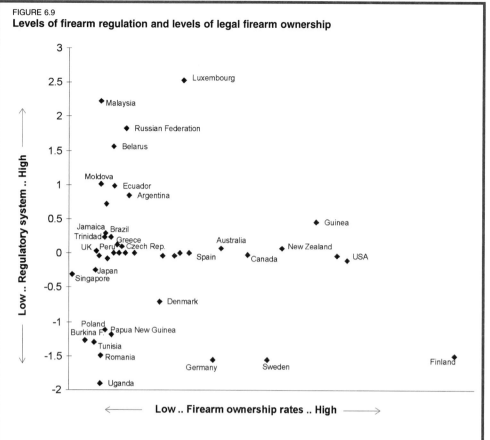

FIGURE 6.9
Levels of firearm regulation and levels of legal firearm ownership

Source: UNFRS, 1997. Note: this scale of firearm regulation is based on the levels of prohibition on firearms (see Table 6.2) and the existence or otherwise of regulations limiting the uses which may be made of firearms (e.g., private security, antique collections etc.) and regulations imposed on the storage and transport of firearms.

computers for data administration and maintenance; closer supervision of firearms dealers; creation of new registers of information on firearms and firearms owners; training of law enforcement officers in ballistics and firearms identification; and cooperation between law enforcement agencies (e.g., employment of services of the United States Bureau of Alcohol, Tobacco and Firearms). Specific firearms units or firearms divisions were created in Canada, Japan and South Africa to improve coordination and effectiveness; Finland plans to establish a Firearm Administration Centre to maintain statistics and coordinate survey and training efforts.

Twenty-one countries reported the existence of initiatives to promote public awareness of firearm regulations and the safe use of firearms. Official governmental initiatives to promote public awareness appear to be few in number. The responses from Australia, Canada and Japan indicate the existence of truly active national campaigns to promote public awareness. South Africa and the

United Kingdom noted the use of amnesty periods to encourage the public to turn in illegally held firearms, which served to promote awareness. In Mexico, teachers have been provided with material for inclusion in school curricula in order to prevent the illegal use, possession and carrying of firearms. Various rifle associations or firearm control lobby groups were also cited as sources of public awareness campaigns.

Twenty-seven countries reported the occurrence of one or more incidents involving criminal use of firearms which have served to raise public concern and to focus the attention of government.

Evaluating civilian firearm regulation

While it is difficult to summarize the exhaustive collection of information that the UN survey has produced, one of the key questions is to what extent does the regulation of firearms actually work to reduce the level of firearm-related problems. In order to address this question it is first necessary to define what is meant by greater and lesser levels of regulation. Next, it is necessary to define and measure what is meant by firearm-related problems, and finally, somehow, it is necessary to compare the two to determine if, in fact, any relationship exists.

None of these steps is, in fact, easy. The UNFRS has provided a great deal of data, but there are missing responses to many questions. As in so many other areas of public policy, certain forms of regulation may be effective in some circumstances, ineffective in some, and completely unnecessary in others. For example, as Figure 6.9 shows, most high firearm ownership countries are developed countries, and while the UN survey suggests that many developed countries have come to believe that tough firearm regulation is necessary to reduce the harms caused by firearms, similar regulation may have little or no impact in low income countries where low incomes make legitimate firearm ownership rare. Several of those

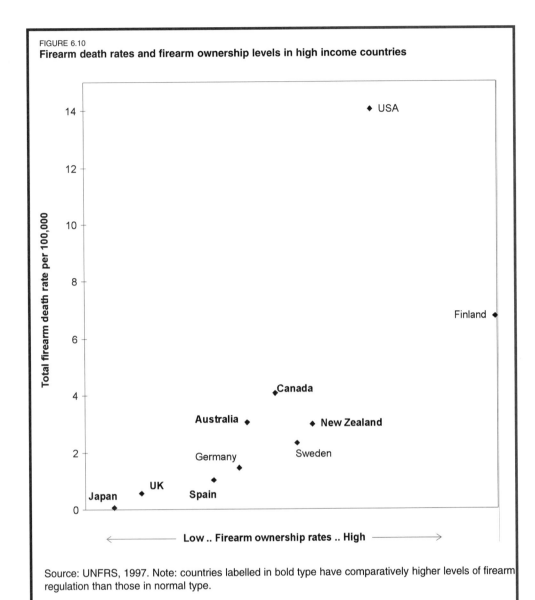

FIGURE 6.10
Firearm death rates and firearm ownership levels in high income countries

Total firearm death rate per 100,000

◆ USA

Finland ◆

◆Canada

Australia ◆

◆ **New Zealand**

Germany

Sweden

UK

Japan   **Spain**

Low .. **Firearm ownership rates** .. High

Source: UNFRS, 1997. Note: countries labelled in bold type have comparatively higher levels of firearm regulation than those in normal type.

...regulation may have little or no impact in low income countries where low incomes make legitimate firearm ownership rare.

countries with lower per capita incomes which have nevertheless chosen a relatively restrictive firearm regulation system appear to have done so as a result of recent major incidents (Trinidad), or major political change (e.g., Belarus, Moldova, Russian Federation).

Similarly, as the International Crime Victim Surveys show, firearm ownership levels are generally higher in rural areas (particularly those where hunting is a common way of life) than in large cities, and hence high rates of firearm ownership also may be a consequence of low levels of urbanization rather than low levels of regulation. One cannot therefore compare levels and types of regulation without taking such factors into account. A sophisticated statistical analysis

of the data is out of the question. However, the following analysis may provide some interesting insights.

Figure 6.10 compares the rates of total firearm death (from Figure 6.1) with the scale of civilian firearm ownership (as described in Figure 6.7) for high income countries. While there appears to be a clear increase in firearm related death rates with higher rates of firearm ownership, there is also some support for the idea that, in developed countries, tougher regulatory systems may help to reduce firearm related deaths. Because of the small number of countries in this chart, it cannot necessarily be regarded as conclusive. Researchers have pointed out also that reducing ownership rates may not necessarily reduce firearm deaths, as other means can be used for both suicides and homicides.

If the *proportion* of homicides committed with firearms is analyzed instead of the rate, there is a positive correlation for the low income countries as well as for the high income ones. So, as firearm ownership rises in low income countries, the proportion of homicides committed using a firearm increases without necessarily increasing the overall homicide rate.

These graphs support the contention that, in countries where average incomes are sufficiently high to support a high rate of firearm ownership, restrictive regulatory systems can be successful in reducing firearm related homicides.

Restrictive systems are not however a *necessary* condition for low firearm homicide rates, since some responding countries in the less restrictive categories also had low firearm homicide rates. Restrictive systems are, equally, not a *sufficient* condition for low homicide rates since both Belarus and Trinidad have low ownership rates concurrent with high homicide rates.

To conclude, we can say that the data obtained from the UNFRS have allowed us to explore a number of interesting and potentially policy relevant aspects of firearms abuse and regulation from an international perspective. As sources of data are improved, it may be possible to reach more definite and extensive conclusions in order to identify appropriate policy responses to the problems posed by improper use of firearms. It is clear that policy alternatives concerning firearms use and abuse at both the national and international levels will benefit greatly as more member countries provide information to the UNFRS.[5]

BOX 6.4

Firearms for law enforcement?

An examination of the *International Factbook of Criminal Justice Systems* reveals that most countries authorize their law enforcement agents to carry firearms. Only a small number of countries do not generally permit their police officers to carry firearms (e.g., England and Wales and Sri Lanka). Of those countries that do authorize their police officers to carry firearms, the rules regulating the use and firing of the firearms vary widely. A few countries (e.g., Singapore, Poland, Russia, Bulgaria, Ukraine and China) explicitly mention that firing a firearm is authorized and regulated by the law and then list criteria that allow a firearm to be used. For example, in Bulgaria the police may use firearms only in self-defense, or if they are attacked or threatened by others with firearms, or in arrest situations, or to prevent a suspect, who has been warned, from fleeing. Police may never use firearms against pregnant women or children.

However, most countries that authorize their law enforcement agents to carry firearms do not explicitly list what factors would allow firearms to be used. Some countries (e.g., Romania) just list circumstances that would permit the use of force to be used without distinguishing firearms from other weapons. For instance, Slovenia, which arms its police officers with various firearms, allows its police officers to use "force" as a last resort to restore peace and order. Deadly force may be used for self-defense in extreme cases. There are no explicit guidelines that state exactly when the use of firearms is permitted.

Thus, while many countries have detailed rules and regulations which govern the use of firearms by civilians, no such comparable criteria exist with regard to official government use of firearms. The United Nations, however, has established guidelines for the use of weapons by law enforcement officials (Box 6.5).

Source: Freilich (Original paper, 1997), from the *International Factbook of Criminal Justice Systems*

BOX 6.5

Basic Principles on the Use of Force and Firearms by Law Enforcement Officials

General provisions. Governments and law enforcement agencies shall adopt and implement rules and regulations on the use of force and firearms against persons by law enforcement officials and keep associated ethical issues constantly under review.

Development and deployment of non-lethal incapacitating weapons should be carefully evaluated to minimize the risk of endangering uninvolved persons, and use should be carefully controlled.

In carrying out their duty, law enforcement officials shall as far as possible apply nonviolent means before resorting to force and firearms. They may use force and firearms only if other means remain ineffective or without any promise of achieving the intended result.

Whenever lawful use of force and firearms is unavoidable, law enforcement officials shall:

a) Exercise restraint and act in proportion to the seriousness of the offence and the legitimate objective;

b) Minimize damage and injury, and respect and preserve human life;

c) Ensure that assistance and medical aid are rendered to any injured or affected persons at the earliest possible moment;

d) Ensure that relatives or close friends of the injured or affected person are notified at the earliest moment.

Where injury or death is caused by the use of force and firearms by law enforcement officials, they shall report the incident promptly to their superior.

Governments shall ensure that arbitrary or abusive use of force and firearms by law enforcement officials **is** punished as a criminal offence under their law.

Exceptional circumstances, such as internal political instability or any other public emergency, may not be invoked to justify any departure from these basic principles.

Special provisions. Law enforcement officials shall not use firearms against persons except in self-defense or defense of others against the imminent threat of death or serious injury, to prevent the perpetration of a particularly serious crime involving grave threat to life, to arrest a person presenting such a danger and resisting their authority, or to prevent his or her escape, and only when less extreme means are insufficient to achieve these objectives.

In the circumstances provided for under the above principle, law enforcement officials shall identify themselves as such and give a clear warning of their intent to use firearms, with sufficient time for the warning to be observed, unless to do so would unduly place the law enforcement officials at risk or would create a risk of death or serious harm to other persons, or would be clearly inappropriate or pointless in the circumstances of the incident.

Rules and regulations should include guidelines that:

a) Specify the circumstances under which law enforcement officials are authorized to carry firearms and prescribe the types of firearms and ammunition permitted;

b) Ensure that firearms are used only in appropriate circumstances and in a manner likely to decrease the risk of unnecessary harm;

c) Prohibit the use of firearms and ammunition that cause unwarranted injury or present an unwarranted risk;

d) Regulate the control, storage and issuing of firearms, including procedures for ensuring that law enforcement officials are accountable for the firearms and ammunition issued to them;

e) Provide for warnings to be given, if appropriate, when firearms are to be discharged;

f) Provide for a system of reporting whenever law enforcement officials use firearms in the performance of their duty.

Qualifications, training and counselling. All law enforcement officials are to be selected by proper screening procedures, have appropriate moral, psychological and physical qualities for effective exercise of their functions and receive continuous professional training. Their continued fitness to perform should be subject to periodic review.

Law enforcement officials are to be trained and tested in accord with appropriate proficiency standards in the use of force. Those required to carry firearms should be authorized to do so only upon completion of special training in their use.

Questions of police ethics and human rights shall be given special attention in the training of law enforcement officials, including the peaceful settlement of conflicts, the understanding of crowd behaviour, and methods of persuasion, negotiation and mediation. Law enforcement agencies should review their training programmes and operational procedures in the light of particular incidents.

Reporting and review procedures. Effective reporting and review procedures are to be established for all incidents where use of force or firearms causes injury or death or when firearms are used in the performance of law enforcement. An effective review process is to be available and independent administrative or prosecutorial authorities are to be in a position to exercise jurisdiction in appropriate circumstances. In cases of death and serious injury or other grave consequences, a detailed report shall be sent promptly to the competent authorities.

Persons affected by the use of force and firearms or their legal representatives shall have access to an independent process, including a judicial process. In the event of the death of such persons, this provision shall apply to their dependents.

Superior officers are to be held responsible if they know, or should have known, that law enforcement officials under their command are resorting, or have resorted, to unlawful use of force and firearms, and they did not take all measures in their power to prevent, suppress or report such use.

No criminal or disciplinary sanction is to be imposed on law enforcement officials who, in compliance with the Code of Conduct for Law Enforcement Officials and these basic principles, refuse to carry out an order to use force or firearms, or who report such use by other officials.

Obedience to superior orders shall be no defense if law enforcement officials knew that an order to use force and firearms resulting in the death or serious injury of a person was manifestly unlawful and had a reasonable opportunity to refuse to follow it. In any case, responsibility also rests on the superiors who gave the unlawful orders.

Source: Adopted by the Eighth United Nations Congress on Prevention of Crime and Treatment of Offenders, Havana, 27 August-7 September 1990; report produced by the Secretariat (UN pub. sales no. E.91.IV.2), Chap. I, Sect. B.

SUMMARY

THINGS IN COMMON	THINGS DIVERSE
• In general, countries that have higher firearm ownership rates also have higher firearm related death rates, including homicide rates.	• Some countries have strong regulation and high firearm related homicides. Others have low regulation and low firearm related homicides.
• Firearms are commonly used in domestic disputes where fatalities occur.	• The rate of firearm related death (accidents, homicides and suicides) varies widely throughout the world.
• In contrast, firearms are hardly ever used in the commission of sexual assault.	
• There is broad international concern for the control and regulation of firearms.	• Countries differ widely in how they translate concern about firearm ownership into public policy and legislation.
• Most countries prohibit the ownership of firearms for civilians with a criminal record or a record of domestic violence.	
• Horrific incidents around the world have heightened awareness of firearms and their danger.	• A few countries have been spurred to legislate firearm control as a result of firearm tragedies.
• Most countries use some form of registry in order to trace lost or stolen firearms.	• The rate of firearm ownership around the world varies from less than one percent of households owning a firearm to as many as 50% of all households.
• The majority of countries prohibit the import and export of some firearms.	• Bilateral or international agreements concerning the regulation of firearms trade tend to be limited in scope.
• The majority of countries regulate the manufacture of firearms and their components.	• Countries in post-conflict situations often become the source of large numbers of illicit weapons, and become a centre of illegal smuggling of weapons to criminals in neighbouring countries
• Prison, usually for a term of more than five years, is the most common punishment for the smuggling of firearms.	
• A common reason given for owning a handgun is for protection against crime.	

CHAPTER 7

Drugs and drug control

Contributing author: Graham Farrell

The influence of drugs and drug control upon crime and criminal justice

In the global picture of crime and justice, it is difficult to overstate the role of drugs and drug control. They are arguably the domain in which the most widespread, substantial and influential changes have taken place in recent years. Two key factors account for these changes. The first is the substantial overall increase in illicit drug manufacture, trafficking and consumption, leading to commensurate increases in related crime problems. The second is the increased emphasis upon illicit drug-related crime by law enforcement agencies (resulting in increased reporting and detection), often accompanied by an increased certitude and severity of formal criminal sanctions. When combined, these factors have seen illicit drug-related crimes increase disproportionately in the last two decades in both absolute and relative terms when compared to most crime-related phenomena.

This chapter has two main aims. The first is to delineate the relationship between drugs, drug control, crime and criminal justice. This includes examining how the current global picture of drugs and drug control has been greatly influenced by the many different aspects of increasing globalization and international interdependence that have occurred in recent years. The second aim is to build an empirical picture of the influence of drugs and drug control upon crime and criminal justice, at the global level and using specific country or regional case studies of interest.

Drug-related crime

Drug-related crime is difficult to clearly define. This is because of the many different aspects of the illicit drug trade and the overlapping issues of offenders and criminal organizations producing crime and victimization that can be directly or indirectly related to drugs in different ways. Drugs and drug control are issues that are directly entwined with many of the other issues discussed in this report. Victims and victimization, guns and gun control are often drug-related. Persons charged with drug-related offences, or who have committed offences in some way related to the drug trade, are brought to justice and the resources of criminal justice systems are expended upon them. In addition, the resources of health and social services and other areas of public and private policy are also increasingly focused upon drug-related crime and drug-related issues. The end result is that a clear typology of drug-related crime does not and, perhaps, should not exist. The list presented as Table 7.1 could have used alternative categorizations, and is not intended as an exhaustive inventory of the drugs-crime nexus.

The global spread of illicit drugs and related crime

While it is commonly asserted that illicit drug use has spread far and wide across the globe, there are relatively few solid indicators of which drugs arrived where and when. Individual accounts or anecdotal evidence are often all that is available. A simple but useful indicator of the speed and extent of the expansion of different illicit drugs across the world is a count of the number of countries seizing different types of drugs. Although this measure is imperfect, as with almost all indicators related to illicit drugs and crime, it is reasonably good because national law enforcement agencies typically record drug seizures for their own opera-

Drug-related crimes have increased disproportionately in the last two decades when compared to other crime-related phenomena.

TABLE 7.1
Drug related crimes

Direct violations of drug laws

◊ Cultivation

◊ Production

◊ Manufacturing

◊ Trafficking (of drugs and precursors)

◊ Distribution and dealing

⇒ in drug street markets

⇒ in bars and clubs

⇒ in private distribution networks (e.g. parties, "dial-a-dope" delivery networks)

◊ Consumption

◊ Violation of drug hindrance laws: possession of drug paraphernalia

---

Violation of other laws, to facilitate the illicit drug trade

◊ Diversion of precursors produced legally

◊ Diversion of drugs produced legally

◊ Theft of drugs produced legally (from producers and distributors, pharmacists, doctors, hospitals)

◊ Illicit production of precursors

Violence to facilitate the illicit drug trade

◊ Violence related to cultivation and manufacture: threats by traffickers upon farmers, by traffickers upon criminal justice and law enforcement officials, between rival manufacturing and trafficking groups,

◊ Violence related to trafficking: (e.g. to keep secrecy among workers; to eliminate competitors; to eliminate law enforcement)

◊ Gang-related violence ("turf" wars)

◊ Drug-market related violence (robbery, assault and threats)

Corruption of officials by the drug trade

◊ Corruption of law enforcement officials

◊ Corruption of other criminal justice officials

◊ Corruption of other government officials

Acquisitive crime to get money for drugs

◊ Property Crime

⇒ burglary (residential and commercial)

⇒ shoplifting

⇒ other theft

⇒ acquisitive car crimes

⇒ fraud and embezzlement (e.g. credit card crimes)

◊ Violent crime

⇒ street robbery

⇒ commercial robbery

◊ Other crime

⇒ drug dealing

⇒ prostitution

Crime attracted to and facilitated by drug markets

◊ Robbery

◊ Assaults and threats

◊ Prostitution

Pharmacological effects of drugs upon crime

◊ Violence precipitated by some drugs in some instances (e.g. cocaine, amphetamine-type stimulants)

◊ Violence reduced by some drugs in some instances (e.g. cannabis, heroin, tranquilizers)

◊ Impaired driving and machine operating ability increases risk of accidents

---

tional purposes. In contrast, there are relatively few countries that keep centralized and internationally comparable records of illicit drug consumption. At the very least, the count of countries where law enforcement has made drug seizures shows the *minimum* number of countries affected by specific illicit drugs. While there are variations in the number of countries in the world as well as in law enforcement recording and reporting practices, the consistency of the trends and the fact that they concord with other more fragmentary indicators and evidence, suggests that the trends in the global spread of illicit drugs may be fairly representative of actual events.

Since the arrival of illicit drugs in a new country or market drives up the level of other types of drug-related crime, notably those related to drug markets and acquisitive crime to fund drug use, then Figure 7.1 is also a valuable indirect indicator of how other types of drug crime will have increased in global coverage.

Cannabis has long been and remains the most prevalent global illicit drug according to this indicator. Estimates of global consumption, discussed later in this chapter, suggest that sedatives are the most prevalent illicit drug in terms of the global population (rather than countries), but otherwise conform roughly to the indicator used here.[1] By 1994, around two-thirds of countries in the world had been affected by cannabis. However, the gap between cannabis and the next two most prevalent illicit drugs — heroin and cocaine — has narrowed rapidly. This measure of the global spread of illicit drugs supports indirect evidence of increases in the volume of heroin and cocaine production and consumption, and suggests about half of all countries are affected by these illicit drugs in the 1990s.

Though having similar levels of coverage in 1980, opium trafficking has spread at a much slower pace than heroin, as might be expected since it is a more unwieldy substance. This suggests that the patterns and trends of Figure 7.1 are not artifacts created by changes in the reporting or recording practices of law enforcement activity. Both LSD and sedatives (mainly benzodiazapine, tranquilizers and barbiturates) appear to have been stable or falling in their global coverage. The global coverage of amphetamine-type stimulants (ATS) increased by about half in the decade between the mid 1980s and 1990s, though they have still infiltrated far fewer countries than cannabis, heroin and cocaine. About a quarter of countries worldwide are affected by amphetamine-type stimulants. There is ample reason to believe that the spread of ATS, including MDMA (methylenedioxymethamphetamine, known as "ecstasy") and its derivatives, will continue. As stimulants, they are cheaper per "hit" and have a far longer duration than cocaine. They have a relatively benign public image, and since the drugs are often produced in developed countries, the distributors experience lower barriers to market entry than drugs from other regions (Pietschmann,1997).

The current geographical origins of many types of illicit drugs are relatively well known and in many cases are used to focus drug control efforts. Cannabis can be, and is, grown virtually anywhere. However, it is concentrated in some areas of Africa and Asia from which trafficking takes place to more lucrative markets, particularly Europe. A large part of the cannabis consumption in North America is believed to derive from domestic growth, supplemented by trafficking from Latin America. In industrialized countries there is increasing use of indoor cannabis plots to avoid detection, and of hydroponic techniques to speed growth times. Heroin is produced in and around the main areas in which the opium poppy is grown, in Southeast and Southwest Asia, and increasingly in the Andean region of South America. From there it is transported to the major markets in Europe and North America by an increasingly diverse number of routes and methods. Some of these are discussed in more detail later. Coca leaf and paste are produced from coca bush cultivation primarily in the Andean countries of Peru, Bolivia and Colombia, though the manufacture of cocaine is disproportionately concentrated in Colombia. From here it is trafficked to North America overland and by air and ship through a range of routes including the Caribbean basin. Cocaine shipments to Europe increased rapidly as the North American market became increasingly saturated in the mid 1980s. Trafficking is by air and sea shipments and couriers, sometimes via transit states as far off as

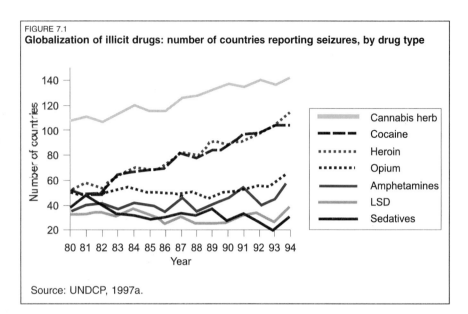

FIGURE 7.1
Globalization of illicit drugs: number of countries reporting seizures, by drug type

Source: UNDCP, 1997a.

Africa if the use of a different apparent origin of the shipment is believed to reduce the risks involved.

The number of types of illicit drugs has increased and their nature diversified in recent years. The increased manufacture and production of the amphetamine-type stimulants and synthetic and designer drugs during the last decade has been located primarily in industrialized countries. This is a marked geographical change from that of the "traditional" illicit drugs of choice. It also means that trafficking often originates within the confines of the geographical and economic boundaries of the consumer market. Thus, drug control law enforcement must be more diverse than sealing the borders.

Increased global coverage by the illicit drug traffic has been supported by increased volume of traffic in those areas where it already existed. Seizures of different drug types around the world (Figures 7.2 and 7.3) suggest strong increases in the volume of illicit drug trafficking. Global illicit production of different drugs has increased greatly over the last decade according to available estimates. Estimated potential illicit opiate production more than trebled in the decade prior to 1996, mainly in the late 1980s. About a third of this is estimated to be consumed as

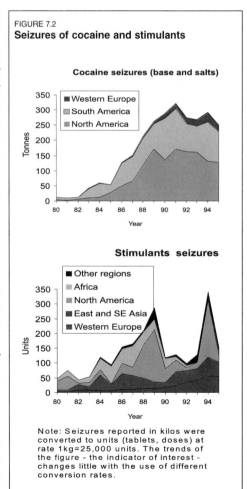

FIGURE 7.2
Seizures of cocaine and stimulants

Source: United Nations (1997b). See Notes to Figures for tabular data.

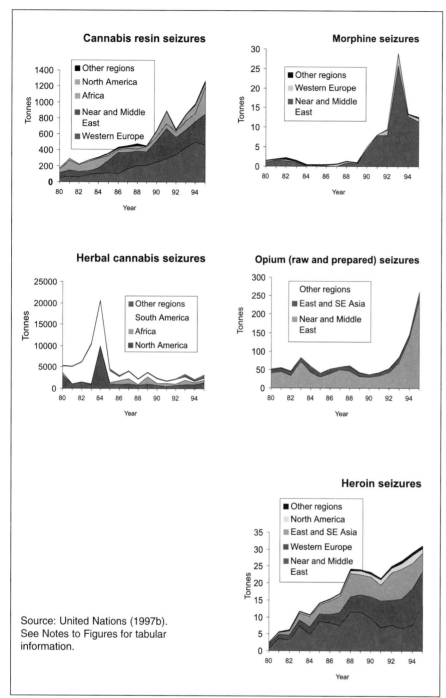

FIGURE 7.3
Seizures of cannabis and opiates

Cannabis resin seizures

Legend: Other regions, North America, Africa, Near and Middle East, Western Europe

Morphine seizures

Legend: Other regions, Western Europe, Near and Middle East

Herbal cannabis seizures

Legend: Other regions, South America, Africa, North America

Opium (raw and prepared) seizures

Legend: Other regions, East and SE Asia, Near and Middle East

Heroin seizures

Legend: Other regions, North America, East and SE Asia, Western Europe, Near and Middle East

Source: United Nations (1997b).
See Notes to Figures for tabular information.

opium, so that potential annual heroin manufacture has been around 300 tons for much of the 1990s. About 1,000 tons of cocaine could have been produced from estimated coca production in 1996, the figure having remained relatively stable during the 1990s after doubling in the second half of the 1980s. These estimates are based on ground and satellite surveys of crops from which the drugs are produced. While being imperfect estimates, they remain firmer than esti-

mates of potential production of most other illicit drugs, for which there are relatively few indicators. Seizures provide some imperfect evidence of trends in production, although the trend in production is probably less steep since seizures also reflect increased law enforcement emphasis.

"Globalization" and illicit drug-related crime

Many seemingly innocuous factors related to technological, socio-economic and political change and advancement have inadvertently provided opportunities for expansion of the illicit drug industry. In turn, expansion of the illicit drug industry drives the range of drug-related crime (Box 7.5). Rapid economic development and the process of globalization in the late twentieth century mean that the world in which drug trafficking now takes place is quite different from that in which many of the global drug control systems were developed. Though the relative contributions of different factors cannot be quantified with methodological accuracy, some of them are listed in Table 7.2 in relation to the different stages and aspects of the illicit drug industry.

At the same time as increasing opportunities become available to the illicit drug industry, technological developments have also improved law enforcement efforts in many ways. Those related to the illicit drug industry include remote sensing satellite technology, infrared and x-ray detection equipment, computing, communications, weaponry and transportation. The role of drug control and other law enforcement in preventing drug-related crimes is discussed in the following sections.

International drug control treaties

An increasing number of countries around the world are bound by the international drug control conventions of 1961 (as amended by the 1972 Protocol), 1971 and 1988. By 1997, over two-thirds of countries in the world were bound by the 1988 UN drug control convention. The number and proportion of countries signing and ratifying the treaties is increasing (Figure 7.4), which in time will reduce the number of havens left open to different aspects of the

TABLE 7.2
Globalization and illicit drug-related crime

Crop cultivation
Technological change
Agricultural improvements (fertilizers; land management techniques; hydroponics; selective breeding). *Effect:* Increased yield per hectare
Clandestine manufacturing
Technological change
◊ Improved scientific equipment, techniques, availability of know-how (e.g. via Internet) and training. *Effect:* More and better equipment; more and better chemists, improved extraction techniques.
◊ Chemical product diversification (medical and non-medical). *Effect:* New psychoactive drugs entering the market.   *Socio-economic and political change*
◊ Increased licit trade in precursors. *Effect:* More sources from which precursors can be obtained or diverted.
Diversion of drugs from licit channels
Socio-economic and political change
◊ Increased global availability of drugs for medical purposes. *Effect:* Increased opportunity for diversion to illicit channels.
Trafficking
Technological change
◊ Cheaper and faster transportation.
◊ Postal system distribution improvements. *Effect:* facilitator to trafficking.   *Socio-economic and political change*
◊ General trade liberalization particularly in developing countries. *Effect:* Increased trade provides cover and markets for trafficking.
◊ Increased shipping (trade and tourism)
◊ Increased aviation (trade and tourism)
◊ Trade agreements (EC, NAFTA). *Effect:* Increased flow of licit trade and reduced border checks both reduce risk to trafficking.
◊ Political integration (Eastern Europe and CIS, South Africa). *Effect:* Increased trade to new markets gives increased routes, cover and markets for traffickers.
◊ Increased migration. *Effect:* Family networks, ties and cover for trafficking and distribution networks
Demand for drugs
Technological change
◊ Increased media communications. *Effect:* Increased awareness of and demand for illicit drugs   *Socio-economic and political change*
◊ Increased public awareness of risks and harms associated with illicit drug use. *Effect:* Loss of credibility of zero-tolerance approaches.
◊ General political shift towards freedom of individual choice in most public policy arenas. *Effect:* Apparent contrast with drug policy.
Money laundering
Technological change
◊ Improved computer technology. *Effect:* Facilitates rapid and large cash transactions in layering stages of money laundering   *Socio-economic and political change*
◊ Increased global communications and financial transactions. *Effect:* Provides increased opportunity and cover for international money laundering.

Source: Keh and Farrell, 1997.

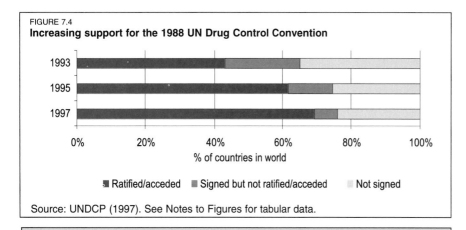

FIGURE 7.4
Increasing support for the 1988 UN Drug Control Convention

% of countries in world

■ Ratified/acceded ■ Signed but not ratified/acceded □ Not signed

Source: UNDCP (1997). See Notes to Figures for tabular data.

BOX 7.1

Economic development, drug control and illicit drug crop cultivation

Sustainable economic growth in developing countries is an aim of national and international economic and social policies, irrespective of the goals of drug policy. However, the notion that the level of economic development of a country is the principal or root cause of illicit cultivation and of the extraction and production of drugs is often overstated: there are many developing countries where illicit cultivation does not occur; there are developed countries where extensive illicit cultivation occurs; and the illicit production of many synthetic drugs has increased in many developed as opposed to developing countries. In addition, while economic growth may indirectly benefit health, education and other areas of social policy, including drug policy, it can also facilitate different aspects of illicit drug trafficking.

There appear to be two mechanisms whereby economic growth can promote drug control. The first would be activated if state control over previously isolated areas of cultivation is increased by improved road and communications infrastructure, which facilitates law enforcement and eradication. The second would be activated if economic growth creates competitive economic opportunities that restrain others from taking up illicit cultivation, or induce migration of labor and farmers away from areas of illicit cultivation. If the relinquished hectarage and the possible gap in the illicit market are not offset by the activities of other farmers, then a reduction in illicit hectarage is the result.

From a drug control perspective, the diversionary aspect of general economic growth is subject to constraints of economic competitiveness, which are determined by the higher and more flexible prices of illicit crops and the subsequent higher income that can be earned by farmers. In negotiating arrangements for reducing illicit cultivation, general economic assistance carries less weight than targeted alternative development assistance. While there is evidence that economic depression in the licit sector may cause workers to migrate to illicit cultivation, as in Bolivia during the 1980s, there is less evidence that economic boom in the licit sector causes a reversal when illicit cultivation has already been adopted. In the Andean region, the workers who are tempted to migrate back to licit economic activity would be more likely to be the migrant subsidiary workers of the coca trade — leaf pickers and stompers — instead of farmers who had become accustomed to more regular and higher income, and had made some investment in the area. Consequently, economic growth would be expected to have only a marginal indirect impact upon the area of illicit cultivation. Once farmers are established in coca bush cultivation, the long-term effect of substantial migration to urban areas might be primarily to increase the marginal cost of seasonal migrant labor in the production process.

The human development index (HDI) gives a crude cross-national comparative indicator of development. Of the major countries of illicit cultivation, Colombia, Mexico, Thailand and the United States are rated at a high level of human development; member states of the CIS in central Asia are rated at either a high or a medium level of human development; Bolivia, China, Jamaica, Lebanon, Morocco, Peru, South Africa and Vietnam are rated at a medium level of human development; and Afghanistan, India, Lao People's Democratic Republic, Myanmar and Pakistan are rated at a low level of human development. The HDI is a composite indicator which cannot reflect variation in the levels of development within a country. However, at the national level, there is no significant correlation between the HDI index, HDI rankings or gross domestic product, on the one hand, and the total or crop-specific area of illicit cultivation, on the other, even when only countries with significant areas of illicit cultivation are considered.

Source: Abridged from UNDCP (1996b)

---

illegal drug trade.

In essence, the conventions set broad parameters within which countries define their national drug control laws. The United Nations International Drug Control Programme (UNDCP) provides technical and legal assistance to implement the treaties, monitor and evaluate their effectiveness, and assist national drug control law enforcement agencies. The International Narcotics Control Board (INCB) works primarily to implement, monitor and evaluate those parts of the treaties pertaining to the licit international trade in drugs and precursors. The most comprehensive and accessible account of the international drug control treaties, illicit drug use and types of drug control is given in the recent World Drug Report (UNDCP, 1997b). The present chapter of this report concentrates upon crime and criminal justice in relation to drugs and drug control.

Global illicit consumption

Global estimates of illicit drug consumption have recently been developed. This is a landmark in drug-related research. The estimates developed by UNDCP were based upon a basket of indicators including local and national user surveys, rapid assessments based on other indicators including health and social service indicators, health-related data, law enforcement seizure and arrest data, and other available sources.

UNDCP estimates that, in any one year, slightly over one in 1,000 persons illicitly use heroin or other opiates, and two in 1,000 illicitly use cocaine. Illicit use of cannabis is estimated to be 17 times more prevalent than that of opiates, and over ten times as prevalent as that of cocaine. Sedatives (primarily barbiturates, benzodiazapines and methaqualone) are estimated to be the most prevalent illicitly used drugs, although the estimate is believed to be high. The illicit use of sedatives is concentrated in South American countries as well as countries in southern Africa.

Figures 7.5 and 7.6 present the same global consumption data in different ways. A small fraction of the world's population uses drugs illicitly (Figure 7.5). Prevalence rates of illicit drug use are, overall, characterized by the similarity of the rarity of use. However, when illicit drug users only are examined (Figure 7.6), variation in the prevalence of illicit drug use is apparent between drug types.

Of those persons who use illicit drugs in any given year, a proportion experience drug use that is problematic in terms of health, and a proportion become addicted, with the proportions varying by drug type and circumstances. Of those who become addicted, some will cease drug use at varying rates, and a proportion will turn to crime to fund their continued drug use. These addicts will also cease drug use over time, at a relatively low annual rate, and a "maturing out" of illicit drug use is apparent.

The types of crime committed by drug addicts are listed in Table 7.1, and are primarily acquisitive, including street robbery, burglary, fraud, prostitution, theft and other robberies. The proportion of overall crimes that these persons commit is not known (although see Box 7.4 for one study), but it is commonly believed to be disproportionate to the level of illicit drug users involved in crime.

Preventing drug-related crime

The strategies and tactics used to tackle drug-related crimes are as varied as the types of drug-related crime themselves. Measures to tackle drug supply at different levels, to tackle demand, and measures to prevent crime by drug users are the main categories. Strategies can overlap to differing de-

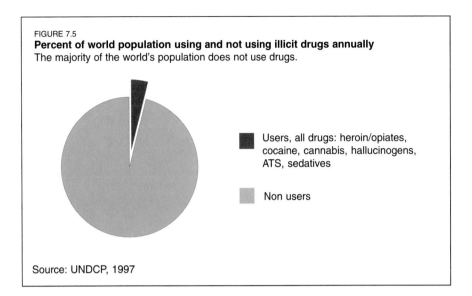

FIGURE 7.5
Percent of world population using and not using illicit drugs annually
The majority of the world's population does not use drugs.

■ Users, all drugs: heroin/opiates, cocaine, cannabis, hallucinogens, ATS, sedatives

▨ Non users

Source: UNDCP, 1997

grees, so that measures to reduce demand and to treat drug users are assumed, if successful, to reduce drug-related crime indirectly.

Supply reduction efforts to reduce illicit cultivation in some producer countries range from eradication to crop substitution and alternative development programs. A recent global review of these efforts concluded that some success can be achieved in reduction of narcotic crop production (Box 7.2). However, the balloon effect, in which reduction in one area has resulted in increases in other areas, has thus far prevented production at the global level from declining in absolute terms.

The effectiveness of drug demand reduction efforts has been recently reviewed at the global level (UNDCP, 1996c). The re-

More and more countries around the world are bound by international drug control conventions.

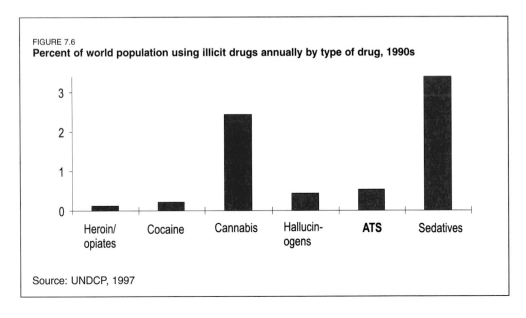

FIGURE 7.6
Percent of world population using illicit drugs annually by type of drug, 1990s

Source: UNDCP, 1997

Global review of crop eradication, crop substitution and alternative development

A recent United Nations global review of efforts to reduce illicit crop cultivation concluded that "only two instances of absolute reductions in illicit cultivation have been recorded at the national level, in Thailand and Turkey, both cases occurring prior to severalfold increases in global cultivation of opium poppy. The reduction in opium poppy cultivation in Turkey in the 1970s coincided with increases in the opium supply from Mexico (for the heroin market in the United States) and from parts of Asia. The reductions in opium cultivation in Thailand have been more than accounted for at the global level by increases in neighbouring Myanmar. Hence, even the impact of those cases of absolute reduction at the national level was greatly diluted at the global level. The other major supplier that came close to absolute reductions at the national level due to intense eradication efforts was Mexico in the mid 1970s, which by the 1990s had substantial areas of illicit cultivation. Large increases in illicit cultivation in Afghanistan may partly account for reductions in illicit cultivation in Pakistan due to decreased competitiveness. At both the national and the global level, the adaptability of the illicit market caused by robust economic incentives is reflected in the 'balloon effect,' or the displacement and replacement of illicit crops, and has served to reduce the overall efficacy of measures to reduce illicit cultivation. Nevertheless, successful efforts at the national level to eliminate or reduce illicit cultivation may have helped to curb the rise in total global production.

Of the five Asian countries where opium cultivation was tackled by United Nations alternative development efforts, partial reductions were recorded, in some instances, in three. In Thailand, the major reductions occurred before the bulk of United Nations drug control investment in alternative development was made, and decreases in Pakistan were largely due to law enforcement and reduced opium prices, although alternative development may have sustained reduction efforts in some areas. Of two programmatic activities in the Lao People's Democratic Republic, one recorded no reductions in illicit cultivation, and the other recorded some decrease within the context of general reductions for the country as a whole. There is no evidence that the progressive limited reduction of coca bush within project areas in Latin America have had an effect in the aggregate. In Lebanon, illicit cultivation of opium poppy and cannabis plant was reduced in the 1990s through eradication, whereas alternative development efforts in Morocco did not reduce cannabis cultivation" (UNDCP, 1996b:28).

Source: Edited and abridged from UNDCP (1996b:28).

view of demand reduction programs suggested that primary prevention (preventing initiation) and secondary prevention (treatment and rehabilitation of drug users) were being widely supplemented by tertiary prevention (controlling health risks to users). Other treatment efforts such as medical prescription of hard drugs to users, with a view to removing the economic incentive to commit crimes to fund drug use, operate in different countries and contexts with varying degrees of success. Prescription has long been known as the "British model" after the presumed origins and continued use of the medical model in that country, a practice that still exists within the general policy of harm reduction in the UK. A recent experiment in prescription that utilized a scientific evaluation method is detailed in Box 7.3.

The extensive demand reduction program known as DARE (Drug Abuse Resistance Education) undertaken initially in schools in the United States and now elsewhere, was comprehensively evaluated in the 1990s. The evaluators concluded that "The effectiveness of the program has yet to be demonstrated ...DARE had no statistically significant main effects on drug use behaviors and had few effects on attitudes or beliefs about drugs" (Rosenbaum *et al.*, 1994: 10). A review of drug education in over 100 schools in Scotland, UK, drew similar conclusions, noting that "A series of process measures suggested that pupils have some positive perceptions of drug education. However, the outcome measures showed little impact of drug education" (Coggans *et al.*, 1996: 12). In keeping the focus of this chapter upon crime and criminal justice, however, the full range of demand reduction and treatment measures will not be reviewed here. As well, most credible evaluations of demand reduction programs have been conducted in industrialized countries, giving the current state of knowledge a rather ethnocentric appearance.

Efforts to prevent crime by drug users pose a different problem to drug supply reduction. In large part, the prevention of the criminal act is subsumed under the general topic of crime prevention and is discussed in Chapter 8. Demand reduction and treatment of drug users have the indirect aims of preventing drug crime, since it is assumed that acquisitive crime will cease if drug use ceases.

Law enforcement efforts to reduce drug supply indirectly influence drug consumption. This is because, as with any economic product, a reduction in supply causes a rise in the price. When the price of a product increases, then the number of persons willing to purchase it decreases. Therefore, when law enforcement efforts reduce supply, the principal mechanism by which consumption is reduced is the price mechanism of the illicit retail market. Variations in the impact, depending upon the change in demand that a change in price produces, are discussed later in relation to organized crime. Trends in the retail prices of heroin and cocaine in the two major illicit consumer markets — Europe and North America — are shown in Figure 7.7. The price of each drug has fallen dramatically in both major markets. This is primarily because, despite increased law enforcement interception efforts, the supply of drugs to consumers has greatly increased as a result of increased illicit production and manufacture. The retail price trends give a composite indicator of the overall impact of drug control law enforcement efforts, and the rate at which law enforcement efforts intercept illicit drugs is reviewed in the following section.

The law enforcement "10 percent rule" is dead — the global interception rate (GIR)

A universal rule of thumb long used by almost all involved in drug control was that ten percent of illicit drugs were assumed to be intercepted and seized by law enforcement agencies. It was based on hearsay and anecdotes, but may have served as a heuristic aid to thinking about trafficking and enforcement. Debunking the myth utilized a conceptually simple methodology: comparing annual estimates of total drug production for opium and cocaine to the total amount of those drugs seized around the world. From this, a crude measure of the proportion intercepted — termed the global interception rate (GIR) — can be estimated. As a measure, the GIR is subject to the limitations of the global estimates of production and seizures (Reuter, 1994, 1996), and the rate presented here uses midpoint estimates that lie within a possible range for each year. However, if errors in production and seizures are reasonably consistent over time, then trends in the GIR can be assumed to be fairly accurate representations of what has occurred. The global interception rate of opiates and cocaine between 1980 and 1994 is shown in Figure 7.8.

The global rate of interception of cocaine appeared to change markedly during the 1980s, but less so for opiates. While the rate of interception of cocaine was far below that of opiates in the early 1980s, it rose rapidly during the mid 1980s to reach levels almost double those of the opiates during the 1990s. These changes may well reflect the increased emphasis upon the interception of cocaine by law enforcement efforts across the Americas.

Like most indicators related to crime and criminal justice, the GIR is partial. It gives

Crime reduction through medical treatment of drug users in Switzerland

Crime by drug users has long been known to be a problem. The prescription of drugs to addicted users to reduce their economic incentive to commit crime was long known as the "British model" of drug control because of its apparent origins and continued use in that country. More recently, while maintaining a clear drug control policy against the use of illicit drugs, in 1993 the government of Switzerland began an experimental prescription programme in several cities with the aim of reducing the volume of crime committed by addicted hard drug users.

The relationship between drug use and crime is difficult to determine in terms of whether or not one causes the other. However, it is clear that drug addicts often account for a disproportionate amount of street robberies and other acquisitive crimes. A baseline study using three years of data from the Zurich police department in Switzerland suggested that over two-thirds of street robbery, between a third and a half of burglary, 20 to 40 percent of other types of robbery (e.g., of bank and commercial establishments) and almost ten percent of vehicle thefts, were consistently committed by drug addicts (the 1995 data are shown in the accompanying Figure).

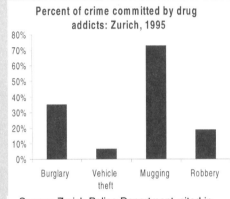

Percent of crime committed by drug addicts: Zurich, 1995

Source: Zurich Police Department, cited in

A programme of measures was introduced to reduce the economic incentive of drug addicts to commit drug crime. The main components of the treatment were the prescription of heroin and the provision of employment opportunities. Persons were eligible for the program if they had a proven history of heroin addiction and of failure in other drug treatment programs. Rates of offending of programme participants were measured before and after treatment, and compared to those of a control group (a comparable group of addicts who were not given the same treatment), using interviews, police arrest records and conviction records. The programme evaluation showed that the volume of crime committed by the drug addicts had reduced substantially in many but not all instances. Both the number of offenders and the number of criminal offences decreased by about 60 percent during the first six months of treatment. Court convictions dropped among those treated, and there were positive indicators of greater social integration. Illicit heroin and cocaine use decreased rapidly, whereas benzodiazapine use decreased slowly and cannabis consumption hardly declined at all. A minority of patients continued to use cocaine (five percent) and benzodiazapine (nine percent). The Netherlands is beginning a similar test of these methods of reducing crime and drug use by addicts, and the methods are being considered by other governments. It is clear that there remains a need for further research to determine if these findings would be replicated under different circumstances.

Sources: Edited and abridged from Killias and Uchtenhagen (1996); Killias and Rabasa (1997); Uchtenhagen (1997).

a "success rate" in terms of interception, and suggests that positive gains have been made. Yet as a partial indicator it does not reflect the fact that while interception rates have been stable or increasing, the amount of opiates and cocaine passing through the enforcement net has increased. This is because illicit production and manufacture has increased several fold. The net result is that despite the improved performance of law enforcement, far larger amounts of illicit

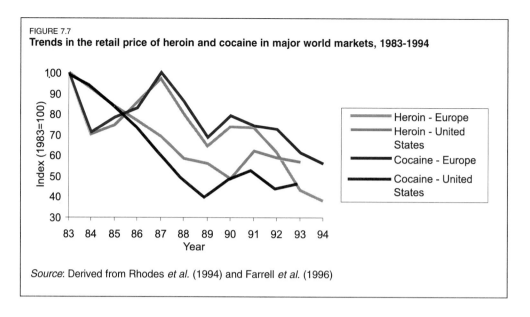

FIGURE 7.7

Trends in the retail price of heroin and cocaine in major world markets, 1983-1994

Heroin - Europe
Heroin - United States
Cocaine - Europe
Cocaine - United States

Source: Derived from Rhodes *et al.* (1994) and Farrell *et al.* (1996)

The rapid replacement and substitution of one criminal organization with a new or altered one, makes preventing drug-related organized crime a daunting task.

opiates and cocaine are being consumed than was the case in previous years.

Organized crime and drug control

A range of organized crime groups is involved in the illicit manufacture, diversion, trafficking and distribution of drugs. Organized crime is most simply defined as any ongoing criminal enterprise. Organizations vary widely in geographical scope and level of organization, from small loose-knit networks — "disorganized crime" (Reuter, 1983) — which may include organizations and gangs in a particular town or city, through national organizations perhaps with international connections, to regional, international and transnational criminal organizations. The most infamous organized criminal organizations involved in the illicit drug trade include the Colombian Cartels, Chi-

nese Triads, (Italian) Mafia or La Cosa Nostra, Jamaican posses, Japanese Jakuza, Mexican Cartels, Nigerian criminal organizations, and Russian organized crime. Within countries there are organized groups involved in distribution, such as the motorcycle gangs on the west coast of the USA, street gangs and other loosely organized or small scale distribution networks.

Defining characteristics suggested for the large scale organizations include their large size, wealth, political power and enforcement resistance. The main driving force for organized crime is economic profit, but each organization differs in structure and scope, and whether or not it is involved in a range of legal or criminal activity in addition to the illicit drug trade: not all organized crime is drug-related, and not all of the illicit drug trade is organized.

The activities of organized crime are influenced by law enforcement activities aimed directly at the organizations but also by enforcement aimed at other aspects of the illicit drug trade. Increased general drug enforcement, as opposed to that targeted at organized crime, can give organized crime groups and networks a relative competitive advantage, because their capacity for violence and corruption helps protect them against ordinary enforcement actions.[2] Similarly, assuming that increased en-

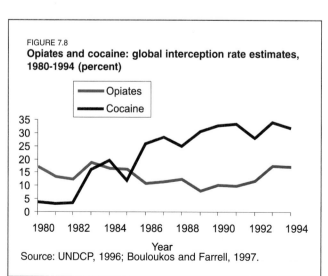

FIGURE 7.8

Opiates and cocaine: global interception rate estimates, 1980-1994 (percent)

Opiates
Cocaine

Source: UNDCP, 1996; Bouloukos and Farrell, 1997.

forcement succeeds in raising the costs of drug dealing and, consequently, the retail price of the drugs, consumption will tend to decrease. However, if prices rise and consumption increases less, in percentage terms, than prices rise, then the overall money to be made in the illicit drug market will, ironically, increase. The key determinant is the change in consumption brought on by a change in retail price, known as the price elasticity of demand. Since some drugs, particularly the more addictive ones, exhibit low elasticity (demand falls less than proportionately compared to a price rise), then increased drug law enforcement can reduce drug consumption while at the same time increasing the profit of organized criminal groups.

Different types of drug law enforcement have different effects. Retail-level enforcement will have most effect upon the number and aggressiveness of retail drug dealers rather than on drug prices. This causes a drop in consumption, due to increased time and risk in making a purchase, producing an unambiguous reduction in the profit of organized crime (Kleiman, 1994).

There has been a range of drug control enforcement crackdowns against organized crime involved in the drug trade. The arrest and incarceration of many key figures in the Colombian cartels was heralded as a significant success. However, the economic incentives of the illicit drug trade serve to make organized trafficking extremely durable. The rapid replacement and substitution or of one organization with a new one or an altered one, make preventing drug-related organized crime a different prospect than much crime prevention work. While many types of crime, even organized crime, can be prevented without much displacement, the prospect is more daunting when it comes to organized crime involved in the illicit drug trade (Bouloukos and Farrell, 1996).

Possession and trafficking offences in the global criminal justice system

Of the different types of crime related to illicit drugs, those that can most clearly be traced in relation to the operations of criminal justice systems are drug trafficking and possession cases. These are more often recorded as separate crime categories, whereas

---

BOX 7.4

Drug using offenders detected during problem-oriented policing initiative

Two case studies of prolific offenders committing crime to fund drug use, who were detected as part of an anti-burglary initiative in West Yorkshire in the United Kingdom in 1996, are presented below. They demonstrate how such prolific offenders, while the exception rather than the norm for drug addicts, can influence the crime rate of a local area. They also show how drugs can be part of "everyday" experiences of crime and policing: a fascinating aspect is that the problem-oriented policing initiative during which they were apprehended was aimed at reducing burglary rather than illicit drug use. The detail related to remand on bail in the second case study also illustrates some of the complexities of what happens when such cases enter the criminal justice system. The public housing estate in which the case studies are set was low level, primarily semi-detached housing built in the 1940s. The details were provided by police constables Gareth Walker and Ian Poskitt, and Sergeant Paul Dixon, the officers involved in the local initiative.

Case Study 1 — Drug-Using Offender. The identified burglar was a male, age 20, who lived in the target area. He was known to have a heroin habit with an estimated cost of £100 (US$ 160) per day. He had been linked to over 100 offences of burglary between 1992 and 1995, of which there was sufficient evidence to pursue about half.

The first stage in the detection process was based on local knowledge of the officer involved and was to realize the connection between the release of the known offender from a custodial sentence and the emergence of a pattern of bogus official-type burglaries (burglary artifice) on the housing estate. Further research by the police officers involved showed that there were similarities between the type of victims chosen (elderly) whose descriptions of the perpetrator were similar. These facts, combined with the relative rarity of burglary artifice as a *modus operandi*, made it statistically likely that these burglaries were committed by the same offender or group of offenders. The key second step of the investigation was to examine the record of previous activities of the suspect. Some of the recently victimized targets had been previously burgled by the same offender. Combined with the fact that the pattern emerged once the known offender had been released, this presented good circumstantial evidence.

The nail in the coffin was to tie the offender irrevocably to the location of at least some of the burglaries. The third step of the process therefore involved taking fingerprints from the houses of recent burglary victims for comparison to the fingerprints of the suspect. These were on record due to his previous convictions. It resulted in three positive identifications. The offender was known to use several addresses, at which he was sought and arrested. For the three offences he received a custodial sentence of five years. The pattern of burglaries on the estate came to an abrupt end, and the offender involved indicated his involvement in an additional 150 offences.

Case Study 2 — Drug-Using Offender. This male was also resident on the estate and had a known heroin and amphetamine habit estimated to cost £100-£150 (US$ 160-240) per day. Between May 1994 and December 1995, this offender had been arrested 17 times. Upon this occasion he was arrested leaving the scene of a handbag snatch in an area where a series of similar offences had occurred.

One of the key elements of this case was that he was remanded in custody. This can be a critical element in terms of crime prevention. Many offenders commit crimes while remanded on bail awaiting trial. One of the initiatives undertaken by West Yorkshire police was to place an emphasis upon remand in custody, thereby removing a spell during which offenders are known to often be particularly prolific. An alleged loophole (from one perspective) of the British criminal justice system is that offences committed while on bail are not usually considered at trial, particularly if they are of the same type as the trial offence. The offender can ask for these offences to be "taken into consideration" upon sentencing, but they rarely have a significant effect upon sentence. This can make bail criminogenic, and act as a reward to offending on bail. In this case, the case presented by the police was sufficiently strong to ensure the offender was remanded in custody.

At trial, this offender was given a three and a half year prison sentence. When interviewed in prison, he admitted to 150 additional crimes, primarily in the project area and surrounding beats.

Source: West Yorkshire Police. Adapted and abridged from Applied Criminology Group (1997).

BOX 7.5
Regional case study — the influence of commerce and trade upon drug trafficking in Europe

While it is well known that increases in global trade, commerce and related economic, technological and political changes have inadvertently facilitated the illicit drug trade (see Table 7.2), the influence of variation in trade and commerce at any one point in time is less intuitively obvious. How do variations in trade and commerce between countries influence patterns of drug trafficking and consumption at any one point in time? This is important because it is possible that variations in illicit drug use and market conditions are sometimes attributed to variations in national drug policies when they would be more properly related to extraneous economic conditions. The relationship between spatial variations in trade, commerce and illicit drug trafficking and use can be examined by comparing patterns in both at a single point in time.

The volume of commercial trade passing through different European seaports varies widely. If the level of drug trafficking per shipment unit is the same, then this would produce variations in drug trafficking equal to the variation in shipments. The same is true of air transportation carrying potential drug couriers. Commercial and passenger air and sea traffic, in addition to overland, are the major *modus operandi* for shipping drugs into Europe. Similarly, since drugs are moved to and from ports and airports by road transportation, drug trafficking is facilitated by the level of road transportation.

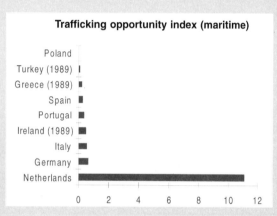

If the same volume of shipments is going into two countries, one of which is ten times larger than the other, then the level of shipments per unit area of the smaller country will be ten times greater. The land surface area of a country serves as a crude proxy indicator of opportunity for trafficking. Combining maritime trade and land area gives an indicator of the expected "funneling" effect, here called the Trafficking Opportunity Index (TOI), caused by different volumes of trade going into different countries (see accompanying Figure). The suggestion is that there are wide variations in opportunities for trafficking into different countries. Using this indicator, it would be expected that, independent of policy or enforcement activity, the volume of illicit drug trafficking would vary greatly between countries.

Differences in the level of commerce and trade between countries can complicate the evaluation of drug control policy and practice. Discrepancies in drug trafficking, consumption and related crime are obviously not solely attributable to differences in drug control law enforcement practices or differences in drug control policy. There may be a benefit to be gained if policy analysis begins to take account of economic differences and variation in a similar manner to which it takes account of cultural, political and social differences between countries.

there is a de facto, if not an actual, decriminalization of small scale or "simple" possession of some soft drugs, particularly cannabis. In other countries such as the UK, the same can also be true for possession of small amounts of hard drugs including heroin and cocaine. This can be for practical operational reasons related to policing. For example, an arrest for possession results in police officers being tied up in lengthy paperwork. In the aggregate this can be a severe drain upon police resources in some areas. The introduction of formal cautioning can speed up processing while producing a formal contact with the criminal justice system for the arrested individual. Such practices can greatly influence the number of cases that enter the front end of the criminal justice system. The data presented here consider only those cases that enter the criminal justice system.

While the fragmented nature of reports to the UNCJS is a constraint to analysis, the UNCJS remains the principal reference point for the development of internationally comparable criminal justice data. The rider is that the specific details of the analysis should be read as being open to revision if and when further information becomes available. There are sometimes also inconsistencies within individual country reports, perhaps reflecting counting and definitional problems in relation to the concepts being measured. Countries sometimes reported more prosecutions for trafficking and possession than there were suspects, more convictions than prosecutions, or more prison admissions than convictions. Such discrepancies were excluded where necessary, but this did not preclude other information from that country from being included elsewhere in the analysis. Since some of the apparent variation in the data cannot be obviously explained, the analysis and interpretation presented here is extremely tentative.

The analysis focuses upon the most recent available information for 1994. The primary focus is upon examining patterns and variations in the overall levels of attrition at different stages in the criminal justice system, from arrest and formal contact with the criminal justice system as a suspect, through prosecution, conviction and prison admission.

other drug-related crimes are typically recorded by the specific type of crime, such as assault or homicide, corruption or fraud, so that the connection to drugs is more difficult to trace.

Definitional and recording differences at the national level mean that cross-national comparisons of drug-related criminal justice data are not without difficulty. Different countries utilize different definitions of both drug trafficking and possession, with variation between drug types. In many countries

The proportion of the global criminal justice system dedicated to trafficking and possession crimes

What proportion of all crimes entering the global criminal justice system are drug trafficking and possession, and how does this vary between stages of the criminal justice system? From the available information, it appears that drug trafficking and possession play an increasingly important role in the later stages of the criminal justice system, particularly imprisonment. Whereas drug crimes account for less than four percent of recorded crimes, eight percent of suspects and prosecutions, and around nine percent of convictions, they account for over 13 percent of all prison admissions. This suggests that on average in 1994, for those countries that made the information available, drug trafficking and possession cases were more likely than the average crime to proceed to each subsequent stage of the global criminal justice system and to result in a sentence of imprisonment (Figure 7.9). Perhaps surprisingly, however, it seems that drug possession offences play an increasingly greater role than drug trafficking offences at the later stages of the criminal justice system. Two main explanations may account for this. The first and most likely is that it is an artifact of the fragmentary nature of the available data. The second is that it is a real difference, and the explanation lies in the workings of the various criminal justice systems. A possible partial explanation for the finding that possession is more likely to result in imprisonment than is trafficking might be found in the fact that some countries use capital punishment for drug trafficking, although this might not be expected to make a significant difference at the global level.

Attrition rates in the global criminal justice system

While the proportion of drug trafficking and possession cases appears to increase in magnitude relative to other crimes at each stage of the global criminal justice system, the number of such cases decreases in absolute magnitude. This is because some cases are dropped for various reasons between each stage. In fact, it seems that ten percent of

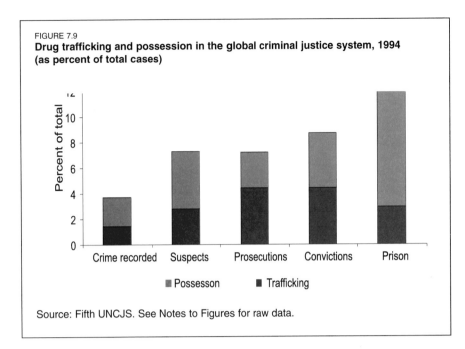

FIGURE 7.9
Drug trafficking and possession in the global criminal justice system, 1994 (as percent of total cases)

Source: Fifth UNCJS. See Notes to Figures for raw data.

those originally apprehended as trafficking and possession suspects go to prison (Figure 7.10).

The greatest absolute number of cases not proceeding to the next stage is between being formally processed as a suspect and being prosecuted. However, in terms of rates the picture is slightly different. Slightly less than half of all cases proceed to prosecution, and two-thirds of those prosecuted are convicted, but only one-third of those convicted are sentenced to imprisonment. In terms of rates, the greatest attrition is at the stage of sentencing, when the available data suggests that two-thirds of cases are given a non-incarceration sentence.

Combining the two elements of analysis of the criminal justice system so far, some comment can also be made on the respective roles of drug possession and trafficking cases compared to other types of crime. The two indicators have gone in different directions: only ten percent of drug trafficking and possession suspects go to prison, but the proportion of trafficking and possession cases at each stage of the criminal justice system increases in relation to other crimes. This implies that a drug trafficking or possession case is more likely than the average case to be retained by the criminal justice system.

The analysis so far shows that trafficking and possession cases are important in the aggregate picture of criminal justice.

...drug trafficking and possession cases were more likely than the average crime to proceed to each subsequent stage of the global criminal justice system and to result in a sentence of imprisonment.

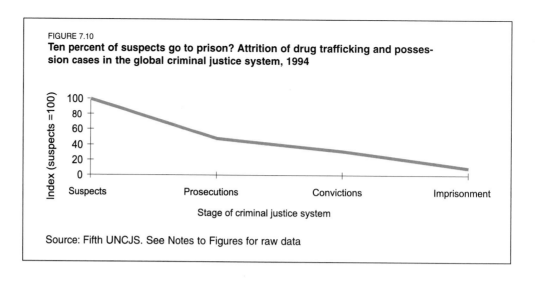

FIGURE 7.10

Ten percent of suspects go to prison? Attrition of drug trafficking and possession cases in the global criminal justice system, 1994

Source: Fifth UNCJS. See Notes to Figures for raw data

...a drug trafficking or possession case is more likely than the average case to be retained by the criminal justice system.

These aggregates will mask the fact that such cases are disproportionately concentrated in some countries as opposed to others. Drug-related arrest rates have increased rapidly in recent years in some countries to the extent that they have placed great strain upon their respective criminal justice systems. The response in the United States of America has been to introduce experimental dedicated "drug courts" to speed the processing of these cases (although this pertains in large part to cases for drug using offenders and dealers rather than trafficking and possession) and reduce the drain of resources away from other non-drug related crimes. This case study is shown in Box 7.6.

The analysis presented so far must be viewed with caution. While it is based on data for all countries which provided the relevant information, this is only a sample of the global total. The patterns and trends might need to be revised as additional information becomes available. Having gained this snapshot of criminal justice processing of trafficking and possession cases at the global level, the following sections examine each stage of the process in more detail, and present available information relating to particular countries. Sections are presented in the sequential order of the justice system, from arrest through to prison admissions.

Suspects per crime

Comparing the number of formal suspects to the number of crimes committed would not indicate the success of law enforcement since offending, like victimization, is highly skewed. A small proportion of offenders commits a large proportion of offences for any given crime type. However, making the large assumptions that the distribution of offending among offenders is relatively constant across countries, and that other factors are also constant, then cross national comparison of the number of suspects arrested per crime committed could be a partial and relative performance indicator. The two key processes on which it might shed light are the performance of law enforcement (in making arrests), or the rate of cautioning or other process which does not lead to a formal arrest being recorded.

In fact, from the available data, this measure is almost certainly not as indicative of actual criminal justice processes pertaining to drug trafficking and possession crimes as it is for other offences. This is because drug trafficking and possession offences are less likely to be recorded than other offences. Unlike burglaries, car crimes and other property offences that are often reported to the police for insurance purposes, or personal crimes where there is a clearly definable victim, drug trafficking and possession offences are unlikely to be reported to the police. The main source of official and quantifiable information relating to offences is from arrests made, and so the difference between the two would not be expected to be great in many instances. In what follows, countries that reported more suspects than crimes were excluded. Tables 7.3, 7.4 and 7.5 present country-level data on the number of arrests per recorded crime for drug trafficking and possession com-

Drug courts in the United States of America

In the United States of America there has been a growing reliance upon an increasing number of dedicated "drug courts" as a means of coping with the increasing volume of drug-related cases entering the criminal justice system. Whereas medical treatment models (see e.g. Box 7.3) typically aim to reduce the number of drug using offenders entering the criminal justice system, the use of drug courts is aimed at diverting drug using offenders from the mainstream criminal justice system. Defendants are referred to a drug court after being charged with drug offences, and must be eligible for court-ordered rehabilitation through probation, diversion or pretrial supervision. Drug courts separate drug cases from non-drug cases in order to process the large volume of drug cases more efficiently and more quickly.

The number of recorded drug-related arrests in the US increased by 360 percent between 1970 and 1996 (see Figure below). The period of most dramatic increase was in the mid to late 1980s, coinciding with the estimated increases in global production, trafficking and seizure of cocaine and the opiates, as well as significant increases in expenditure upon drug control law enforcement effort by the US government. However, while the number of drug trafficking and possession arrests has nearly doubled since 1985, expenditure upon domestic law enforcement

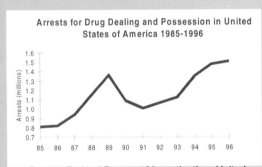

Arrests for Drug Dealing and Possession in United States of America 1985-1996

Source: Federal Bureau of Investigation, United States of America: The Uniform Crime Reports.

efforts has increased over sixfold (see Figure above right).

Two main types of drug courts have evolved: (1) Speedy Trial and Differentiated Case Management (DCM), and (2) Dedicated Drug Treatment. The earlier drug court models focused on case processing procedures to speed the disposition of drug cases. Assigning judges, prosecutors and public defenders to drug courtrooms enables them to use their expertise on drug cases and therefore process the cases faster and more efficiently. Another goal of the DCM model drug court is to relieve pressures on non-drug caseloads by diverting drug cases out of mixed calendar courtrooms.

The dedicated drug treatment model is used under a diversion, deferred prosecution or deferred sentencing arrangement to attempt to treat the drug-using offender. Most of the drug courts today are this model because their main goal is to reduce crime by changing the defendant's

drug-using behaviour. In this model, just after being charged, defendants waive their right to a speedy trial and enter a treatment program. Defendants who fail to complete the program have their charges adjudicated, while those who complete the program are not prosecuted further or have their charges dismissed.

Drug courts emerged in the late 1980s in a response to the rising number of crack cocaine (and other drug) cases. Drug courts were set up in four of New York City's five boroughs in 1987. These drug courts were called "Narcotics Parts." The main goal in these new courts was to expedite the processing of the increased drug cases. Then, in June 1989, Dade County, Florida, began using drug courts. They were the first court to incorporate drug treatment into their programme. Dade County drug court has become a model for other

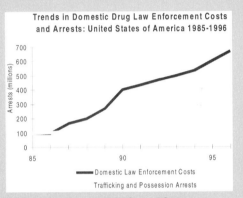

Trends in Domestic Drug Law Enforcement Costs and Arrests: United States of America 1985-1996

Source: US National Drug Control Strategy, several years; Federal Bureau of Investigation, United States of America: The Uniform Crime Reports.

efforts to divert drug offenders into treatment.

The number of drug courts in the United States has increased since the creation of the first one in Dade County. As of March 31, 1997, there were 161 drug courts in operation (40 percent of these located in Florida and California). Over $125 million has been made available for the planning or evaluation of drug courts from different funding sources since 1989. Although courts vary from state to state, each drug court has a single drug court judge and a dedicated staff. It is as yet undetermined whether drug courts are effective in reducing participants' recidivism or subsequent drug use, although they appear to have expedited case processing.

Source: Box prepared by Kim Steiner. Summarized and abridged from: *GAO Report to the Committee on the Judiciary*, US Senate, and the Committee on the Judiciary, House of Representatives. *Drug Courts — Overview of Growth, Characteristics, and Results.* July 1997; The Bureau of Justice Assistance — *Special Drug Courts Program Brief.* November 1993; "Drug Courts: GAO Withholds Judgement on Effectiveness," *Justice Bulletin*, National Criminal Justice Association, 17, 9, 1997.

bined and individually.

In general, the proportion of arrests per crime recorded was high, as might be expected. The lack of reporting of trafficking and possession cases to the police by victims may well also explain why a large number of countries appeared to report more arrests than crimes for trafficking and possession. Median and mean global arrest rates were close together, suggesting little skew in the distribution of results across countries. All three data points relating to crimes and arrests for trafficking and possession were available for 12 countries (Table 7.6). Swe-

TABLE 7.3

Trafficking and possession suspects per trafficking and possession crime recorded, 1994

Malaysia	1.00
Singapore	1.00
Jamaica	0.99
Chile	0.99
Finland	0.98
Denmark	0.97
Austria	0.93
Syrian Arab Rep	0.91
Azerbaijan	0.88
Rep of Moldova	0.88
Kyrgyzstan	0.82
Japan	0.74
Lithuania	0.73
Mauritius	0.73
Canada	0.72
Ukraine	0.72
Kazakhstan	0.70
Croatia	0.69
Georgia	0.66
Belarus	0.66
Russian Federation	0.64
Latvia	0.43
Ecuador	0.38
Estonia	0.33
Western Samoa	0.28
Sweden	0.26
Marshall Islands	0.12
Egypt	0.10
Median	0.72
Mean	0.69

Source: Fifth UNCJS. Note: Turkey, Costa Rica, Qatar, Malta, the Former Yugoslav Republic of Macedonia, Greece, Madagascar, the Republic of Korea, Nicaragua, Bahamas, Italy, Romania, Slovenia, Cyprus, India, Colombia, Hong Kong, Slovakia, France and Hungary all reported more suspects than drug crimes.

TABLE 7.4

Trafficking suspects per trafficking crime recorded, 1994

Malaysia	1.00
Singapore	1.00
Jamaica	1.00
Ecuador	1.00
Egypt	0.97
Chile	0.97
Austria	0.93
Denmark	0.91
Kyrgyzstan	0.82
Canada	0.78
Kazakhstan	0.78
Georgia	0.42
Sweden	0.22
Median	0.92
Mean	0.83

Source: Fifth UNCJS. Note: Malta, Ukraine, Syrian Arab Republic, Qatar, the Former Yugoslav Republic of Macedonia, Nicaragua, France, Costa Rica, Italy, Hong Kong, Madagascar, Slovenia, Romania, Japan, and the Republic of Moldova, all reported more trafficking suspects than crimes.

TABLE 7.5

Possession suspects per possession crime recorded, 1994

Malaysia	1.00
Singapore	1.00
Jamaica	1.00
Ecuador	1.00
Chile	1.00
Marshall Islands	1.00
Denmark	0.97
France	0.96
Austria	0.93
Japan	0.87
Rep of Moldova	0.85
Kazaskstan	0.78
Georgia	0.71
Canada	0.69
Ukraine	0.63
Western Samoa	0.51
Kyrgyzstan	0.50
Sweden	0.32
Median	0.90
Mean	0.82

Source: Fifth UNCJS. Note: Costa Rica, Madagascar, Nicaragua, Malta, the Former Yugoslav Republic of Macedonia, Egypt, Hong Kong, and Slovenia all reported more possession suspects than crimes.

The lack of reporting of trafficking and posses-sion cases to the police by victims may well explain why a large number of countries appeared to report more arrests than crimes for trafficking and possession.

den appeared to have unusually low num-bers of suspects per crime recorded. It might have been expected that offences recorded for drug trafficking were more likely to re-sult in a formal suspect being charged than cases recorded for possession. This did not seem to be the case. There was virtually no difference in the mean number of suspects per crime between the two types of drug-related offences. A possible explanation, as discussed earlier, is the large expected error factor in the number of recorded trafficking and possession crimes.

Prosecutions per suspect

What proportion of apprehended suspects are prosecuted for drug trafficking and pos-session? The apparent likelihood of prosecu-tion appears to vary between countries from

virtually certain to extremely rare. Table 7.7 shows the available country-level informa-tion for trafficking and possession com-bined, and Table 7.8 that for trafficking only. Of the 20 countries for which the combined information was available, the likelihood of

186

prosecution for trafficking or possession appears fairly evenly distributed across the range, with five countries in each quartile of the distribution. For drug trafficking cases only, the median prosecution rate (0.72) is substantially higher than the mean (0.41), suggesting a skewed distribution with more countries having higher than lower prosecution rates for trafficking offenses.

Convictions per prosecution

What is the likelihood that a drug trafficking or possession prosecution results in a conviction? There appears to be wide variation across countries (Table 7.9 and Table 7.10). The average rate of success of convictions across the 25 countries reporting was 62 percent. Drug possession cases that were prosecuted appeared to have a higher likelihood of conviction at 71 percent, although the different samples could well influence this finding. This may be connected to the possibility that a smaller proportion of possession cases reach prosecution, so that those that do are prosecuted more successfully.

TABLE 7.7
Prosecutions per suspect (prosecution rates) for drug trafficking and possession, 1994

Estonia	1.00
Bahamas	1.00
India	0.99
Hong Kong	0.87
Rep of Moldova	0.83
FYRM	0.69
Hungary	0.67
Russian Federation	0.60
Italy	0.55
Cyprus	0.53
Egypt	0.44
Singapore	0.44
Slovakia	0.43
Finland	0.31
Croatia	0.30
Canada	0.18
Columbia	0.09
Slovenia	0.05
Kazakhstan	0.03
Belarus	0.02
Median	0.48
Mean	0.50

Source: Fifth UNCJS. Note: Estonia and Bahamas reported 11 and 997 cases respectively for each of suspects and prosecutions. Western Samoa, Sweden, the Republic of Korea, Turkey, Latvia and Japan all reported more prosecutions than suspects.

TABLE 7.6
Suspects per crime for trafficking, possession, and all drug crimes, 1994: cases where all three data points were available

Country	Trafficking suspects per crime	Possession suspects per crime	Suspects per trafficking and possession crime
Malaysia	1.00	1.00	1.00
Singapore	1.00	1.00	1.00
Jamaica	1.00	1.00	0.99
Ecuador	1.00	1.00	0.38
Chile	0.97	1.00	0.99
Austria	0.93	0.93	0.93
Denmark	0.91	0.97	0.97
Kyrgyzstan	0.82	0.50	0.82
Canada	0.78	0.69	0.72
Kazakhstan	0.78	0.78	0.70
Georgia	0.42	0.71	0.66
Sweden	0.22	0.32	0.26
Median	0.92	0.95	0.91
Mean	0.82	0.83	0.79

Source: Fifth UNCJS

TABLE 7.8
Drug trafficking prosecutions per suspect (prosecution rates)

Kyrgyzstan	0.93
Georgia	0.90
Hong Kong	0.90
Singapore	0.72
FYRM	0.71
Italy	0.55
Canada	0.13
Slovenia	0.06
Median	0.72
Mean	0.41

Source: Fifth UNCJS. Note: Malaysia, Sweden and Chile reported more prosecutions than suspects and were excluded.

Imprisonment rates for drug trafficking and possession

There are a number of different ways of measuring and comparing cross national imprisonment rates. One simple way of looking at the level of usage of imprisonment between countries is to see what proportion of convictions result in imprisonment. This is problematic if cases reaching sentencing are qualitatively different between countries. While this will undoubtedly be the case to some extent, it is not unreasonable to assume at least some degree of seriousness for a trafficking or possession case to have passed through all the prior stages of the criminal justice system.

TABLE 7.9

Convictions per prosecution (conviction rates) for drug trafficking and possession, 1994

Country	Conviction rate
Finland	0.97
Estonia	0.91
Hong Kong	0.90
Northern Ireland	0.88
South Africa	0.87
Scotland	0.87
Cyprus	0.86
Slovenia	0.83
Germany	0.83
England & Wales	0.81
Israel	0.79
Croatia	0.78
Japan	0.66
Slovakia	0.56
Italy	0.56
Hungary	0.53
Latvia	0.51
Portugal	0.48
Netherlands	0.41
Czech Rep	0.37
FYRM	0.32
Sweden	0.30
Rep of Korea	0.24
India	0.23
Andorra	0.12
Median	0.66
Mean	0.62

Source: Fifth UNCJS. Note: countries were included only if they reported both the number of prosecutions and convictions. Nine countries reported more convictions than prosecutions and were excluded.

TABLE 7.10

Convictions per prosecution (conviction rates) for drug possession, 1994

Country	Conviction Rate
Hong Kong	0.98
Scotland	0.92
Northern Ireland	0.91
South Africa	0.91
England & Wales	0.89
Germany	0.77
Denmark	0.49
FYRM	0.29
Portugal	0.26
Median	0.83
Mean	0.71

Source: Fifth UNCJS. Note: countries were included only if they reported both prosecution and conviction data for possession. Canada reported more convictions than prosecutions and was excluded. Slovenia reported five cases of each. The Former Yugoslav Republic of Macedonia reported 17 prosecutions and five convictions.

Making this assumption, differences in the proportion of convictions resulting in imprisonment may reflect two main factors. First, since the only available data relates to an aggregate of both trafficking and possession, the proportions of each in the total may vary. If the likelihood of imprisonment varies between trafficking and possession, then this will influence the aggregate results. A second explanation is that judicial practices vary between countries in the use of a sentence of imprisonment for crimes of a similar nature.

The relevant information was only made available by a relatively small number of countries. From the available information, European countries appear to have lower than average rates of imprisonment for offenders convicted of drug trafficking and possession (Table 7.11). Six of the seven European countries for which data were available imprisoned around one or two in ten of offenders convicted for these drug crimes, a rate which is half or less than half of the mean imprisonment rate. Of those countries that made the data available, Egypt has by far the lowest rate of imprisonment of offenders convicted for drug trafficking and possession. This could be because Egypt uses capital punishment for some drug-related crimes, which could produce a lower rate of imprisonment relative to other countries.

A common cross national comparative measure of the use of prison is imprisonments per capita population. These rates are shown alongside rates per conviction in Table 7.11 for countries where both data points were available. For the 15 countries where both data points were available, there was no significant correlation between imprisonments per conviction and imprisonments per capita (Pearson r=0.183). Both theory and data suggest that population does not serve as a good proxy in the denominator for the calculation of a rate of imprisonment (Pease, 1995). Of those countries that made the information available, South Africa appeared by far the most punitive in 1994 when measured in terms of imprisonments per capita. In terms of imprisonments per conviction, South African imprisonment rates were less than those in Slovenia and the Sudan, and not as far removed from rates of other countries as it might appear using a measure based on population.

TABLE 7.11

Imprisonments per conviction and per capita for drug trafficking and possession, 1994

Country	Imprisonments per conviction	Imprisonments per 1000 pop.
Slovenia	0.95	0.01
Sudan	0.80	0.16
South Africa	0.70	0.60
Greece	0.61	0.06
Indonesia	0.48	0.00
Japan	0.45	0.04
Rep of Moldova	0.31	0.02
Cyprus	0.30	0.03
Sweden	0.22	0.14
Switzerland	0.21	0.27
Scotland	0.17	0.17
Denmark	0.15	0.18
England & Wales	0.14	0.07
Northern Ireland	0.13	0.04
Egypt	0.01	0.00
Median	0.30	0.06
Mean	0.38	0.12

Source: Fifth UNCJS. Note: six countries (Italy, the Former Yugoslav Republic of Macedonia, the Republic of Korea, Belgium, Hong Kong and Georgia) reported more imprisonments than convictions for systemic drug crimes, and were excluded. See Notes to Tables for additional tabular information.

Drug-related crime: the need for further data collation and analysis

While there is an ever expanding and improving knowledge base related to the illicit drug industry, knowledge related to other drug-related crimes, including street crimes and drug markets, remains extremely fragmented at the international level. Information relating to the progress of drug users through and in the criminal justice system is almost nonexistent, primarily because these categories of information are typically not recorded. Information relating to the drug trafficking and possession cases in the criminal justice system is extremely fragmented, almost certainly in part because of wide variation in legal definitions and recording practices between countries. There is a need for a more systematic collation of governmental and non-governmental reports produced at the national and local levels to be used to supplement methodologically standardized data collection instruments such as the UNCJS.

The global picture of the influence of drugs and drug control upon crime and criminal justice is fragmented. What is clear is that drugs and drug control have come to play an increasingly significant role in the overall picture of crime and criminal justice in recent years. The global coverage of drug-related crime has increased. The overall volume of drug-related crime has increased in those countries where it was already established. While law enforcement activities have increased and appear to have improved in many ways, they have been faced with overwhelming odds. Relative improvements in enforcement efficiency have taken place alongside absolute reductions in effectiveness. The overall influence upon criminal justice systems of drug-related offending is not readily apparent at the global level, since only data pertaining to drug trafficking and possession cases are available. It is likely that the role of drug-using offenders has concurrently increased at each stage of the criminal justice system. The increases in drug-related crime and the increased strain placed upon criminal justice systems have seen the emergence of innovative approaches to managing the problems, including medical prescriptions for addicts, and dedicated courts for drug-related cases. While trends in illicit drug production and trafficking appear, for some drug types, to have stabilized during the 1990s, it remains to be determined whether drug-related crime and pressure upon the criminal justice system globally will experience similar trends.

There is a need for a more systematic collation of government and non-governmental reports produced at the national and local levels to be used to supplement methodologically standardized data collection instruments such as the UNCJS.

SUMMARY

THINGS IN COMMON	THINGS DIVERSE
• In any one year, slightly over one in a thousand persons illicitly use heroin or other opiates, and two in a thousand illicitly use cocaine.	• A small fraction of the world's population uses drugs illicitly.
• The number of types of illicit drugs has increased and their nature diversified in recent years.	• While cannabis has long been the most prevalent global illicit drug, sedatives (primarily barbiturates, benzodiazapines and methaqualone) are estimated to be as prevalent if not more so.
• Drug-related crimes have increased disproportionately in the last two decades when compared to other crime-related phenomena. Types of crime committed by drug addicts are primarily acquisitive.	• There are relatively few countries that keep centralized and internationally comparable records of illicit drug consumption.
• The number of countries supporting the 1988 United Nations drug control convention has continued to increase over the last four years.	• The balloon effect, in which crop reduction in one area has resulted in increases in other areas, has thus far prevented production at the global level from declining in absolute terms.
	• Proper evaluations of demand reduction and drug education programmes are still few and far between.
• The price of heroin and cocaine has fallen dramatically in recent years. This is primarily because, despite increased law enforcement interception efforts, the supply of drugs to consumers has greatly increased as a result of increased illicit production.	• In many countries there is a de facto, if not an actual, decriminalization of small scale or "simple" possession of some soft drugs, particularly cannabis.
• The economic incentives of the illicit drug trade serve to make organized trafficking extremely durable.	
• Drug trafficking and possession cases were more likely than the average crime to proceed to each subsequent stage of the global criminal justice system and to result in a sentence of imprisonment.	• The available data suggest that two thirds of offenders in drug crime cases are given a non-incarceration sentence

CHAPTER 8

 # International trends in crime prevention: Cost-effective ways to reduce victimization

Contributing authors: Irvin Waller and Brandon Welsh

Introduction

Most nations are faced with unacceptable levels of delinquency and violent crime. Despite slight decreases in the rates of crime recorded by the police in many industrialized countries, these rates are two to three times those of 30 years ago. And we saw in Chapter 1 that when crime is measured by citizens' reports of victimizations, the rates are even much higher, leaving no country untouched by crime.

Street and domestic crime create loss, inflict physical and psychological wounds, undermine the safety of communities, and take lives. The efforts to stem the tide have been insufficient, costly and sometimes threatening to basic human rights. Crime and insecurity also cost the general public and so endanger sustainable development. They exact an economic toll in growing expenditures for security and health. They accelerate community decay and scare away investment. The failure to use the best know-how to reduce crime slows human and economic development, particularly in the large and fast-growing cities that are the economic motors of most countries.

The leaders of the government agencies responsible for public security remain captive to increased spending on law enforcement and prisons. Are there more affordable and more effective solutions that are waiting to be put to work? Can government deficits be reduced while reducing crime? How can more effective solutions be implemented?

In this chapter, crime has been defined as those criminal acts which are of a personal or household nature. These include such crimes as murder, attempted murder, rape, various degrees of sexual assault, assault, robbery, burglary, theft of and from

vehicles, theft from the person, and vandalism. Excluded are traffic, organized and transnational crimes (the latter two crimes are examined in the following chapter).

We define crime prevention as anything that reduces delinquency, violent crime and insecurity by successfully tackling the scientifically identified causal factors. It gives special attention to activities that are "problem solving partnerships." That is, measures developed as a result of a careful effort to identify causal factors while mobilizing the agencies able to influence those factors.

Academics divide crime prevention into approaches either focused on victims or offenders. They refine these categories with reference to whether the strategy applies to all persons in a community, only those "at-risk," or those who have already been involved in offences. Typically the approaches would be summarized as follows:

- *Social development* — reducing the social factors that predispose young persons to become persistent offenders — often focusing on potential offenders;
- *Opportunity reduction* — making crime more difficult, more risky, or less rewarding to potential offenders — often focusing on potential victims.

Later in this chapter specific examples are provided of prevention projects that have reduced crime. These have been grouped into pragmatic categories that have to do with the type of prevention and the delivery mechanism. They were chosen on the basis of what is working in prevention. They involve initiatives by central and local government, as well as the activities of the private sector: those in city management, urban planning, policing, the judiciary, schools, housing, social services, youth services, women's affairs, public health, universities and the media.

Can government deficits be reduced while reducing crime? How can more effective solutions be implemented?

The prevention and elimination of all forms of violence against women was one of the key objectives of the declaration.

Many persons involved in law enforcement, courts, prisons and legislating criminal policy confine prevention to the use of deterrence, incapacitation, education or rehabilitation. While crime reductions may, in some cases, be due to these activities, they are more rare than often believed. So, this chapter does not include these in its definition of prevention, unless the sanction is used to tackle a causal factor. Further, we do not provide a synopsis of the positive results of specialized programmes such as focused police patrols or correctional programmes tackling risk factors. Reviews of such programmes are available elsewhere (see e.g., Sherman, Gottfredson, MacKenzie, Eck, Reuter and Bushway, 1997).

This chapter examines international trends in crime prevention by a) reviewing the main instruments that have been adopted by the United Nations and other inter-governmental agencies for prevention to make communities safer from crime; b) reviewing the central strategies to foster crime prevention, drawing particular attention to seven developed countries; c) recounting a number of crime prevention successes; d) assessing some selected economic costs of crime and the economic benefits of crime prevention; e) reviewing trends in the means that are used to facilitate effective crime prevention; f) noting a number of present and future issues facing crime prevention; and, finally, g) drawing some conclusions and proposing an action plan to achieve more effective and cost-effective crime prevention globally.

International instruments recommend prevention to make communities safer from crime

Calls for more effective prevention to reduce crime have come from major international meetings in Strasbourg in 1986, Barcelona in 1987, Montreal in 1989, Paris in 1991 and, more recently, Vancouver in 1996. Mayors, police executives, judges, community leaders, governmental representatives and crime prevention experts and practitioners from the developed, developing and transitional nations were the delegates who set out a common vision.

Their declarations seeking ways for the UN crime programme to be more effective were welcomed by the Eighth UN Congress on the Prevention of Crime and the Treatment of Offenders (Havana, 1990), the Ministerial Meeting on the Creation of an Effective United Nations Crime Prevention and Criminal Justice Programme (Paris, 1991), and the Ninth UN Congress on the Prevention of Crime and the Treatment of Offenders (Cairo, 1995). In addition, the UN Commission on Crime Prevention and Criminal Justice has made the prevention of crime in urban areas, juvenile delinquency and violent crime one of its three priorities for its long-term work programme.

The United Nations and other inter-governmental agencies have adopted a number of instruments urging prevention in order to make communities safer from crime.

The United Nations Centre for International Crime Prevention (UNCICP) and selected UN action to facilitate more effective crime prevention

Since assuming the position of Secretary-General of the United Nations, Mr. Kofi Annan has embarked on a deliberate and important reform effort that has touched all aspects of the United Nations organization. As part of this programme of reform, the Secretary-General has established the Office for Drug Control and Crime Prevention (ODCCP) as the locus for the integrated efforts of the United Nations in drug control, crime prevention and combating international terrorism in all its forms. The ODCCP is constituted by the United Nations Drug Control Programme (UNDCP) and the United Nations Centre for International Crime Prevention (UNCICP). The UNCICP is a new entity which integrates the functions of the former Crime Prevention and Criminal Justice Division.

Located at the United Nations Office in Vienna, the UNCICP serves as the secretariat to the Commission on Crime Prevention and Criminal Justice, which is the chief policy-making body on crime and justice matters within the UN.

The UNCICP "implements policy decisions of the Commission, formulates policy options and coordinates crime prevention and criminal justice activities within the United Nations system and at the international level" (United Nations, 1996). The UNCICP is also responsible to member states for:

- promoting the application and use of UN instruments and resolutions and facilitating their implementation;
- providing technical assistance, advisory services and specialized training programmes; and,
- exchanging information.

Information activities are central to the work of the UNCICP. The Centre also maintains the UN Crime and Criminal Justice Information Network (UNCJIN) — an Internet service which provides access to UN data bases (e.g., country crime statistics).

In recent years, the United Nations has formulated a number of instruments which call for active prevention policies to match policing and criminal justice as a world wide priority. These emphasize national policies as well as community programmes that reinforce common values and social and community development, and reduce opportunities for offending as ways of making communities safer.

Habitat II

Also known as the United Nations Conference on Human Settlements, Habitat II (Istanbul, June 1996) was the 20 year follow-up to Habitat I, held in Vancouver. Habitat II aimed to confront the emerging urban crisis and make cities safe and sustainable. Habitat's Global Plan of Action set out a brief yet important agenda for governments at all levels in partnership with key stakeholders to work towards the prevention, reduction and ultimate elimination of violence and crime.

The action plan strongly emphasized the need for preventive action by tackling the scientifically established early risk factors of delinquency and later criminal offending (e.g., poverty, inequality). In addition it recommended reducing opportunities for crime through improved city design, greater individual responsibility and improved educational awareness, more use of alternatives to incarceration without widening the social control net, and making policing services more efficient and accountable to crime victims and the larger community.

Habitat II proved to be a milestone event, bringing together for the first time at a UN sponsored conference city leaders and heads of member states. A best practices exposition showcased some important crime and violence prevention schemes from around the world.

Other major inter-governmental conferences

In the last few years, the United Nations has been responsible for organizing a number of important global conferences which have focused directly or indirectly on the prevention of crime and violence. Two UN conferences are the focus of this discussion: the Ninth Congress on the Prevention of Crime and the Treatment of Offenders, held in Cairo in 1995, and the Fourth World Conference on Women, held in Beijing in 1995.

Importantly, the UN Crime Congress acknowledged the limited resources which federal and central governments spend on crime prevention relative to criminal justice. It recommended that governments take innovative steps to strengthen crime prevention by reallocating existing criminal justice resources to prevention. Many governmental studies on crime prevention have recommended similar funding mechanisms (see e.g., Home Office Standing Conference on Crime Prevention, 1988; Horner Committee, 1993; Task Force on Crime Prevention, 1993; see also the section below under the heading "Sustainable funding").

Informing the public about practical crime prevention measures (that are proven effective) was another important issue at the Congress. It recommended that a citizen's manual on preventing crime be prepared to guide states in the development of national public awareness programmes (United Nations, 1995b). Earlier in 1993, Crime Concern had published *A Practical Guide to Crime Prevention for Local Partnerships*, which acts as a step-by-step guide to the development of locally-based crime prevention initiatives, drawing on the successes of similar approaches.

Entitled *Action for Equality, Development and Peace*, the Fourth World Conference on Women (United Nations, 1995c) was an opportunity to take stock of ten years of action since the third conference in

The Platform for Action of the Beijing Conference

United Nations Fourth World Conference on Women

1. We, the governments participating in the Fourth World Conference on Women:

2. Gathered here in Beijing in September 1995, the year of the fiftieth anniversary of the founding of the United Nations,

4. Acknowledging the voices of all women everywhere and taking note of the diversity of women and their roles and circumstances, honouring the women who paved the way and inspired by the hope present in the world of youth,

reaffirm our commitment to:

8. The equal rights and inherent human dignity of women and men and other purposes and principles enshrined in the Charter of the United Nations, to the Universal Declaration of Human Rights and other international human rights instruments, in particular the Convention on the Elimination of All Forms of Discrimination against Women and the Convention on the Rights of the Child, as well as the Declaration on the Elimination of Violence against Women and the Declaration on the Right to Development;

9. Ensure the full implementation of the human rights of women and of the girl child as an inalienable, integral and indivisible part of all *human* rights and fundamental freedoms;

10. Build on consensus and progress made at previous United Nations conferences and summits on women in Nairobi in 1985, on children in New York in 1990, on environment and development in Rio de Janeiro in 1992, on human rights in Vienna in 1993, on population and development in Cairo in 1994 and on social development in Copenhagen in 1995 with the objective of achieving equality, development and peace;

12. The empowerment and advancement of women, including the right to freedom of thought, conscience, religion and belief, thus contributing to the moral, ethical, spiritual and intellectual needs of women and men, individually or in community with others and thereby guaranteeing them the possibility of realizing their full potential in society and shaping their lives in accordance with their own aspirations.

We are convinced that:

13. Women's empowerment and their full participation on the basis of equality in all spheres of society, including participation in the decision-making process and access to power, are fundamental for the achievement of equality, development and peace;

14. Women's rights are human rights;

15. Equal rights, opportunities and access to resources, equal sharing of responsibilities for the family by men and women, and a harmonious partnership between them are critical to their well-being and that of their families as well as to the consolidation of democracy;

18. Local, national, regional and global peace is attainable and is inextricably linked with the advancement of women, who are a fundamental force for leadership, conflict resolution and the promotion of lasting peace at all levels.

We are determined to:

29. Prevent and eliminate all forms of violence against women and girls;

30. Ensure equal access to and equal treatment of women and men in education and health care and enhance women's sexual and reproductive health as well as education.

38. We hereby adopt and commit ourselves as governments to the Platform for Action, ensuring that a gender perspective is reflected in all our policies and programmes. We urge the United Nations system, regional and international financial institutions, other relevant regional and international institutions and all women and men, as well as non-governmental organizations, with full respect for their autonomy, and all sectors of civil society, in cooperation with governments to fully commit themselves and contribute to the implementation of this Platform for Action.

Source: Edited and abridged from Report of the Fourth World Conference on Women (Beijing, 4-15 September 1995) A/CONF-177/20. 17 October 1995. Adopted at the 16th plenary session on 15 September 1995.

Nairobi, which adopted the *Forward-looking Strategies for the Advancement of Women to the Year 2000,* and to chart a path for the continued advancement of women into the new millennium.

The Platform for Action of the Beijing Conference (United Nations, 1995c; see Box 8.1) identified a number of critical issues which present obstacles to the advancement of women and strategies to counter these obstacles. Strategies were proposed for immediate action by governments, the international community, non-governmental organizations, the private sector and individuals. The prevention and elimination of all forms of violence against women was one of the key objectives of the declaration. Its importance was further signified by the recent placement of the issues of violence against women and sexual harassment on the global agenda.

Montreal, Paris, and Vancouver international conferences

Montreal, Paris and Vancouver were the sites of milestone events which helped to strengthen the global cause to get more effective crime prevention into action.

In 1989, Montreal was the host to the first European and North American Conference on Urban Safety and Crime Prevention. It represented the first global attempt to bring direction and greater political action to an effort that was still very much in its infancy. The conference's final declaration, the *Agenda for Safer Cities* (European Forum for Urban Safety, Federation of Canadian Municipalities, and The US Conference of Mayors, 1989), set out a programme of concrete action to prevent crime and victimization and lessen feelings of insecurity in cities across the world. It enunciated four key crime prevention principles, which still stand today as benchmarks for effective crime prevention policy and practice:

- the community is the focal point of crime prevention;

- any response to crime needs to go beyond the criminal justice system and be part of a long-range approach that is also responsive to immediate needs;

- crime prevention must bring together those responsible for housing, social services, schools, policing and justice to tackle the situations that breed crime; and,

- partnerships need to be developed at local and national levels (European Forum for Urban Safety *et al*., 1989).

Shortly thereafter, the Agenda for Safer Cities was adopted at the Eighth UN Congress in Havana in 1990. It became known as the Prevention of Urban Crime resolution (United Nations, 1990), which was the first UN resolution to articulate the global importance of the need for striking a greater balance between repression and prevention.

In 1991, Paris was the site of the Montreal conference follow-up. More than 1,600 crime prevention practitioners and experts, mayors, governmental representatives and police from 65 countries were in attendance. Like its predecessor, the Paris Final Declaration (European Forum for Urban Safety, Federation of Canadian Municipalities, and The US Conference of Mayors, 1991) set out a hard-hitting action programme to bring about concrete change in safety in cities and communities (Box 8.2). The declaration called for:

- government investment to meet the needs of at-risk and disadvantaged populations;
- governments to establish national crime prevention structures which invest in cities, provide training and undertake research and evaluation;
- cities to set up crime prevention structures to mobilize key stakeholders;
- public education programmes to inform and mobilize citizens to take part in grassroots crime prevention; and,
- support for the establishment of an international crime prevention centre to harness the world's crime prevention know-how to reduce crime, increase community safety, and enhance civic vitality (European Forum for Urban Safety *et al*., 1991).

Notwithstanding the achievements of the first two global crime prevention conferences, crime prevention remained more rhetoric than action. In most industrialized countries, government spending on crime prevention changed little, remaining at less than one percent of criminal justice levels;

BOX 8.2

FINAL DECLARATION

II International Conference on Urban Safety, Drugs and Crime Prevention (Paris, November 18-20, 1991)

Following the conference of Barcelona organized by the Council of Europe, the first conference on urban safety and prevention of crime was held in Montreal in 1989 and established the "Agenda for Safer Cities," which was adopted at the 8th United Nations Congress in its resolution on the Prevention of Urban Crime.

More than 1,600 mayors, councillors, police executives, social development leaders and government representatives from 65 countries came to Paris to exchange experiences and decide how to better implement the Agenda for Safer Cities. Major delegations represented Europe, North America, Latin America, Asia and Africa. The outcome of the meeting produced a series of recommendations.

Seven Steps to Make World Communities Safer.

1. Governments must invest now to meet socioeconomic and urban needs, particularly the needs of alienated groups such as young persons at risk.

2. Governments must establish national crime prevention structures to recommend improved national policies, undertake research and development, and foster the implementation of effective crime prevention programmes, particularly by cities.

3. Municipalities must establish crime prevention structures to mobilize the local officials who control policies relating to housing, schooling, youth, families, social services, policing and justice.

4. The public must be encouraged by local, regional and national governments, international agencies and non-governmental groups to participate in comprehensive crime prevention and to understand the importance to urban development of implementing effective ways of making communities safer from crime.

5. Developed countries should support the creation of an International Centre for the Prevention of Crime, consistent with the objectives of the United Nations and which might become affiliated with it.

6. The United Nations Ministerial Meeting on Effective International Cooperation on the Prevention of Crime and the Treatment of Offenders is requested to make comprehensive prevention of crime a visible and important part of the programme in the next decade. In particular, they are asked to:

(i) place greater emphasis on the prevention of crime in relation to arrest, detention and sentencing;

(ii) ensure that the resources available for the United Nations efforts on crime prevention are equivalent to those available for efforts on drug abuse and control;

(iii) ensure that the 1995 United Nations Congress on the Prevention of Crime and the Treatment of Offenders does, in fact, stress the prevention of crime as a major theme.

7. The European Forum of Local Authorities on Urban Safety, The United States Conference of Mayors and the Federation of Canadian Municipalities will adopt ways to implement this Declaration.

Source: Edited and abridged from European Forum for Urban Safety *et al.* (1991)

---

little of the voluminous scientific findings on the causes of criminal offending was translated into preventive action; and crime prevention decision-making and coordination continued to operate at bureaucratic, not community, levels. The International Conference for Crime Prevention Practitioners (see Pearcey, Welsh, Waller and French, 1996), held in Vancouver in 1996, was about changing this situation. In short, the conference set out to move "beyond political rhetoric and scientific conclusions to the practical projects and activities that will reduce crime and violence" (Pearcey *et al.*, 1996).

The conference plan of action outlined a number of important steps to achieve its principal aim of getting more of what works in preventing crime into action:

- support for an international network of crime prevention practitioners to facilitate the exchange of ideas cross-culturally and develop training and skill building;
- exchange of best and promising practices via the International Centre for the Prevention of Crime's Best Practices Bureau;
- development of crime prevention guidelines and standards and a greater emphasis on evaluation; and,
- development of innovative strategies for attracting sustainable funding from the private sector and the promotion of closer working ties with the media to convey practical solutions to crime problems.

Council of Europe

The Council of Europe, an inter-governmental agency which promotes the advancement of European countries, has played an instrumental role in the development of crime prevention policy and practice within and beyond its continental boundaries. The council's first entrance into the crime prevention arena came in 1983, with the adoption of a policy paper on the participation of the public in crime policy (Waller, 1989). Social and situational crime prevention were key components of this policy.

In the same year, the council set up a committee of experts on the "Organization of Crime Prevention." A number of important recommendations were made, among

them that crime prevention should be a permanent feature of government programmes for controlling crime, with the necessary funding (Waller, 1989).

The Council of Europe's Standing Conference of Local and Regional Authorities of Europe followed up the expert committee's recommendations and initiated a number of international conferences to strengthen crime prevention in Europe (e.g., Strasbourg in 1986 and Barcelona in 1987). In 1987, the Standing Conference created the European Forum for Urban Safety (*Forum Européan pour la Sécurité Urbaine*) to act as the permanent crime prevention structure for Europe. Its members presently include the mayors of the cities of Europe that are at the forefront of crime prevention and urban safety. Its work programme is chiefly founded on strengthening city partnerships for the prevention of crime.

Central strategies to foster crime prevention

Governments within the context of the United Nations have adopted guidelines on the prevention of crime (United Nations, 1995d). They call for crime prevention to be implemented locally, following problem solving approaches. They emphasize that central authorities — consistent with the competence of the agency — should provide active support, assistance and encouragement to the local efforts, as well as coordinate national strategies and work with relevant central administrations (United Nations, 1995a; United Nations, 1995g; United Nations, 1995h; United Nations, 1995i; United Nations, 1997b).

This section focuses predominantly on central strategies to foster crime prevention from seven developed countries: Australia, Belgium, Canada, England and Wales (hereafter referred to as England), France, the Netherlands and USA. It represents a synthesis of a larger piece of research being carried out by the International Centre for the Prevention of Crime (Waller, Welsh and Sansfaçon, 1997). These seven countries represent some of the countries presently most advanced in the prevention of crime. Information is also presented on the activities of a number of developing countries and

Central authorities should provide active support, assistance and encouragement to the local efforts at crime prevention.

TABLE 8.1
Crime prevention secretariats

Country	Responsible Entity	Department	Rank below top official	Mandate	Budget (per year) (per capita)	Other orders of government (only in federal governmental systems)
Australia	National Campaign Against Violence and Crime (1996)	Attorney General	3	To develop and implement best practice in crime prevention - including capacity building, community education, and coordination.	US$3 million US$0.17	South Australia, New South Wales, Tasmania, Queensland, Victoria and Western Australia have their own entities.
Belgium	Permanent Secretariat for Prevention Policy (1993)	Ministry of the Interior	2	To coordinate the implementation of a national prevention policy.	US$55 million US$5.50	
Canada	Crime Prevention Secretariat and National Crime Prevention Council (1994)	Department of Justice and Ministry of the Solicitor General	4	To implement the crime prevention and community safety strategy, provide crime prevention policy development and liaise horizontally across all departments, with provinces/territories, municipalities and NGOs.	US$2.2 million US$0.07	Some provinces have entities to encourage prevention with small budgets.
England	Crime Prevention Unit (1984) - Crime Prevention Agency (1996)	Home Office	4	To promote crime prevention, including the management of the CPU and Crime Prevention Agency, coordinate key players, disseminate good practice, research and development, and provide strategic advice.	US$19 million US$0.35	
France	Prevention Pole (DIV) (1989)	City Secretariat (DIV)	2	To integrate crime prevention into urban development policies and practices.	US$45 million US$1.28	
Netherlands	Department of Prevention, Youth and Sanctions (Justice, 1989) and Public Order and Safety (Interior, 1993)	Ministries of Justice and Interior	3	To coordinate policy and programme development and research and evaluation as well as implementation of the Integrated Safety and Security Policy.	US$12 million US$1.25	
USA	Office of Juvenile Justice and Delinquency Prevention (1984), Bureau of Justice Assistance, Office of Justice Programs	Department of Justice	3	To provide national leadership, coordination and resources to develop, implement and support effective methods to prevent juvenile delinquency.	US$200 million US$0.75	All States and criminal justice planning boards fund criminal justice programmes, including crime prevention.

countries in transition, although in a less systemic and rigorous fashion. This section does not, however, include any detailed analysis of central efforts by state or provincial governments in federal systems.

Six elements have been identified as important for the success of a central strategy that will foster effective local crime prevention. "Effective" refers to activities that are likely to reduce delinquency, violent crime and insecurity (see below under the heading "Crime prevention best practice"). For each element, we provide a commentary based on the comparative experience, and, in one instance, a short illustration from one of the seven countries. The six elements, divided into two categories, are 1) *characteristics of the central secretariat*: staff, reporting to a senior official, with a budget for development; capacity to mobilize key partners, harness effective methods and set priorities; and able to propose strategies based on analysis of crime problems and prevention practices; 2) *delivery possible through*: collaboration with other government departments; development of local problem-solving partnerships; and involvement of citizens.

Commentators talk about crime prevention as a fourth pillar in government action against crime added to the three traditional pillars of policing, courts and prisons.

Secretariats that foster crime prevention centrally

Most of the entities that foster crime prevention in these seven countries had their origins in secretariats, offices, and a council set up in the early 1980s. Scandinavian countries were really the precursor to this development, with national crime prevention councils set up in Denmark in 1971, Sweden in 1974 and Norway in 1980. In France, from 1983 to 1988, the National Crime Prevention Council was chaired by the prime minister. Council members included members of parliament, mayors, and representatives from trade unions, employers and community organizations. The council was able to generate considerable momentum around the creation of municipal crime prevention councils, so that there are more than 850 today with representation from all the key agencies, such as justice, social services, housing and education, and the not-for-profit sector.

Table 8.1 overviews the crime prevention secretariats of seven countries, focusing on: responsible entity; governmental department in which the secretariat is located; rank below top official; mandate; budget[1]; and other orders of government with active crime prevention institutions.

As can be seen in Table 8.1, most secretariats report to an official between two and four levels down from the top public servant. On a per capita basis, the maximum resources allocated are only $5.50.[2]

In Belgium, the Permanent Secretariat for Crime Prevention Policy was created in 1993. While the budget for crime prevention was five million BF in 1989, it has increased to 1.7 billion BF in 1996 (approximately $55 million or $5.50 per capita). This funding capacity has allowed the secretariat to develop and fund Prevention and Security Contracts with cities (now over 60 contracts). These contracts involve the creation of a local crime prevention council organized around the diagnosis of the problem and the definition and implementation of preventive actions.

In the year prior to Belgium's initiative, New Zealand set up a crime prevention unit in the highest level of political hierarchy: the Department of the Prime Minister and Cabinet. The role of the unit was to act as principal advisor to the government in the formulation of crime prevention strategies, monitor functions in the maintenance and growth of the national crime prevention strategy, and promote the development of Safer Community Councils based on a comprehensive crime prevention model. The councils were to perform two key roles: coordinating existing community crime prevention programmes, and planning for and encouraging the development of new programmes within the context of a local community crime prevention plan (Crime Prevention Unit, 1994).

Less well known perhaps is the work of the People's Republic of China, which in 1984 established, within the Ministry of Justice, the Institute of Crime Prevention and Criminal Reform. Divided into six divisions, the institute's Research Division on Crime Prevention undertakes analyses of crime trends and the characteristics of crime and its causes, as well as exploring effective strategies in the prevention and reduction of crime.

Some of the other countries that have set up specialized crime prevention secretariats within government include: Argentina, Finland, Germany (as part of the National Police), Iceland, Israel, Japan and Saudi Arabia. Many countries, particularly countries in transition, are in the process of establishing governmental crime prevention units. Some of these include Brazil, Chile and South Africa. Estonia, Czech Republic and Mexico have recently established national councils for crime prevention, which maintain a semi-autonomous standing from government.

Crime prevention strategies encouraged

For the seven countries under study, crime prevention actions undertaken by the secretariats generally focus on only one of the types of crime prevention, such as designing out crime, increasing social control, or investing in youth. Issues of enhancing responsibility, such as regulating the use of firearms or drugs, are dealt with by other agencies. None of the fostering secretariats has adopted a comprehensive approach including all the types of successful crime prevention identified below under the heading "Crime prevention best practice."

Most of the secretariats focused initially on crime prevention that is implemented by the police and citizens. France focused at the beginning on cities and justice agencies. The USA focused more on the causes of youth violence, and still does today. All have some type of link with inter-departmental bodies and increasingly with the range of key partners, including cities.

Analysis of crime problems and prevention practices

Four countries have been active in conducting research and development studies: Australia, England, the Netherlands and the USA. In these countries, significant resources have been allocated to research and development, and in at least two cases — the Netherlands and the USA — systematic programmes of project development and evaluation have been implemented.

In England, research conducted by the Home Office Research Unit played a role in the creation of the Home Office Crime Prevention Unit in the early 1980s. The Dutch crime prevention secretariat influenced other departmental activities and countries — this occurred when its head reported directly to the senior official. The Directorate for Crime Prevention of the Ministry of Justice allocated ten percent of its annual resources to research and evaluation. In Australia, developing and disseminating best practices is one of the key mandates of the newly formed National Campaign Against Violence and Crime.

Commentators talk about crime prevention as a fourth pillar in government action against crime — added to the three traditional pillars of policing, courts and prisons. Most secretariats do not undertake an explicit analysis of crime or what their role is in relation to other pillars of criminal justice policy. The original French national crime prevention council had a mandate to examine crime trends and recommend preventive solutions. In the USA, the Office of Juvenile Justice and Delinquency Prevention (OJJDP) writes its comprehensive strategy using an analysis of juvenile crime trends and accumulated research knowledge from the USA.

Influence over economic and social policies that prevent crime

Fostering economic and social policies that prevent crime is a goal of some of the central crime prevention secretariats. However, it is rarely specified how they pursue this objective or what results are achieved. Policy areas most often targeted are housing, health, youth, children and municipal government.

In the Netherlands, for example, the national public safety and security policy includes the coordination of the ministries involved: Justice and the Interior. Next to this policy the National Platform for Crime Control promotes cooperation between the ministries of Justice, the Interior, Economic Affairs, Transport and Finance, and the business community (insurance, banking, retail, etc.). Justice and Interior are able to bring results from the evaluation of successful projects to this forum to interest the other ministries in taking on particular programmes that could reduce crime. The development of the Police Secured Housing Label has involved close coordination between Justice, Interior and Physical Planning, with a view to influencing private sector practices to include crime prevention as one of their concerns in developing new homes and renovating existing ones.

Encouraging problem-solving partnerships and involving and informing citizens

Some crime prevention secretariats have focused on fostering partnerships by local authorities and problem-oriented policing. Some have instituted programmes to promote national standards for new residences that will provide protection from residential burglary.

Partnerships with local authorities are growing. In France, Belgium, England, the Netherlands and the USA, local problem-solving partnerships are evolving with many of the essential ingredients, which are described below in the section on successful projects of crime prevention.

These partnerships have been helped by a variety of non-governmental groups. For example, the European Forum for Urban Safety provides technical assistance, devel-

Some secretariats have instituted programmes to promote national standards for new residences that will provide protection from residential burglary.

ops pilot and demonstration projects, disseminates information, and prepares training courses and conferences. A similar forum has recently been created in Belgium. In England, Crime Concern was created in 1988 with the mission to work with local partners to prevent crime and create safer communities. It has set up 25 local community safety partnerships and provided consulting services to 100 local authorities and other agencies. It has developed guidelines on reducing crime in high crime neighborhoods, using examples of successes.

Several secretariats promote campaigns to provide citizens with information on how to protect themselves that may or may not be based on a rigorous analysis of what works. Education campaigns are conducted through publications, electronic media and other channels to enhance citizen responsibility and encourage their involvement. Others have encouraged programmes such as Neighbourhood Watch.

Crime prevention best practice

This section shows that many different types of projects in different countries have reduced levels of delinquency and violent crime by tackling the causes — whether those that are conducive to victimization or those that generate criminal behaviour — and by forming real partnerships at the local level.

In recent years, attempts at illustrating

crime prevention best practice have been the focus of much attention, particularly in the western world. The published literature has ranged from books and journal articles (Clarke, 1992, 1995, 1997; Mulvey, Arthur and Reppucci, 1993; Tremblay and Craig, 1995; Yoshikawa, 1994; Zigler, Taussig and Black, 1992), to reports of national commissions (Reiss and Roth, 1993), to government sponsored reports (Hurley, 1995; Safe Neighbourhoods Unit, 1993; Van Limbergen, Walgrave and Dekegel, 1996), to agency sponsored studies (Farrington, 1996b; Graham and Bennett, 1995; Grabosky and James, 1995; Waller and Welsh, 1995). This section draws from and builds upon that work.

There are a variety of approaches to crime prevention and crime reduction, perhaps the most innovative at the moment being what has become known as "situational crime prevention." While beginning in such small projects as designing out crime, this approach has developed into a broadly encompassing set of practical techniques for preventing crime (Box 8.3). In the first part of this section, we show the extent to which crime is reduced by five different types of crime prevention projects: designing out crime; promoting social control; investing in youth and families; promoting responsibility; and breaking the cycle of violence against women and children. In the second part, we present some results from crime prevention partnerships that are based on city action along with innovative police and justice cooperation with other agencies.

A recent report for the US Congress by Sherman *et al.* (1997) demonstrated the extent to which scientific evaluations provided conclusions on traditional and problem-oriented approaches to reduce crime. They noted how few evaluations exist of traditional policing and incarceration programmes. However, where they exist, they do not usually show positive results.

In selecting the projects presented here, we have not limited the discussion to projects where scientific evaluations have demonstrated a reduction in crime

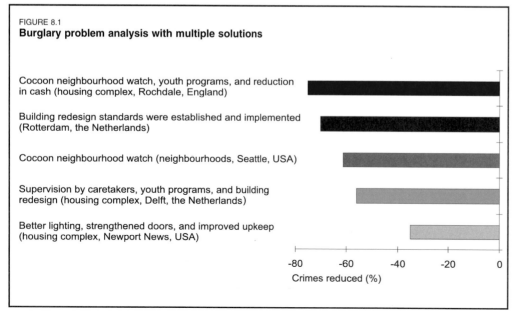

FIGURE 8.1
Burglary problem analysis with multiple solutions

Cocoon neighbourhood watch, youth programs, and reduction in cash (housing complex, Rochdale, England)

Building redesign standards were established and implemented (Rotterdam, the Netherlands)

Cocoon neighbourhood watch (neighbourhoods, Seattle, USA)

Supervision by caretakers, youth programs, and building redesign (housing complex, Delft, the Netherlands)

Better lighting, strengthened doors, and improved upkeep (housing complex, Newport News, USA)

Crimes reduced (%)

-80   -60   -40   -20   0

"beyond reasonable doubt." Instead, we have included projects where the "balance of probabilities" is that they reduced crime, or where the project undertook some analysis of the problem before implementing the solution.

Designing out crime

We selected five projects spread over two continents to illustrate (see Figure 8.1) the extent to which residential burglary can be reduced. Each of these projects evolved from an analysis of the causes of crime in which public and private agencies with the solutions were involved. No significant displacement of the crimes to the surrounding areas was found. However, some diffusion of benefits occurred where households in the surrounding area began to adopt the same procedures and so got some additional reductions.

Beginning in 1986, a project team of city officials, police, social workers, and university faculty and students undertook to tackle repeat victimization on the Kirkholt housing estate of Rochdale, England, by analyzing the nature of the problem and then implementing solutions (Forrester, Frenz, O'Connell and Pease, 1990). They offered burglary victims: ways to remove coin-operated electric and gas meters; target hardening by upgrading home security with improved locks and bolts; and a "cocoon" neighbourhood watch programme in which six or more residents surrounding a victimized dwelling were asked to participate by watching and reporting anything suspicious to prevent repeat victimization. A scientific evaluation showed a 58 percent reduction in burglaries in the first year and 75 percent by the end of the third year.

In 1991, the Dutch safe housing label was initiated by police in the triangle Rotterdam-Leiden-The Hague. It was introduced nationally in 1996. When housing project developers or housing associations apply for a Police Secured Label, their

BOX 8.3
Situational crime prevention: a scientific approach to crime reduction and prevention

Situational crime prevention is a systematic approach to solving specific crime problems. Crime prevention specialists carefully analyze the situation and context within which a particular crime problem occurs, then employ a number of opportunity reducing techniques to solve the problem. Usually, a combination of the techniques listed in the table below is employed. The success of this approach depends on the skill and experience of the crime prevention analyst as well as the ability of the local authorities and organizations (such as police, urban or housing planners, transportation officials, etc., depending on the type of crime) to work together in implementing a complete crime prevention strategy.

Increasing Perceived Effort	Increasing Perceived Risks	Reducing Anticipated Rewards	Removing Excuses
1. Target hardening Slug rejecter device Steering locks Bandit screens	**5. Entry/exit screening** Automatic ticket gates Baggage screening Merchandise tags	**9. Target removal** Removable car radio Women's refuges Phonecard	**13. Rule setting** Customs declaration Harassment codes Hotel registration
2. Access control Parking lot barriers Fenced yards Entry phones	**6. Formal surveillance** Red light cameras Burglar alarms Security guards	**10. Identifying property** Property marking Vehicle licensing Cattle branding	**14. Stimulating conscience** Roadside speedometers "Shoplifting is stealing" "Idiots drink and drive"
3. Deflecting offenders Bus stop placement Tavern location Street closures	**7. Surveillance by employees** Pay phone location Park attendants CCTV systems	**11. Reducing temptation** Gender-neutral listings Off-street parking Rapid repair	**15. Controlling disinhibitors** Drinking age laws Ignition interlock V-chip
4. Controlling facilitators Credit card photo Gun controls Caller-ID	**8. Natural surveillance** Defensible space Street lighting Cab driver ID	**12. Denying benefits** Ink merchandise tags PIN for car radios Graffiti cleaning	**16. Facilitating compliance** Easy library checkout Public lavatories Trash bins

Source: Clarke (1997) Table reproduced with permission, Harrow and Heston, Publishers

project and its environment must be approved by the police as meeting standards relating to residents' participation and responsibility, neighbourhood management and home watch, as well as building design features such as orientation of living rooms, low roof, main entrance and target hardening. A simple before-after design showed a

70 percent reduction in burglaries between those new houses involved in the programme and those not in Rotterdam (Scherpenisse, 1997).

In 1972, the mayor created the Law and Justice Planning Office in the city hall of Seattle, USA. In 1973, a Community Crime Prevention Program was initiated to tackle burglary problems through: residential security inspection services; marking personal property during the home security inspection, and displaying decals warning burglars that property has been marked; "cocoon-type" block watches involving ten to 15 families; and public education campaigns to promote citizen awareness and prevention of the burglary problem. A before-after evaluation using victimization surveys showed a 61 percent reduction in residential burglaries in the targeted areas (Waller, 1982).

In 1985, officials of the city of Delft, the Netherlands, mobilized local partners to launch a programme aimed at reducing crime problems and community decay in a public housing project. The programme included efforts focused on: organizing recreational activities for young people and providing a street worker to coordinate activities; hiring seven caretakers to intensify surveillance; and altering physical design features to encourage surveillance and decrease building vulnerability to vandalism. A before-after evaluation confirmed a 56 percent drop in reported crime in the housing complex after two years (Willemse, 1994).

In the mid 1980s in Newport News, USA, the chief of police appointed 12 officers to a task force charged with the responsibility of analyzing the nature and causes of the most pervasive crime problems. To address the problems of burglary, they scanned and grouped individual-related incidents and defined them as part of a pattern of problems. When this traditional information was seen to be insufficient, they turned to local residents. From there onwards, co-ordinated, cooperative and systematic action programmes began. These actions involved partnerships with the police, city and state agencies and tenants, along with some opportunity reduction measures. What had been an abandoned housing complex was gradually revamped, with assistance from the Housing and Urban Development fed-

A before-after evaluation confirmed a 56 percent drop in reported crime in the housing complex after two years.

eral department. In the housing complex where one in four units had been broken into each year, a before-after design showed a reduction of 35 percent in burglaries (Spelman and Eck, 1987).

Promoting social control

Successful measures have also been developed to reduce crime by providing social control. In some cases, the government or the city have hired persons off unemployment to undertake the task, and in some cases, it has been done through fixed closed circuit television cameras (CCTVs).

To deal with the problems of fare-dodging, vandalism and aggression in the Dutch public transport system, young people, mostly unemployed, were hired to act as ticket inspectors and carry out formal surveillance. Started in Rotterdam and expanded to Amsterdam and The Hague, the project involved approximately 1,200 young persons. A one year before-after evaluation found reductions in fare-dodging in all three cities, with Amsterdam showing the largest reduction in all three modes of public transport: tram 17.7 percent to 9 percent; metro 23.5 percent to 6.5 percent; and bus 9.2 percent to 1.7 percent. Pooling the results gives an approximate overall reduction of 68 percent in fare-dodging (van Andel, 1989).

In England, experience has shown that CCTV is most effective when it forms part of a package of crime prevention measures. Since 1992, the city of Newcastle has used CCTVs to help address crime and disorder problems. The major benefits of using the camera system include: discrete surveillance of troublesome areas or incidents; coordination of more rapid and targeted responses; and the capacity to produce hard copies (e.g., photos) and record the video surveillance for use in court or to identify potential witnesses. A before-after evaluation showed a 57 percent drop in the average monthly burglary totals in the area where cameras were installed after 15 months. Similar results were shown for criminal damage (-34 percent), thefts of vehicles (-47 percent) and theft from vehicles (-50 percent) (Brown, 1995).

The *Stadswacht* or City Guard programme began in 1989 in the city of Dordrecht. Drawn from the long-term unemployed, individuals receive eight weeks of first-aid/law/security training and perform the following tasks: provide police with reports on crime and disorder problems; provide municipal departments with reports on graffiti and street lighting problems; and provide tourists with information and/or directions. In 1996, the Dutch government earmarked resources to create 20,000 jobs over the next four years. A simple evaluation showed a reduction of 17 percent in reported crime (Hauber, Hofsta, Toornvliet and Zanderbergen, 1994).

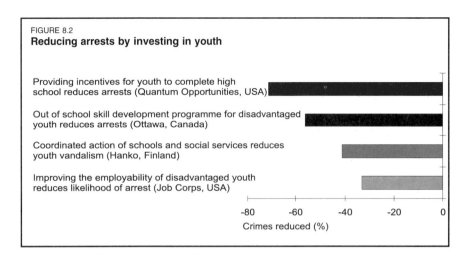

FIGURE 8.2
Reducing arrests by investing in youth

Investing in youth and family

Socio-economic deprivation and difficulties for young persons growing up are some of the strongest predictors of delinquency and violent crime. Figure 8.2 illustrates three successful programmes that target those risks.

For four years (1989-1993), the Quantum Opportunities Program (QOP) offered disadvantaged teenagers in five US cities (San Antonio, Philadelphia, Milwaukee, Saginaw and Oklahoma City) after school activities for which they received hourly stipends ($1 to $1.33 per hour) and a matching amount of funds in a college-fund account. The youths were encouraged to complete school through activities such as computer-assisted instruction, peer tutoring, homework assistance, community service and public event projects, and developmental activities such as curricula on life/family skills and college and career planning.

In each city, an equal number of youths (N=50) were randomly assigned to either a programme group that received the intervention or a control group that did not. The programme achieved a 71 percent reduction in arrests after four years (Hahn, 1994).

From 1980 to 1982, the Participate and Learn Skills (PALS) programme developed the skills of disadvantaged children (age 5-15 years) in a low-income housing complex in Ottawa, Canada. Participating children were offered free non-school skill-development programmes (including: swimming, judo, ballet, scouting, orienteering and co-operative games), and children were actively recruited into the programme. Compared to a matched control site, children who participated in PALS fared better in a number of areas, but the strongest programme effect was a 56 percent reduction in delinquency (Jones and Offord, 1989).

In the mid 1970s, the US Job Corps was established as a federal training programme for disadvantaged/unemployed youths. It aimed to improve employability and reduce crime by helping disadvantaged youths achieve stable and long-term employment opportunities. The programme now operates in over 100 centres, enrolls approximately 100,000 participants (age 16-24 years) a year, and provides the following in a residential setting: job training, classroom courses (permitting the attainment of graduate equivalent degrees), health care, counseling and job placement services.

In an evaluation (Long, Mallar and Thornton, 1981) which included approximately 5,100 youths, Job Corps members who had been out of the programme for a maximum of two years were compared with a matched group of non-participating youths, and an 18 month follow-up period was provided. Evaluation findings showed that participating youths were one-third less likely than non-participants to have been arrested one or more times. As well, 75 percent of Job Corps members moved on to full-time study or stable employment where earnings were 15 percent higher than non-participants who were employed.

In 1991, a multidimensional programme was created in Hanko, Finland, to tackle the factors which were responsible for young persons accounting for 65 percent of the criminal offences solved that year. The Shadow Side Work Group focused on im-

Pooling the results gives an approximate overall reduction of 68 percent in fare-dodging.

In Canada, gun control legislation was found to have reduced homicides by approximately 55 percent between 1977 and 1993.

proving the social status of disadvantaged young people and their families, and targeting various associated problems and at-risk groups by: developing non-institutionalized child care options; implementing a night life street patrol programme; and involving youth in pro-social activities like youth employment and apprenticeship programmes.

In the following two years, there was a reduction of 41 percent in property offences (largely vandalism and larceny) committed by juveniles, a 50 percent reduction in costs relating to municipal child welfare, and a significant increase of youth involvement in community organized activities (Shadow Side Work Group, 1994).

In 1977, the city of Turin, Italy, began offering programmes which reach out to young people and adolescents at risk of involvement in delinquency and later criminality. The programme seeks to make institutions and the adult world aware of young people's problems, as well as to provide a range of prevention programmes, in concert with other stakeholders (e.g., the city, schools, private institutions, community groups, young people's clubs). One of the successful activities has included the training of adults responsible for youth sports teams. Adults are trained to detect early signs of delinquency, intervene with the young people, and make referrals to community services. Another initiative that has shown some promise in improving the quality of life of young people and the community at-large is the establishment of a micro-enterprise business run by young people. Part of the revenue generated from sales of the crafts market goes to fund a youth-driven, urban restoration programme.

Promoting responsibility

Projects designed to promote responsibility have successfully reduced various forms of crime. Projects in this area are, to a larger degree than in other domains, influenced by a public health approach to the prevention of crime. Unfortunately, many of the more promising programmes such as peer mediation in schools, *Maison de justice* in France, and action plans do not yet have any evaluations.

In the Netherlands, the HALT programme was created to respond to the

problem of youth vandalism. It provided a variety of measures such as reparation of the damage, volunteer work as an alternative to prosecution, and assistance in resolving the underlying problems of youth. Using a control group method, the programme evaluation found that vandalism had stopped or decreased in over 60 percent of the participants, while it had stopped or decreased in only 25 percent of the control group (Kruissink, 1990).

In 1992, approximately 150,000 people received public-funded drug and alcohol treatment services in California. Treatment services were offered in the following major treatment programme types: residential therapeutic communities; residential social model; outpatient drug-free; and outpatient methadone. An evaluation of the treatment programmes involving a representative sample of 1,900 persons revealed that the overall rate of recidivism among treated individuals was reduced by 72 percent (Gerstein, Johnson, Harwood, Fountain, Suter and Malloy, 1994)

Canada adopted its first gun control legislation in 1977, later amended and strengthened in 1991 and 1995. The 1977 Firearms Control Initiative involves two components. The legislative component includes the Firearms Acquisition Certificate which is required before an individual can take possession of a firearm, while the programme component includes safety courses on the safe handling and use of firearms.

The Department of Justice of Canada conducted a rigorous evaluation of the 1977 legislative component's effects, conducting three types of analyses: exploratory, time-series, and structural modelling (Department of Justice Canada, 1996). In reviewing the levels of homicides, both involving firearms and not, it found a clear effect of the gun control legislation on the structural model: homicides were reduced by approximately 55 percent between 1977 and 1993.

In 1988, an initiative was undertaken in Belgium to reduce violence in football stadiums. An integrated strategy, including the following key elements, was implemented to tackle the problem: fan coaches (e.g., street workers) attended games to help defuse potential violent incidents; the infrastructure and social control in stadiums was improved, and, with judicial approval, a system of alternative sanctions was created for young hooligans; and programmes and social workers were provided to help young fans solve their individual problems. As a result, hooliganism was reduced by 45 percent over an unspecified period of time (Van Limbergen *et al.*, 1996).

Throughout France, neighbourhood justice "houses" and "offices" have been set up by the Ministry of Justice and local associations to address minor crimes and other legal problems through alternative justice approaches. Staff are trained to provide victim-offender mediation and are legally empowered to deal with cases. It is reported, although not proven, that everywhere they have been set up, they have relieved the courts and settled cases faster. By improving the community's access to justice using restorative justice approaches, the houses have also had an impact on reducing recidivism and enhancing citizen responsibility and citizenship.

Breaking the cycle of violence

Figure 8.3 reports on the findings of evaluations of four programmes which have set out to break the cycle of violence by investing in families, children and re-education.

In 1962, a preschool programme was introduced in Ypsilanti, Michigan, to increase cognitive abilities and school achievement among disadvantaged children, and to reduce the potential for future delinquency and criminal behaviour. The programme was evaluated using a longitudinal, experimental design. The 123 children were randomly assigned to either a programme group that received the intervention (N=58) or a matched control group (N=65) that did not. The programme group received high quality preschool education for two years, home visits by a child's teacher to promote parental involvement in child development, and monthly group meetings for parents to exchange views and support each other's efforts in child rearing. The programme reduced the mean number of arrests by 50 percent (2.3 for programme group vs. 4.6 for control) 23 years after programme

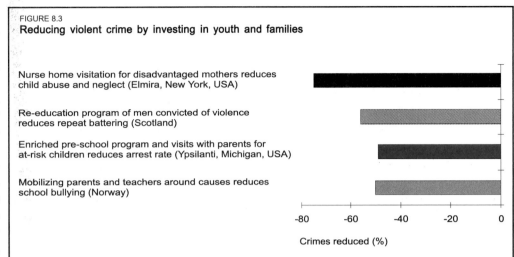

FIGURE 8.3
Reducing violent crime by investing in youth and families

completion (Schweinhart, Barnes, and Weikart, 1993).

In 1980, a programme was initiated in Elmira, New York, for nurses to visit homes to provide support to poor and unmarried teenage mothers during their pregnancies and in the first two years of their children's lives. In attempting to improve the quality of child care and the personal development of the women and their children, nurse home visitors provided: parental education to promote healthy pregnancies, and child health and development; and assistance in improving participants' access and use of both informal and formal neighbourhood support and medical services until the children reached the age of two years.

The longitudinal, clinical trial randomly assigned 400 pregnant women to one of four treatment conditions. The experimental group received all four treatments. At two years post-intervention, compared to the matched control group which did not receive post-natal home visits, the experimental group showed impressive results across a range of outcomes, including reducing child abuse and neglect by more than 75 percent (4% of programme group vs. 19% of control) (Olds, Henderson, Chamberlin and Tatelbaum, 1986).

In the early 1990s, a programme was launched in the United Kingdom which provided men convicted of violence against their female partners with a re-education programme as a condition of a probation order – involving weekly group sessions over a period of six to seven months. A quasi-experimental design assessed the effectiveness of the programme against other

...the experimental group showed impressive results across a range of outcomes, including reducing child abuse and neglect by more than 75 percent.

criminal sanctions (e.g., prison, probation, fines). At one-year post-intervention, female partners of men in the re-education programme (N=27) reported a much lower prevalence (occurrence of at least one incident – 33 percent vs. 75 percent) and frequency (five or more incidents – 7 percent vs. 37 percent) of violence perpetrated by their male partners compared to female partners of men who did not receive the intervention (N=59). This translates into a 56 percent decrease in the prevalence of violence and an 81 percent decrease in frequency (Dobash, Dobash, Cavanagh and Lewis, 1996).

In 1983, a national elementary school programme was initiated in 42 schools in Norway to reduce bully/victim problems. Key components of this collaborative programme included: school personnel, who received a 32 page booklet describing bully/victim problems and how to intervene effectively; parents, who received information and advice; the public, who were provided with access to a 25 minute video on bullying and its impact; and periodic questionnaires which were administered to school children to identify the nature and extent of bully/victim problems. The project reduced the prevalence of bullying by 50 percent over two years, and also decreased rates in theft, vandalism and truancy (Olweus, 1991).

City action

Cities are strategically placed to bring together the agencies that can reduce delinquency, violent crime and insecurity (European Forum for Urban Safety *et al.*, 1989, 1991). They have traditionally taken responsibility for urban planning and often have or can make links to school authorities, housing agencies, public health agencies and social service boards, as well as to police and justice services. In Europe, local authorities are increasingly playing a role in police and justice issues.

Cities in different world regions are pioneering strategies to involve key agencies in diagnosing and tackling causes, often with citizen and private sector involvement. These include safer cities, business forums on public safety, community action plans, crime prevention councils and public health for violence prevention.

In 1988, the Home Office in the United Kingdom funded multi-agency project teams under the Safer Cities Programme in 20 cities or boroughs to tackle a range of local crime problems. The programme has since supported 4,400 crime prevention projects in 30 inner-city and urban areas at a cost of over £29 million ($46.4 million). A steering committee involving representatives from the local agencies (local authority and police) and from the voluntary sectors was responsible for overseeing each city project with a paid local coordinator. The Home Office provided £250,000 ($400,000) per year per city. By 1992, residential burglary was targeted by nearly 300 initiatives under the programme. Specific measures employed included: target-hardening through door and window improvements, alarms and security lighting; community action through Neighbourhood Watch and property marking programmes; and other activities such as the distribution of leaflets and small house-to-house surveys.

A large-scale impact evaluation of the residential burglary schemes (240 in total) showed that risk of residential burglary was ten to 30 percent lower than expected, depending on the targeted areas and specific programme used. Also, the programme more than paid for itself through reduced costs to victims and the state alone (Ekblom, Law and Sutton, 1996).

In France, the focal point for crime prevention is local municipal crime prevention councils, which bring together elected officials, experts and persons in charge of governmental and community organizations. Councils administer funds for local projects through funding supplied under contract by the central government. The municipal councils are required to carry out: a detailed crime analysis; a review of current strategies to prevent crime; and a systematic plan for future action. Today, there are over 850 local councils, and most of them have had substantial impacts on the local crime situation (Bousquet, 1996).

Formal empirical evaluations of the councils have not been conducted. During the period from 1983 to 1987, crime fell by 10.5 percent across France. In one very active and successful city, Lille, there was a fall of almost 12 percent between 1985 and 1986 (Ville de Lille, 1992). Crime also fell

In England, a large-scale impact evaluation of the residential burglary schemes (240 in total) showed an overall reduction of 21 percent in the prevalence of residential burglary.

in the first cities to use the approach in comparison to increases in similarly situated cities.

In the summer of 1993, the city of Houston in the United States created a coalition of 60 members. It was one of the seven major cities involved in the Texas City Action Plan to Prevent Crime (T-CAP) (National Crime Prevention Council, 1994). Coalitions were created from diverse sectors of the city under the leadership of the mayor. The process was designed to include: an assessment of city needs; development of both long-term and short-term goals; use of in-depth, subject-specific task forces to involve additional residents and draw on specialized expertise; a process for official approval; and a specific plan for implementation. Recommendations included: education plans focused on cultural sensitivity and safer learning environments; plans to prepare youth for employment and create stronger links with employers; health/environment plans to refer high-risk individuals to available services and prevent street gang activities; and recreation plans to develop youth problem-solving and communication skills.

Rates of police-reported crime decreased in all seven of the T-CAP cities from 1992 to 1994. The largest T-CAP city, Houston, reported a 14 percent fall in total crime over this two year period (National Crime Prevention Council, 1995).

Under the leadership of the mayor, the city of Cali, Colombia, implemented a comprehensive violence prevention programme (DESEPAS), which viewed violence as a preventable social and public health problem (Eastman, Carrion and Cobo, 1995). Targeted at the most violent communities in the city, the programme's three main areas of action — social development, education for peace and police accountability — hinged on strong community leadership and participation. Social development stressed such areas as primary health care, education and self-built housing, which was achieved through micro-enterprise development. Early evaluation results from the implementation of the programme in a violent community showed promising reductions in crime rates and a greater responsibility on the part of the residents for the peace of their community.

In 1994, the city of Villa María, located in the province of Cordoba, Argentina, established a multi-disciplinary prevention committee to harness the expertise of the many local groups involved in crime prevention activities and implemented a coordinated city-wide plan to prevent delinquency and violent crime. One of the first initiatives of the partnership-based committee was the establishment of a police-youth branch. Other programmes being planned by the committee include a training programme in parenting skills and the construction of more than ten parks and playgrounds across the city, which offer recreation services for young people. The prevention committee is also working to establish similar committees in secondary schools, working closely with students and teachers.

Innovative policing and justice approaches

In the last decade, problem-oriented policing has been touted as a way for the police to focus on ways to tackle the underlying problems that create repeated demands for service (Box 8.4). It is based on the theory that there will be a rigorous process of problem solving: identification, analysis, response and evaluation.

In San Diego, California, in the late 1980s, the police department initiated a number of problem-oriented policing strategies to deal with drug offences and the associated violence and public disorder. Police, with the support of local businesses, initiated a plan involving increased surveillance and enhanced foot patrol. After nine months, reported crimes in the targeted areas had decreased by 45 percent, and calls for service fell by 63 percent in 12 months (Capowich and Roehl, 1994).

What began as a demonstration project to test the effectiveness of implementing problem-oriented policing on an agency-wide scale in the city of Newport News, USA, soon turned into a model of best practice. In just three months, following a multi-agency effort on the part of the police, a state agency and local businesses, prostitution-related robberies were reduced by 39 percent (Spelman and Eck, 1987). Eighteen months after the scheme had ended, neither

In just three months, following a multi-agency effort on the part of the police, a state agency and local businesses, prostitution-related robberies were reduced by 39 percent in Newport News, USA.

BOX 8.4

Japan's Koban: a tradition of community policing for crime prevention

Japan is said to be one of the safest countries in the world. This is largely attributable to the Japanese community police system based on Koban or police boxes. The "community" police officers (renamed from "patrol" officers in 1992) account for about 40 percent of the total police strength in Japan. The 1996 statistics show that community police officers caught some 80 percent of the total penal code offenders, handled about 50 percent of traffic violations and 60 percent of traffic accidents, and helped local residents solve 18,500 civil problems nationwide through counseling service. Koban forms part of the local community, functioning as a "Community Safety Center." Major Koban duties are:

Administrative service. This service includes response to people visiting the Koban. For instance, Koban officers give directions to those unfamiliar with the area (the most common task in big cities), handle lost and found articles, take care of stray children, provide counseling service for residents, etc.

Initial response to incidents and accidents. Koban officers initially respond to various incidents and accidents. For example, once Koban officers know a criminal case is imminent or taking place, they immediately rush to the scene, arrest suspects, find eyewitnesses, take care of victims or close off the site. Then they hand over the case to criminal investigators who soon arrive at the scene from the police station.

Prevention of crimes and accidents. Koban officers routinely visit houses and work places on their beat to raise awareness of the prevention of crimes and accidents. They talk with residents and workers face-to-face to learn what they are troubled by and to give useful information about incidents and accidents. In addition, a community relations meeting is often held at Koban. Community volunteers participate in it to talk about community problems.

A typical Koban officer and his daily duty. Mr. Yamada, a typical Koban officer, finished a ten month pre-service training course at a prefectural police academy two years ago, and he was assigned to a police station. The station is made up of six sections: administration, crime prevention, criminal investigation, traffic, security and community police. The total personnel numbers around 400. Almost half of them are assigned to the community police section, under which ten Koban and five patrol cars operate.

The working pattern of Koban is based on the three-day rotation system. Officer Yamada, for example, works from 8:30 AM on the first day to 8:30 AM on the second day. Then, he gets a day off on the second day. After that, he works from 8:30 AM to 5:15 PM on the third day. This is the basic pattern, but the working hours a week are limited to 40 hours.

Officer Yamada lives in a dormitory attached to the police station. He shares his room with a colleague. He gets up at 6:30 AM and takes breakfast at a dining facility in the dormitory. At 8:30 AM he goes to an auditorium in the police station. About 40 officers in all, who will be assigned to each Koban on this day, assemble there. A chief of the station checks out their uniforms and equipment, and gives general directions. After the morning formation, Officer Yamada and two other policemen go to "Ekimae Koban" by bicycle, a kilometer away from the police station.

At 9 AM Officer Yamada and his mates take over the responsibility from members of an outgoing group. A police sergeant, Koban leader of the day, gives them specific instructions, such as to be especially watchful for burglaries.

At 10 AM Officer Yamada goes out of the Koban to patrol. He pays special attention to apartment houses which are likely to be targeted by offenders. At 10:30 AM he gets a radio report of a traffic accident in the neighbourhood. He rushes to the scene, rescues victims and controls the traffic there, until traffic police officers come from the police station.

At 11 AM Officer Yamada goes back to the Koban and carries out his duties there until 12:00 noon. He orders a lunch box by phone from a restaurant which has delivery service. The lunch box comes in ten minutes. He eats it in a rear room of the Koban and takes a break until 1 PM.

From 1 to 2 PM, Officer Yamada stands just in front of the Koban and gives directions to more than ten strangers, while his mates are eating lunch.

At 2 PM Officer Yamada starts to make routine visits to houses and offices on his beat by bicycle. He visits eight houses and two offices for two hours, and tells the residents and the office workers about burglaries which recently occurred nearby. He also hears from them about what they want the police to do.

At 4:10 PM a little girl visits the Koban accompanied by her mother to turn in a wallet she found at a park. Officer Yamada receives the wallet from her, checks what is in it, and makes out the "Found Property Report." He explains to her mother that she can claim a reward of from five to 20 percent of its value if its owner is identified. In case the owner does not appear in six months and 14 days, the law says that the wallet will be awarded to her.

At 7 PM Officer Yamada eats a bowl of noodles delivered by a noodle shop and takes a break at the day room for one hour.

At 8 PM Officer Yamada goes out on foot patrol with his partner. Around 8:50 at a narrow street, a suspicious-looking man makes an about-face and tries to run away as soon as the man recognizes the police. They dash up to the man and ask several questions. Consequently, they find the man carrying a handgun illegally. In Japan, the possession of a handgun is almost totally banned by the law. The man is immediately put under arrest for violating the Firearms and Swords Control Law. They take the suspect to the police station and hand him over to criminal investigators. After transferring the suspect to the detectives, they return to their patrol.

Officer Yamada is supposed to have a few hours of sleep in the rear room until 5 AM. But at 3:15 AM there is a fire report from a nearby resident. He is awakened by his partner, rushes to the scene, and helps people escape to safety. The fire is put out in 30 minutes and no one is injured. At 4 AM he returns to the Koban and takes a rest until 6 AM.

At 7:30 AM Officer Yamada stands at a busy intersection to help school children cross the street on their way to school. He loves the school kids, because they always say to him, "Good morning, Officer! Thank you very much for the good job."

At 9 AM members of an incoming party arrive at the Koban and take over the duty. After some paper work at the police station, Officer Yamada goes back to the dormitory, takes a quick shower, and goes to bed.

Source: Hirota (Original paper, 1997)

prostitution activity nor reported incidences of robbery showed signs of returning to pre-intervention levels. Also, through a stepped-up police enforcement strategy, thefts from cars in a shipyard parking lot were reduced by 53 percent after only a few months (Spelman and Eck, 1987).

In June 1993, in the Netherlands, a Commercial Robbery Task Force of five individuals representing the police, local and central government, and the national associations of banks and shopkeepers was created for a term of three years to analyze the problem of commercial robbery and recommend solutions. The following strategies were identified to tackle the problem: regional coordination for tracking offenders; opportunity reduction prevention (e.g., CCTVs); social prevention (e.g., education and work programmes for young people at-risk of delinquency and later criminal offending); and victim assistance (e.g., training of coordinators and volunteers to assist victims of robbery). It is reported to have achieved a 28 percent reduction in commercial robberies in one year (Jammers, 1995, 1996).

In Sydney, Australia, a systematic analysis of the car theft problem led to police partnerships with the key stakeholders (motorists, car manufacturers, insurance companies, repair shops and local government) to improve liaison with police and implement a wide array of public education and opportunity-based preventive measures (e.g., more secure parking facilities). The scheme cut car theft by 25 percent in one year (Grabosky, 1995).

In response to high levels of victimization against women and under-reporting and inaction on the part of the police in Sao Paulo, Brazil, all-female police stations were set up across the city (Eluf, 1992). The police stations were empowered to investigate and counter such crimes by: attending to victims; writing official complaint reports; working to deter male violence directed at women; and providing counselling services and emergency shelter for battered women and their children. In the two years following the introduction of an all-female police station in Rio de Janeiro, reported threats against women dropped by 63 percent and reported rapes fell by 37 percent (Jornal Do Brasil, 1991; see also Box 8.6).

Economic costs of crime and benefits of crime prevention

In Europe, North America and other regions of the world, governments have been forced to find ways of reducing expenditures, restructuring government departments, and identifying which investments will best meet the needs of their citizens. Major reforms have been implemented in areas vital to citizens such as health and education. For crime control the strategic issues have yet to be faced.

Nevertheless, the payoffs from alternative expenditures to reduce delinquency, violent crime and insecurity are and will be important. This section first presents data on the economic costs of crime and criminal justice. The next section examines the conclusions from various efforts by scientists to identify the quantitative monetary benefits from different investments in crime prevention as well as the comparative cost advantages of prevention projects and programmes.

Economic costs of crime

Over the last few years in developed countries, particularly Australia (Walker, 1992, 1995, 1997), Canada (Brantingham and Easton, 1996; Spigelman, 1996; Welsh and Waller, 1995), England and Wales (Home Office Standing Conference on Crime Prevention, 1988), France (Godefroy and Lafargue, 1993), and the United States (Cohen, 1988; Miller, Cohen and Rossman, 1993; Miller, Cohen and Wierseman, 1996), research into the economic consequences of crime has generated considerable interest among decision-makers and practitioners in the crime and justice field. It has provided another piece of evidence, perhaps stronger, which calls into question the continued reliance on a reactive criminal justice approach to deal with crime.

For the purpose of costing crime, a comprehensive categorization is necessary. In their estimation of the costs of personal and household crime in the USA in 1992, Mandel, Magnusson, Ellis, DeGeorge and Alexander (1993) used a six-part scheme:
- criminal justice system (police, courts and corrections);
- private security (alarms, private guards

BOX 8.5

Estimating the cost of crime in Australia

Estimating the financial and economic costs of crime involves the use of sophisticated methodology plus a pinch of guesswork. Neither *financial costs* nor *economic costs* of crime are easy to define or measure.

Financial costs are those costs which are not, in the eyes of economists, losses to the community, but are illegal transfers of purchasing power from victims to offenders. Thus the thief who steals $100 is better off by that amount, cancelling out the loss incurred by the victim. Yet we intuitively count these as costs of crime; this report follows that intuition.

Economic costs of crime arise when crime causes society to divert time, energy and resources from more productive purposes. These include the diversion of scarce medical resources to the treatment of victims of crime, the quality of life losses incurred by victims, and the time spent by victims assisting police with inquiries, as well as the more obvious costs of public and private resources used against crime.

Long-term and indirect costs of crime are often particularly difficult to define. For example, serious victimization which causes severe emotional stress can in affect employability and therefore career earnings. These costs can have economic "multiplier effects" in which the victims' families, relatives, business associates and even whole communities also suffer losses. Where do we draw the line? The criminal justice system itself costs taxpayers several billion dollars each year, yet its many employees contribute to taxation revenues. Arguably only the net costs, not the total costs, of this should count.

Caveat. It must be stressed that these figures can at best be regarded as estimates only. They vary considerably in the extent to which they include "intangible" and long term costs. While comparisons between these estimates for 1996 and those for 1992 will inevitably be taken as indicating likely changes over this four year period, this interpretation should be used with great caution as, in some cases, the basis for estimation has changed significantly owing to improved data sources.

Example: robbery and extortion. Estimates derived from the NCVS suggest that at least 229,500 robberies occurred in Australia from 1992 to 1993, of which 52.1 percent (119,570) were reported to police. These may include robberies of commercial premises where the business, not the survey respondent was the victim. Such incidents, according to police data, would involve much greater losses than robberies of individuals (Victoria Police 1996). By contrast, the NCVS suggests only 12,765 robberies were reported to police in 1993, 13,983 in 1994 and 16,466 in 1995, including both personal and business robberies.

There are clearly major problems with the definition of the word "robbery," which is commonly used by victims when, technically, a theft or a burglary, not a robbery, has taken place — the difference being that no violence was used or threatened. So police data must be regarded as the more reliable for reported crime.

Using the NCVS figure of 52.1 percent reporting rate suggests that 15,139 unreported robberies would have occurred in 1995 in addition to the 16,466 that were reported.

Victoria Police data for 1995-96 suggest an average cost per reported robbery of $2,042. Combining these cost data and National Injury Surveillance and Prevention Project estimates of the costs of injury suggests current costs of only $37 million.

A further complication is the extent to which stolen property is recovered or other economic damage is caused. No information has been found to provide meaningful estimates of this.

Some rare cases of extortion (for example, instances involving tampering with food products on supermarket shelves) for which few statistics of any sort are available, not only involve very large amounts demanded from the victim, but often the full cost includes considerable lost sales. In addition, anecdotal evidence exists of significant underreporting of extortion amongst some migrant communities in our cities. Total costs of robbery and extortion may therefore be considerably greater than the costs indicated here.

Source: Edited and abridged from Walker (1997)

and security systems);

- urban decay (lost jobs and relocation of residents — urban flight);
- property loss (stolen goods);
- medical care (treating crime victims); and,
- shattered lives (pain, suffering and lost quality of life of crime victims and their families).

Although this classification scheme is by no means exhaustive (see Cohen, Miller and Rossman, 1994), it takes into account the vast range of public and private costs. Most importantly, it accounts for the full impact of crime on victims — an area that has, until recently, been neglected in the study of the costs of crime.

Using part of this categorization scheme, Figure 8.4 presents the costs of crime in six industrialized countries: Australia, Canada, England, France, the Netherlands and the USA.[3] This figure is not for comparison purposes, but rather to illustrate the magnitude of the costs of crime. Certainly, the data sources used to estimate costs are not uniform across these countries and, in some cases, different years have been used.

In all six countries police expenditures account for over 60 percent of the criminal justice costs, except in the USA where they are approximately 40 percent due to high corrections costs. It must be noted that some of the police costs go to maintain order and some to deterring and coping with delin-

Major Category	One Year Estimate of Current Costs	% of Grand Total
Homicide	maximum $323 million	1.6
Assaults, including Sexual Assaults	minimum $979 million	5.0
Robbery & Extortion	$37 million	0.2
Breaking and Entering	$1193 million	6.1
Fraud/ forgery/ false pretences	$3000 million - $3500 million	15.3 -17.9
Theft /illegal use of motor vehicle	$654 million	3.3
Shoplifting	$1020 million - $2460 million	5.2 - 12.6
Stealing from the Person	$545 million	2.8
Other Theft	$659 million	3.4
Property Damage/ Environmental	minimum $510 million	2.4
Drug Offences	$2000 million	10.2
Total Crime	**$10920 million - $12860 million**	**55.6 - 65.5**
Police & Law Enforcement	$2858 million	14.6
Courts & Administration of Justice	$817 million	4.2
Corrective Services	$747 million	3.8
Other CJS	$2011 million	10.3
Total Criminal Justice System	maximum $6433 million	32.8
Other	minimum $1300 million	6.6
Grand Total	**$18 653 - $20 593 million**	**100.0**

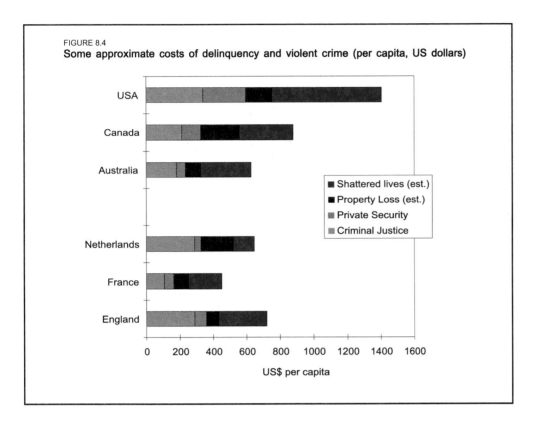

FIGURE 8.4
Some approximate costs of delinquency and violent crime (per capita, US dollars)

Legend:
- Shattered lives (est.)
- Property Loss (est.)
- Private Security
- Criminal Justice

X-axis: US$ per capita (0, 200, 400, 600, 800, 1000, 1200, 1400, 1600)

Countries: USA, Canada, Australia, Netherlands, France, England

quency and violent crime. The estimates here do not make this distinction. In Australia, Canada, the Netherlands and the USA, the costs of crime account for more than five percent of the gross domestic product (GDP), a figure comparable to spending on public education.

Scientists have quantified the costs of lost quality of life, pain, suffering and fear of crime to victims based on what a civil court would pay or what the public would willingly pay for additional security. These costs have been brought together for the first time in Figure 8.4. As a proportion of all costs measured, the costs of shattered lives generally account for the largest share. They are the highest in France, Australia, England and the USA, accounting for more than 40 percent of the costs of crime.

Economic benefits of crime prevention

In most of the countries where research into the costs of crime has been carried out, attention has also turned to measuring the economic benefits of crime prevention. In part, this attention has come as a result of the present fiscal situation which confronts these countries. With governments down-sizing and cutting back on many public services, governments have become more in tune with cost-effectiveness thinking.

Cost to benefit ratios from crime prevention programmes

Few crime prevention programmes have carried out economic evaluations (e.g., cost-benefit, cost-effectiveness). An economic evaluation is largely concerned with "aggregating all the gains and losses from a programme in such a way that the net gain from one programme can be compared to that of an alternative" (Barnett and Escobar, 1987). In Figure 8.5, findings of the economic evaluations of crime prevention programmes which have used large samples of persons and communities have been presented as cost-to-benefit ratios, which are an expression of the value received by the public from a one monetary unit investment in a programme. Programmes which have a cost-benefit ratio over one monetary unit produce an economic gain; those which have a ratio below one unit produce a loss.

High intensity areas in the Safer Cities Programme in the United Kingdom (over £13 or $22 per household spent on burglary prevention) were found to be more cost-effective than lower intensity areas and areas without schemes. When averaged over the

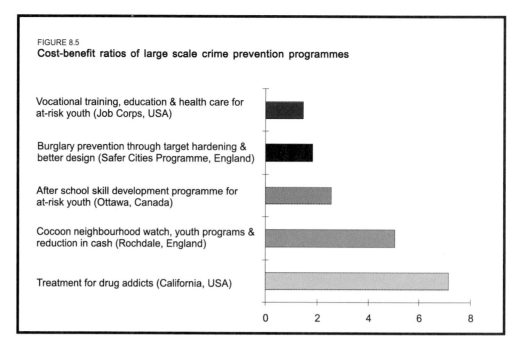

FIGURE 8.5
Cost-benefit ratios of large scale crime prevention programmes

Vocational training, education & health care for at-risk youth (Job Corps, USA)

Burglary prevention through target hardening & better design (Safer Cities Programme, England)

After school skill development programme for at-risk youth (Ottawa, Canada)

Cocoon neighbourhood watch, youth programs & reduction in cash (Rochdale, England)

Treatment for drug addicts (California, USA)

approximately 240 burglary schemes evaluated, the average return to the public was close to double the initial investment (Ekblom *et al.*, 1996). Equally impressive was an experimental evaluation of the US Job Corps programme in the late 1970s (Long *et al.*, 1981), which found that each dollar spent resulted in a $1.45 return.

Another large scale prevention programme which resulted in substantial savings to the public was the California Drug and Alcohol Treatment Assessment (Gerstein *et al.*, 1994), which involved a sample of 1,900 persons receiving various forms of substance abuse treatment. It produced a strong cost-benefit ratio ($7.14), meaning that taxpayers received over a 700 percent return on their one dollar investment. Participate and Learn Skills (PALS) – an after school, skill development programme in a large public housing community in Ottawa, Canada – produced a 255 percent return on the initial investment (Jones and Offord, 1989). A burglary prevention project on the Kirkholt housing estate, which had more than 2,000 households, produced a 500 percent return on the initial investment (Forrester *et al.*, 1990).

Other studies which have assessed costs and benefits include:

- Perry Preschool (United States) returned to the public $7.16 for each dollar spent on the programme (Barnett, 1993);
- a cost-benefit evaluation of the Quantum Opportunities Program – run in five cit-

ies across the USA – found that for each dollar invested a return of $3.68 was produced (Hahn, 1994);

- a nurse home visitation programme in Elmira, New York, covered programme costs for low income families (Olds, Henderson, Phelps, Kitzman and Hanks, 1993); and,
- a business-led scheme to reduce robberies in Victoria, Australia, produced close to a 200 percent return on the initial investment (Clarke and McGrath, 1990).

Two other identified programmes, which have presented cost data, show the economic benefits of investing in crime prevention:

- Hawaii Healthy Start – a state-wide home visitation programme for disadvantaged families – saved $1.3 million in child protection services alone from 42 fewer cases of child abuse and neglect (Earle, 1995); and,
- The Syracuse University Family Development Research Program (United States), which provided enriched child care and support for parents, found that the estimated cost from involvement with the justice system was $186 per programme group member and $1,985 per control (Lally, Mangione and Honig, 1988).

Economic benefits from reduced crime in the form of fewer victims and savings to the criminal justice system often account for a large proportion of the total savings from crime prevention programmes. Property loss, lost wages, increased insurance fees and lost quality of life are just some of the many direct and indirect costs which crime victims incur. However, economic benefits from crime prevention programmes are often not limited to savings from reduced crime, but are also produced from other improved life course outcomes such as reduced dependence on welfare and increased educational achievement and earnings.

Economics of alternative strategies to reduce crime

A recent study by RAND in the United States (Greenwood, Model, Rydell and Chiesa, 1996) estimated the number of crimes that would be saved by a one million dollar investment in various strategies to tackle delinquents before or after they become chronic offenders. For our purposes here, estimates produced by the original study on the percentage of serious crime reduced per year by intervention type have been presented as a cost per household to reduce crime by ten percent per year[4] (see Figure 8.6).

As illustrated in Figure 8.6, it is estimated that a ten percent reduction in serious crime per year can be achieved by increasing taxes per household by $228 to pay for prison (California's Three Strike Law — a third felony brings life imprisonment), $118 for delinquent supervision, $48 to pay for parent training, or $32 for graduation incentives. By opting for the two social prevention schemes over incarceration, the public is getting between a five and seven fold return on their tax dollars, with no loss in crime reduction effectiveness.

In 1994, the newly elected government of the Netherlands dedicated an annual budget of 160 million guilders ($100 million) for local crime prevention efforts to tackle the early risk factors of delinquency and later criminal offending. This decision was based largely on scientific research carried out by the Dutch Ministry of Justice (van Dijk, 1997). A simulation model using historical crime and crime control trends was developed to forecast the effects of four hypothetical scenarios on government spending on public safety: (1) extrapolating current trends (doing nothing); (2) adding 1,000 extra police officers to a force of 27,620 officers; (3) increasing investment in situational prevention by 30 percent; and (4) strengthening social prevention to achieve a ten percent decrease in crime.

As shown in Figure 8.7, over time[5], social prevention was predicted to have the strongest effect on reducing police/justice spending. The study estimated that after seven years, by the year 2000, adding more police would not reduce crime — in fact violent crime alone was expected to grow by six percent after three years — and would cost the government 100 million guilders ($63 million) more than had they done nothing at all. Also, situational prevention would have already begun to pay for itself by reduced crime and modest savings to government.

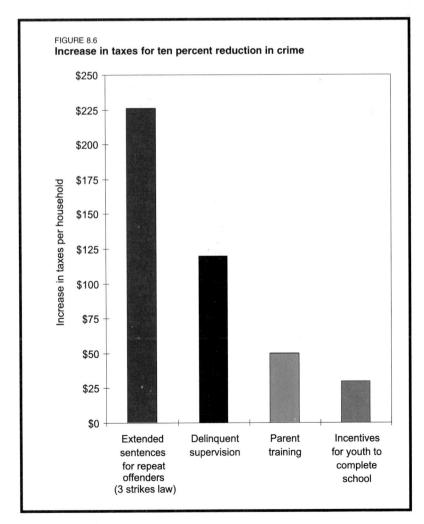

FIGURE 8.6
Increase in taxes for ten percent reduction in crime

Source: Adapted from Greenwood *et al.*, (1996)

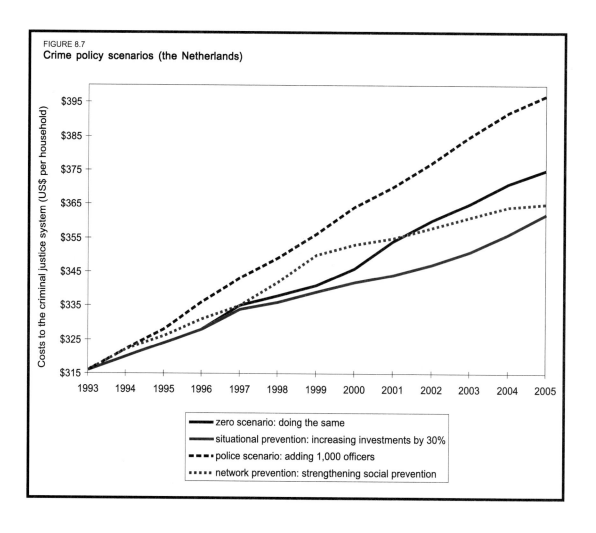

FIGURE 8.7
Crime policy scenarios (the Netherlands)

- zero scenario: doing the same
- situational prevention: increasing investments by 30%
- police scenario: adding 1,000 officers
- network prevention: strengthening social prevention

Crime prevention that works is grounded in scientific research. It is not founded on intuition or guess work.

Reallocating shrinking resources

Developing countries and countries in transition allocate between nine and 14 percent of their government budgets to criminal justice responses to crime (United Nations, 1996), severely depleting funds for critical human development sectors, such as health, education and employment. In developed countries the proportion of government budgets spent on criminal justice ranges from two to three percent (United Nations, 1996). In the USA, since 1985, state spending on corrections has outpaced all other budgetary components (Irwin and Austin, 1994).

In health care – an area vital to citizens – hospital spaces are being curtailed and capped, so that doctors have to set priorities on which patients will be admitted to hospitals. Maybe for crime reduction – an area also vital – prison expansion could be curtailed and capped, so that courts have to set priorities to ensure that this scarce resource is used for the most dangerous, most morally repugnant, and most appropriate cases.

RAND (Greenwood, Rydell, Abrahamse, Caulkins, Chiesa, Model and Klein, 1994) estimates that the full implementation of California's Three Strikes Law would cost taxpayers $5.5 billion a year. By the year 2002, the state of California's corrections budget will have doubled to 18 percent of total government spending, while at the same time spending on higher education will have shrunk from 12 percent to one percent and "other" government spending (e.g., environmental protection) will have all but disappeared.

Means used to facilitate effective crime prevention

Crime prevention that works is grounded in scientific research. It is not founded on intuition or guesswork. Longitudinal and victimization studies carried out across the world inform us of where our crime prevention efforts and resources should be directed to most effectively reduce later criminal offending and crimes. Scientific research on criminal justice agencies, particularly the police and prisons, has also helped to inform more effective crime reduction policy and practice. This research, which has largely exposed what does not work in reducing crime, has contributed to a greater understanding of the need to move away from a reliance on a criminal justice approach to crime and to strike a greater balance between repression and prevention.

This section reviews trends in the means that are used to facilitate effective crime prevention, such as some of the accumulated knowledge about the causes of crime, crime prevention legislation, community crime prevention planning, contracting and training, and the work of the Canadian International Centre for the Prevention of Crime.

Factors which predispose children to growing up as delinquents

Police officers, prosecutors, judges and corrections personnel are aware that there are some offenders that come back again and again, monopolizing significant resources. In England, the Netherlands and the USA scientists have completed several longitudinal studies of children growing up. A typical study collects extensive data from birth to young adulthood on a sample of several hundred children born in a particular year. The scientists are then able to test whether there are particular early or late childhood experiences which are associated with more youth getting involved in delinquency and violent crime.

These longitudinal studies confirm that there is a group of persistent offenders — fewer than five percent of males born in a particular year that account for as many as 70 percent of offences. Further, offending peaks during late adolescence, diminishing significantly in the early twenties. These studies show that persistent offenders tend to come from families who experienced: socio-economic deprivation, poor housing and disorganized inner-city communities; inconsistent and uncaring child-rearing techniques; and parental conflict (Farrington, 1996b). The children who are more likely to become persistent offenders are highly impulsive and hyperactive, with low intelligence and school attainment, and drop-outs from school (Farrington, 1996b).

Australia (National Committee on Violence, 1990) established a major commission to examine what was known about violence from across the world. They appointed scientists, leaders of business and the women's movement, and trade unionists to the commission, with a budget and staff to bring the scientific studies together. The following factors were the first six in order of priority as increasing violence: (1) families as the training ground for violence (one-quarter of abused kids grow up to abuse their kids); (2) society valuing violence (e.g., through sport); (3) economic inequalities; (4) gender inequalities; (5) cultural disintegration; and (6) substance abuse.

Situations in which people get victimized

Several of the national statistical agencies undertake extensive surveys of households to be able to compare those who have and who have not been victims of selected crimes. Scientists have undertaken a number of specialized studies to identify factors that are associated with victimization. These show that persons are more likely to be victims of:

- violent offences at the hands of a family member or close acquaintance, than a stranger, particularly for homicide and rape;
- offences involving alcohol and firearms, the more alcohol and firearms are available;
- property offences, the more they own goods that are easy to transport and sell — for instance, cars, bicycles, televisions and computers;
- burglary, the more they leave their residence; and,
- an offence a second time than they were for the first offence.

Legislation on crime prevention

There is a need for legislation that clarifies the importance of improving the safety and security of persons and property, and provides direction for the long term. Legislation can be achieved through a modification of the mandate of ministries of the interior to make them ministries of public

The International Centre for the Prevention of Crime (ICPC) offers a Best Practice Bureau to identify, compile, and diffuse information on successful crime prevention.

safety and security. Revisions need also to be made to criminal codes and laws governing police and judges to clarify their responsibility for pursuing prevention in collaboration with agencies that can influence the causes of crime. In the Canadian province of Ontario, model legislation has made the safety and security of persons and property the first principle of policing, and mandates the police to work with the community in its achievement (Ministry of the Solicitor General of Ontario, 1991).

Planning for effective crime prevention

Effective crime prevention at the community level begins with a rigorous planning model. It is characterized by: a systematic analysis of the crime problem and the conditions that generate it; a review of the services and activities in place to tackle those conditions and ways to improve them; implementation of the programme; and evaluation of the programme's impact on crime and its implementation so that improvements can be made, including a cost-benefit analysis (Ministry of the Solicitor General of Canada, 1984; Prairie Research Associates, 1996).

There is a need for this planning model to include efforts to forecast developments in crime, policing and the social demography in which these occur. In North America, environmental scanning and crime mapping have become the "buzz words" for these approaches as police forces, local authorities and others have adopted the methodology. It is also important that these exercises are themselves inter-sectoral so that the agencies that can influence the undesirable trends are involved from the beginning of the process.

Contracting and training

Most of the pioneer countries use contracting and training as ways of encouraging increased use of effective crime prevention methods. In countries such as Belgium, France, the Netherlands and the United Kingdom, the use of contracting has become a part of the process for ensuring that crime prevention is effective.

There is an urgent need to train the political leaders, executives and practitioners

who would implement the policies, programmes and projects that will reduce crime. The European Forum for Urban Safety is attempting to set up a practical training course on local crime prevention policies, designed mainly for prevention coordinators in cities throughout Europe (United Nations, 1995a). The regional institutes of the Arab world, Africa, Asia, Europe and Latin America already offer training courses on general criminal justice issues. Efforts are underway to include a component targeted more toward crime prevention, with priority attention to the coordinators responsible for these issues in the cities. Crime Concern and the University of the West of England offer a long distance education course leading to a certificate as a crime prevention coordinator.

Canadian International Centre for the Prevention of Crime

The International Centre for the Prevention of Crime (ICPC) was established in 1994 with the mission of assisting cities and countries to reduce delinquency, violent crime and insecurity. It is a not-for-profit, non-governmental organization which collaborates with local, national, regional and specialized entities to harness prevention experience and know-how from around the world to solve local crime problems.

It is governed by a board of directors combining the competencies of cities, prevention experts, the private sector, and specialized institutes from around the world. It is supported by the governments of Belgium, Canada, France, the Netherlands, United Kingdom and the province of Quebec, which make up an Advisory and Policy Committee.

Its creation was in response to calls for action from local authorities, first articulated at the Paris Conference in 1991, as the fifth step necessary to create safer, more sustainable communities (European Forum for Urban Safety et al., 1991).

The ICPC offers:
- a Best Practice Bureau to: identify, compile and disseminate information on successful crime prevention; and design and facilitate training courses on the adaptation of international best practice to local action;

- technical assistance to: help urban entities develop public safety diagnoses and community wide crime prevention strategies; provide needs assessments and work plans to use international know-how and experience; and support countries and regions with the development of strategies to foster effective crime prevention;

- an exchange of expertise through cross-national meetings to encourage more extensive implementation of effective crime prevention; and,

- tools to raise awareness of the impact of crime prevention, which stress the importance of leadership, the affordability and cost-benefit of crime prevention, and the contribution of crime prevention strategies and programmes to the sustainable development of cities and countries.

The ICPC supports the work of the UN agencies on crime prevention, particularly in the context of the preparation and follow-up to events such as the Ninth UN Crime Congress and Habitat II.

Issues facing crime prevention and community safety: present and future

This section examines a number of the key issues which face crime prevention and community safety now and in the future. These include: public attitudes toward crime and its prevention; prevention of violence against women; public health and private sector involvement in preventing crime; and sustainable funding.

Public attitudes toward crime and its prevention

The public see crime as an important concern in their communities and on the national agenda. In recent years in many developed countries, crime as a national priority has reached, and in some cases surpassed, the levels of some of the more traditional issues (e.g., unemployment, government deficit). A 1995 survey, which questioned 18,000 people in 21 European countries and presented them with 15 different areas of national concern, found that crime ranked second only to joblessness as the most important national concern (Helgadottir, 1995). Crime is the top priority in England and the

Netherlands; in France, crime ranks third behind unemployment and AIDS.

In South Africa, close to one out of every two citizens (45.6 percent) view crime as the most serious current problem facing the country. Unemployment ranked second with 18.1 percent (Schlemmer, 1996).

Crime is also a very real concern to community leaders. A survey of 135 mayors from every continent, carried out by the United Nations Development Programme (1994), found that delinquency and violent crime ranked as the fourth "most severe" problem facing the world's cities.

In Canada and the USA, surveys of the public consistently show a greater level of support for the use of preventive measures to reduce crime compared to criminal justice strategies. In a nationally representative sample, 61 percent of Canadians supported limited government resources being spent on preventive measures to reduce crime; 35 percent felt that such resources should be used for criminal justice (Environics, 1994) (see Figure 8.8). In the USA, 54 percent of the public believe that increased spending on social and economic problems is more effective in the fight against crime, compared to 31 percent who prefer spending on police, judges and prisons (Gerber and Engelhardt-Greer, 1996).

In a survey by the National League of Cities (1994), US mayors overwhelmingly supported crime prevention measures as the most effective approaches to reduce crime in their communities. Almost two-thirds (64

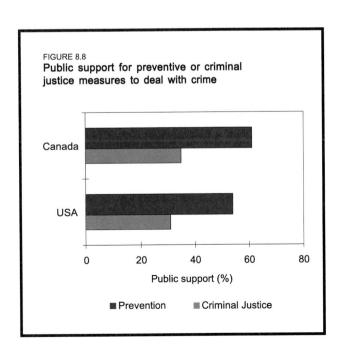

FIGURE 8.8
Public support for preventive or criminal justice measures to deal with crime

Preventing violence against women in Sao Paulo, Brazil

The challenge. In 1983, the State Council on the Status of Women made it clear that scores of Brazilian women had been subjected to violence while offenders escaped sanctions due to chronic under-reporting and police inaction.

The response. A response was to create police stations run entirely by women officers to reduce and prevent violence against women by deterring offenders and offering support services to victims. Beginning in 1985 in Sao Paulo (approx. population 15.8 million), the new police stations were empowered to investigate and counter such crimes by:

• attending to victims, writing official complaint reports and detailed police inquiry reports, and attempting to deter male violence directed at women; and

• providing victimized women with social/psychological support services, emergency shelter in appropriate cases, and organizing courses for abusive male partners to develop respect for women's right to safety.

The impact. Reporting of violence against women at the first women's police station in Sao Paulo increased from 2,000 complaints in 1985 to over 7,000 in 1989. Though the hidden nature of violence against women makes it difficult to attribute changes to the introduction of the women's police stations, in the two years (1987-1989) following the introduction of such a station in Rio de Janeiro, reported threats against women dropped by 63 percent and reported rapes fell by 37 percent. These reductions have not been confirmed by independent scientific evidence.

Key partners. The Sao Paulo State Council on the Status of Women led the initiative with the support of the Brazilian Bar Association and various non-governmental women's organizations. While the state government has provided most of the funding, the municipal government of Sao Paulo has contributed office space and some personnel.

Final note. That Brazilian mothers often send their abused daughters back to their husbands with the proverb *Ruim com ele, pior sem ele* (It's bad with him, but worse without him) underlines the pressing need to intervene, and the creation of 70 such police stations across Brazil demonstrates police agreement with all female police stations.

Sources. Adapted from the International Centre for Prevention of Crime web site, and Eluf (1992); *Jornal do Brasil* (1991)

---

percent) said strengthening and supporting family stability was the most effective crime reduction strategy. Half (49 percent) supported jobs and targeted economic development, while adding more police was supported by less than 40 percent. In a survey of US police chiefs, six out of ten (60 percent) ranked as number one increased investment in Head Start and youth programmes as the strategy most effective in reducing delinquency and violent crime; hiring more police received only 17 percent support (Fight Crime: Invest in Kids, 1996).

Prevention of violence against women

The Centers for Disease Control and Prevention in the USA have been a world leader in the prevention of criminal violence.

Violence against women continues to be one of the most critical public safety and health concerns shared by all regions of the world. In the most disadvantaged of countries, women are at even higher risk of victimization and receive little or no protection under the law. Victimization survey research reveals that the most serious acts of violence against women continue to be the most unreported of criminal incidents (van Dijk and Mayhew, 1992; Zvekic and Alvazzi del Frate, 1995; Alvazzi del Frate and Patrignani, 1995).

Many countries have made much progress toward the prevention of and ultimate goal of ending violence against women. Australia has established a national committee on violence against women. In the United States, the 1994 Crime Act established the Office for the Prevention of Violence Against Women, with a one billion dollar budget over five years. In Mexico, legislation has been passed with the aim of protecting women from violence and promoting the creation of crisis centres for women victimized by their partners. In Brazil, new police stations were created staffed entirely by female officers with the aim of reducing and preventing violence against women (Box 8.6).

Recent international conferences and research have also helped to strengthen the global effort towards ending violence against women. In 1991, in Brussels, the first conference of European ministers on physical and sexual violence against women was held to help establish a continent-wide action plan to end violence against women (Bruynooghe, Carmen, Hutsebaut and Vansteenwegen, 1991). In 1993, in The Hague, the United Nations Development Fund for Women (UNIFEM) and the Netherlands Ministry of Foreign Affairs convened a conference, Calling for Change: International Strategies to End Violence Against Women (Kerr, 1994). Key research and information on best practices internationally have included *Strategies for Confronting Domestic Violence: A Resource Manual* (United Nations, 1993), and UNIFEM's book, *Freedom from Violence: Women's Strategies from Around the World* (Schuler, 1992).

Public health involvement in crime prevention

The entrance of the public health community in recent years to the multitude of sectors working on the problem of crime and violence has been a welcome addition. The public health approach to criminal violence is characterized by viewing crime as an intentional injury within the wider context of health problems, focusing on primary prevention, the complex causes of crime, and a grounding in science and attention to rigorous research methodologies (Gabor, Welsh and Antonowicz, 1996; Mercy, Rosenberg, Powell, Broome and Roper, 1993). The Center for Disease Control and Prevention in the USA has been a world leader in the prevention of criminal violence, funding demonstration projects to prevent violence against women and youth, carrying out research into the prevention of firearm morbidity and mortality, and advocating for a greater balance between repression and prevention in US crime policy.

With the exception of the USA, however, the public health community's involvement in the prevention of criminal violence throughout the western world has been relatively passive. Less is known about developing countries and countries in transition. Recent events, however, have shown promise in changing this situation. In 1994, the Pan American Health Organization (PAHO) convened an Inter-American Conference on Health, Violence, and Society in Washington, DC. Participants included ministers, legislators, mayors, public health doctors, emergency physicians and leading experts in other human development fields. It issued a declaration urging greater national, regional and international commitment to the prevention of violence through the public health approach (Pan American Health Organization, 1994).

Private sector involvement in crime prevention

The involvement of the private sector in the prevention of crime has been, like public health, a recent and welcome event. Its emergence on the scene can, in part, be explained by three key trends: (1) research has shown that businesses suffer from a high level of victimization and resulting economic losses (van Dijk and Terlouw, 1996); (2) the business community has taken a greater interest in the wider community it serves; and (3) the declining resources of governments makes it difficult to fund prevention.

In the United Kingdom, private sector involvement in crime prevention is well established. Crime Concern has been a leader in mobilizing businesses to be an active partner and investor in community crime prevention, which has included everything from in-kind support from businesses' vast resources, to sponsorship of conferences and public launchings, to direct funding for research and community programmes. Business giants like Marks and Spencer and British Airways make significant yearly investments in local crime prevention efforts.

In South Africa, the National Business Initiative (NBI), known for its role in mediating the transition from the de Klerk to the Mandela government, has played a lead role in the design of a national crime prevention strategy for South Africa. Under the management of NBI, Business Against Crime is spearheading and coordinating an initiative that is drawing upon the collective contribution of South African companies to prevent crime and increase community safety.

Sustainable funding

Sustainable funding has been and will continue to be one of the most important issues facing crime prevention and community safety. Few governments fund crime prevention programmes beyond the initial start-up year or invest in longitudinal research into the causes and protective factors of crime (see e.g., Farrington, 1996a, on the United Kingdom). Crime prevention practitioners and researchers know all too well the difficulties in trying to achieve lasting funding, even for programmes with demonstrated successes.

Finding alternatives to shrinking government resources and a government reorientation to short-term projects and process goals has brought about a great deal of innovation in the field of crime prevention. Advocates argue for getting needed funding from existing criminal justice budgets through a process of reallocation. In 1993, a Canadian parliamentary committee investigating crime prevention unanimously recommended that one percent of criminal justice spending be allocated to crime prevention, an allotment which is to increase to five percent after five years (Horner Committee, 1993). In the same year, the Task Force on Crime Prevention (1993) recommended an equivalent mechanism to fund crime prevention in the province of Quebec.

It is time to invest in a comprehensive action plan that will pay dividends in both the short- and long-term.

Conclusion: beyond the rhetoric

In the last decade, crime prevention has achieved a prominent position in crime reduction thinking and practice around the world. Designing out crime, promoting social control and responsibility, investing in youth and family, breaking the cycle of violence, city action and innovative policing and justice approaches have become synonymous with best practice in crime reduction. In many crime-ridden communities where these forms of prevention have been implemented, substantial and lasting reductions in crime have been achieved, a greater quality of life has been realized, and community and economic growth has flourished. There is indeed much to celebrate.

However, crime prevention remains more rhetoric than action. Government investment in crime prevention is extremely low – less than one percent of criminal justice spending in most industrialized countries, and nonexistent in most developing countries and countries in transition. The traditional, reactive approach to dealing with crime – police, courts and corrections – continues to dominate national crime policies. Little attention has been paid to the scientific conclusions and the international consensus on what works to reduce crime.

This rhetoric has meant that citizens must continue to put up with unacceptable levels of crime. It is time to move beyond rhetoric and invest in a comprehensive plan that will pay dividends in both the short and long-term.

The proposed plan is grounded in the various declarations and resolutions of the UN, the Council of Europe, the ICPC and international and regional meetings of community leaders and crime and justice experts which identify the causes of crime and point to specific steps that must be taken to implement effective crime prevention strategies. It calls for immediate action to:

(1) *support national crime prevention structures* which promote collaboration between agencies which influence the factors that generate crime;

(2) *provide financial and technical support to local authorities* to form and promote multi-disciplinary coalitions and partnerships;

(3) *be rigorous in implementing prevention* using (i) experience gained with projects that have been proven effective in reducing crime, (ii) long-term action that is responsive to short-term needs, and (iii) sustainable measures that take advantage of scientific knowledge in a systematic manner;

(4) *seek the support of policing and justice agencies for prevention* by introducing guidelines and legislation that clarify that the goal of policing and justice is safety and security of persons and property, particularly through collaboration with citizens, local authorities and social agencies able to tackle the causes of crime;

(5) *reallocate resources to meet socioeconomic and urban needs*, particularly the needs of vulnerable groups such as children, women and minorities, with priority to the prevention of violence and neglect in early childhood;

(6) *encourage individual citizens to participate* in comprehensive crime prevention and to understand the importance to community development of implementing effective ways of making communities safer from crime; and,

(7) *promote global cooperation to limit access to facilitators of violence*, such as firearms, trafficking of illicit drugs, or media programmes that encourage violence and the sexual abuse of women and children.

Governmental investment in crime prevention is less than one percent of criminal justice spending in most industrialized countries, and nonexistent in most developing countries and countries in transition.

CHAPTER 9

Emerging Issues: Transnational crime and its control

Contributing author: Phil Williams

Defining and measuring transnational crime

During the 1990s transnational organized crime has increased in scope, intensity and sophistication. The end of the Cold War, the collapse of state authority in some countries and regions, and the process of globalization – of trade, finance, communications and information – have all provided an environment in which many criminal organizations find it profitable and preferable to operate across national borders rather than confine their activities to one country. In some cases, these cross-border activities are regional; in others they are global in scope. Whatever the geographic scope of the criminal operations, however, it is clear that organized crime is no longer simply a local or domestic activity. More often than not it is transnational in scope and character. Indeed, from the perspective of organized crime in the 1990s Al Capone was a small-time hoodlum with restricted horizons, limited ambitions and merely a local fiefdom. Criminal enterprises in the 1990s in contrast merge corporate and criminal cultures and in many cases have developed into sophisticated transnational businesses generating huge profits. The range of activities pursued by criminal organizations has also broadened significantly. These developments have been accompanied by a marked expansion in both illicit markets and informal economies. With the revival of very familiar forms of crime such as maritime piracy and the development of relatively new forms of criminal enterprise such as highly organized software piracy, transnational criminal enterprises have not only become more pervasive but have also grown in both power and wealth.

Few observers would dispute these observations. Providing empirical confirmation of the major trends in transnational criminal activity, however, remains elusive. As was noted in the introductory chapter to this report, providing quantitative indicators for traditional crimes is difficult, but finding hard data on illicit enterprises of transnational scope is close to impossible. There are several reasons for this, not the least of which is that illicit enterprises, by their very nature, are successful only when their activities remain invisible or immune to law enforcement. Yet, like traditional crime, most of the figures that are available stem from law enforcement successes. This poses all kinds of difficulty. Estimates of the drug trade or nuclear trafficking, for example, depend in large part on what assumptions are made about the percentage of the overall trade that is represented by seizures. The ratio between failures and successes, however, is an unknown. Consequently, estimates can vary widely. The other problem is that highly reliable national statistics are rare. In many countries there are no serious efforts to collect data about transnational organized crime – partly because of a lack of resources and expertise. Moreover, there are very few efforts to coordinate collection efforts and to combine national statistics about organized crime activity. In some respects this is not surprising, as the practical difficulties are formidable. Definitions of what constitutes organized criminal activity, for example, vary from one country to another, with the result that combining national data is often problematic at best.

When the dynamism and opportunism of transnational organized crime are added to the equation, great care has to be taken to avoid the provision of data that is potentially misleading. Indeed, measuring the value of the global trade in drugs or illicit armaments, estimating the number of illegal aliens who enter destination countries or remain in transit states, and determining the amount of

In many countries there are no serious efforts to collect data about transnational organized crime.

Crime, law and justice at the international level

On 12 July 1985 a squad of French security service agents sunk in the Auckland Harbor, New Zealand, the British-registered vessel *Rainbow Warrior*, owned by a non-governmental environmental organization Greenpeace. One crew member drowned.[1] Two French agents were arrested and charged by New Zealand authorities with conspiracy to commit arson, the use of explosives to intentionally sink the vessel, and the murder of one of its crew. Although no extradition treaty existed with France, New Zealand police issued warrants of arrest and requested the extradition of other agents. France requested extradition of the arrested agents, arguing that they could not be charged with any crime because they acted according to official governmental orders.

Although New Zealand was willing to return the French agents, it wanted France's assurance that they would continue to serve the imprisonment to which they were sentenced in New Zealand. France, however, noted that under its law, an individual can only be imprisoned as a result of a judgement rendered by a French court, or as a result of provisions in an international treaty relating to the transfer of prisoners. New Zealand did not agree, adding that the defense of "superiors' orders" was not recognized in New Zealand law.

Both countries submitted their case for arbitration by the United Nations Secretary-General. The Secretary-General ruled that France violated international law and that both apology and compensation were due by France to New Zealand. Equally important, however, was the ruling that New Zealand release the two agents to French authorities, but that those agents be immediately transferred to the island of Hao in French Polynesia and kept in the French military facility there for a period of three years without the benefit of any contact with the outside world. At the request of New Zealand, the ruling also included a provision that any disagreement concerning its implementation should be ruled on by a specially established tribunal. Reportedly, the two sentenced agents had comfortable living conditions, some military duties, normal pay and family visits unrestricted in number or duration. "This was represented by some French authorities as being equivalent to their release, while the New Zealand government insisted that they remained prisoners."[2] The two agents were eventually returned to France.

In reviewing the case, the special tribunal found France in breach of its obligations toward New Zealand. However, the tribunal did not grant New Zealand the financial compensation it had requested. The only satisfaction New Zealand received from the tribunal was the declaration that France had breached its obligations. Finally, the tribunal recommended that France make an initial contribution equivalent to two million US dollars to a joint fund to promote harmonious and friendly relations between France and New Zealand.

Source: Redo (1998). See Notes to Boxes for additional information.

"dirty money" that enters the global economy are inherently difficult undertakings. The whole point of money laundering, for example, is to ensure that illicit proceeds are indistinguishable from licit business profits. In these circumstances, completely accurate estimates of the amount of money laundered every year are virtually impossible.

The other problem, of course, is to determine what is truly transnational crime. The concept has gradually come to mean "criminal activities extending into, and violating the laws of several countries" (Mueller, 1998). This is different from both international crimes (i.e., crimes recognized as such by international law such as war crimes) and local crimes which can be in-

fluenced by factors beyond the boundaries of the affected jurisdiction, but which are, in effect, limited to one jurisdiction (Mueller, 1998). The case described in Box 9.1 illustrates this difficulty, as well as highlighting the problem of dealing with cases at the international level.

If there is sometimes uncertainty about the precise categorization of particular criminal activities, however, the most common and distinctive feature of transnational crime is that it involves the crossing of borders or national jurisdictions. The border crossing itself can involve either the actual or potential perpetrators of crime – who cross borders in the course of their activities (crossing borders in order to commit acts of terror or violence, for example) or in efforts to evade law enforcement – the illicit products, or the proceeds of illicit activity. Increasingly, it can also involve the transmission of information and what is, in effect, a "virtual" as opposed to a physical border crossing.

There is also some uncertainty about the crimes themselves. After all, different national jurisdictions criminalize different activities and punish them in different ways. Nevertheless, a significant number of activities are dealt with in international conventions, without which it would be close to impossible to apply justice with any satisfaction to international cases (Box 9.1). These conventions – the most famous of which is probably the UN Convention of 1988 against Illicit Trafficking in Narcotics Drugs and Psychotropic Substances, which covers money laundering and precursor chemicals as well as drugs themselves – represent a shared understanding among states that certain activities need to be regulated, prohibited or criminalized.

Although these issues pose serious problems for research on transnational organized crime, they are certainly not prohibitive. After all, not all criminal activities are clandestine or covert. Terrorist attacks, for example, are generally very public, as are incidents of piracy at sea. Moreover, even in cases where the criminal activities are less visible, it is possible to identify some of the activities and to make some assessments of their scale and scope. It is also possible to identify qualitative as well as quantitative trends. Indeed, in some cases, such as nuclear material trafficking, the quality of the material being trafficked is probably the most important single indicator of the seriousness of the crime, at least in terms of its impact on national and international security. Accordingly, this chapter aims to assess the scope of transnational criminal activities in particular areas and, where possible, to identify and elucidate trends both quantitatively and qualitatively. Concentrating not on criminal organizations but on criminal activities, and accepting that there are no perfect indices of such activities, it nevertheless seeks to identify useful indicators. The focus is on a variety of transnational activities ranging from terrorism to software piracy and money laundering. Due to limitations of space, only brief mention will be made of some transnational activities, particularly those for which hard data is lacking. As noted above, however, because there are no hard data does not mean that these crimes are any less serious in their outcomes or extent. The reader will, no doubt, be able to identify other crimes that are not mentioned in this chapter, but which have a transnational character or transnational implications. The transnational crimes mentioned in this chapter, including those dealt with in boxes are: illegal migration, trafficking in women and children, trafficking in body parts, corruption, theft and illegal export of cultural property, theft and trafficking in automobiles, fauna and flora trafficking, computer crimes, software piracy, nuclear material theft and trafficking, and international terrorism. Money laundering and trafficking in drugs and firearms will not be examined, as these are topics dealt with in Chapters 6 and 7 respectively. Because of space limitations, reviews of control measures will be made only for those at the international level. There are, of course, measures that may be taken within affected countries, but these will be noted only if they have international implications.

Illegal migration

As globalization and interdependence have become dominating characteristics of economies and societies at the end of the twentieth century, it is only natural that cross-border migration should also become more substantial. Such migration is driven by push factors such as ethnic conflict and poverty, as well as pull factors stemming in part from transnational familial linkages and the prospect of economic betterment. Although there is not the opportunity here for a comprehensive discussion of migration dynamics, it is clear that these dynamics are enormously powerful and difficult to reduce or contain. At the same time, governments in many of the advanced industrial and post-industrial economies have attempted to restrict the flow of immigrants. The results have been predictable. As the Director General of the International Organization for Migration has noted: "The combination of increased freedom of movement, pursuit of better opportunities, diminished legitimate migration possibilities, and demand for foreign labour have resulted in a profound rise in the level of illegal migration."[1]

These conditions have also resulted in the rise of criminal networks and organizations which ruthlessly exploit the desire of many people to achieve greater personal security or economic advancement through migration. Indeed, these networks profit from what is sometimes described as a trade in human misery, with many immigrants traveling under appalling conditions and often putting at risk not only their health and well-being but their very lives. There are also numerous cases in which the traffickers take the money and leave the would-be migrants stranded at some point en route. In mid 1994, for example, it was reported that over 100 trafficked migrants from Pakistan had been abandoned and stranded in Kazakhstan and Russia.[2]

For all its ruthlessness, illegal migrant trafficking has become "a global business, generating huge profits for traffickers and organized crime syndicates, creating serious problems for governments of the countries involved and potentially exposing migrants to abuse and exploitation."[3] The criminal groups that arrange and facilitate such trafficking are highly dynamic and adaptable. Some of them at least have moved from drug trafficking to people trafficking, partly because of the lower risks and lower penalties (Smith, 1997). The following data provides some insight into the dimensions of this particular form of transnational crime:

- The International Center for Migration Policy Development suggested that alien smugglers might have earned as much as

Networks profit from what is sometimes described as a trade in human misery, with many immigrants traveling under appalling conditions.

BOX 9.2

Illegal aliens in the Netherlands

The largest groups of illegal aliens in the Netherlands are from Africa (52.6 percent; including Morocco, 15.3 percent), followed by Indonesia (11.4 percent), the Middle East (10.8 percent) and Eastern Europe (9.2 percent).

Detention of illegal aliens falls under the jurisdiction of the Immigration and Naturalization Service of the Ministry of Justice. The first detention center, the *Grenshospitium*, built specifically for the purpose of housing illegal aliens awaiting deportation, was opened in Amsterdam in 1992. This was followed by the conversion of a former military barracks, *Kazerne Willem II*, with a cell capacity of 400, into an alien detention center (Jenezon). By the end of 1996, 11 institutions or sections within already existing facilities were used to detain this population.[1]

As of December 1996 there were 887 usable cells[2] and approximately 850 illegal aliens in detention awaiting deportation (Jenezon, 1996). These detention facilities are used for foreigners without legal residence papers, those awaiting deportation after hearings, or "undesirable aliens." Police *razzias* in search of illegal foreigners do not occur in the Netherlands.[3] Foreigners often enter a facility after having been caught at one of the borders (or directly at Schipol International Airport) without proper identification after having committed a criminal offence. A decision may be made by the public prosecution department to drop charges for a non-serious offence in favor of deportation proceedings. In the case of serious offences, an individual must first serve his or her sentence before being deported.

Foreigners can be detained if they present a threat to public order or national security. This allows for the detention of any foreigner who may go "underground" to avoid deportation, whose criminal background indicates a potential threat, or who enters the country illegally and fails to register with the proper authorities. Further grounds for detention are the disposal of identification documents, failure to aid in identification, or having perpetrated fraud by attempting to apply for residence status in various places using different information on the application forms.

Officially, illegal aliens may only be detained if there is a realistic probability that they will or can be deported. This is easier said than done. A consulate or embassy must often initiate an investigation, then recognize the individual as a citizen of its country and must issue a passport before the individual can be deported. This happens in approximately half of the cases. In some cases the individual's identity is known but the country refuses to issue the proper paperwork because the individual is considered an "undesirable" (Jenezon, 1996).

Officially, illegal aliens may only be detained in the majority of detention centres for a maximum period of six months. Because of the "sober conditions"[4] in two institutions, the maximum period is two months. In practice, detentions may last longer under the premise that the individual "is not cooperating in the identification or deportation process" (Jenezon, 1996).

Illegal foreigners in detention, 797 persons, comprise almost 6.8 percent of the total correctional population. The 797 incarcerated persons awaiting deportation (official statistics for September 1996; *Dienst Justitiële Inrichtingen*, based upon land of birth), represents a 21.8 percent increase over the 623 detainees of a year earlier. The largest majority, 52.6 percent (N=419), were born in Africa – 37.3 percent (N=297) in "other Africa" and 15.3 percent (N=122) in Morocco. The second largest group, 11.4 percent (N=91), are from Indonesia, followed by 10.8 percent (N=86) from the Middle East, and 9.2 percent (N=73) from Eastern Europe. Various other groups comprise the remainder of the illegal aliens in detention.

The current deportation policy has come under heavy criticism for its time-consuming processes. Deportation has met with limited "success." It remains to be seen whether the individuals can be identified, the process can be expedited and countries can be motivated to aid in the repatriation of their citizens.

Source: Aronowitz (Original paper, 1997). See also Box 4.1 and Notes to Boxes for additional information.

$9.5 billion in 1994.[4]

- There are an estimated half a million to two million illegal migrants in South Africa, arousing concern among the indigenous population about a loss of jobs and the growth of crime.[5]

- *The Economist* estimates that about 300,000 people are smuggled into Western Europe each year (as opposed to around two million legal migrants). In 1994, 43,302 people from 74 states were caught trying to cross the German-Czech border illegally.[6]

- There are an estimated half a million illegal immigrants in Thailand, 334,000 of whom are Burmese and provide labour for the construction industry and women for the service and sex industries (Robinson, 1994).

- Russian authorities estimate that up to two million illegal immigrants from Asia and Africa are in Russia. The Federal Migration Service estimates that there are about 500,000 Chinese illegal immigrants in Siberia and the Russian Far East, while other estimates suggest that the figure might be as high as one million.[7]

There are, of course, regional variations on this pattern of global migration. Nevertheless, the wealthier countries of the G-7 are usually the final destination.[8]

Control. Governments in many destination countries have been vigorous in their response to a problem that directly challenged all efforts to regulate immigration. In October 1995, for example, it was reported by Itar Tass that illegal immigration had recently been declared a national security threat by the Russian Security Council. In the United States too, the issue has received top-level attention. On February 7, 1995 President Clinton instructed the State and Justice Departments to establish a new structure to coordinate efforts to deter alien smuggling. Yet governments such as the United States and Russia have been hindered by the fact that in many transit countries alien smuggling is not illegal, and as well by gross variations in law enforcement capabilities to respond to the activity where it is illegal. Some initiatives have been taken to alter this situation in Central America, with Panama and Nicaragua joining Honduras in imposing criminal penalties for alien trafficking.[9] Harmonization of criminal legislation, however, important though it is, can only be one part of a more comprehensive response. Indeed, there is broad agreement that law enforcement and interdiction efforts have to be increased and refocused. Where possible, there is a need for more extensive cooperation between sending and destination states, the active support of transit states, and greater education efforts, especially in source countries and regions (Winer, 1997). Long term initiatives need to be taken to harmonize legal frameworks among different countries while, in the short term, more effective and systematic information exchanges would enhance efforts to disrupt the trafficking networks (Siemens, 1996).

Trafficking in women

Trafficking in women for prostitution is a crime where statistics are sparse, but where a few path-breaking surveys have been done, especially by the International Organization for Migration. Trafficking in women occurs when a woman in a country other than her own is exploited by another person against her will and for financial gain. The trafficking element may – cumulatively or separately – consist of: arranging legal or illegal migration from the country of origin to the country of destination; deceiving victims into prostitution once in the country of destination; or enforcing victims' exploitation through violence, threat of violence or other forms of coercion.[10] Thailand, Brazil and Philippines head the list of countries with significant numbers of women working overseas in the sex trade. It has been estimated, for example, that there are about 40,000 to 50,000 Thai women staying illegally in Japan where they work as prostitutes (Robinson, 1994). An important study has also been done of women from the Dominican Republic, about 50,000 of whom work abroad in the sex trade – mainly in Austria, Curacao, Germany, Greece, Haiti, Italy, Netherlands, Panama, Puerto Rico, Spain, Switzerland, Venezuela and the West Indies.[11]

There has also been a substantial growth in trafficking of women from Eastern Europe to Western Europe. Women from the Russian Federation, Ukraine and other parts of the former Soviet Union have been trafficked to Australia, Dubai, Israel, Macao and the United States (Pope, 1997). Estimates suggest that between 200,000 and half a million women are working as sex workers illegally in the European Union; in Germany

75 percent of prostitutes are foreigners, while the figure in Milan is 80 percent (Mugar, 1996). In Italy one study suggests that there are between 19,000 and 25,000 foreign prostitutes, approximately 2,000 of whom have been trafficked, with 70 to 80 percent of these being used for street prostitution.[12]

The pattern in Austria is of women being trafficked mainly from Central and Eastern Europe. In Vienna in 1990 there were 800 registered prostitutes and 2,800 illegal prostitutes; by 1995 only 670 were registered while the number of unregistered prostitutes had increased to 4,300.[13] The number of cases of trafficking increased by six times from 1990 to 1994 (with a dip in 1993), but the number of convictions has lagged far behind.[14] This is reflected in Figure 9.1.

Of the 751 victims of trafficking identified in Austria in an 18 month period from January 1994 to the end of June 1995, 48 percent were from the Czech and Slovak republics and another 16 percent were from the Dominican Republic.[15] Most women are under 25 and many are in the 15 to 18 age range. Sentences against traffickers are light, and there have been few successful convictions. A similar picture exists elsewhere in

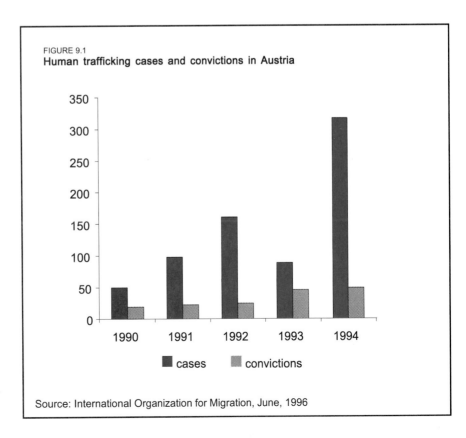

FIGURE 9.1
Human trafficking cases and convictions in Austria

Source: International Organization for Migration, June, 1996

BOX 9.3

A "modern" transnational crime: trafficking in children and child prostitution

Global nature of the crime. There is no part of the world that is truly free of this crime. In the United States, for example, estimates of the number of child prostitutes range from 100,000 to 300,000. In Asia, the problem is extensive, and UNICEF estimates that the number of children exploited for commercial sex is 200,000 in Thailand, over 650,000 in the Philippines, and 400,000 in India. The phenomenon is less extensive in Africa, although even here there is a growing problem, partly due to poverty, migration from rural to urban areas, and increased tourism. In Zimbabwe, the problem is related to the sex trade near the border. The Sudan, Kenya and Libya are all on the list of countries facing the challenge. Algeria has been reported as a place of transit for traffickers. In Mauritania, there are reports of foreign pedophiles at work and an increase in boy victims of prostitution. In Ghana, young girls are tricked into prostitution in the belief that they will be housemaids. Visible increases of children in sexual exploitation are noted in Cote d'Ivoire and Burkina Faso. The problem is even greater in Central and South America, where there are large numbers of street children, many of whom become involved in prostitution. Child victims of prostitution are present in large numbers in such countries as Bolivia, Brazil, Chile, Colombia, Ecuador, Mexico and Peru. In Brazil estimates range from 200,000 to 500,000, revealing both the difficulty of data collection, and the extent of the problem. Children taken to the mining towns for prostitution are virtually held as slaves. And in Peru, it is estimated that about half of the one million adult prostitutes are in fact minors working with false identification cards. The average age of the children is between 13 and 17, although cases of much younger children have been documented in Brazil. In Chile, there is a close link between drug addiction and child prostitution: traffickers and pimps will addict the children to inhalants such as benzene gum and glue. The children taking these inhalants are as young as nine, ten, or eleven years old. They are kept addicted.

Transnational aspect of the crime. Children are increasingly sold and trafficked across frontiers — between developing and developed countries, among developing countries, and among developed countries. The spread of child prostitution world wide is part and parcel of the less positive aspects of globalization. Trafficking in children from Nepal to India and from Myanmar to Thailand are two of the most obvious examples. Abduction, false documentation and sham marriages are all used to facilitate this movement.

International customers. As one INTERPOL report noted: "The incredible escalation of child prostitution over the last ten years is directly caused by the tourism trade. Child prostitution is the newest tourist attraction offered by developing countries. The parallel to this phenomenon in the Western countries is the explosion of a huge underground trade in child pornography in videos and magazines. Since laws against child prostitution are stringently enforced in most affluent countries, pornographic films and photographs often have their origin in countries where child prostitution has become a temporary escape from poverty for struggling rural people." For example, in 1996, police officers in Szczecin (Poland) detained a man who allegedly managed a "matchmaking" agency for pedophiles. During the search of the suspect's home a list of 800 customers was found, not only from Poland, but Belgium, Canada, Germany and the Netherlands.

Borderless trafficking in child pornography. The advent of the Internet has erased the borders of countries trying to keep out child pornography. Pornography can be easily transported from one country to another to international customers simply by sending the images electronically via the Internet. Although countries are passing new laws to cope with this international trade, it is still difficult for one country to police the activities of a pornographer in a foreign country which may have different laws and procedures concerning these crimes.

The international response. International efforts to deal with prostitution more generally date back to the beginning of the twentieth century and encompass several conventions dealing with slavery and sexual exploitation. In addition, the International Labour Organization (ILO) has been instrumental in pressing for international legislation against forced labour, thereby covering also child prostitution. In 1930, the Forced Labour Convention (No. 29) was adopted, later reinforced in 1957 by the Abolition of Forced Labour Convention (No. 105). An important instrument relating to sexual exploitation was the 1949 Convention on the Suppression of Traffic in Persons and of the Exploitation of the Prostitution of Others, which targeted those who procured and exploited prostitutes rather than the prostitutes themselves. The 1979 Convention on the Elimination of All Forms of Discrimination Against Women provides in Article 6 that "States Parties shall take all appropriate measures, including legislation, to suppress all forms of traffic in women and exploitation of prostitution of women." Children were specifically addressed in the 1959 United Nations Declaration on the Rights of the Child, and subsequently the 1989 Convention on the Rights of the Child, Article 34 of which obligates state parties to undertake to protect the child from all forms of sexual exploitation and sexual abuse. Now that the UN has initiated a significant program of reform under the leadership of Secretary-General Kofi Annan, the prevention of trafficking in children has become a special concern of the UNCICP in Vienna and the UNICRI in Rome. Both offices will diligently pursue work on this important issue, just as they did for the Sixth UN Commission on Crime Prevention and Criminal Justice in 1997 in Vienna, where the elaboration of an international convention against trafficking in children was discussed (United Nations, 1997b).

Some positive developments that have occurred are:

• *End Child Prostitution in Asian Tourism (ECPAT)*, a non-governmental organization, which was established in 1991 by welfare groups in Thailand, Taiwan, Sri Lanka and the Philippines and has done a great deal both to focus attention on the problem and to pressure states to pass legislation dealing with extraterritorial child sex abuse.

• *Programme of Action for the Prevention of the Sale of Children, Child Prostitution and Child Pornography*, adopted by the United Nations Commission on Human Rights in 1992.

• *World Tourism Organization Tourist Code* (1985) exhorted both tourist professionals and tourists themselves to refrain from exploiting others for prostitution purposes.

• *INTERPOL Working Party on Offences Committed against Minors*.

• *African Charter on the Rights of the Child, 1987* calls for protection of the child from exploitation. Similarly, the Council of Europe in 1991 adopted the Recommendation on Sexual Exploitation, Pornography and Prostitution of and Trafficking of Children and Young Adults, which emphasised expansion of national jurisdiction to cover the misdeeds of nationals abroad, exchange of information, and more research on the link between the sex industry and organized crime.

• *First World Congress Against the Commercial Sexual Exploitation of Children*, held in Stockholm in 1996. The Congress placed great emphasis on ways in which existing commitments could be translated into actions designed both to stop the supply and eliminate the demand.

Source: Edited and abridged from Williams (1997) and Adamski (Original paper, 1997).

Western Europe.[16]

Control. There is a strong case for strengthening and modernizing international legal instruments, since the most detailed convention in this area is almost 50 years old. Less emphasis should be placed on immediate deportation of the women themselves and more encouragement and opportunities provided for them to press charges against those who have been benefiting most from their activities. This requires expanded witness protection and special care programmes as well as other programmes designed to rescue, rehabilitate and return the women to their home countries.[17]

Corruption

The extent of corruption is even more difficult to estimate than the proceeds of most transnational crimes. Traditionally, there has been marked divergence among commentators on both the causes and consequences of corruption. In contrast, there is broad agreement on the essence of corruption even though definitions of the phenomenon vary in both emphasis and complexity. "[Corruption] is a transaction that enables private actors to have access to public resources (contracts, financing, decision-making, etc.) by giving them an unfair advantage, because there is neither transparency nor competition" (Della Porta, 1997). More simply, corruption is widely understood as "abuse of public office for private gain." Please see Boxes 9.4 and 9.5 for a brief overview of the causes of corruption.

Control. The various measures that are needed can be categorized as administrative, judicial, cultural and international.[18] The international measures are:

• *Enhanced data collection.* Although corruption has become a global problem, it still tends to be understood in national and regional terms. Greater efforts need to be made to develop more comprehensive and comparative analyses that highlight the most effective measures to prevent and control corruption. As one expert group noted, a database needs to be developed on national legislation, investigation techniques, and best practices in this area.[19]

• *International cooperation.* Efforts to combat corruption also need to be transnational in scope. States should be prepared to help

---

BOX 9.4

Corruption: an old crime in a new world

Corruption around the world. Although corruption has always existed, the 1990s are witnessing an "eruption of scandals" that do not appear to respect national borders. The BCCI (Bank of Credit and Commerce International) affair has epitomized a new type of "global scandal," as it embarrassed many countries around the world (Passas, 1995, 1996; see also Box 0.11). Older stereotypes portray developing countries as plagued by widespread and systemic corruption.

We have no shortage of scandals in Asia and Latin America. We have seen the indictment of a third of India's cabinet and of two former South Korean presidents as well as parliamentary investigations into abuses by the heads of state in Pakistan and Turkey. The presidents of Peru and Guatemala dissolved or closed down their Congresses and judicial bodies on allegations of corruption. Mexico's president resigned after his brother was charged for receiving kickbacks, while the presidents of Brazil and Venezuela were impeached for abusing their offices and illicit enrichment. Colombia's president fought allegations that his election campaign received funds from drug traffickers. Finally, IBM Argentina has been the subject of bribery investigations. Countries in transition from planned to market economies and from communist rule to parliamentary democracies are particularly hard hit by both corruption and the rising opportunities for "frontier capitalism" and organized crime (Shelley, 1994; White, 1996).

Scandals have also shaken up industrialized countries. The most sensational revelations of extensive networks of illicit influence and funding of political parties, corruption, and organized crime are still coming from Italy (Arlacchi, 1995; *Tribunali di Milano e Napoli*, 1996). Scandals of illegal political funding, corrupt payments, and general "sleaze" have had serious effects in France, Germany, the United Kingdom, Spain and Portugal (della Porta and Meny, 1995; Jamieson, 1996; Ridley and Doig, 1996; Remer, 1996). Implicated in all of these scandals were prominent politicians and business people. Unholy alliances between professional criminals and prominent politicians or political parties have brought down a number of prime ministers in Japan (*Economist*, 1992a, 1992b; Kerbo and Inoue, 1990; Yayama, 1990). Israel's prime minister faced allegations of corrupt practices. In the USA, the White House has been fighting allegations of improper political campaign payments from foreign concerns and a special prosecutor's investigation into the Whitewater affair. No administration has escaped corruption scandals (Chambliss, 1988).

Causes of corruption and its growth. In a world of relative turmoil produced by radical changes in the Post-Cold War era, there are new opportunities and incentives to engage in corrupt practices. Challenged by recent revelations is the assumption that "free markets" and non-interventionism are the remedy against corruption. It now appears that each socio-political and economic system produces its own version of corrupt practices and that no system is completely corruption-free. A cursory look at countries prominent in the promotion of free trade and democratic governance serves as a cautionary note to those who might consider market liberalization and Western-style democratic governance a panacea in the fight against corruption (Passas, 1994; Phythian, 1996).

The problem of corruption is systemic rather than individual. Firstly, it occurs in monopolistic or oligopolistic situations, in which one or a handful of companies control a given market. The state may wish to engage private companies to perform specific tasks or provide services or public works. To the extent that only a very small number of companies can practically carry out the work, the ground is fertile for corrupt practices (e.g., overcharging, low quality work, delays, etc.). Such a condition obtains, for example, in the field of defense projects. In this field, oligopolistic conditions may be even desired: no one wishes proliferation of certain types of weapons or technology that affect national and international security. In this field, then, it is warranted to devote special attention and have special bodies overseeing the transactions.

Secondly, very wide discretionary powers in the hands of individuals or organizations can generate temptations and motives for corrupt practices. Whenever there are few or no mechanisms of "checks and balances," people will have plenty of opportunities to take undue advantage of their power. An example is the power conferred to people with extremely specialized skills and knowledge. By definition, there are not too many of them and therefore their powers are to a large extent unchecked. Again, the defense industry may be a concrete illustration of this situation.

Finally, lack of transparency reduces the ability to control those in positions of authority. This lack of transparency may be caused by factors ranging from secrecy in banking to dictatorial regimes disallowing the questioning of authority.

Source: Passas (Original paper, 1997)

Corruption at the highest level

Public corruption is not a new phenomenon in Latin America. Recently, however, this problem has given rise to political and social consequences previously unknown in the region. In the majority of countries, public opinion surveys reveal that the citizenry ranks corruption and public safety among the top five most important problems facing their country. These surveys also reveal that the public ranks the justice system among the most corrupt institutions of government and seriously questions the ability of the administration of justice to do anything about it. The result of these concerns is a widespread distrust in almost all government institutions.

Complaints about the level of corruption in the justice system have served to justify the abolition of Congress and the Supreme Court by Peru's President Fujimori in 1993. Although this move was classified as an unconstitutional coup, the President's move received widespread popular support. Shortly thereafter, Guatemala's President Serrano unsuccessfully attempted a similar purge in his country, basing his attempt on the corruption of the justice sector. His successor launched a constitutional reform that resulted in the abolition of the sitting Congress and Supreme Court. In 1992, two attempted military coups were applauded by a large proportion of the population, and were also justified on the basis of eliminating public corruption generally, but more specifically in the judiciary. Following the first attempted coup, seven of the 15 members of the Supreme Court resigned. Finally, in Bolivia, the President and Vice-President of the Supreme Court were impeached in 1994 on charges of accepting bribes.

The judiciary has not been the only target of reformers. Thus, Brazil's President Collor de Mello was impeached in 1993 for corruption and now resides in Miami. Venezuela's sitting President Carlos A. Pérez was likewise impeached in the same year on similar charges and served a term of imprisonment under house arrest while charges were also filed against former President Lusinchi. Former President Jorge Blanco was likewise convicted on corruption charges in the Dominican Republic and serves a prison term. Mexico's former President Salinas currently wanders the world while facing investigations of massive corruption charges that have already resulted in the imprisonment of his brother. The Vice-President of Ecuador, Alberto Dahik, was also removed from office and still faces charges while the subsequent President is exiled in Panama following similar accusations.

Another target of the anticorruption movement have been traditional political parties unable to adapt to the shift in public opinion that has given rise to the emergence of new reformist parties, such as *Causal Radical* in Venezuela and Fujimori's party in Peru. The creation of these new parties is a result of popular discontent with traditional parties and a desire to elect leaders without any political alliances. For example, in Colombia, a son of Lithuanian immigrants, Anthanas Mockus, a philosopher and mathematician, was elected mayor of Bogota even though he was not a member of any political party, was classified as an eccentric, and only invested $40 in his electoral campaign. He is currently a candidate for the presidency of that country. The most notable example of the impact of the anticorruption mood on traditional parties is the PRI in Mexico, which enjoyed the longest rule of any party in Latin America (67 years in control of the government) and is now undergoing its most serious internal crisis following the investigations into the widespread corruption of President Salinas' administration. The crisis has been aggravated by the emergence of an armed guerrilla movement, the Zapatista Army, and deteriorating economic conditions.

Finally, one of the gravest consequences of popular distrust in government institutions, and especially in the administration of justice, is resort to vigilantism and self-help methods as people seek to take justice into their own hands.

Popular discontent arising from the concern over corruption has been fueled by a widespread perception that the justice system is unwilling and incapable of addressing the problem. This conclusion arises from the lack of successful prosecution and the impunity that is enjoyed by corrupt public officials.

Source: Salas (Original paper, 1997)

---

one another in identifying, seizing and returning the proceeds of corruption, in gathering evidence for corruption investigations, and where necessary extraditing perpetrators. On occasion, multinational task forces can be important in combating cases that span several jurisdictions.

- *Establishing conditionality.* As a final step, financial aid and assistance to developing countries and states in transition should be made contingent upon more serious efforts to combat corruption and devise forms of governance that are effective, efficient, legitimate and honest. There is evidence that this form of conditionality is being introduced. The World Bank in its recent efforts at "radical renewal" has acknowledged the need to combat corruption, and along with other donor agencies is going much further than in the past in linking national anti-corruption efforts to the willingness of the international donor community to provide economic aid and assistance.[20]

- *Increased technical cooperation.* The international donor community, as part of its efforts at enhancing state capacity, should provide greater training in anti-corruption measures.

- *Elaboration of an international convention.* One of the most important functions of conventions is that they provide an established standard of conduct that states strive towards and that can be used to measure progress. Such an initiative would build on the International Code of Conduct for Public Officials adopted by the General Assembly of the United Nations.

Theft and illegal export of cultural property

The theft of cultural property is another illicit transnational business that is flourishing. Although looting of art treasures has long been a feature of warfare and conquest, in recent years it has also become a major peacetime phenomenon. Indeed, there has been a vast increase in theft of art and antiquities in all their forms, crime "with the potential for denuding entire cultures and nations of their cultural heritage" (Mueller, 1998). Such crime has several analytically distinct but closely related dimensions:

Controlling public corruption in Latin America

Public corruption is a highly complex criminal event that can seldom be addressed by resort to traditional criminal legislation. Recently, countries have begun to enact reforms aimed at defining and sanctioning the "illicit enrichment" of public officials. These criminal statutes have generally been complemented by civil forfeiture laws that permit the government to seize and dispose of assets resulting from corruption. Another new type of criminal conduct recently defined in several countries deals with the failure to file financial statements that adequately reflect the assets of the declarant.

In addition to the necessity for substantive criminal law reform there is also an urgent need to replace antiquated codes of criminal procedure that are characterized by inefficiency and delay. Some of the most serious impediments to successful prosecution are: bans on electronic surveillance, plea bargaining and negotiations of sentences, limitations on the use of testimony of informants, absence of whistle blowing statutes and witness protection, exclusion of confessions as evidence, and the secrecy of bank records.

Lack of coordination is an almost insurmountable barrier to a successful prosecution of corruption cases in which the bulk of the evidence lies in multinational financial institutions and records of transactions. Since neither the investigative police agency nor the judges or prosecutors have qualified staff to adequately review financial records they are incapable of interpreting evidence supplied by banks or regulatory agencies. Financial institutions or their regulators, on the other hand, are unskilled in the evidentiary requirements necessary for convictions.

Recently, there has been recognition that public corruption cannot be prosecuted in the same manner as other crimes. Thus, for example, the Attorney General and Controller General of Venezuela established joint task forces to investigate public corruption. These task forces were critical in the successful prosecution of a sitting president and other high-level political figures. In Bolivia, the creation of a specialized investigative unit was called for in recent money laundering and anti-corruption legislation.

While the struggle to prosecute public corruption is inhibited by a number of technical and legal deficiencies, the absence of political will remains the most serious obstacle. Even in those cases in which an activist attorney general or chief judge has instituted prosecutions, this activism has seldom been embraced by his successor, and the failure to institutionalize reforms has let many of these agencies slide into the practices of the past.

The most serious problem for the judiciary, and for most public officials, is the absence of accountability for their actions as reflected in the absence of adequate controls for the prevention or sanction of judicial misconduct. No specialized corps of functionaries dedicated to investigative complaints against the judiciary generally exist. Likewise, no information is available to the public about the method or institution to which they could direct complaints.

Although these obstacles to change appear insurmountable, there are encouraging signs. International organizations such as the OAS and development agencies have identified public corruption as a serious challenge to the consolidation of democracy in the hemisphere and are proposing national and international compacts and strategies to combat it.

The media in Latin America, often criticized for its passivity in the face of corruption, has been at the forefront of efforts to expose corruption. While some of this new activism can be attributed to the influence of political parties in media circles, investigative reporting has begun to emerge as an important specialization within journalist circles, and there is a recognition that media has matured in Latin America as it seeks to define its role within a democratic society.

Popular dissatisfaction with traditional institutions has contributed to the rise of citizen groups (*Poder Popular* in Argentina, for example) and non-government organizations (Transparency International, for example) that focus on the prevention and sanctioning of corruption. The pressure that they can bring upon the government cannot be underestimated.

Perhaps the most encouraging sign of change is the current political will, in some countries, to prosecute and imprison corrupt public officials. While normative and operational reforms are necessary, public confidence will not be restored until citizens see public officials being dragged away to prison. The fact that high-level public officials are being removed from office through democratic means for the first time in the region is the most positive sign in the struggle against public corruption.

Source: Salas (Original paper, 1997)

- the illegal excavation of antiquities, many of which are subsequently exported;

- illegal export of art and antiquities when there are statutes intended to preserve the national cultural heritage by prohibiting such exports;

- theft of antiquities from historical sites, museums, antique businesses and galleries;

- theft of art from museums and private collections.

The international trade in stolen, smuggled and looted art is estimated at $4.5 billion to $6 billion per year.[21] The illicit market is populated by a mix of criminal organizations, individual thieves, fences and unscrupulous collectors, but also depends to a surprising extent on the tacit connivance of apparently legitimate individuals and institutions such as auction houses and antique dealers.

The well-organized nature of the illicit market for art and antiquities is perhaps most strikingly demonstrated by the fact that only around five percent of all stolen art is recovered.[22] Clearly, organized crime of various kinds is involved. Transnational networks have grown up involving links between local villagers in the areas where antiquities have been discovered and dealers who violate national legislation prohibiting their illegal export and smuggle them to countries where they are purchased by other

Model Treaty for the Prevention of Crimes that Infringe on the Cultural Heritage of Peoples in the Form of Movable Property

For the purposes of this Treaty, movable cultural property shall be understood as referring to property which, on religious or secular grounds, is specifically designated by a State Party as being subject to export control by reason of its importance for archaeology, prehistory, history, literature, art or science.

This Treaty applies to movable cultural property stolen in or illicitly exported from the other State Party after the coming into force of the Treaty.

General principles. Each State Party undertakes:

a) To take necessary measures to prohibit the import and export of movable cultural property which has been stolen in the other State Party or which has been illicitly exported from the other State Party;

b) To take the necessary measures to prohibit the acquisition of, and dealing within its territory with, movable cultural property which has been imported contrary to the above prohibitions;

c) To legislate to prevent persons and institutions within its territory from entering into international conspiracies with respect to movable cultural property;

d) To provide information concerning stolen movable cultural property to an international data base agreed upon between the States Parties;

e) To take measures to ensure that the purchaser of stolen movable cultural property which is listed on the international data base is not considered to have purchased such property in good faith;

f) To introduce a system whereby the export of movable cultural property is authorized by issue of an export certificate;

g) To use all means, including the fostering of public awareness, to combat illicit import and export, theft, illicit excavations and illicit dealing in movable cultural property.

Each State undertakes to take the necessary measures to recover and return, at the request of the other State Party, any movable cultural property which is covered in subparagraph a) above.

Sanctions. Each State Party undertakes to impose sanctions upon:

a) Persons or institutions responsible for illicit import or export of movable cultural property;

b) Persons or institutions that knowingly acquire or deal in stolen or illicitly imported movable cultural property;

c) Persons or institutions that enter into international conspiracies to obtain, export or import movable cultural property by illicit means.

Procedures. Requests for recovery and return shall be made through diplomatic channels. All expenses incidental to the return and delivery of the movable cultural property shall be borne by the requesting State Party, and no persons or institution shall be entitled to claim any form of compensation from the State Party returning the property claimed. Neither shall the requesting State Party be required to compensate in any way such persons or institutions as may have participated in illegally sending abroad the property in question, although it must pay fair compensation to any person or institution that in good faith acquired or was in legal possession of the property.

Both parties agree not to levy any customs or other duties on such movable property as may be discovered and returned in accord with the present Treaty.

Source: Adopted by the Eighth Crime Congress and welcomed by the United Nations General Assembly in resolution 45/121

dealers and private collectors. According to one report, the illicit trade in stolen and/or illegally exported cultural objects has grown so large that INTERPOL now believes it to be one of the most prevalent categories of international crime.[23] Moreover, it is one dependent for its success, in large part, upon close links between the black market and the licit sector.[24]

In African countries such as Mali, the purchase for export of cultural objects and the widespread looting of archaeological sites have increased rapidly since the 1970s. Among the most recent trends, however, has been the theft of Nigerian art treasures to supply dealers in London and New York.[25] Something similar is happening in South Africa,[26] Asia,[27] Latin America and former Soviet bloc countries.[28]

Trafficking in cultural property is pervasive in Western countries as well. A Mafia pentiti recently admitted to the theft of a Caravaggio in Palermo in 1969. Not surprisingly, Italy has been a prime target with "no less than 253,000 recorded art thefts ... during the period 1970-90" (Brooks, 1992). In a more recent case, police in Italy recovered 1,273 stolen works of art and disrupted an art theft ring that included a priest and an expert in gold leaf restoration and was responsible for thefts of paintings, furniture and religious relics worth a total of $4.2 million and apparently destined for clandestine art markets in Japan and the United States.[29] Another target has been the United Kingdom where according to one assessment the losses of insured fine art and antiques are somewhere on the order of $600 million to $750 million per annum, with uninsured losses bringing the total to around $1.5 billion.[30]

Control. There are several things that have been done and are being done in response to this problem. The importance of preserving cultural property was recognized in the Hague Convention for the Protection of Cultural Property in the Event of Armed Conflict (1954),[31] and the 1970 UNESCO Convention on the Means of Prohibiting and Preventing the Illicit Import, Export and Transfer of Ownership of Cultural Property.[32] The European Community, as it moved towards the creation of a single market has issued several directives and regulations in a similar vein.

In June 1995 a Convention on the International Return of Stolen or Illegally Exported Cultural Objects was adopted by the International Institute for the Unification of Private Law (UNIDROIT), an independent intergovernmental organization based in Rome. The aim of the convention is to establish "a unified code whereby claimants in countries that are party to the convention may sue in the courts of other signatory countries for the return of stolen or illegally exported cultural objects."[33] (See also the United Nations Model Treaty for prevention of cultural theft, Box 9.7.)

Several organizations also collect and disseminate information about stolen cultural objects. These include UNESCO, the International Council of Museums (ICOM), the International Foundation for Art Research (IFAR), Trace, and the International Art and Antique Loss Register (London and New York). The Art Loss Register maintained in New York has a database of around 80,000 items (including paintings, sculptures, ceramics, Asian art items, icons, etc.) known to have been stolen. It estimates that the recovery rate is approximately ten to 15 percent, although this increases dramatically when the art object is well-known. Since 1991 there has been a significant increase in the number of items added to the list, but this could well be attributable to the spread of knowledge about the database and the subsequent increase in reporting, rather than to an increase in the number of art crimes per se. The items that were valued on this list (about 20 percent are reported without any value attached) come to about 650 million dollars.[34]

Theft and trafficking in automobiles

Vehicle theft has long been a domestic problem and one that often involved individuals or small groups of teenagers who were engaged in little more than joyriding. Cars were stolen locally and often found locally some time later. In recent years, however, the theft of cars has increasingly been a prelude to transporting them to another country or countries. Smuggling cars to "far-flung destinations" is facilitated by insufficient cooperation among law enforcement agencies, legislative discrepancies with regard to bona fide ownership, divergent vehicle registration practices and the like.[35] All of these factors make "illicit trafficking in motor vehicles a criminal activity that, although considered low-risk, generates high profits."[36] The pattern of this trade is very clear: it goes from advanced economies where luxury cars are plentiful to developing state or states in transition where they are far less common, but where demand is high.

In many respects these illicit flows can be understood as the reverse of patterns of migration — supplier and recipient states are transposed. Indeed, states in which market economies have been introduced such as Russia and China have become major customers for luxury cars from the West. Not surprisingly, therefore, this area of crime is no longer the province of teenagers engaged in random acts of theft. It is now well-organized, often employing sophisticated technology including electronic decoders to disarm alarm systems.[37]

The same kind of pattern of organization is evident elsewhere. On the US-Mexican border sport utility vehicles such as Chevrolet Suburbans and Jeep Cherokees are sometimes stolen only to be mounted with weapons and used by drug trafficking organizations.[38] Russian organized crime groups in northern California have been shipping automobiles out of Seattle and Oakland, while it was reported in December 1994 that a separate group of emigres from the former Soviet Union, operating in Los Angeles, had shipped 200 stolen cars with a total value of about ten million dollars to Russia, Ukraine and Central America.[39] In Toronto, Chinese gangs have used fake credit cards to rent cars which were subsequently sent to China and the Middle East. Some of the major transnational flows of stolen cars are as follows:

- *Western Europe to Eastern Europe and Russia*. Among the most popular cars stolen from Western Europe are Volkswagen Golfs. The most important targets, however, are luxury cars such as S-class Mercedes which are greatly in demand in the Russian, Ukrainian and Albanian black markets. Some transit through the Balkan route to the Middle East while others go through Poland, the Czech Republic or Hungary to the CIS countries.[40]

- *Hong Kong to China*. In 1992 there were six car thefts a day, a threefold increase on 1991. Moreover, the business was very well organized with luxury cars such as Mercedes and Rolls Royce being transported to China on *tai feis*, power boats with four very powerful engines.[41]

- *The United States to Mexico, Central America and the Caribbean as well as the Middle East*. Like just about every other American industry, the growth area for the car-theft industry is overseas. The Middle

The pattern in illicit auto trafficking is very clear: it goes from advanced economies where luxury cars are plentiful to developing states or states in transition where they are far less common, but where demand is high.

Maritime piracy: an old modern crime

Piracy in many respects appears to be an anachronism. Certainly until the late 1970s it appeared to be a relic of the past. In the late 1970s and early 1980s, there was an upsurge of incidents, but this seemed to be an aberration as the number of incidents declined again until the late 1980s.

As in many other areas, however, there are questions here about the extent to which such incidents are accurately reported. As one knowledgeable analyst has commented: "Shippers may be reluctant to report incidents which might imply negligence, and even more reluctant to delay and disrupt a voyage in order that crews may testify and provide evidence to local authorities." There are also some difficult definitional issues. The United Nations Convention on the High Seas (1958) and Law of the Sea Convention (1982) defined piracy as "an attack mounted for private ends on a ship, involving violence, illegal detention of persons or property, or the theft or destruction of goods." Significantly, this definition did not extend to similar actions undertaken in territorial waters. The International Maritime Bureau has offered a broader definition that does not exclude territorial waters and is more congruent with what is actually happening. In its view piracy is "any act of boarding any vessel with the intent to commit theft or other crime, and with the capability to use force in the furtherance of the act."

The 1990s has been a decade in which piracy appears to be flourishing once more. From 1990 to mid 1992 there was a significant increase in the incidence of piracy, especially in Southeast Asia. Choke points are always attractive to pirates and in this period the Strait of Malacca and the Phillip Channel south of Singapore and north of the islands of Batam and Bintan became a particularly dangerous region for merchant ships. Indeed, from 1990 to mid 1992 about 200 pirate attacks are estimated to have taken place in this area. Although pressure on Indonesia led to a respite in the second half of 1992, the number of incidents remains relatively high. In part, this may reflect greater accuracy as the result of the opening of a reporting center in Kuala Lumpur in October 1992. It also suggests, however, that piracy is undergoing a resurgence. Whatever the case, in the seas around Indonesia there were 22 incidents of piracy in 1994, 33 in 1995 and 53 in 1996. The other area in which piracy became more prevalent was around China, Hong Kong and Macao, which witnessed four incidents in 1994 and 31 in 1995. While there were only nine incidents in this area during the first half of 1996, there were 13 incidents in the seas off Thailand.

The overall trend in piracy in the mid 1990s was very disturbing, with 92 reported cases in 1994 almost doubling to 170 in 1995. This high trend continued during 1996 with 175 incidents reported during the year (see accompanying Figure).

As for responses, a variety of things are possible. At the most basic level, shipowners and captains can simply increase precautions. This has certainly been done in passenger ships. In accordance with International Maritime Organization standards most passenger ships have developed security plans, appointed a security officer and devised systems to prevent unlawful boarding. Similar precautionary measures can be extended to cargo ships. Port security, however, still has many weaknesses, partly because, as the Maritime Security Council has noted, it is "focused on preventing goods leaving a port rather than preventing unauthorized people and their weapons getting to the ship. In many ports, access to a ship is completely open, and in some cases Port Authorities even insist that this is a traditional right of their citizens." Raising the security standards of ports requires both pressure and systematic oversight by governments. Greater pressure also needs to be exerted by the international community on any state where there is evidence of collusion between government officials or military forces on the one side and the pirates on the other. Pressure on coastal states to strengthen patrols in the most dangerous areas, as well as hot pursuit agreements between regional states would also enhance the prospects for reducing the incidence of piracy. Such initiatives, however, will only occur after states recognize that piracy is a serious – if geographically circumscribed – threat that carries with it an increased danger of collision at sea which could all too easily result in environmental disaster.

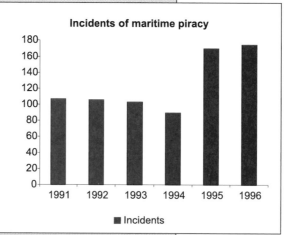

Incidents of maritime piracy

Source: Williams (1997)

East has become a hot market for stolen BMWs, Lincoln Town Cars and Cadillacs.[42]

- *Argentina and Brazil to Bolivia.* Cars are transported either through Paraguay, or in the case of Brazil through Paraguay and Argentina, to Bolivia. From 1993 through June 1996 Argentina recovered 2,422 cars at its border crossings broken down as follows – 1993: 975; 1994: 540; 1995: 537; and in the first half of 1996: 370.[43]

- *Europe to West Africa via Britain.* Although not as large as some of the other trafficking flows there has been a flow of stolen Mercedes to Britain, and from there to West Africa.[44]

The scale of this is also significant. As one commentary observed, "The professionals have taken over, and they have developed global markets for stolen cars and parts. If the car-theft industry were organized as a single company, its revenue would make it the 56th largest US corporation."[45] Not surprisingly, this has implications for the prospects of the owner recovering the vehicle. According to a report by the National Insurance Crime Bureau, in 1970, an American who reported a car stolen had an 84 percent chance of driving the car again.[46] The current figures are much lower. Moreover, although the rates of theft have been declining in recent years the costs to the consumers are around $7.5 billion a year – 134 percent more than in 1970 – partly because cars are more expensive – but also because fewer are recovered.[47] Part of the reason is simply the difficulty of reclaiming a car that has been taken overseas, especially as in many countries if the owner bought it legitimately he or she is entitled to retain possession.

Control. Responses to this problem occur at a variety of levels.[48] International efforts remain mostly at the law enforcement level. These include the creation of national task forces to deal with the problem, as has been done in Australia, and the inclusion of stolen cars on the agenda of cooperative international agencies such as Europol. Indeed, INTERPOL has established an Automatic Search Facility International Stolen Vehicle Database that can be accessed by member states in their efforts to identify and where possible recover stolen vehicles. This database, however, needs to be augmented by national databases and by information sharing arrangements at the bilateral, regional and sub-regional levels. [49]

The United States has signed a treaty with Mexico which led to the tracking down of 5,000 stolen cars in one year, half of which were returned. This has provided a model for further treaties with countries in Central America and the Caribbean (Belize, Costa Rica, Dominican Republic, El Salvador, Guatemala, Honduras, Nicaragua and Panama) which should help to "identify, recover, and return stolen vehicles to the United States."[50] The United States has also provided training for customs and enforcement officials in Panama, El Salvador, Honduras and Venezuela and is extending this to other parts of the world. Enhancing the capacity of destination states to respond to this problem is a priority not only for the United States, but also for the states of the European Union, and would make it more likely that border guards in the former Soviet bloc countries could identify false registration documents.

Higher recovery rates would also be facilitated by a tightening up of national registration procedures and the development of an international standard for documentation. Efforts to harmonize legislation regarding the return of stolen and exported vehicles to the country of origin are also essential.[51] In this connection, the United Nations has formulated a Model Treaty for the return of stolen or embezzled vehicles.[52] None of these measures will be able to stop the problem; but they should at least reduce it and increase the percentage of cars which are retrieved.

Fauna and flora trafficking

One form of transnational crime that has received increasing attention in recent years is fauna and flora smuggling. This is partly because of a widespread acknowledgment of the importance of bio-diversity and a recognition that certain species of animals and plants are in danger of extinction. This has been enshrined in the Convention on International Trade in Endangered Species of Wild Flora and Fauna (CITES).

In spite of this recognition, however, there are large and flourishing black markets in a variety of rare species ranging from Siberian tigers to Thai orchids. The demand side of this trade stems from collectors who want to own rare animals, breeders who want them for profit, those who want to use particular animal parts in herbal medicines or aphrodisiacs, and those who want to use parts such as skins or ivory tusks for various forms of ornamentation. Moreover, the scale of this trade is enormous. INTERPOL figures suggest that in the United States trafficking of animals is worth $1.2 billion a year in some 90,000 unauthorized shipments while the global trade is estimated "to be in the vicinity of five billion dollars per year. It is the largest black market trade after narcotics."[53] Moreover, it is a highly profitable trade which, according to a World Wildlife Fund report, produces from $2 billion to $3 billion in profits per year.[54]

The supply chains for animals and animal products start with villagers and hunters, but also involve transnational criminal networks. Indeed, it has been claimed that Asian criminal organizations are significant participants in trade in rhinoceros horns and tiger parts while in Europe the Neapolitan Camorra is deeply involved in trafficking of animals.[55] Not surprisingly the prices paid for these products increase significantly as they near the consumer. The initial suppliers obtain very little of the profits. Illicit trafficking occurs in rare birds,[56] turtles and reptiles,[57,58] and bears and elephants.[59]

Control. Apart from control efforts within countries[60] international efforts have been attempted in order to disrupt the supply chain. In Holland, for example, in 1995, several measures were taken to disrupt smuggling networks. Penalties were increased to six years in jail, and surveillance of ports and airports was strengthened.[61] Periodic clamp-downs at border crossings can also have at least a temporary impact. In March 1996, for example, the US Fish and Wildlife Service, US Customs, and the Immigration and Naturalization Service cooperated in a search and seizure effort at the port of entry border town of San Ysidro, California, confiscating not only animals but also products from animals protected by CITES. Similar efforts have been initiated in Vancouver and other Canadian ports of entry.[62]

In the United States trafficking of animals is worth $1.2 billion a year.

Trafficking in human organs

One of the most controversial areas of transnational crime is human organ trafficking. It is controversial, partly because of the inherent ethical issues involved, partly because in some cases it appears that there is government involvement — or at the very least connivance — in the harvesting of organs from executed prisoners, and partly because the issue is sometimes used as a political tool. The United States Information Agency, in a survey, found that most accounts of organ trafficking stemmed from sensational journalism and either had very little basis in fact, or involved deliberate lies and distortions. One report even suggested that organ trafficking was "the global lie that cannot be silenced."[1] Indeed, the United States government has been very skeptical and, in some cases, openly critical of such accounts, especially those related to the kidnapping of children for organ transplants.

Accepting that the kidnapping of babies in Latin America for organ transplants in the United States is an unfortunate urban myth, however, does not imply that black markets in human organs in various parts of the world are completely absent. In countries such as Brazil there have been persistent reports suggesting that there is a thriving black market in human organs.[2] Other accounts suggest that in parts of Africa, including Zambia, there have been instances in which people have been arrested for the trade in human organs.[3] There has also been considerable speculation about the case of a journalist for *Le Figaro,* who in October 1996 was found hanged. It was claimed that he had been investigating the execution of Bosnian POWs for their organs and was including this in a book on the conflict in Yugoslavia. His father asserted that "in less than six hours the organs from the concentration camp were in a private clinic in Trieste."[4]

One response, of course, is that grim as these specific cases are they are no more than horrible but isolated aberrations, providing little evidence of organized transnational trafficking. At the same time, there are good grounds for concluding that a black market in human organs does exist, and that because of differential levels of wealth among nations has a transnational dimension. One of the most important cases was that of Montese de Oca, a state run mental institution in Lujan near Buenos Aires. There were 12 arrests and it appeared that in the period from 1976 to 1991 1,321 patients had died and about 1400 had disappeared, with their relatives being informed that they had escaped. Another significant case occurred in June 1995 when police in Bangalore arrested four physicians and two middlemen for organ theft and trafficking. They had apparently obtained kidneys from unemployed labourers, which were then sold to buyers from Saudi Arabia, the Gulf, Turkey and Europe.[5] What sets this case apart from other transactions in India is that it was involuntary. There have been many well-documented cases in India of people selling kidneys. As one study has observed: "India has become known as the organ capital of the world. Several reasons have been identified for this reputation. The first is that there is an over-abundance of poor people in India who are willing to sacrifice their kidneys for cash. Second, there are hospitals and clinics that will perform transplant operations, but not always for humanitarian reasons alone. Finally, there are the business-minded middlemen who have pounced upon the opportunity to bring recipients, donors and clinics together for the chance of making a profit."[6] In 1995, Indian authorities moved to clamp down on illegal transplants. The fact that this led Nepal to impose more stringent regulations on transplant clinics to preempt a form of displacement of regional trafficking along what is a largely open border provides an indicator of the extent of the illicit trade.

Control. Organ trafficking can be understood at one level in simple demand and supply terms. In the United States, for example, where there is very stringent legislation and oversight, in 1992 just over 16,000 organs were transplanted, while there were 40,000 people waiting, 2,500 of whom died. As many as one-fifth of all those needing transplants die waiting.[7] In other countries the same kind of market dynamic can combine with a much more permissive approach to encourage the growth of illicit trading. In some cases, of course, governments are moving vigorously against this and are trying to conform with the World Health Organization resolution of May 1989 exhorting member state to legislate against the trafficking of organ and to enforce this legislation. Indonesia, Russia and Sri Lanka, for example, have made commercial organ trade illegal and in October 1996, President Samper of Colombia ordered the creation of a new police unit — *Humanitas* — to clamp down on child kidnapping, body part trafficking and "social cleansing operations." Similarly, Turkey, in December 1996, in passing legislation against money laundering included organ trafficking as one of the predicate offences.

Source: Williams (1997)

Ensuring that more and more states not only become parties to CITES but that they are vigorous in enforcement is something that also needs to be done more vigorously and systematically than hitherto. The 18 office global TRAFFIC Network, in conjunction with its parent organizations, World Wildlife Fund and the World Conservation Union (IUCN), is continuing to investigate the medicinal trade in imperiled species. What might be particularly helpful in focusing attention on this issue, however, is an annual assessment of the extent to which both signatories and non-signatories are in accordance with CITES.

Computer crimes

As computers and connected information systems have become more prevalent so too have the opportunities for criminal activities both exploiting and targeting such systems increased significantly. There are several crimes that have become closely associated with connected computer systems. These are:

- *Hacking.* The illegal intrusion into computer networks for fun or profit.[63]

- *Distribution of child pornography* on the World Wide Web. This has become an extensive problem, and one related closely to trafficking in children discussed above. It is something, however, on which it is difficult to get definitive data given the constantly changing number and location of web sites.

- *Extortion using threats to destroy computer and information systems.* This area of activity is also one in which definitive evidence is hard to obtain, largely because banks and other financial institutions are reluctant to provide or confirm details of extortion incidents, partly because of concerns that this could undermine the confidence of their customers and partly because of a belief that the greater the publicity the greater the likelihood that the crimes will encourage imitation.[64]

- *Penetration of computer systems for theft or fraud.* There have been cases in which raids on data banks have made it possible to obtain credit card numbers and other information that could subsequently be used for fraud.[65]

Control. Because computer networks,

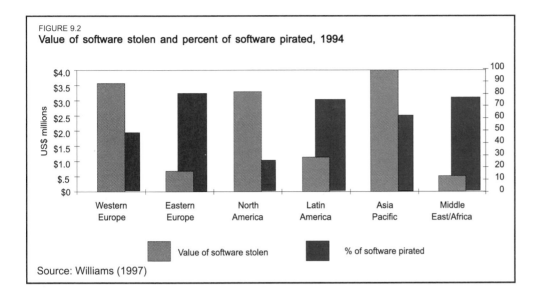

FIGURE 9.2
Value of software stolen and percent of software pirated, 1994

Source: Williams (1997)

particularly the Internet, do not recognize national boundaries, the transnational significance of computer crime is self evident. One of the responses of law enforcement has been to create special units which focus exclusively on computer crimes. One of the oldest of these is the US Air Force Office of Special Investigations which created a dedicated computer crime unit in 1978. The difficulty that such law enforcement agencies face, however, is that even when they can find hackers in the virtual world that does not mean that they can find them in the real world. Moving from the electronic to the geographical is fraught with difficulty, given the inadequacy of many national laws in what is a relatively new area of criminal activity. Offenders may reside in any country. Even if identified and caught, extradition of criminals cannot be guaranteed because of the complex and poorly developed systems of extradition treaties existing among countries around the world (see Box 9.11). It is clear that this is an area demanding both the creation of more dedicated units at the national level and the development of much more intensive and extensive cooperation among national and international agencies.

Software piracy

There are several forms of transnational crime that do not fit neatly into any category. Software piracy, for example, could be viewed as an aspect of computer crime, as counterfeiting, or as the theft of intellectual property. This section will examine only software piracy.

If maritime piracy is one of the oldest forms of transnational crime, one of the most modern is software piracy. This exists at several levels, from the individual who copies software for friends and colleagues to the organized groups which, in effect, engage in large scale counterfeiting. It is also something that has been studied extensively by two industry watchdog associations, the Software Publishers Association and the Business Software Alliance.[66] The global figures for losses involving business software are shown in Figure 9.2 with a regional breakdown by amount. The figure also shows the value of the percentage of software that was pirated in each region in 1995. What stands out from this figure is that software piracy is far greater in terms of percentage where the market is smaller and less developed, but that the losses are greatest where the markets are most developed.

In some senses, the real problems are in Russia, China and Thailand, where piracy rates are over 90 percent – although in terms of revenue losses the leaders are Japan and the United States. Eastern Europe had the highest overall piracy rates, with an average of 83 percent. The lowest regional piracy rate was seen in North America, with an average 27 percent rate. Individual countries with high rates of piracy in 1995 include Vietnam (99 percent), El Salvador (97 percent), China (96 percent), Oman (96 percent) and Russia (94 percent). By contrast, individual countries with lower software piracy rates include the United States (26 percent), Australia (35 percent), the United Kingdom (38 percent), New Zealand (40

If maritime piracy is one of the oldest forms of transnational crime, one of the most modern is software piracy.

BOX 9.10

Regulation of counterfeit goods in Korea

Introduction. The market for counterfeit goods has emerged in the process of economic development and industrialization. In many countries, as the economic level rises, consumption patterns change, manufacturing technology accumulates, and famous brand names are frequently imported. These circumstances create ideal conditions for the emergence of a market in counterfeit goods.

In Korea, counterfeit goods markets have formed – near US Army bases and popular tourist destinations – where foreign travelers are able to find counterfeit goods easily. Recently, these markets have expanded into other major cities in Korea, as well as Seoul, the capital city.

Korean markets for counterfeit goods prevail across the nation. Since the illicit dealings of those goods are clandestine, the challenge to law enforcement is considerable. It is not easy to discover either the quantity of domestic counterfeit goods or their point of origin, or the scale of imported goods and their distribution.

In the past, Korean counterfeiters copied foreign brands, but today there is a new trend, especially in Asian countries, to copy famous Korean brands illegally, as Korean brands are perceived as more valuable in international markets.

The Korean Public Prosecutor's Office exerts a constant effort to regulate those illicit dealings and to protect intellectual property rights by imposing harsh punishment. In 1996 alone, 15,166 violators were booked by the police and prosecutor's offices and 1,106 were detained in prison.

However, intellectual property rights continue to be violated by illicitly duplicating well-known brand labels and copying books and computer software, although the number of violations is now decreasing. In fact, the Public Prosecutor's Office is considering even more drastic monitoring and control.

Meaning and legal restriction of counterfeit goods. Counterfeit goods are commercial products with counterfeit trademarks. A trademark is a symbol used by individuals or companies in the process of producing, manufacturing or packaging their own goods. Symbols identify and distinguish their products from other goods. The main purposes of using a trademark are to display the product's originality, such as product name, company name, place of production, and so on; to warrant products, such as expiration dates, business ID, warranty periods, and so on; and to advertise products. Conceptually speaking, the product label can be distinguished from the trademark. However, in many cases the product label is used as a trademark in the business community. If a certain trademark meets all the above conditions and is legally registered, it can be protected from counterfeiting by trademark laws. In addition, there is the law on the prevention of unfair competition to assure that regulation on trademarks is properly enforced.

Current situation of counterfeit goods regulation in Korea. According to the Korean Public Prosecutor's Office statistics on intellectual property rights violations in 1995, 13,683 people were booked by the police and prosecutors and, among them, 843 people were detained in prison facilities. In 1996, 15,166 people were booked and among them 1,106 people were detained in prison facilities. The number of those booked by the police and prosecutors increased by 10.8 percent and those who were detained in-

creased by 31.2 percent in one year.

In 1996, among 4,166 cases of violation of the trademark law and unfair competition prevention law, 4,170 people were booked and 755 people are detained in prison facilities. From January 1 to May 31, 1997, 6,507 people were booked by the police and prosecutors due to the violation of the intellectual property rights law. Among them, 6,499 cases were booked and 378 people were detained. Compared with statistics of the same period in the previous year, the booking rate was increased 20.8 percent and the detention rate was decreased 15.3 percent in 1997. In cases of violation of the trademark law or unfair competition prevention law, 1,526 people among 1,524 cases were booked and 168 people were detained.

The above statistics are limited to criminal cases. Those of civil cases are excluded in this article because the solutions of civil cases are generally made by the concerned party.

The characteristics of counterfeiters Because Korean consumers are eager to buy foreign products with famous brand names, clandestine counterfeiting networks have arisen and become highly complex and thus very difficult to control and regulate through regular counterfeiting laws. Regulation is difficult for a number of reasons. First, it is difficult to trace the origins of counterfeit goods through retailers because their methods of distribution become clandestine and intellectual. Second, it is difficult to detect the authenticity of counterfeit goods since print technology is highly developed. Third, even when detected, it is hard for authorities to prove illegal dealings when retailers or wholesalers insist that they did not purchase counterfeit goods; and even in cases where the purchase of illicit goods is shown, it is difficult to prove whether the dealings are intentionally illicit or not.

Future prospects. To control counterfeit goods effectively and practically, Korean prosecutor's offices are considering several countermeasures.

First, the collection of information related to counterfeiting is necessary. Collecting information requires cooperation between government and retailers and manufacturers of brand name products, associations of market vendors, and the Office of Patents. Furthermore, information can be obtained by using psychology – vendors will sometimes give information about competitors to grab more opportunities in their particular market. In brief, in order to regulate these violations, it is essential to obtain the cooperation of other government agencies and foster extensive information exchange.

Second, along with customs officers, prosecutors supervise and regulate counterfeit goods in the process of custom services. Under Korea's "parallel importing system," products with certain labels are imported, while others are produced in domestic markets. In contravention of this system, local manufacturers illegally order certain products through third country subcontractors, which are then exported to Korea, again illegally. To detect these counterfeit goods, customs officials are in need of support from prosecutor's offices.

Third, it is necessary to pay more attention to goods imported from China, many of which are counterfeit, by using already existing customs service data.

Finally, by advertising the necessity and justification of protection of intellectual property rights, it is necessary to attract civilians' voluntary participation in crime reports. For those who report intellectual property rights violation, provision of monetary rewards would be appropriate.

Source: Jin-Sup Jung (Original paper, 1997)

percent) and Germany (42 percent).[67]

According to the Business Software Alliance (BSA), piracy of computer software in Gulf Arab states is among the highest in the world, costing legitimate firms nearly $68 million in lost revenues in 1996. Oman had a piracy rate of 95 percent — the highest in the Middle East and Africa — while Bahrain had 90 percent, Kuwait and Qatar 89 percent and Saudi Arabia 79 percent. Indeed, "levels of software piracy in the Middle East and Africa remain among the highest in the world with revenue losses estimates at $511 million in 1996."[68]

Nuclear material theft and trafficking

One of the most disturbing of all transnational crimes is the theft of radioactive materials. This is something that has really emerged as a serious problem since the end of the Cold War and the collapse of the Soviet Union. It is also a problem that could all too easily feed into extortion and terrorist actions likely to inflict large casualties and have significant environmental impact. There is an important distinction to be made, however, between trafficking in radioactive materials in general and trafficking in nuclear weapons grade materials that might facilitate nuclear proliferation. Although trafficking in the first category has been widespread the number of what William Potter has termed "proliferation significant" incidents remains very small.[69]

Figure 9.3 is based on a chronology of incidents drawn from open sources from July 1991 onwards.[70] The difficulty, of course, is interpreting these figures. The decline after 1994 could reflect a real decline, an effort to give the issue less publicity, or a move in the business away from Germany where law enforcement was effective and the chances of interdiction relatively high, to the southern routes from Russia to the Middle East through the Caucasus and Central Asia where law enforcement capacity was very limited and the prospects for interception much lower. In fact, it might well represent a combination of these factors.

It might also reflect some of the efforts made by the international community to respond to the phenomenon of nuclear material trafficking. These include initiatives to improve security at storage sites, laborato-

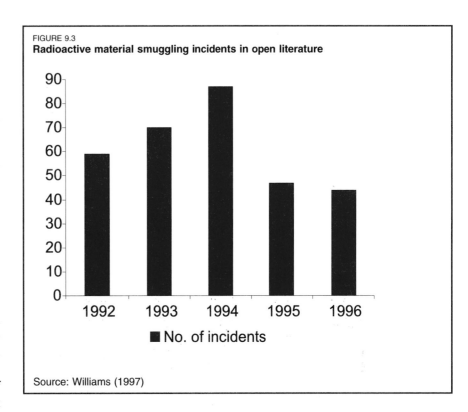

FIGURE 9.3
Radioactive material smuggling incidents in open literature

■ No. of incidents

Source: Williams (1997)

ries and other installations, a process greatly assisted by the United States through its Protection, Monitoring, Control and Accountability Program.[71] The issue has been discussed at G-7 or P-8 meetings and agreements have been reached to facilitate the sharing of information among law enforcement and intelligence agencies in key nations.[72]

International terrorism in all its forms

Terrorism is an area where, quantitatively, there is good news, but this is offset to some extent by some rather disturbing qualitative trends. According to statistics collected and published by the US Department of State, international terrorist incidents reached a peak of 667 in 1987 and have been, more or less, falling ever since.[73] There are several reasons for this including the end of the Cold War, the loss of much state sponsorship for terrorist activities, and the peace process in the Middle East. The decline has not been even, of course, and in 1993 and 1995 there was a temporary increase as a result of one or two groups. Moreover, the figures could have been much more substantial in 1995 had a plan to bomb United States airlines over the Pacific not been discovered in

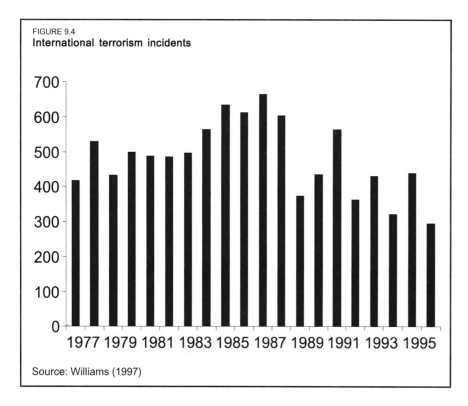

FIGURE 9.4
International terrorism incidents

700
600
500
400
300
200
100
0

1977 1979 1981 1983 1985 1987 1989 1991 1993 1995

Source: Williams (1997)

time.[74] The number of international terrorist incidents is reflected in Figure 9.4

The number of deaths and wounded, of course, depends largely on the kinds of targets chosen by terrorist organizations. "The total number of fatalities from international terrorism worldwide declined from 314 in 1994 to 165 in 1995, but the number of persons wounded increased by a factor of ten – to 6,291 persons."[75] This was explicable largely as a result of the Sarin gas attack on the Tokyo subway carried out by Aum Shinrikyo. Although there were only 12 fatalities, over 5,500 people were injured by the gas, in some cases very seriously. "During 1996 there were 296 acts of international terrorism, the lowest annual total in 25 years and 144 fewer than in 1995. In contrast, the total number of casualties was one of the highest ever recorded: 311 persons killed and 2,652 wounded. A single bombing in Sri Lanka killed 90 persons and wounded more than 1,400 others."[76]

Control. In terms of the response of governments, terrorism has been recognized as a problem rather longer than transnational organized crime. Consequently, there are more measures in place to deal with the terrorist threat. Many countries have national legislation against terrorism and can invoke emergency powers in certain specified circumstances. Precautions taken at airports have also reduced the number of plane hijackings very dramatically. In the last few years, however, efforts have also been made to develop a coordinated international approach using bodies such as the P-8 which have provided an excellent forum for the advanced industrialized nations to cooperate with one another and with Russia. Among the efforts that have been given priority are: the sharing of intelligence on terrorism; measures to prevent the terrorist use of nuclear, chemical and biological materials; inhibiting the movement of terrorists by enhancing measures to prevent or identify the falsification of documents; depriving terrorists of funds; an increase in mutual legal assistance; and additional measures to protect aviation, maritime and other transportation systems and assets. Moreover, the P-8 is trying to ensure universal adherence to international treaties and conventions on terrorism by the year 2000.[77]

Money laundering

Of all areas of criminal activity money laundering is one of the most elusive to measure. While it is difficult to make estimates regarding the value of illicit trade in particular markets, efforts to determine the total amount of money laundered every year are even more problematic. In essence, they require an attempt to add figures which are inherently uncertain. Moreover, when estimating the amount of money laundered there is a certain amount of elasticity in the definition, with some observers using the term as a synonym for criminal earnings as a whole and others employing it only in relation to money that is moved in an effort to hide its origin or ownership and to put it beyond the reach of law enforcement. Not surprisingly, estimates range from 200 billion dollars in the United States and another 100 billion or so worldwide each year, to claims that as much as one trillion dollars are laundered annually. In one of the few really systematic efforts to assess the scale of money laundering at the national level – in this case Australia – one well-informed analyst concluded that a range of between $1,000 and $4,500 million was a sensible interpretation with some confidence that it was around $3,500 million.[78]

Part of the difficulty is knowing what kinds of profits are yielded by various illicit activities and how much criminal organizations actually make. This depends in part on the amount that has to be used to sustain the criminal enterprise itself. Although production and transportation costs tend to be low, the cost of corruption to ensure both safe havens and safe passage can be significant. Moreover, some money is likely to be reinvested in further criminal activities. Of the remainder, a considerable portion might be devoted to the acquisition of possessions such as luxury homes and cars. In effect, what is left at the end of all this is the only money that, strictly speaking, is laundered. Some of this might simply be set aside as personal assets of high ranking criminals whereas some of the laundered profits might be used to infiltrate and purchase licit businesses.

This can be illustrated in Figure 9.5 with a series of concentric circles highlighting the possible breakdown of the profits of crime. If determining the overall amount of money laundered is difficult, it is possible to identify several qualitative trends regarding the manner in which money is laundered. These include the use of specialists or professional money brokers,[79] use of trade and free trade zones, use of non-bank financial institutions such as check-cashing establishments, use of cash businesses such as restaurants, food delivery establishments and casinos,[80] use of electronic transfers,[81] exploitation of offshore banking,[82] use of new financial instruments such as futures and derivatives, use of the states in transition where regulation is modest and organized crime has infiltrated the banking system, and the use of informal or underground banking systems. As well as these well-documented trends it is clear that new opportunities for money laundering are emerging with such innovations as smart cards and cyber-banking. Smart cards, in particular, will make it even more difficult to police currency exchange regulations and therefore are likely to be used extensively to transfer the proceeds of crime.

Control. International anti-money laundering efforts include: the UN Convention Against Illicit Traffic in Narcotic Drugs and Psychotropic Substances of 1988; the Basle Committee on Banking Regulations and Supervisory Practices Statement of Principles of December 1988; the Financial Action Task Force (FATF) Report of April 1990 (with its 40 recommendations for action); the Council of Europe Convention on Laun-

dering, Search, Seizure and Confiscation of Proceeds of Crime of September 8, 1990; the 61 recommendations of the Caribbean Drug Money Laundering Conference of June 1990; the agreement on EC legislation by the European Community's Ministers for Economy and Finance of December 17, 1990; the Organization of American States Model Regulations on Crimes Related to Laundering of Property and Proceeds Related to Drug Trafficking of March 1992; and the FATF supplementary recommendations issued in 1996. Moreover, several countries have set up specialized anti-money laundering units with a specific mandate to combat money laundering. These include FINCEN in the United States and AUSTRAC in Australia. The difficulty, however, is that large parts of the world have either no anti-money laundering legislation, or, in some cases, token legislation, which there is little effort to implement or enforce. The result in these circumstances is simply to push money laundering activities from relatively high risk areas to low risk locations.

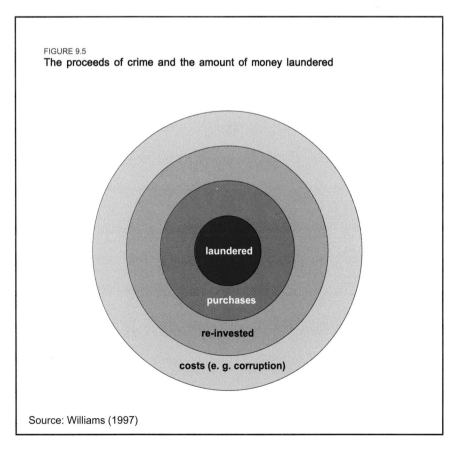

FIGURE 9.5
The proceeds of crime and the amount of money laundered

laundered

purchases

re-invested

costs (e. g. corruption)

Source: Williams (1997)

International crime control through extradition treaties and conventions

Recently, a delegation of Chinese investigators arrived in New York to gather evidence to convict two suspects in China who had planned to collect a ransom from a victim's family. This was a historic moment for Chinese investigators and the New York Police Department to participate in a cooperative effort to fight crime across the globe. While this represents an example of aggressive forging of links between various law enforcement agencies of the global community, historically countries cooperated with each other in matters pertaining to crime control by exchanging wanted criminals and fugitive offenders.

Extradition. The practice of exchanging wanted criminals in contemporary history is primarily guided by extradition treaties. Extradition generally refers to the surrender by one state to another of a person accused or convicted of a crime "by virtue of a treaty, reciprocity or comity as between the respective states" (Bassiouni, 1974: 2). Extradition treaties specifically address the attempts of two or more countries to resolve crime problems where the offender from one country commits a crime in his/her country and takes refuge in another country; or the offender from one country commits a crime in another country and slips back into his/her own country. Not all countries have extradition treaties with the rest of the world. Some such as the US have treaties with more countries than others.

Extradition arrangements may exist in the form of bilateral or multilateral treaties and conventions. According to Bassiouni (1974), the two most important features that distinguish modern extradition treaties include the purpose of returning a person to the competent authority to exercise jurisdiction over him or her; and a body of rules imposed by international law and municipal law that governs extradition process.

Extradition treaties include either an *enumerative method* or an *eliminative method*. A treaty that follows the enumerative method lists and defines the crimes for which extradition will be granted. In the eliminative or "no list" method extraditable offences are defined in terms of their punishability according to the laws of the two countries by a minimum standard of severity (Shearer, 1971: 134). Though each of these methods has shortcomings, the latter appears to have become a more popular method in recent years (Shearer, 1971). Despite the differences, both methods observe the rule of double criminality; that is, both the requesting and the requested states shall extradite only such acts that are considered crimes in both countries (Shearer, 1971: 137).

Extradition treaties. Treaties usually address one or more of four areas: judicial and/ or legal assistance (e.g., search and seizure, documents relevant to criminal acts, etc.), penal matters (e.g., cooperative efforts to fight crime), illicit traffic in narcotic drugs, and treaties to fight terrorism. Examples of major treaties are as follows:

1. Pact of the League of Arab States. This pact was signed in Cairo on March 22, 1945 by Egypt, Iraq, Trans-Jordan, Lebanon, Saudi Arabia, Syria and Yemen. Only Egypt, Jordan and Saudi Arabia ratified the treaty, which has been operative since August 23, 1954 (Bassiouni, 1974: 20).

2. The Benelux Extradition Convention. This treaty concerning extradition and mutual assistance in criminal matters was signed in Brussels on June 27, 1962 by Belgium and Luxembourg, on the one hand, and Belgium and the Netherlands on the other hand. This convention became effective on May 15, 1968.

3. The Commonwealth Scheme. The Scheme Relating to the Rendition of Fugitive Offenders Within the Commonwealth was conceived at a meeting of the Commonwealth Law Ministers in London in 1966. This scheme was based on the Fugitive Offenders Act of 1881, which provided for the surrender of fugitive criminals between British possessions.

4. European Convention on Extradition. The European Convention on Extradition was signed in Paris on December 13, 1957, and became effective on April 18,1960. The members included Austria, Czech Republic, Denmark, France, Germany, Greece, Ireland, Israel, Italy, Luxembourg, Netherlands, Norway, Portugal, Spain, Sweden, Switzerland, Turkey and United Kingdom and Northern Ireland. As of 17 November, 1997, the following countries have also signed and ratified this convention: Belgium, Bulgaria, Croatia, Cyprus, Estonia, Finland, Hungary, Iceland, Latvia, Liechtenstein, Lithuania, Malta, Moldova, Poland, Rumania, Slovakia and Slovenia.

5. Convention between the UK, Australia, New Zealand, South Africa, India and Portugal. This supplementary to the extradition treaty of October 17, 1892 was signed in Lisbon, January 20, 1932.

Continued on next page

Conclusion

It is clear that most – although certainly not all – transnational crimes involve trafficking in some kind of illicit products and services, or in licit products that have been obtained through illegal means. Against this background there are several observations that can be made about these illicit markets.

- The dynamics of illicit markets are easy to identify but difficult to contain. In most cases, supply chains come into being in order to meet demand.

- Most of these markets are populated by a complex mix of actors with transnational criminal organizations playing a large but not exclusive role. In the case of prostitution of both women and children, for example, criminal organizations control a significant portion of the business and are instrumental in maintaining supply. Yet supply would be more problematic were it not for the collusion of villagers willing to sell their children. Furthermore, the business would not be nearly as profitable without the connivance of segments of the tourist industry to provide sex tours to countries such as Thailand. Similar connivance can be found in the art and antiquities business.

- Most of the markets have become global in scope and generally involve trafficking of illicit products from the developing world or states in transition to the developed world. The exceptions are arms and cars. Luxury motor vehicles in particular go from the countries of Western Europe to states in transition in Eastern Europe and the former Soviet Union and to developing states in Africa. Similarly cars stolen from the United States often end up in Central and South America. This is an interesting reversal of the direction of most illicit flows.

- There is some overlap among the various markets, partly because some criminal organizations traffic in a variety of products. Once the trafficking infrastructure is in place, the product line is virtually irrelevant.

- There has to be an acknowledgment that in many of the sectors of activity examined above, there is no sharp disconnect between licit business activities and illicit

BOX 9.11 CONTINUED

International crime control through extradition treaties and conventions

6. Montevideo Convention on Extradition. The Montevideo Convention on Extradition was signed on December 26, 1933, and went into effect on January 25, 1935. The participating countries include Argentina, Chile, Colombia, Dominican Republic, Ecuador, El Salvador, Guatemala, Honduras, Mexico, Nicaragua, Panama and the United States. However, Article 21 provides that the convention does not affect existing treaties between individual states.

7. The Nordic States Scheme. Denmark, Finland, Iceland, Norway and Sweden were parties to this extradition treaty of 1962 (Bassiouni, 1974: 20-21).

8. The OCAM Convention. On September 12, 1961, 12 of the 14 former French territories in equatorial and west Africa formed the *Union Africaine et Malgache* and signed a convention on judicial cooperation at Tananarive. The Union was subsequently renamed the *Organisation Communale Africaine et Malgache* (OCAM) and was enlarged by the accession of Togo (Bassiouni, 1974: 22-23).

Conventions on judicial / legal assistance

1. European Convention on Mutual Assistance in Criminal Matters. The European Convention on Mutual Assistance in Criminal Matters was signed in Strasbourg on April 4, 1959. As of 17 November, 1997, the states which have ratified the agreement include: Austria, Belgium, Bulgaria, Czech Republic, Denmark, Estonia, Finland, France, Germany, Greece, Hungary, Iceland, Ireland, Israel, Italy, Latvia, Lithuania, Luxembourg, Netherlands, Poland, Portugal, Slovakia, Spain, Sweden, Turkey and the UK.

2. European Convention on the Transfer of Proceedings in Criminal Matters. This convention was signed in Strasbourg on May 15, 1972 and became effective on March 30, 1978. The parties which have ratified this convention include: Austria, Czech Republic, Denmark, Estonia, Netherlands, Norway, Slovakia, Spain, Sweden, Turkey and Ukraine. The following states have signed, but not ratified the convention: Belgium, Iceland, Greece, Liechtenstein, Lithuania, Luxemburg and Portugal.

The Implementation of Model Treaties

One of the most important services provided to the international community by the UN has been the drafting of standards and norms in crime prevention and criminal justice (United Nations, 1992b). Of course, these standards and norms are not binding on the nations of the world; rather, they provide the framework for developing bilateral and multilateral agreements between nations which are interested in improving their cooperation in criminal matters and in achieving greater efficacy in crime prevention. To assist nations as they negotiate bilateral and multilateral conventions, the UNCICP has produced implementation guides such as the one for the Model Treaty on Extradition and the Model Treaty on Mutual Assistance in Criminal Matters (United Nations, 1995j). Beyond the preparation of implementation guides, the UNCICP also provides technical assistance and training to criminal justice officials in those countries which seek to implement a model treaty. For instance, the UNCICP and UNDCP jointly organized a training seminar in Grand-Bassam, Ivory Coast, in September of 1997. The purpose of the training seminar was to assist criminal justice officials from the 16 member states of the Economic Community of Western African States (ECOWAS) in the practical implementation of conventions developed on the basis of UN model treaties, including Conventions on Extradition and Mutual Assistance in Criminal Matters of ECOWAS and relevant provisions of the UN Conventions Against Illicit Traffic in Narcotic Drugs and Psychotropic Substances of 1988 (United Nations, 1997c). This training seminar, and others like it around the world, underscore the commitment of the UN to provide the international community with guidelines for the creation of bilateral and multilateral agreements on matters related to criminal justice and, just as importantly, the resources and technical assistance to implement those agreements at the operational level.

Source: Nalla (Original paper, 1997)

---

or criminal activities. There are significant grey areas populated by unscrupulous entrepreneurs who move from the licit to the illicit and back again as circumstances and opportunities dictate.

- Several criminal activities, such as trafficking in people, have spawned lucrative cottage industries or service industries especially in forging of documents, end user certificates and the like.

- The overall impression from this analysis is that although governments are responding to transnational criminal organizations and transnational criminal activities, they are doing too little too late. Efforts need to be expanded especially in the area of reliable and uniform data collection. More sophisticated methodologies need to be devised and greater use made of the information available in the private sector. As

a matter of urgency a central clearing house needs to be established with a focus on illicit market activities of all kinds and a recognition of the cross-linkages and synergies that are being developed.

References

Note: The original papers written for this report are not included in this reference list. They are placed in a separate listing directly after the references.

Albrecht, Hans-Jörg.1996. Sanctions and their implementation. Paper presented at the twenty-first Criminological Research Conference. Strasbourg: Council of Europe PC-CRC(96)5.

Al-Sagheer, Mohamed Faleh. 1994. Diyya legislation in Islamic Shari'a and its application in the Kingdom of Saudi Arabia. In Uglješa Zvekic (Ed.), *Alternatives to Imprisonment in Comparative Perspective*. Chicago: Nelson-Hall.

Alvazzi del Frate, A. 1996. *Manual for International Crime (Victim) Survey*. Rome: UNICRI.

Alvazzi del Frate, A. 1997. Preventing crime: citizens' experience across the world. *Issues and Reports* no. 9. Rome: UNICRI

Alvazzi del Frate, A. and Angela Patrignani. 1995. *Women's Victimisation in Developing Countries*. Rome: UNICRI.

Alvazzi del Frate, A., Uglješa Zvekic and Jan J.M. van Dijk. (Eds.). 1993. *Understanding Crime: Experiences of Crime and Crime Control*. Rome: UNICRI.

Amnesty International. 1997a. *The Death Penalty: List of Abolitionist and Retentionist Countries. July 1997*. London, UK.

Amnesty International. 1997b. *The Death Penalty World Wide: Developments in 1996*. London, UK.

Anderson, David, Sylvia Chenery and Ken Pease. 1994. *Biting Back: Tackling Repeat Burglary and Car Crime*. Crime Detection and Prevention Series, no. 58. London: Home Office Police Department.

Angus G., K. Wilkinson, and P. Zabar. 1994. *Child Abuse and Neglect, Australia 1990-91*. Attorney General's Department, 1995, Portfolio Budget Measures Statements 1994-95, various papers. Canberra: Australian Institute of Health and Welfare.

Anyebe, A.P. 1985. *Customary Law: The War Without Arms*. Enugu, Nigeria: Fourth Dimension Publishing Co. Ltd.

Applied Criminology Group. 1997. Evaluation report of the Boggart Hill anti-burglary initiative. *Report to the Multi-Agency Panel*. University of Huddersfield, UK.

Arlacchi, P. 1995. *Political Corruption and Organized Crime in Contemporary Italy*. Collected Works of the Seventh International Anti-Corruption Conference. Beijing.

Aromaa, K and M. Lehti. 1996. *Foreign Companies and Crime in Eastern Europe*. Helsinki.

Australian Bureau of Statistics. 1994. *Crime and Safety Australia*. ABS Cat. no. 4509.0, Canberra.

Australian Bureau of Statistics. 1995. *Implicit Price De-flators of Gross Domestic Product*. Table 61 of *National Income, Expenditure and Product, June Quarter, 1995*. ABS Cat. no. 5206.0, Canberra.

Australian Bureau of Statistics. 1996a. *Australian National Classification Offences, 1985*. ABS Cat. no. 1234.0, Canberra.

Australian Bureau of Statistics. 1996b. *Women's Safety, Australia*.

Australian Bureau of Statistics. 1997. *National Crime Statistics January to December 1995*. ABS Cat. no. 4510.0, Canberra.

Australian Federal Police. 1997. *Annual Report 1995-96*. Canberra: Australian Federal Police.

Aye Maung, N. 1995. Survey design and interpretation of the British Crime Survey. In M.Walker (Ed.), *Interpreting Crime Statistics*. Oxford: Oxford University Press.

Barnett, W.S. 1993. Cost-benefit analysis. In L.J. Schweinhart, H.V. Barnes and D.P. Weikart, *Significant Benefits: The High/Scope Perry Preschool Study Through Age 27*. Ypsilanti, Michigan: High/Scope Press.

Barnett, W.S. and C.M. Escobar. 1987. The economics of early educational intervention: a review. *Review of Educational Research*, 57, 4: 387-414.

Bassiouni, Cherif M. 1974. *International Extradition and World Public Order*. Dobbs Ferry, NY: A.W. Sijthoff-Leyden Oceana Pub.

Bennett, Richard R. 1991. Development and crime: a cross-national time series analysis of competing models. *The Sociological Quarterly*, 32: 343-363.

Bennett, Richard R. and Lynch, James P. 1990. Does a difference make a difference? Comparing cross-national crime indicators. *Criminology*, 28, 1: 153-181.

Biles, David. 1997. Private prisons: welcome or not? *Australian Journal of Forensic Sciences*, vol. 29.

Biles, David. and Richard Harding. 1994. *Correction in Asia and the Pacific: Record of the Fourteenth Asia and the Pacific Conference of Correctional Administrators*. Darwin, Australia.

Block, Richard. 1993. Measuring victimizations risk: The effects of methodology, sampling, and fielding. In Anna Alvazzi del Frate, Uglješa Zvekic and Jan J.M. van Dijk (Eds.), *Understanding Crime: Experiences of Crime and Crime Control*. Rome: UNICRI.

Bouloukos, Adam C. and Graham Farrell. 1996a. Taking a bite out of organized crime? Probability theory and criminal organisation as a means of conceptualising the relationship between situational crime prevention and displacement. Paper presented at the meeting on the Theoretical and Philosophical Foundations of Situational Crime Prevention and Rational Choice, 10-14 April, INTERCENTER, Messina, Italy.

Bouloukos, Adam C. and Graham Farrell. 1996b. Organized crime and drug trafficking: Efforts of the United Nations. In *Criminalitee Organisee et Ordre dans la Societe*. Marseilles, France: University D'Aix-en Provence.

Bousquet, R. 1996. Social development and cities: Preventing crime in France. Paper presented at the International Conference for Crime Prevention Practitioners, March 31-April 3, 1996, Vancouver.

Brantingham, P.J. and S.T. Easton. 1996. *The Crime Bill: Who Pays and How Much?* Vancouver: The Fraser Institute.

Brown, B. 1995. *CCTV in Town Centres: Three Case Studies*. London: Home Office Police Research Group.

Bruinsma, G.J.N., H. G. van de Bunt and F.J.P. Fiselier. 1991. Hoe onveilig is Nederland? Enkele theoretische en methodische kanttekeningen bij een international vergelijkend victimologisch onderzoek. *Tijdschrift voor Criminologie*, 32, 2: 138-155.

Bruynooghe, R., I. Carmen, F. Hutsebaut and A. Vansteenwegen. 1991. *Physical and Sexual Violence Against Women: Situation in Europe*. Brussels: Secretary of State for the Environment and Social Emancipation.

Bucke, T. 1995. *Policing and the Public: Findings from the 1994 British Crime Survey.*

Butler, W.E. 1992. Crime in the Soviet Union: early glimpses of the true story. *British Journal of Criminology,* 32: 144-159.

Canadian Centre for Justice Statistics. 1994. *A Review of the Alternative Measures Survey: 1991-92.* Ottawa: Statistics Canada.

Canadian Centre for Justice Statistics. 1996. *Annual Youth Court Statistics 1994-95.* Ottawa: Statistics Canada.

Cannon-Brooks, P.C. 1992. The movement, location and tracing of cultural property. *Museum Management and Curatorship,* 11: 3-18.

Capowich, G.E. and J.A. Roehl. 1994. Problem-oriented policing: actions and effectiveness in San Diego. In D.P. Rosenbaum (Ed.), *The Challenge of Community Policing: Testing the Promises.* London: Sage.

Centraal Bureau voor de Statistiek. 1996. *Gevangenisstatistiek 1995.* Voorburg / Heerlen.

Centraal Bureau voor de Statistiek. 1997. *Statistisch Jaarboek 1997.* Voorburg / Heerlen.

Chalidze, Valery. 1977. *Criminal Russia: Essays on Crime in the Soviet Union.* Translated from the Russian by P.S. Falla. New York: Random House.

Chambliss, W.J. 1988. *On the Take: From Petty Crooks to Presidents.* Bloomington: Indiana University Press.

Chermak, S.M. 1995. *Victims in the News.* Boulder, CO: Westview Press.

Christie, Nils. 1993. *Crime Control as Industry.* London: Routledge.

Clarke, R.V. (Ed.). 1992. *Situational Crime Prevention: Successful Case Studies.* Albany, New York: Harrow and Heston, Publishers.

Clarke, R.V. 1995. Situational crime prevention. In M. Tonry and D.P. Farrington (Eds.), *Building a Safer Society: Strategic Approaches to Crime Prevention.* Chicago: University of Chicago Press.

Clarke, R.V. (Ed.). 1997. *Situational Crime Prevention: Successful Case Studies,* 2nd Edition. Albany, New York: Harrow and Heston, Publishers.

Clarke, R.V. and G. McGrath. 1990. Cash reduction and robbery prevention in Australian betting shops. *Security Journal,* 1, 3: 160-163.

Coggans, N. *et al.* 1994. *National Evaluation of Drug Education in Scotland, ISDD Research Monograph,* 4. London: Institute for the Study of Drug Dependence.

Cohen, M.A. 1988. Pain, suffering, and jury awards: a study of the cost of crime to victims. *Law and Society Review,* 22: 537-555.

Cohen, M.A., T.R. Miller and S.B. Rossman. 1994. The costs and consequences of violent behavior in the United States. In A.J. Reiss and J.A. Roth (Eds.), *Understanding and Preventing Violence, Volume 4, Consequences and Control.* Washington, DC: National Academy Press.

Cole, George. 1989. *The American System of Criminal Justice,* 5th Edition. Pacific Grove, CA: Brooks/Cole.

Collins, D.J. and H.M. Lapsley. 1991. *Estimating the Economic Costs of Drug Abuse in Australia.* Canberra: Dept. of Community Health and Services.

Commonwealth Giants Commission. 1990. *Report on General Revenue Grant Relativities, 1990.* Canberra: Commonwealth Giants Commission.

Corkery, J. 1994. *The Theft of Firearms.* Home Office Research and Planning Unit Paper 84.

Council of Europe. 1987. *European Prison Rules.* 12 February.

Council of Europe. 1992. *European Rules on Community Sanctions and Measures.* Recommendation R (92): 16 October.

Council of Europe. 1996. *Penological Information Bulletin. No. 19 and 20.* December 1994-1995.

Crime Concern. 1993. *A Practical Guide to Crime Prevention for Local Partnerships.* London: Home Office.

Crime Prevention Unit, Department of the Prime Minister and Cabinet. 1994. *The Crime Prevention Unit – A Fact Sheet.* Wellington, New Zealand: Crime Prevention Unit.

Crouch, B.M. 1993. Is incarceration really worse? Analysis of offenders'

preferences for prison over probation. *Justice Quarterly,* 10, 1: 67-88.

Dagger, D. 1993. *Persons in Juvenile Corrective Institutions,* no. 56 and 59. Canberra: Australian Institute of Criminology.

David, Rene and John E.C. Brierley. 1985. *Major Legal Systems of the World Today: An Introduction to the Comparative Study of Law,* 3rd Edition. London, England: Stevens and Sons.

De Leeuw, E.D. and J. van der Zouwen. 1988. Data quality in telephone and face-to-face surveys: a comparative meta-analysis. In R.M. Groves, P.P. Biemer, L.E. Lyberg, J.T. Masset, W.L. Nicholls II and J. Wakesberg (Eds.), *Telephone Survey Methodology.* New York: Wiley.

della Porta, D. 1997. Introduction: democracy and corruption. In D. della Porta and Yves Meny (Eds.), *Democracy and Corruption in Europe.* London: Pinter.

della Porta, D. and Y. Meny (Eds.). 1995. *Democratie et Corruption en Europe.* Paris: La Dicouverte.

Department of Justice Canada. 1996. *A Statistical Analysis of the Impacts of the 1977 Firearms Control Legislation.* Ottawa: Research, Statistics and Evaluation Directorate, Department of Justice.

Devlin, Patrick. 1960. *The Criminal Prosecution in England.* London: Oxford University Press.

Dhokalia, R.P. and K. Narayana Rao (Eds.). 1988. *Terrorism and International Law.* New Delhi: Indian Society of International Law.

Dienst Justitiële Inrichtingen. Department of Correctional Services. Ministry of Justice, the Hague. Data and information obtained per letter to Alexis Aronowitz.

Directions for Australia. 1990. Final report of the national committee on violence. Canberra: Australian Institute of Criminology.

Dobash, R., R. Dobash, K. Cavanagh and R. Lewis. 1996. *Research Evaluation of Programmes for Violent Men.* Edinburgh: The Scottish Office Central Research Unit.

Dunmore, J. 1996. *Review of Comparative Costs and Performance of Privately and Publicly Operated Prisons.* Prison Service Report no.2, Research and Statistics Directorate, Home Office.

Earle, R.B. 1995. Helping to prevent child abuse – and future consequences: Hawaii Healthy Start. *Program Focus,* October. Washington, DC: National Institute of Justice.

Eastman, A.C., F. Carrion and G. Cobo (Eds.). 1995. *Ciudad y Violencias en America Latina.* Quito: Programa de Gestión Urbana.

Ebbe, Obi N. I. 1996. Criminal procedure in Nigeria. In *Comparative and International Criminal Justice Systems: Policing, Judiciary, and Corrections.* Boston: Butterworth/Heinemann.

Ebbe, Obi N.I. 1985. Power and criminal law: criminalizing conduct norms in a colonial regime. *International Journal of Comparative and Applied Criminal Justice,* Winter, 9, 2: 113-121.

Ebbe, Obi N.I. 1989. Crime and delinquency in metropolitan Lagos: a study of crime and delinquency area theory. *Social Forces.*

Economist. 1992a. Dirty dozen. Sept. 5-11: 36, 38.

Economist. 1992b. Money, gangsters and politics: an everyday story of Japan. Sept. 26-Oct. 2: 31-32.

Economist. 1997. April 19: 21-23.

Ekblom, P., H. Law and M. Sutton. 1996. *Safer Cities and Domestic Burglary Schemes.* London: Home Office.

Ellsberg, M., R. Pena, A. Herrera, J. Liljestrand and A. Winkvist. 1996. *Confites en el Infierno: Prevalencia y Caracteristicas de Violencia Conyugal hacia las Mujeres en Nicaragua.* Managua: Asociacion de Mujeres Profesionales.

Eluf, L.N. 1992. A new approach to law enforcement: the special women's police stations in Brazil. In M. Schuler (Ed.), *Freedom From Violence: Women's Strategies From Around the World.* New York: United Nations Development Fund for Women.

Environics. 1994. Focus on crime and justice. *Focus Canada,* March. Ottawa: Author.

European Committee on Crime Problems. 1996. Report on responses to developments in the volume and structure of crime in Europe in a time of change. In *Project Group Europe in a time of change: Crime policy and criminal law, Final activity report*, 3-7 June 1996, appendix IV. Strasbourg: Council of Europe.

European Forum for Urban Safety, Federation of Canadian Municipalities, and the US Conference of Mayors. 1989. *Agenda for Safer Cities: Final Declaration*. European and North American Conference on Urban Safety and Crime Prevention, October 10-13, Montreal.

European Forum for Urban Safety, Federation of Canadian Municipalities, and the US Conference of Mayors. 1991. *Final Declaration*. Second International Conference on Urban Safety and Crime Prevention, November 18-20, Paris.

European Union. 1996. *Situation report on organised crime in the EU 1995*. 10555/1/96 Brussels.

Evans, R. and R. Ellis. 1997. Police cautioning in the 1990s. *Home Office Research Findings*, 52. London: Home Office.

Fairchild, Erika S. 1993. *Comparative Criminal Justice Systems*. Belmont, CA: Wadsworth.

Farrell, Graham, Melissa Tullis and Kashfia Mansur. 1996. Heroin and cocaine in Europe 1983-1993: a cross-national comparison of trends in trafficking and prices. *British Journal of Criminology*, 36, 2: 255-281.

Farrell, Graham. 1995. The global rate of interception of cocaine and the opiates 1980-1994. *Transnational Organized Crime*, 1, 4: 134-149.

Farrington, D.P. 1996a. Quantitative criminology in the United Kingdom in the 1990s: a brief overview. *Journal of Quantitative Criminology*, 12, 3: 249-263.

Farrington, D.P. 1996b. *Understanding and Preventing Youth Crime*. York: Joseph Rowntree Foundation.

Felson, M. 1994. *Crime and Everyday Life; Insights and Implications for Society*. Thousand Oaks: Pine Forge Press.

Fight Crime: Invest in Kids. 1996. Police chiefs say more government investments in kids are key to fighting crime: survey findings. Washington, DC: Author.

Fijnaut *et al.* (Eds.). 1995. *Changes in society, crime and criminal justice in Europe II: international, organised and corporate crime*. The Hague.

Fiselier, J.P.S. 1978. *Slachtoffers van delicten. Een onderzoek naar verborgen criminaliteit*. Utrecht: Ars Aequi Libri.

Forrester, D., S. Frenz, M. O'Connell and K. Pease. 1990. *The Kirkholt Burglary Prevention Project: Phase II*. Crime Prevention Unit Paper 23. London: Home Office.

Gabor, T., B.C. Welsh and D.H. Antonowicz. 1996. The role of the health community in the prevention of criminal violence. *Canadian Journal of Criminology*, 38, 3: 317-333.

Gabriel-Stet, Mugur. 1996. Europe-women: social measures urged to end women trafficking. *Inter Press Service English News Wire*, June17.

Garland, David. 1990. *Punishment and Modern Society*. London: Oxford University Press.

Garland, David. 1996. The limits of sovereign state. *The British Journal of Criminology*. 36, 4: 445-471.

Garland, David. 1997. Probation and the reconfiguration of crime control. In R. Burnett. (Ed.), *The Probation Service: Responding to Change. Probation Studies Unit Report No.3/97*. Oxford: Centre for Criminological Research.

Geason, S. and P. Wilson. 1992. *Preventing Retail Crime*. Canberra: Australian Institute of Criminology.

Gerber, J. and S. Engelhardt-Greer. 1996. Just and painful: attitudes toward sentencing criminals. In T.J. Flanagan and D.R. Longmire (Eds.), *Americans View Crime and Justice: A National Public Opinion Survey*. Thousand Oaks, California: Sage.

Gerstein, D.R., R.A. Johnson, H.J. Harwood, D. Fountain, N. Suter and K. Malloy. 1994. *Evaluating Recovery Services: The California Drug and Alcohol Treatment Assessment. CALDATA*. General Report. Sacramento, California: California Department of Alcohol and Drug Programs.

Godefroy, T. and B. Lafargue. 1993. *Les Coûts du Crime en France. Les*

Dépense de Sécurité. Données pour 1988 à 1991. Paris: Ministère de Justice, Centre de Recherches Sociologiques sur le Droit et les Institutions Pénales.

Goldstein, Jeffrey H. 1986. *Aggression and Crimes of Violence*. New York: Oxford University Press.

Gottfredson, M.R. and T. Hirschi. 1990. *A General Theory of Crime*. Stanford: Stanford University Press.

Government Computing. Solving the time crime. July, 1997, vol. 11, no. 6.

Government Statistician's Office. 1992. *Crime Victims Survey, Queensland 1991*. Brisbane.

Graber, F. 1980. *Crime News and the Public*. NY: Praeger.

Grabosky, P. 1995. Preventing motor vehicle theft in New South Wales. In P. Grabosky and M. James (Eds.), *The Promise of Crime Prevention: Leading Crime Prevention Programs*. Canberra: Australian Institute of Criminology.

Grabosky, P. and M. James, (Eds.). 1995. *The Promise of Crime Prevention: Leading Crime Prevention Programs*. Canberra: Australian Institute of Criminology.

Graham, J. and B. Bowling. 1996. *Young People and Crime*. Home Office Research Study No. 145, London.

Graham, J. and T. Bennett. 1995. *Crime Prevention Strategies in Europe and North America*. Helsinki: European Institute for Crime Prevention and Control.

Greenwood, P.W., C.P. Rydell, A.F. Abrahamse, J.P. Caulkins, J. Chiesa, K.E. Model and S.P. Klein. 1994. *Three Strikes and You're Out: Estimated Costs and Benefits of California's New Mandatory-Sentencing Law*. Santa Monica, California: RAND.

Greenwood, P.W., K.E. Model, C.P. Rydell and J. Chiesa. 1996. *Diverting Children from a Life of Crime: Measuring Costs and Benefits*. Santa Monica, California: RAND.

Groves, W. Byron, Graeme Newman and Charles Corrado. 1987. Islam, modernization and crime: a test of the religious ecology thesis. *Journal of Criminal Justice*, 13: 23-29.

Gunningham, N., J. Norberry and S. McKillop (Eds.). 1995. *Environmental Crime*. Canberra: Australian Institute of Criminology.

Hahn, A. 1994. *Evaluation of the Quantum Opportunities Program (QOP): Did the Program Work?* Waltham, Massachusetts: Brandeis University.

Hamai, Koichi *et al.* (Eds.). 1995. *Probation Round the World: A Comparative Study*. UNICRI. London: Routledge.

Harding, Richard. 1995. Prison privatisation in Australia, New Zealand. *Overcrowded Times*, October.

Hauber, A.R., L.J. Hofsta, L.G. Toornvliet and J.G.A. Zanderbergen. 1994. *Stadswachten*. The Hague: Ministry of Justice.

Heise, L. 1994. Violence against women: a neglected public health issue in less developed countries. *Social Science and Medicine*, 39, 9: 1165-1179.

Heise, L., L. Pitanguy and A. Germain. 1994. *Violence Against Women: The Hidden Health Burden*. Washington, DC: World Bank Discussion Paper no. 255.

Helgadottir, B. 1995. Do Europeans share common ideals? *The European*, 26 October-1 November: 11.

Henderson, R. 1972. *The King in Every Man: Evolutionary Trends in Onitsha-Ibo Society and Culture*. New Haven: Yale University Press.

Hoffman, Vincent. 1997a. Interviews with members of the Ministry of Public Security, People's Republic of China, April 21, China Police Investigation College, Shenyang, China.

Hoffman, Vincent. 1997b. Stress among police officers in China. Paper presented at the Annual Meeting of the American Society of Criminology, November 17, Boston, MA.

Home Office Standing Conference on Crime Prevention. 1988. *Report of the Working Group on the Costs of Crime*. Home Office, London.

Hood, Roger G. 1990. The death penalty: a world-wide perspective. A report to the United Nations Committee on Crime Prevention and

Control. Oxford, UK: Clarendon Press; NY: Oxford University Press.

Hood, Roger G. 1996. *The Death Penalty: A World-Wide Perspective.* 2nd Edition. London: Oxford Clarendon Press.

Horlow, Robert E. *et al.* 1995. The severity of intermediate sanctions: a psychological scaling approach for obtaining community perceptions. *Journal of Quantitative Criminology,* 11, 1: 71-95.

Horner Committee. Standing Committee on Justice and the Solicitor General. 1993. *Crime Prevention in Canada: Toward a National Strategy.* Ottawa: House of Commons.

Hsieh, C.C. and M.D. Pugh. 1993. Poverty, income inequality, and violent crime: a meta-analysis of recent aggregate data studies. *Criminal Justice Review,* 18, 2: 182-202.

Huang, W.S. Wilson. 1993. Are international murder data valid and reliable? Some evidence to support the use of INTERPOL data. *International Journal of Comparative and Applied Criminal Justice,* 17, 1: 17-29.

Huang, W.S. Wilson and Charles F. Wellford. 1989. Assessing indicators of crime among international crime data series. *Criminal Justice Policy Review,* 3, 1: 28-48.

Hurley, J. 1995. *Delinquency Prevention Works.* Washington, DC: National Institute of Justice, US Department of Justice.

Ingraham, Barton L. 1987. *The Structure of Criminal Procedure: Laws and Practices of France, the Soviet Union, China and the United States.* New York: Greenwood.

Insurance Council of Australia. 1994. *Insurance Fraud in Australia.* Sydney.

International Victim Survey. 1997. Home Office, London.

InterView. 1991. A response experiment in Belgium and the USA. Amsterdam: InterView.

Irwin, J. and J. Austin. 1994. *It's About Time: America's Imprisonment Binge.* Belmont, California: Wadsworth.

Jamieson, A. 1996. Political corruption in Western Europe: judiciary and executive in conflict. March 1996. *Conflict Studies,* no. 288. Research Institute for the Study of Conflict and Terrorism.

Jammers, V. 1995. Commercial robberies: the business community as a target in the Netherlands. *Security Journal,* 6, 1: 13-20.

Jammers, V. 1996. Commercial robbery in the Netherlands: changing trends. Paper presented at the First International Conference for Crime Prevention Practitioners, March 31-April 3, 1996, Vancouver.

Japanese Ministry of Justice. 1996. Summary of White Paper on Crime.

Jenezon, M. 1996. Van niets naar nergens. *Contrast,* Jaargang 3, 40, December: 1-2.

Jones, M.B. and D.R.Offord. 1989. Reduction of antisocial behaviour in poor children by nonschool skill-development. *Journal of Child Psychology and Psychiatry,* 30, 5: 737-750.

Jornal Do Brasil. 1991. Trabalho das assistentes foi pionero. *Jornal Do Brasil,* Rio de Janeiro, March 8: 6.

Joutsen, Matti. 1996. *The Status of Firearms Control in Europe.* Helsinki: HEUNI Newsletter.

Joutsen, Matti and Uglješa Zvekic. 1994. Non-custodial sanctions: comparative overview. In Uglješa Zvekic (Ed.), *Alternatives to Imprisonment in Comparative Perspective.* UNICRI. Chicago: Nelson Hall.

Junger-Tas, Josine, Gert-Jan Terlouw and Malcolm Klein (Eds.). 1994. *Delinquent Behavior of Young People in the Western World — First Results of the International Self-report Delinquency Study.* Amsterdam: Kugler Publications.

Kalish, Carol B. 1988. *International Crime Rates.* Washington, DC: Bureau of Justice Statistics.

Keh, Douglas and Graham Farrell. 1997. Trafficking drugs in the global village. *Transnational Organized Crime,* 3, 2.

Kerbo, H. R. and M. Inoue. 1990. Japanese social structure and white collar crime: recruit cosmos and beyond. *Deviant Behavior,* 11: 139-154.

Kerr, J. (Ed.). 1994. *Calling for Change: International Strategies to End Violence Against Women.* Publication no. 8. The Hague: Development Cooperation Information Department, Ministry of Foreign Affairs.

Kerry, J. 1992. The BCCI Affair. Report to the Senate Foreign Relations Committee. Subcommittee on Terrorism, Narcotics and International Operations. Washington, DC: GPO.

Killias, M. 1989. *Les Suisses Face au Crime.* Grusch, Switzerland: Ruegger.

Killias, M. 1993. Gun ownership, suicide and homicide: an international perspective. In Alvazzi del Frate *et al., Understanding Crime.* Rome: UNICRI.

Killias, M. and Ambros Uchtenhagen. 1996. Does medical heroin prescription reduce delinquency among drug-addicts? On the evaluation of the Swiss heroin prescription projects and its methodology. *Studies on Crime and Crime Prevention,* 5, 2: 245-255.

Killias, M. and Juan Rabasa. 1997. Less crime in the cities through heroin prescription? Paper presented to the Sixth International Conference on Environmental Criminology and Crime Analysis, Oslo, Norway, June.

Kim, K. and Y. Cho. 1992. Epidemiological survey of spousal abuse in Korea. In E. Viano (Ed.), *Intimate Violence: Interdisciplinary Perspectives.* Washington, DC: Hemisphere Publishing.

Kinand T. 1994. Technology and people — the importance of a united approach. Paper presented to Retail Loss Prevention Symposium, National Conference Services, Sydney.

Kleck, G. 1995. Guns and violence: an interpretive review. *Social Pathology,* 1, 1: 12-47.

Kleiman, Mark A.R. 1994. Organized crime and drug abuse control. In Robert J. Kelly, Ko-Lin Chin and Rufus Schatzberg (Eds.), *Handbook of Organized Crime in the United States.* Connecticut: Greenwood Press.

Koss, P. 1996. The measurement of rape victimisation in crime surveys. *Criminal Justice and Behaviour,* 23: 55-69.

Kress, Jack M. 1976. Progress and prosecution. *Annals of the American Academy of Political and Social Science,* 423: 99-116.

Kruissink, M. 1990. The HALT program: diversion of juvenile vandals. *Dutch Penal Law and Policy.* The Hague: Research and Documentation Centre, Ministry of Justice.

Kudriavtzev, Vladimir N. 1990. Introduction. In United Nations Interregional Crime and Justice Research Institute, *Soviet Criminology Update.* Rome: United Nations Publication.

Kuhn, André. 1992. Attitude toward punishment. In A. Alvazzi del Frate *et al.* (Eds.), *Understanding Crime: Experiences of Crime and Crime Control.* Rome: UNICRI.

Kuhn, André. 1996. Incarceration rates: Europe versus USA. *European Journal on Criminal Policy and Research.* 4, 3: 46-73.

Kury, H. 1991. Victims of crime: results of a representative telephone survey of 5000 citizens of the former Federal Republic of Germany. In A. Alvazzi del Frate, A.U. Zvekic and Jan J.M. van Dijk (Eds.), *Understanding Crime: Experiences of Crime and Crime Control.* Rome: UNICRI.

Kvashis, Vitaly Y. 1996. Current tendencies and prospects of the use of the death penalty in Russia. Paper presented to the Annual Meeting of the American Society of Criminology.

Laffargue, Bernard and Thierry Godefroy. 1989. Economic cycles and punishment: unemployment and imprisonment. *Contemporary Crises,* 13: 371-404.

Lally, J.R., P.L. Mangione and A.S. Honig. 1988. The Syracuse University Family Development Research Program: Long-range impact of an early intervention with low-income children and their families. In D. Powell (Ed.), *Parent Education as Early Childhood Intervention: Emerging Directions in Theory, Research and Practice.* Norwood, New Jersey: Ablex.

Larrain, S. 1993. *Estudio de Frecuencia de la Violencia Intrafamiliar y la Condicion de la Mujer en Chile.* Santiago, Chile: Pan-American Health Organization.

Lee, R. and J. Klipin. 1997. The human factor: public confidence and crime prevention. *Crime and Conflict*, no. 8, University of Natal, South Africa.

Lempert, R. 1992. A Jury for Japan? *The American Journal of Comparative Law*, 40, 1: 37-71.

Lenton, Rhonda L. 1995. Power versus feminist theories of wife abuse. *Revue Canadienne de criminologie*.

Lezhikov, Gennady L. 1995. Statistical information on crime and its use in crime control. Paper presented at the Ninth United Nations Congress on the Prevention of Crime and the Treatment of Offenders. Cairo, Egypt, May, 1995.

Lian, Changgang. 1997. Comparisons between policing in China and the US. Research paper presented at the School of Criminal Justice, Michigan State University.

Lippman, Matthew, S. McConville and M. Yerushalmi. 1988. *Islamic Criminal Law and Procedure*. New York: Praeger.

Liukkonen, M. 1997. *Motor vehicle theft in Europe*. HEUNI Paper no. 9, Helsinki.

Lloyd, S., G. Farrell and K. Pease. 1994. *Preventing Repeated Domestic Violence: A Demonstration Project on Merseyside*. Crime Prevention Unit Paper 49. London: Home Office.

Long, D.A., C.D. Mallar and C.V.D. Thornton. 1981. Evaluating the benefits and costs of the Job Corps. *Journal of Policy Analysis and Management*, 1, 1: 55-76.

Louw, A. 1997. Bad news? Crime reporting: trends and effects. *Crime and Conflict* no. 8, University of Natal, South Africa.

Louw, A. and M. Sekhonyane. 1997. Violence to democracy? KwaZulu-Natal's slow road. *Crime and Conflict*, no. 8, University of Natal, South Africa.

Lynch, James P. 1993. Secondary analysis of international crime survey data. In A. Alvazzi del Frate, Uglješa Zvekic and Jan J.M. van Dijk (Eds.), *Understanding Crime: Experiences of Crime and Crime Control*. Rome: UNICRI.

Maguire, Kathleen and Ann L. Pastore. 1995. *Sourcebook of Criminal Justice Statistics*. Washington DC: US Department of Justice.

Maguire, M. and J. Pointing (Eds.). 1988. *Victims of Crime: A New Deal?* Oxford University Press.

Mandel, M.J., P. Magnusson, J.E. Ellis, G. DeGeorge and K.L. Alexander. 1993. The economics of crime. *Business Week*, December 13.

Mantius, P. 1995. *Shell Game*. New York: St. Martin's Press.

Maxwell, G. and A. Morris. 1993. *Families, Victims and Culture: Youth Justice in New Zealand*. Wellington: Department of Social Welfare and Institute of Criminology.

Maxwell, G. and A. Morris. 1996. Research on family group conferences with young offenders in New Zealand. In J. Hudson, A. Morris, G. Maxwell and B. Galaway (Eds.), *Family Group Conferences: Perspectives in policy and practice*. Annandale, NSW: Federation Press.

Mayhew, P. and Jan. J.M. van Dijk. 1997. *Criminal Victimisation in Eleven Industrialised Countries; Key Findings from the 1996 International Crime Victims Survey*. The Hague: WODC, Ministry of Justice.

Mayhew, P. and P. White. 1997. The 1996 international crime victimisation survey. *Research Findings* 57, Home Office, London.

Melossi, Dario. 1994. The effect of economic circumstances on the criminal justice system. In Council of Europe, *Crime and Economy, Proceedings*. Reports presented to the Eleventh Criminological Colloquium.

Mercy, J.A., M.L. Rosenberg, K.E. Powell, C.V. Broome and W.L. Roper. 1993. Public health policy for preventing violence. *Health Affairs*, 12, 4: 7-29.

Merryman, John H. 1985. *The Civil Law Tradition*, 2nd Edition. Stanford, CA: Stanford University Press.

Miller, T.R., M.A. Cohen and S.B. Rossman. 1993. Victim costs of violent crime and resulting injuries. *Health Affairs*, 12, 4: 186-197.

Miller, T.R., M.A. Cohen and B. Wiersema. 1996. *Victim Costs and Consequences: A New Look*. Washington, DC: National Institute of Justice.

Ministry of the Solicitor General of Canada. 1984. *Working Together to Prevent Crime: A Practitioner's Handbook*. Ottawa: Minister of Supply and Services.

Ministry of the Solicitor General of Ontario. 1991. Bill 107: An act to revise the Police Act and amend the law relating to police services. Fact sheet. Toronto: Queen's Printer for Ontario.

Mirrlees-Black, C. and A. Ross. 1995a. Crime against retail premises in 1993. *Research Findings* 26, Home Office, London.

Mirrlees-Black, C. and A. Ross. 1995b. Crime against manufacturing premises in 1993. *Research Findings* 27, Home Office, London.

Moley, Raymond. 1929. *Politics and Criminal Prosecution*. New York: Minton, Balch and Co.

Moore, W.E. 1974. *Social Change*. Englewood Cliffs: Prentice-Hall Inc.

Morris, A. and G. Maxwell. 1997. *Family Group Conferences and Convictions*. Occasional Papers in Criminology New Series, no.5, Institute of Criminology, Wellington.

Morrison, S. and I. O'Donnell. 1994. *Armed Robbery*. Occasional Paper 15, University of Oxford Centre for Criminological Research.

Moyer, S. *et al.* 1996. *A Profile of the Juvenile Justice System in Canada: Report to the Federal-Provincial-Territorial Task Force on Youth Justice*. Ottawa: Department of Justice.

Msamba, Sita, G. Wilson Edanyu and D. Ayigale Aliobe. 1996. *The Prison Back Home: Social Rehabilitation as a Social Process. The Uganda Experience*. UNAFRI and Uganda Prison Service.

Mueller, G.W.O. 1998. Transnational crime; an experience in uncertainties. *Uncertainty Scenarios*, 1, 1.

Mulvey, E.P., M.W. Arthur and N.D. Reppucci. 1993. The prevention and treatment of juvenile delinquency: a review of the research. *Clinical Psychology Review*, 13: 133-167.

Nalla, Mahesh K. 1996. Criminal justice system in Singapore. In Graeme Newman, Debra Cohen and Adam C. Bouloukos (Eds.), *International Factbook of Criminal Justice Systems*. Bureau of Justice Statistics: http://www.ojp.usdoj.gov/pub/bjs/ascii/wfbcjsin.txt

Nalla, Mahesh K. and Donald Hummer. 1996. Relations between police and security in Michigan: an executive summary. School of Criminal Justice, Michigan State University, East Lansing, MI.

Nalla, Mahesh K. and Graeme Newman. 1993. Is white collar policing, policing? *Policing and Society*.

Nalla, Mahesh K. and Vincent J. Hoffman. 1996. Security training needs: a study of the perceptions of security guards in Singapore. *Security Journal*, 7: 287-293.

Nalla, Mahesh K., Vincent J. Hoffman and Kenneth E. Christian. 1996. Security guards' perceptions of their relationship with police officers and the public in Singapore. *Security Journal*, 7: 281-286.

National Committee on Violence. 1990. *Violence: Directions for Australia*. Canberra: Australian Institute of Criminology.

National Correctional Services Statistics Unit. 1996. *Prisoners in Australia 1994*. Melbourne: Australian Bureau of Statistics.

National Crime Prevention Council. 1994. *Taking the Offensive to Prevent Crime: How Seven Cities Did It*. Washington, DC: Author.

National Crime Prevention Council. 1995. Crime declines in T-CAP cities! *T-CAP RECAP*, 14: 8.

National League of Cities. 1994. *Rethinking Public Safety: The 1994 Futures Report*. Washington, DC: Author.

Neapolitan, J. 1995. Differing theoretical perspectives and cross-national variations in thefts in less developed nations. *International Criminal Justice Review*, 5: 17-31.

Nelson, E. and C. Zimmerman. 1996. *Household Survey on Domestic Violence in Cambodia*. Phnom Penh: Ministry of Women's Affairs and Project Against Domestic Violence.

Newman, Graeme. 1976. *Comparative Deviance: Perception of Law in Six Cultures*. New York: Elsevier.

Newman, Graeme. 1994. *Just and Painful: A Case for the Corporal Punishment of Criminals*. NY: Harrow and Heston Publishers.

Newman, Graeme and Eduardo Vetere. 1977. International crime statistics: an overview from a comparative perspective. *Abstracts in Criminology and Penology*, 17, 3: 251-273.

Newman, Graeme and Adam C. Bouloukos. 1996. What is a criminal justice system? A view from the *International Factbook of Criminal Justice Systems*. Paper presented at the annual meeting, American Society of Criminology, Chicago, IL, November.

Newman, Graeme, Debra Cohen and Adam C. Bouloukos, (Eds.). 1996. *International Factbook of Criminal Justice Systems*. Published electronically by the US Bureau of Justice Statistics: http://www.ojp.usdoj.gov/bjs/abstract/wfcj.htm.

NSW Women's Coordination Unit. 1991. *Costs of Domestic Violence*. Sydney: NSW Women's Coordination Unit.

Olds, D.L., C.R. Henderson, C. Phelps, H. Kitzman and C. Hanks. 1993. Effects of prenatal and infancy nurse home visitation on government spending. *Medical Care*, 31, 2: 155-174.

Olds, D.L., C.R. Henderson, R. Chamberlin and R. Tatelbaum. 1986. Preventing child abuse and neglect: a randomized trial of nurse home visitation. *Pediatrics*, 78: 65-78.

Olweus, D. 1991. Bully/victim problems among school children: basic facts and effects of a school based intervention program. In D.J. Pepler and K.H. Rubin (Eds.), *The Development and Treatment of Childhood Aggression*. Hillsdale, NJ: Lawrence Erlbaum Associates.

Packer, Herbert. 1968. *The Limits of the Criminal Sanction*. Stanford, CA: Stanford University Press.

Pan American Health Organization. Declaration. Inter-American Conference on Society, Violence and Health, Washington DC, November 16-17, 1994.

Passas, N. 1993. Structural sources of international crime: policy lessons from the BCCI affair. *Crime, Law and Social Change*, 20, 4: 293-305.

Passas, N. 1994. European integration, protectionism and criminogenesis: a study on farm subsidy frauds. *Mediterranean Quarterly*, 5, 4: 66-84.

Passas, N. 1995. The mirror of global evils: a review essay on the BCCI affair. *Justice Quarterly*, 12, 2: 801-829.

Passas, N. 1996. Accounting for fraud: auditors' ethical and legal dilemmas in the BCCI affair. In W. M. Hoffman, J. Kamm, R. E. Frederick, and E. Petry (Eds.), *The Ethics of Accounting and Finance*. Newport, CO: Quorum Books.

Passas, N. 1997. Anomie, reference groups, and relative deprivation. In N. Passas and R. Agnew (Eds.), *The Future of Anomie Theory*. Boston: Northeastern University Press.

Pavlovic, Zoran. 1994. International Crime Survey in Ljubljana. Telephone versus face-to-face survey method. In Kirchhoff *et al.* (Eds.), *International Debates of Victimology*. Moenchengladbach: World Society of Victimology.

Pearcey, P., B.C. Welsh, I. Waller and S. French (Eds.). 1996. *Setting the Stage for Community Safety: Report on Progress Towards World Change*. Final report of the First International Conference for Crime Prevention Practitioners, March 31-April 4, Vancouver. Ottawa: Correctional Service Canada.

Pease, Ken. 1994. Cross-national imprisonment rates: limitations of method and possible conclusions. *The British Journal of Criminology*, 34, special issue: 116-130.

Pease, Ken. 1995. The future of imprisonment and its alternatives. Report for the Fifth Conference on Crime Policy /CDPC (95) 85. Council of Europe.

Penal Reform International. Making standards work: report of an international conference. The Hague, Netherlands, November 17-19, 1994.

Penal Reform International. 1995. Making standards work: An international handbook on good prison practice. The Hague: Author.

Petersilia, Joan and Elizabeth Piper Deschenes. 1994. What punishes? Inmates rank the severity of prisons vs. intermediate sanctions. *Federal Probation*, 58, 1: 3-8.

Phythian, M. 1996. *Arming Iraq: How the U.S. and Britain Secretly Built Saddam's War Machine*. Boston: Northeastern University Press.

Pietschmann, Thomas. 1997. Economic forces driving manufacture, trafficking and consumption of amphetamine-type stimulants. In H. Klee (Ed.), *Amphetamine Misuses: International Perspectives on Current Trends*. Switzerland: Harwood Press.

Pope, Victoria. 1997. Trafficking in women. *US News and World Report*, April 7, pp. 38-44.

Potas, I. *et al.* 1990. *Young People and Crime. Costs and Prevention*. Canberra: Australian Institute of Criminology.

Prairie Research Associates. 1996. *Building A Safer Canada: A Community-Based Crime Prevention Manual*. Ottawa: Department of Justice, Canada.

Preliminary findings from the Violence and Threats of Violence Against Women in America Survey. Personal communication with P. Tjaden, Center for Policy Research, Denver, Colorado.

Profamilia. 1990. *Encuestra de Prevalencia, Demografia y Salud*. Bogata: Demographic and Health Survey.

Raghavan, R.K. and Mangai Natarajan. 1996. India. In Graeme Newman, Debra Cohen and Adam C. Bouloukos (Eds.), *International Factbook of Criminal Justice Systems*. Bureau of Justice Statistics: http://www.ojp.usdoj.gov /pub/bjs/ascii/wfbcjsin.txt

Ramsay M and J. Spiller. 1997. Drug misuse declared in 1996: key results from the British Crime Survey. *Research Findings* 56, Home Office, London.

Redo, Slawomir. 1986. The United Nations crime trends surveys: comparative criminology in the global context. *International Annals of Criminology*, 24: 163f.

Redo, Slawomir. 1998. International criminal cases in the territorial and cyberspace context: extradition and other forms of justice administration from the United Nations perspective (forthcoming).

Regemer, W. 1996. La justice allemande et la corruption. *Diviance et Sociiti*, 20, 3: 275- 290.

Reichel, Philip L. 1994. *Comparative Criminal Justice Systems: A Topical Approach*. Englewood Cliffs, NJ: Prentice Hall.

Reiner, R. 1985. *The Politics of the Police*. Brighton: Wheatsheaf.

Reiss, A.J. and J.A. Roth (Eds.). 1993. *Understanding and Preventing Violence*. Washington, DC: National Academy Press.

Reloj Delictivo. 1997. Direccion General de Politica y Estadistica Criminal, Procuraduria General de Justicia del Distrito Federal, Mexico, DF. Paper presented at the Ad Hoc Expert Group Meeting on Criminal Justice Management and Information Projects: Improving National and International Data Collection and Exchange, Buenos Aires, Argentina, March.

Research and Training Institute. 1990. *Summary of the White Paper on Crime*. Tokyo: Ministry of Justice.

Research Institute for the Ministry of the Interior. 1996. Publication regarding the functions of the Chief Information Center, received through personal correspondence to William Pridemore from Vyatcheslav Knyazev.

Reuter, Peter. 1983. *Disorganized Crime: The Economics of the Visible Hand*. Cambridge, MA: MIT Press.

Reuter, Peter. 1994. The organization and measurement of the international drug trade. In *The Economics of the Narcotics Industry Conference Report*. Washington DC: US State Department.

Reuter, Peter. 1996. The mismeasurement of the international drug trade: the implications of its irrelevance. In Susan Pozo (Ed.), *Exploring the Underground Economy: Studies of Illegal and Unreported Activity*. Kalamazoo, MI: W.E. Upjohn Institute for Employment Research.

Rhodes, William, Raymond Hyatt and Paul Scheiman. 1994. The price of cocaine, heroin and marijuana 1981-1993. *Journal of Drug Issues*, 3, 383: 402.

Ridley, F.F. and A. Doig. 1996. *Sleaze: Private Interests and Public Reactions*. Oxford: Oxford University Press.

Robert H. Jackson. 1940. *Journal of American Judicature Society*, 24: 18.

Robinson, Court. 1994. The International Conference on Transnational Migration in the Asia-Pacific Region: Problems and Prospects. ARCM January-December Newsletter Selections.

Rodgers, K. 1994. Wife assault: the findings of a survey. Canadian Centre for Justice Statistics, *Juristat* 14, 9.

Rosenbaum, Dennis P., L. Robert, Susan L. Flewelling *et al.* 1994. *Journal of Research in Crime and Delinquency,* 31, 1: 3-31.

Rosner, Lydia S. 1986. *The Soviet Way of Crime: Beating the System in the Soviet Union and the USA.* South Hadley, MA: Bergin and Garvey Publishers, Inc.

Rusche, Otto and George Kirkheimer. 1939. *Punishment and Social Structure.* New York: Russel and Russel.

Safe Neighbourhoods Unit. 1993. *Crime Prevention on Council Estates.* London: HMSO.

Sanders, A. 1993. From suspect to trial. In M.Maguire *et al., Oxford Handbook of Criminology.* Oxford: Clarendon.

Saris, W.E. and A. Scherpenzeel. 1992. Effecten van vraagformulering en data-verzamelingsmethoden in slachtofferenquêtes. (On the effects of the phrasing of questionnaire items and methods of data collection in victimisation surveys.) Amsterdam: Universiteit van Amsterdam.

Savona, E., S. Adamoli and P. Zoffi. 1995. Organised crime across the borders. Helsinki: HEUNI papers no. 6.

Scherpenisse, R. 1997. The police label for secured housing: initial results in the Netherlands. Paper presented at the European Union Conference, Crime Prevention: Towards A European Level, Noordwijk, the Netherlands.

Schlemmer, L. 1996. *National Survey on Crime.* Johannesburg: The Nedcor Project.

Schuler, M. (Ed.). 1992. *Freedom from Violence: Women's Strategies from Around the World.* New York: UNIFEM.

Schweinhart, L.J., H.V. Barnes and D.P.Weikart. 1993. *Significant Benefits: The High/Scope Perry Preschool Study Through Age 27.* Ypsilanti, MI: High/Scope Press.

Secretaria de Justicia. 1996. *Hacia un Plan Nacional de Politica Criminal.* Buenos Aires: Ministry of Justice.

Serio, Joseph. 1992. *USSR Crime Statistics and Summaries: 1989 and 1990.* The Office of International Criminal Justice, The University of Illinois at Chicago.

Shadow Side Work Group. 1994. *It Really Works! Improving the Social Status of Children, Young People, and Young Families.* Turku, Finland: Sampo-Group.

Shearer, I.A. 1971. *Extradition in International Law.* Manchester, UK: Manchester University Press, Oceana Publications.

Shelley, L. 1994. Post-soviet organized crime. *Demokratizatsiya,* 2, 3: 341-358.

Shelley. L. 1981. *Crime and Modernization; the Impact of Industrialization and Urbanization on Crime.* Carbondale: Southern Illinois University Press.

Sherman, L.W., D. Gottfredson, D. MacKenzie, J. Eck, P. Reuter and S. Bushway. 1997. *Preventing Crime: What Works, What Doesn't, What's Promising.* Report to the United States Congress. Washington, DC: National Institute of Justice.

Shrader-Cox, E. and R. Valdez-Santiago. 1992. *La violencia hacia la mujer Mexicana como problema de salud publica: la incidencia de la violencia domestica en una microregion de Ciudad Nexahualcoyotl.* Mexico City: Centro de Investigacion y Lucha Contra la Violencia Domestica.

Siemens, Maria A. 1996. European responses to the phenomenon of illegal migration: national and international initiatives. Paper presented at ISPAC International Conference on Migration and Crime: Global and Regional Problems and Responses, Courmayeur, October 5-8.

Smith, J.C. 1996. *Smith and Hogan: Criminal Law.* London: Butterworth.

Smith, M.D. 1989. Woman abuse: the case for surveys by telephone. *Journal of Interpersonal Violence,* 4: 308-324.

Smith, Paul J. 1997. Chinese migrant trafficking: a global challenge. In

Paul J. Smith (Ed.), *Human Smuggling: Chinese Migrant Trafficking and the Challenge to America's Immigrant Tradition.* Washington: Center for Strategic and International Studies.

Soros Foundation Center for Crime, Communities and Culture. 1997. *Pathfinder on Domestic Violence in the United States.* New York: Open Society Institute.

Souryal, Sam S. *et al.* 1994. The penalty of hand amputation for theft in Islamic justice. *Journal of Criminal Justice,* 22, 3: 249-265.

Souryal, Sam S. 1987. The religionisation of a society: the continuing application of Shariah law in Saudi Arabia. *Journal for the Scientific Study of Religion,* 26: 429-449.

South African Police Service. 1997. *The Incidence of Serious Crime,* 1, 97. Pretoria: Crime Management Information Centre.

Sparks, R.F., H.G. Genn and D.J. Dodd. 1977. *Surveying Victims. A Study of the Measurement of Criminal Victimization.* Chicester, New York: Wiley and Sons.

Spelman, W. and J.E. Eck. 1987. Problem-oriented policing. *Research in Brief,* January. Washington, DC: US Department of Justice.

Spigelman, M. 1996. *Money Well Spent: Investing in Preventing Crime.* Ottawa: National Crime Prevention Council.

Standing Committee on Justice and Legal Affairs. 1997. *Renewing Youth Justice.* House of Commons, Canada.

Stangeland, P. 1995. *The Crime Puzzle: Crime Patterns and Crime Displacement in Southern Spain.* IAIC. Malaga: Gomez Ediciones.

Sydney Law Reform Commission of Victoria. 1990. *Report No. 40. Homicide.* Melbourne: LRCV.

Task Force on Crime Prevention. 1993. *Partners in Crime Prevention: For a Safer Québec. Report of the Task Force on Crime Prevention.* Quebec City: Minister of Public Security.

Thomas, C.W. 1997. *Private Adult Correctional Facility Census.* Private Corrections Project, Center for Studies in Criminology and Law, University of Florida.

Toft, S. 1986. *Domestic Violence in Papua New Guinea.* Law Reform Commission Occasional Paper 19, Port Morseby, Papua New Guinea.

Törnudd, Patrik. 1994. Sentencing and punishment in Finland. *Overcrowded Times,* 5, 6: 1-16.

Tournier, Pierre. 1997. Detention stocks, and flows and durations: modes of turnover of prison populations in Europe. Paper presented at International Seminar on Prison Population in Europe and North America. Helsinki, Finland, March, 1997.

Travis, G., S. Egger, B. O'toole, D. Brown, R. Hogg and J. Stubbs. 1995. The international crime surveys: some methodological concerns. *Current Issues in Criminal Justice,* 6: 346-361.

Travis, Lawrence F. *et al.* 1992. *Corrections: Issues and Approach,* Third Edition. Cincinnati, OH: Anderson Publishing.

Tremblay, R.E. and Craig, W.M. 1995. Developmental crime prevention. In M. Tonry and D.P. Farrington (Eds.), *Building a Safer Society: Strategic Approaches to Crime Prevention,* Crime and Justice, vol. 19. Chicago: University of Chicago Press.

Tribunali di Milano e Napoli. 1996. *Le Mazzette della Fininvest.* Milano: Kaos Edizioni.

Truell, P. and L. Gurwin. 1992. *False Profits.* Boston and New York: Houghton Mifflin.

Uchtenhagen, A. 1997. Summary of the Synthesis Report. In A.Uchtenhagen, F. Gutzwiller and A. Dobler-Mikola (Eds.), *Programme for a Medical Prescription of Narcotics: Final Report of the Research Representatives.* Zurich, Switzerland: Institute for Social and Preventive Medicine at the University of Zurich.

UNCICP. 1997. United Nations international study on firearms regulation (draft). Report to the Commission on Crime Prevention and Criminal Justice, Sixth Session, Vienna, 28 April - 9 May. Document E/CN.15/1997/CRP.6.

UNDCP. 1996a. Crops from which drugs are extracted and appropriate strategies for their reduction. Report of the Secretariat to the Commission on Narcotic Drugs. Document E/CN.7/1996/9.

UNDCP. 1996b. Illicit drug trafficking. Report of the Secretariat to the Commission on Narcotic Drugs. Document E/CN.7/1996/11.

UNDCP. 1997a. Illicit drug trafficking. Report of the Secretariat to the Commission on Narcotic Drugs. Document E/CN.7/1997/4.

UNDCP. 1997b. *World Drug Report.* UK: Oxford University Press.

UNDP. 1992. *Human Development Report.* UK: Oxford University Press.

UNDP. 1994. *International Colloquium of Mayors on Social Development.* New York: Author.

UNDP. 1995. *Human Development Report.* UK: Oxford University Press.

United Nations Interregional Crime and Justice Research Institute. 1995. *Criminal Victimization in the Developing World.* Publication no. 55, Rome.

United Nations. 1955. *The Standard Minimum Rules for the Treatment of Prisoners.* Resolution of First United Nations Congress on the Prevention of Crime and the Treatment of Offenders. 30 August.

United Nations. 1975. *Declaration on the Protection of All Persons from Being Subject to Torture and Other Cruel, Inhuman or Degrading Treatment or Punishment.* General Assembly Resolution 3452 (XXX). 9 December.

United Nations. 1986. *Safeguards Guaranteeing Protection of the Rights of Those Facing the Death Penalty.* Economic and Social Council Resolution 1984/50, 25 May.

United Nations. 1990a. *Prevention of Urban Crime.* Report of the 8th United Nations Congress on the Prevention of Crime and The Treatment of Offenders. A/CONF.144/28, 5 October.

United Nations. 1990b. *Standard Minimum Rules for Non Custodial Measures.* General Assembly Resolution 45/110, 14 December.

United Nations. 1992a. *Trends in Crime and Criminal Justice, 1970-1985, in the Context of Socio-economic Change.* New York: United Nations.

United Nations. 1992b. Compendium of United Nations standards and norms in crime prevention and criminal justice. United Nations: New York. United Nations Publication Sales No. E.92.IV.1.

United Nations. 1993. *Strategies for Confronting Domestic Violence: A Resource Manual.* New York: Author.

United Nations. 1995a. Crime prevention strategies, in particular as related to crimes in urban areas and juvenile and violent criminality, including the question of victims: assessment and new perspectives. Background paper for the workshop on urban policy and crime prevention, Ninth UN Congress on the Prevention of Crime and The Treatment of Offenders, Cairo, April 29 - May 8, 1995. A/CONF.169/10.

United Nations. 1995b. *Report of the Ninth United Nations Congress on the Prevention of Crime and the Treatment of Offenders.* Cairo, April 29-May 8, 1995. A/CONF.169/16. 12 May.

United Nations. 1995c. *Report of the United Nations Fourth World Conference on Women.* Beijing, September 4-15, 1995. A/CONF.177/20. 17 October.

United Nations. 1995d. UN action against organised crime. V.95-52525, Ninth UN Congress, Cairo.

United Nations. 1995e. *Compendium of Human Settlements Statistics 1995.* United Nations Publication no. E.95.XVII.11, United Nations: New York.

United Nations. 1995f. Guidelines for the prevention of urban crime. ECOSOC 1995/9.

United Nations. 1995g. Crime prevention strategies, in particular as related to crimes in urban areas and juvenile and violent criminality, including the question of victims: assessment and new perspectives. Background paper for the workshop on the prevention of violent crime. Ninth UN Congress on the Prevention of Crime and the Treatment of Offenders, 29 April-8 May, 1995, Cairo. A/CONF.169/11.

United Nations. 1995h. Crime prevention strategies, in particular as related to crimes in urban areas and juvenile and violent criminality, including the question of victims: assessment and new perspectives. Background paper for the workshop on mass media and crime prevention. Ninth UN Congress on the Prevention of Crime and the Treatment of Offenders, 29 April-8 May, 1995, Cairo. A/CONF.169/9.

United Nations. 1995i. Crime prevention strategies, in particular as related to crimes in urban areas and juvenile and violent criminality, including the question of victims: assessment and new perspectives. Working paper prepared by the Secretariat. Ninth UN Congress on the Prevention of Crime and the Treatment of Offenders, 29 April-8 May, 1995, Cairo. A/CONF.169/7.

United Nations. 1995j. Manual on the Model Treaty on Extradition and Manual on the Model Treaty on Mutual Assistance in Criminal Matters: an implementation guide. *International Review of Criminal Policy*, 45, 46: 1-55.

United Nations. 1996a. *Human Development Report.* New York: United Nations.

United Nations. 1996b. Economic and Social Council. United Nations standards and norms in the field of crime prevention and criminal justice: capital punishment and implementation of the safeguards guaranteeing the protection of the rights of those facing the death penalty. Report of the Secretary General. 27 March 1996. E/CN15/1996/19.

United Nations. 1996c. Economic and Social Council. United Nations standards and norms in the field of crime prevention and criminal justice: use and application of the standard minimum rules for the treatment of prisoners. 22 March. E/CN15/1996/16/Add.1.

United Nations. 1996d. *The United Nations and Crime Prevention: Seeking Security and Justice for All.* New York: Department of Public Information, United Nations.

United Nations. 1997a. Use and application of United Nations standards and norms in crime prevention and criminal justice. Commission on Crime Prevention and Criminal Justice, Sixth Session, Vienna, 28 April-9 May, 1997. E/CN15/1997/14/Add.1.

United Nations. 1997b. Strategies for crime prevention and control, particularly in urban areas and in the context of public security: measures to prevent trafficking in children. Commission on Crime Prevention and Criminal Justice, Sixth Session, Vienna, 28 April-9 May, 1997, E/CN15/1997/12.

United Nations. 1997c. Joint training seminar on the practical implementation of the ECOWAS Conventions on Extradition and Mutual Assistance in Criminal Matters: report of the seminar. Vienna: United Nations Center for International Crime Prevention.

Upham, Frank K. 1987. *Law and Social Change in Postwar Japan.* Cambridge, MA: Harvard University Press.

US Department of State. 1994. *Treaties in Force: A List of Treaties and Other International Agreements of the United States in Force on January 1, 1994.* Washington DC: United States Government Printing Office.

US Government. 1995. China CIA Fact Sheet. http./www.odci.gov/cia/publications/95fact/ch.html

van Andel, H. 1989. Crime prevention that works: the care of public transport in the Netherlands. *British Journal of Criminology*, 29, 1: 47-56.

van den Berg, G.P. 1985. *The Soviet System of Justice: Figures and Policy.* Durdrecht, Netherlands: Martinus Nijhoff.

van Dijk, Jan J.M. 1991. On the uses of local, national and international crime surveys. In G. Kaiser, H. Kury and H.J. Albrecht (Eds.), *Victims and Criminal Justice: Victimological Research: Stocktaking and Prospects.* Freiburg: Max-Planck Institut.

van Dijk, Jan J.M. 1994a. *Opportunities of Crime: A Test of the Rational-interactionist Model.* Report for the Symposium on Economics and Crime of the Permanent Committee on Crime Problems of the Council of Europe, Strasbourg, November 28-31..

van Dijk, Jan J.M. 1994b. Understanding crime rates: on the interactions between the rational choices of victims and offenders. *British Journal of Criminology*, 34, 2: 105-121.

van Dijk, Jan J.M. 1994c. Who is afraid of the crime victim: criminal victimisation, fear of crime and opinions on crime in an international perspective. Paper presented at the World Society of Victimology Symposium, Adelaide, Australia, August 21-26.

van Dijk, Jan J.M. 1997a. Towards a research-based crime reduction policy; crime prevention as a cost-effective policy option. Paper presented at the European Union Conference, Crime Prevention: Towards a European Level, Noordwijk, the Netherlands.

van Dijk, Jan J.M. 1997b. Criminal victimisation and victim empowerment in an international perspective: key results on fifty nations of the international crime victims surveys 1989-1996. Keynote address at the opening session of the Ninth International Symposium on Victimology, Amsterdam, August 25-29.

van Dijk, Jan J.M. and G.J. Terlouw. 1996. An international perspective of the business community as victims of fraud and crime. *Security Journal*, 7, 3: 157-167.

van Dijk, Jan J.M. and J.N. van Kesteren. 1996. The prevalence and perceived seriousness of victimisation by crime; some results of the international crime victim survey. *European Journal of Crime, Criminal Law and Criminal Justice*, January: 48-71.

van Dijk, Jan J.M. and Jaap de Waard. 1991. A two-dimensional typology of crime prevention projects: with a bibliography. *Criminal Justice Abstracts*, 23, 3: 483-503.

van Dijk, Jan J.M. and Pat Mayhew. 1992. *Criminal Victimization in the Industrialized World: Key Findings of the 1989 and 1992 International Crime Surveys*. The Hague: Ministry of Justice, Directorate for Crime Prevention.

van Dijk, Jan J.M., Pat Mayhew and Martin Killias. 1990. *Experiences of Crime across the World: Key Findings of the 1989 International Crime Survey*. Deventer: Kluwer Law and Taxation.

Van Limbergen, K., S. Walgrave and I. Dekegel. 1996. *Promising Practices, Crime Prevention in Belgium: Ten Examples*. Brussels: The Permanent Secretariat for Prevention Policy, Ministry of the Interior.

Victoria Police. 1996. *Crime Statistics 1995-1996*. Melbourne.

Ville de Lille. 1992. Conseil Communal de prévention de al délinquance. *L'implication communautaire dans la prévention de la délinquance*. Lille, France: Author.

Walker, J. 1992. Estimates of the costs of crime in Australia. *Trends and Issues in Crime and Criminal Justice*, 39. Canberra: Australian Institute of Criminology.

Walker, J. 1993. *Crime in Australia*. Canberra: Australian Institute of Criminology.

Walker, J. 1994. *The First Australian National Survey of Crimes against Businesses*. Canberra: Australian Institute of Criminology.

Walker, J. 1995a. Crimes against businesses in Australia. *Trends and Issues*, no. 45. Canberra: Australian Institute of Criminology.

Walker, J. 1995b. Estimates of the costs of crime in Australia: revised 1995. Paper prepared for the Commonwealth Law Enforcement Board.

Walker, J. 1995c. *Estimates of the Extent of Money Laundering in and through Australia*. Sydney: AUSTRAC.

Walker, J. 1997. Estimates of the costs of crime in Australia in 1996. *Trends and Issues in Crime and Criminal Justice*, no. 72, August, Australian Institute of Criminology.

Walker, J. and D. Dagger. 1993. *National Corrections Management Information 1991-92*. Canberra: Australian Institute of Criminology.

Waller, I. 1982. What reduces residential burglary: action and research in Seattle and Toronto. In H.J. Schneider (Ed.), *Victim in International Perspective*. New York: de Gruyter.

Waller, I. 1989. *Current Trends in European Crime Prevention: Implications for Canada*. Ottawa: Department of Justice, Canada.

Waller, I. and B.C. Welsh. 1995. *International Trends in Crime Prevention: An Annotated Bibliography*. Montreal: International Centre for the Prevention of Crime.

Waller, I., B. Welsh and D. Sansfacon.1997. *Crime Prevention Digest: Trends and Payoffs for Selected Countries*. International Centre for the Prevention of Crime.

Walmsley, Roy. 1996. *Prison Systems in Central and Eastern Europe: Progress, Problems and the International Standards*. Helsinki, Finland: HEUNI.

Welsh, B.C. and I. Waller. 1995. *Crime and Its Prevention: Costs and Benefits*. Ottawa: Department of Criminology, University of Ottawa.

Wemmers, Jo-Anne. 1995. *Victims in the Criminal Justice System: A Study into the Treatment of Victims and its Effects on their Attitudes and Behaviour*. Amsterdam: Kugler Publications.

White, G. 1996. Corruption and the transition from socialism in China. *Journal of Law and Society*, 23, 1: 149-169.

Willemse, Hans.M. 1994. Developments in Dutch crime prevention. In R.V. Clarke (Ed.), *Crime Prevention Studies*, Volume 2. Monsey, New York: Criminal Justice Press.

Willemse, Hans M. and Jaap de Waard. 1993. Crime analysis and prevention: perspectives from experience in the Netherlands. *Security Journal*, 4, 4.

Wilson, Margo and Martin Daly. 1993. An evolutionary psychological perspective on male sexual proprietariness and violence against wives. *Violence and Victims*, 8, 3: 271-294.

Winer, Jonathon. 1997. Alien smuggling: elements of the problem and the US response. *Transnational Organised Crime*, 3, 1: 48-56.

Women's Aid Organization. 1992. Draft Report of the National Study on Domestic Violence. Kuala Lumpur, Malaysia.

World Bank. 1997. *World Development Report 1997*. New York: Oxford University Press.

Yayama, T. 1990. The recruit scandal: learning from the causes of corruption. *Journal of Japanese Studies*, 16: 93-114.

Yoshikawa, H. 1994. Prevention as cumulative protection: effects of early family support and education on chronic delinquency and its risks. *Psychological Bulletin*, 115, 1: 28-54.

Zigler, E., C. Taussig and K. Black. 1992. Early childhood intervention: a promising preventative for juvenile delinquency. *American Psychologist*, 47, 8: 997-1006.

Zvekic, Uglješa and A. Alvazzi del Frate. 1993. Victimisation in the developing world: an overview of preliminary key findings from the 1992 International Crime Survey. In Alvazzi del Frate *et al.* (Eds.), *Understanding of Crime*. Rome: UNICRI.

Zvekic, Uglješa and A. Alvazzi del Frate. 1995. *Criminal Victimisation in the Developing World*. Rome: UNICRI.

Zvekic, Uglješa and Takashi Kubo. 1988. Main trends in research on capital punishment (1979-1986). In *The Death Penalty: A Bibliographical Research*. Rome: UNSDRI.

Zvekic, Uglješa. 1996. The International Crime (Victim) Survey; issues of comparative advantages and disadvantages. *International Criminal Justice Review*, 6: 1-21.

Original Papers

The following papers were written especially for the Global Report and have been used as the basis for boxes. In some cases they have been reproduced in full for the Box; in others they have been edited and abridged.

Acker, James. 1997. The death penalty in the United States. School of Criminal Justice, University at Albany.

Adamski, Andrej. 1997. International trading in girls.

Aronowitz, Alexis A. 1997. Foreigners in Dutch Prisons. International Police Institute Twente, University of Twente the Netherlands.

Bayley, David. 1997. Policing as peacekeeping in Bosnia. Dean and Professor, School of Criminal Justice, University at Albany.

Beattie, Rick and Karen Mihorean. 1997. A model criminal. Justice statistics reporting system in Canada. Canadian Centre for Justice Statistics.

Biles, David. 1997. Private prisons in Australia. Criminologist, Coordinator, Asian and Pacific Conference on Correctional Administrators.

Boraine, Alex. 1997. South African Truth and Reconciliation Commission. Vice chairperson, South African Truth and Reconciliation Commission.

Burnham, R.W. 1997. History of world crime surveys. US National Institute of Justice Fellow.

Chavez, Jorge. 1997. Media reporting of crime in Argentina. School of Criminal Justice, University at Albany.

Chavez, Jorge. 1997. Official crime statistics and the media. School of Criminal Justice, University at Albany.

Ebbe, Obi. 1997. Informal customary justice in Nigeria. State University of New York at Brockport.

Ebbe, Obi. 1997. Formal customary justice in Nigeria. State University of New York at Brockport.

El-Kassas, Madhy and Mahesh K. Nalla. 1997. A day in an Egyptian prison. Mansoura University, Egypt and School of Criminal Justice, Michigan State University.

Farrell, Graham. 1997. Economic development, drug control, and illicit drug crop cultivation.

Farrell, Graham. 1997. Global review of crop eradication, crop substitution and alternative development.

Farrell, Graham. 1997. Crime reduction through medical treatment of drug users in Switzerland.

Farrell, Graham. 1997. Drug using offenders detected during problem-oriented policing initiative.

Farrell, Graham. 1997. Regional case study – the influence of commerce and trade upon drug trafficking in Europe.

Farrell, Graham. 1997. Drug courts in the United States of America. Center for Crime Prevention, Rutgers University.

Freilich, Josh. 1997. Most victimized groups by country according to the *International Factbook of Criminal Justice Systems*. School of Criminal Justice, University at Albany.

Freilich, Josh. 1997. Police use of guns around the world according to the *International Factbook of Criminal Justice Systems*. School of Criminal Justice, University at Albany.

Freilich, Josh. 1997. Ages of criminal responsibility around the world. School of Criminal Justice, University at Albany.

Friday, Paul, Akira Yamagami and John P.J. Dussich. 1997. Threshold of violence in Japan and the US. University North Carolina at Charlotte, and Tokyo Medical and Dental College, Tokiwa University.

Guo, Jianan. 1997. Rights of victims in China. Chief and Professor, Research Division of Crime Prevention, Institute for Crime Prevention, Ministry of Justice, P.R. China.

Guo, Jianan. 1997. Changes in criminal law in response to environmental crime. Chief and Professor, Research Division of Crime Prevention, Institute for Crime Prevention, Ministry of Justice, P.R. China.

Henshaw, C. and K. Pease. 1997. Making an arrest in England. Sergeant in W. Yorks Police, England, and University of Huddersfield.

Hill, Gary. 1997a. The anatomy of a technical assistance project : Bosnia and Herzegovina and the Republic of Srpska.

Hill, Gary. 1997b. The training of police and prison personnel in UN and international standards and norms.

Hill, Gary. 1997c. How an NGO influenced punishment practice in two countries.

Hirota, Toshikazu. 1997. A day in the life of a Tokyo police officer. National Police Agency of Japan.

Hoffman, Vince. A day in life of police officer in China. Michigan State University, School of Criminal Justice.

Howard, Gregory J. and Graeme Newman. 1997. Rape as a most reported crime. School of Criminal Justice, University at Albany.

Howard, Gregory J., Josh Freilich and Graeme Newman. 1997. Reliability of the UNCJS. School of Criminal Justice, University at Albany.

Hwang, Heechul. 1997. Integrated criminal justice information systems in South Korea. Supreme Prosecutor's Office, Ministry of Justice, South Korea.

Ifkovich, S. 1997. Lay criminal justice personnel. Graduate Program, Harvard Law School.

Johnson, Holly. 1997. Domestic violence in particular countries. Canadian Centre for Justice Statistics.

Joutsen, Matti. 1997. The stabilisation of crime trends in Western Europe: statistical artifact or reality? HEUNI.

Joutsen, Matti. 1997. Prison rates in Eastern Europe. HEUNI.

Jung, Jin-Sup. 1997. Counterfeit good in South Korea. Vice President, Korean Institute of Criminology.

Junger Tas, Josine. 1997. Delinquent behavior of young people in the western world. University of Leiden.

Kangaspunta, Kristiina. 1997. Reduction of prison population in Finland. HEUNI.

Kress, Jack. 1997. The US District Attorney: a prosecutor of diverse legal, national and cultural origins.

Lewis, Chris. 1997. Police technology and crime recording. Research and Statistics Directorate, Home Office, UK.

Lewis, Chris. 1997. Offences allegedly committed by members of the Aum Shinrikyo cult.

Lewis, Chris. 1997. Status of firearms control in Europe.

Lewis, Chris. 1997. Self-report surveys of offending.

Lewis, Chris. 1997. Commercial victimisation surveys.

Lewis, Chris. 1997. Organised crime in Europe.

Lewis, Chris. 1997. Good practice in collecting and analysing recorded crime data.

Lewis, Chris. 1997. Public confidence and crime prevention.

Lewis, Chris. 1997. The International Crime Victim Survey (ICVS): another count of crime.

Lewis, Chris. 1997. Difficulties in interpreting recorded crime statistics.

Marongiu, Pietro and Sandro Norfo. 1997. Organized crime in Italy. Department of Forensic Medicine, University of Cagliari, Italy, and Public Prosecutor at the General Attorney's Office of the Court of Appeal of Cagliari, Italy.

Morris, Allison and Gabrielle Maxwell. 1997. Family group conferences and restorative justice in New Zealand. Institute of Criminology, Victoria University of Wellington.

Mrkic, Srdjan. 1997. Comparing crime in urban and rural areas: problems and an illustration. UN Statistics Division.

Mueller, G.W.O. and Freida Adler. Gauging transnational criminality: a new challenge for the United Nations Survey of Crime Trends and the UNCJS. Professors, School of Criminal Justice, Rutgers University.

Mukherjee, Satyanshu. 1997. Intermediate sanctions: Electronic monitoring and house arrest. Australian Institute of Criminology.

Mukherjee, Satyanshu. 1997. Case attrition in New South Wales, Australia. Australian Institute of Criminology.

Nalla, Mahesh. 1997. Private policing in India. Michigan State University, School of Criminal Justice.

Nalla, Mahesh. 1997. Extradition. Michigan State University, School of Criminal Justice.

Nimsombun, Thakoon. 1997. Day in the life of a Thai police investigator. Michigan State University, School of Criminal Justice.

Passas, Nikos. 1997. Corruption: a world view. Temple University, Department of Criminal Justice.

Passas, Nikos. 1997. BCCI and money laundering: a multi-crime crime. Temple University, Department of Criminal Justice.

Pridemore, William Alex. 1997. Generation of crime statistics in Russia. School of Criminal Justice, University at Albany.

Pridemore, William Alex. 1997. The death penalty in Russia. School of Criminal Justice, University at Albany.

Reichel, P. 1997. World legal traditions. University of Northern Colorado.

Rivera, Craig. 1997. Victim status in different countries. School of Criminal Justice, University at Albany.

Rogel, Noga. 1996-97. Compulsory national service and policing in Israel. *Innovation*, Winter, no. 6. Jerusalem, Israel. Reprinted with permission.

Salas, Luis. 1997. Corruption in Latin America. Professor, School of Public Affairs, Florida International University, Miami, Florida.

Trevathan, S. and B. MacKillop. Diversion and alternative measures. Canadian Centre for Justice Statistics.

van Dijk, Jan J.M. 1997. The International Crime Victim Survey (ICVS): another count of crime.

Weiss, Michael. 1997. Police training and qualifications around the world. School of Criminal Justice, University at Albany.

Weiss, Michael. 1997. Police equipment and technology. School of Criminal Justice, University at Albany.

Weiss, Michael 1997. Police technology in different countries. School of Criminal Justice, University at Albany.

Wilson, Paul. 1997. Day in a Thailand prison. Dean of Humanities and Social Sciences, Bond University, Australia.

Notes

Notes to Boxes

Introduction

Box 0.5 The generation of crime statistics in the Russian Federation

NOTE 1
The Russian Ministry of the Interior also collects information from the Commonwealth of Independent States, the Baltic States, and the Republic of Georgia, providing the same services to these states as it does to its own Russian agencies.

NOTE 2
The Prosecutor-General's Office collects information on the activities and results of investigating and prosecuting agencies. The Ministry of Justice uses these data to analyze criminal court proceedings and the characteristics of offenders (Lezhikov, 1995).

Box 0.6 Rape: the most reported crime by countries in the UNCJS

Method of Computation. The crimes considered in this box, all for 1994, include committed intentional homicide, total drug offenses, rape, total assault, robbery and total theft. The provision of data for these crime types by countries responding to the Fifth UNCJS was assessed at four levels of the criminal justice system: initial recording of a crime by the police, arrests, prosecutions and convictions. For each stage, a country was coded as 1 if it provided data about a particular crime and as 0 if data were missing for a particular crime. The number of countries providing data about a particular crime (i.e., those coded as 1) at each level was divided by the number of responding countries to the Fifth UNCJS (n=91) to yield the proportion of countries furnishing data on a particular crime at each level. Raw data are presented in the following tables.

Table B0.1. Crimes recorded by the police in 1994

Country	Homicide	Drugs	Rape	Robbery	Assault	Theft
Andorra	.00	.00	.00	.00	.00	.00
Australia	1.00	.00	1.00	1.00	.00	.00
Austria	1.00	1.00	1.00	1.00	1.00	1.00
Azerbaijan	1.00	1.00	1.00	1.00	1.00	1.00
Bahamas	1.00	1.00	1.00	1.00	.00	.00
Belarus	1.00	1.00	1.00	1.00	1.00	1.00
Belgium	1.00	1.00	1.00	1.00	1.00	1.00
Bermuda	1.00	1.00	1.00	1.00	1.00	1.00
Bolivia	.00	1.00	1.00	1.00	.00	1.00
Brazil	.00	.00	.00	.00	.00	.00
Brunei Daruss.	.00	.00	.00	.00	.00	.00
Bulgaria	1.00	.00	1.00	1.00	1.00	1.00
Canada	.00	1.00	1.00	1.00	1.00	1.00
Chile	.00	.00	1.00	1.00	1.00	1.00
Colombia	1.00	1.00	1.00	1.00	1.00	1.00
Costa Rica	1.00	1.00	1.00	1.00	1.00	1.00
Croatia	1.00	1.00	1.00	1.00	1.00	1.00
Cyprus	1.00	1.00	1.00	1.00	1.00	1.00
Czech Republic	.00	.00	.00	.00	.00	.00
Denmark	1.00	1.00	1.00	1.00	1.00	1.00
Ecuador	1.00	1.00	1.00	1.00	1.00	1.00
Egypt	1.00	1.00	1.00	1.00	1.00	1.00

Country	Homicide	Drugs	Rape	Robbery	Assault	Theft
El Salvador	.00	.00	.00	.00	.00	.00
England & Wales	.00	.00	1.00	1.00	1.00	1.00
Estonia	1.00	1.00	1.00	1.00	1.00	1.00
Finland	1.00	1.00	1.00	1.00	1.00	1.00
France	1.00	1.00	1.00	1.00	.00	1.00
Georgia	1.00	1.00	1.00	1.00	1.00	1.00
Germany	.00	.00	.00	.00	.00	.00
Greece	1.00	1.00	1.00	1.00	1.00	1.00
Guyana	.00	.00	.00	.00	.00	.00
Hong Kong	1.00	1.00	1.00	1.00	1.00	1.00
Hungary	1.00	1.00	1.00	1.00	1.00	1.00
India	1.00	1.00	1.00	1.00	.00	1.00
Indonesia	.00	1.00	1.00	1.00	1.00	.00
Israel	1.00	1.00	1.00	1.00	1.00	1.00
Italy	1.00	1.00	1.00	1.00	1.00	1.00
Jamaica	1.00	1.00	1.00	1.00	1.00	1.00
Japan	1.00	1.00	1.00	1.00	1.00	1.00
Jordan	1.00	.00	1.00	1.00	1.00	1.00
Kazakhstan	.00	1.00	1.00	1.00	1.00	1.00
Kiribati	.00	.00	.00	.00	.00	.00
Kuwait	1.00	1.00	1.00	1.00	1.00	1.00
Kyrgyzstan	.00	1.00	1.00	1.00	1.00	1.00
Latvia	1.00	1.00	1.00	1.00	1.00	1.00
Liechtenstein	.00	.00	.00	.00	.00	.00
Lithuania	1.00	1.00	1.00	1.00	1.00	1.00
Luxembourg	.00	.00	.00	.00	.00	.00
Macau	1.00	1.00	1.00	1.00	1.00	1.00
Madagascar	1.00	1.00	1.00	1.00	1.00	1.00
Malaysia	1.00	1.00	1.00	1.00	1.00	1.00
Malta	1.00	1.00	1.00	1.00	1.00	1.00
Marshall Islands	1.00	1.00	1.00	1.00	1.00	1.00
Mauritius	1.00	1.00	1.00	1.00	1.00	1.00
Mexico	.00	.00	.00	.00	.00	.00
Morocco	1.00	1.00	1.00	.00	1.00	1.00
Myanmar	.00	.00	.00	.00	.00	.00
Netherlands	.00	.00	.00	.00	.00	.00
Nicaragua	1.00	1.00	1.00	1.00	1.00	1.00
Northern Ireland	1.00	1.00	1.00	1.00	1.00	1.00
Panama	.00	1.00	1.00	1.00	1.00	1.00
Peru	.00	.00	.00	.00	.00	.00
Philippines	.00	.00	1.00	1.00	.00	.00
Portugal	.00	.00	.00	.00	.00	.00
Qatar	1.00	1.00	1.00	.00	1.00	1.00
Rep. of Korea	1.00	1.00	1.00	1.00	1.00	.00
*"FYRM"	.00	1.00	1.00	1.00	1.00	1.00
Rep. of Moldova	1.00	1.00	1.00	1.00	1.00	1.00
Romania	1.00	1.00	1.00	1.00	1.00	1.00
Russian Fed.	1.00	1.00	1.00	1.00	.00	1.00
Saint V. & Gren.	.00	.00	1.00	1.00	.00	.00
Sao Tome & P.	1.00	.00	.00	.00	1.00	1.00
Scotland	1.00	1.00	1.00	1.00	1.00	1.00
Singapore	1.00	1.00	1.00	1.00	1.00	1.00
Slovakia	1.00	1.00	1.00	.00	1.00	1.00
Slovenia	1.00	1.00	1.00	1.00	1.00	1.00
South Africa	.00	.00	.00	.00	.00	.00
Spain	1.00	.00	1.00	1.00	1.00	1.00
Sudan	1.00	1.00	1.00	1.00	.00	.00
Sweden	1.00	1.00	1.00	1.00	1.00	1.00
Switzerland	1.00	1.00	1.00	1.00	1.00	1.00
Syrian Arab Rep.	1.00	1.00	1.00	1.00	1.00	1.00
Turkey	.00	1.00	1.00	1.00	1.00	1.00
Uganda	.00	.00	.00	.00	.00	.00
Ukraine	1.00	1.00	1.00	1.00	.00	.00
USA	.00	.00	1.00	1.00	1.00	1.00
Uruguay	.00	1.00	.00	1.00	1.00	1.00
Western Samoa	1.00	1.00	1.00	1.00	1.00	1.00
Yugoslavia	.00	.00	.00	.00	.00	.00
Zambia	1.00	1.00	1.00	1.00	1.00	.00
Zimbabwe	.00	1.00	1.00	1.00	1.00	1.00
Mean	**.637**	**.703**	**.780**	**.758**	**.659**	**.703**

*"The Former Yugoslav Republic of Macedonia"

Table B0.2. Arrests (or formal contact with the criminal justice system) in 1994

Country	Homicide	Drugs	Rape	Robbery	Assault	Theft
Andorra	.00	.00	.00	.00	.00	.00
Australia	.00	.00	.00	.00	.00	.00
Austria	.00	1.00	1.00	1.00	1.00	1.00
Azerbaijan	1.00	1.00	1.00	1.00	1.00	1.00
Bahamas	1.00	1.00	1.00	1.00	1.00	1.00
Belarus	.00	.00	.00	.00	.00	.00
Belgium	.00	.00	.00	.00	.00	.00
Bermuda	.00	.00	.00	.00	.00	.00
Bolivia	.00	.00	.00	.00	.00	.00
Brazil	1.00	.00	1.00	1.00	1.00	1.00
Brunei D.	.00	1.00	1.00	1.00	1.00	1.00
Bulgaria	.00	1.00	1.00	1.00	1.00	1.00
Canada	1.00	1.00	1.00	1.00	1.00	1.00
Chile	1.00	1.00	1.00	1.00	1.00	1.00
Colombia	.00	1.00	1.00	1.00	1.00	1.00
Costa Rica	1.00	1.00	1.00	1.00	1.00	1.00
Croatia	.00	.00	.00	.00	.00	.00
Cyprus	1.00	1.00	1.00	1.00	1.00	1.00
Czech Republic	1.00	1.00	1.00	1.00	1.00	1.00
Denmark	1.00	1.00	1.00	1.00	1.00	1.00
Ecuador	.00	.00	.00	.00	.00	.00
Egypt	1.00	1.00	1.00	1.00	1.00	1.00
El Salvador	1.00	1.00	1.00	1.00	1.00	.00
England & Wales	1.00	1.00	1.00	1.00	1.00	1.00
Estonia	1.00	1.00	1.00	1.00	1.00	1.00
Finland	.00	.00	.00	.00	.00	.00
France	.00	1.00	1.00	1.00	1.00	1.00
Georgia	.00	.00	.00	.00	.00	.00
Germany	1.00	1.00	1.00	1.00	1.00	1.00
Greece	1.00	1.00	1.00	1.00	.00	1.00
Guyana	.00	.00	.00	.00	.00	.00
Hong Kong	.00	.00	.00	.00	.00	.00
Hungary	1.00	1.00	1.00	1.00	1.00	1.00
India	1.00	1.00	1.00	1.00	1.00	1.00
Indonesia	1.00	1.00	1.00	1.00	1.00	1.00
Israel	1.00	1.00	1.00	1.00	.00	1.00
Italy	.00	1.00	1.00	1.00	1.00	1.00
Jamaica	.00	.00	.00	.00	.00	.00
Japan	.00	.00	.00	.00	.00	.00
Jordan	.00	1.00	1.00	1.00	1.00	1.00
Kazakhstan	1.00	1.00	1.00	1.00	1.00	1.00
Kiribati	.00	.00	.00	.00	.00	.00
Kuwait	1.00	1.00	1.00	1.00	1.00	Theft
Kyrgyzstan	.00	.00	.00	.00	.00	.00
Latvia	1.00	1.00	1.00	1.00	1.00	1.00
Liechtenstein	1.00	1.00	1.00	1.00	1.00	1.00
Lithuania	1.00	1.00	1.00	1.00	1.00	1.00
Luxembourg	1.00	1.00	1.00	1.00	1.00	1.00
Macau	1.00	1.00	1.00	1.00	1.00	1.00
Madagascar	.00	.00	.00	.00	.00	.00
Malaysia	.00	.00	.00	.00	.00	.00
Malta	.00	.00	.00	.00	.00	.00
Marshall Islands	.00	.00	.00	.00	.00	.00
Mauritius	1.00	1.00	1.00	1.00	1.00	1.00
Mexico	.00	.00	.00	.00	.00	.00
Morocco	.00	.00	.00	.00	.00	.00
Myanmar	.00	.00	.00	.00	.00	.00
Netherlands	.00	.00	.00	.00	.00	.00
Nicaragua	1.00	1.00	1.00	.00	1.00	1.00
Northern Ireland	1.00	1.00	1.00	1.00	.00	.00
Panama	.00	1.00	1.00	1.00	1.00	1.00
Peru	1.00	1.00	1.00	1.00	.00	.00
Philippines	1.00	1.00	1.00	1.00	.00	1.00
Portugal	.00	.00	1.00	1.00	.00	.00
Qatar	1.00	1.00	1.00	1.00	1.00	1.00
Rep. of Korea	.00	.00	.00	.00	.00	.00
*"FYRM".	1.00	1.00	1.00	1.00	1.00	1.00
Rep. of Moldova	.00	1.00	1.00	1.00	1.00	1.00
Romania	1.00	1.00	1.00	1.00	1.00	1.00
Russian Fed.	.00	.00	.00	.00	.00	.00
Saint V.& Gren.	.00	1.00	1.00	1.00	1.00	1.00
Sao Tome & P.	.00	.00	.00	.00	.00	.00
Scotland	1.00	1.00	1.00	1.00	1.00	1.00
Singapore	.00	.00	.00	.00	.00	.00
Slovakia	1.00	1.00	1.00	1.00	1.00	1.00
Slovenia	.00	1.00	1.00	1.00	1.00	1.00
South Africa	.00	1.00	1.00	1.00	1.00	1.00
Spain	.00	.00	.00	.00	.00	.00
Sudan	1.00	1.00	1.00	1.00	.00	.00
Sweden	.00	.00	.00	.00	.00	.00
Switzerland	.00	1.00	1.00	1.00	1.00	1.00
Syrian Arab Rep.	.00	.00	.00	.00	.00	.00
Turkey	.00	.00	.00	.00	.00	.00
Uganda	.00	.00	.00	.00	.00	.00
Ukraine	.00	.00	.00	.00	.00	.00
USA	1.00	1.00	1.00	1.00	1.00	1.00
Uruguay	.00	.00	.00	.00	.00	.00
Western Samoa	.00	.00	.00	.00	.00	.00
Yugoslavia	.00	.00	.00	.00	.00	.00
Zambia	.00	.00	.00	.00	.00	.00
Zimbabwe	1.00	1.00	1.00	1.00	.00	.00
Mean	**.429**	**.549**	**.582**	**.571**	**.484**	**.516**

*"The Former Yugoslav Republic of Macedonia"

Table B0.3. Prosecutions in 1994

Country	Homicide	Drugs	Rape	Robbery	Assault	Theft
Andorra	1.00	1.00	1.00	1.00	1.00	1.00
Australia	.00	.00	.00	.00	.00	.00
Austria	.00	.00	.00	.00	.00	.00
Azerbaijan	1.00	.00	1.00	1.00	1.00	1.00
Bahamas	.00	1.00	1.00	1.00	1.00	1.00
Belarus	.00	.00	.00	.00	.00	.00
Belgium	.00	.00	.00	.00	.00	.00
Bermuda	.00	.00	.00	.00	.00	.00
Bolivia	.00	.00	.00	.00	.00	.00
Brazil	1.00	.00	1.00	1.00	1.00	1.00
Brunei D.	.00	1.00	1.00	1.00	1.00	1.00
Bulgaria	.00	.00	1.00	1.00	.00	.00
Canada	.00	1.00	1.00	.00	.00	1.00
Chile	.00	.00	.00	.00	.00	.00
Colombia	.00	1.00	1.00	1.00	1.00	1.00
Costa Rica	1.00	1.00	1.00	1.00	1.00	1.00
Croatia	1.00	1.00	1.00	1.00	.00	.00
Cyprus	1.00	.00	1.00	1.00	.00	1.00
Czech Republic	.00	.00	.00	.00	.00	.00
Denmark	.00	1.00	1.00	1.00	1.00	1.00
Ecuador	1.00	1.00	1.00	1.00	1.00	1.00
Egypt	1.00	1.00	1.00	1.00	1.00	1.00
El Salvador	1.00	1.00	1.00	1.00	1.00	1.00
England & Wales	.00	.00	.00	.00	.00	.00
Estonia	.00	.00	1.00	1.00	.00	.00
Finland	1.00	1.00	1.00	1.00	1.00	1.00
France	.00	.00	.00	.00	.00	.00
Georgia	.00	.00	.00	.00	.00	.00
Germany	1.00	1.00	1.00	1.00	1.00	1.00
Greece	1.00	1.00	1.00	1.00	.00	1.00
Guyana	.00	1.00	1.00	1.00	.00	.00
Hong Kong	1.00	1.00	1.00	1.00	1.00	1.00
Hungary	1.00	1.00	1.00	1.00	1.00	1.00
India	.00	.00	.00	.00	.00	.00
Indonesia	.00	1.00	1.00	1.00	1.00	.00
Israel	.00	.00	.00	.00	.00	.00
Italy	.00	1.00	1.00	1.00	.00	.00
Jamaica	.00	.00	.00	.00	.00	.00
Japan	.00	.00	.00	.00	.00	.00

Country	Homicide	Drugs	Rape	Robbery	Assault	Theft
Jordan	.00	.00	1.00	1.00	.00	.00
Kazakhstan	.00	1.00	1.00	1.00	.00	1.00
Kiribati	.00	.00	.00	.00	.00	.00
Kuwait	.00	.00	.00	.00	.00	.00
Kyrgyzstan	.00	.00	.00	.00	.00	.00
Latvia	.00	.00	.00	.00	.00	.00
Liechtenstein	.00	.00	1.00	1.00	.00	.00
Lithuania	.00	.00	.00	.00	.00	.00
Luxembourg	.00	.00	.00	.00	.00	.00
Macau	.00	.00	.00	.00	.00	.00
Madagascar	.00	.00	.00	.00	.00	.00
Malaysia	.00	.00	.00	.00	.00	.00
Malta	.00	.00	.00	.00	.00	.00
Marshall Islands	.00	1.00	1.00	1.00	1.00	1.00
Mauritius	.00	.00	.00	.00	.00	.00
Mexico	.00	.00	.00	.00	.00	.00
Morocco	1.00	1.00	1.00	1.00	1.00	1.00
Myanmar	.00	.00	.00	.00	.00	.00
Netherlands	1.00	1.00	1.00	1.00	1.00	1.00
Nicaragua	.00	.00	.00	.00	.00	.00
Northern Ireland	.00	1.00	1.00	1.00	1.00	1.00
Panama	.00	1.00	1.00	1.00	.00	.00
Peru	.00	.00	.00	.00	.00	.00
Philippines	1.00	1.00	1.00	1.00	1.00	1.00
Portugal	.00	.00	.00	.00	.00	.00
Qatar	1.00	1.00	1.00	1.00	1.00	1.00
Rep. of Korea	1.00	1.00	1.00	1.00	1.00	1.00
*"FYRM".	1.00	1.00	1.00	1.00	1.00	1.00
Rep. of Moldova	.00	1.00	1.00	1.00	1.00	1.00
Romania	.00	1.00	1.00	1.00	1.00	1.00
Russian Fed.	1.00	1.00	1.00	1.00	1.00	1.00
Saint V.& .Gren.	1.00	1.00	.00	1.00	.00	.00
Sao Tome & P.	1.00	1.00	.00	1.00	.00	1.00
Scotland	1.00	1.00	.00	.00	1.00	1.00
Singapore	.00	.00	.00	.00	.00	.00
Slovakia	.00	.00	.00	.00	.00	.00
Slovenia	.00	1.00	1.00	1.00	1.00	1.00
South Africa	.00	1.00	1.00	1.00	1.00	1.00
Spain	.00	.00	.00	.00	.00	.00
Sudan	.00	.00	.00	.00	.00	.00
Sweden	1.00	1.00	1.00	1.00	1.00	1.00
Switzerland	.00	.00	.00	.00	.00	.00
Syrian Arab Rep.	.00	.00	.00	.00	.00	.00
Turkey	.00	1.00	1.00	1.00	1.00	1.00
Uganda	.00	.00	.00	.00	.00	.00
Ukraine	.00	.00	.00	.00	.00	.00
USA	1.00	1.00	1.00	1.00	1.00	1.00
Uruguay	1.00	1.00	1.00	1.00	1.00	1.00
Western Samoa	1.00	1.00	1.00	1.00	1.00	1.00
Yugoslavia	.00	.00	.00	.00	.00	.00
Zambia	1.00	1.00	1.00	1.00	1.00	1.00
Zimbabwe	.00	1.00	1.00	1.00	.00	.00
Mean	**.330**	**.484**	**.549**	**.538**	**.385**	**.429**

*"The Former Yugoslav Republic of Macedonia"

Table B0.4. Convictions in 1994

Country	Homicide	Drugs	Rape	Robbery	Assault	Theft
Andorra	1.00	1.00	1.00	1.00	.00	.00
Australia	.00	.00	.00	.00	.00	.00
Austria	.00	1.00	1.00	1.00	1.00	1.00
Azerbaijan	.00	1.00	1.00	1.00	1.00	1.00
Bahamas	.00	.00	.00	.00	.00	.00
Belarus	1.00	1.00	1.00	1.00	1.00	1.00
Belgium	1.00	1.00	1.00	1.00	1.00	1.00
Bermuda	.00	.00	.00	.00	.00	.00
Bolivia	.00	.00	.00	.00	.00	.00
Brazil	.00	.00	.00	.00	.00	.00
Brunei D.	.00	.00	.00	.00	.00	.00
Bulgaria	1.00	1.00	1.00	1.00	.00	1.00
Canada	.00	1.00	1.00	1.00	1.00	1.00
Chile	.00	.00	1.00	1.00	1.00	.00
Colombia	1.00	1.00	1.00	.00	.00	1.00
Costa Rica	1.00	1.00	1.00	1.00	1.00	1.00
Croatia	1.00	1.00	1.00	1.00	1.00	1.00
Cyprus	1.00	1.00	1.00	1.00	1.00	1.00
Czech Republic	1.00	1.00	1.00	1.00	.00	.00
Denmark	1.00	1.00	1.00	1.00	1.00	.00
Ecuador	.00	.00	1.00	.00	.00	.00
Egypt	1.00	1.00	1.00	1.00	.00	.00
El Salvador	.00	.00	.00	.00	.00	.00
England & Wales	1.00	1.00	1.00	1.00	1.00	1.00
Estonia	1.00	1.00	1.00	1.00	1.00	1.00
Finland	1.00	1.00	1.00	1.00	1.00	1.00
France	.00	.00	.00	.00	.00	.00
Georgia	.00	1.00	1.00	1.00	1.00	1.00
Germany	1.00	1.00	1.00	1.00	1.00	1.00
Greece	1.00	1.00	1.00	1.00	.00	1.00
Guyana	.00	.00	.00	.00	.00	.00
Hong Kong	1.00	1.00	1.00	1.00	1.00	1.00
Hungary	1.00	1.00	1.00	1.00	1.00	1.00
India	1.00	1.00	1.00	1.00	.00	.00
Indonesia	1.00	1.00	1.00	1.00	.00	.00
Israel	1.00	1.00	1.00	1.00	1.00	1.00
Italy	1.00	1.00	1.00	1.00	1.00	1.00
Jamaica	1.00	.00	1.00	1.00	.00	.00
Japan	1.00	1.00	1.00	1.00	1.00	1.00
Jordan	1.00	1.00	1.00	.00	1.00	.00
Kazakhstan	.00	1.00	1.00	1.00	1.00	1.00
Kiribati	.00	.00	.00	.00	.00	.00
Kuwait	.00	.00	.00	.00	.00	.00
Kyrgyzstan	.00	.00	.00	.00	.00	.00
Latvia	.00	1.00	1.00	1.00	1.00	1.00
Liechtenstein	.00	.00	.00	.00	.00	.00
Lithuania	.00	1.00	1.00	1.00	1.00	1.00
Luxembourg	.00	.00	.00	.00	.00	.00
Macau	.00	.00	.00	.00	.00	.00
Madagascar	.00	.00	.00	.00	.00	.00
Malaysia	.00	.00	.00	.00	.00	.00
Malta	.00	.00	.00	.00	.00	.00
Marshall Islands	.00	.00	.00	.00	.00	.00
Mauritius	.00	.00	.00	.00	.00	.00
Mexico	1.00	1.00	1.00	1.00	1.00	.00
Morocco	.00	.00	.00	.00	.00	.00
Myanmar	1.00	1.00	1.00	1.00	.00	.00
Netherlands	.00	1.00	1.00	1.00	1.00	1.00
Nicaragua	.00	.00	.00	.00	.00	.00
Northern Ireland	1.00	1.00	1.00	1.00	1.00	1.00
Panama	.00	.00	1.00	1.00	.00	1.00
Peru	.00	.00	.00	.00	.00	.00
Philippines	.00	.00	.00	.00	.00	.00
Portugal	1.00	1.00	1.00	1.00	1.00	1.00
Qatar	.00	1.00	1.00	1.00	1.00	1.00
Rep. of Korea	.00	1.00	1.00	1.00	1.00	1.00
*"FYRM".	.00	1.00	1.00	1.00	1.00	1.00
Rep. of Moldova	.00	1.00	1.00	1.00	1.00	1.00
Romania	.00	.00	.00	.00	.00	.00
Russian Fed.	1.00	1.00	1.00	1.00	1.00	1.00
Saint V.& Gren.	.00	.00	.00	.00	.00	.00
Sao Tome & Pr.	.00	.00	.00	.00	.00	.00
Scotland	1.00	1.00	1.00	1.00	1.00	1.00
Singapore	1.00	.00	1.00	1.00	1.00	1.00
Slovakia	1.00	1.00	1.00	1.00	1.00	1.00
Slovenia	.00	1.00	1.00	1.00	1.00	1.00
South Africa	1.00	1.00	1.00	1.00	1.00	1.00
Spain	.00	.00	.00	.00	.00	.00
Sudan	.00	.00	1.00	.00	.00	.00
Sweden	.00	1.00	1.00	1.00	1.00	1.00
Switzerland	1.00	1.00	1.00	1.00	1.00	1.00
Syrian Arab Rep.	.00	.00	.00	.00	.00	.00

Country	Homicide	Drugs	Rape	Robbery	Assault	Theft
Turkey	.00	.00	.00	.00	.00	.00
Uganda	.00	.00	.00	.00	.00	.00
Ukraine	.00	.00	.00	.00	.00	.00
USA	.00	1.00	1.00	1.00	1.00	1.00
Uruguay	1.00	.00	1.00	.00	.00	.00
Western Samoa	.00	.00	.00	.00	.00	.00
Yugoslavia	1.00	.00	1.00	1.00	1.00	1.00
Zambia	.00	.00	.00	.00	.00	.00
Zimbabwe	.00	.00	.00	.00	.00	.00
Mean	.407	.516	.604	.560	.473	.495

*"The Former Yugoslav Republic of Macedonia"

Box 0.7 The reliability of the United Nations Survey on Crime Trends and Criminal Justice Systems: the case of homicide

Definitions of Homicide. Each of the official data sources on homicide define the crime in slightly different manner. However, all three seem to agree that homicide is any intentional taking of a human life by another human. It should be noted that there are differences in terminology between the data sources with INTERPOL referring to the intentional killing of another human being as murder while the United Nations and WHO refer to the same action as homicide. Because the concern of this box is to compare the United Nations data to other official sources of data on crime, the term used by the United Nations survey is adopted for purposes of clarity in the text. The specific definitions of homicide offered by each official data source are given below:

1. *United Nations Survey of Crime Trends and Criminal Justice Systems:* "Intentional homicide refers to death deliberately inflicted on a person by another person, including infanticide." This definition is identical over all five United Nations surveys.

2. INTERPOL: "Any act performed with the purpose of taking human life, no matter in what circumstances. This definition excludes manslaughter and abortion but not infanticide." From 1978 forward, manslaughter is not explicitly excluded from the definition.

3. WHO: "Homicide and injury purposely inflicted by other persons." Importantly, legal interventions are also sometimes included in this definition.

Method of Computation. The homicide rate per 100,000 population was calculated by dividing the total number of intentional homicides reported by the United Nations Survey of Crime Trends and Operation of Criminal Justice Systems, INTERPOL and WHO for 1974, 1978, 1984, 1988 and 1993 by the total population of each country for each year as reported in the United Nations *Demographic Yearbook* and multiplying by 100,000. This homicide rate includes attempts for both the United Nations and the INTERPOL data. Where the data were available, a similar measure of the homicide rate was calculated which excluded attempts from the United Nations and INTERPOL measures. The method of computation is identical to the one reported above, save the number of attempted homicides was removed from the total number of intentional homicides.

Sample of Countries. Only those countries with homicide rates available for each of the three data sources for each year were included in the analysis. Importantly, the sample of countries varies from year to year so one must resist the temptation to assess these data in a longitudinal sense. In other words, conclusions about the comparability of the United Nations data to the other official data sources must be limited to specific years only. The homicide rates for each nation by year and data source are reported below.

Table B0.5. Homicide rates per 100,000 population in 1974

Country	United Nations*	INTERPOL*	WHO
Austria	3.00	3.04	1.54
Chile	14.26	7.17	2.25
Denmark	.69	2.02	.73
Egypt	3.50	3.46	1.09
England & Wales	1.98	2.24	.98
Germany	4.40	4.47	1.17

Country	United Nations*	INTERPOL*	WHO
France	.40	2.72	.94
Greece	.30	.86	.57
Italy	3.10	2.97	1.12
Japan	1.74	1.74	1.26
New Zealand	1.10	1.53	1.46
Norway	.50	.50	.63
Philippines	6.22	2.68	1.31
Singapore	2.70	2.79	2.16
Spain	5.00	.66	.35
Sweden	1.53	3.37	1.25
Trinidad & Tobago	5.42	10.56	6.54
Venezuela	7.18	7.17	8.97
Median	2.852	2.758	1.208
Mean	3.501	3.331	1.907

* Note: United Nations and INTERPOL data in these columns should include attempts.

Table B0.6. Homicide rates per 100,000 population in 1978

Country	United Nations*	INTERPOL*	INTERPOL**	WHO
Australia	2.62	2.79	N/A	1.81
Austria	1.98	1.98	1.05	1.41
Denmark	2.82	2.76	.67	.53
England & Wales	.33	1.97	N/A	.82
Germany	4.86	4.86	2.42	3.01
Fiji	4.18	4.18	1.38	1.21
Finland	1.25	1.20	.45	.71
Greece	5.50	1.60	N/A	1.63
Israel	1.62	1.62	N/A	1.14
Japan	4.83	1.75	N/A	1.17
Kuwait	1.32	2.51	1.90	1.86
New Zealand	.86	.76	N/A	.74
Norway	1.80	1.76	N/A	1.67
Scotland	.58	.72	N/A	.92
Singapore	1.50	4.60	1.52	.99
Spain	6.03	5.56	5.23	.33
Sweden	24.21	25.47	N/A	20.40
Syria	1.46	1.46	1.08	1.25
Thailand	10.29	10.29	N/A	9.11
Venezuela	5.41	.93	N/A	1.51
Median	2.301	1.976	1.377	1.226
Mean	4.173	3.939	1.744	2.61

* Note: United Nations and INTERPOL data in these columns should include attempts.
** Note: INTERPOL data in this column should not include attempts.

Table B0.7. Homicide rates per 100,000 population in 1984

Country	United Nations*	INTERPOL*	INTERPOL**	WHO
Australia	1.68	3.43	N/A	1.92
Austria	2.44	2.44	1.32	1.77
Belgium	3.27	3.27	N/A	1.66
Canada	2.51	6.37	2.67	2.32
Denmark	5.77	5.77	1.17	1.02
Germany	4.52	4.52	3.02	1.24
Finland	2.19	5.63	2.27	2.74
France	4.94	4.62	N/A	1.32
Greece	1.83	1.83	1.00	.94
Hong Kong	1.63	1.63	1.56	1.70
Hungary	3.72	3.72	1.90	2.61
Japan	1.47	1.47	.78	.94
Malta	.91	4.23	.91	.30
Netherlands	12.24	1.19	1.19	.95
New Zealand	1.24	2.57	1.67	1.18
Portugal	4.66	4.57	3.02	1.69

Country	United Nations*	INTERPOL*	INTERPOL**	WHO
Scotland	1.36	1.38	N/A	1.63
Singapore	2.73	2.73	2.53	2.73
Spain	2.09	2.12	N/A	1.18
Sweden	1.39	5.75	1.38	1.10
Switzerland	2.24	2.24	1.10	.93
Trinidad & Tobago	8.38	8.38	6.32	5.38
United States	7.89	7.89	N/A	8.23
Median	**2.436**	**3.433**	**1.556**	**1.632**
Mean	**3.525**	**3.814**	**1.99**	**1.979**

* Note: United Nations and INTERPOL data in these columns should include attempts.
** Note: INTERPOL data in this column should not include attempts.

Table B0.8. Homicide rates per 100,000 population in 1988

Country	United* Nations	United** Nations	INTERPOL*	INTERPOL**	WHO
Australia	1.93	N/A	4.47	2.26	2.39
Austria	1.80	.87	1.83	.87	1.22
Canada	5.31	2.08	5.45	2.23	1.88
Denmark	4.83	.97	5.17	1.33	1.11
Germany	4.14	2.27	4.14	1.32	1.07
Finland	6.19	2.43	.67	N/A	2.79
Greece	1.91	.94	1.75	.86	1.07
Hungary	3.81	1.97	3.81	1.97	2.71
Italy	4.95	2.22	2.18	N/A	1.86
Japan	1.18	.61	1.18	.63	.75
Norway	2.00	1.05	2.00	1.05	1.16
Portugal	4.59	3.03	4.67	3.11	1.39
Singapore	2.19	2.12	2.08	N/A	1.92
Sweden	7.22	1.73	7.24	1.74	1.39
Switzerland	2.26	1.20	2.26	1.20	1.21
Median	**3.811**	**1.852**	**2.26**	**1.321**	**1.387**
Mean	**3.621**	**1.677**	**3.259**	**1.547**	**1.596**

* Note: United Nations and INTERPOL data in these columns should include attempts.
** Note: United Nations and INTERPOL data in these columns should not include attempts.

Table B0.9. Homicide Rates per 100,000 Population in 1993

Country	United* Nations	United** Nations	INTERPOL*	INTERPOL**	WHO
Austria	2.29	1.00	2.30	1.01	1.33
Azerbaijan	8.26	6.52	8.26	6.52	41.44
Bulgaria	10.80	5.78	20.79	11.14	4.93
Canada	1.92	N/A	5.59	2.18	1.82
Croatia	9.33	4.56	9.33	4.56	4.77
Denmark	4.80	1.37	4.80	1.37	1.21
Estonia	21.62	18.59	21.62	18.59	25.77
Finland	8.25	2.57	.61	N/A	3.28
France	4.89	2.63	4.89	2.63	1.08
Greece	2.45	1.45	2.45	1.45	1.28
Hong Kong	1.32	1.22	1.55	1.45	1.23
Hungary	4.52	2.89	4.48	2.89	4.09
Israel	4.92	2.68	1.82	N/A	2.32
Japan	.99	.53	.99	.54	.65
Latvia	16.59	14.97	16.59	14.97	24.67
Malta	3.84	1.92	3.84	1.92	1.64
Mauritius	2.28	1.91	2.37	2.01	2.28
Norway	2.44	.90	2.53	.95	.97
Poland	3.02	2.35	3.02	N/A	2.70
Rep. of Korea	1.83	1.80	1.83	N/A	1.64
Russian Fed.	19.72	18.28	19.72	N/A	30.42
Singapore	2.02	2.02	2.02	N/A	1.88

Country	United* Nations	United** Nations	INTERPOL*	INTERPOL**	WHO
Slovenia	3.57	1.31	3.57	1.31	1.36
Sweden	8.75	1.98	8.77	2.02	1.30
Switzerland	2.51	1.50	2.51	1.50	1.59
Median	**3.836**	**2.001**	**3.566**	**2.005**	**1.817**
Mean	**6.116**	**4.197**	**6.25**	**4.158**	**6.626**

* Note: United Nations and INTERPOL data in these columns should include attempts.
** Note: United Nations and INTERPOL data in these columns should not include attempts.

CORRELATIONS

A. 1974 (Attempts should be included in the United Nations and INTERPOL Data)

	INTERPOL	UN	WHO
INTERPOL	1.00	– –	– –
UN	0.6409**	1.00	– –
WHO	0.793**	0.4176*	1.00

* $p < .05$ (two-tailed test)
** $p < .01$ (two-tailed test)

B. 1978 (Attempts should be included in the United Nations and INTERPOL Data)

	INTERPOL	UN	WHO
INTERPOL	1.00	– –	– –
UN	0.9479**	1.00	– –
WHO	0.9627**	0.943**	1.00

* $p < .05$ (two-tailed test)
** $p < .01$ (two-tailed test)

C. 1984 (Attempts should be included in the United Nations and INTERPOL Data)

	INTERPOL	UN	WHO
INTERPOL	1.00	– –	– –
UN	0.3304	1.00	– –
WHO	0.6445**	0.4297*	1.00

* $p < .05$ (two-tailed test)
** $p < .01$ (two-tailed test)

D. 1988 (Attempts should be included in the United Nations and INTERPOL Data)

	INTERPOL	UN	WHO
INTERPOL	1.00	– –	– –
UN	0.5628*	1.00	– –
WHO	-0.0033	0.3249	1.00

* $p < .05$ (two-tailed test)
** $p < .01$ (two-tailed test)

E. 1993 (Attempts should be included in the United Nations and INTERPOL Data)

	INTERPOL	UN	WHO
INTERPOL	1.00	– –	– –
UN	0.9051**	1.00	– –
WHO	0.6566**	0.7398**	1.00

* $p < .05$ (two-tailed test)
** $p < .01$ (two-tailed test)

F. 1978 (Attempts should be excluded from the INTERPOL Data)

	INTERPOL	WHO
INTERPOL	1.00	– –
WHO	0.5726*	1.00

* p < .05 (two-tailed test)
** p < .01 (two-tailed test)

G. 1984 (Attempts should be excluded from the INTERPOL Data)

	INTERPOL	WHO
INTERPOL	1.00	– –
WHO	0.8639**	1.00

* p < .05 (two-tailed test)
** p < .01 (two-tailed test)

H. 1988 (Attempts should be excluded from the United Nations and INTERPOL Data)

	INTERPOL	UN	WHO
INTERPOL	1.00	– –	– –
UN	0.9045**	1.00	– –
WHO	0.55	0.4643	1.00

* p < .05 (two-tailed test)
** p < .01 (two-tailed test)

I. 1993 (Attempts should be excluded from the United Nations and INTERPOL Data)

	INTERPOL	UN	WHO
INTERPOL	1.00	– –	– –
UN	0.971**	1.00	– –
WHO	0.6939**	0.7417**	1.00

* p < .05 (two-tailed test)
** p < .01 (two-tailed test)

Box 0.9 The International Crime Victim Survey (ICVS): another count of crime

NOTE 1

The working group was comprised of Jan van Dijk, Pat Mayhew and Martin Killias (Lausanne University, Switzerland). After the first round, the United Nations Interregional Crime and Justice Research Institute (UNICRI) in Rome expressed an interest in carrying out similar surveys in developing countries and countries in transition. Thereafter the working group reformed, consisting of Jan van Dijk (Ministry of Justice/University of Leiden, the Netherlands; overall co-ordinator), Pat Mayhew (Home Office, United Kingdom) and Ugljesa Zvekic and Anna Alvazzi del Frate of UNICRI.

The second ICVS took place in 1992/94, and the third in 1996/97. In industrialized countries, each country has met its own survey costs, although much of the administrative overheads of the ICVS programme has been borne by the Dutch Ministry of Justice, which also sponsored survey activities in almost all developing countries and countries in transition. Further financial assistance was provided by the Dutch Ministry of Foreign Affairs, the Home Office, UK, the Department of Justice Canada, the European Institute for Crime Prevention and Control, affiliated with the United Nations (HEUNI) and UNDP.

NOTE 2

The data from the surveys have been integrated and processed by John van Kesteren of the Criminological Institute, Faculty of Law of the University of Leiden in the Netherlands.

NOTE 3

Methodology of the survey is summarized in the following table.

Table B0.10. Overview of participation, methodology and languages used in the International Crime Victim Survey

First ICVS - 1989	Date	Sample	Urban	Rural	Method	Language
Industrialized countries						
Australia	1989	2,012	706	1,306	CATI	English
Belgium	1989	2,060	123	1,937	CATI	Frch/Flem
Canada	1989	2,074	968	1,106	CATI	Engl/Frch
England & Wales	1989	2,006	628	1,378	CATI	English
Finland	1989	1,025	222	803	CATI	Finnish
France	1989	1,502	347	1,155	CATI	French
Japan	1989	2,411			CATI	Japanese
Netherlands	1989	2,000	386	1,614	CATI	Dutch
Northern Ireland	1989	2,000		2,000	F/F	English
Norway	1989	1,009	145	864	CATI	Norwegian
Scotland	1989	2,007	484	1,523	CATI	English
Spain	1989	2,041	895	1,146	CATI-F/F	Spanish
Switzerland	1989	1,000	128	872	CATI	Frch/Ger.
USA	1989	1,996	390	1,606	CATI	English
(West) Germany	1989	5,274	1,523	3,751	CATI	German
Developing countries						
Indonesia (Surabaya)	1989	600		600	F/F	Bah. Indon.
Countries in transition						
Poland (Warsaw)	1989	500		500	F/F	Polish

Second ICVS - 1992	Date	Sample	Urban	Rural	Method	Language
Industrialized countries						
Australia	1992	2,006	1,471	535	CATI	English
Belgium	1992	1,485	242	1,243	CATI	Frch, Flemish
Canada	1992	2,152	683	1,469	CATI	Eng., French
England & Wales	1992	2,001	496	1,505	CATI	English
Finland	1992	1,655	420	1,235	CATI	Finnish
Italy	1992	2,024	550	1,474	CATI	Italian
Netherlands	1992	2,000	409	1,591	CATI	Dutch
New Zealand	1992	2,048	557	1,491	CATI	English
Spain (Malaga)	1993	1,634	842	792	CATI+F/F	Spanish
Spain (Malaga)	1994	1,505	920	585	CATI	Spanish
Sweden	1992	1,707	327	1,380	CATI	Swedish
USA	1992	1,501	354	1,147	CATI	English
Developing countries						
Argentina (Buenos Aires)	1992	1,000	1,000		F/F	Spanish
Brazil (Rio de J.)	1992	1,017	1,017		F/F	Port.
China (Beijing)	1994	2,000	2,000		F/F	Chinese
Costa Rica	1992	983	707	276	F/F	Spanish
Egypt (Cairo)	1992	1,000	1,000		F/F	Arabic
India (Bombay)	1992	1,040	1,040		F/F	Eng/Hind
Indonesia	1992	3,239	2,139	1,100	F/F	Bah.Ind.
Papua New G.*	1992	1,583	1,010	573	F/F	English (Orally translated into Pidgin, Motu or Tokples)
Philippines (Manila)	1992	1,503	1,503		F/F	Eng/Filip.
South Africa (Johannesburg)	1993	988	988		F/F	Eng/Afrik.
Tanzania (Dar Es Salaam)	1992	1,004	1,004		F/F	Swahili
Tunisia (Tunis)	1993	1,087	1,087		F/F	Arabic
Uganda (Kampala)	1992	1,023	1,023		F/F	Eng/Luga.
Countries in transition						
Czechoslovakia: Czech **	1992	1,262	237	1,025	F/F	Czech/Slovak
Czechoslovakia: Slovak **	1992	508	21	487	F/F	Czech/Slovak

Second ICVS - 1992	Date	Sample	Urban	Rural	Method	Language
Estonia	1993	1,000	457	543	F/F	Estonian
Georgia	1992	1,395			F/F	Russian
Poland	1992	2,033	666	1,367	F/F	Polish
Russia (Moscow)	1992	1,002	1,002		F/F	Russian
Slovenia (Ljubljana)	1992	1,000	1,000		CATI/CAPI***	Sloven.

* Data set not available
** Sample from the survey carried out in the former Czechoslovakia was broken down into Czech and Slovak
*** Computer assisted personal interview

Third ICVS - 1996/97	Date	Sample	Urban	Rural	Method	Language
Industrialized countries						
England & Wales	1996	2,171	559	1612	CATI	English
Scotland	1996	2,194	353	1841	CATI	English
Northern Ireland	1996	1,042	262	780	F/F	English
Netherlands	1996	2,008	434	1574	CATI	Dutch
Switzerland	1996	1,000	110	890	CATI	Frch/Ger
France	1996	1,003	199	804	CATI	French
Finland	1996	3,830	977	2853	CATI	Finnish
Sweden	1996	1,000	234	766	CATI	Swedish
Austria	1996	1,507	433	1074	CATI	German
USA	1996	1,003	193	810	CATI	English
Canada	1996	2,134	702	1432	CATI	Eng/Frch
Malta	1997	999	543	456	F/F	Maltese
Developing countries						
Argentina (Buenos Aires)	1996	1,000	1,000		F/F	Spanish
Bolivia (La Paz)	1996	999	999		F/F	Spanish
Botswana (Gaborone)	1997	644	644		F/F	English/ Steswana
Brazil (Rio de Janeiro)	1996	1,000	1,000		F/F	Port.
Colombia (Bogota)	1997	1,000	1,000		F/F	Spanish
Costa Rica	1996	1,000	701	299	F/F	Spanish
India (Bombay)	1996	1,200	999	201	F/F	Eng/Hindi
Indonesia (Jak., Surab.)	1996	1,400	1,200	200	F/F	Bah. Ind.
Paraguay	1996	587	587		F/F	Spanish

Third ICVS - 1996/97	Date	Sample	Urban	Rural	Method	Language
South Africa (Johannesburg)	1996	1,006	1,006		F/F	Eng/Afrikaans
The Philippines (Manila)	1996	1,500	1,250	250	F/F	Eng/Filipino
Uganda (Kampala)	1996	1,197	997	200	F/F	Eng/Luganda
Zimbabwe (Harare)	1996	1,006	1,006		F/F	English/Shona
Countries in transition						
Albania (Tirana)	1996	1,200	983	217	F/F	Albanese
Belarus (Minsk)	1997	999	999		F/F	Belorussian/ Russian
Bulgaria (Sofia)	1997	1,076	1,076		F/F	Bulgarian
Croatia (Zagreb)	1997	994	994		F/F	Croatian
Czech Republic	1996	1,801	717	1,084	F/F	Czech
Estonia	1995	1,173	364	809	F/F	Russian/ Estonian
Georgia	1996	1,137	567	570	F/F	Russian
Hungary (Budapest)	1996	756	756		F/F	Hungarian
Kyrgyzstan	1996	1,750	1,494	256	F/F	Kyrgyz/ Russian/Uzbeck
Latvia	1996	1,411	1,011	400	F/F	Lat./Russ.
Lithuania	1997	1,176	656	520	F/F	Lith./Russ.
*"FYRM" (Skopje)	1996	700	700		F/F	Macedonian
Mongolia (Ulan Baatar)	1996	1,200	1,053	147	F/F	Mongolian
Poland	1996	3,483	2,410	1,073	F/F	Polish
Romania (Bucharest)	1996	1,091	1,000	91	F/F	Romanian
Russia (Moscow)	1996	1,018	1,018		F/F	Russian
Slovakia (Bratislava)	1997	1,105	1,105		F/F	Slovak
Slovenia (Ljubljana)	1997	2,053	1,107	946	CATI	Slovenian
Ukraine (Kiev)	1997	1,000	1,000		F/F	Ukr./Russ.
Yugoslavia (Belgrade)	1996	1,094	1,094		F/F	Serbian

*"The Former Yugoslav Republic of Macedonia"

Chapter 1. The experience of crime and justice

Box 1.3. The threshold of violence: a comparative study of the US and Japan

Table B1.1. Threat scenarios by response by country in percent

	I. Threat outside		II. Breaks in		III. Knife threat		IV. Grabs girl	
Response	US	Japan	US	Japan	US	Japan	US	Japan
Leave	1.6	5.1	14	15.3	2.1	9.2	.5	3.2
Obey	0	0	0	0	2.8	1.2	.2	.3
Call neighbor	4.3	2.1	3	1.3	7.2	9.7	1.9	2.8
Call police	.5	5.1	.7	6.8	1.9	7.1	.9	5.1
Ask to stop	91.8	80	45	63.3	24.9	48.5	11.9	25.7
Yell profanity	.7	5.9	.2	2.4	0	4.1	0	1.9
Threaten	.2	.3	11.7	3.5	11.2	5.1	4.2	5.6
Hit	.5	1.1	6.7	5.2	8.4	3.7	.22	19.8
Use weapon	.5	.2	18.8	2.2	41.5	11.3	58.3	35.5

Table B1.2. Difference of means test escalating scenes

Scene	Mean	Median	Mode	t	Sig.
1 Threat outside					
US	4.05	4	4	.984	.325
Japan	4.00	4	4		
2 Offender breaks in					
US	5.17	4	4	9.823	.000
Japan	3.96	4	4		
3 Offender threatens					
US	6.68	7	9	15.131	.000
Japan	4.68	4	4		
4 Grabs daughter					
US	7.91	9	9	9.480	.000
Japan	6.65	8	9		

Table B1.3. Outside the home threats and response

Response	Yells Threats Percent	Pushes/shoves Percent	Threat-Weapon Percent
1 Do nothing			
US	2.9	0.2	8.4
Japan	3.8	2.9	3.5
2 Walk away			
US	74.4	49.9	27.9
Japan	32.7	12.7	11.8
3 Stare down			
US	3.9	2.3	2.1
Japan	14.0	13.3	4.2
4 Get police			
US	8.8	20.0	47.2
Japan	7.6	13.6	45.8
5 Talk back			
US	9.2	8.6	4.2
Japan	40.4	46.5	24.7
6 Shove/hit			
US	0.5	16.5	2.3
Japan	1.6	10.8	5.2
7 Threaten w/ weapon			
US	0	1.2	2.1
Japan	0	0.1	2.0
8 Use weapon			
US	0.2	1.4	5.8
Japan	0	0.1	2.8

$X^2 = 236.971$, p<.000 $X^2 = 359.855$, p<.000 $X^2 = 141.279$, p<.000

Table B1.4. Impact of weapon ownership on response to threats

Stranger Pushes/shoves	US Own	US Not Own	Japan Own	Japan Not Own
Retreat reaction	78 (44.8%)	146 (57.3%)	10 (38.5%)	245 (28.7%)
Get police	33 (19.0%)	53 (20.8%)	3 (11.5%)	117 (13.7%)
Talk back	14 (8.0%)	23 (9.0%)	7 (26.9%)	402 (47.0%)
Physical response	49 (28.2%)	33 (12.9%)	6 (23.1%)	91 (10.6%)
	174	255	26	855

$X^2 = 15.877$, p<.001 $X^2 = 6.661$, p<.084

Chapter 2. Police records of crime

Box 2.2 Definitions of recorded crime used in the 5th United Nations Survey of Crime Trends and Operations of Criminal Justice Systems

Definitions taken from the instructions which are part of the questionnaire of the 5th UNCJS.

Box 2.8 Comparing crime in urban and rural areas: problems and an illustration

NOTE 1

The category "crime per 1,000 population" refers to all crimes reported to the police. The respondents (in this case national statistical authorities) were asked to provide the total number of all crimes reported to the police and further to break this figure down into six general categories (against life and limb, property, economy, public traffic, sexual integrity and drug related). In some cases these breakdowns were provided, but in others only the total number of crime was reported to us. For additional details the reader is referred to Table 21 in the *Compendium of Human Settlements Statistics 1995* (United Nations, 1997).

Table B2.1. All crimes reported to the police, per 1,000 pop.

	Urban	Rural
El Salvador	5	2
Cyprus	6	4
Russian Fed.	8	8
Ukraine	9	5
Lithuania	13	10
Latvia	14	19
Bulgaria	24	16
Ireland	32	20
Hungary	52	27
Norway	70	106
Poland	92	9
Netherlands	99	44
Finland	185	125
Sweden	381	92

Table B2.2. Property crime and violent crime reported to police, per 1,000 pop.

	Property crime Urban	Property crime Rural	Violent crime Urban	Violent crime Rural
El Salvador, 1989	2.2	1.7	1.2	0.9
Cyprus, 1990	5.1	2.8	0.2	0.2
Bulgaria, 1991	22.2	13.1	0.2	0.2
Finland, 1989	57.9	22.9	6.3	3.3
Hungary, 1991	43.1	20.2	1.1	1.0
Ireland, 1991	12.7	10.2	0.3	0.3
Lithuania, 1991	10.5	7.1	0.2	0.3
Netherlands, 1990	84.2	34.5	2.7	1.1
Norway, 1991	42.0	52.6	2.2	3.1
Poland, 1990	27.6	6.8	0.5	0.3
Sweden, 1991	296.9	69.7	13.4	3.3

Box 2.10 Self-report surveys of offending

NOTE 1

Results now becoming available for various countries show that very high rates of offending are not unusual. However, direct comparison between different countries for these surveys can be misleading because of the lack of common methodology in the conducting of the surveys.

Box 2.11 Measuring organized crime in Europe

NOTE 1

Comparative data on crime is not only available from the UN, but more and more from groupings of countries which come together for a common purpose (e.g., security, culture or economic advancement).

Box 2.12 Measuring organized crime in Italy

NOTE 1

The Sicilian Mafia. Originating in the local management of the huge estates of the landed nobility in the feudal Sicily of the 19th century, the Mafia subsequently developed as a new social category and a structured criminal organization after the abolition of feudal privileges in 1812 (Marongiu and Newman, 1987: 127-128).

In the last decades the Mafia has progressively moved from its traditional rural context and activities to the city (particularly Palermo, the capital of Sicily), always adapting itself to the evolution and modification of political and economic power and following the creation and development of new and more profitable criminal opportunities to accumulate wealth, power and status. Among the fields of operation that promise a fast profit now are international drug trafficking, extortion, ordinary and political corruption, illegal property (real estate) speculation, and illegal contracting for state-sponsored public works (such as public buildings, bridges, highways etc.).

Using illegal profits for legal investments is common in all Italian criminal organizations, and the Mafia shows great flexibility in shifting from one sector to another, always being inclined to use its typical criminal methods (violence and intimidation) even when running a legal business.

Although the Mafia displays such a differentiation in activities in time and place, some essential features of its structure, mentality and prescribed style of behavior remain basically constant. These features essentially are:

a) ethnic homogeneity (almost all members are Sicilians, with very few recent exceptions, due to important business reasons);

b) secret, esoteric initiation and rigid division among the various hierarchical and operative components of the organization;

c) pyramidal structure with strict and widespread control of the areas of influence and their resources;

d) deep rootedness in the Sicilian society; and

e) systematic interference and infiltration in the political system (both at regional and national level).

The basic unit of Cosa Nostra has always been and still is the "famiglia" (family), whose structure is either biological or associative. More territorially adjacent families constitute a "mandamento." The chiefs of the "mandamenti" on a provincial basis (the Sicilian region is administratively divided into nine provinces) are members of the " commissione provinciale" (provincial commission). The chiefs of the provincial commissions form the "commissione regionale" (regional commission).

The Mafia, therefore, appears to be a sort of parallel illegal state, with its own legal system and territory which is carefully controlled and divided into districts.

Each family is formally independent and free to operate in its area of influence, except for important questions of common interest (such as the assassination of prominent government officials) that are decided by the pertinent commission.

Recent history and development. From the mid 1970s on the progressive conversion of the traditional Mafia activities into the more remunerative drug business led to a ferocious conflict between families, responsible for hundreds of killings and eventually resulting in the supremacy of the Corleone family (from the rural town of Corleone, not far from Palermo).

The rise of the corleonesi involved some deprivation of power and authority of the commissioni, many important decisions being made by the dominant group. The aggressive policy of the corleonesi (also due to the necessity of accumulating a large amount of capital to support the international drug trafficking) brought about an expansion of Mafia activities in other Italian regions (especially the richer areas of the north).

A distinctive feature of the corleonesi is the systematic use of extreme violence both to fight other families (to force them out of competition by physical destruction or subjugation) and to limit the interference of criminal justice officials in Mafia affairs. The resort to terrorist-like strategies, such as making use of high potential explosives, has been recurrent in recent years, as in the spectacular 1992 bombings which led to the death of Giovanni Falcone and Paolo Borsellino, two important judges who were beginning to get results in a series of investigations on Mafia crime.

This situation produced a counteraction from the state (as well as a growing protest from large sectors of the Italian public and institutions, such as the Roman Catholic Church) leading to the successful trial and conviction of many important Mafia leaders, who have been fugitives (though often hiding in Palermo) for many years. The most important of these operations has been the arrest (on January 15, 1993), prosecution and conviction (life sentence) of the "boss of all bosses" (capo di tutti i capi) Toto' Riina, absolute leader of the Corleone family. Very recently (June 1997) Toto' Riina's underboss, Pietro Aglieri, allegedly in charge after Riina's capture, was apprehended.

The success of the state intervention against the Mafia is undoubtedly, at least in part, due to the widespread utilization both in the investigation and prosecution stages of the so-called "collaboratori di giustizia" (collaborators of justice), who are former members of the Mafia that agree to cooperate with the authorities by producing useful evidence in order to fight the organization. This, in turn, had the effect of increasing Mafia secrecy in recruitment and operations to reduce the risks of detection and apprehension. Violence to eliminate or intimidate witnesses and opponents has also been increased.

The current position of relative weakness of the Mafia is also revealed by the rise of new criminal organizations in the Sicilian territory, such as the Stidda, whose members were expelled from Cosa Nostra. The Sicilian Mafia also has to meet the competition of the other growing Italian criminal organizations (Camorra, 'Ndrangheta and Sacra Corona Unita).

The Camorra. A centuries old organization (with secret, esoteric initiation) that presumably originated as a self-help association of the convicts inside the Neapolitan prisons and subsequently developed as an important criminal organization (almost as powerful as the Sicilian Mafia), with the creation in the 1970s of the Nuova Camorra Organizzata, founded by "Don" Raffaele Cutolo. Under Cutolo's leadership the Nuova Camorra utilized the prison as a favorable place for criminal recruitment and as the organization's headquarters, expanding its influence over all the Campania region.

The traditional source of the Camorra income has been the extensive use of extortion at business enterprises' expense. In turn a number of businessmen, especially building contractors, took advantage of their relationship with the Camorra, obtaining cheap labor, control of the unions, forced collection of credit, etc. In the 1980s, the Camorra almost monopolized illegal contracting for state-sponsored public works for reconstruction, making huge amounts of money. Illegal gains are utilized to finance other criminal activities such as loan-sharking, prostitution rings, cigarette smuggling, etc., and to support the families of the members of the organization who are in prison. Systematic infiltration in local administration through corruption and control of the voters to facilitate illegal activities in the territory has also been extensive. After Raffaele Cutolo's sentence to life imprisonment, the Nuova Camorra Organizzata has shown a progressive decline, partly due to the state intervention and thousands of arrests (also using the information provided by the "collaborators of justice") and partly due to the rise of a competing criminal organization, the Nuova Famiglia, whose leaders were also associated with Cosa Nostra. A clear sign of the Sicilian influence on the Camorra is the strong involvement in the international drug trafficking, previously abhorred by Cutolo.

The current situation of the Camorra is characterized by relative weakness and dispersion also due to a strong competition among many groups which constantly struggle (especially in the metropolitan area of Naples) for the control of relatively small portions of the territory.

The 'Ndrangheta. The basic unit of this criminal organization, which controls large portions of the territory in Calabria, is the "locale," a village clan consisting of an extended patriarchal family whose succession in terms of leadership and distribution of power is patrilinear, thus reducing the likelihood of defections which might result in cooperation with the authorities (collaboratori di giustizia). The affiliation is, like in the Sicilian Mafia and the Camorra, also secret and esoteric. Given the large dimensions of the clans and the small size of most territorial administrative jurisdictions in Calabria, they are easily infiltrated by the 'Ndrangheta. As a result, many local officials in Calabria (but also in Sicily and Campania) were under investigation and a number of city councils and other local administrations have been dismissed.

Each "locale" is distinctly independent from the others. The 'Ndrangheta as a whole can be seen as a federation of autonomous clans. Recently, the creation of a central structure above the clans has been made necessary by the current situation of constant ferocious conflict among them. (The common resort to extreme violence is a distinctive feature of the 'Ndrangheta, as shown by the great numbers of killings of opponents, including police officers and magistrates.) According to law enforcement officials, this would have led to a relative weakening of the organization.

A traditional criminal activity of this organization has been and (to an increasingly minor extent) still is ransom kidnapping, given the control of the clans over the rural territory of internal Calabria (where there is an established practice of illegal intermediation in farm labor). In ransom kidnapping, hostages were seized in many Italian regions (especially from the north) but almost always held in this area, hundreds of miles away from the place of capture. Like the other main Italian criminal organizations in recent times, the 'Ndrangheta has been deeply involved in the international drug business, showing a greater mobility in comparison with both Mafia and Camorra and expanding its activities in other countries (even in Australia), nevertheless keeping regular contacts with the original clans in Calabria. By investing a large amount of illegal capital in legal business, the 'Ndrangheta is also in a position of great advantage in comparison with any other legitimate business in the area; there is no need to resort to bank credit (not to mention the classic intimidation methods commonly utilized to force out the competition). Recent developments of the 'Ndrangheta show an increasing connection with a number of illegal Masonic lodges (whose members not infrequently turned out to be prominent bosses of the organization) in order to take advantage of the Masonic network to infiltrate all levels of the public administration.

The Sacra Corona Unita. There are several independent criminal organizations on an ethnic basis in Puglia, all of recent origin (less than 20 years old), the Sacra Corona Unita being the first and most important of them. It was created in the late 1970s on the model of the Neapolitan Camorra. Raffaele Cutolo at that time, indeed, made an attempt to expand his influence in Puglia by creating the Nuova Camorra Pugliese. The Sacra Corona Unita is a centralized structure with its own secret, esoteric initiation rites, a collective body (consisting of the most important members) and hierarchical decision making. The iconography of the organization in fact shows a crown (corona) representing a circle of affiliates circumscribing a cup (representing the top commanding unit).

Following the model of the Sacra Corona Unita, other independent criminal organizations were subsequently created in the same region. They are the Sacra Corona Autonoma, the Rosa dei Venti, the Remo Lecce Libera, and the Nuova Famiglia Salentina.

The preferred fields of criminal operation of all criminal organizations in Puglia are largescale international drug and military weapons trafficking. This has been facilitated by establishing organic links with the Montenegrin (Yugoslav) underworld, which has become increasingly influential and aggressive, especially after the recent collapsing of the Yugoslav State.

NOTE 2

Additional sources are as follows:

General headquarters of the Carabinieri Force. Annual reports on carabinieris' operational activities. Years 1992, 1993, 1994, 1995, 1996. Rome, 1993, 1994, 1995, 1996, 1997. (Comando Generale dell'Arma dei Carabinieri, resoconti annuali, in "Attivita' Operativa dell'Arma dei Carabinieri." Anni 1992, 1993, 1994, 1995, 1996. Roma, 1993, 1994, 1995, 1996, 1997.)

General headquarters of the Finance Guard. "Guardia di Finanza" (annual reports). Years 1993, 1995, 1996. Rome, 1994, 1996, 1997. (Comando Generale della Guardia di Finanza, resoconti annuali, in "Guardia di Finanza." Anni 1993, 1995, 1996. Roma, 1994, 1996, 1997.)

Marongiu, Pietro and Mario Biddau. 1996. *The World Factbook of Criminal Justice Systems.* Italy: Bureau of Justice Statistics. Web site http://www.ojp.usdoj.gov/bjs/abstract/wfcj.htm.

Marongiu, Pietro and Graeme Newman. 1987. *Vengeance: The Fight Against Injustice.* Totowa, NJ: Rowman and Littlefield.

Ministry of the Interior, Police Department. "State Police" (annual reports). Years 1993-1997. Rome, 1993-1997. (Ministero degli Interni, Dipartimento della Pubblica Sicurezza , resoconti annuali, in "Polizia di Stato." Anni 1993-1997. Roma, 1993-1997.)

Official Gazette, April 24, 1993 n. 95. Government's Decree, March 29, 1993 n. 119. (Decreto Legge 28 marzo 1993 n.119, in Gazzetta Ufficiale, 24 aprile 1993 n. 95.)

Official Gazette, August 7, 1992, n. 185. Statute Law August 7, 1992 n. 365. (Legge 7 agosto 1992, n. 365, in Gazzetta Ufficiale, n. 185.)

Official Gazette, December 17, 1994 n. 294. Government's Decree, November 24, 1994 n. 687. (Decreto Legge 24 Novembre 1994 n. 687, in Gazzetta Ufficiale, 17 dicembre 1994 n. 294.)

Official Gazette, January 15, 1991, n. 12. Government's Decree, January 15, 1991 n.8. (Decreto Legge 15 gennaio 1991 n. 8, in Gazzetta Ufficiale, 15 gennaio 1991 n. 12.)

Official Gazette, January 20, 1992 n. 15. Statute Law, Januaty 20, 1992 n. 8. (Legge 20 gennaio 1992 n. 8, in Gazzetta Ufficiale, 20 gennaio 1992 n. 15.)

Official Gazette, June 5, 1965 n. 138. Statute Law (with subsequent modifications), May 31, 1965 n. 575. (Legge 31 maggio 1965, con successive modificazioni, in Gazzetta Ufficiale, 5 giugno 1965 n. 138.)

Official Gazette, May 13, 1991 n. 110. Government's Decree, May 13, 1991 n. 152. (Decreto Legge 13 maggio 1991 n. 152, in Gazzetta Ufficiale, 13 Maggio 1991 n. 110.)

Per Aspera ad Veritatem: J*ournal of Intelligence and Professional Culture*, n. 1 (supplement), January-April 1995, Proceedings of the 1st European Seminar "Falcon One" on organized crime, Rome, April 26-28, 1995. (Atti del Primo Seminario Europeo "Falcon One" sulla Criminalita' Organizzata, Roma 26-28 Aprile 1995. In Per Aspera ad Veritatem: Rivista di Intelligence e Cultura professionale, n.1 (supplemento), gennaio-aprile 1995.)

Superior Council of the Judiciary: proceedings of the meeting on "The crimes of criminal organizations: criminological, juridical and procedural profiles." Unpublished paper. (Consiglio Superiore della Magistratura: Atti dell' Incontro di Studio sul tema "I delitti di criminalita' organizzata: profili criminologici, sostanziali e processuali." Frascati (Rome), May 13-17, 1996.)

Box 2.13 Offences allegedly committed by members of the Aum Shinrikyo cult

NOTE 1

This box gives another example of the difficulties in measuring organized crime, even when it is very much in the public eye.

Chapter 3. Bringing to justice

Box 3.4 Age of criminal responsibility around the world

Table B3.1. Minimum age of criminal responsibility around the world

Country	Minimum age	Age of full adult responsibility
Albania[1] (#1)	14	18 (#2)
Armenia (#2)	16 (14)[2]	18
Australia[3] (#1)	7[4]	16
Austria (#3)	14	20[5]
Azerbaijan (#2)	16 (14)[6]	18
Bahamas (#3)	7	18
Belarus (#2)	16 (14)[7]	18
Belgium (#2)	18 (16)[8]	18
Bermuda (#3)	under 16	16 and over
Bolivia (#3)	15	21
Bulgaria (#1, #2, #3)	14[9]	18
Canada (#1, #2, #3)	12	18
Chile (#3)	under 18	18 or over
China (#1)	under age 16[10]	over age 16 [11]
Colombia (#3)	under 18	18 or over
Costa Rica (#1)	12[12]	18
Croatia (#3)	14	18
Cyprus (#3)[13]	under 17	17 or over
Czech Republic (#2)	15	18
Denmark (#3)	15	18
Ecuador (#3)	under 18	18 and over
Egypt (#3)	under 18	18 and over
England & Wales (#1)	10[14]	18
Estonia (#2, #3)	13[15]	18
Finland (#3)	14[16]	21

Country	Minimum age	Age of full adult responsibility
France (#3)	13	19[17]
Georgia (#3)	14	18
Germany (#1, #2)	14	18[18]
Ghana (#1)	under 18	18 and over
Greece (#3)[19]	under 17	17 and over
Hong Kong (#3)	7	21
Hungary (#2, #3)	14	18
Iceland (#2)	15	18
India (#3)[20]	under 16[21]	16 and older[22]
Indonesia (#3)	under 21[23]	21 and over[24]
Ireland (#2)	7 (14)[25]	18[26]
Northern Ireland (#1)	under 17[27]	17 and over
Israel (#2)	12	18
Italy (#1, #2)[28]	14	18
Jamaica (#2)	12	18
Japan (#3)	14	20[29]
Jordan (#3)	under 18	18 and over
Kazakhstan (#2)	16 (14)[30]	18
Kenya (#1)	7	18
Kyrgystan (#2)	16 (14)[31]	18
Latvia (#2, #3)	16 (14)[32]	18
Liechtenstein (#3)	14	19
Lithuania (#2, #3)	16 (14)[33]	18
Former Yug. Rep. Maced. (#2)	14	18
Madagascar (#3)	under 18	18 and over
Malta (#1, #2)	9 (14)[34]	18
Mauritius (#3)	under 18	18 and over
Micronesia (#1)	under 16[35]	16 and over
Moldova (#2)	16 (14)[36]	18
Morocco (#3)	under 16	16 and over
Netherlands (#1, #2)	12	18[37]
New Zealand (#1)	10[38]	18
Nicaragua (#3)	under 16	16 and over
Nigeria (#1)	7[39]	17
Norway (#2)	15	18
Papua New Guinea (#1)	7[40]	18
Peru (#3)	under 18	18 and over
Poland (#2)	17 (16)	18
Portugal (#2)	16	20
Qatar (#3)	under 18	18 and over
Republic of Korea (#1, #3)	14	20[41]
Romania (#1, #2, #3)	14[42]	18
Russian Fed. (#1, #2, #3)	16 (14)[43]	18
Saint V. & the G. (#3)	8	15
Western Samoa (#3)	under 18	18 and over
Sao Tome & Principie (#3)	16	18
Scotland (#2)	8 (16)[44]	21
Singapore (#1)	7[45]	17
Slovakia (#2, #3)	15	18
Slovenia (#1, #2)	14	18[46]
Spain (#1, #2)	16	18[47]
Sri Lanka (#1)	6[48]	17
Sudan (#3)	under 18	18 and over
Sweden (#1, #3)	15	21[49]
Switzerland (#2)	7 (15)[50]	18
Syria (#3)	under 18	18 and over
Tajikistan (#2)	16 (14)[51]	18
Turkey (#2)	11	18
Ukraine (#1, #2)	16 (14)[52]	18
USA (#3)	under 18	18 and over
Uruguay (#3)	under 18	18 and over
Venezuela (#1)	under 18	18 and over
Yugoslavia (#3)	14	18
Zambia (#3)	under 18	18 and over

[1]All information listed in this table was obtained from the following sources: *International Factbook of Criminal Justice Systems* (1996, herein #1); Kangaspunta, Kristiina (Ed.) (1995). *Crime and Criminal Justice in Europe and North America*. Helsinki, Finland: European Institute for Crime Prevention and Control (herein #2); 5th UNCJS(herein #3).

[2]For serious crimes such as homicide, rape, theft and intentional grievous bodily injury, the minimum age is 14.

[3]The ages vary according to the individual states and territories of Australia (#1).

[4]In all jurisdictions any child above the age of criminal responsibility who is charged with homicide can be tried in adult court (#1).

[5]However, #2 states that the age of full adult responsibility is 19.

[6]See F.N. 2 (#2).

[7]See F.N. 2 (#2).

[8]The age limit may be lowered to 16 in some cases where specific juvenile measures are deemed inadequate (#2).

[9]Only if the juvenile was able to understand the nature of his/her act and govern his/her own behavior (#1).

[10]The age of responsibility is 16; under age 16, an offender is not punished, but the head of the family or guardian is ordered to subject the offender to discipline. However, an offender aged 14-16 who commits homicide, infliction of serious bodily injury, robbery, arson, habitual theft or any other crime which seriously undermines the social order bears full criminal responsibility but the severity of punishment is lighter or mitigated (#1).

[11]However, the death penalty may not be imposed on a person under 18 (#1).

[12]Under age 12, the offender is not sent to a juvenile facility; rather, no punitive action is taken and he/she is referred to social agencies (#1).

[13]#2 states that the minimum age is 12 and that the age of full adult responsibility is 16.

[14]#2 states that the age is 10 only if it is shown that in the circumstances of the case the offender is capable of distinguishing right from wrong; otherwise, the age is 14.

[15]It varies by year but ages 13 to 17 is the widest range (#3).

[16]However, #1 and #2 list the minimum age as 15 and the adult age as 18.

[17]However, #2 lists the adult age as 18.

[18]Young adults aged 18-21 upon mitigating circumstances may be dealt with by a juvenile court and institutionalized in a juvenile facility until age 25 (#1).

[19]However, #2 states that the minimum age is 12 and the adult age is 18.

[20]However, #1 states that the age of criminal responsibility is age 7. But, any child 7-12 who would otherwise be criminally liable is free from liability if it is proved that the child had not attained sufficient maturity of understanding to judge the nature and consequences of his/her conduct on the occasion in question. In addition, courts exist for handling juvenile delinquency. Under certain circumstances a person under 21 who is convicted of an offense punishable by a fine or with imprisonment for 7 years or less may be released on probation.

[21]Under 16 is for males, for females it is under 18 (#3).

[22]For females it is 18 and older (#3).

[23]And unmarried (#3).

[24]Or any married person (#3).

[25]A child between 7-14 is presumed not to have reached the age of discretion. But this assumption is rebuttable (#2).

[26]But #1 states that full criminal responsibility is reached at age 14.

[27]However, #2 states that the minimum age is 10.

[28]However, #3 states that minimum age is under 18 while the adult age is 18 and over.

[29]The death penalty may not be imposed on a juvenile below age 18 (#1).

[30]See F.N. 2 (#2).

[31]See F.N. 2 (#2).

[32]See F.N. 2 (#2).

[33]See F.N. 2 (#2, #3).

[34]Between ages 9-14 a person is presumed to be incapable of forming malicious intent but criminal responsibility may be established if it is proved that the person acted with mischievous discretion (#1).

[35]The age varies by regions. In some regions the minimum age is under 18 and the age of full responsibility is 18 and over (#1).

[36]See F.N. 2.

[37]However, judicial discretion may be exercised when taking into account the seriousness of the offense and the personality of the offender. For example a judge can order a person aged 16-18 to be dealt with under adult criminal law. Similarly judicial discretion will allow a young adult offender 18-21 to be subject to juvenile criminal law (#1).

[38]However, children under 14 are rarely prosecuted (#1).

[39]7-11 are considered children, 12-16 are considered juveniles. Offenses

of both children and juveniles are handled by juvenile courts (#1).

[40]There is a presumption that a child 7-14 is not capable of committing an offense unless it can be proved that the child knew he/she was doing wrong (#1).

[41]Individuals under 18 may not be sentenced to capital punishment or life imprisonment (#1).

[42]One can only be criminally responsible ages 14-16 if it is proved one committed the offense deliberately (#1). However, #2 states that between ages 14-16 the judge must establish whether the minor has reached a sufficient age of maturity to be considered responsible for his/her action.

[43]See F.N. 2 (#1, #2).

[44]Criminal prosecution of an offender aged 8-16 can only proceed with the consent of the Lord Advocate (#2). However, children under 16 are rarely prosecuted (#1).

[45]However, a child 7-12 who in view of the judge does not have sufficient understanding is exempt from criminal responsibility (#1).

[46]Juveniles 18-21 have full criminal responsibility, but depending on the circumstances educational measures may be used instead of punishment (#1). However, #3 lists the age of full responsibility as 19.

[47]However #3 states that under 16 is a juvenile offender while 16 and over is an adult offender.

[48]Children 6-12 are not punished unless the magistrate finds they have sufficient maturity (#1).

[49]However, #2 lists the age of full adult responsibility as 18.

[50]Children aged 7-14 are brought before special authorities which are similar to child welfare offices while minors aged 15-17 are subject to juvenile criminal justice authorities (#2).

[51]See F.N. 2 (#2).

[52]See F.N. 2 (#2).

Chapter 4. Punishment

Box 4.1. Foreigners in Dutch correctional facilities

Note 1

The following are the complete tabular data. See also Box 9.2 concerning illegal aliens for additional information.

Table B4.1. Individuals incarcerated by place of birth and year (by percentage)

	1990	1991	1992	1993	1994	1995
EUROPE	66	67	65	64	63	62
Netherlands	55	56	53	52	50	50
Germany	1	1	1	1	1	1
Turkey	5	4	5	6	5	5
AFRICA	8	10	10	11	12	13
Morocco	6	7	8	8	7	8
ASIA	5	4	4	4	4	4
Middle-East	1	1	1	2	2	2
S AMERICA	19	18	18	19	19	18
Surinam	11	11	11	11	11	10
Netherlands (Antilles)	5	5	5	6	6	6
OTHER AMERICA	0	1	1	1	1	1
UNKNOWN	2	1	2	0	1	1
Total	6,892	7,302	7,495	8,037	8,737	10,329

Source: Gevangenisstatistie1995; Centraal Bureau voor de Statistiek, 1996; Table 4.3; page 44.

Table B4.2. Incarcerated individuals by place of birth and age, 1995

	Total %	15-24 %	25-29 %	30-39 %	40 %
EUROPE	62	58	62	61	69
Netherlands	49	46	48	50	56
Germany	1	1	1	1	2
Turkey	5	5	6	5	4
AFRICA	14	20	16	11	6
Morocco	8	13	9	7	3
ASIA	4	3	4	4	5
Middle-East	2	2	2	3	1
SOUTH AMERICA	18	16	16	21	19
Surinam	10	8	9	12	13
Netherlands (Antilles)	6	7	6	7	4
OTHER AMERICA	1	1	1	1	1
UNKNOWN	1	1	1	1	0
Total	9,889	2,531	2,399	3,303	1,656

Source: Gevangenisstatistie1995; Centraal Bureau voor de Statistiek, 1996; Table 4.3; page 44.

Table B4.3. Incarcerated individuals by place of birth and offence, 1995

	N	Violent offences %	Property offences %	Destruction of property; public order offences %	Other serious offences %	Violations of traffic law %	Violations of opium law %	Other offences %	Unknown %
EUROPE	6,412	36	33	5	3	1	13	1	7
Netherlands	5,114	37	37	5	3	1	10	1	6
Germany	125	30	28	2	4	2	26	1	8
Turkey	521	42	10	4	7	0	31	1	5
AFRICA	1,387	27	27	4	2	0	10	1	29
Morocco	838	33	33	3	2	0	10	1	18
ASIA	408	28	23	7	2	0	14	1	25
Middle-East	198	25	27	8	1	1	11	-	28
SOUTH AMERICA	1,894	38	24	3	3	0	27	1	5
Surinam	1,073	38	26	3	3	0	23	1	5
Netherlands Antilles	661	43	23	2	2	0	25	1	4
OTHER AMERICA	131	18	16	4	3	1	40	-	18
UNKNOWN	97	18	11	4	5	-	2	1	59
Total	10,329	34	30	5	3	1	15	1	11

Source: Gevangenisstatistie1995; Centraal Bureau voor de Statistiek, 1996; Table 4.17; page 50.

Box 4.3 Fluctuations in prison rates in Central and Eastern Europe

Table B4.4. Prison rates in Central and Eastern Europe

Country	1985 rate per 100,000	1990 rate per 100,000	1995N	1995 rate per 100,000	Date on which 1995 data are based
Albania	30**	90**	3,177*	95*	1 Sep 1995
Belarus	310**	140**	52,033	505	1 Dec 1995
Bosnia-Herzeg.	n.a.	n.a.	6,761	85	30 Nov 1995
Bulgaria	170**	125**	9,684	110	1 Jan 1996
Croatia	75**	30**	2,572	55	1 Jan 1996
Czech Republic	270	80	19,508	190	1 Sep 1995
Estonia	455	220	4,034	270	1 Sep 1995
Hungary	220	120	12,455	120	1 Sep 1995
Latvia	640	320	9,608	375	1 Sep 1995
Lithuania	405	230	13,228	360	1 Sep 1995
a"FYRM"	n.a.	n.a.	1,278*	60*	1 Sep 1995
Moldova	520**	275**	10,363	275	1 Jan 1996
Poland	270	120	65,819	170	31 Aug 1995
Romania	260	110	45,309	200	31 Dec 1995
Russian Fed.	n.a.	470**	1,017,372	690	1 Jan 1996
Slovakia	225	70	7,979	150	1 Sep 1995
Slovenia	70	40	630	30	1 Sep 1995
Ukraine	340**	185**	203,988	600	1 Sep 1995

a"The Former Yugoslav Republic of Macedonia"
Source: Walmsley 1997, pp. 5 and 7.
*May be unreliable since they are inconsistent with information from other sources.
**Figures taken from the country reports in Walmsley 1997, and are approximate figures. For Ukraine, the first figure is for 1986.
Additional sources:
 Roy Walmsley: *Prison Systems in Central and Eastern Europe. Progress, problems and the international standards*. HEUNI publication no. 29, Helsinki 1996.
 Roy Walmsley: *Prison Populations in Europe and North America. Some Background Information*. HEUNI Paper no. 10, Helsinki 1997.

Box 4.10 Intermediate sanctions: electronic monitoring and house arrest

Sources used in preparation of this box:

Baumer, T., M. Maxfield and R. Mendelsohn. 1993. A comparative analysis of three electronically monitored home detention programs. *Justice Quarterly*, 10, 1: 121-142.

Byrne, J., A. Lurigio and J. Petersilia (Eds.). 1992. *Smart Sentencing: The Emergence of Intermediate Sanctions*. Newbury Park, CA: Sage Publications.

Fay-Stephen, J. 1993. The rise and fall of tagging as a criminal justice measure in Britain. *International Journal of the Sociology of Law*, 21, 4: 301-317.

Fay-Stephen, J. 1995. Electronically monitored justice: a consideration of recent evidence as to its effectiveness. *Anglo-American Law Review*, 24, 4: 397-425.

Figgis, H. 1996. *The Home Detention Bill 1996: Commentary and Background*. Sydney: New South Wales Parliamentary Library.

Latessa-Edward, J. and H.E. Allen. 1997. *Corrections in the Community*. Cincinnati, OH: Anderson Publishing Co.

Lilly, J.R. 1993. Electronic monitoring in the US: an update. *Overcrowded Times*, 4, 5: 4, 15.

Mair, G. 1993. Electronic monitoring in England and Wales. *Overcrowded Times*, 4, 5: 5, 12.

Northern Territory. 1990. *Criminal Law (Conditional Release of Offenders) Amendment Act*. N.T. Government Printing.

Roy, S. 1997. Five years of electronic monitoring of adults and juveniles in Lake County, Indiana: a comparative study on factors related to failure. *Journal of Crime and Justice*, 20, 1: 141-160.

Chapter 5. Resources in criminal justice

BOX 5.1 Informal customary justice in Nigeria

NOTE 1
Women have never been judges in either the formal or the informal customary criminal courts in Nigeria. The informal customary justice, until recently, has always been patriarchal. Today, a community of women can hold an informal court session to try another female offender, but this is an *ad hoc* customary court for women. However, they can impose penalties that are strictly enforced.

NOTE 2
Village chiefs who have the means, may construct two courts (Obis), with one located inside the walls of the compound and another outside the walls. The one surrounded by the walls of the compound is for settling family matters, and the one outside the walls, located close to the wall's exit gate, is for settling cases from the village and from outside the village.

NOTE 3
Under the customary law of the Ibos of Nigeria, every sexual intercourse outside the confines of marriage is rape. At the customary court, the rapist must marry his victim because no other man in Ibo culture will marry a woman he knows has been defiled by another man. It is the parents of the woman who sue for rape.

Box 5.2 Private police in emerging markets: a quiet revolution

NOTE 1
The US Department of Commerce lists 18 countries while others have expanded the list to include another eight countries. Emerging markets include: Argentina, Brazil, Brunei Darussalam, Chile, China, the Czech Republic, Greece, Hungary, Hong Kong, India, Indonesia, Israel, Malaysia, Mexico, the Philippines, Poland, Portugal, the Russian Federation, Singapore, South Africa, Thailand, Taiwan, Turkey, Venezuela and Vietnam.

NOTE 2
For example, the Security Guards Board for Greater Bombay and Thane District constituted under Section 6 (1) of the Maharastra Private Security Guards (Regulation of Employment and Welfare) Act of 1981.

NOTE 3
Research in Singapore (Nalla, Hoffman and Christian, 1996) and in India suggests that the relationship between private security and the police is very similar to conditions in the US (e.g., Nalla and Hummer, 1996). That is, police officers do not have a positive view of security guards. Part of the problem stems from inadequate guard training. Guards in Singapore and India overwhelmingly echoed the sentiments of security personnel in the US regarding the need for government-sponsored training. Respondents believed training would enhance the professionalism of the security industry which in turn would foster positive relationships with the police and increased public acceptance.

Box 5.6 Private prisons in Australia

NOTE 1
For a more detailed discussion on this and other aspects of prison privatization see Richard Harding, *Private Prisons and Public Accountability*, United Kingdom: Open University Press, 1997.

Chapter 6. Firearm abuse and regulation

Box 6.1 Domestic violence around the world

1. Heise, L. 1994. Violence against women: a neglected public health issue in less developed countries. *Social Science and Medicine*, 39, 9: 1165-1179.

2. One forum that serves to connect researchers working in this area is the International Research Network on Violence Against Women with a secretariat centred in Washington, DC. A current project of this group is to develop and test a manual to assist researchers in resource-poor settings to undertake scientifically sound surveys.

3. The varying methodologies and sampling and definitions of violence against wives are summarized as follows.

Survey	Geographic frame	Sample Size	Mode of Interviewing	Prevalence rates	Definition of spousal assault
Canada Violence Against Women Survey, 1993	Ten provinces (excludes the northern territories)	12,300 women age 18 and over	Telephone	29% ever assaulted by a spouse	Sexual and physical violence by spouses
United States Violence and Threats of Violence Against Women in America Survey, 1996	National	8,000 women and 8,000 men age 18 and over	Telephone	21% ever assaulted by a spouse	Sexual and physical violence by spouses
Australia Women's Safety Survey, 1996	National	6,300 women age 18 and over	Combination of telephone and face-to-face	23% ever assaulted by a spouse	Sexual and physical violence by spouses
England and Wales British Crime Survey, 1996	England and Wales		Self-completed face-to-face interviews	1% assaulted by a spouse in 1995	A module of questions on physical violence by spouses among questions about other types of crimes.
Nicaragua City of Leon	City of Leon, population 195,000	488 women age 15-49	Face-to-face	52% ever assaulted by a spouse	Physical violence by spouses
Mexico Mexico City, 1992	Mexico City	342 women age 15 or older	n/a	33% ever assaulted by a spouse; 6% marital rape	
Chile City of Santiago	City of Santiago	1,000 women age 22-55 in a relationship for 2 years or more	n/a	26% severe physical violence by current spouse	Physical violence by current spouse
Colombia Part of Colombia's Demographic and Health Survey, 1990	National	3,272 urban women and 2,118 rural women	n/a	20% physical violence by current spouse 10% marital rape	Sexual and physical violence by current spouse
Korea	National	707 women and 609 men living with a partner for at least 2 years	Face-to-face	37% physical violence in past year; 12% severe violence	Physical violence by current spouse
Cambodia Household Survey on Domestic Violence in Cambodia, 1995	Six provinces and Phnom Penh	1,374 women and 1,286 men, currently or previously married	Face-to-face	16% physical violence by current spouse	Physical violence by current spouse
Malaysia National Study on Domestic Violence, 1989	National	713 women and 508 men over 15 years of age	n/a	39% physical violence in past year	Physical violence by current spouse
Papua New Guinea	National with stratified urban/rural sample	715 rural and 397 urban women; 736 rural and 546 urban men	Face-to-face	67% of rural women 56% of urban low-income 62% of urban elites	Physical violence by spouses

Chapter 7. Drugs and drug control

Box 7.5 Regional case study – the influence of commerce and trade upon drug trafficking in Europe

The figure was constructed from data in Table B7.1 which was in turn constructed from Table B7.2.

Table B7.1. Maritime trafficking opportunity index (tonnes of maritime trade per km² land area)

Country	"Funneling Index" (Tonnes of maritime trade per km²)
Netherlands	11.06
Germany	0.63
Italy	0.57
Ireland (1989)	0.52
Portugal	0.36
Spain	0.26
Greece (1989)	0.25
Turkey (1989)	0.07
Poland	0.05

Table B7.2. International goods transport in Europe: goods unloaded 1990 (millions of tonnes) and land surface area

	*Maritime transport 1993	**Road transport 1990	***Land surface area: Europe 1992 (000's km2)
Austria	—	11	83
Belgium	230	52.6	—
Czechoslovakia	—	2.2	—
Denmark	—	7.5	42
Finland	—	0.5	305
France	—	61.5	550
Germany	222	89.6	350
Greece	32	1(1989)	129
Ireland	36	1.1(1989)	69
Italy	167	34.8	294
Luxembourg	—	1.6 (1986)	—
Netherlands	376	60.2	34
Norway	—	2.6	307
Poland	16	1.2	304
Portugal	33	2.9	92
Spain	130	14.9	499
Sweden	—	8.4	412
Switzerland	—	4.7	40
Turkey	57	3 (1989)	770
United Kingdom	—	12.3	242

*Source: UN Statistical Yearbook 1995

**Source: Statistical Trends in Transport 1965-1990 by European Conference of Ministers of Transport (ECMT, OECD, 1995)

***Source: UNDP 1995. Human Development Report. Geneva, UNDP

Chapter 9. Crime prevention

Box 9.1 Crime, law and justice at the international level

1. For a more account of the case see: Jose A. Baez, An international crimes court: further tales of the king of Corinth, *Georgia Journal of International Comparative Law*, 23, 289: 289-325, 1993; and J. Scott Davidson, The Rainbow Warrior: arbitration concerning the treatment of the French agents Mafart and Prieur, *International and Comparative Law Quarterly*, 40: 446-457, 1991, on the basis of which the case is summarized herein. See also: Matsuura, K., Joachim W. Müller and Karl P. Sauvant. 1992. *Chronology and Fact Book of the United Nations. Annual Review of the United Nations Affairs*. Dobbs Ferry, NY: Oceana Publications; and electronic home page with related assessment of the role of the Secretary-General, by Edward Newman, International Civil Servants and the International Power Structures: the Secretaryship-General and Pérez de Cuéllar (http://snipe.ukc.ac.uk/international/papers.dir/newman.html).

2. Keesing's Contemporary Archives. Weekly Diary of World Events, Vol. XXXII, August 1986, p. 34568.

Box 9.2 Illegal aliens in the Netherlands

1. Information obtained in a letter dated 21 April 1997 from the Department of Correctional Services, *Dienst Justitiële Inrichtingen*, Ministry of Justice.

2. Information obtained in a letter dated 21 April 1997 from the Department of Correctional Services, *Dienst Justitiële Inrichtingen*, Ministry of Justice.

3. Infomation obtained in a letter dated 21 April 1997 from the Department of Correctional Services, *Dienst Justitiële Inrichtingen*, Ministry of Justice.

4. "Sober conditions" indicate minimum standards of comfort and care.

Box 9.9 Traficking in human organs

1. Organ Trafficking Myths, paper by Todd Leventhal, USIA Senior Policy Officer; and UNOS Paper on Organ Theft Myths.

2. Brazil opens probe of alleged organ-trafficking Mafia. *Agence France Presse*, April 21 1996. For more specific reports see old news *Eubios Ethics Institute* (http://www.biol.tsukuba.ac.jp/~macer/index.html).

3. Chela, Fred. Vodoo trade in human organs on the increase in Africa. *Deutsche Presse- Agentur*, April 18, 1996.

4. Journalist probing organ trade may have been slain. *Houston Chronicle*, May 28 1996.

5. Crooked doctors in India steal kidneys from poor, newspaper says. *Deutsche Presse-Agentur*, April 2 1995.

6. Chang, Dae H. A new form of international crime: the human organ trade. *International Journal of Comparative and Applied Criminal Justice*, 19, 1: 5.

7. Information obtained from Center for Organ Recovery and Education, Pittsburgh

Notes to Chapters

Chapter 1. The experience of crime and justice

1. The members of this working group are: Jan Van Dijk (chair), Pat Mayhew and Ugljesa Zvekic.

2. Computerized data are at present available at the Criminological Institute of Leiden University on 60 nations. The number of countries included in this chapter may depend on the particular data set used, as new countries are continuously added into the data set.

3. **Data collection of the ICVS**

   Industrialized countries

   In all developed countries except Spain and Northern Ireland, interviews were done by telephone. Interviewers used computers from which they read the questions and recorded answers – a procedure known as computer assisted telephone interviewing (CATI).

   InterView was appointed as overall contractor for the 1996 surveys, as was the case in 1989 and 1992. Fieldwork was subcontracted to survey companies in the countries taking part. Interviews began in January 1996 and lasted six to seven weeks. An average interview lasted about 15 minutes, depending mainly on the extent of victimization experience reported.

   To keep costs in check and encourage as full participation as possible, samples in all sweeps of the ICVS have been relatively modest. In industrialized countries, samples were usually of between 1,000 and 2,500 respondents. In each country, a regionally well spread sample of households was taken. Within each household, one randomly selected respondent aged 16 or more was questioned. The respondent was generally selected by the Troldahl-Carter method. No substitution of the selected respondent was allowed. Selected respondents were recalled at least four times. Those who refused or were not available were recontacted one week later.

   Results for the developed countries in this chapter are based on data which have been weighted to make the samples as representative as possible of national populations aged 16 or more in terms of gender, regional population distribution, age and household composition. The iterative weighting procedures in the 1996 surveys are the same as those used previously and details can be found in van Dijk and Mayhew (1992).

   Developing countries

   Fieldwork in developing countries and countries in transition included the undertaking of feasibility/training missions and the carrying out of pilot studies in the countries which were participating in the ICVS for the first time.

   The main aim of the missions was to pass on experience and provide advice as to the technical and organizational aspect of the ICVS, with the assistance of the "Manual" developed by UNICRI for this purpose (Alvazzi del Frate, 1996). Details regarding sampling, translation of the questionnaire into local language(s), organization of the project, selection and training of the interviewers, data collection method, data entry procedure, data analysis, and the structure of the national report were discussed and mutually agreed upon. Training on the conduct of the face-to-face survey and on the use of the ICVS data entry software developed by the University of Leiden was provided to selected members of the local team who, in turn, provided further training to the interviewers.

   In principle, pilots were carried out in all countries that were newcomers to the ICVS. The results of the pilots carried out in Albania, Bolivia, Mongolia, Romania, Zimbabwe, and in late 1995 were used for the drafting of the revised version of the questionnaire adopted by the 1996-97 ICVS and for necessary modifications taking into account local conditions.

   In developing countries and countries in transition, samples of 1,000 respondents were generally drawn from the population of the largest city, although in a few countries the survey covered either several cities with or without the addition of a small rural sample (Estonia, Georgia, Indonesia, Kyrgyzstan, Latvia) or a national sample (Czech Republic, Poland).

   Full standardization of the sampling designs was not feasible. The manual lays down some basic principles of random-stratified sampling. Sampling designs were prepared by local experts and approved by UNICRI. The procedures are explained in the reports of the national coordinators. The samples were stratified geographically on the basis of administrative zones in the cities. Where possible the sample was also stratified according to the social status of the zones (higher status, middle status, lower status). This criterion was not always applicable in the countries in transition where the social status of areas is often mixed.

   The respondents in the selected areas were chosen by a step-by-step procedure aimed at identifying 1) streets, 2) blocks, 3) households, and 4) the person aged 16 or more whose birthday is next. (The questionnaire opens with a few questions for the primary respondent in the household and then continues with questions for the member of the household whose birthday is next.) The households were selected at random (e.g., through random walk techniques or the selection of each tenth household starting from a randomly chosen start address). Interviewers were instructed to recontact the selected address or person at least twice. No substitution of the address or of the selected respondent was allowed. In some countries it was difficult to contact sufficient numbers of young males. In these countries quota sampling was used to ensure a more equal representation of gender and age groups.

   The data were in all cases weighted to make the samples representative in terms of household size, gender and age (three groups).

   In developing countries the survey was carried out face-to-face. In most countries the survey was carried out by an ad hoc team of interviewers, whereby the national coordinators relied on senior students. In some countries, data collection was subcontracted to survey companies (Estonia, Bolivia, Costa Rica, Czech Republic, Georgia, Hungary, Kyrgyzstan, Poland, Russia) whose work was supervised by the national coordinator.

   In addition to a local language or dialect requirement, in some countries it was important to match interviewers and respondents in terms of ethnicity, tribal affiliation or other such characteristics. Some other traits needed to be taken into account. For example, in some cultures male respondents were not willing to talk with female interviewers, and vice versa. Customs precluded the use of male interviewers to interview female respondents particularly for such sensitive issues as sexual victimization. On average, face-to-face interviews lasted 30 minutes and could generally be understood by illiterate respondents.

In most of the developing countries and countries in transition the full-fledged survey was administered during the period January-March 1996. However, due to certain problems in terms of funding in some countries, the survey was carried out somewhat later in the year.

Data collection lasted from eight to ten weeks in each country and was followed by the data entry and logical validation process. On average, fieldwork lasted four months, including translation of the questionnaire, sampling, data collection and preparation of the data set for delivery. A final report was prepared by each national coordinator.

Response rates

Industrialized countries

In the 11 industrialized countries in the 1996 ICVS taken as a whole, 67 percent of the respondents selected for interview agreed to take part. This was an improvement on the overall response rate of 60 percent for the 12 countries in the 1992 sweep for which response details are available, and on the 43 percent response rate in 1989 (14 countries with details). To try and improve response after the first sweep, three pilot studies were carried out in 1991 to test whether people who initially refused to cooperate could be persuaded to participate when approached again after two to three weeks. In a second phase of fieldwork, then, all initial refusals and those not contacted the first time were called back. All exercises resulted in the response rate being substantially increased (by 10-22 percentage points). This procedure was used in most countries in the second and third sweeps of the ICVS. In 1996, response varied from 40 percent (in the USA) to 80 percent or more in Austria, Finland and Northern Ireland.

Developing countries

Information on the response rate was provided by the national coordinators in their final reports. The response rate was generally higher than 85 percent and in no country lower than 75 percent. It was observed that in some countries in transition the refusal rate was higher due to recent war conflicts which increased the suspicion of strangers at the door.

In some countries the interview was announced through a letter to the household in order to improve participation.

Special methodological issues

While many of the methodological features of the ICVS relate to crime surveys in general, some have particular pertinence because of the comparative nature of the ICVS, and the possibility of *differential* effects. The main issues for the ICVS are as follows.

Survey company performance

Although survey administration was in the main centrally organized, the performance of the individual survey companies or research teams conducting fieldwork in different countries could have differed, affecting what respondents were (and were not) prepared to tell interviewers. This problem applies to any survey conducted in different sites or at different times, where survey companies vary. In the case of the ICVS, InterView tried to standardize company performance as far as possible, while UNICRI, by providing a standard "Manual" and on-site training, also attempted to standardize the data collection procedure. Nevertheless, it must be underlined that the level of standardization as regards sampling and data collection procedure was higher in all the countries in which CATI was used. Therefore, more caution is needed in the interpretation of the victimization levels for the developing world and countries in transition.

Response rates

Getting an adequate representative cross-section of the population is always difficult, and it is problematic to the extent that those who are not successfully interviewed may differ from those who are. Not all ICVS surveys have produced high response rates — although they have generally improved over time.

The effect of response levels on measured victimization is important for the ICVS. The main question is whether variability in response levels upsets comparability.

To consider this issue, analysis was carried out for the large number of surveys in industrialized countries in the three sweeps of the ICVS.

In terms of overall response levels (for which 37 surveys in industrialized countries could be examined), there was no statistically robust correlation between victimization risks and the proportion of eligible contacts who responded. (The correlation between response rates and overall "last year" victimization rates suggests that high response rates were associated with lower victimization, but the result was not statistically robust: r= -0.200; n = 37; ns.) This result is not out of line with other tests looking at response levels in relation to victimization counts. These have provided some support for the notion that surveys with poorer response have higher counts, although the differences in risks have been generally modest, or differences in other test conditions (e.g., mode of interview) have made sound comparisons difficult. Some early research in the Netherlands (Fiselier, 1978) and Switzerland (Killias, 1989) on the basis of mail questionnaires showed that victimization rates were slightly higher among those who first responded than among those who did not initially do so — though the differences were small. A similar result was evident in a re-contact test in Belgium and the USA in 1991 in the context of the ICVS, though again differences were marginal (InterView, 1991). The ICVS survey in Malaga (Spain) had a split sample design, with some respondents interviewed by phone and some face-to-face. Telephone interviews conducted later with about half of those who had initially refused to participate in a personal interview produced an overall victimization rate slightly lower than the main telephone sample — again suggesting that they had "less to say" (Stangeland, 1995). In an independently organized victimization survey in Germany in 1990 response was higher than in the 1989 ICVS, and the overall victimization rate lower (Kury, 1991).

As mentioned, the response rates of the studies in developing countries and the countries in transition — where face-to-face interviewing was applied — were a good deal higher. In some of these countries the victimization rates are relatively high and in others relatively low.

In sum, there is no overriding evidence from the ICVS that countries with low response levels have either inflated or deflated counts of victimization relative to other countries. It cannot be ruled out that response effects work differently in different countries (such that a low response rate in one country influences the victimization count in a way that does not occur in another), but the overall burden of the ICVS evidence does not indicate substantial bias due to variable response rates.

Sample sizes

Sample sizes in the ICVS are small by the standards of the most "bespoke" national crime surveys. However, the decision to accept relatively modest samples was carefully made. It was considered simply unrealistic to assume sufficient countries would participate if costs were too high (especially as some countries had their own "bespoke" surveys). The value of the ICVS rests on the breadth of countries which have participated; this would have been considerably reduced if costs had been higher.

Modest sample sizes produce relatively large sampling error, but for straightforward comparisons of national risks, samples of 1,000 or more suffice to judge broad variations in levels of crime across the country. This is even more true for city or urban area only samples. Modest samples, however, restrict the scope for analysis issues about which a small proportion of the sample would provide information.

Telephone and face-to-face interviewing

Telephone interviewing, and in some instances the specific computer assisted (CATI) variant of it, has been increasingly used in victimization surveys — in Canada, the Netherlands, Switzerland and the USA, for example. For the ICVS, CATI was accepted as a sound technique for industrialized countries where telephone penetration is high. Cost was a major consideration, since central telephoning avoids the costs of getting interviewers to a large number of households across the country. Just as important, though, is that CATI allows much tighter standardization of questionnaire administration. It also enables samples to be drawn which are geographically unclustered because some variant of random digit dialing is used based on full coverage of telephone owners, including those with unlisted numbers.

There are two main issues for the ICVS. The first is whether telephone interviews produce different results than would be the case with face-to-face (personal) interviews. Methodological work has generally shown little difference in responses to telephone and face to-face interviews (see Leeuw & Zouwen [1988] for a review of 28 studies). With respect to crime victimization, the general consensus also is that the two modes produce similar results, as long as the same standards of fieldwork are applied, although Smith (1989) has argued that telephone interviews provide a higher degree of confidentiality and minimize interviewer effects for more sensitive topics, such as sexual victimization. Tests in the context of the ICVS have produced mixed results about the "productivity" of telephone versus personal interviews, but they have not provided any overridingly strong evidence that victimization counts are affected by interview mode. One test was in the Netherlands. Three ICVS questions were used in an experimental test of the CATI technique and self-assisted telephone interviewing through a modem, which allows the respondent to answer questions at his/her own pace (more similar to face-to-face interviewing). No significant differences in victimization rates emerged (Saris and Scherpenzeel, 1992). In a second test, Pavlovic (1994) used the ICVS questionnaire in a survey in Ljubljana, Slovenia, using split samples of 700 telephone interviews and 300 personal interviews. Refusal rates were very low in both modes, and no differences were found as regards victimization levels, bearing in mind the relatively small samples. The split sample design used in the ICVS survey in Malaga, Spain, had rather larger samples (Stangeland, 1995). The overall victimization rate in the personal interviews was higher than in the telephone interview, but the response rate was appreciably lower. The difference in response rates in the two modes complicates conclusions about which mode is more "productive" in terms of victimization counts. Finally, in an experiment by Kury et al. (1991), mailed interviews using the ICVS questionnaire produced significantly higher overall prevalence rates than personal interviews. Here, again, the lower response rate of the mailed questionnaire complicates the interpretation. It cannot entirely be discounted, however, that some differences in results across country reflect differences in the acceptability of being questioned by phone.

The second issue regarding telephone interviewing is whether there is bias in the results because non-telephone owners are omitted. At the time of the first ICVS, telephone penetration was lower in some countries than it was in 1996, thus allowing the possibility of bias both as regards counting victimization and measuring attitudes. While it is impossible to say conclusively whether this was the case, levels of telephone ownership in the 1989 ICVS did not relate to the experience of different crimes in any consistent way (van Dijk et al., 1990). It is also the case that the characteristics of non-telephone owners (most of which will be related to income) may be more akin to those of respondents with whom it is harder to achieve a personal interview (cf. Aye Maung, 1995).

Response error

It is well established that crime surveys are prone to various response errors. For one, certain groups (e.g., the better educated) seem more adept at remembering and articulating incidents of victimization. Second, and more important, is that respondents' memories are imperfect, and they may fail to report all relevant incidents that happened in the period asked about, or may "telescope in" incidents outside this period. In a study in the Netherlands, based on a check of victimization survey data against police data (forward record check), respondents tended to "telescope in" incidents into the last year reference period which had actually taken place in the previous year (van Dijk, 1991). In the ICVS, the initial screening question reference period of five years is meant to reduce the forward time telescoping that can occur when respondents are asked about the last year. In a test of the screening questions used in the ICVS, it was found that the omission of the five year reference period screener produce significantly higher one year rates (Saris and Scherpenzeel, 1992). Some people may also fail to realize that an incident is relevant, or may be reticent to talk about some incidents, for instance sexual incidents or those involving people they know. These factors probably mean, on balance, that the ICVS undercounts crime. It certainly means that it only measures those crimes that respondents are prepared to reveal to interviewers.

A critical issue is whether response errors are constant across countries. There is little way of knowing for certain. The tendency to forget more trivial incidents of crime may be relatively universal, as may "forward telescoping" of more salient incidents. Some types of differential "response productivity" may also be constant, at least within the industrialized world. Whether respondents differ across countries in their preparedness to talk to interviewers about victimization is difficult to

say. Cultural sensitivity may possibly apply most to some forms of assaults, and to sexual incidents, where the ICVS has been particularly criticized (Travis et al., 1995; Koss, 1996).

A criticism of the ICVS has been that respondents in different countries may have different cultural thresholds for defining certain behaviours as crime, thus differentially "defining in" or "defining out" certain sorts of antisocial behaviour in response to the questions put to them (Bruinsma et al., 1992). For industrialized countries, this may have been overstated to the extent that the increasing number of cross-cultural features, as well as the globalization of markets and mass media information, lead to fairly universal definitions about most convention crimes (e.g., Gottfredson and Hirschi, 1990). This also applies to urban settlements across the world, although some differences may have been preserved. Certainly, what is now known from the ICVS is that victims across western countries hold strikingly similar views about the relative seriousness of different offence types about which they are asked. Results on seriousness assessments, presented in this chapter, showed that there was consensus on the ranking of types of crime across countries.

4. The regional rates are the mean rates of the participating countries per region. National rates will not necessarily always conform to the regional pattern but they usually do. No urban rates are available for Japan.

5. The rates of car owners victimized by car crimes are less divergent. The ownership rates are 48.7 for Western Europe, 48.5 for the New World, 49.6 for Latin America, 47.9 for Central and Eastern Europe, 28.9 for Asia and 55.9 for Africa. Although more cars per 100,000 inhabitants are stolen in the industrialized countries, the risks of owners are higher in African and Central or Eastern European cities.

6. In the survey respondents are asked whether they have been a victim of a broadly defined sexual incident and/or a broadly defined incident of non-sexual physical aggression, including threats. The rates for violence are derived from information given on the last incident that happened over five years. The rates give a minimum estimate since victims who reported more than one incident of sexual aggression or non-sexual aggression might have been the victim of actual violence on one of the previous occasions. Since the same counting rules were used, comparability across countries is not affected.

7. Interviewers were instructed to include incidents of violence of a sexual nature under assault. No special question about such offences was put to male respondents.

8. Data are available for 52 countries which participated in the second and/or third sweeps of the ICVS.

9. The lowest correlation is that between the ranking of the victims in Tanzania and the over all ranking (.44; p= < 0.10). The highest correlations are shown by Costa Rica (.92), Finland (.92), and Ukraine (.92). The number of victims for some crime types are fairly small and sampling error might be considerable. This makes the strength of the correlations more remarkable.

10. The analysis of the determinants of car crimes showed that the level of car crimes is most strongly related to the level of car ownership (beta=.87).

11. Analysis is as follows (next page):

Table N1.1. Results of a stepwise, multiple regression analysis with the national rates of more serious crimes as dependent variable (n=49)

step	MultR	Rsq	AdjRsq	F(Egn)	SigF	RsaCh	Fch	SigCh	Variable	BetaIn	Corrwel
1	.6908	.4773	.4651	39.261	.000	.4773	39.261	.000	urban mean	.6908	.6908
2	.7238	.5239	.5012	23.105	.000	.0466	4.110	.049	going out	.2208	.0656
3	.7545	.5693	.5378	18.063	.000	.0454	4.323	.044	strain	.2944	.5216

Variables in the equation:

variable	B	SE B	Beta	T	Sig T
urban mean	2.877442	.661036	.572341	4.353	.0001
strain	.500237	.240603	.294393	2.079	.0439
going out	4.895261	1.790132	.309560	2.735	.0092
(constant)	-12.933051	6.044654		-2.140	.0384

Path analyses, carried out with the programme Lisrel VI, showed that the inverse relationship between affluence and more serious crimes is mediated by the variables "economic strain" and "going out." In the model urbanization is inversely related to affluence. This statistical relationship is an artifact of the sampling design, because in developing countries the samples were drawn from large cities rather than from the national population. Urbanization is strongly related to high levels of serious crimes. A path analysis of the relationships of the variables just mentioned among the inhabitants of large cities across the world also produced a model with strain and affluent life-styles as mediatory variables between affluence and level of serious crime.

12. The USA is one of the most extreme examples of a country where a high level of gun ownership is accompanied by high levels of contact crimes. If this case is deleted from the analysis, the correlation is not altered (r=.316; p=<.02; n= 52).

13. Analysis is as follows:

Table N1.2. Correlation coefficients between national rates of gun ownership and rates of contact crimes

	handgun	contact crime	robbery	sexual offence	assault/ threat	assault/ threat with gun
handgun	1.0000	0.3200	0.3715	0.3131	0.0816	0.5801
	(53)	(53)	(52)	(53)	(53)	(37)
		p=.020	p=.007	p=.022	p=.561	p=.000

14. The item on the use of a weapon was included only in the 1996 survey.

15. Analysis is as follows:

Table N1.3. Results of a stepwise, multiple regression analysis with the national rates of contact crimes as dependent variable (n=49)

step	MultR	Rsq	AdjRsq	F(Egn)	SigF	RsaCh	Fch	SigCh	Variable	BetaIn	Corrwel
1	.6307	.3978	.3838	28.400	.000	.3978	28.400	.000	urban mean	.6307	.6307
2	.6957	.4840	.4595	19.700	.000	.0863	7.022	.011	strain	.3758	.6230
3	.7842	.6149	.5868	21.825	.000	.1309	13.938	.001	going out	.3996	.0866
4	.8113	.6583	.6241	19.261	.000	.0433	5.071	.030	education	-.2139	-.3715
5	.8390	.7039	.6659	18.542	.000	.456	6.011	.019	handgun	.2617	.2821
6	.8261	.6824	.6507	21.490	.000	-.215	2.825	.101	urban mean		.6307

Variables in the equation

variable	B	SE B	Beta	T	Sig T
handgun	.173530	.048565	.344920	3.567	.0010
strain	.605817	.084794	.721484	7.145	.0000
going out	2.247591	.811387	.287621	2.770	.0854
education	-1.150953	.362920	-.298180	-3.171	.0029
(constant)	-.937914	3.525658		-.266	..7916

16. Analysis is as follows:

Table N1.4. Results of a stepwise, multiple regression analysis with the national rates of violence against women as dependent variable (N=44)

step	MultR	Rsq	AdjRsq	F(Egn)	SigF	RsaCh	Fch	SigCh	Variable	BetaIn	Corrwel
1	.5416	.2933	.2765	17.431	.000	.2933	17.431	.000	strain	.5416	.5416
2	.6154	.3788	.3485	12.499	.000	.0855	5.641	.022	divorced females	.2977	.1851
3	.6623	.4387	.3966	10.421	.000	.0599	4.271	.045	educ. women mean	-.2704	-.2168

Table continued next page

Variables in the equation

variable	B	SE B	Beta	T	Sig T
strain	.281349	.060646	.564487	4.639	.0000
educ. women mean	-.588408	.284717	-.270438	-2.067	.0453
divorced females	.266377	.086674	.401642	3.073	.0038
(constant)	2.294248	1.536517		1.493	.1432

17. The dependent variable of the regression analysis was the decision to report theft from cars, burglary with entry, robbery, sexual incidents and assaults/threats (N=24,081). The variables chosen in the equation were income, seriousness, age, education, gender and life-style (outdoor visits). The multiple R was .27.

18. The multiple R was .92 (N=7,081).

19. Data are available for 43 countries which participated in the 1996 survey. Contact crimes include robberies, sexual incidents and threats/assaults.

20. Contact crimes here include robberies, sexual assaults and assaults.

21. Data are as follows:

Table N1.5. Percentage of victims of burglary, violence against women and contact crimes who would have appreciated receiving help from a specialized agency, results of the International Crime Victim Survey, 1996

	All	Africa	Asia	Central and Eastern Europe	Latin America	New World	Western Europe
Number of countries	43	3	3	19	6	2	10
Burglary	64.7	91.1	84.0	80.3	66.7	29.2	36.9
N	4085	538	118	1633	794	231	772
Contact crimes	64.9	80.7	90.6	75.3	57.2	45.2	40.4
N	7395	738	237	2960	2037	217	1206
Violence against women	75.3	86.9	99.3	78.4	71.5	66.5	49.4
N	1376	140	61	553	374	39	208

Chapter 2. Police records of crime

1. The results shown in Figure 2.9 may differ from those of the Global Snapshot on page 50 because (a) the countries included in each figure differed, (b) the figures were estimated for Figure 2.9 for least developed countries because of low reporting rates, and (c) the Snapshot did not distinguish between least developed and developing countries, so that a number of least developed countries were included in the non-industrial or developing countries group.

Chapter 3. Bringing to justice

1. See Kangaspunta, K. (Ed.) 1995. *Crime and Criminal Justice in Europe and North America 1986-1990.* Helsinki: European Institute for Crime Prevention and Control Affiliated with the United Nations; and Mukherjee, S. and D. Dagger. 1995. *Crime Trends in Asia and the Pacific: The Fourth United Nations Survey.* Tokyo and Canberra: UNAFEI and AIC.

Chapter 4. Punishment

1. In the survey questionnaire, "Deprivation of liberty includes various forms of detention, including security measures, combined or split sentence (where at least one part of the sentence involves deprivation of liberty) and all other sanctions involving deprivation of liberty (i.e., where the person is forced to stay at least one night in an institution of any kind) ... Control of freedom includes a probation order, a conditional sentence with additional supervision requirement and other forms of so-called controlled liberty (i.e., cases where the person is required to fulfil special requirements with regards to supervision) ... Warning and admonition includes suspended sentences, conditional sentences, findings of guilty without sanctions, formal admonitions, formal warnings, imposing of duties without control, conditional dismissal and conditional discharge." (Survey questionnaire, p.26)

2. This premise is rather too presumptive, since a minor punishment can be imposed for a serious crime. Although it is necessary theoretically to analyze the relationship between the crime type and the adjudi-

cated punishment, such information is not available for this analysis.

3. Hierarchical cluster analysis is used for countries that provided more than three sentencing options. Countries that responded "not applicable" or that had missing data for other sentencing options are treated as zero.

4. "Violent crime" includes homicide, major assaults, rape and robbery.

5. Selected results of the correlation analysis is as follows:

	All sentencing	Deprivation of liberty	Control in freedom	Fine
Total crime rate	.0403 P=.984	-.1458 P=.468	.0821 P=.690	.0624 P=.468
Violent crime rate	-.2138 P=.379	-.1540 P=.517	-.0800 P=.745	-.1893 P=.424
Theft	.0330 P=.876	-.1864 P=.372	.0184 P=.932	.0563 P=.789

6. The UN Crime Survey includes several indices prepared by the United Nations Development Programme (UNDP). The UNDP major world aggregates (DEVELP) indicate the industrial development of a country as "least developed," "developing" or "industrialized." UNDP human development aggregates (HUMDEV) rank the country's situation of human development in three: low, middle and high.

The Human Development Index (HDI) is "based on three indicators: longevity, as measured by life expectancy at birth; educational attainment, as measured by a combination of adult literacy (two-thirds weight) and combined primary, secondary and tertiary enrolment ratios (one-third weight); and standard of living, as measured by real GDP per capita (PPS$)" (United Nations, Human Development Report 1996: 106). Countries with "low human development" are those which score HDI 0.500 or less, the "middle" countries score from 0.500 to 0.799, and those with "high" human development have an HDI of 0.800 and more. UNDP income aggregate (INCOMEAG) measures a country's financial situation. Low income means that the GNP per capita is 695 US dollars or less, middle income refers to GNP per capita that ranges from 696 dollars to 8625 dollars, and high income means GNP per capita above $ 8625. For the regional grouping, the category employed by the International Crime Victim Survey (ICVS), rather than the UNDP category, was used. The ICVS category divides the world into six regions: Western Europe, New World (Australia, Canada, the United States of America and New Zealand), countries in transition (Eastern and Central Europe), Asia and the Pacific, Africa and Latin America. It indeed presents a less precise division than the UNDP category, which includes nine categories (Sub-Saharan Africa, Arab States, East Asia, Southeast Asia and the Pacific, South Asia, Latin America and the Caribbean, North America, Eastern Europe and the Commonwealth of Independent States, and Western and Southern Europe). Nevertheless, the ICVS category is favoured because the large amount of missing responses obscures the explanatory power of precise grouping. These indicators would provide quite a handy tool for assessing the relationship between the level of development and status of the country and the use of punishment. Therefore, they will be used throughout the chapter to analyze the relationship between various punishment indicators and socio-economic situations of the countries.

7. The ANOVA technique was used to explore the relationship between imprisonment rate and development indices used in the UNCJS. The following tables show the results.

Table C4.1. Total prisoners by UNDP Major World Aggregates

Category	Mean	N
Least developed	124.0165	6
Developing	119.4616	20
Industrialized	170.8425	31

Source	Sum of squares	d.f	Mean Square	F	Sig.
Between Groups	35914.4929	2	17957.2464	1.1785	.3155
Within Groups	822833.3308	54	15237.6543		
	Eta = .2045 Eta Squared = .0418				

Table C4.2. Total prisoners by UNDP Human Development Aggregates

Category	Mean	N
Low	120.6491	5
Middle	167.3411	15
High	143.6780	37

Source	Sum of squares	d.f	Mean Square	F	Sig.
Between Groups	10041.9345	2	5020.9672	.3195	.7279
Within Groups	848705.8892	54	15716.7757		
	Eta = .1081 Eta Squared = .0117				

Table C4.3. Total prisoners by UNDP Income Aggregates

Category	Mean	N
Low Income	109.3456	8
Middle Income	172.4063	28
High Income	129.8718	21

Source	Sum of squares	d.f	Mean Square	F	Sig.
Between Groups	35532.5517	2	17766.2759	1.1654	.3195
Within Groups	823215.2719	54	15244.7273		
	Eta = .2034 Eta Squared = .0414				

Table C4.4. Convicted prisoners by UNDP Major World Aggregates

Category	Mean	N
Least developed	52.3146	6
Developing	68.2550	21
Industrialized	118.0260	30

Source	Sum of squares	d.f	Mean Square	F	Sig.
Between Groups	41576.5338	2	20788.2669	2.8378	0673
Within Groups	395576.8225	54	7325.4967		
	Eta = .3084 Eta Squared = .0951				

Table C4.5. Convicted prisoners by UNDP Human Development Aggregates

Category	Mean	N
Low	34.6068	5
Middle	113.0896	17
High	91.2133	35

Source	Sum of squares	d.f	Mean Square	F	Sig.
Between Groups	24018.6288	2	12009.3144	1.5697	.2175
Within Groups	413134.7275	54	7650.6431		
	Eta = .2344 Eta Squared = .0549				

Table C4.6. Convicted prisoners by UNDP Income Aggregates

Category	Mean	N
Low Income	44.6254	9
Middle Income	114.0399	28
High Income	84.6638	20

Source	Sum of squares	d.f	Mean Square	F	Sig.
Between Groups	34842.7959	2	17421.3980	2.3384	.1062
Within Groups	402310.5604	54	7450.1956		
	Eta = .2823 Eta Squared = .0797				

8   The ANOVA technique was used to explore the relationship between prison admission rate and UN developmental aggregates.

Table C4.7. Total prison admissions by UNDP Major World Aggregates

Category	Mean	N
Least developed	222.2573	6
Developing	257.1258	21
Industrialized	231.3083	29

Source	Sum of squares	d.f	Mean Square	F	Sig.
Between Groups	10238.7708	2	5119.3854	.0816	.9217
Within Groups	3324207.0497	53	62720.8877		
	Eta = .0554 Eta Squared = .0031				

Table C4.8. Total prison admissions by UNDP Human Development Aggregates

Category	Mean	N
Low	225.4892	5
Middle	173.4535	19
High	281.8145	32

Source	Sum of squares	d.f	Mean Square	F	Sig.
Between Groups	141143.4389	2	70571.7195	1.1713	.3179
Within Groups	3193302.3816	53	60250.9883		
	Eta = .2057 Eta Squared = .0423				

Table C4.9. Total prison admissions by UNDP Income Aggregates

Category	Mean	N
Low Income	199.7921	9
Middle Income	237.3553	29
High Income	264.4274	18

Source	Sum of squares	d.f	Mean Square	F	Sig.
Between Groups	25493.3929	2	12746.6965	.2042	.8160
Within Groups	3308952.4276	53	62433.0647		

Eta = .0874 Eta Squared = .0076

Table C4.10. Prison admissions by conviction by UNDP World Development Aggregates

Category	Mean	N
Least developed	126.9182	4
Developing	105.8769	10
Industrialized	193.0802	13

Source	Sum of squares	d.f	Mean Square	F	Sig.
Between Groups	45700.3424	2	22850.1712	1.4932	.2448
Within Groups	367270.3030	24	15302.9293		

Eta = .3327 Eta Squared =.1107

Table C4.11. Admission by convictions by UNDP Human Development Aggregates

Category	Mean	N
Low	100.5251	3
Middle	173.6458	10
High	145.6037	14

Source	Sum of squares	d.f	Mean Square	F	Sig.
Between Groups	13179.1392	2	6589.5696	.3956	.6776
Within Groups	399791.5062	24	16657.9794		

Eta = .1786 Eta Squared = .0319

Table C4.12. Admission by convictions by UNDP Income Aggregates

Category	Mean	N
Low Income	86.8613	5
Middle Income	193.3977	15
High Income	105.8876	7

Source	Sum of squares	d.f	Mean Square	F	Sig.
Between Groups	61778.1436	2	30889.0718	2.1109	.1431
Within Groups	351192.5018	24	14633.0209		

Eta = .3868 Eta Squared = .1496

9. Such a claim may be invalid due to deviations from the basic assumptions of statistical theory: random sampling and normality of distribution. Hence, this should be considered an exploratory practice rather than a conclusive comment.

10. The UN Crime Survey provides inconsistent data. Some countries provide "total number of prisoners," which is different from the total of all prisoner types listed in the survey. Some provide numbers for each category, but do not provide a total number of prisoners. The data from the countries which provide matching data between provided total and calculated total number are used in this analysis.

11. This section is based on United Nations (1996c).

12. For instance, see: Penal Reform International (1994).

13. Based on replies from 49 countries.

14. Changes are based on the increase or decrease in the number of countries that provide either positive or negative answers. It might not reflect pure "qualitative" changes within a country.

15. For the prohibition of torture and other cruel punishment, see United Nations (1975). On the distinction between corporal punishment and torture, see Newman (1994).

16. For the explanation of corporal punishment, and especially of hand amputation for the crime of theft, see: Souryal, Sam S. et al. (1994). See also Newman (1994) for a discussion of the comparative utility of corporal punishment as a deterrent compared to retributive use.

17. For an extensive collection of research results on the death penalty, see Zvekic and Kubo (1988).

18. See United Nations (1996b).

19. "Control in freedom includes a probation order, a conditional sentence with additional supervision requirement and other forms of so-called controlled liberty (i.e., cases where the person is required to fulfil special requirements with regard to supervision)."

20. "Warnings and admonition include suspended sentences, conditional sentences, findings of guilt without sanctions, formal admonitions, formal warnings, imposing duties without control, conditional dismissal, conditional discharge."

21. The number of persons on probation per given day was also requested by the United Nations Survey of Crime Trends and Criminal Justice Systems, but there were too few responses to make this measure usable.

22. For an in-depth comparative analysis, see Hamai, Koichi et al. (1995).

23 However, there is a need to make a fine distinction between popular support and "well-informed opinion" as is the case with the death penalty. As Roger Hood underlined: "Public opinion polls can prove to be a misleading indicator, the responses depending greatly on the nature and specificity of the question posed, their order and sequence of questioning, the context in which the survey takes place, the alternative measures suggested, and the socio-economic, race and gender composition of the sample" (Hood, 1996).

24. Canada, England and the United States are good examples.

25. The question was as follows: "People have different ideas about the sentences which should be given to offenders. Take for instance the case of a man 21 years old who is found guilty of a burglary for a second time. This time he stole a colour TV. Which of the following sentences do you consider the most appropriate for such a case: fine, prison, community service, suspended sentence or any other sentence?" If the interviewee opted for imprisonment, he/she was asked to specify the length.

26. In a stepwise regression analysis on the regional level, among the four chosen predictors of the preference for imprisonment, "anglophone countries" was positively related with a beta of 0.43. (van Dijk 1994c).

27. Notwithstanding the net-widening effect of such punitive non-custodial sanctions, the introduction of such sanctions might create some confusion concerning the concept of, and feelings about, the hierarchy of punishment, especially since the introduction of such punitive sanctions has led to some degree of intrusion in people's personal lives. Horlow et al. (1995) showed that informed citizens rated such "intermediate sanctions" as "intensively supervised probation" and "electronic monitoring," as ones that are literally situated in an intermediate position between the prison sentence and probation. However, the perception of the offender may be different. Several studies have come to a very interesting conclusion (i.e., that the offender considers imprisonment less serious than intensively supervised probation). Therefore, the main question such as "Do offenders generally share the state's punitiveness in the ranking of criminal sanctions?" (Crouch, 1993; Petersilia and Deschenes, 1994) should be considered. Such research suggests that the conventional order of "seriousness" of punishment also needs to be critically analyzed.

28. Further consequences of the risk-management orientation of the criminal justice system are to be found in that the "Modern criminal law relies essentially on the concept of 'endangering offences,' a technique widely used today in criminal legislation to ensure e.g. traffic safety, a proper natural environment, the well-being of economy, public health, internal security and ultimately feelings of safety...With risk management and the concept of endangering offences a mechanism is initiated which among others influences the type of sanctions used" (Albrecht, 1996).

29. To these one should add that public opinion and mass-media pressure and/or isolation and adverse publicity orders appear to possess greater deterrent as well as sanctioning power when applied to corporate actors rather than individuals in modern society; effcts perhaps similar to peer and community pressure in traditional socities or small groups.

Chapter 5. Resources in criminal justice

1. The number of lay judges per 100,000 population in 1994 was calculated by dividing the total number of lay judges reported by each country for 1994 in the Fifth UNCJS by each country's 1994 population as reported by the United Nations in *World Population Prospects 1950-2050 (The 1996 Revision)* and then multiplying by 100,000. An identical procedure was used to obtain the number of lay judges per 100,000 in 1990. The percent change in lay judges per 100,000 was calculated in the following manner. For each country, the number of lay judges per 100,000 in 1994 was subtracted from the number of lay judges per 100,000 in 1990. The difference was then divided by the number of lay judges per 100,000 in 1990 and multiplied by 100. The resulting data were as follows.

Table C5.1. Number of lay judges 1990, 1994 (per 100,000 pop.)

Country	Lay Judges per 100,000 1990	Lay Judges per 100,000 1994	Percent change 1990-1994
Belarus	.00	.00	N/A
Belgium	19.75	21.54	9.08
Costa Rica	.04	.00	-100.00
Croatia	N/A	139.92	N/A
Cyprus	.00	.82	N/A
Czech Rep	174.05	85.16	-51.07
England & Wales	56.70	58.43	3.05
Estonia	.00	.00	N/A
Finland	42.12	79.98	89.90
Hong Kong	.19	.18	-5.87
Hungary	130.32	119.69	-8.16
Indonesia	.00	.00	N/A
Israel	.00	.00	N/A
Jamaica	1.57	1.52	-3.25
Japan	.00	.00	N/A
Kiribati	N/A	142.86	N/A
Latvia	6.29	7.30	16.06
Liechtenstein	34.48	32.26	-6.45
Lithuania	.00	.00	N/A
Luxembourg	N/A	.00	N/A
Malta	1.69	1.92	13.46
Portugal	.00	.00	N/A
Rep of Moldova	.00	.00	N/A
Russian Fed.	.00	.00	N/A
Scotland	87.70	82.63	-5.78
Singapore	.00	.00	N/A
Slovakia	174.86	108.04	-38.21
Slovenia	343.39	301.49	-12.20
Sudan	13.20	11.75	-11.04
Sweden	N/A	91.12	N/A
Turkey	.00	.00	N/A
Uruguay	2.84	4.61	62.08
USA	.19	.18	-4.32
Zambia	.00	.05	N/A
Median	**.19**	**1.17**	**-5.78**
Mean	**36.31**	**37.98**	**-3.10**

2. The data were as follows:

Table C5.2. Prosecutors by level of development (1994, per 100,000 pop.)

Country	Prosecutors per 100,000 Pop.	Level of Economic Development
Colombia	10.56	Developing
Costa Rica	2.51	Developing
Cyprus	9.67	Developing
Egypt	1.24	Developing
El Salvador	4.11	Developing
Indonesia	2.79	Developing
Madagascar	2.39	Developing
Malaysia	.62	Developing
Panama	1.63	Developing
Peru	3.51	Developing
Philippines	2.37	Developing
Qatar	5.19	Developing
Rep of Korea	2.08	Developing
Sao Tome&Principe	4.80	Developing
Singapore	2.08	Developing
Sudan	.59	Developing
Turkey	3.85	Developing
Western Samoa	9.15	Developing
Zambia	.55	Developing
Australia	3.84	Industrial
Austria	2.49	Industrial
Azerbaijan	16.49	Industrial
Belarus	14.44	Industrial
Belgium	7.68	Industrial
Bulgaria	6.98	Industrial
Czech Rep	8.16	Industrial
Denmark	7.42	Industrial
England & Wales	4.06	Industrial
Estonia	8.21	Industrial
Finland	6.56	Industrial
Georgia	7.04	Industrial
Germany	6.60	Industrial
Greece	3.76	Industrial
Hungary	11.24	Industrial
Japan	1.68	Industrial
Kazakhstan	18.60	Industrial
Kyrgyzstan	11.73	Industrial
Latvia	15.62	Industrial
Lithuania	15.80	Industrial
Luxembourg	6.73	Industrial
Portugal	10.33	Industrial
Rep of Moldova	10.74	Industrial
Russian Federation	19.27	Industrial
Scotland	4.85	Industrial
Slovakia	10.47	Industrial
Spain	3.28	Industrial
Sweden	8.17	Industrial
Andorra	4.62	NA
Bermuda	11.11	NA
Croatia	6.97	NA
Liechtenstein	9.68	NA
Macau	2.15	NA
**"FYRM"	5.56	NA
Slovenia	7.31	NA
Median	**6.58**	
Mean	**6.84**	

*"Former Yugoslav Republic of Macedonia"

3. Pearson correlation coefficient = .51 (p=.000). See notes to figure 5.5 for data.

4. The number of corrections staff in adult institutions per 100,000 population in 1994 was calculated by summing the corrections personnel (management, custodial, treatment and others) in adult institutions reported by each country for 1994 in the Fifth UNCJS to yield the total number of corrections personnel in 1994. For each country, the total number of corrections personnel in 1994 was then divided by the population in 1994 as reported by the United Nations in *World Population Prospects 1950-2050 (The 1996 Revision)* and multiplied by 100,000 to yield the number of corrections personnel in adult institutions per 100,000 population in 1994. An identical procedure was followed to obtain the number of corrections personnel in adult institutions per 100,000 in 1986 and 1990, save that data were taken from the Fourth UNCJS to compute the figure for 1986. The resulting data were as follows.

Table C5.3. Corrections personnel 1986, 1990, 1994, per 100,000

	1986	1990	1994
Austria	43.72	42.26	43.76
Belgium	41.28	45.20	48.99
Bulgaria	30.54	30.43	31.91
Cyprus	52.44	30.84	29.43
Denmark	68.72	67.12	74.76
El Salvador	23.64	4.85	6.10
Finland	51.06	52.31	52.62
Hungary	29.33	49.00	.92
Jamaica	44.32	69.11	67.63
Japan	12.65	13.78	13.65
Malta	16.86	13.56	32.97
Netherlands	36.12	54.58	61.42
Portugal	31.69	38.99	41.97
Rep Of Korea	18.69	24.99	25.20
Russian Federation	64.57	122.40	147.24
Singapore	43.46	55.23	57.78
Turkey	39.33	40.41	39.18
Median	**39.34**	**42.27**	**41.97**
Mean	**38.14**	**44.42**	**45.62**

5. For more on the application of the Standard Minimum Rules for the Treatment of Prisoners, see Penal Reform International, 1995; United Nations, 1997a.

6. See *UN Crime and Criminal Justice Newsletter*, 32/33, June 1997 for a special issue on non-governmental organizations.

Chapter 6. Firearm abuse and regulation

1. Resolution 9, entitled, "Firearms regulation for the purposes of crime prevention and public safety."

2. Subsequently, the Secretary-General invited all remaining member states to participate in the project through the *Note Verbale* of 10 October 1996, as decided by the ECOSOC in its resolution 1996/28, adopted on the recommendation of the Fifth Session of the Commission on Crime Prevention and Criminal Justice. Responses to the survey were obtained through a "national consultant" in each country. The representatives of regional institutes coordinated the surveys within their regions and answered the follow-up questions of national consultants as required. Responses were coded into a database, a draft report was prepared, and a data validation process commenced. This involved firstly discussions with participants in the Expert Group Meeting of 10-14 February 1997 in Vienna, in which those who had been involved in preparing their country's response to the survey were asked to clarify their responses and to comment on their interpretations of the survey questions. Subsequently, *all* country respondents were sent copies of the tables from the draft report, together with some clarifications of terminology, providing an opportunity for respondents to add to or amend their original responses.

3. See also *Report of the Third United Nations Survey of Crime Trends, Operations of Criminal Justice Systems and Crime Prevention Strategies* (A/CONF.144/6; 27 July 1990) for a salient review of the difficulties and problems encountered in the comparison of international crime (and public health) statistics.

4. Although there have been significant changes in many countries in the last few decades in the way the criminal justice system treats violence in the home (or "domestic violence"), often involving the use of civil injunctions in addition to criminal sanctions, few countries as yet have recording systems which would identify persons with a record of domestic violence. See also Box 6.1.

5. A final report containing responses from 69 countries will be published in 1998 by the United Nations in English, French and Spanish.

Chapter 7. Drugs and drug control

1. The difference might be explained if sedatives were extremely concentrated in a small number of countries or if law enforcement operations or recording practices did not emphasize sedatives to the extent of the other drug types.

2. Much of this section is based on Kleiman (1994).

Chapter 8. Crime prevention

1. Throughout, national currencies have been expressed in US dollars (US$). At the time of writing, the exchange rates (the cost of purchasing one US$) were: Australia, A$1.4; Belgium, BF31; Canada, C$1.4; England, £0.6; France, 5.1FF; Netherlands, 1.6 guilders (dfl).

2. This budget does not include the recurring budget items that are paid to law enforcement agencies who may include in the tasks of their officers some responsibility for crime prevention. Nor does it include funds allocated by Ministries of Education or Social Services for programs such as preschool programs or employment training for young persons.

3. More information on the methodology used is available on request from the authors. Criminal justice costs were calculated on the basis of figures provided by the various countries. These figures are generally comparable in so far as they refer to police, courts and prison expenditures. Private security costs and property losses must be interpreted with caution as definitions vary between countries. Shattered lives has been calculated using the definition provided by Mandel *et al.* (1993), and the figure they provide for the USA has been used. For Australia, Canada, England and the Netherlands, the cost of shattered lives was calculated using their index, relative to the country specific victimization level. In France, the figure collected by CESDIP almost annually since 1972 was used.

4. RAND presented data for five strategies, showing the percentage of serious crime reduced and the corresponding program costs: 3 Strikes (21.4 percent, $5.5 billion); delinquent supervision (1.8 percent, $0.2 billion); parent training (6.6 percent, $0.4 billion); graduation incentives (15.5 percent, $0.6 billion); and home visits/day care (5.5 percent, $3.2 billion). We used these figures to estimate the costs to achieve a ten percent reduction in crime, as well as the percentage of the cohort treated (total cohort population in California multiplied by the proportion treatable in a full-scale program). Aggregate costs were then divided by the estimated total number of households in California (11.3 million). We have not reproduced the analysis for day care/home visits, as our estimates would be based on targeting day care/home visits to a smaller proportion of the cohort who would be at risk and so would have given a lower cost for this strategy. Also, the data were judged to be unreliable as they were based on: few experimental longitudinal trials upon which assumptions about effect size were based; not accounting for reductions in child abuse and neglect by parents in home visitation programs; and methodological uncertainties concerning the scale-up and decay functions used by the study.

5. The study used 1992 constant guilders (dfl), hence controlling for inflation. The figure is presented in US$ per household.

Chapter 9. Transnational crime

1. Statement by James N. Purcell, Jr., Director General, International Organization for Migration, at the European Conference on Trafficking in Women Organized by the European Commission and the International Organization for Migration (IOM) Vienna, 10-11 June, 1996

2. *Trafficking in Migrants Quarterly Bulletin,* No. 4, Sept 1994, p. 3.

3. *Ibid.*

4. US migration: passport smugglers earn billions for their wares. *Inter Press Service English News Wire,* New York, Dec. 16 1996.

5. Hill, Michael. 1995. Immigration crisis grows in S. Africa. *The Baltimore Sun,* February 6, 1995. See also: South Africans claim illegal immigrants steal jobs. *Migration News* 2, 3, March, 1995.

6. The new trade in humans. *The Economist*, 336, 7926: 45.

7. *Migration News,* 1, 11, December, 1994. See also: CIS: One in 30 residents of former USSR is migrant. Moscow INTERFAX in English, 1326 GMT 13 Oct 96 FBIS-SOV-96-200. Document type: daily report; document date: 13 Oct 1996. Other useful sources are: Andrei Nikolayev, Threat to Russia: what is it, *Soviet Press Digest,* November 23, 1994; Jan Cienski, Russia unable to deal with flock of refugees, *Deutsche Presse-Agentur*, November 17, 1994;and Anatoli Yelizarov, Illegal aliens in Russia, *Argumenty I Fakty, No. 29.*

8. The United States, for example, estimates that between 50,000 and 120,000 Chinese illegally enter the country every year. (The Presidential Initiative to Deter Alien Smuggling: Report of the Interagency Working Group puts the figure at 50,000 but other estimates are much higher.) While some of these migrants arrive on ships which are in poor repair and have appalling conditions for the passengers, about 90 percent of them come in by air, paying $30,000 to $35,000 to those who arrange for their passage. Although the seaborne Chinese immigrants have received a lot of publicity, the number of them who are seized is actually very small. DeStefano, Anthony M. Destination: Queens — The Traffic In Human Cargo, *Newsday*, June 3, 1996, p. A07.

Table N9.1. Illegal immigrants detained by US Coast Guard

Fiscal Year	Chinese Migrants	Dominican Migrants
1996	38	N/A
1995	455	3,387
1994	291	232
1993	2,517	873
1992	607	588
1991	138	1,007
1990	0	1,426

9. Central America: Anti-trafficking initiatives, *Trafficking in Migrants Quarterly Bulletin,* No. 13, December 1996.

10. *Trafficking and Prostitution: the Growing Exploitation of Migrant Women from Central and Eastern Europe.* (Geneva: International Organization for Migration, June 1996).

11. In most cases, the proceeds from prostitution were used to support parents or children. For those women really concerned about providing such support, opportunities in the licit economy were very limited in a society where $80 a month is the minimum salary for domestic work. Those coming to Europe traveled first to Denmark or Italy where visas were not required. The majority knew what they were involved in and were not deceived by being contracted as dancers. Significantly, however, many of those who returned to the Dominican Republic did so with mental disorders. *Trafficking in Women from the Dominican Republic for Sexual Exploitation* (Geneva: International Organization for Migration, June 1996).

12. Particularly alarming is the fact that some of the victims were as young as 14 when first brought to Italy. They were recruited by "deception, physical threats or payments made by the women's families." Nigerian women in particular are easily controlled because their families are forced to repay a huge debt, and many of them have never even attended school. Women from the former Yugoslavia and from Albania also loomed large. In Italy the number of people charged with trafficking women for sexual exploitation increased from 285 in 1990 to 737 in 1994 (258 of whom were foreigners with 158 from Central and Eastern Europe and 57 from Africa including 18 from Nigeria). *Trafficking in Women to Italy For Sexual Exploitation* (Geneva: International Organization for Migration, June 1996).

13. *Trafficking in Women to Austria for Sexual Exploitation* (Geneva: International Organization for Migration, June 1996).

14. *Ibid.*

15. *Ibid.*

16. *Trafficking and Prostitution: The Growing Exploitation of Migrant Women.* In the Netherlands in 1994, for example, nearly 70 percent of trafficked women were from Central and Eastern Europe. In Belgium, at least 10-15 percent (200-300) of the 2,000 foreign prostitutes are victims of trafficking. Women in the former Soviet bloc are particularly vulnerable. In the Russian Federation in 1992, for example, women made up 52 percent of the labor force but 71 percent of the unemployed. It is easier and cheaper to bring these women to Western Europe rather than those from developing countries. There are some variations in trafficking patterns: in the Netherlands, women are mostly recruited by friends and acquaintances, while in Belgium from 1990 to 1993 the majority was recruited by "impresario or agent." Whatever the initial lure, however, these women become extremely dependent on, or intimidated by, the traffickers, with the result that in the Netherlands only 12 of 155 cases went to court and only four resulted in convictions. From *Central and Eastern Europe, op. cit.*

17. This paragraph draws heavily on the recommendations of the International Organization for Migration in the various publications cited above.

18. For administrative, cultural and legislative measures, please see the *Report of the Secretary-General on Promotion and Maintenance of Rule of Law and Good Governance: Action Against Corruption,* Commission on Crime Prevention and Criminal Justice Sixth Session, Vienna, 28 April-9 May, 1997, as well as the addendum containing the *Report of the Expert Group Meeting on Corruption* held at Buenos Aries from 17 to 21 March 1997. They also draw heavily on *Governance and the Economy in Africa.*

19. See *Report of the Secretary-General on Promotion and Maintenance of Rule of Law and Good Governance: Action Against Corruption,* Commission on Crime Prevention and Criminal Justice Sixth Session Vienna 28 April-9 May 1997 as well as the addendum containing the *Report of the Expert Group Meting on Corruption* held at Buenos Aries from 17 to 21 March 1997.

20. Saving the World Bank. *The Washington Post,* April 19 1997, p. A20.

21. Riding, Alan. Art theft is booming, bringing an effort to respond, *The New York Times*, Nov 20, 1995, Security: C Cultural Desk: p.11.

22. *Ibid.*

23. *Sunday Times* (London), January 8, 1995.

24. Barker Godfrey and Laura Stewart. The salesman's job: the art of the possible (Sotheby's inquiry into "smuggling"). February 7, 1997 on Museum-Security Web Site (http://museum-security.org). See also Coggins, C., Illicit traffic of Pre-Colombian antiquities, *Art Journal*, 29 (1969): 94-98; Department: letter from Istanbul: a smuggler's den of antiquities, *Business Week,* April 15 1996; Younge, Gary, Stealing beauty from Africa, May 23, 1997 on Museum-Security Web Site.

25. Younge, Gary. Stealing beauty from Africa, May 23, 1997 on Museum-Security Web Site.

26. Thieves rob South Africa of its cultural heritage, *Cape Argus,* May 26, 1997.

27. Murphy, J.D. 1994. The People's Republic of China and the illicit trade in cultural property, *International Journal of Cultural Property,* 2, 3: 227-

242. See also, Vietnam: market reform opens doors to smuggling of relics, *IPS*, 15 May 1997.

28. *New York Times*, April 12, 1994. See also, Russia police: art smuggling grows, *Moscow News* 17 Apr 1997.

29. *La Republica* 30 Mar 1997.

30. Protecting cultural objects through international documentation standards, Getty Museum Web Site. See also: Doug Morrison, Auctioneers join police to fight art fraud, 4 November 1996, on Museum-Security Web Site.

31. *Hague Convention for the Protection of Cultural Property in the Event of Armed Conflict* (1954).

32. 1970 *UNESCO Convention on the Means of Prohibiting and Preventing the Illicit Import, Export, and Transfer of Ownership of Cultural Property.*

33. Protecting Cultural Objects Through International Documentation Standards: Background Part One: The Response of the International Community. While 37 countries voted in favor there were five against and 17 abstaining, and there was considerable opposition from art and antiquities dealers. Although such conventions are not always fully implemented, they have helped to publicize the problem and encouraged law enforcement agencies to recognize "illicit trade in cultural objects as a major category of international crime."

34. All information obtained from the *Art Loss Register.*

35. Report of the Secretary-General to the Commission on Crime Prevention and Criminal Justice, Sixth Session, Vienna, 28 April-9 May, 1997. *International Cooperation in Combating Transnational Crime: Illicit Trafficking in Motor Vehicles* E/CN.15/1997/9 February 24 1997, p. 3.

36. *Ibid.*

37. As one analysis of the situation in Europe noted, "Free-lance theft is on the decrease while thefts to order, carried out through established channels, are growing. Such thefts are conducted in an organized manner, from the theft itself, the forging of plates and documentation, transporting the car to its destination, right through to its sale. Cars stolen in European towns and cities have been ordered previously from Moscow, Warsaw, Prague, Kiev, Uzhgorod, Tirana, or Mostar, Sarajevo, Zenica, Belgrade, or even Tripoli. The biggest profits are reaped by the organisers." BANKA International, *Eastern European black markets: Car thieves.*

38. Rotella, Sebastian. Both sides of Mexico drug wars adore stolen 4x4s. *Los Angeles Times,* May 22, 1994, p. A-1.

39. Banerjee, Neela. International: Russian organized crime goes global; gangs use skills honed in former police state. *Wall Street Journal*, Dec 22, 1994 Sec: A p: 10.

40. According to one analysis "Over two-thirds of these cars end up on the Eastern European market, some of them in Croatia. Poland, where 37.5 percent of cars stolen in Europe are sold, is Europe's biggest black market. Next are Hungary (12.2 percent), the Czech Republic (12.6 percent), and Italy (10.4 percent). These figures, particularly in the case of Poland, do not reflect the real situation, because a large portion of stolen cars eventually find their way to the Russian and Ukrainian markets, after undergoing the necessary transformation, which includes laundering documentation" (Eastern European black markets, *op. cit.*).

41. Wright, Robin and Ronald J. Ostrow. Crime without borders. There is a dark side to globalization, one that has hit nearly every nation. And law enforcement is trying to cope. *Los Angeles Times,* April 27, 1993, Home Edition World Report, p. 1.

42. Christian, Nicole M. Autos: new generation of car thieves restructures the business. *Wall Street Journal*, July 19, 1995, Sec B, p: 1.

43. Escobar, Gabriel. Smuggling profitable in Andes; Argentina, Bolivia trade coca and cars. *The Washington Post,* September 17 1996, p. A11.

44. Many of these had been hired using stolen credit cards in Europe, after which they were driven to Britain and then sent to West Africa along with a variety of licit export products. In effect, as one British law enforcement officer noted "Britain is effectively being used as a clearing house for stolen prestige vehicles."

45. Christian, *op cit.*

46. *Ibid.*

47. *Ibid.*

48. At the simplest is the employment of additional protective devices by the car owners. Although anti-theft devices are far from foolproof, they do pose added complications for thieves. A step up from this is for more built-in anti-theft mechanisms and identification devices when the car is assembled. These include electronic devices which have to be present before the car will move, devices that are increasingly being embedded in ignition keys. As technology moves forward "smart keys" will become even more prevalent as will electronic immobilizers. Another initiative in the United States (which was part of the Federal Anti-Car Theft Act of 1992) is that from 1997 all new cars have to have vehicle identification numbers on 14 major components such as the engine, transmission and doors. Christian, *op cit.* See also Sean Malinowski, Eastern Europe battles transnational auto theft problems, *Criminal Justice Europe.*

49. Liukkonen, Markku. *International Cooperation in Combating Transnational Crime: Illicit Trafficking in Motor Vehicles.*

50. Stolen Cars Initiative. Office of International Criminal Justice, US Department of State Bureau For International Narcotics and Law Enforcement Affairs.

51. Liukkonen, Marrku. *International Cooperation in the Prevention and Control of the Illicit Trafficking in Motor Vehicles.* Submitted to HEUNI Sept 1996.

52. *International Cooperation in Combating Transnational Crime: Illicit Trafficking in Motor Vehicles.*

53. *Deutsche Presse-Agentur,* November 17, 1994.

54. *Inter Press Service,* July 21, 1995.

55. *Ibid.*

56. Those that survive bring high prices. Parrots that cost $15 in Mexico sell for $250 to $1500 in the United States. Profits are even greater on particularly rare species such as hyacinth macaws, which are smuggled from South America to the United States and can bring as much as $15,000 to $20,000 per bird. Indeed, it has been reported that "in Colombia alone, official figures indicate that an average of 600,000 wild animals are illegally exported from the country each year, at least 200,000 of which are primates headed towards research centers and laboratories." *Inter Press Service,* July 21, 1995.

57. Rare tortoise species threatened by thieves, on World Wildlife Fund Web Site.

58. Rare Madagascar reptiles seized, on World Wildlife Fund Web Site. See also *The Orlando Sentinel*, 17 August 1996 and US Department of Justice News Release, 22 August 1996.

59. *Zhongguo Xinwen She News Agency*, Beijing, in English 2 Dec 94, as reported by BBC Summary of World Broadcasts December 6, 1994.

60. In some African countries such as Swaziland there has been considerable success. Although Swaziland was rife with rhino poaching by commercial traffickers from 1988 to 1992 (losing one rhino every two weeks) arrests led to the breakup of a regional poaching syndicate and not a single rhino has been lost since December 1995.

61. As trade in endangered species increases, Dutch strengthen enforcement, *op cit.*

62. "Reportedly, more than 211,000 illicit items, whose ingredients contained or were purported to contain endangered species derivatives, were seized at Canada's west coast port in 1995, compared to only 1,200 items seized in 1987." *Agence France Presse*, 28 June 1996.

63. For example, according to a report by the US General Accounting Office the Department might have experienced as many as 250,000 attacks or intrusions in 1995, most of which were undetected and even when detected were unreported. *Information Security: Computer Attacks at Department of Defense Pose Increasing Risks* GAO/AIMD-96-84 (Washington: General Accounting Office, May 22, 1996).

64. Nevertheless, there was a report in June 1996 in *The Times* that companies in London, in other financial centers in Western Europe and in New York had paid up to 400 million pounds in response to threats to destroy computer and information systems. According to what was a

well researched analysis, there had been 40 attacks on financial institutions since 1993 using such devices as logic bombs and encrypted threats which demonstrated the capacity to penetrate the system. It was suggested that in some of the incidents a Russian criminal group was involved. City surrenders 400M pounds to gangs, *The Sunday Times* 2 June 1996 p.1.

65. Slatem, Steven. Secret incidents of hackers' attacks upon Czech banks and release of Czech citizens' personal information. *CEESSS*, 12 Nov 1996.

66. The subsequent analysis draws heavily on the news release: More than $13 billion lost worldwide to software piracy joint BSA/SPA survey reveals, (December 18, 1996) and *Software Publishers Association's 1995 Report on Global Software Piracy*.

67. *Ibid.*

68. Piracy in Middle East, Africa still high. *Reuters,* May 16, 1997.

69. Potter, William. Nuclear leakage from the post-Soviet states. Oral presentation before the Permanent Subcommittee on Investigations, US Senate Committee on Governmental Affairs March 13, 1996.

70. Woessner, Paul. Chronology of Nuclear Smuggling Incidents. In *Transnational Organized Crime,* 3, 2 (forthcoming).

71. *Global Proliferation of Weapons of Mass Destruction Part II.* Hearings before the Committee on Governmental Affairs, United States Senate, March 13, 20, 22, 1996.

72. *Ibid.*

73. *1995 Patterns of Global Terrorism.* 1996. Washington: US Department of State.

74. *Ibid.*

75. *Ibid.*

76. *Patterns of Global Terrorism, 1996.* 1997. Washington: US Department of State.

77. Gray, Herb. Solicitor General of Canada, *Statement on National Security*, May 14, 1996.

78. Walker, John. *Estimates of the Extent of Money Laundering in and through Australia.* Paper prepared for the Australian Transactions Reports and Analysis Center.

79. See *International Narcotics Strategy Report: Executive Summary.* Washington: State Department, March, 1996 (hereafter cited as INCSR).

80. *Money Laundering: Rapid Growth of Casinos Makes Them Vulnerable.* Washington: General Accounting Office Report.

81. *Ibid.* Funds are moved almost anywhere in the world with speed and ease. The global financial system includes not only banks but stock exchanges and other financial institutions that allow anonymous trading and thereby make it possible to obscure both origin and ownership. Moreover, the capacity to move money freely and easily across national jurisdictions makes it difficult for law enforcement to seize such assets.

82. See section on *Challenges Posed by a Changing Banking World*, International Narcotics Control Strategy Report 1996. Washington: State Department, March.

Notes to Figures

Introduction

Figures 0.1-0.3 Responsiveness to the United Nations Survey of Crime Trends and Criminal Justice Systems

Method of Computation. First, the number of responding countries was established for each of the five United Nations Survey of Crime Trends and Criminal Justice Systems (UNCJS). There were 72 responding countries for the First UNCJS, 88 for the Second, 93 for the Third, 101 for the Fourth, and 103 for the Fifth, although only 91 of these are considered in this volume since 12 of the responses were received too late for inclusion. These numbers are reported in Figure 1.

Next, the number of countries providing some information for a variety of specific data requests (described below) was determined for each of the five UNCJS by obtaining frequencies for the data of interest and choosing the year with the most non-missing responses. The number of non-missing cases, obtained for each data request in each UNCJS, was then divided by the respective number of responding countries to yield the percentage of countries providing some information to the specific data requests for each UNCJS. These percentages are reported in Figure 2.

The specific data requests were defined and, where different from that described above, operationalized for this analysis in the following manner.

1. Total Crimes: All crimes recorded by the police. Countries were not asked to provide a total recorded crime figure in the Fourth UNCJS.

2. Crimes by Type: The UNCJS asks the survey respondents to provide the number of crimes recorded by the police broken down into separate categories, including homicide, assault, rape, robbery, theft, burglary, fraud, embezzlement, drugs, bribery and/or corruption, and other. A country was considered a respondent to this type of data request if it provided information for at least one of these categories. Thus, frequencies for all of the crime types were examined for each year, and the year which had the most non-missing cases in each UNCJS, regardless of the crime type, was identified. The number of non-missing cases for this year and crime type in each UNCJS was then divided by the respective number of responding countries to yield the proportion of countries providing some information about recorded crime by type.

3. Total Arrests: The total number of persons brought into formal contact with the criminal justice system, whether arrested, suspected, or otherwise.

4. Arrests by Age: In the First, Second, and Fifth UNCJS, the responsiveness of countries to this data request was determined by the number of non-missing responses for a given year to a question asking about the total number of juveniles brought into formal contact with the criminal justice system. In the Third and Fourth UNCJS, the responsiveness of countries was determined by the number of non-missing responses for a given year to a question asking about the total number of juvenile males brought into formal contact with the criminal justice system.

5. Arrests by Gender: Countries were not asked to provide data on formal contact with the criminal justice system by gender in the First and Second UNCJS. In the Third and Fourth UNCJS, the responsiveness of countries was determined by the number of non-missing responses for a given year to a question asking about the number of adult males brought into formal contact with the criminal justice system. In the Fifth UNCJS, the responsiveness of countries was determined by the number of non-missing responses for a given year to a question asking about the total number of males brought into formal contact with the criminal justice sys-tem.

6. Total Convictions: The total number of persons convicted at the national level in criminal court.

7. Convictions by Crime: The UNCJS asks the survey respondents to provide the number of persons convicted in criminal court at the national level broken down into separate categories, including homicide, assault, rape, robbery, theft, burglary, fraud, embezzlement, drugs, bribery and/or corruption, and other. A country was considered a respondent to this type of data request if it provided information for at least one of these categories. Thus, frequencies for all of the crime types were examined for each year, and the year which had the most non-missing cases in each UNCJS, regardless of the crime type, was identified. The number of non-missing cases for this year and crime type in each UNCJS was then divided by the respective number of responding countries to yield the proportion of countries providing some information about the number of persons convicted in criminal court by crime type.

8. Prison Population: The total number of convicted prisoners held in prison.

9. Number of Police: The total number of police personnel.

10. Number of Professional Judges: The total number of professional judges or magistrates.

11. Number of Prison Personnel: In the First, Second, and Fifth UNCJS, a question on the total number of prison personnel was used to assess responsiveness to this data request. In the Third and Fourth UNCJS, the responsiveness of countries was determined by the number of countries which provided non-missing responses for a given year to questions asking about the total number of managerial and custodial staff in prisons.

Figure 0.4 Comparison between police data and victim surveys

This material has been compiled from the results of International Crime Victim Survey from 1988 to 1995 and is compared with data collected by the UK Research and Statistics Directorate (International Crime Survey 1997).

Table F0.1. Change in crime reported to the police and reported to the ICVS, 1988-1995

	Police figures	Victimization figures
England and Wales	+33.6%	+84.0%
Netherlands	+1.4%	+24.0%
Finland	+10.6%	+24.0%
USA	-7.9%	-24.0%
Canada	+0.7%	-9.0%

Chapter 1. The experience of crime and justice

Figure 1.1

Table F1.1. Percentage of the public victimized by car crimes, burglary, other theft, contact crimes, violence against women and violence against men over five years in urban areas of six global regions; results of the International Crime Victim Survey, 1989-1996

	Africa	Asia*	Central and Eastern Europe	Latin America	New World	Western Europe
number of countries	6	4	20	6	4	15
number of respondents	8,180	10.49	21.972	8.015	5,951	12.828
any crime	74.0	45.0	62.0	76.6	65.3	61.2

*Except Japan

Rates (percentages) are calculated from percent of those reporting victimization over the past five years. Data have been combined from three sweeps of surveys conducted in different countries at different points in time from 1988 through 1996. Please see notes to Chapter 1 for further details on the data collection of the ICVS. Individual country and national rates are presented in Table F1.2.

Table F1.2: Percentage of the public victimized by car crimes, burglary, other theft, contact crimes, violence against women and violence against men and any crime over five years in the urban areas of six global regions; results of the International Crime Victim Surveys, 1989-1996

	number of countries	number of cases	car crimes[1]	burglary + attempts	other thefts[2]	contact crimes[3]	assaults (women)[4]	assaults (men)[5]	any crime
all	55	67364	29.7	20.4	32.3	20.4	7.4	6.2	63.7
Western Europe									
Austria		413	28.7	6.5	28.5	16.2	6.5	6.3	53.9
Belgium		345	33.1	14.6	25.0	10.6	3.9	1.0	56.1
England & Wales		1700	42.3	22.5	21.1	16.7	4.5	6.6	63.4
Finland		1660	27.2	4.6	28.4	18.5	10.0	10.0	55.8
France		482	43.6	21.0	31.8	15.9	3.6	4.5	69.5
Germany (West)		1389	36.8	11.7	30.2	18.0	3.6	3.7	62.4
Italy		554	45.0	20.1	26.9	15.4	3.4	1.2	65.9
Malta		549	46.1	7.1	10.0	12.3	2.7	4.0	55.3
Netherlands		1225	40.5	25.2	48.7	22.3	5.7	6.9	77.0
Northern Ireland		176	33.1	10.9	19.8	13.8	3.3	8.1	54.8
Norway		164	35.9	15.3	20.1	16.3	10.4	3.4	56.2
Scotland		821	38.2	18.9	16.0	13.8	4.7	5.7	58.2
Spain		2615	43.8	11.7	20.9	19.2	3.1	4.0	63.5
Sweden		548	34.8	15.1	42.0	18.7	6.7	7.4	67.2
Switzerland		187	23.1	11.0	36.8	9.1	2.9	1.6	59.0
New World									
Australia		2174	42.8	25.6	22.2	18.3	5.5	9.2	64.1
Canada		2282	41.6	19.7	28.9	18.5	7.7	6.0	64.3
New Zealand		554	48.6	24.6	26.9	24.0	12.9	11.2	68.7
USA		941	45.4	23.4	28.5	19.8	5.7	7.0	64.1
Central and Eastern Europe									
Albania		983	9.6	15.5	35.0	12.7	6.0	1.6	52.6
Belarus		999	17.4	10.5	25.7	16.6	5.5	7.2	50.1
Bulgaria		1076	44.9	31.4	35.8	21.5	6.9	6.4	77.2
Croatia		930	29.9	8.1	20.0	15.2	5.3	5.4	53.4
Czech Rep.		1010	35.9	18.8	38.5	14.0	8.3	6.6	68.8
Estonia		842	26.8	27.1	31.7	22.3	6.4	8.7	64.0
Georgia		567	32.6	25.1	29.3	22.7	5.4	4.5	66.2
Hungary		756	34.6	16.6	24.2	10.3	1.8	3.6	57.4
Kyrgyzstan		1494	14.0	19.6	36.1	22.4	13.1	8.3	60.4
Latvia		1011	21.5	18.7	31.4	15.7	4.4	5.0	58.6
Lithuania		654	32.8	21.2	28.5	16.0	5.4	7.3	62.1
"Former Yugoslav Rep. Macedonia"		700	35.0	11.8	23.0	11.6	3.8	5.6	52.6
Mongolia		1053	12.3	28.1	44.0	18.7	5.8	8.7	68.2
Poland		1622	30.2	13.4	31.9	16.3	4.8	7.2	61.3

	number of countries	number of cases	car crimes[1]	burglary + attempts	other thefts[2]	contact crimes[3]	assaults (women)[4]	assaults (men)[5]	any crime
Romania		1000	20.7	10.7	29.8	18.1	7.3	9.7	56.1
Russia		2020	23.9	17.1	32.6	22.2	8.4	8.2	62.8
Slovenia		1126	37.8	16.5	38.4	7.2	2.0	1.4	66.1
Slovenia		2035	40.7	15.6	29.1	18.1	7.2	6.2	64.6
Ukraine		1000	15.6	18.6	42.8	19.5	5.6	7.4	64.8
Yugoslavia		1094	40.5	14.8	29.9	24.2	7.5	9.9	72.2
Asia									
China		2000	1.9	9.1	44.2	12.9	3.7	2.7	52.2
India		2039	6.6	9.9	28.5	14.6	8.7	2.2	43.7
Indonesia		3928	15.6	16.7	25.5	13.0	5.5	2.8	43.8
Philippines		2523	5.8	9.8	23.1	11.3	1.2	2.1	40.1
Africa									
Egypt		1000	20.0	22.0	35.5	32.0	8.9	3.6	68.9
South Africa		1994	24.2	23.1	24.7	28.7	11.5	12.8	64.2
Tanzania		1002	25.4	46.4	47.4	29.8	17.9	2.9	76.5
Tunisia		1086	25.9	32.0	46.0	31.4	7.2	7.6	76.5
Uganda		2020	24.3	56.1	53.7	39.8	21.2	7.8	87.8
Zimbabwe		1006	14.9	32.7	42.7	29.4	8.8	12.4	70.1
Latin America									
Argentina		2000	44.1	28.2	53.0	36.8	18.6	8.8	86.7
Bolivia		999	15.7	43.6	45.0	30.0	5.2	10.2	76.6
Brazil		2017	22.4	13.5	30.5	44.9	23.1	10.4	68.0
Colombia		1000	44.5	39.1	54.0	50.6	15.9	8.3	87.1
Costa Rica		1412	24.6	33.7	35.5	30.7	13.6	5.7	71.5
Paraguay		587	28.2	36.3	36.5	23.7	9.1	4.4	69.9

1. Car theft, theft from car and car damage.
2. Motorcycle theft, bicycle theft and other personal theft.
3. Robbery, sexual offences, threats and assaults.
4. Sexual assault and non-sexual assault.
5. Assault.

Figure 1.2

Table F1.3. Percentage of men and women victimized by violence over five years in urban areas of six global regions; results of the International Crime Victim Surveys, 1989-1996

	all	Africa	Asia	Central and Eastern Europe	Latin America	New World	Western Europe
assaults (women)	7.4	12.6	4.8	6.0	14.3	8.0	5.0
assaults (men)	6.2	7.9	2.4	6.5	8.0	8.4	5.0
any crime	63.7	74.0	45.0	62.0	76.6	65.3	61.2

Rates (percentages) are calculated from percent of those reporting victimization over the past 5 years. Data have been combined from three sweeps of surveys conducted in different countries at different points in time from 1988 through 1996. Please see notes to Chapter 1 for further details on the data collection of the ICVS.

Figure 1.5

Table F1.4. Percentages of offences victims say they reported to the police in six global regions; results of the International Crime Victims Surveys, 1989-1996, burglaries and violence against women

report to the police	all	Africa	Asia	Central and Eastern Europe	Latin America	New World	Western Europe
number of countries	55	6	4	20	6	4	15
N burglary	8152	1795	799	2251	1309	866	1131
% report burglary	66.8	62.6	41.5	64.6	45.3	86.3	81.5
N violence women	2880	577	239	807	680	225	351
% report violence women	29.7	31.3	21.9	27.3	17.5	44.6	35.2

Figure 1.6

Table F1.5. Percentage of victims satisfied with the police after reporting burglaries and contact crimes respectively, in six global regions, results of the International Crime Victim Survey, 1996

	all	Africa	Asia	Central and Eastern Europe	Latin America	New World	Western Europe
number of countries	43	3	3	19	6	2	10
burglary	47.2	29.0	44.5	35.4	24.5	76.5	73.5
N	3398	387	94	1365	445	248	861
contact crimes	53.2	45.3	59.4	41.0	36.6	69.8	67.2
N	2966	231	99	1022	510	267	836
violence women	55.1	44.7	57.4	45.8	50.8	68.2	63.7
N	551	65	23	199	61	53	150

Figure 1.7

Table F1.6. Percentages of victims of burglaries, contact crimes and violence against women respectively who received help from a specialized agency; results of the International Crime Victim Surveys, 1996

	all	Africa	Asia	Central and Eastern Europe	Latin America	New World	Western Europe
number of countries	43	3	3	19	6	2	10
burglary	4.1	3.0	4.3	3.2	1.4	2.5	10.1
N	5455	670	315	2244	1050	253	923
contact crimes	6.9	4.7	2.8	4.0	3.5	15.9	10.4
N	10232	1074	573	4196	2705	274	1410
violence women	10.4	6.8	1.6	3.6	5.5	28.2	16.9
N	1901	225	125	738	488	55	269

Chapter 2. Police records of crime

Figures 2.1-2.3

Raw data are as follows:

Table F2.1 Reported crime rates (homicide, theft, assault, rape and robbery), 1994

The figures in this table have been derived from the reported crime figures for 1994 in the 5th UNCJS for homicide, theft, assaults, rape and robbery. Reported figures have been divided by the population figure for the same country as reported in the United Nations *Demographic Yearbook*. Results have been rounded. The theft figures are expressed in rates per 10,000, and all other rates are per million population.

Country	Homicide rate/mill.	Theft rate/10,000	Assault rate/mill.	Rape rate/mill.	Robbery rate/mill.
Australia	49	-	-	783	802
Austria	35	19	4208	69	305
Azebaijan	89	6	56	10	39
Bahamas	828	-	-	717	1813
Belarus	99	70	310	65	674
Belgium	34	275	3333	90	145
Bermuda	133	261	10200	317	1550
Bolivia	234	39	-	314	1603
Bulgaria	113	193	128	107	785
Canada	20	344	7727	1085	989
Chile	45	13	3242	69	5147
Colombia	786	19	833	56	826
Costa Rica	96	51	661	95	5183
Croatia	82	95	260	21	86
Cyprus	17	16	1394	10	20
Denmark	51	397	1900	93	938
Ecuador	185	24	264	83	1948

Country	Homicide rate/mill.	Theft rate/10,000	Assault rate/mill.	Rape rate/mill.	Robbery rate/mill.
Egypt	15	0	2	0	6
Estonia	257	165	274	1987	-
Finland	104	226	3889	76	416
France	-	447	-	113	1271
Georgia	143	11	104	9	60
Greece	29	55	728	25	78
Hong Kong	16	51	1180	16	1028
Hungary	46	132	1075	80	249
India	79	3	-	14	26
Israel	72	18	2843	102	83
Italy	53	233	365	15	524
Jamaica	297	52	5542	428	2184
Japan	3	21	198	13	22
Jordan	573	13	2874	7	96
Kazakhstan	157	59	358	109	701
Latvia	165	109	424	50	457
Lithuania	151	23	258	45	218
Macau	-	58	2060	63	1205
Madagascar	4	2	81	3	2
Malaysia	-	2624	145	49	311
Malta	28	102	208	25	82
Mauritius	33	101	11692	31	697
Morocco	18	3	90	35	-
Nicaragua	256	17	2043	300	3028
Panama	124	63	1063	112	1408
Philippines	95	-	-	37	137
Qatar	24	12	444	28	-
Rep Korea	101	-	-	139	103
Rep Moldova	94	33	293	61	520
Romania	76	46	297	61	183
Russia	232	89	-	94	1003
St Vincent	160	-	-	-	-

Country	Homicide rate/mill.	Theft rate/10,000	Assault rate/mill.	Rape rate/mill.	Robbery rate/mill.
San Marino	-	-	-	-	-
Sao Tome	-	1	-	-	-
Singapore	18	93	-	-	-
Slovakia	39	111	113	15	153
Slovenia	58	83	-	112	655
Sudan	35	-	-	21	29
Sweden	119	576	6098	205	606
Syria	13	15	5	7	1
*"FYRM"	38	32	250	18	63
S Africa	666	194	5219	1073	2913
Turkey	29	12	527	8	25
Ukraine	97	-	-	33	627
UK-E and W	14	487	4092	98	1162
UK-Scot	22	67	1160	112	1039
UK-NI	213	208	2270	130	979
USA	90	363	4265	392	2371
Uruguay	-	166	2181	-	960
Zambia	152	-	-	37	357
Zimbabwe	160	148	6089	278	1115

*"Former Yugoslav Republic of Macedonia"

Table F2.2. Reported crime rates (burglary, fraud, drugs and embezzlement), 1994 (per million population)

The figures in this table have been derived from the reported crime figures for 1994 in the 5th UNCJS for burglary, fraud, drug-related crime and embezzlement. Reported figures have been divided by the population figure for the same country as reported in the United Nations *Demographic Yearbook*.

Country	Burglary	Fraud	Drugs	Embezzlement
Austria	11270	4032	1495	403
Azebaijan	158	59	298	-
Bahamas	1473	540	2490	-
Belarus	1974	149	139	283
Belgium	15466	607	1496	-
Bermuda	18900	6283	6900	4500
Bolivia	-	914	16	1062
Bulgaria	-	536	-	193
Canada	13283	3535	2075	-
Chile	-	262	628	351
Colombia	247	59	400	0
Costa Rica	4098	746	136	136
Croatia	4052	775	190	53
Cyprus	1844	588	193	26
Denmark	20450	1959	3012	201
Ecuador	707	488	1439	78
Egypt	100	48	1439	78
Estonia	-	523	22	134
Finland	19344	3057	1162	725
France	8404	1747	934	-
Georgia	-	23	202	-
Greece	3570	49	243	-
Hong Kong	2215	340	757	-
Hungary	7658	2553	25	445
India	13225	34	22	18
Israel	547	-	1631	-
Italy	-	710	669	-
Jamaica	584	717	2358	24
Japan	1981	416	184	15
Jordan	312	105	-	4
Kazakhstan	9	160	564	-
Kuwait	970	111	1318	19
Kyrgystan	2031	139	553	288
Latvia	-	303	111	82
Lithuania	1988	226	90	63
Macau	-	378	643	-

Country	Burglary	Fraud	Drugs	Embezzlement
Madagascar	90	19	22	1
Malaysia	1105	106	531	65
Malta	4773	93	615	3
Mauritius	873	1049	1711	436
Morocco	-	108	557	-
Nicaragua	27	424	224	-
Panama	-	415	1145	303
Qatar	590	94	34	106
Rep Korea	23	2824	39	455
Rep Moldova	1962	111	66	186
Romania	1339	534	12	-
SaoTome	60	4650	-	-
Singapore	848	663	636	224
Slovakia	8126	957	17	226
Slovenia	5485	2152	214	58
Spain	3599	306	-	111
Sudan	2700	1589	61	2
Sweden	16054	5675	3498	1046
Syria	118	34	195	0
*"FYRM"	4539	316	55	59
S Africa	7848	1549	1171	-
Turkey	-	37	38	-
Ukraine	-	222	547	183
UK-E & W	24473	2540	-	-
UK-Scot	17332	4293	3781	70
UK-NI	10564	3188	804	-
USA	10394	-	-	-
Zambia	1418	313	-	528
Zimbabwe	5220	-	-	-

*"Former Yugoslav Republic of Macedonia"

Figure 2.1 World homicide rates, 1994

The homicide rates from the raw data reported above (Table F2.1) have been used. Some extreme high values were excluded, both because of the likelihood of error and because their inclusion would adversely affect the colour-coding of the map.

Figure 2.2 World theft rates, 1994

The theft rates from the raw data reported above (Table F2.1) have been used. Some extreme high values were excluded, both because of the likelihood of error and because their inclusion would adversely affect the colour-coding of the map.

Figure 2.3 Crime reported in the UNCJS, 1994

This broad categorization of the amount of each type of crime was estimated from the 5th UNCJS figures for 1994. Estimation was necessary because not every country reported each type of crime. Broadly speaking, countries which reported all types of the crimes in Figure 2.3 were included and the amounts of reported crime for each such country was summed to make a total. This summation gave the following percentages of total crime reported to the UN in 1994:

Theft	50%
Burglary	20%
Assault	7%
Robbery	6%
Fraud	7%
Drug-related	7%
Other	3%

Figure 2.4 Percentage of countries reporting a fall in crime, 1990-1994

The figure has been created from the data in the table that follows and arranged in order of the percentage of countries showing a fall in reported crime over the period 1990 to 1994.

Raw Data (next page)

Table F2.3. Changes in UN reported crime, 1990-1994

	Countries showing a decrease	Countries showing an increase	Countries showing stability
Total Crime	17	48	4
Homicide	15	40	5
Assaults	12	42	2
Rape	17	42	8
Robbery	26	32	2
Theft	25	34	2
Burglary	20	30	4
Fraud	17	44	3
Embezzlement	18	22	2
Drugs-related	7	52	2

Table F2.4. Percentage of countries reporting a fall in crime, 1990-1994

Drug-related crime	11%
Assaults	21%
Homicide	25%
Total crime	25%
Fraud	27%
Rape	30%
Burglary	37%
Theft	41%
Robbery	43%

Figure 2.5 Countries reporting changes in homicides, thefts and rapes, 1986-1994

The following tables have used reported crime numbers from the 4th UNCJS for 1986 and the 5th UNCJS for 1994. The changes in crime have been calculated and arranged into six categories in the chart:

A fall of more than 10%
Stable (i.e. less than 10% rise or fall)
10% to 50% increase
50% to 100% increase
100% to 300% increase
Over 300% increase

Table F2.5. Change in number of homicides reported to UN 1986-1994

Fall of more than 10%: Canada, Costa Rica, Denmark, Egypt, Japan, Madagascar, Philippines, Singapore, Syria. [9]
Stable (change between -10% and +10%): England and Wales, Hungary, Italy, Mauritius. [4]
Change between +10% and +50%: Austria, Bermuda, Cyprus, Finland, Greece, Hong Kong, Romania, Slovenia. [8]
Change between +50% and +100%: Jamaica, Malta, Moldova, Qatar, Sweden. [5]
Change between +100% and +300%: Australia, Bulgaria, Chile, India, Jordan, Kyrgystan, Latvia, Lithuania, Russia, Slovakia. [10]
Change over +300%: Israel, Kuwait, Rep of Korea. [3]

Table F2.6. Change in number of rapes reported to UN 1986-1994

Fall of more than 10%: Austria, Denmark, Egypt, Hungary, Mauritius, Madacasgar, Slovakia. [7]
Stable (change between -10% and +10%): Japan, Jordan, Moldova, Slovenia, Syria. [5]
Change between +10% and +50%: Bermuda, Bulgaria, Chile, Costa Rica, Cyprus, Finland, Hong Kong, Italy, Korea, Kuwait, Latvia, Lithuania, Malaysia, Scotland, Russia, Jamaica. [16]
Change between +50% and +100%: Canada, India, Israel, Kyrgystan, Romania, Sweden. [6]
Change between +100% and +300%: Philippines, Qatar, England and Wales. [4]
Change over +300%: Australia, Malta, Turkey. [3]

Table F2.7. Change in number of thefts reported to UN 1986-1994

Fall of more than 10%: Bermuda, Chile, Cyprus, Denmark, Egypt, Hong Kong, Madagascar, Slovenia. [8]
Stable (change between -10% and +10%): Austria, Canada, India, Malaysia, Malta, Sweden. [6]
Change between +10% and +50%: Finland, Italy, Japan, Jamaica, Lithuania, Mauritius, Qatar, England and Wales, Scotland. [9]
Change between +50% and +100%: Moldova, Romania, Singapore, Turkey. [4]
Change between +100% and +300%: Hungary, Russia. [2]
Change over +300%: Bulgaria, Greece, Jordan, Kyrgystan, Latvia, Slovakia. [6]

Figure 2.6 Median reported crime rates by region, 1994

The data have been obtained from Table F2.1 and Table F2.2. For each individual offence group, the rates for each country have been arranged by UNDP region, and the median values for each region have been calculated. Regions where fewer than three countries reported data for a particular crime in 1994 have been excluded.

Table F2.8. Median reported crime rates (rape, assault, homicide and robbery) by region, 1994 (per million population)

UNDP Region	Rapes	Assaults	Homicides	Robberies
Eastern Europe	63	274	98	432
Western Europe	83	1394	35	416
North America	392	7727	90	1550
Latin America	112	1553	210	1813
Africa (sub-Sahara)	34	6089	151	697
Arab States	7	267	24	29
South Asia	65	2843	72	90
South East Asia	49			
East Asia	63			1028

Raw data are as follows:

Table F2.9. Reported rape rates, 1994

Countries reporting	63
Median reported rate	65 per million population
Rates of 90% of countries	Between 7 and 780
Rates of 75% of countries	Between 15 and 300
Median reported rates in UNDP regions:	
Eastern Europe	63 per million population
Western Europe	83 per million population
North America	392 per million population
Latin America	112 per million population
Africa (sub-Sahara)	34 per million population
Arab States	7 per million population
South Asia	14 per million poplulation
South East Asia	49 per million population
East Asia	63 per million population

Table F2.10. Reported assault rates, 1994

Countries reporting	52
Median reported rate	780 per million population
Rates of 90% of countries	Between 80 and 7700
Rates of 75% of countries	Between 140 and 4200
Median reported rates in UNDP regions:	
Eastern Europe	274 per million population
Western Europe	1394 per million population
North America	7727 per million population
Latin America	1553 per million population
Africa (sub-Sahara)	6089 per million population
Arab States	267 per million population
South Asia	2843 per million population

Table F2.11. Reported homicide offences, 1994

Countries reporting 62
Median reported rate .... 79 per million population
Rates of 90% of countries .... Between 14 and 590
Rates of 75% of countries .... Between 18 and 230
Median reported rates in UNDP Regins:
    Eastern Europe .... 98 per million population
    Western Europe .... 35 per million population
    North America .... 90 per million population
    Latin America .... 210 per million population
    Africa (sub-Sahara) .... 151 per million population
    Arab States .... 24 per million population
    South Asia .... 72 per million population

Table F2.12. Reported robbery offences, 1994

Countries reporting 61
Median reported rate .... 524 per million population
Rates of 90% of countries .... Between 20 and 2350
Rates of 75% of countries .... Between 40 and 1550
Median reported rates from UNDP regions:
    Eastern Europe .... 432 per million population
    Western Europe .... 416 per million population
    North America .... 1550 per million population
    Latin America .... 1813 per million population
    Africa (sub-Sahara) .... 697 per million population
    Arab States .... 29 per million population
    South Asia .... 54 per million population
    East Asia .... 1028 per million population

Figure 2.7 Median reported crime rates by region, 1994

The data have been obtained from Table F2.1 and Table F2.2. For each individual offence group, the rates for each country have been arranged by UNDP Region, and the median values for each region have ben calculated. Regions where fewer than three countries reported data for a particular crime in 1994 have been excluded.

Table F2.13. Median reported crime rates (burglary, fraud, drug-related and embezzlement) by region, 1994 (per million population)

UNDP Region	Burglary	Fraud	Drug-Related	Embezzlement
Eastern Europe	2010	450	139	184
Western Europe	11270	710	934	151
North America	13283	456		
Latin America	838	1049	448	136
Africa (sub-Sahara)	1145	105	1171	436
Arab States	312	206	376	3
South Asia			184	
East Asia	1981	378	643	

Table F2.14. Reported theft offences, 1994

Countries reporting 59
Median reported rate .... 59 per 10,000 population
Rates of 90% of countries .... Between 3 and 560
Rates of 75% of countries .... Between 12 and 260
Median reported rates in UNDP Regions:
    Eastern Europe .... 59 per 10,000 population
    Western Europe .... 217 per 10,000 population
    North America .... 344 per 10,000 population
    Latin America .... 39 per 10,000 population
    Africa (sub-Sahara) .... 50 per 10,000 population
    Arab States .... 2 per 10,000 population
    South Asia .... 21 per 10,000 population

Table F2.15. Reported burglary offences, 1994

Countries reporting 53
Median reported rate .... 1962 per million population
Rates of 90% of countries .... Between 30 and 19000
Rates of 75% of countries .... Between 150 and 13300
Median reported rates in UNDP Regions:
    Eastern Europe .... 2010 per million population
    Western Europe .... 11270 per million population
    North America .... 13283 per million population
    Latin America .... 838 per million population
    Africa (sub-Sahara) .... 1145 per million population
    Arab States .... 312 per million population
    East Asia .... 1981 per million population

Table F2.16. Reported fraud offences, 1994

Countries reporting 62
Median reported rate .... 450 per million population
Rates of 90% of countries .... Between 34 and 4293
Rates of 75% of countries .... Between 59 and 2824
Median reported rates in UNDP Regions:
    Eastern Europe .... 450 per million population
    Western Europe .... 710 per million population
    Latin America .... 456 per million population
    Africa (sub-Sahara) .... 1049 per million population
    Arab States .... 105 per million population
    South East .... 206 per million population
    East Asia .... 378 per million population

Table F2.17. Reported drug-related offences, 1994

Countries reporting 57
Median reported rate .... 531 per million population
Rates of 90% of countries .... Between 22 and 3012
Rates of 75% of countries .... Between 38 and 1631
Median reported rates in UNDP Regions:
    Eastern Europe .... 139 per million population
    Western Europe .... 934 per million population
    Latin America .... 448 per million population
    Africa (sub-Sahara) .... 1171 per million population
    Arab States .... 376 per million population
    South Asia .... 184 per million population
    East Asia .... 643 per million population

Table F2.18. Embezzlement offences, 1994

Countries reporting 43
Median reported rate .... 122 per million population
Rates of 90% of countries .... Between 1 and 1046
Rates of 75% of countries .... Between 4 and 450
Median reported rates in UNDP Regions:
    Eastern Europe .... 184 per million population
    Western Europe .... 151 per million population
    Latin America .... 136 per million population
    Africa (sub-Sahara) .... 436 per million population
    Arab States .... 3 per million population

Figure 2.8 Homicide and robbery rates for 35 cities, 1994

These figures are taken from the homicide and robbery numbers for reported crime for the Fifth UNCJS, together with the population of these cities as reported to the Fifth UNCJS for 1994. The raw data are reproduced below.

Table F2.19. Reported homicide rates by city, 1994

	Homicide rate/million 1994
Bogota	714
Kingston	628
La Paz	317
Guayaquil	288
Tallinn	261
Almorty	218
New York	213
Stockholm	209
Managua	186
Riga	178
Helsinki	145
Zagreb	144
Zurich	115
Sofia	104
Antananarivo	99
Copenhagen	87
San Jose	84
Seoul	84
Ljubljana	63
Minsk	63
Bratislava	62
Vienna	53
Budapest	52
Skopje	41
Bombay	41
Istanbul	40
Rome	40
Santiago	31
Toronto	28
London	23
Qatar	21
Hong Kong	16
Tokyo	15
Nicosia	12
Cairo	7

Table F2.20. Reported robbery rates by city, 1994

	Robbery rate/million 1994
New York	9896
San Jose	8651
New Providence	8539
Santiago	8117
Managua	6987
La Paz	5544
Madrid	5239
Kingston	5180
Lima	4596
London	3443
Bogota	3301
Tallinn	3152
Stockholm	2691
Chisinau	2160
Zurich	2065
Toronto	1782
Guayaquil	1755
Almorty	1534
Sofia	1458
Helsinki	1355
Copenhagen	1298
Kuala Lumpur	1235
Vienna	1067
Hong Kong	1034
Minsk	1020
Rome	802
Riga	784
Bratislava	731

	Robbery rate/million 1994
Paris	676
Moscow	547
Budapest	476
Ljubljana	433
Vilnius	289
Zagreb	271
Jackarta	237
Seoul	110
Skopje	102
Istanbul	88
Tokyo	54
Bombay	52
Atananarivo	18
Nicosia	12
Cairo	9

Figure 2.9 Homicide and theft rates by income and economic development, 1994

The data on homicide and theft have been obtained from Table F2.1. Median rates for homicide and theft have been calculated for:

a) Countries classified by the UNDP as High Income (GNP per capita above $8,625 in 1993), Medium Income (GNP per capita $696 to $8625 in 1993) and Low Income (GNP per capita $695 and below in 1993) (UNDP *Human Development Report 1996*).

b) Countries classified by the UNDP as Industrial, Developed and Least Developed (UNDP *Human Development Report 1996*).

Table F2.21. Classification of countries by income and development levels

Country	Income	Development	Country	Income	Development
Australia	High	Industrial	Austria	High	Industrial
Azerbaijan	Medium	Industrial	Bahamas	High	Developing
Belarus	Medium	Industrial	Belgium	High	Industrial
Bermuda	n/a	n/a	Bolivia	Medium	Developing
Bulgaria	Medium	Industrial	Canada	High	Industrial
Chile	Medium	Developing	Colombia	Medium	Developing
Costa Rica	Medium	Developing	Croatia	n/a	n/a
Cyprus	High	Developing	Denmark	High	Industrial
Ecuador	Medium	Developing	Egypt	Low	Developing
Estonia	Medium	Industrial	Finland	High	Industrial
France	High	Industrial	Georgia	Medium	Industrial
Greece	Medium	Industrial	Hong Kong	High	Developing
Hungary	Medium	Industrial	India	Low	Developing
Israel	High	Industrial	Italy	High	Industrial
Jamaica	Medium	Developing	Japan	High	Industrial
Jordan	Medium	Developing	Kazakhstan	Medium	Industrial
Latvia	Medium	Industrial	Lithuania	Medium	Industrial
Macau	n/a	n/a	Madagascar	Low	Least developed
Malaysia	Medium	Developing	Malta	Medium	Industrial
Mauritius	Medium	Developing	Morocco	Medium	Developing
Nicaragua	Low	Developing	Panama	Medium	Developing
Philippines	Medium	Developing	Qatar	High	Developing
Rep Korea	Medium	Developing	Rep Moldova	Medium	Industrial
Romania	Medium	Industrial	Russia	Medium	Industrial
St Vincent	Medium	Developing	San Marino	n/a	n/a
Sao Tome	Low	Least dev.	Singapore	High	Developing
Slovakia	Medium	Industrial	Slovenia	Medium	Industrial
Sudan	Low	Least dev.	Sweden	High	Industrial
Syria	Medium	Developing	"FYRM"*	n/a	n/a
Turkey	Medium	Developing	Ukraine	Medium	Industrial
UK-E & W	High	Industrial	UK-Scot	High	Industrial
UK-NI	High	Industrial	USA	High	Industrial
Uruguay	Medium	Developing	Zambia	Low	Least developed
Zimbabwe	Low	Developing			

Table F2.22. Median homicide rates per million population by income status of country

```
High ....................... 42
Medium ................... 98
Low ........................ 79
```

Table F2.23. Median homicide rates per million population by development status of country

```
Industrial ................. 90
Developing .............. 87
Least developed ....... 26
```

Table F2.24. Median theft rates per 10,000 population by income status of country

```
High ...................... 208
Medium ................... 48
Low .......................... 2
```

Table F2.25. Median theft rates per 10,000 population by development status of country

```
Industrial ................ 122
Developing ............. 19
```

Crime rates and Human Development Index. Statistical analysis was applied to the data reported in Table F2.26 and Table F2.1 producing no significant relationship between HDI and crime rate. The Human Development Index figures used are from the UNDP *Human Development Report 1996* and are listed below.

Table F2.26. Classification of countries by the UNDP Human Development Index

Country	HDI 1990	Country	HDI 1990	Country	HDI 1990
Australia	0.971	Austria	0.950	Bahamas	0.875
Belgium	0.950	Bolivia	0.394	Bulgaria	0.865
Canada	0.982	Chile	0.863	Colombia	0.758
Costa Rica	0.842	Cyprus	0.912	Denmark	0.953
Ecuador	0.641	Egypt	0.385	Finland	0.953
France	0.969	Greece	0.901	Hong Kong	0.913
Hungary	0.893	India	0.297	Israel	0.939
Italy	0.922	Jamaica	0.722	Japan	0.981
Jordan	0.586	Madagascar	0.325	Malaysia	0.789
Malta	0.854	Mauritius	0.793	Morocco	0.429
Nicaragua	0.496	Panama	0.731	Philippines	0.600
Qatar	0.802	Rep Korea	0.871	Romania	0.733
St Vincent	0.693	Sao Tome	0.374	Singapore	0.848
Sudan	0.157	Sweden	0.976	Syria	0.665
South Africa	0.674	Turkey	0.671	UK-E & W	0.962
USA	0.976	Uruguay	0.880	Zambia	0.315
Zimbabwe	0.397				

Figure 2.10 Monthly deaths caused by political violence: Kwa-Zulu-Natal, South Africa

The data are taken from the article by Louw (1997).

Table F2.27. Monthly recorded number of deaths caused by political violence, 1993-1996

	1993	1994	1995	1996
January	100	161	100	38
February	120	170	78	43
March	115	310	65	58
April	122	330	79	57
May	150	110	80	47
June	145	80	74	52
July	210	82	80	39
August	188	78	83	35
September	180	76	51	40
October	210	70	53	38
November	215	84	47	36
December	220	80	74	47

Chapter 3. Bringing to justice

Figure 3.1 Percent distribution of world's legal systems

Legal system	Number of countries
Islamic	6
Common	35
Civil/Common	20
Civil/Islamic	10
Common/Islamic	9
Socialist	5
Civil	88

Figure 3.2 The world's legal systems

The following listing excludes countries for which no data were available. These classifications have been derived from *The International Factbook of Criminal Justice Systems* and Reichel (1994)

Country	Legal system
Afghanistan	Islamic & combinations
Albania	Civil
Algeria	Islamic & combinations
Andorra	Civil
Angola	Civil
Antigua and Barbuda	Common
Argentina	Civil/Common
Armenia	Civil
Australia	Common
Austria	Civil
Azerbaijan	Civil
Bahamas	Common
Bahrain	Islamic & combinations
Bangladesh	Common
Barbados	Common
Belorussia	Civil
Belgium	Civil
Belize	Common
Benin	Civil
Bhutan	Common
Bolivia	Civil
Bosnia and Herzegovina	Civil
Botswana	Civil
Brazil	Civil
Brunei	Islamic & combinations
Bulgaria	Civil
Burkina Faso	Civil
Burundi	Civil
Cambodia	Other

Cameroon	Civil	Madagascar	Civil
Canada	Civil/Common	Malawi	Common
Cape Verde	Other	Malaysia	Common
Central African Republic	Civil	Maldives	Islamic & combinations
Chad	Civil	Mali	Civil
Chile	Civil	Malta	Civil/Common
China	Socialist	Marshall Islands	Other
Colombia	Civil/Common	Mauritania	Islamic & combinations
Comoros	Islamic & combinations	Mauritius	Civil/Common
Congo	Civil	Mexico	Civil/Common
Costa Rica	Civil	Micronesia	Other
Croatia	Civil	Moldavia	Civil
Cuba	Socialist	Monaco	Civil
Cyprus	Civil/Common	Mongolia	Civil
Czech Republic	Civil	Morocco	Islamic & combinations
Denmark	Civil	Mozambique	Civil
Djibouti	Islamic & combinations	Namibia	Civil
Dominica	Common	Nepal	Common
Dominican Republic	Civil	Netherlands	Civil
Ecuador	Civil	New Zealand	Common
Egypt	Islamic & combinations	Nicaragua	Civil
El Salvador	Civil/Common	Niger	Civil
Equatorial Guinea	Civil	Nigeria	Islamic & combinations
Estonia	Civil	Norway	Civil/Common
Ethiopia	Other	Oman	Islamic & combinations
Fiji	Common	Pakistan	Islamic & combinations
Finland	Civil	Palau	Other
France	Civil	Panama	Civil
Gabon	Civil	Papua New Guinea	Common
Gambia	Islamic & combinations	Paraguay	Civil
Georgia	Civil	Peru	Civil
Germany	Civil	Philippines	Civil/Common
Ghana	Common	Poland	Civil
Greece	Civil	Portugal	Civil
Greenland	Civil	Puerto Rico	Common
Grenada	Common	Qatar	Islamic & combinations
Guam	Common	Romania	Civil
Guatemala	Civil	Russian Federation	Civil
Guinea	Civil	Rwanda	Civil
Guinea-Bissau	Other	Saint Lucia	Common
Guyana	Common	Saint Vincent and the Grenadines	Common
Haiti	Civil	San Marino	Civil
Honduras	Civil/Common	Sao Tome and Principe	Civil
Hong Kong	Common	Saudi Arabia	Islamic & combinations
Hungary	Civil	Senegal	Civil
Iceland	Civil	Seychelles	Civil/Common
India	Common	Sierra Leone	Common
Indonesia	Civil	Singapore	Common
Iran	Islamic & combinations	Slovakia	Civil
Iraq	Islamic & combinations	Slovenia	Civil
Ireland	Common	Solomon Islands	Common
Israel	Common	Somalia	Islamic & combinations
Italy	Civil	South Africa	Civil/Common
Ivory Coast	Civil	Spain	Civil
Jamaica	Common	Sri Lanka	Islamic & combinations
Japan	Civil/Common	Sudan	Islamic & combinations
Jordan	Islamic & combinations	Surinam	Civil
Kazakhstan	Civil	Swaziland	Civil
Kenya	Islamic & combinations	Sweden	Civil
Kyrgyzstan	Civil	Switzerland	Civil
Korea, Dem.Peoples Rep.	Socialist	Syria	Islamic & combinations
Rep. of Korea	Civil/common	Tadzhikistan	Civil
Kuwait	Islamic & combinations	Taiwan	Civil/Common
Laos	Socialist	Tanzania	Common
Latvia	Civil	Thailand	Civil/Common
Lebanon	Civil	Togo	Civil
Lesotho	Civil/Common	Trinidad and Tobago	Common
Liberia	Common	Tunisia	Islamic & combinations
Libya	Islamic & combinations	Turkey	Civil
Liechtenstein	Civil	Turkmenistan	Civil
Lithuania	Civil	U.S. Virgin Islands	Common
Luxembourg	Civil	Uganda	Common
"FYRM"	Civil	Ukraine	Civil

United Arab Emirates .... Islamic & combinations
United Kingdom .... Common
United States .... Common
Uruguay Civil
Uzbekistan Civil
Vanuatu .... Civil/Common
Vatican City Civil
Venezuela Civil
Vietnam .... Socialist
Western Sahara .... Other
Western Samoa .... Common
Yemen .... Islamic & combinations
Yugoslavia Civil
Zaire Civil
Zambia .... Common
Zimbabwe .... Civil/Common

Figure 3.3 and Figure 3.4 Offender processing rates, 1994 (per 100,000 population)

Figures are based on Table F3.1.

Table F3.1. Raw data on suspects and prosecutions

| | Suspects | | | | | Prosecutions | | | | |
	1990	1991	1992	1993	1994	1990	1991	1992	1993	1994
Belarus	42400	43925	52300	58743	66073	3253	3142	3641	4254	5794
Croatia	29937	25470	56616	39948	37710	44642	31793	24836	28196	27459
Cyprus	2801	2926	3434	3423	3935	931	824	983	841	1074
Denmark	148683	143107	156389	155704	147094	143093	115439	156915	157548	164794
Egypt	16528	19041	21737	21117	19149	6098005	6836232	3889841	7679047	7177073
Estonia	5230	5157	6951	9956	9316	5230	5157	6951	9956	9316
Finland	289217	222305	223006	209511	211791	98188	102567	100196	97296	88870
Hungary	112254	122835	132644	122621	119494	72267	104733	113598	104640	102875
Italy	547288	628180	680851	717991	744892	348127	506280	561230	550354	601369
Japan	378217	380907	357037	371640	376988	123938	120080	114085	119105	118721
Latvia	12879	12719	15231	15262	13350	7481	8256	10967	12622	11633
Rep.Mold.	17356	18058	15946	16007	17850	12114	13404	13310	15556	16647
Slovakia	37670	42495	43457	51746	48803	30563	34659	36899	40612	42436
Slovenia	27555	28899	37737	32332	31787	13070	11571	11640	10920	9320
*"FYRM"	15252	15874	23236	23550	24076	12957	13170	14321	15864	14832
Turkey	144249	150034	168908	232762	250969	1175149	1354527	1322920	1422139	1651851
Hong Kong	44013	44059	41780	45042	49784	31122	29148	27665	29125	33742

*"Former Yugoslav Republic of Macedonia"

| | Convictions | | | | | Imprisonments | | |
	1990	1991	1992	1993	1994	1990	1992	1994
Belarus	29840	32814	36990	47610	53401	16004	23875	37629
Croatia	25346	19146	15015	18015	18546	1487	1371	1637
Cyprus	665	680	793	656	766	193	188	142
Denmark	27010	25088	25625	25953	27471	2322	2309	2584
Egypt	3261887	3809527	3920671	3914733	4264130	22762	28343	32257
Estonia	3532	3954	5036	6274	7276	3529	2912	2595
Finland	94521	98859	96624	93781	85460	2923	2994	2642
Hungary	47694	65647	77481	74481	78324	8819	11424	8944
Italy	118116	158264	177362	193275	206631	11030	19855	25630
Japan	58603	55339	55235	57313	58889	39938	37293	37482
Latvia	7159	7372	9097	11280	11295	7308	6492	6901
Rep of Moldova	10429	11983	11863	13274	15233	7001	7557	7267
Slovakia	11821	22878	23634	25667	25442	2874	5054	5509
Slovenia	10839	9354	8733	7966	7316	505	603	537
*"FYRM"	8942	8452	8113	8399	8266	890	794	1149
Turkey	466228	630944	646989	670516	751147	29506	13193	20926
Hong Kong	21536	20415	19904	21562	25663	10980	9875	10781

*"Former Yugoslav Republic of Macedonia"

	1990 (E)	1992 (E)	1994 (E)	1990	1992	1994
Suspects	534.9794	574.0847	601.8509	624.2831	672.4956	710.365
Prosecutions	2349.736	1806.29	2791.149	714.1811	840.8708	956.6683
Convictions	1201.768	1448.178	1563.51	317.1158	406.5604	455.4985
Imprisonments	48.04335	49.0691	56.66933	48.90237	48.64368	56.84307

Figure 3.5 Number of adult male suspects per adult female suspects, 1994

Table F3.2. Number of adult male suspects per adult female suspects, 1994

Method of computation. Derived from Table 3.2.

Bolivia	1.97
Jamaica	2.54
Sudan	4.04
Austria	4.07
Denmark	4.25
United States of America	4.30
Sao Tome & Principe	4.54
Japan	4.54
Morocco	4.69
Canada	4.87
Sweden	4.87
Ukraine	5.04
Hong Kong	5.50
France	5.68
Bermuda	6.15
Russian Federation	6.22
Rep of Korea	6.45
Slovenia	6.99
Madagascar	7.09
Lithuania	7.20
Kyrgyzstan	7.33
Saint Vincent & The Grenadines	7.44
Hungary	8.39
Rep of Moldova	9.44
Latvia	9.72
Bulgaria	9.76
Nicaragua	9.95
Ecuador	10.11
Romania	10.32
Slovakia	12.50
Syrian Arab Republic	13.96
Cyprus	14.18
Chile	14.28
Azerbaijan	14.51
Yugoslavia	14.56
Georgia	15.19
Colombia	15.67
Bahamas	16.89
Croatia	19.48
Marshall Islands	20.74
Qatar	21.33
India	23.79
Indonesia	54.55
Western Samoa	91.00
Average	**12.41**

Figure 3.6. Number of juvenile male suspects per juvenile female suspects, 1994

Table F3.3. Number of juvenile male suspects per juvenile female suspects, 1994

Method of computation. Derived from Table 3.2.

Jamaica	2.00
Bolivia	2.28
United States of America	3.02
Romania	3.05
Sao Tome & Principe	3.34
Syrian Arab Rep	3.42
Madagascar	3.50
Sudan	3.85
Canada	3.98
Japan	4.05
Sweden	4.34
Morocco	4.62
India	4.96
Hong Kong	5.15
Austria	5.50
Chile	5.56
Denmark	5.57
Nicaragua	6.24
Bermuda	6.29
Saint Vincent & The Grenadines	7.35
France	9.51
Slovenia	11.18
Russian Federation	11.27
Hungary	11.61
Ukraine	12.18
Bahamas	12.67
Rep of Moldova	12.69
Latvia	13.64
Kyrgyzstan	13.71
Ecuador	13.93
Lithuania	14.73
Colombia	15.67
Rep of Korea	15.68
Slovakia	18.82
Bulgaria	19.76
Yugoslavia	27.34
Croatia	30.17
Qatar	57.33
Azerbaijan	73.00
Indonesia	78.88
Georgia	79.44
Average	**15.64**

Figure 3.7 Number of adult male convictions per female convictions, 1994

Table F3.4 Number of adult male convictions per female convictions, 1994

Method of computation. Data derived from Table F3.6

Qatar	167.24
Kazakhstan	28.43
Chile	27.51
Azerbaijan	20.45
Turkey	18.55
Slovakia	18.37
Lithuania	17.70
Rep of Macedonia	16.37
Cyprus	15.53
Estonia	13.16
Rep of Moldova	12.23
Bulgaria	12.23
Rep of Korea	11.54
Croatia	11.11
Japan	11.02
Czech Republic	10.36
Hungary	10.29
Portugal	9.66
Malaysia	9.66
Russian Federation	9.46
Latvia	9.27
Israel	8.24
Netherlands	8.11
Northern Ireland	8.02
South Africa	7.42
Canada	7.25
Slovenia	6.94
Switzerland	6.61
Greece	6.51
England & Wales	6.49
Scotland	6.32
Belarus	5.85
Finland	5.47
Sweden	5.37
Hong Kong	5.23
Italy	5.20
Germany	4.45
Austria	4.37
Average	**14.95**

Figure 3.8 Number of juvenile male convictions per juvenile female convictions, 1994

Table F3.5. Number of juvenile male convictions per juvenile female convictions, 1994

Method of computation. Derived from Table F3.6.

Finland	4.44
Italy	4.50
Canada	4.87
Sweden	5.05
Switzerland	5.63
Hong Kong	7.82
England & Wales	7.90
South Africa	7.90
Slovenia	8.09
Germany	8.24
Austria	8.68
Northern Ireland	9.06
Chile	9.40
Malaysia	10.44
Estonia	11.91
Rep of Moldova	12.05
Latvia	12.80
Netherlands	13.16
Turkey	13.88
Czech Republic	13.90
Belarus	15.18
Scotland	15.50
Russian Federation	15.56
Hungary	15.64
Portugal	16.12
Kazakhstan	16.37
Lithuania	17.02
Japan	19.08
Israel	22.60
Greece	24.65
Bulgaria	29.77
Croatia	31.76
Rep of Korea	36.86
"Former Yugoslav Rep. Macedonia"	38.54
Azerbaijan	51.42
Slovakia	80.79
Average	**17.41**

Table F3.6. Number of convictions by gender and age and rate of all convictions per 100,000 population, 1994

Country	Adult Males	Adult Females	Juvenile Males	Juvenile Females	Total	Rate
Austria	53824	12312	3003	346	69485	865.21
Azerbaijan	11024	539	617	12	12192	163.17
Belarus	40412	6905	5708	376	53401	515.70
Bulgaria	8132	665	655	22	9474	112.21
Canada	83622	11536	61360	12609	169127	578.25
Chile	34332	1248	141	15	35736	255.37
Croatia	15903	1431	1175	37	18546	411.77
Cyprus	590	38	38	0	666	90.74
Czech Rep	41857	4040	5629	405	51931	502.57
Estonia	5670	431	1084	91	7276	485.39
Finland	64648	11826	7333	1653	85460	1677.33
Germany	360273	81040	53574	6498	501385	615.88
Greece	68454	10517	4658	189	83818	803.93
Hungary	63601	6180	7084	453	77318	753.51
Israel	29001	3520	2260	100	34881	647.98
Italy	170195	32748	3018	670	206631	361.29

Country	Adult Males	Adult Females	Juvenile Males	Juvenile Females	Total	Rate
Japan	53769	4879	229	12	58889	47.19
Kazakhstan	48466	1705	1228	75	51474	302.31
Latvia	9124	984	1101	86	11295	443.29
Lithuania	13472	761	2196	129	16558	444.99
Malaysia	51690	5351	376	36	57453	294.80
Netherlands	67197	8283	5660	430	81570	530.36
Portugal	26549	2747	4885	303	34484	350.80
Qatar	2843	17	61	0	2921	540.93
Rep.Korea	111777	9683	7593	206	129259	290.78
Rep.Moldova	12502	1022	1578	131	15233	350.18
Russian Fed.	735433	77703	104710	6728	924574	624.72
Slovakia	21181	1153	3070	38	25442	475.82
Slovenia	5497	792	914	113	7316	376.73
South Africa	39123	5271	29171	3692	77257	191.06
Sweden	104061	19386	24667	4882	152996	1742.55
Switzerland	64109	9698	6999	1244	82050	1172.98
*"FYRM"	6337	387	1503	39	8266	385.90
Turkey	680032	36657	32142	2316	751147	1227.71
Eng.& Wales	188253	28999	91596	11600	320448	622.96
Hong Kong	20326	3890	1283	164	25663	423.41
Northern Ireland	6821	850	607	67	8345	511.39
Scotland	44098	6979	124	8	51209	997.76
Totals					4311176	509.84

*"Former Yugoslav Republic of Macedonia"

Figure 3.9 Suspect rates and GNP per capita, 1994 (US dollars, per 100,000 population)

The relationship between rates at which suspects are taken by the police and income levels of countries are presented in Figure 3.9. In this display the rate of suspects per 100,000 population (1994) is shown against Gross National Product per capita (1995). The countries have been arranged in ascending order of GNP per capita. The left axis represents GNP per capita in US$ in 1995 and the right axis presents suspect rate per 100,000 population. The chart appears to show that except for Japan all the countries with high GNP per capita tend to have high suspect rate. The trend line show that the suspect rate rose slowly until about Croatia in the x-axis and thereafter a faster increase occurred. The trend data could be very helpful in developing an appropriate research strategy to investigate the link between crime and suspect rate and income level thoroughly.

Chapter 4. Punishment

Figure 4.1 Types of punishments applied to adult convicted persons (34 countries, percent of total, 1994)

The base numbers are persons and not cases, since they are records of sanctions imposed upon the convicted person. It should be noted that when a country did respond to the survey but did not provide information for a certain type of punishment, this could either mean that such type of sentencing does not exist in the country, or that it is not utilized in sentencing practice, or that data are not available.

Method of computation. The percentages of each adjudication punishment to the total sentence number was calculated. Data were provided by Fifth UNCJS. Some countries are excluded from analysis, because of their irregular data.

The number of total adults sentenced should match the summing up of different kinds of sentencing to adults, namely: total adults receiving life imprisonment, total adults receiving corporal punishment, total adults receiving sentence of deprivation of liberty, total adults receiving control in freedom, total adults receiving warning, total adults receiving fine, total adults receiving community service order, and total adults receiving other sentences.

The following countries provided data in which either the total sentencing exceeds summation of all types of sentence options or the summation of all types of sentencing options exceeds provided total sentencing.

1. Andorra: Original total exceeds added total by 1;
2. Belgium: Added total exceeds original total by 2327;
3. Bulgaria: Added total exceeds original total by 5122;
4. Canada: Original total exceeds added total by 710;
5. Germany: Original total exceeds added total by 177;
6. Hungary: Added total exceeds original total by 17575;
7. Kyrgyzstan: Original total exceeds added total by 5124;
8. Latvia: Original total exceeds added total by 4200;
9. Qatar: Added total exceeds original total by 18;
10. Russian Fed: Added total exceeds original total by 57052;
11. Singapore: Added total exceeds original total by 309;
12. Slovakia: Added total exceeds original total by 2031;
13. Switzerland: Added total exceeds original total by 3170;
14. FYR of Macedonia: Original total exceeds added total by 2608.

Among them, we excluded countries in which the summation of all types of sentencing options exceeds the provided total sentencing. Then, we incorporated countries which provided for a discrepancy of less than 1,000.

Table F4.1. Types of punishments applied to all adult convicted persons (percent of total, 1994)

Country	Life Sentence	Corporal Punishment	Depriv. Liberty	Control in Freedom	Warning	Fine	Community Service	Other
Colombia	0.00	0.00	100.00	0.00	0.00	0.00	0.00	0.00
Greece	0.02	0.00	95.91	0.00	0.00	4.07	0.00	0.00
Mexico	0.00	0.00	92.29	0.00	0.00	6.58	0.00	1.13
Rep of Moldova	0.13	0.00	83.05	0.00	0.00	16.82	0.00	0.00
Italy	0.02	0.00	60.03	0.00	0.00	39.95	0.00	0.00
South Africa	0.00	7.18	56.76	0.01	22.51	7.78	0.00	5.75
Georgia	–	–	53.17	7.77	19.12	7.49	11.63	0.82
Hong Kong	0.09	0.00	47.93	5.84	12.75	31.19	2.19	0.00
Portugal	0.00	0.00	44.94	0.17	29.88	24.58	0.43	1.42
Netherlands	0.00	0.00	44.52	0.00	0.04	46.82	8.63	0.00
Lithuania	0.03	0.00	44.41	51.43	0.00	4.11	0.00	0.02
Zambia	0.91	26.55	41.04	5.67	9.44	12.50	0.00	3.89
Kazakhstan	0.00	0.00	40.10	0.00	51.06	8.84	0.00	0.00
Azerbaijan	0.00	0.00	39.89	35.48	0.10	6.98	12.83	4.71
Costa Rica	0.00	0.00	37.38	42.11	0.00	20.51	0.00	0.00
Cyprus	0.32	0.00	35.67	2.87	28.82	32.32	0.00	0.00
Belarus	0.00	0.00	33.14	11.02	46.12	9.15	0.00	0.57
Turkey	0.03	0.00	32.10	0.00	16.67	45.07	0.00	6.13
Canada	0.00	0.00	29.80	28.16	2.58	38.65	–	0.14
Estonia	0.00	0.03	27.27	0.00	40.80	31.50	0.00	0.39
Rep of Korea	0.06	0.00	24.03	54.40	1.26	18.01	0.00	2.23
Scotland	0.06	–	22.21	8.13	11.35	48.51	7.01	2.93
Czech Rep	0.00	0.00	21.97	66.25	0.00	11.15	0.00	0.63
Egypt	0.02	0.24	21.86	–	0.22	77.66	–	–
Northern Ireland	0.23	–	20.69	8.80	35.26	28.26	6.02	0.73
Myanmar	0.02	0.00	16.83	0.38	0.28	82.49	0.00	0.00
Slovenia	0.00	0.00	14.58	0.00	73.67	11.75	0.00	0.00
Andorra	0.00	0.00	14.42	42.94	0.00	31.56	0.00	10.93
Israel	0.03	–	11.95	52.02	0.00	26.78	1.94	7.27
Austria	0.02	0.00	9.87	18.96	0.54	70.61	0.00	0.00
Finland	0.01	0.00	9.54	0.00	15.66	72.90	1.89	0.00
Germany	0.02	0.00	6.87	13.92	0.84	78.31	0.00	0.00
England & Wales	0.02	–	4.41	7.07	7.98	79.33	–	1.19
Japan	0.00	–	1.95	0.43	2.69	94.93	–	0.00
Mean	**0.06**	**1.21**	**36.49**	**14.06**	**12.64**	**33.15**	**1.75**	**1.54**

Figure 4.2 Types of serious punishments applied to all adult convicted persons (34 countries, percent of total, 1994)

Method of computation. For the countries selected in Table F4.1, total number of life imprisonment, corporal punishment, deprivation of liberty and control of freedom is calculated, then the percentage of each type of punishment in the above-mentioned total was calculated as follows in Table F4.2.

Table F4.2. Selected "serious" punishments applied to all adult convicted persons (percent of total, 1994)

Country	Life Sentence	Corporal Punishment	Depriv. of Liberty	Control in Freedom
Colombia	0	0	100	0
Kazakhstan	0	0	100	0
Mexico	0	0	100	0
Netherlands	0	0	100	0
Slovenia	0	0	100	0
Greece	0.02	0	99.98	0
Italy	0.03	0	99.97	0
Turkey	0.08	0	99.92	0
Finland	0.11	0	99.89	0
Estonia	0	0.12	99.88	0
Rep of Moldova	0.15	0	99.85	0
Portugal	0	0	99.63	0.37

Country	Life Sentence	Corporal Punishment	Depriv. of Liberty	Control in Freedom
Egypt	0.1	1.08	98.83	–
Myanmar	0.09	0	97.68	2.23
Cyprus	0.82	0	91.8	7.38
Hong Kong	0.18	0	88.98	10.84
South Africa	0	11.22	88.75	0.02
Georgia	–	–	87.24	12.76
Japan	0.17	–	81.89	17.94
Belarus	0	0	75.05	24.95
Scotland	0.19	–	73.06	26.75
Northern Ireland	0.79	–	69.61	29.61
Zambia	1.23	35.8	55.33	7.64
Azerbaijan	0	0	52.92	47.08
Canada	0.01	0	51.41	48.59
Costa Rica	0	0	47.02	52.98
Lithuania	0.03	0	46.33	53.64
England & Wales	0.16	–	38.34	61.5
Austria	0.07	0	34.22	65.71
Germany	0.09	0	33.02	66.89
Rep of Korea	0.08	0	30.62	69.3
Andorra	0	0	25.13	74.87
Czech Rep	0	0	24.9	75.1
Israel	0.04	–	18.68	81.28
Mean	**0.13455**	**1.72214**	**73.8215**	**25.3767**

Figure 4.3 Incarceration rate by world regions, 1994 (per 100,000 population)

Method of computation. Average incarceration rate and convicted prisoner rate for each region were calculated from numbers reported for Table T4.2 and Table T4.3 (see Notes to Tables Chapter 4). Each country was labeled according to geographical region. Average figures of each region were computed by SPSS (one-way ANOVA, list-wise deletion of missing data). Calculated data are shown in Table F4.3. There was a significant statistical relationship ($p<.05$) which permits the rejection of the null hypothesis (all regions have equal incarceration rates and convicted prisoner rates).

Table F4.3. Incarceration rate by world regions, 1994 (per 100,000 population)

Region	Convicted Prisoners	Total Prisoners
New World	189.38	255.44
Countries in Transition	148.23	214.13
World Average	96.14	149.17
Africa	39.31	144.79
Latin America	70.63	142.78
Asia	96.35	121.92
Western Europe	57.37	85.05

Figure 4.4 Change in prison admission by convicted prisoners; Western and Eastern Europe.

Method of computation. Because of the problem mentioned in the explanation for computation at Table T4.5 (see Notes to Tables Chapter 4), the one-way ANOVA analysis failed to reject the null hypothesis, "average number of total prison admission and prison admission by convicted prisoners are equal" for all world regions. Consequently, Western European countries and Eastern and Central European countries, which provided more samples and produced a significant difference, were deliberately chosen. Averages of each group were computed by SPSS. Calculated figures are shown in Table F4.4 below.

Table F4.4. Change in prison admission by convicted prisoners; Western and Eastern Europe 1990-1994 (per 10,000 population)

	1990	1991	1992	1993	1994
Western Europe	51.73	51.93	53.86	56.52	54.01
Countries in Transition	154.49	150.89	174.27	186.19	211.27

Figure 4.5 Change in prison population rate in world regions; 1990, 92, 94

Method of computation. Average incarceration rates for 1990, 1992 and 1994 for each region were calculated from numbers of Table T4.2 (see Notes to Tables Chapter 4) by labeling each country according to the region to which it belongs. Average figures for each region were computed by SPSS (one-way ANOVA), and it was decided to include this in the chapter because there was a significant statistical relationship ($p<.05$) which permits the rejection of the null hypothesis (all regions have equal incarceration rates and convicted prisoner rates). Calculated data are shown in Table F4.5.

Table F4.5. Change in prison population rate in world regions; 1990, 92, 94

Region	1990	1992	1994
New World	219.71	240.04	255.44
Countries in Transition	153.59	189.23	214.13
World Average	130.7	138.45	149.17
Africa	140.36	135.22	144.79
Latin America	153.03	141.35	142.78
Asia	129.25	121.93	121.92
Western Europe	78.81	82.38	85.05

Figure 4.6 Percentage of convicted and remand prisoners by world regions, 1994

Method of computation. Percentages of convicted prisoners and remand prisoners are calculated for each country by dividing the respective numbers by total prison population. Then the average percentage of each category was aggregated according to the world region to which the country belongs. It produced a statistically significant relationship which permits the rejection of the null hypothesis (all world regions have the same average convicted or remand prisoners rate). Calculation was made by ANOVA method on SPSS, and data are shown in Table F4.6.

Table F4.6 Percentage of convicted prisoners and remand prisoners by world regions, 1994

Region	Convicted	Remand
New World	84.62	13.51
Asia and the Pacific	71.63	24.84
Countries in Transition	66.03	23.82
Western Europe	65.15	31.34
World Average	60.51	33.67
Latin America	43.49	47.89
Africa	35.89	63.76

Figure 4.7 Percentage of convicted and remand prisoners by development aggregate, 1994

Method of computation. Percentages of convicted prisoners and remand prisoners are calculated for each country by dividing respective numbers by total prison population. Then the average percentage of each category was aggregated according to the developmental stage labeled by UNDP to which the country belongs. It produced a statistically significant relationship which permits the rejection of the null hypothesis (all world regions have the same average convicted or remand prisoners rate). Calculation was made by ANOVA method on SPSS, and data are shown in Table F4.7.

Table F4.7. Percentage of convicted prisoners and remand prisoners by development aggregate, 1994

Development Aggregate	Convicted	Remand
Least Developed	35.89	63.78
Developing Countries	53.37	39.34
Industrial Countries	69.07	24.87

Figure 4.8 Variations in parole, total prisoners, convicted prisoners, total admissions, sentences to prison (rates per 100,000) and average time spent in prison (weeks), 1990-1994: selected countries

Method of computation. Selection of countries was based on data availability. For each country, numbers are taken from existing tables (total prisoner rate from Table T4.2, convicted prisoner rate from Table T4.3, total prison admission from Table T4.4 and parole rate from Table T4.6 — for each table, see Notes to Tables Chapter 4) except for average effective sentence and adults sentenced to imprisonment. Average effective sentence was directly adopted from the Fifth UNCJS data, whereas the adults sentenced to imprisonment was calculated by dividing the reported number of adults sentenced to deprivation of liberty by 100,000 population of each country as reported in the United Nations *Demographic Yearbook*.

Table F4.8. Variations in parole, total prisoners, convicted prisoners, total admissions, sentences to prison (rates per 100,000) and average time spent in prison (weeks), 1990-1994: England, Finland, Japan, Latvia and Belarus

England & Wales	1990	1992	1994
Total prisoner rate	88.06	89.01	95.02
Convicted prisoner rate	68.97	68.85	68.48
Total prison admission rate	256.01	279.95	304.26
Rate of imprisonment sentence (adult)	81.46	83.59	101.41
Parole rate	25.46		3.84
Average time spent in prison (week)	28	29	25

Finland	1990	1992	1994
Total prisoner rate	67.79	69.52	62.37
Convicted prisoner rate	58.62	59.38	51.85
Total prison admission rate	177.12	195.38	170.97
Rate of imprisonment sentence (adult)	223.89	214.88	143.22
Parole rate	119.66		106.87
Average time spent in prison (week)	33	37	37

Japan	1990	1992	1994
Total prisoner rate	37.93	36.29	36.96
Convicted prisoner rate	32.33	30.02	30.04
Total prison admission rate	36.31	35.91	38.57
Rate of imprisonment sentence (adult)	19.1	17.64	17.86
Parole rate	15.37		13.15
Average time spent in prison (week)	85	90	90

Latvia	1990	1992	1994
Total prisoner rate	326.69	313.53	359.69
Convicted prisoner rate	273.61	246.66	270.84
Total prison admission rate	147.29	141.22	163.07
Rate of imprisonment sentence (adult)	246.57	198.06	257.34
Parole rate	13.79		46.59
Average time spent in prison (week)	234	234	234

Belarus	1990	1992	1994
Total prisoner rate	204.07	314.76	477.78
Convicted prisoner rate	155.98	231.5	363.39
Total prison admission rate	97.73	152.21	207.27
Rate of imprisonment sentence (adult)	75.44	95.93	151.41
Parole rate	7.27		46.94
Average time spent in prison (week)	4	4	5

Figure 4.9 Capital punishment around the world

Data are taken from Amnesty International (1997a). Bolivia reports its status as abolitionist in the Fifth UNCJS. However, Amnesty International classifies Bolivia as "de facto" abolitionist since its Penal Code extends capital punishment to treason, parricide, homicide, etc. (see Hood, 1996). Amnesty International classifies South Africa as abolitionist for ordinal crimes only. Hood (1996) contends it can be categorized as totally abolitionist. Amnesty International (1997b) reports that Bahamas, Bahrain, Comores, Guatemala and Thailand resumed executions in 1996.

Figure 4.10 Abolitionist and retentionist countries in 1988 and 1996

1988 data are taken from Hood (1996) p.9, Table 1. 1996 data are taken from Amnesty International (1997a).

Figure 4.11 and Figure 4.12 Favoured sentence by region and development status (ICVS, 1996)

Method of computation. The 1996 International Crime Victim Survey data, on which both figures are based, are as shown in Table F4.9.

Table F4.9. Favoured sentence by region and development status

	Fine	Prison	Community	Suspended
Global region				
Western Europe	9.9	28.7	46.2	7.7
New World	6.9	53	22.7	5.3
Countries in Transition	10.2	38.9	32.3	7.5
Asia	7.7	71	9	1.9
Africa	9.9	72.6	10.2	2.5
Latin America	6.3	49.8	30.4	5.1
Status				
Industrialized Countries	8.4	40.8	34.5	6.5
Countries in Transition	10.2	38.9	32.3	6.5
Developing Countries	8	64.5	16.5	3.2

Chapter 5. Resources in criminal justice

Figure 5.1 Median distribution of personnel in the criminal justice workforce, 1986, 1994 (27 countries)

Table F5.1. Percent corrections, court and police personnel, 1994 (Fifth UNCJS)

Country	% Corrections Personnel 1994	% Court Personnel 1994	% Police Personnel 1994
Austria	10.10	5.14	84.75
Belgium	11.86	4.74	83.40
Colombia	6.67	6.73	86.59
Costa Rica	.32	.08	99.60
Croatia	6.09	4.02	89.89
Cyprus	5.15	3.29	91.56
England & Wales	15.08	1.44	83.48
Estonia	26.13	3.32	70.55
Finland	17.01	8.01	74.97
Greece	4.33	4.03	91.63
Hungary	.28	10.01	89.71
Japan	6.06	1.76	92.18
Latvia	13.15	4.09	82.75
Liechtenstein	19.54	12.64	67.82
Lithuania	15.38	3.38	81.24
Madagascar	34.63	7.90	57.47
Malaysia	8.59	.21	91.20
Rep of Korea	10.78	2.05	87.17
Rep of Moldova	17.91	5.20	76.90
Russian Federation	10.52	1.98	87.50
Scotland	16.98	1.70	81.32
Singapore	5.08	.44	94.48
Slovenia	6.74	7.03	86.24
Sweden	14.88	3.64	81.48
*"FYRM"	5.93	6.65	87.41
Turkey	16.21	5.22	78.57
Zambia	15.20	1.84	82.96
Median	**10.78**	**4.01**	**84.75**
Mean	**11.88**	**4.32**	**83.81**

*"Former Yugoslav Republic of Macedonia"

Table F5.2. Percent corrections, court and police personnel, 1986 (Fourth UNCJS)

Country	% Corrections Personnel 1986	% Court Personnel 1986	% Police Personnel 1986
Austria	10.03	5.20	84.76
Botswana	28.69	1.40	69.91
Costa Rica	72.88	11.91	15.20
Cyprus	7.85	2.56	89.60
Ethiopia	.00	50.50	49.50
Finland	16.67	6.39	76.94
Hong Kong	9.28	.40	90.32
Hungary	5.70	5.22	89.08
Italy	12.95	3.08	83.97
Latvia	6.04	2.60	91.37
Lesotho	17.47	.19	82.34
Lithuania	10.61	1.73	87.66
Mauritius	11.93	.17	87.90
Myanmar	.00	4.14	95.86
Nepal	5.64	13.84	80.52
Netherlands	11.74	2.77	85.49
Norway	20.64	4.15	75.21
Philippines	.00	2.77	97.23
Rep. of Korea	9.72	1.85	88.43
Rwanda	7.25	53.12	39.63
Singapore	11.58	.92	87.51
Slovenia	7.32	7.89	84.79
Swaziland	31.90	1.41	66.69
Sweden	15.12	7.10	77.78
Syria	5.19	.53	94.28
Turkey	19.78	6.79	73.43
Ukraine	3.63	1.44	94.93
Median	**10.03**	**2.78**	**84.79**
Mean	**13.32**	**7.41**	**79.27**

Method of Computation. The distribution of personnel in the criminal justice workforce was calculated in the following manner. For each country, the number of police, prosecutors and professional judges, and corrections personnel (management, custodial, treatment and others) in adult facilities were summed to yield the total size of the criminal justice workforce in 1986 (Fourth UNCJS) and 1994 (Fifth UNCJS). The percentage of the criminal justice workforce in policing was obtained for each year by dividing the number of police by the total criminal justice workforce and multiplying by 100. The percentage of the workforce in courts was obtained for each year by dividing the number of court personnel (prosecutors and professional judges) by the total criminal justice workforce and multiplying by 100. The percentage of the workforce in adult corrections was obtained for each year by dividing the number of corrections personnel (management, custodial, treatment and others) in adult facilities by the total criminal justice workforce and multiplying by 100. The data in Figure 5.1 represent the median percentage of personnel in each sector of the criminal justice workforce.

Figure 5.2 Proportion of personnel in police, courts and corrections functions, 1994

Definitions for each occupational category may be found in Appendix 1. Raw Data: see Table F5.1.

Method of Computation. See notes to Figure 5.1 for method of computing the proportion of personnel in police, courts and corrections functions in 1994.

Figure 5.3 Number of police per 100,000 population, selected countries, 1986-1994

Table F5.3. Number of police 1986, 1990, 1994 (per 100,000)

Country	1986	1990	1994
Canada	273.26	283.49	249.00
Greece	394.29	387.12	383.02
India	134.77	134.98	134.12
Madagascar	29.60	30.70	21.31
Philippines	183.18	184.34	155.02
Rep of Korea	170.06	202.96	203.72

Method of Computation. See notes to Table 5.1 for method of calculating the number of police per 100,000 population in 1994. An identical procedure was used to calculate the figures for 1986 and 1990, save that data from the Fourth UNCJS were used for 1986.

Figure 5.4 Policing rate by crime rate, 1994 (per 100,000 population)

See Appendix 1 for definitions of crime categories.

Table F5.4. Police, thefts and homicides, 1994 (per 100,000 population)

Country	Police per 100,000 Pop.	Thefts per 100,000 Pop.	Intentional Homicides per 100,000
Australia	274.65	N/A	1.65
Austria	367.00	1582.32	1.10
Bahamas	743.43	N/A	18.98
Belgium	344.37	2732.98	1.19
Bermuda	796.83	2485.71	9.52
Canada	249.00	3430.40	N/A
Chile	275.62	125.60	N/A
Colombia	274.91	233.25	78.44
Costa Rica	36.34	520.84	5.93
Croatia	669.60	690.08	3.17
Cyprus	522.89	134.88	.95
Denmark	237.69	3963.07	1.44
Egypt	37.16	3.04	.40
England & Wales	346.69	4863.56	N/A
Estonia	436.22	1649.03	20.15
Finland	231.91	2261.71	2.89
France	349.28	4455.77	2.43
Greece	383.02	550.00	1.28
Hong Kong	639.89	513.71	1.52
Hungary	292.77	1321.70	3.05
India	134.12	33.05	4.20
Japan	207.62	1049.80	.56
Jordan	468.81	126.34	3.79
Kazakhstan	778.66	591.57	N/A
Latvia	463.46	1067.94	13.66
Lithuania	544.99	1036.82	12.50
Madagascar	21.31	23.74	.42
Malaysia	429.65	262.50	1.72
Malta	507.14	1125.00	.82
Marshall Islands	268.52	5.56	3.70
Morocco	100.38	6.88	.69
Nicaragua	145.15	173.94	12.47
Northern Ireland	520.46	2036.56	5.09
Panama	432.75	629.89	N/A
Rep of Korea	203.72	N/A	1.30
Rep of Moldova	241.20	334.05	7.63
Romania	214.16	457.57	3.41
Russian Federation	1224.58	888.39	20.21
Scotland	359.64	4641.75	2.12
Singapore	1074.68	919.56	1.71
Slovakia	352.23	1099.81	1.98
Slovenia	412.05	811.69	2.11
Spain	128.70	184.74	.68
Sweden	281.99	5770.41	1.81
*"FYRM"	317.79	314.33	N/A
Turkey	189.89	122.67	N/A
Ukraine	418.61	N/A	8.14
USA	300.06	3613.68	N/A
Uruguay	830.88	1563.85	N/A
Western Samoa	283.54	218.90	.00
Zambia	106.81	N/A	9.04
Median	**344.37**	**750.88**	**2.28**
Mean	**381.82**	**1318.01**	**6.52**

*"Former Yugoslav Republic of Macedonia"

Pearson r for theft by policing=.002

Pearson r for murder by policing=.14 with Colombia included, .53 with Colombia excluded.

Method of Computation. See notes to Table 5.1 for method of calculating the number of police per 100,000 population. The theft rate for 1994 was computed by dividing the total number of thefts reported by each country in the Fifth UNCJS by each country's 1994 population as reported by the United Nations in *World Population Prospects 1950-2050 (The 1996 Revision)* and multiplying by 100,000. The murder rate for 1994 was calculated by dividing the total number of intentional homicides reported by each country in the Fifth UNCJS by each country's 1994 population as reported by the United Nations in *World Population Prospects 1950-2050 (The 1996 Revision)* and multiplying by 100,000.

Figure 5.5 Corrections staff and convicted prisoners, 1994 (per 100,000 population)

Table F5.5. Number of corrections personnel and convicted prisoners, 1994 (per 100,000 population)

Country	Corrections Personnel	Adult Convicted Prisoners
Australia	55.69	132.59
Austria	43.76	62.00
Belarus	28.67	351.97
Belgium	48.99	37.34
Bermuda	314.29	309.52
Brunei Darussalam	75.17	196.15
Bulgaria	31.91	67.74
Chile	44.47	62.59
Colombia	21.19	40.27
Costa Rica	52.69	192.54
Croatia	45.38	36.35
Cyprus	29.43	19.35
Czech Rep	78.49	94.67
Denmark	74.76	49.64
Egypt	1.44	55.76
El Salvador	6.10	29.74
England & Wales	62.63	58.37
Estonia	161.57	170.85
Finland	52.62	49.19
Georgia	34.96	138.05
Greece	18.12	36.21
Guyana	37.58	117.58
Hong Kong	55.42	148.29
Hungary	60.36	83.32
Indonesia	12.00	14.64
Japan	13.65	30.01
Kuwait	30.99	.19
Kyrgyzstan	50.37	300.26
Latvia	73.67	250.20
Lithuania	103.17	193.68
Luxembourg	46.13	75.56
Macau	74.46	47.73
*"FYRM"	21.57	48.32
Madagascar	12.84	50.44
Malaysia	40.47	79.69
Marshall Islands	14.81	27.78
Mexico	31.61	48.33
Northern Ireland	179.49	87.02
Panama	16.11	40.50
Portugal	41.97	62.58
Rep of Korea	25.20	75.82
Rep of Moldova	56.16	209.59
Russian Federation	147.24	558.08
Sao Tome&Principe	31.20	16.80
Scotland	75.07	73.75
Singapore	57.78	222.76
Slovenia	32.18	27.65
Sudan	43.50	187.19
Sweden	51.49	58.54
Switzerland	39.09	63.40
Turkey	39.18	33.19
Ukraine	41.57	234.64
Zambia	19.57	94.94
Median	**41.97**	**63.40**
Mean	**52.81**	**108.55**

*"Former Yugoslav Republic of Macedonia"

Method of Computation. The number of corrections staff in adult facilities per 100,000 population in 1994 was calculated by dividing the total number of corrections workers (management, custodial, treatment and others) in adult facilities reported by each country for 1994 in the Fifth UNCJS by each country's 1994 population as reported by the United Nations in *World Population Prospects 1950-2050 (The 1996 Revision)* and multiplying by 100,000. The number of convicted adult prisoners per 100,000 population in 1994 was computed by dividing the total number of convicted adult prisoners reported by each country for 1994 in the Fifth UNCJS by each country's 1994 population as reported by the United Nations in *World Population Prospects 1950-2050 (The 1996 Revision)* and multiplying by 100,000.

Figure 5.6 Number of corrections staff per 100,000 population, selected countries, 1986-1994

Table F5.6. Number of corrections personnel, 1986, 1990, 1994 (per 100,000 population)

Country	1986	1990	1994
Austria	43.72	42.26	43.76
Bulgaria	30.54	30.43	31.91
El Salvador	23.64	4.85	6.10
Japan	12.65	13.78	13.65
Rep of Korea	18.69	24.99	25.20
Singapore	43.46	55.23	57.78

Method of Computation. See notes to Figure 5.5 for method of computing the number of corrections staff in adult institutions per 100,000 population in 1994. An identical method was used to calculate the number of corrections staff in adult institutions per 100,000 population in 1986 and 1990, save that data for the 1986 figure were obtained from the Fourth UNCJS.

Figure 5.7 Corrections staff and convicted prisoners, 1990-1994 (per 100,000 population)

Table F5.7. Percent change adult convicted prisoners and corrections personnel, 1990-1994

Country	% change Adult Convicted Prisoners	% change Corrections Personnel
Austria	10.38	3.53
Belarus	135.61	89.67
Belgium	22.11	8.38
Brunei Daruss.	-12.78	4.43
Bulgaria	-34.67	4.86
Colombia	-16.82	5.53
Croatia	16.78	11.54
Cyprus	-16.08	-4.57
Denmark	9.89	11.37
Egypt	29.07	.35
El Salvador	233.23	25.70
Finland	-12.07	.60
Greece	6.42	7.60
Guyana	-16.81	-7.68
Hungary	3.05	23.2
Japan	-7.10	-.91
Latvia	4.96	-38.63
Lithuania	.05	3.53
Madagascar	-25.98	-27.70
Marshall Islands	112.96	-57.41
Mexico	12.76	80.49
Portugal	1.53	7.66
Rep of Korea	12.04	.84
Sao Tome & P.	60.57	2.51
Singapore	65.14	4.62
Slovenia	10.28	6.28
Sudan	9.04	-4.89
Switzerland	14.46	26.25
Rep of Macedonia	24.20	-10.37
Turkey	-35.28	-3.06
Ukraine	36.97	18.63
Zambia	10.13	-12.21
Hong Kong	-7.49	13.49
Northern Ireland	.15	-3.94
Scotland	17.55	13.73
Macau	-56.05	75.32
Bermuda	-18.97	-13.64
Median	**6.42**	**3.53**
Mean	**12.92**	**3.89**

Method of Computation. See notes to Figure 5.5 for method of computing the number of corrections staff in adult institutions per 100,000 population in 1994. An identical method was used to calculate the number of corrections staff in adult institutions per 100,000 population in 1986 and 1990, save that data for the 1986 figure were obtained from the Fourth UNCJS. Also, see notes to Figure 5.5 for method of computing the number of convicted adult prisoners in 1994. An identical method was used to calculate the number of convicted adult prisoners in 1986 and 1990, save that data for the 1986 figure were obtained from the Fourth UNCJS.

Figure 5.8 Proportion of the criminal justice workforce that were female, 1994

Table F5.8. Percent personnel by level of development

Country	%Female Corrections Per. 1994	%Female Judicial Per. 1994	%Female Prosecution Per. 1994	%Female Police Per. 1994	Level of economic development
Austria	12.46	18.57	16.00	13.56	Industrial
Cyprus	4.17	8.96	33.80	5.00	Non-Industrial
Greece	10.16	37.04	17.09	5.64	Industrial
Latvia	36.23	70.97	57.54	17.55	Industrial
Liechtenstein	5.88	.00	33.33	3.39	N/A
Lithuania	23.73	42.58	34.35	11.06	Industrial
Madagascar	19.60	46.75	45.32	9.28	Non-Industrial
Rep Korea	5.45	4.57	.87	1.34	Non-Industrial
Rep Moldova	29.27	27.27	14.13	3.63	Industrial
Russian Fed.	30.14	56.63	33.31	21.33	Industrial
Singapore	18.02	23.53	29.51	5.65	Non-Industrial
Slovenia	18.08	56.47	45.07	20.26	N/A
Sweden	34.00	30.77	31.94	33.32	Industrial
*"FYRM"	12.77	40.60	31.09	5.32	N/A
Turkey	5.24	5.19	9.97	2.67	Non-Industrial
Zambia	14.67	16.17	23.53	13.11	Non-Industrial
Scotland	9.32	6.57	45.78	23.40	Industrial
Median	**14.67**	**27.27**	**31.94**	**9.29**	
Mean	**17.01**	**28.98**	**29.57**	**11.50**	

*"Former Yugoslav Republic of Macedonia"

Method of Computation. The percent female police in 1994 was calculated by dividing the number of female police reported by each country for 1994 in the Fifth UNCJS by the total number of police reported by each country for 1994 in the Fifth UNCJS and multiplying by 100. The percent female prosecutors in 1994 was calculated by dividing the number of female prosecutors reported by each country for 1994 in the Fifth UNCJS by the total number of prosecutors reported by each country for 1994 in the Fifth UNCJS and multiplying by 100. The percent female professional judges in 1994 was calculated by dividing the number of female professional judges reported by each country for 1994 in the Fifth UNCJS by the total number of professional judges reported by each country for 1994 in the Fifth UNCJS and multiplying by 100. The percent female corrections workers in adult institutions in 1994 was calculated by dividing the number of female corrections workers in adult institutions reported by each country for 1994 in the Fifth UNCJS by the total number of corrections workers in adult institutions reported by each country for 1994 in the Fifth UNCJS and multiplying by 100. The percent female criminal justice workers in 1994 was calculated by summing the number of female police, prosecutors, professional judges, and corrections workers (management, custodial, treatment, and others) in adult institutions reported by each country for 1994 in the Fifth UNCJS and dividing this sum by the total number of police, prosecutors, professional judges, and corrections workers (management, custodial, treatment, and others) reported by each country for 1994 in the Fifth UNCJS and multiplying by 100. See notes to Table 5.7 where the method by which countries were classified as industrial or non-industrial is explained.

Figure 5.9 Expenditure per capita on all levels of criminal justice, 1994 (US dollars)

Table F5.9. Expenditure per capita on criminal justice system.

Country	Expenditure on entire criminal justice system (US$) per capita 1994
Colombia	25.05
Finland	162.44
Hungary	23.20
Japan	63.44
Madagascar	.12
Netherlands	308.42
Rep of Korea	77.45
Singapore	125.07
Slovenia	132.33
Switzerland	467.55
Turkey	12.98
Median	**77.45**
Mean	**127.10**

Method of Computation. Expenditure per capita (US$) on all levels of criminal justice in 1994 was calculated in the following manner. First, total expenditures on police, prosecution, courts and corrections reported by each country in local currency for 1994 in the Fifth UNCJS were summed to yield the total expenditures on criminal justice. These expenditures in local currency were then converted to US dollars using exchange rates (local currency per US dollar) reported by the United Nations. For each country, the total criminal justice expenditure in local currency was multiplied by a conversion value (1.000/exchange rate) to yield the country's total criminal justice expenditure in US currency. This figure was then divided by the 1994 population for each country reported by the United Nations in *World Population Prospects 1950-2050 (The 1996 Revision)* to yield the expenditure per capita (US$) on all levels of criminal justice in 1994 for each country.

Figure 5.10 Expenditure on criminal justice functions, 1994 (per capita US dollars)

Table F5.10. Expenditure on criminal justice functions, 1994 (per capita US dollars)

Country	Exp. on Police	Exp. on Court	Exp. on Corrections	Level of Econ.Dev.
Colombia	18.72	1.82	1.62	Non-Industrial
Costa Rica	7.42	3.33	3.70	Non-Industrial
Cyprus	136.59	.62	7.60	Non-Industrial
Finland	112.23	36.68	9.30	Industrial
Hong Kong	185.65	11.75	42.03	Non-Industrial
Hungary	6.09	7.99	8.15	Industrial
Japan	18.40	23.16	14.37	Industrial
Madagascar	.05	.03	.04	Non-Industrial
Malta	77.09	12.03	7.59	Industrial
Northern Ireland	575.47	34.47	137.66	Industrial
Rep of Korea	54.27	8.56	7.67	Non-Industrial
Singapore	100.94	2.02	21.37	Non-Industrial
Slovenia	98.13	21.98	8.79	N/A
Median	**77.09**	**8.56**	**8.16**	
Mean	**107.00**	**12.65**	**20.76**	

Method of Computation. The expenditure by each country on courts per capita (US$) was calculated by multiplying the expenditure (salaries and fixed assets) on courts reported by each country in local currency for 1994 in the Fifth UNCJS by the conversion value (1.000/exchange rate) described in the computational notes for Figure 5.9 and then dividing this product, which represents each country's expenditure on courts in US currency, by the 1994 population for each country reported by the United Nations in *World Population Prospects 1950-2050 (The 1996 Revision)*. Similarly, the expenditure by each country on corrections per capita (US$) was calculated by multiplying the expenditure (salaries and fixed assets) on corrections (penal and correctional institutions) reported by each country in local currency for 1994 in the Fifth UNCJS by the conversion value (1.000/exchange rate) described in the computational notes for Figure 5.9 and then dividing this product, which represents each country's expenditure on corrections in US currency, by the 1994 population for each country reported by the United Nations in *World Population Prospects 1950-2050 (The 1996 Revision)*. The expenditure by each country on police per capita (US$) was calculated by multiplying the expenditure (salaries and fixed assets) on police reported by each country in local currency for 1994 in the Fifth UNCJS by the conversion value (1.000/exchange rate) described in the computational notes for Figure 5.9 and then dividing this product, which represents each country's expenditure on police in US currency, by the 1994 population for each country reported by the United Nations in *World Population Prospects 1950-2050 (The 1996 Revision)*. See notes to Table 5.7 where the method by which countries were classified as industrial or non-industrial is explained.

Figure 5.11 Police expenditure by gross domestic product, 1994 (per capita US dollars)

Table F5.11. Raw data police expenditure by gross domestic product, (per capita US dollars)

Country	GDP (US$) per cap.	Expenditure on Police (US$) per capita
Colombia	1847	18.72
Costa Rica	2463	7.42
Croatia	3867	20.57
Cyprus	9754	136.59
Denmark	28245	145.28
Finland	19048	112.23
France	24608	148.90
Greece	7465	60.01
Hong Kong	22590	185.65
Hungary	4072	6.09
India	309	.20
Japan	36782	18.40
Jordan	1095	15.42
Madagascar	208	.05
Malta	7394	77.09
Netherlands	21536	204.09
Romania	1274	4.13
Saint V.& Grenadines	2248	41.45
Singapore	23556	100.94
Slovenia	7206	98.13
Spain	12201	27.73
Sweden	22499	157.29
Switzerland	36096	299.53
Turkey	2227	9.66
Median	**7429.50**	**50.73**
Mean	**12441.25**	**78.98**

Pearson r= .733

Method of Computation. See notes to Figure 5.10 for method of computing the expenditure by each country on police per capita in 1994 (US$). Gross domestic product per capita in 1994 (US$) was obtained from the United Nations *Statistical Yearbook, Forty-first issue.*

Figure 5.12 Corrections expenditure by gross domestic product, 1994 (per capita US dollars)

Table F5.12. Corrections expenditure by gross domestic product, 1994 (per capita US dollars)

Country	GDP	Exp. on Corrections
Austria	24823	11.15
Belgium	21765	5.89
Canada	18635	46.14
Colombia	1847	1.62
Costa Rica	2463	3.70
Croatia	3867	.45
Cyprus	9754	7.60
Czech Rep	3498	8.43
Denmark	28245	32.24
Finland	19048	9.30
Guyana	655	.64
Hong Kong	22590	42.03
Hungary	4072	8.15
Israel	14333	.99
Japan	36782	14.37
Luxembourg	27611	33.16
Madagascar	208	.04
Malta	7394	7.59
Netherlands	21536	48.57
Nicaragua	433	.48
Panama	2550	1.16
Philippines	965	.07
Portugal	8822	14.05
Singapore	23556	21.37
Slovakia	2331	2.96
Slovenia	7206	8.79
Switzerland	36096	71.10
Turkey	2227	1.12
Uruguay	4199	1.20
Median	**7394.00**	**7.60**
Mean	**12327.97**	**13.94**

Method of Computation. See notes to Figure 5.10 for method of computing the expenditure by each country on corrections per capita in 1994 (US$). Gross domestic product per capita in 1994 (US$) was obtained from the United Nations *Statistical Yearbook, Forty-first issue*.

Figure 5.13 Expenditure on corrections by industrial and non-industrial countries, 1994 (per capita US dollars)

Table F5.13. Expenditure on corrections by industrial and non-industrial countries, 1994 (per capita US dollars)

Country	Expenditure on Corrections	Level of Development
Austria	11.15	Industrial
Belgium	5.89	Industrial
Bermuda	174.91	N/A
Canada	46.14	Industrial
Colombia	1.62	Non-Industrial
Costa Rica	3.70	Non-Industrial
Croatia	.45	N/A
Cyprus	7.60	Non-Industrial
Czech Rep	8.43	Industrial
Denmark	32.24	Industrial
England & Wales	36.03	Industrial
Finland	9.30	Industrial
Guyana	.64	Non-Industrial
Hong Kong	42.03	Non-Industrial
Hungary	8.15	Industrial
Israel	.99	Industrial
Japan	14.37	Industrial
Luxembourg	33.16	Industrial
Madagascar	.04	Non-Industrial
Malta	7.59	Industrial
Netherlands	48.57	Industrial
Nicaragua	.48	Non-Industrial
Northern Ireland	137.66	Industrial
Panama	1.16	Non-Industrial
Philippines	.07	Non-Industrial
Portugal	14.05	Industrial
Rep of Korea	7.67	Non-Industrial
Singapore	21.37	Non-Industrial
Slovakia	2.96	Industrial
Slovenia	8.79	N/A
Switzerland	71.10	Industrial
Turkey	1.12	Non-Industrial
Uruguay	1.20	Non-Industrial
Scotland	34.10	Industrial
Median	**8.29**	
Mean	**23.37**	

Method of Computation. See notes to Figure 5.10 for method of computing the expenditure by each country on corrections per capita in 1994 (US$). See notes to Table 5.7 where the method by which countries were classified as industrial or non-industrial is explained.

Chapter 6. Firearm abuse and regulation

Figure 6.1 Deaths caused by a fatal wound inflicted by a firearm (aggregate estimate comprised of firearm suicides, firearm accidents and firearm homicides; rate per 100,000 population)

Method of computation. This estimated total firearm death rate represents the summation of its component parts (i.e., firearm suicides, homicides and accidents) and may be composed of figures from different years; international comparisons should be made with caution. The following table presents the data from which Figures 6.1, 6.2 and 6.3 are derived.

Table F6.1. Raw data for Figures 6.1–6.3

Country	Firearm homicide rate per 100,000	Number of firearm homicides	Firearm suicide rate per 100,000	Number of firearm suicides	Firearm accident rate per 100,000	Number of accidents involving firearms	Aggregate firearm death rate
Argentina	1.5	45	n.a.	n.a.	n.a.	n.a.	
Australia	0.56	96	2.38	420	0.11	20	3.05
Austria	0.53	43	n.r.	n.r.	n.r.	n.r.	
Belarus	n.r.a.	n.r.a.	n.r.a.	n.r.a.	0.23	24	
Belgium	n.a.	n.a.	n.a.	n.a.	n.a.	n.a.	
Brazil	25.78	41000	0.44	700	0.75	1200	26.97
Burkina Faso	n.a.	n.a.	0.14	15	0.05	5	
Canada	0.6	176	3.35	975	0.13	38	4.08
China	n.r.	n.r.	n.r.	n.r.	n.r.	n.r.	
Costa Rica	2.57	88	1.61	55	0.29	10	4.47
Czech Republic	0.92	94	1.01	104	0.07	7	2.00
Denmark	n.r.a.	n.r.a.	n.r.a.	n.r.a.	n.r.a.	n.r.a.	
Ecuador	n.r.	n.r.	n.r.	n.r.	n.r.	n.r.	
Estonia	6.12	91	3.63	54	0.4	6	10.15
Finland	0.87	44	5.78	294	0.12	6	6.77
Germany	0.21	168	1.23	1004	0.03	25	1.47
Greece	0.55	58	1.3	136	0.02	2	1.87
Guinea	0.03	2	n.r.a.	n.r.a.	n.r.a.	n.r.a.	
Hungary	0.47	47	0.88	89	n.a.	n.a.	
India	n.r.a.	n.r.a.	0.06	586	0.26	2375	
Jamaica	18.23	450	0.36	9	0.12	3	18.72
Japan	0.03	34	0.04	49	0.01	10	0.07
Luxembourg	n.a.	n.a.	n.a.	n.a.	n.a.	n.a.	
Malaysia	0.2	41	0.005	1	0.08	16	0.29
Mexico	n.r.	n.r.	n.r.	n.r.	n.r.	n.r.	
Moldova	0.63	28	n.a.	n.a.	n.a.	n.a.	
New Zealand	0.22	8	2.45	84.2	0.29	10	2.97
Papua New Guinea	n.a.	n.a.	n.a.	n.a.	n.a.	n.a.	
Peru	1.06	253	0.1	24	0.02	5	1.18
Philippines	3.61	2496	n.r.a.	n.r.a.	n.r.a.	n.r.a.	
Poland	0.27	104	0.16	62	0.01	5	0.44
Romania	0.12	27	n.r.a.	n.r.a.	n.r.a.	n.r.a.	
Russian Federation	n.a.	n.a.	n.a.	n.a.	n.a.	n.a.	
Singapore	0	0	n.a.	n.a.	n.a.	n.a.	
Slovakia	0.36	19	0.58	31	n.a.	n.a.	
South Africa	26.63	11044	n.a.	n.a.	n.a.	n.a.	
Spain	0.19	76	0.55	219	0.26	101	1.01
Sweden	0.31	27	1.95	169	0.05	4	2.31
Tanzania	0.5	150	0.02	5	0.02	5	0.53
Trinidad & Tobago	3.42	44	0.08	1	0.54	7	4.04
Tunisia	n.r.	n.r.	0.02	2	0.00	0	
Uganda	n.a.	n.a.	n.a.	n.a.	n.a.	n.a.	
United Kingdom	0.13	72	0.33	193	0.02	12	0.48
United States	6.24	16524	7.23	18940	0.58	1521	14.05
Vietnam	0.12	85	0.02	16	0.04	30	0.18
Zambia	5.37	434	0.15	12	0.02	2	5.54
Summary							
Minimum	0	0	0.005	1	0.00	0	0.07
Maximum	26.63	41000	7.23	18940	0.75	2375	26.97
Average	3.28	–	1.28	–	0.17	–	4.90
No response	4	4	4	4	4	4	–
Not available	6	6	9	9	11	11	–
Not reasonably available	3	3	5	5	4	4	–
Count	33	33	28	28	27	27	23

This estimated total firearm death rate represents the summation of its component parts (i.e., firearm suicides, homicides, and accidents) and may be composed of figures from different years; international comparisons should be made with caution. Notation: *nr: no response; na: not available; nra: not reasonably available; npa: not publicly available*

Figure 6.4 Homicide victims killed by a firearm (per 100,000 population)

Method of computation. The information presented here represents the most recent annual statistics available, which differ by country. Statistics have been converted into rates per 100,000 inhabitants, so as to facilitate international comparison of data. Also, note that differences exist in record-keeping methodologies, and international comparisons must be made cautiously. For example, with regard to homicide, some countries compile statistics that include *attempted* homicides in their count of homicides, as no disaggregated information is available. Again, see *Report of the Third United Nations Survey of Crime Trends, Operations of Criminal Justice Systems and Crime Prevention Strategies* (A/CONF.144/6; 27 July 1990) for a salient review of the difficulties and problems encountered in the comparison of international crime (and public health) statistics.

Figure 6.5 Percent of crime types in which guns are used

Table F6.2. Raw data for Figure 6.5

Country	Year	Domestic /family homicide rate (per 100,000)	Number of domestic/family homicides	Domestic/ family firearm homicide rate (per 100,000)	Number of domestic/ family firearm homicides	% of domestic family homicides using firearms
Argentina	1993	1.20	36.00	0.83	25.00	69.44
Australia	1992	0.73	127.00	0.21	37.00	29.13
Brazil	1995	0.82	1300.00	0.38	600.00	46.15
Canada	1995	0.68	200.00	0.17	50.00	25.00
Malaysia	1995	0.17	34.00	0.01	2.00	5.88
Moldova	1996	1.12	50.00	0.07	3.00	6.00
New Zealand	1995	0.56	20.00	0.22	8.00	40.00
Peru	1996	0.02	5.00	0.02	4.00	80.00
Poland	1995	0.75	289.00	0.03	12.00	4.15
Singapore	1995	0.30	10.00	0.00	0.00	0.00
Trinidad & Tobago	1995	2.10	27.00	0.31	4.00	14.81
United Kingdom	1994	0.48	270.00	0.03	15.00	5.56
United States	1994	1.38	3646.00	0.75	1997.00	54.77
Vietnam	1995	0.14	105.00	0.02	13.00	12.38
Zambia	1995	0.32	26.00	0.04	3.00	11.54
Median						**14.81**
Mean						**26.99**

Country	Year	Theft/robbery rate (per 100,000)	Number of thefts /robberies	Firearm theft/ robbery rate (per 100,000)	Number of firearm thefts/robberies	% of theft/ robbery using firearms
Australia	1995	92.16	16466.00	11.53	2060.00	12.51
Austria	1995	26.33	2118.00	1.84	148.00	6.99
Belgium	1995	61.62	6240.00	17.63	1785.00	28.61
Brazil	1995	141.50	225000.00	127.35	202500.00	90.00
Burkina Faso	1995	1.20	126.00	0.00	0.00	0.00
Canada	1995	102.96	30273.00	22.76	6692.00	22.11
Estonia	1995	46.64	694.00	11.96	178.00	25.65
Germany	1995	77.79	63470.00	7.66	6251.00	9.85
Guinea	1995	1.21	89.00	0.04	3.00	3.37
Hungary	1995	26.29	2657.00	0.83	84.00	3.16
Jamaica	1995	179.25	4424.00	97.69	2411.00	54.50
Malaysia	1995	269.30	53861.00	3.45	605.00	1.28
Moldova	1995	66.42	2947.00	3.70	164.00	5.56
New Zealand	1995	55.10	1962.00	6.43	229.00	11.67
Poland	1995	69.38	26750.00	4.11	1584.00	5.92
Singapore	1995	23.72	789.00	0.21	7.00	0.89
Spain	1995	237.94	94289.00	10.54	4176.00	4.43
Tanzania	1995	25.16	7554.00	2.32	698.00	9.24
Trinidad & Tobago	1995	300.54	3868.00	102.56	1320.00	34.13
Tunisia	1996	384.27	35157.00	1.33	122.00	0.35
United Kingdom	1994	115.71	65300.00	7.72	4359.00	6.68
Vietnam	1995	2.63	1944.00	0.18	132.00	6.79
Zambia	1995	45.98	3716.00	43.57	3521.00	94.75
Median						**6.99**
Mean						**19.06**

Country	Year	Sexual assault rate (per 100,000)	Number of sexual assaults	Firearm sexual assault rate (per 100,000)	Number of firearm sexual assaults	% of sexual assaults using firearms
Australia	1995	71.69	12809	0.12	21	0.16
Brazil	1995	6.6	10500	1.32	2100	20
Burkina Faso	1995	0.58	61	0	0	0
Estonia	1995	7.06	105	0	0	0
Germany	1995	16.28	13280	0.24	193	1.45
Jamaica	1995	65.03	1605	11.67	288	17.94
Moldova	1995	5.27	234	0	0	0
Poland	1995	5.88	2267	0.09	33	1.46
Singapore	1995	33.6	1118	0	0	0
Trinidad & Tobago	1995	24.01	309	1.01	13	4.21
United Kingdom	1994	59.36	33500	0.04	22	0.07
Median						**0.16**
Mean						**4.117273**

Figure 6.6 Reported lost or stolen firearms, 1995 (rates per 100,000 firearms owned)

Table F6.3. Raw data for Figure 6.6

Country	Number of firearms owned by civilians	Reports of lost/ stolen firearms	Reports lost/ stolen per 100,000 firearms owned
Japan	410417.00	10.00	2.44
Belarus	170858.00	43.00	25.17
Finland	2100000.00	932.00	44.38
Spain	2563490.00	1389.00	54.18
United Kingdom	2124000.00	1433.00	64.47
Sweden	2167581.00	1400.00	64.59
Malaysia	142038.00	123.00	86.60
Tanzania	69840.00	62.00	88.77
Hungary	146911.00	136.00	92.57
Estonia	42500.00	57.00	134.12
Moldova	29313.00	50.00	170.57
Russian Federation	3636000.00	7125.00	195.96
Canada	7100000.00	14610.00	205.77
Philippines	472991.00	1234.00	260.89
Czech Republic	283009.00	776.00	274.20
Trinidad & Tobago	7801.00	28.00	358.93
South Africa	3500000.00	17492.00	499.77
Jamaica	18145.00	138.00	760.54
Argentina	1446145.00	15317.00	1059.16
Median			**134.12**

Figure 6.7 Comparative rates of legal civilian firearm ownership

Table F6.4. Raw data for Figure 6.7 . Estimated numbers of licensees, firearms owners, firearms, and percent of households with at least one firearm. (Please see method of construction of ownership rate following the table.)

Country	Number of licensees	Rate of licenses per 1000	Number of firearm owners	Rate of owners per 1000	Estimated no. of firearms *	Rate of firearms per 1000	% houses with at least one firearm
Argentina	450000	12.94	n.a.	n.a.	1446145	41.59	n.r.
Australia	1046931	58.60	n.a.	n.a.	3500000	195.90	16
Austria	330000	41.02	n.a.	n.a.	n.a.	n.a.	n.a.
Belarus	n.r.	n.r.	n.r.a.	n.r.a	170858	16.50	n.r.a.
Belgium	458162	n.r.	n.r.	n.r.	n.r.	n.r.	n.r.
Brazil	n.r.	n.r.	1300000	8.18	n.r.	n.r.	n.r.
Burkina Faso	> 1000	> 0.10	n.r.	n.r.	> 2500	> 0.24	0.06
Canada	600000	20.41	3000000	102.03	7100000	241.48	26
China	n.r.a	n.r.a	n.r.a	n.r.a	n.r.	n.r.	n.r.a
Costa Rica	152923	44.66	152923	44.66	225822	65.95	n.a.
Czech Republic	n.app.	n.app.	180170	17.56	283009	27.58	4.3
Denmark	21000	4.02	n.r.	n.r.	850000	162.74	8
Ecuador	n.r.	n.r.	n.r.	n.r.	200000	17.45	5
Estonia	31000	20.83	n.a.	n.a.	42500	28.56	9
Finland	1100000	215.39	n.r.	n.r.	2100000	411.20	50
Germany	2000000	24.51	10000000	122.56	n.a.	n.a.	10
Greece	3180	0.30	3150	0.30	805000	77.00	n.a.

Country	Number of licensees	Rate of licenses per 1000	Number of firearm owners	Rate of owners per 1000	Estimated no. of firearms *	Rate of firearms per 1000	% houses with at least one firearm
Guinea	n.r.	n.r.	800000	108.86	n.r.a	n.r.a	n.r.a
Hungary	84022	8.31	n.a.	n.a.	146911	14.54	n.a.
India	n.r.a	n.r.a	n.r.a	n.r.a	n.r.a	n.r.a	n.r.a
Jamaica	16000	6.48	16000	6.48	18145	7.35	n.a.
Japan	239380	1.91	239380	1.91	410417	3.28	0.57
Luxembourg	18000	44.23	18000	44.23	n.a.	n.a.	n.r.
Malaysia	142038	7.05	142038	7.05	142038	7.05	0.007
Mexico	n.r.a.	n.r.a.	n.r.a.	n.r.a.	n.r.a.	n.r.a.	n.r.a.
Moldova	26626	6.00	26626	6.00	29313	6.61	0.76
New Zealand	250000	70.20	400000	112.33	1100000	308.90	20
Papua New Guinea	n.r.	n.r.	50000	11.63	50000	11.63	n.a.
Peru	180000	7.65	140000	5.95	180000	7.65	6
Philippines	358934	5.29	n.r.a.	n.r.a.	472991	6.97	n.r.a.
Poland	131249	3.40	n.a.	n.a.	204437	5.30	n.a.
Romania	61238	2.69	61238	2.69	67388	2.97	n.r.a.
Russian Federation	n.r.	n.r.	3200000	21.55	3636000	24.49	n.a.
Singapore	795	0.24	795	0.24	795	0.24	n.a.
Slovakia	n.r.a.	n.r.a.	91429	17.13	170357	31.91	n.r.a.
South Africa	1800000	43.41	1800000	43.41	3500000	84.41	5
Spain	2500000	63.09	n.r.	.50	2563490	64.69	n.a.
Sweden	781521	88.93	800000	91.03	2167581	246.65	20
Tanzania	69840	2.33	69840	2.33	69840	2.33	n.r.
Trinidad & Tobago	7715	5.99	7715	5.99	7801	6.06	3
Tunisia	3408	0.38	3408	0.38	3408	0.38	0.2
Uganda	n.r.a.	n.r.a.	n.r.a.	n.r.a.	2770	0.14	n.a.
United Kingdom	861958	14.84	861958	14.84	2124000	36.58	4
United States	n.app.	n.app.	n.a.	n.a.	n.a.	n.a.	41
Vietnam	n.r.	n.r.	n.r.	n.r.	n.r.	n.r.	n.r.
Zambia	n.r.a.	n.r.a.	n.r.a.	n.r.a.	n.r.a.	n.r.a.	n.r.a

Summary	Total	Range	Total	Range	Total	Range	Range
	13.9 mill.	0.1-215	23.4 m.	0.2-122	33.9 m.	0.1-411	.007 - 50%
Non-responses (all)	17	17	22	22	13	13	27

* In most cases, the numbers supplied are of legally owned firearms. Some figures may have included estimated numbers of illegal firearms. See also notes on following page.

Notation: *nr: non-response, left blank; na: not available, does not exist, not known; nra: not reasonably available; npa: not publicly available; n app: not applicable.*

Additional Notes

Canada, *number of licenses*: current estimate of the number of individuals who are holders of a Firearms Acquisition Certificate, which is required only for the purchase of firearms, not for possession.

Jamaica, *percent of households*: figure represents total persons licensed x 100 out of population of 2,509,800.

Slovakia, *number of firearm owners*: 91,429 persons; 2,975 corporate bodies.

Trinidad & Tobago, *number of firearm owners*: licensed Firearm User's License holders (unlicensed firearm owners undetermined); *percentage of households*: The Firearm Act was promulgated by the president in 1970. Following the destruction of the records in 1990, they were updated. The new figures revealed that 7,715 Firearm User's Licenses were issued between 1990 and 1996 by the Commissioner of Police. This figure is then related to the estimated number of households in the country, 300,000.

United Kingdom, *number of licensees and number of owners*: in total 174,000 firearm certificates and 722,600 shotgun certificates were on issue in England, Wales and Scotland on 31 December 1995. In addition 88,200 certificates covering firearms, shotguns and air weapons were on issue in Northern Ireland; some individuals will hold both firearm and shot gun certificates. There are no current statistics, but an estimate made in 1972 suggested that 17 percent of shotgun certificate holders also held a firearms certificate. *Percentage of households*: the estimate is taken from the International Crime Survey for England and Wales in 1992, and is the percentage of all households which owned a firearm. Information for Scotland was not collected in 1992, but was shown, in the earlier 1989 survey, to be the same as for England and Wales. There is no separate estimate for Northern Ireland but the figure of about 4 percent is consistent with an estimate derived from comparing the total number of certificates with the number of households in the UK.

USA. The following definition of National Firearms Act (NFA) firearms was provided: "The types of firearms that must be registered in the National Firearm Registration and Transfer Record are defined in the NFA and in 27 CFR part 179." Some examples of the types of firearms that must be registered are: machine guns; the frames or receivers of machine guns; any combination of parts designed and intended for use in converting weapons into machine guns; any part designed and intended solely and exclusively for converting a weapon into a machine gun; any combination of parts from which machine guns can be assembled if the parts are in the possession or under the control of a person; silencers and any part designed and intended for fabricating a silencer; sawed-off rifles; sawed-off shotguns; destructive devices; and, "any other weapons." A few examples of destructive devices are: Molotov cocktails; anti-tank guns (over caliber .50); bazookas; and mortars. A few examples of "any other weapon" are: H&R Handyguns; Ithaca Auto-Burglar guns; cane guns; and gadget-type firearms and "pen" guns which fire fixed ammunition. Source: Department of the Treasury, Bureau of Alcohol, Tobacco and Firearms, *Federal Firearms Regulation Reference Guide* (Washington, DC: BATF, 1995) p. 109.

Construction of a combined scale of firearms ownership rates

Because of the gaps in the data on firearms ownership, it is necessary to build a combined scale from the four scales obtained by the survey: numbers of licenses per 1,000 persons, numbers of firearms owners per 1,000 persons, numbers of firearms per 1,000 persons, and the percentage of households with at least one firearm.

Each of these is a valid measure per se, but cannot simply be added or averaged to obtain an overall rate of firearms ownership for each country. Because of different methods of licensing, some countries, such as Canada, appear to have above-average rates if measured by numbers of owners or firearms per 1000 persons, but lower than average rates if measured by numbers of licenses per 1000 persons. Furthermore, most countries were unable to estimate all of the four variables required to calculate these four rates. A more subtle approach is required.

Firstly, each of the four scales is standardized to a mean of zero and a standard deviation of one, using only those countries for which data were provided. The countries included in these calculations vary between the four rates, but it is of little consequence. This means that any country scoring above zero on each of the standardized scales has an above-average firearms ownership rate, compared to the other countries which provided data, and countries scoring below zero have below-average ownership rates, according to the particular measure chosen. Finally, the new scales are averaged for each country to give a combined score, excluding all missing values. The calculations are shown in full in the table below, which also contains the data on firearms homicide rates per 100,000 for comparison.

Using this combined scale, Finland, Guinea, New Zealand and Sweden emerge as having the highest ownership rates of all the responding countries, with Japan and Singapore having the lowest.

Table F6.5. Raw data for Figures 6.7, 6.9, 6.10: standardized measure of firearms ownership

Country	Rate of licensing per 1000		Rate of ownership per 1000		Rate of firearms per 1000		25a: Percentage of households with at least 1 firearm		Average Standardised Ownership Rates	Firearm Homicides per 100,000
	Raw	Standard	Raw	Standard	Raw	Standard	Raw	Standard		
Argentina	13.01	-0.47			41.81	-0.33			-0.40	0.13
Australia	57.88	0.47			193.50	1.01	16.00	0.08	0.52	0.37
Austria	41.41	0.12							0.12	0.54
Belarus					16.85	-0.55			-0.55	
Belgium										
Brazil			8.04	-0.73					-0.73	
Canada	20.36	-0.32	101.82	1.31	240.98	1.43	26.00	0.68	0.77	0.60
Costa Rica	44.66	0.19	44.66	0.06	65.95	-0.12			0.05	2.57
Czech Republic			17.50	-0.53	27.49	-0.45	4.30	-0.62	-0.53	0.91
Estonia	20.26	-0.32			27.78	-0.45	9.00	-0.34	-0.37	5.95
Finland	215.39	3.76			411.20	2.92	50.00	2.12	2.93	0.87
Germany	24.51	-0.23	122.56	1.76			10.00	-0.28	0.42	0.21
Greece	0.30	-0.74	0.30	-0.90	77.03	-0.02			-0.55	0.55
Guinea			119.40	1.69					1.69	0.03
Hungary	8.30	-0.57			14.52	-0.57			-0.57	0.46
India										
Jamaica	6.54	-0.61	6.54	-0.77	7.42	-0.63	0.64	-0.84	-0.71	18.39
Japan	1.91	-0.71	1.91	-0.87	3.28	-0.67	0.57	-0.84	-0.77	0.03
Luxembourg	44.34.	0.18	44.34	0.06					0.12	
New Zealand	69.93	0.72	111.89	1.53	307.69	2.01	50.00	2.12	1.59	0.22
P.N.G.			11.62	-0.65	11.62	-0.59			-0.62	
Peru	7.57	-0.59	5.89	-0.78	7.57	-0.63	6.00	-0.52	-0.63	
Poland	3.42	-0.67			5.33	-0.65			-0.66	0.27
Romania										
Singapore	0.28	-0.74	0.28	-0.90	0.28	-0.69			-0.78	0
Slovakia			17.08	-0.54	31.83	-0.42			-0.48	0.35
South Africa	43.41	0.16	43.41	0.04	84.41	0.05	5.00	-0.57	-0.08	0.10
Spain	63.10	0.57			64.70	-0.13			0.22	0.19
Sweden	89.01	1.12	91.12	1.08	246.88	1.48	20.00	0.32	1.00	0.31
Tanzania	2.35	-0.70	2.35	-0.86	2.35	-0.67			-0.74	0.51
Trinidad & T.	5.91	-0.62	5.91	-0.78	5.97	-0.64	3.00	-0.69	-0.68	3.37
Uganda					0.13	-0.69			-0.69	
United Kingdom							4.00	-0.63	-0.63	0.12
Vietnam										0.11
Zambia										4.59
Mean	35.63		41.71		79.02		14.61			
Std. Dev	47.80		45.95		113.65		16.71			

Chapter 7. Drugs and drug control

Figure 7.1 Globalization of illicit drugs: number of countries reporting seizures of different drug types by year

Table F7.0. Number of countries reporting seizures of different drug types by year

Year	80	81	82	83	84	85	86	87	88	89	90	91	92	93	94
Cannabis	108	111	107	113	120	115	116	126	128	133	138	135	140	137	143
Cocaine	44	49	49	64	66	68	69	81	77	83	86	96	97	103	103
Heroin	51	55	51	61	68	66	69	80	77	88	87	89	96	102	112
Opium	51	48	50	52	56	51	51	50	51	47	51	53	56	56	65
Amphetamines	36	40	41	37	41	40	36	46	37	41	47	55	43	46	63
LSD	32	32	33	30	36	32	24	29	24	24	25	31	33	26	37
Sedatives	38	49	41	34	33	30	32	35	34	39	28	33	27	20	33

Figure 7.2. Seizures of cocaine and stimulants

Table F7.1. Raw data: seizures of cocaine and stimulants (tonnes)

Cocaine

Year	80	81	82	83	84	85	86	87	88	89	90	91	92	93	94	95
North America	4	2	6	9	12	28	50	66	118	170	135	172	163	161	131	126
South America	8	7	6	30	46	24	75	82	88	85	137	132	92	86	129	102
Western Europe	0	0	0	1	1	1	2	4	7	8	17	17	18	19	30	22
Other regions	0	0	0	0	0	0	0	0	0	0	0	1	1	3	1	0

Stimulants

Year	80	81	82	83	84	85	86	87	88	89	90	91	92	93	94	95
Western Europe	3	2	9	8	6	7	10	10	16	13	17	23	37	42	55	55
East and SE Asia	6	6	18	12	54	20	55	49	34	24	18	47	39	40	65	47
North America	30	48	5	14	17	2	33	26	110	176	46	39	8	21	192	25
Africa	8	19	10	20	40	62	50	73	46	37	34	14	9	1	5	13
Other regions	1	1	0	0	4	4	6	7	5	37	4	5	6	25	25	13

Figure 7.3. Seizures of cannabis and opiates (tonnes)

Table F7.2. Raw data: seizures of cannabis and opiates

Heroin

Year	80	81	82	83	84	85	86	87	88	89	90	91	92	93	94	95
Near and Middle East1	4	3	7	5	9	8	8	12	12	10	7	8	7	8	13	
Western Europe	1	1	1	2	2	2	2	4	4	5	6	8	7	9	11	10
East and SE Asia	0	1	1	2	3	3	4	5	7	6	6	5	8	9	8	5
North America	0	0	0	0	0	0	1	1	1	1	1	2	1	2	2	1
Other regions	0	0	0	0	0	0	0	0	1	1	1	0	0	1	1	1

Morphine

Year	80	81	82	83	84	85	86	87	88	89	90	91	92	93	94	95
Near and Middle East1	2	1	1	0	0	0	0	1	1	5	8	8	26	13	11	
Western Europe	0	0	0	0	0	0	0	0	0	0	0	1	3	0	1	
Other regions	0	0	1	0	0	0	0	0	0	0	0	0	0	0	0	

Opium

Year	80	81	82	83	84	85	86	87	88	89	90	91	92	93	94	95
Near &Middle East	41	44	33	71	43	29	38	50	46	32	29	33	42	69	133	238
East and SE Asia	7	10	12	12	16	12	14	7	12	9	7	8	10	14	8	23
Other regions	4	1	1	0	0	0	0	0	4	1	1	1	1	3	3	1

Cannabis resin

Year	80	81	82	83	84	85	86	87	88	89	90	91	92	93	94	95
Western Europe	55	73	60	95	100	111	101	166	209	209	251	292	347	433	510	467
Near and Middle East	55	73	66	46	73	159	272	202	179	166	264	376	209	220	246	383
Africa	45	116	90	114	122	59	28	49	24	68	53	60	74	112	100	331
North America	15	28	5	18	6	20	18	21	45	2	66	156	17	74	109	67
Other regions	3	2	2	6	8	13	20	15	21	9	7	6	15	9	14	20

Herbal Cannabis

Year	80	81	82	83	84	85	86	87	88	89	90	91	92	93	94	95
North America	3073	1042	1366	906	9885	1031	864	1044	828	1092	783	402	764	971	982	1385
Africa	638	48	162	155	48	358	974	1232	156	1668	388	790	316	1042	355	644
South America	1540	3953	4548	9291	10542	2702	984	1685	1115	888	1123	464	1099	726	316	421
Other regions	184	140	186	253	210	529	170	252	133	197	128	144	151	669	552	802

Figure 7.4 Increasing support for the 1988 UN Drug Control Convention

Table F7.3. Percent of countries supporting the 1988 UN Drug Control Convention

Year supported	1997	1996	1995	1994	1993
Ratified/acceded	70	62	61	56	43
Signed but not ratified	7	10	13	16	22
Not signed	24	28	25	28	35

Figure 7.5 Percent of world population using and not using illicit drugs annually

Table F7.4. Percent of world population using and not using illicit drugs annually

Drug type	Heroin & opiates	Cocaine	Cannabis	Hallucinogens	ATS	Sedatives
using	0.14	0.23	2.45	0.44	0.52	3.92
not using	99.86	99.77	97.55	99.56	99.48	96.08

Figure 7.6 Percent of world population using illicit drugs annually by type of drug, 1990s

Table F7.5. Percent of world population using illicit drugs annually by type of drug, 1990s

Drug type	Heroin & opiates	Cocaine	Cannabis	Hallucinogens	ATS	Sedatives
Estimated total (millions)	8	13.3	141.2	25.5	30.2	227.4
in % of total population	0.14	0.23	2.45	0.44	0.52	3.92

Figure 7.7 Trends in the retail price of heroin and cocaine in major world markets, 1983-1994

Table F7.6. Retail price of heroin and cocaine in major world markets, 1983-1994

Year	83	84	85	86	87	88	89	90	91	92	93	94
Heroin - Europe	100.0	70.4	75.0	85.8	97.2	80.5	64.8	73.9	73.6	61.7	43.3	38.2
Heroin - USA	100.0	92.4	83.7	76.8	69.2	58.6	55.9	48.7	62.0	58.9	57.0	
Cocaine - Europe	100.0	70.9	78.6	82.8	100.0	86.2	68.6	79.1	74.5	72.6	61.2	56.0
Cocaine - USAs	100.0	93.9	84.8	73.9	61.8	49.7	39.4	48.5	52.7	43.6	46.4	

Figure 7.8 Opiates and cocaine: global interception rates estimates, 1980-1994

Table F7.7. Opiates and cocaine: global interception rates estimates, percent interception, 1980-1994

Year	1980	1981	1982	1983	1984	1985	1986	1987	1988	1989	1990	1991	1992	1993	1994
Opiates	16.9	13.1	12.2	18.5	16.4	16.1	10.8	11.2	12.4	8	10	9.8	11.7	17.5	17
Cocaine	3.9	3	3.6	16	19.6	12	26	28.3	25	30.6	32.7	33.3	28.2	34.2	31.7

Figure 7.9 Drug trafficking and possession in the global criminal justice system, 1994 (as percent of total cases)

Table F7.8. Drug trafficking and possession in the global criminal justice system, 1994 (as percent of total cases)

	Crime recorded	Suspects	Prosecutions	Convictions	Prison
Trafficking	1.42	2.79	4.44	4.4	2.93
Possesson	2.3	4.49	2.77	4.35	10.26

Figure 7.10 Ten percent of suspects go to prison? Attrition of drug trafficking and possession cases in the global criminal justice system, 1994

Table F7.9. Median and mean processing rates for trafficking and possession at different stages of the global criminal justice system in 1994

	Arrest Rate	Prosecution Rate	Conviction Rate	Imprisonment Rate
All Drug Crimes				
Median	0.72	0.48	0.66	0.30
Mean	0.69	0.50	0.62	0.38
n	28	20	25	15
Trafficking				
Median	0.92	0.72	NR	NR
Mean	0.83	0.41		
n	13	8		
Possession				
Median	0.90	NR	0.83	NR
Mean	0.82		0.71	
n	18		9	

Source: 5th UNCJS.
Note: NR means the information was not requested on the Fifth UNCJS.

Table F7.10. Drug crimes in the global criminal justice system in 1994: proportion due to trafficking and possession

	% of Total Crimes at this Stage	Standard deviation	Minimum % (country)	Maximum % (country)	Number of countries responding (N)
Recorded crime					
Total	3.72	4.68	0.06	27.58	61
(% Possession)	(61.89)	(33.06)	0.00	(100)	(46)
Suspects					
Total	7.28	9.05	0.12	47.78	46
(% Possession)	(61.65)	(31.77)	0.00	(100)	(32)
Prosecutions					
Total	7.21	14.00	0.09	86.00	44
(% Possession)	(38.41)	(33.22)	(0.00)	(100)	(22)
Convictions					
Total	8.75	11.55	0.09	61.35	47
(% Possession)	(49.75)	(31.89)	(5.59)	(100)	(19)
Prison admissions					
Total	13.19	11.17	0.52	41.41	38
(% Possession)	(78.00)	(25.39)	15.81	100	(18)

Source: Fifth UNCJS.

Notes: a. "Total drugs" is not necessarily equal to sum of possession and trafficking if number of reporting countries varies or data reported are not wholly consistent.
b. "% trafficked" shows the proportion of the total "drug crimes" (trafficking and possession) that were drug trafficking. It is calculated for those countries where data are available, which is often less than the number that report a combined figure for trafficking and possession.
Ecuador and Syria excluded. Ecuador reported 88022 drug trafficking and possession offences but only 20957 total crimes, and Syria 2692 and 2282 respectively.

Notes to Snapshots

Global Snapshot. Percent of respondents reporting victimization by assault or threats

One year victimisation rate for assault /threat

	1988	1991	1995
England and Wales	1.9	3.8	5.9
Netherlands	3.3	4.0	4.0
Finland	2.9	4.4	4.1
Western Europe	2.7	4.06	4.66
USA	5.4	4.7	5.7
Canada	4.0	4.8	4.0
North America	4.7	4.75	4.85

Global Snapshot. Intentional homicide reported in each of the five UNCJS

Method of Computation. The homicide rate per 100,000 population was calculated by dividing the total number of intentional homicides reported in the UNCJS for 1974 (First UNCJS), 1978 (Second UNCJS), 1984 (Third UNCJS), 1988 (Fourth UNCJS) and 1993 (Fifth UNCJS) by the total population of each country for each year as reported in the United Nations *Demographic Yearbook*. Level of economic development is derived from the UNDP *Human Development Report 1996*. Raw data are as follows.

Country	Level of economic development	Homicide Rate, 1974	Homicide Rate, 1978	Homicide Rate, 1984	Homicide Rate, 1988	Homicide Rate, 1993
Algeria	Developing	1.40	N/A	N/A	N/A	N/A
Argentina	Developing	13.40	7.15	.69	N/A	N/A
Bahamas	Developing	12.50	10.43	24.45	N/A	82.48
Bahrain	Developing	2.00	1.76	N/A	1.06	N/A
Bangladesh	Developing	N/A	1.93	2.81	N/A	N/A
Barbados	Developing	4.58	4.44	N/A	7.86	N/A
Belize	Developing	N/A	23.33	N/A	N/A	N/A
Botswana	Developing	N/A	N/A	6.62	11.24	N/A
Burundi	Developing	N/A	N/A	.76	N/A	N/A
Chile	Developing	14.26	7.51	N/A	N/A	2.40
China	Developing	N/A	N/A	.86	N/A	N/A
Colombia	Developing	N/A	1.79	N/A	N/A	78.44
Costa Rica	Developing	16.41	5.40	4.01	N/A	9.05
Cuba	Developing	3.73	N/A	N/A	N/A	N/A
Cyprus	Developing	15.40	1.13	1.22	1.89	1.50
Dominica	Developing	N/A	N/A	2.53	N/A	N/A
Ecuador	Developing	1.42	N/A	N/A	N/A	17.94
Egypt	Developing	3.50	N/A	1.49	1.55	1.42
Ethiopia	Developing	N/A	N/A	N/A	10.36	N/A
Fiji	Developing	.71	.33	3.35	N/A	N/A
Guyana	Developing	8.05	N/A	N/A	N/A	N/A
Honduras	Developing	N/A	8.66	4.30	N/A	N/A
Hong Kong	Developing	N/A	N/A	1.63	N/A	1.55
India	Developing	3.17	3.00	N/A	6.21	7.47
Indonesia	Developing	.87	.11	.90	N/A	.79
Iraq	Developing	9.53	8.06	N/A	N/A	N/A
Jamaica	Developing	11.49	N/A	21.23	17.75	27.72
Jordan	Developing	N/A	1.34	2.08	2.03	5.46
Kuwait	Developing	6.06	4.83	1.04	7.20	10.56
Liberia	Developing	N/A	N/A	2.42	N/A	N/A

Country	Level of economic development	Homicide Rate, 1974	Homicide Rate, 1978	Homicide Rate, 1984	Homicide Rate, 1988	Homicide Rate, 1993
Madagascar	Developing	N/A	53.18	N/A	.85	.43
Malawi	Developing	N/A	N/A	2.40	N/A	N/A
Malaysia	Developing	2.07	1.85	1.94	N/A	1.93
Maldives	Developing	N/A	N/A	N/A	1.50	N/A
Mauritius	Developing	3.45	N/A	N/A	2.09	N/A
Morocco	Developing	.90	1.05	N/A	N/A	1.14
Myanmar	Developing	N/A	N/A	N/A	.82	N/A
Nepal	Developing	N/A	.48	1.93	N/A	N/A
Nicaragua	Developing	N/A	N/A	N/A	N/A	21.45
Oman	Developing	2.70	N/A	N/A	N/A	N/A
Pakistan	Developing	7.10	5.43	N/A	N/A	N/A
Panama	Developing	N/A	10.05	N/A	N/A	N/A
Papua New Guinea	Developing	N/A	2.04	N/A	N/A	N/A
Peru	Developing	2.05	N/A	3.21	N/A	N/A
Philippines	Developing	6.22	7.65	N/A	N/A	N/A
Qatar	Developing	3.13	3.00	2.11	2.10	2.04
Rep. of Korea	Developing	1.59	1.31	1.36	N/A	1.47
St Kitts & Nevis	Developing	N/A	N/A	11.11	N/A	N/A
St Vincent & The Grenadines	Developing	N/A	N/A	15.74	N/A	N/A
Western Samoa	Developing	N/A	N/A	N/A	N/A	3.05
Sao Tome & Principe	Developing	N/A	N/A	N/A	N/A	142.40
Saudi Arabia	Developing	.77	.89	N/A	N/A	N/A
Senegal	Developing	N/A	2.53	N/A	N/A	N/A
Seychelles	Developing	N/A	5.00	N/A	N/A	N/A
Singapore	Developing	2.70	1.80	2.73	2.15	1.74
South Africa	Developing	N/A	18.26	N/A	N/A	N/A
Sri Lanka	Developing	7.23	7.67	12.07	25.16	N/A
Sudan	Developing	6.44	5.46	N/A	N/A	3.26
Suriname	Developing	N/A	1.08	32.16	N/A	N/A
Swaziland	Developing	N/A	N/A	N/A	67.62	N/A
Syria	Developing	4.55	6.03	2.22	N/A	2.99
Thailand	Developing	32.95	24.21	N/A	7.59	N/A
Trinidad & Tobago	Developing	5.42	5.04	8.38	N/A	N/A
Turkey	Developing	14.11	N/A	N/A	N/A	N/A
United Arab Emirates	Developing	N/A	3.38	N/A	N/A	N/A
Uruguay	Developing	N/A	3.53	3.68	N/A	5.87
Vanuatu	Developing	N/A	N/A	N/A	.67	N/A
Venezuela	Developing	7.18	10.29	N/A	N/A	N/A
Zambia	Developing	N/A	8.56	N/A	N/A	N/A
Zimbabwe	Developing	N/A	4.94	N/A	N/A	8.95
Australia	Industrial	N/A	2.62	1.68	1.93	3.57
Austria	Industrial	3.00	1.98	2.44	1.80	2.45
Azerbaijan	Industrial	N/A	N/A	N/A	N/A	8.10
Belarus	Industrial	N/A	N/A	N/A	N/A	9.19
Belgium	Industrial	N/A	N/A	3.27	N/A	3.13
Bulgaria	Industrial	4.52	4.27	4.03	3.45	10.54
Canada	Industrial	2.71	2.56	2.51	5.31	1.87
Czechoslovakia	Industrial	N/A	.48	.85	N/A	N/A
Denmark	Industrial	.69	2.82	5.77	4.83	4.90
Estonia	Industrial	N/A	N/A	N/A	N/A	24.35
Finland	Industrial	N/A	4.86	2.19	6.19	10.05
France	Industrial	.40	N/A	4.94	N/A	4.67
Georgia	Industrial	N/A	N/A	N/A	N/A	12.55
Federal Republic of Germany	Industrial	4.40	4.18	4.52	4.14	N/A
Greece	Industrial	.30	1.25	1.83	1.92	2.53
Hungary	Industrial	N/A	N/A	3.72	3.81	4.32
Israel	Industrial	N/A	5.50	N/A	3.60	5.96
Italy	Industrial	3.10	3.33	4.96	4.95	4.71
Japan	Industrial	1.74	1.62	1.47	1.17	1.02
Kazakhstan	Industrial	N/A	N/A	N/A	7.28	14.97
Kyrgyzstan	Industrial	N/A	N/A	N/A	N/A	11.88
Latvia	Industrial	N/A	N/A	N/A	4.16	14.72
Lithuania	Industrial	N/A	N/A	N/A	3.91	14.06
Malta	Industrial	N/A	N/A	.91	.29	2.47
Netherlands	Industrial	N/A	7.99	12.24	13.39	N/A
New Zealand	Industrial	1.10	1.32	1.24	N/A	N/A
Norway	Industrial	.50	.86	.99	2.00	N/A
Poland	Industrial	2.33	1.51	1.76	1.51	N/A

Country	Level of economic development	Homicide Rate, 1974	Homicide Rate, 1978	Homicide Rate, 1984	Homicide Rate, 1988	Homicide Rate, 1993
Portugal	Industrial	N/A	4.01	4.66	4.63	N/A
Moldova	Industrial	N/A	N/A	N/A	N/A	8.78
Romania	Industrial	N/A	N/A	N/A	2.71	5.81
Russian Fed./USSR	Industrial	N/A	N/A	7.45	7.20	21.82
Slovak Republic	Industrial	N/A	N/A	N/A	N/A	2.43
Spain	Industrial	5.00	.58	2.09	1.30	1.64
Sweden	Industrial	1.53	1.50	1.39	7.22	9.53
Switzerland	Industrial	.61	N/A	2.24	2.26	2.30
Ukraine	Industrial	N/A	N/A	4.61	3.91	8.81
UK - England & Wales	Industrial	1.98	1.46	1.56	N/A	N/A
UK - Northern Ireland	Industrial	N/A	N/A	3.99	N/A	20.71
UK - Scotland	Industrial	N/A	5.41	1.36	15.31	14.26
USA	Industrial	9.82	8.94	7.89	N/A	N/A
Developing (Median)		**4.567**	**4.833**	**2.475**	**2.128**	**3.157**
Industrial (Median)		**1.975**	**2.587**	**2.436**	**3.912**	**7.03**

Global Snapshot. Prosecutions reported in the Third, Fourth, and Fifth UNCJS (rates per 100,000)

Method of Computation. The prosecution rates per 100,000 were computed by taking the total number of persons prosecuted at the national level reported in each of the Third, Fourth, and Fifth UNCJS for the appropriate year and dividing this figure by the total population provided by the United Nations *Demographic Yearbook* and multiplying by 100,000. Raw Data data are as follows.

Country	Economic Development	Prosecution Rate 1983	Prosecution Rate 1988	Prosecution Rate 1992
Antigua & Bar.	Developing	1036.00	n/a	n/a
Argentina	Developing	891.67	47.90	n/a
Bahamas	Developing	n/a	n/a	1595.09
Bahrain	Developing	n/a	2219.75	n/a
Bangladesh	Developing	186.21	n/a	n/a
Botswana	Developing	n/a	242.71	n/a
Burundi	Developing	90.89	n/a	n/a
Chile	Developing	n/a	3140.15	3309.43
China	Developing	n/a	36.41	n/a
Colombia	Developing	n/a	n/a	516.60
Costa Rica	Developing	1408.50	1349.98	n/a
Cyprus	Developing	114.95	261.96	139.24
Egypt	Developing	2269.37	n/a	521.23
El Salvador	Developing	n/a	317.98	489.70
Fiji	Developing	1282.14	n/a	n/a
Hong Kong	Developing	n/a	524.28	476.03
India	Developing	684.29	734.02	743.91
Indonesia	Developing	668.17	n/a	23.99
Jamaica	Developing	n/a	1010.42	n/a
Kuwait	Developing	1280.78	n/a	n/a
Malawi	Developing	542.14	n/a	n/a
Maldives	Developing	n/a	290.00	n/a
Mauritius	Developing	n/a	159.44	3956.95
Peru	Developing	n/a	n/a	93.81
Rep. Korea	Developing	1068.67	1244.85	1883.73
St.Kitts & Nevis	Developing	n/a	1363.23	n/a
Saint Lucia	Developing	56.49	n/a	n/a
St V.& Gren.	Developing	2084.11	n/a	n/a
Western Samoa	Developing	n/a	n/a	551.55
Sao Tome & P.	Developing	n/a	n/a	34.17
Seychelles	Developing	n/a	1076.16	n/a
Singapore	Developing	295.84	357.71	346.20
South Africa	Developing	1624.19	1416.26	1219.52
Sri Lanka	Developing	325.09	n/a	n/a
Suriname	Developing	n/a	n/a	n/a
Trinidad & Tob.	Developing	20.98	n/a	n/a
Turkey	Developing	n/a	2547.03	2258.16
Vanuatu	Developing	373.44	n/a	n/a

Country	Economic Development	Prosecution Rate 1983	Prosecution Rate 1988	Prosecution Rate 1992
Azerbaijan	Industrial	n/a	n/a	138.79
Belarus	Industrial	n/a	n/a	35.30
Bulgaria	Industrial	352.55	307.59	127.53
Canada	Industrial	n/a	n/a	n/a
Czech Republic	Industrial	n/a	n/a	645.13
Czechoslovakia	Industrial	882.06	689.92	n/a
Denmark	Industrial	2154.85	2838.42	3035.11
Estonia	Industrial	n/a	n/a	450.19
Finland	Industrial	6492.36	1915.48	1987.23
France	Industrial	n/a	151.97	n/a
Georgia	Industrial	n/a	n/a	20.91
Germany	Industrial	n/a	n/a	723.93
Hungary	Industrial	569.71	667.06	1100.33
Israel	Industrial	n/a	n/a	804.29
Italy	Industrial	973.92	1331.13	987.06
Japan	Industrial	2071.36	1161.85	1019.57
Kazakhstan	Industrial	n/a	n/a	67.62
Kyrgyzstan	Industrial	n/a	n/a	411.71
Latvia	Industrial	n/a	n/a	416.68
Luxembourg	Industrial	n/a	n/a	n/a
Malta	Industrial	107.32	n/a	n/a
Netherlands	Industrial	1525.98	1518.28	1555.78
New Zealand	Industrial	9390.87	n/a	n/a
Norway	Industrial	403.05	407.01	n/a
Poland	Industrial	684.70	n/a	n/a
Portugal	Industrial	n/a	301.16	841.33
Romania	Industrial	n/a	182.38	n/a
Russian Rep.	Industrial	n/a	319.57	377.56
Slovakia	Industrial	n/a	n/a	696.21
Sweden	Industrial	3266.60	2727.66	2640.89
Ukraine	Industrial	n/a	187.69	n/a
UK-Eng.& Wales	Industrial	1064.25	975.24	3924.36
USA	Industrial	18.54	n/a	26.04
UK-N. Ireland	Industrial	553.97	290.45	668.44
UK-Scotland	Industrial	4719.18	1280.02	1279.86
Developing (Median)		**676.232**	**734.021**	**521.23**
Industrial (Median)		**973.925**	**678.492**	**696.208**

Global Snapshot. Known suspects reported in each of the five UNCJS (rates per 100,000)

Method of Computation. The arrest rates per 100,000 were computed by taking the total number of persons brought into formal contact with the criminal justice system, whether by arrest, as a suspect, or in some other capacity, reported in each of the five UNCJS for the appropriate year and dividing this figure by the total population provided by the United Nations *Demographic Yearbook* and multiplying by 100,000. Raw data is as follows.

Country	UNDP Economic Development	Arrest Rate 1974	Arrest Rate 1978	Arrest Rate 1984	Arrest Rate 1988	Arrest Rate 1994
Antigua & Barbuda	Developing	n/a	n/a	1719.74	n/a	n/a
Argentina	Developing	n/a	464.39	14.39	18.70	n/a
Bahamas	Developing	864.00	1550.48	1903.02	n/a	1771.17
Bahrain	Developing	490.80	n/a	n/a	n/a	n/a
Bangladesh	Developing	n/a	192.44	183.41	n/a	n/a
Barbados	Developing	422.92	n/a	n/a	1427.05	n/a
Botswana	Developing	n/a	n/a	4110.82	n/a	n/a
Burundi	Developing	n/a	n/a	26.30	n/a	n/a
Chile	Developing	n/a	557.30	5300.83	4897.17	5011.37
Colombia	Developing	n/a	344.60	n/a	n/a	204.50
Costa Rica	Developing	105.10	n/a	n/a	n/a	335.85
Cyprus	Developing	3167.62	n/a	988.87	n/a	536.10
Ecuador	Developing	64.11	n/a	279.35	53.95	289.53
Egypt	Developing	14.00	n/a	n/a	n/a	33.10
El Salvador	Developing	481.90	n/a	n/a	n/a	n/a
Ethiopia	Developing	n/a	n/a	n/a	130.66	n/a
Fiji	Developing	2106.96	1292.74	1145.48	n/a	n/a
Guyana	Developing	4727.40	n/a	n/a	n/a	n/a
Honduras	Developing	n/a	345.60	132.23	n/a	n/a
Hong Kong	Developing	n/a	n/a	781.60	732.12	821.38
India	Developing	n/a	289.52	n/a	789.18	668.08
Indonesia	Developing	n/a	n/a	n/a	n/a	n/a
Iran	Developing	687.12	n/a	n/a	n/a	n/a
Iraq	Developing	115.94	n/a	n/a	n/a	n/a
Jamaica	Developing	1388.66	n/a	1326.05	1010.42	1405.01
Kuwait	Developing	848.94	n/a	n/a	n/a	n/a
Lebanon	Developing	n/a	n/a	n/a	269.28	n/a
Madagascar	Developing	n/a	n/a	18.52	91.14	43.00
Malawi	Developing	n/a	n/a	320.91	n/a	n/a
Malaysia	Developing	43.00	119.53	154.33	n/a	n/a
Maldives	Developing	988.46	n/a	n/a	n/a	n/a
Mauritius	Developing	2287.24	58.22	n/a	464.83	n/a
Morocco	Developing	448.13	n/a	n/a	n/a	n/a
Myanmar	Developing	n/a	n/a	n/a	101.74	n/a
Nepal	Developing	n/a	39.56	n/a	n/a	n/a
Nicaragua	Developing	n/a	n/a	n/a	n/a	602.86
Oman	Developing	130.54	n/a	n/a	n/a	n/a
Pakistan	Developing	282.02	6.09	n/a	n/a	n/a
Panama	Developing	n/a	n/a	n/a	853.88	n/a
Papua New Guinea	Developing	n/a	n/a	n/a	n/a	n/a
Peru	Developing	342.64	n/a	792.36	362.57	n/a
Philippines	Developing	n/a	1.18	n/a	n/a	n/a
Qatar	Developing	n/a	1600.00	889.97	675.70	945.56
Rep. of Korea	Developing	655.65	2288.38	2015.63	n/a	n/a
Rwanda	Developing	n/a	n/a	n/a	724.39	n/a
St Kitts & Nevis	Developing	n/a	n/a	6356.82	n/a	n/a
St Vincent & Grenadines	Developing	n/a	n/a	2833.03	n/a	n/a
Seychelles	Developing	n/a	n/a	n/a	1271.28	n/a
Singapore	Developing	227.97	417.94	768.37	1117.68	1093.21
Sri Lanka	Developing	n/a	339.32	341.75	237.81	n/a
Sudan	Developing	n/a	n/a	n/a	n/a	1406.45
Suriname	Developing	n/a	285.63	1404.27	n/a	n/a
Swaziland	Developing	n/a	n/a	n/a	2683.81	n/a
Syria	Developing	340.04	n/a	130.37	13.09	322.88
Trinidad & Tobago	Developing	549.07	n/a	1274.62	n/a	n/a
Turkey	Developing	66.61	n/a	n/a	285.25	410.19
Uruguay	Developing	n/a	319.49	3076.73	n/a	n/a
Vanuatu	Developing	n/a	n/a	n/a	n/a	n/a
Venezuela	Developing	n/a	n/a	n/a	436.86	n/a

Country	UNDP Economic Development	Arrest Rate 1974	Arrest Rate 1978	Arrest Rate 1984	Arrest Rate 1988	Arrest Rate 1994
Armenia	Developing	n/a	n/a	n/a	152.54	n/a
Australia	Industrial	n/a	n/a	2180.98	n/a	n/a
Austria	Industrial	2238.45	1700.11	n/a	2256.89	2512.23
Azerbaijan	Industrial	n/a	n/a	n/a	n/a	195.89
Belarus	Industrial	n/a	n/a	511.95	n/a	638.08
Belgium	Industrial	n/a	88.58	n/a	n/a	n/a
Bulgaria	Industrial	n/a	n/a	406.88	386.35	755.98
Canada	Industrial	n/a	n/a	2065.24	2240.99	2401.62
Czech Republic	Industrial	n/a	n/a	n/a	n/a	n/a
Czechoslovakia	Industrial	n/a	1091.08	1041.80	n/a	n/a
Denmark	Industrial	249.76	874.76	843.63	1206.59	2826.01
Estonia	Industrial	n/a	n/a	n/a	n/a	621.48
Finland	Industrial	6915.05	3011.72	n/a	4835.26	4156.84
France	Industrial	585.19	1273.86	1686.60	n/a	1342.27
Georgia	Industrial	n/a	n/a	n/a	n/a	144.69
Germany	Industrial	1158.02	2313.97	2117.26	2139.57	n/a
Greece	Industrial	1194.26	3432.64	2813.12	n/a	2626.51
Hungary	Industrial	n/a	n/a	805.39	788.40	1164.55
Ireland	Industrial	301.67	n/a	n/a	n/a	n/a
Israel	Industrial	n/a	n/a	n/a	1347.97	n/a
Italy	Industrial	794.30	n/a	798.35	977.89	1302.42
Japan	Industrial	344.79	384.26	357.71	403.79	302.09
Kazakhstan	Industrial	n/a	n/a	n/a	n/a	639.49
Kyrgyzstan	Industrial	n/a	n/a	n/a	n/a	453.87
Latvia	Industrial	n/a	n/a	n/a	518.58	523.94
Lithuania	Industrial	n/a	n/a	n/a	348.76	572.16
Malta	Industrial	n/a	n/a	n/a	n/a	390.38
Netherlands	Industrial	n/a	1431.20	1771.75	1689.65	n/a
New Zealand	Industrial	2732.36	4565.95	4862.73	n/a	n/a
Norway	Industrial	210.73	332.48	308.98	407.01	n/a
Poland	Industrial	760.66	677.07	835.65	657.07	n/a
Portugal	Industrial	n/a	n/a	487.98	154.59	n/a
Republic of Moldova	Industrial	n/a	n/a	n/a	n/a	410.34
Romania	Industrial	n/a	n/a	n/a	218.76	768.67
Russian Fed./USSR	Industrial	n/a	n/a	622.69	568.09	974.05
Slovakia	Industrial	n/a	n/a	n/a	n/a	912.72
Spain	Industrial	107.02	n/a	431.58	444.33	586.73
Sweden	Industrial	6888.85	108.14	1114.46	1071.82	1160.50
Switzerland	Industrial	283.14	n/a	n/a	n/a	n/a
Tajikistan	Industrial	n/a	n/a	n/a	162.06	n/a
Ukraine	Industrial	n/a	n/a	444.00	335.02	n/a
UK - England	Industrial	4173.02	n/a	n/a	n/a	n/a
United States	Industrial	2127.21	4260.32	5000.52	n/a	5620.04
UK - Northern Ireland	Industrial	n/a	n/a	n/a	n/a	n/a
UK - Scotland	Industrial	n/a	n/a	n/a	n/a	n/a
Developing (Median)		465.014	339.323	889.967	464.827	602.863
Industrial (Median)		794.297	1273.857	839.639	568.095	762.323

Global Snapshot. Convictions reported in each of the five UNCJS (rates per 100,000)

Method of Computation. The conviction rates per 100,000 were computed by taking the total number of persons convicted in criminal court reported in each of the five UNCJS for the appropriate year and dividing this figure by the total population provided by the United Nations *Demographic Yearbook* and multiplying by 100,000. Raw data are as follows.

Country	UNDP economic development	1972	1976	1982	1988	1992
Argentina	Developing	76.90	92.40	62.56	47.90	n/a
Bangladesh	Developing	10.46	14.42	n/a	n/a	n/a
Belize	Developing	577.69	535.00	n/a	n/a	n/a
Botswana	Developing	n/a	n/a	n/a	171.73	n/a
Brunei Dar.	Developing	n/a	n/a	331.50	n/a	n/a
Chile	Developing	704.84	762.33	117.03	166.64	152.03
China	Developing	n/a	n/a	n/a	33.04	n/a
Colombia	Developing	54.00	48.38	43.59	n/a	41.08
Costa Rica	Developing	n/a	225.54	238.90	266.35	181.76
Cyprus	Developing	78.85	74.43	611.86	1056.15	112.32
Dominica	Developing	n/a	n/a	14.47	n/a	n/a
Ecuador	Developing	33.32	27.03	n/a	n/a	n/a
Egypt	Developing	n/a	n/a	2958.97	4734.66	433.06
Ethiopia	Developing	n/a	n/a	n/a	91.95	n/a
Fiji	Developing	1645.93	980.34	688.24	n/a	n/a
India	Developing	434.29	297.02	453.48	441.60	455.09
Indonesia	Developing	n/a	n/a	n/a	n/a	33.18
Jamaica	Developing	n/a	n/a	n/a	718.90	n/a
Lesotho	Developing	n/a	n/a	n/a	174.21	n/a
Madagascar	Developing	371.98	301.78	n/a	118.78	n/a
Malaysia	Developing	n/a	247.97	n/a	n/a	267.59
Mauritius	Developing	575.65	495.73	n/a	3604.28	3805.14
Mexico	Developing	n/a	n/a	n/a	119.92	114.42
Myanmar	Developing	n/a	n/a	n/a	79.33	20.38
Panama	Developing	n/a	n/a	76.42	90.70	80.18
Peru	Developing	n/a	n/a	33.69	21.67	n/a
Qatar	Developing	796.15	610.00	208.56	n/a	503.00
Rep.Korea	Developing	347.86	234.56	251.97	243.28	301.67
Rwanda	Developing	n/a	n/a	n/a	197.25	n/a
Saint Lucia	Developing	1426.00	1563.64	n/a	n/a	n/a
St V.& Gren.	Developing	n/a	n/a	51.43	n/a	n/a
Senegal	Developing	144.99	126.09	n/a	n/a	n/a
Seychilles	Developing	n/a	n/a	1209.38	n/a	n/a
Singapore	Developing	122.60	175.44	174.07	205.58	198.19
South Africa	Developing	n/a	n/a	n/a	1112.87	939.19
Sudan	Developing	n/a	n/a	n/a	n/a	36.34
Suriname	Developing	4.59	2.97	n/a	n/a	n/a
Swaziland	Developing	n/a	n/a	n/a	1627.76	n/a
Syria	Developing	125.99	72.38	n/a	442.19	n/a
Thailand	Developing	524.19	498.21	n/a	n/a	n/a
Trinidad & Tobago	Developing	n/a	n/a	3.23	n/a	n/a
Turkey	Developing	n/a	n/a	n/a	1562.24	1104.38
Uruguay	Developing	n/a	n/a	n/a	n/a	103.86
Zambia	Developing	1309.29	1195.62	n/a	n/a	436.30
Hong Kong	Developing	n/a	n/a	n/a	421.49	342.46
Bahamas	Developing	863.33	883.33	n/a	n/a	n/a
Armenia	Industrial	n/a	n/a	n/a	112.91	n/a
Austria	Industrial	n/a	n/a	1183.81	892.07	943.92
Azerbaijan	Industrial	n/a	n/a	n/a	n/a	106.56
Belarus	Industrial	n/a	n/a	n/a	n/a	358.67
Belgium	Industrial	n/a	n/a	n/a	n/a	418.87
Bulgaria	Industrial	356.27	335.58	276.23	246.84	126.99
Czech Republic	Industrial	n/a	n/a	n/a	n/a	300.76
Czechoslovakia	Industrial	693.08	591.66	752.38	n/a	n/a
Denmark	Industrial	409.20	467.61	2061.43	n/a	495.65
Estonia	Industrial	n/a	n/a	n/a	n/a	326.17
Finland	Industrial	n/a	1229.34	6689.48	1842.93	1916.38
France	Industrial	1084.41	1051.58	15226.71	989.33	n/a
Georgia	Industrial	n/a	n/a	n/a	n/a	68.17
F.R. Germany	Industrial	n/a	n/a	1253.64	n/a	559.78
Greece	Industrial	n/a	n/a	n/a	n/a	1041.98
Hungary	Industrial	n/a	n/a	594.30	653.07	738.20
Ireland	Industrial	57.48	60.00	n/a	271.00	n/a
Israel	Industrial	1852.25	n/a	n/a	628.66	667.09
Italy	Industrial	149.41	183.41	214.29	182.97	311.93
Japan	Industrial	61.38	58.17	66.82	56.04	44.46
Kazakhstan	Industrial	n/a	n/a	n/a	266.07	231.40
Kyrgyzstan	Industrial	n/a	n/a	n/a	157.43	n/a
Latvia	Industrial	n/a	n/a	n/a	295.64	345.63
Lithuania	Industrial	n/a	n/a	n/a	218.95	308.18
Netherlands	Industrial	483.82	504.68	598.28	533.49	488.00
New Zealand	Industrial	n/a	8102.53	3423.12	n/a	
Norway	Industrial	260.69	248.21	376.01	291.27	n/a
Poland	Industrial	496.24	467.43	409.79	362.26	n/a
Portugal	Industrial	146.88	164.24	n/a	204.07	307.76
Rep.Moldova	Industrial	n/a	n/a	n/a	n/a	272.84
Romania	Industrial	n/a	n/a	n/a	128.77	n/a
Russian Fed	Industrial	n/a	n/a	n/a	290.65	444.82
Slovakia	Industrial	n/a	n/a	n/a	n/a	445.92
Spain	Industrial	n/a	n/a	162.04	n/a	n/a
Sweden	Industrial	4054.08	2508.15	n/a	1930.29	1910.93
Switzerland	Industrial	758.78	788.19	833.72	970.88	1031.64
Ukraine	Industrial	n/a	n/a	n/a	176.50	n/a
UH-Eng. & Wales	Industrial	4185.02	3885.47	1179.41	761.17	653.60
USA	Industrial	2091.74	n/a	14.71	n/a	370.38
UK-N. Ireland	Industrial	312.90	311.49	526.10	n/a	527.43
UK-Scotland	Industrial	810.27	868.96	4174.92	1115.49	1062.65
Developing (Median)		**371.978**	**247.967**	**191.315**	**205.583**	**198.19**
Industrial (Median)		**490.027**	**467.613**	**675.33**	**293.455**	**431.841**

Global Snapshot. Prison rates over twenty years of UN surveys (rates per 100,000)

Method of Computation. The prison rates for each year were calculated using data provided by each of the five UNCJS. For the appropriate year and UNCJS, the total number of convicted people in prison was divided by the relevant total population figure derived from the United Nations *Demographic Yearbook* and this quotient was then multiplied by 100,000. Raw data are as follows.

Country	UNDP Economic Development	Prison rate 1972	Prison rate 1980	Prison rate 1984	Prison rate 1988	Prison rate 1992
Argentina	Developing	30.77	41.12	n/a	4.93	n/a
Bahamas	Developing	361.67	276.19	n/a	n/a	n/a
Bahrain	Developing	140.91	63.80	n/a	n/a	n/a
Bangladesh	Developing	14.55	9.38	32.60	n/a	n/a
Brunei Darussalam	Developing	n/a	n/a	196.76	n/a	218.18
Burundi	Developing	n/a	n/a	17.80	n/a	n/a
Chile	Developing	61.12	45.88	n/a	n/a	51.70
Costa Rica	Developing	n/a	n/a	n/a	n/a	173.88
Cyprus	Developing	n/a	n/a	33.64	23.85	26.29
Dominica	Developing	n/a	n/a	393.67	n/a	n/a
Egypt	Developing	n/a	n/a	35.45	n/a	48.99
El Salvador	Developing	n/a	n/a	n/a	n/a	10.73
Ethiopia	Developing	n/a	n/a	n/a	37.18	n/a
Fiji	Developing	193.70	182.49	n/a	n/a	n/a
Ghana	Developing	n/a	n/a	588.98	n/a	n/a
Guyana	Developing	n/a	n/a	n/a	n/a	98.79
Honduras	Developing	n/a	n/a	3.05	n/a	n/a
Hong Kong	Developing	n/a	n/a	132.31	162.69	162.93
India	Developing	37.01	8.62	n/a	n/a	n/a
Indonesia	Developing	15.13	19.34	.94	n/a	14.79
Jamaica	Developing	n/a	116.22	n/a	120.17	n/a
Kuwait	Developing	85.36	8.31	223.27	n/a	n/a
Lesotho	Developing	n/a	n/a	n/a	174.21	n/a
Madagascar	Developing	n/a	n/a	n/a	n/a	44.05
Malaysia	Developing	46.82	46.95	59.31	83.61	67.86
Mauritius	Developing	142.71	141.15	n/a	169.60	n/a
Morocco	Developing	49.92	48.06	n/a	n/a	n/a
Nicaragua	Developing	n/a	n/a	n/a	n/a	29.02
Papua New Guinea	Developing	n/a	143.89	n/a	n/a	n/a
Peru	Developing	n/a	n/a	107.76	21.67	20.38
Philippines	Developing	n/a	3.19	3.96	2.98	n/a
Qatar	Developing	1367.69	1359.13	90.88	n/a	n/a
Rep. of Korea	Developing	116.69	76.92	n/a	66.74	75.33
Rwanda	Developing	n/a	n/a	n/a	117.45	n/a
St Kitts & Nevis	Developing	n/a	n/a	n/a	322.22	n/a
St. Lucia	Developing	391.00	294.35	n/a	n/a	n/a
St Vincent & Grenadines	Developing	n/a	n/a	256.48	n/a	n/a
Western Samoa	Developing	n/a	n/a	n/a	n/a	146.95
Sao Tome & Principe	Developing	n/a	n/a	n/a	n/a	15.20
Seychelles	Developing	456.00	317.46	355.38	n/a	n/a
Singapore	Developing	115.40	107.66	121.67	168.90	141.50
Sri Lanka	Developing	44.57	33.22	83.21	27.54	n/a
Sudan	Developing	n/a	n/a	n/a	n/a	238.16
Suriname	Developing	n/a	n/a	93.78	n/a	n/a
Swaziland	Developing	n/a	n/a	n/a	132.65	n/a
Syria	Developing	n/a	n/a	27.89	n/a	n/a
Thailand	Developing	163.48	161.60	n/a	n/a	n/a
Trinidad & Tobago	Developing	120.57	75.14	40.00	n/a	n/a
Turkey	Developing	46.50	85.09	57.02	55.45	21.56
Uganda	Developing	48.01	n/a	n/a	15.40	n/a
Uruguay	Developing	16.15	12.70	n/a	n/a	n/a
Vanuatu	Developing	n/a	n/a	37.88	90.16	n/a
Zambia	Developing	n/a	n/a	n/a	n/a	87.64
Australia	Industrial	n/a	n/a	54.89	64.95	n/a
Austria	Industrial	n/a	n/a	87.25	60.10	58.17
Belarus	Industrial	n/a	n/a	n/a	n/a	230.56
Belgium	Industrial	27.84	24.40	28.80	65.86	35.09
Bulgaria	Industrial	147.24	137.37	139.83	131.11	68.71
Canada	Industrial	n/a	n/a	97.38	n/a	n/a
Czech Republic	Industrial	n/a	n/a	n/a	n/a	87.12

Country	UNDP Economic Development	Prison rate 1972	Prison rate 1980	Prison rate 1984	Prison rate 1988	Prison rate 1992
Denmark	Industrial	n/a	n/a	43.13	49.11	44.36
Estonia	Industrial	n/a	n/a	n/a	n/a	182.52
Finland	Industrial	102.69	90.75	72.12	65.91	58.76
France	Industrial	32.22	55.32	35.27	88.27	n/a
Germany	Industrial	60.90	68.29	80.58	n/a	n/a
Greece	Industrial	24.96	25.64	26.05	69.18	39.71
Hungary	Industrial	n/a	n/a	139.58	92.43	111.33
Israel	Industrial	124.76	109.70	n/a	93.97	n/a
Italy	Industrial	20.56	16.29	23.84	23.60	34.72
Japan	Industrial	36.12	35.82	n/a	37.21	29.88
Kazakhstan	Industrial	n/a	n/a	n/a	n/a	275.99
Latvia	Industrial	n/a	n/a	n/a	358.63	204.59
Lithuania	Industrial	n/a	n/a	n/a	265.14	198.71
Luxembourg	Industrial	n/a	n/a	n/a	n/a	64.59
Netherlands	Industrial	16.41	17.12	n/a	n/a	n/a
New Zealand	Industrial	44.97	48.96	86.12	88.94	n/a
Norway	Industrial	45.85	43.98	n/a	50.20	n/a
Poland	Industrial	235.63	225.86	130.13	142.93	n/a
Portugal	Industrial	n/a	36.61	n/a	56.27	62.51
Republic of Moldova	Industrial	n/a	n/a	n/a	n/a	216.57
Romania	Industrial	n/a	n/a	n/a	42.05	n/a
Russian Fed./USSR	Industrial	n/a	n/a	n/a	431.25	n/a
Slovakia	Industrial	n/a	n/a	n/a	n/a	94.52
Spain	Industrial	11.94	19.87	n/a	38.52	n/a
Sweden	Industrial	39.31	4.17	n/a	44.77	50.13
Switzerland	Industrial	n/a	n/a	48.59	n/a	n/a
Ukraine	Industrial	n/a	n/a	n/a	232.67	188.98
UK - England & Wales	Industrial	73.99	n/a	71.33	76.56	69.14
United States	Industrial	n/a	n/a	n/a	n/a	178.10
UK - Northern Ireland	Industrial	n/a	64.54	120.79	100.95	83.46
UK - Scotland	Industrial	n/a	n/a	73.98	n/a	84.19
Developing (Median)		**85.357**	**75.139**	**71.26**	**83.61**	**59.782**
Industrial (Median)		**42.138**	**43.979**	**73.051**	**69.18**	**83.465**

Global Snapshot. Twenty years of policing world wide (rates per 100,000)

Method of Computation. The rate of policing was calculated by taking the total number of police personnel reported in the UNCJS for 1973 (First UNCJS), 1978 (Second UNCJS), 1984 (Third Survey), 1990 (Fourth Survey) and 1994 (Fifith Survey) and dividing the number by the total population reported for each country for the respective years in the United Nations *Demographic Yearbook* and multiplying by 100,000. Countries were classified as developing or industrial according to the UNDP *Human Development Report 1986*. Raw Data are as follows.

Country	UNDP Economic Development	Policing Rate 1973	Policing Rate 1978	Policing Rate 1984	Policing Rate 1990	Policing Rate 1994
Argentina	Developing	n/a	n/a	113.69	n/a	n/a
Bahamas	Developing	n/a	543.04	677.29	n/a	743.43
Bahrain	Developing	1369.57	n/a	n/a	n/a	n/a
Bangladesh	Developing	n/a	72.72	74.05	n/a	n/a
Barbados	Developing	363.33	n/a	n/a	n/a	n/a
Belize	Developing	n/a	348.00	n/a	n/a	n/a
Botswana	Developing	n/a	n/a	209.78	270.68	n/a
Burundi	Developing	n/a	n/a	2.86	n/a	n/a
Chile	Developing	n/a	n/a	n/a	n/a	275.62
China	Developing	n/a	n/a	n/a	72.37	274.91
Colombia	Developing	n/a	171.90	n/a	n/a	n/a
Costa Rica	Developing	n/a	n/a	29.79	16.17	36.34
Cyprus	Developing	517.58	572.42	574.43	576.41	522.89
Dominica	Developing	n/a	n/a	481.01	n/a	n/a
Egypt	Developing	n/a	n/a	968.03	n/a	37.16
Ethiopia	Developing	n/a	n/a	n/a	1.58	n/a
Fiji	Developing	n/a	210.82	n/a	n/a	n/a

Country	UNDP Economic Development	Policing Rate 1973	Policing Rate 1978	Policing Rate 1984	Policing Rate 1990	Policing Rate 1994
Guyana	Developing	490.00	n/a	n/a	n/a	n/a
Honduras	Developing	n/a	n/a	137.05	n/a	n/a
Hong Kong	Developing	n/a	n/a	456.39	545.25	639.89
India	Developing	n/a	98.60	n/a	136.23	134.12
Indonesia	Developing	78.36	n/a	n/a	n/a	n/a
Jamaica	Developing	237.72	n/a	272.19	385.41	n/a
Jordan	Developing	n/a	n/a	n/a	n/a	468.81
Kuwait	Developing	n/a	n/a	n/a	336.27	n/a
Lesotho	Developing	n/a	n/a	76.67	n/a	n/a
Liberia	Developing	n/a	n/a	105.17	n/a	n/a
Madagascar	Developing	n/a	n/a	72.04	30.70	21.31
Malawi	Developing	n/a	n/a	61.25	n/a	n/a
Malaysia	Developing	316.15	n/a	530.33	n/a	429.65
Maldives	Developing	n/a	n/a	n/a	25.12	n/a
Mauritius	Developing	446.16	n/a	n/a	636.10	n/a
Mexico	Developing	n/a	n/a	n/a	n/a	4.61
Morocco	Developing	n/a	n/a	n/a	n/a	100.38
Myanmar	Developing	n/a	n/a	n/a	122.92	n/a
Nepal	Developing	n/a	n/a	133.01	164.03	n/a
Nicaragua	Developing	n/a	n/a	n/a	n/a	145.15
Oman	Developing	285.83	n/a	n/a	n/a	n/a
Pakistan	Developing	186.49	n/a	n/a	n/a	n/a
Panama	Developing	n/a	n/a	n/a	n/a	432.75
Peru	Developing	209.97	159.01	333.62	n/a	429.33
Philippines	Developing	n/a	115.01	n/a	184.34	155.02
Qatar	Developing	n/a	2503.00	n/a	n/a	n/a
Republic of Korea	Developing	n/a	129.56	144.20	202.96	203.72
Rwanda	Developing	n/a	n/a	n/a	7.63	n/a
St Kitts & Nevis	Developing	n/a	n/a	742.22	n/a	n/a
St Vincent & Grenadines	Developing	n/a	n/a	512.04	n/a	598.20
Western Samoa	Developing	n/a	n/a	n/a	n/a	283.54
Senegal	Developing	n/a	104.81	n/a	n/a	n/a
Seychelles	Developing	n/a	981.67	n/a	804.42	n/a
Sierra Leone	Developing	n/a	n/a	n/a	n/a	n/a
Singapore	Developing	n/a	297.68	278.49	295.22	1074.68
South Africa	Developing	n/a	12.35	n/a	n/a	n/a
Sri Lanka	Developing	9.72	116.14	111.41	338.63	n/a
Swaziland	Developing	n/a	n/a	n/a	244.26	n/a
Syria	Developing	n/a	n/a	n/a	205.85	n/a
Thailand	Developing	n/a	245.29	n/a	n/a	n/a
Trinidad & Tobago	Developing	n/a	359.56	414.44	384.70	n/a
Turkey	Developing	n/a	n/a	n/a	148.52	189.89
Uruguay	Developing	n/a	n/a	779.93	n/a	830.88
Vanuatu	Developing	n/a	n/a	n/a	413.23	n/a
Venezuela	Developing	n/a	n/a	n/a	28.38	n/a
Zambia	Developing	n/a	186.65	n/a	n/a	106.81
Zimbabwe	Developing	n/a	n/a	206.55	n/a	n/a
Armenia	Industrial	n/a	n/a	n/a	963.84	n/a
Australia	Industrial	176.67	206.60	223.95	274.56	274.65
Austria	Industrial	344.58	362.17	358.92	358.95	367.00
Belgium	Industrial	n/a	n/a	n/a	n/a	344.37
Canada	Industrial	263.66	278.92	212.60	283.30	249.00
Denmark	Industrial	177.17	219.59	178.95	258.60	237.69
Estonia	Industrial	n/a	n/a	n/a	n/a	436.22
Finland	Industrial	339.34	231.66	239.04	239.49	231.91
France	Industrial	379.00	n/a	359.17	n/a	349.28
Germany	Industrial	330.98	n/a	n/a	311.91	n/a
Greece	Industrial	436.75	381.85	n/a	391.51	383.02
Hungary	Industrial	n/a	n/a	n/a	438.01	292.77
Ireland	Industrial	268.37	283.60	n/a	n/a	n/a
Israel	Industrial	n/a	n/a	n/a	330.95	n/a
Italy	Industrial	n/a	n/a	134.58	347.99	n/a
Japan	Industrial	200.33	175.81	211.21	n/a	207.62
Kazakhstan	Industrial	n/a	n/a	n/a	n/a	778.66
Latvia	Industrial	n/a	n/a	n/a	604.55	463.46
Lithuania	Industrial	n/a	n/a	n/a	848.95	544.99
Luxembourg	Industrial	n/a	n/a	n/a	250.39	n/a
Malta	Industrial	n/a	n/a	371.60	458.04	507.14
Netherlands	Industrial	n/a	n/a	n/a	254.07	n/a
New Zealand	Industrial	175.24	171.38	158.10	n/a	n/a

Country	UNDP Economic Development	Policing Rate 1973	Policing Rate 1978	Policing Rate 1984	Policing Rate 1990	Policing Rate 1994
Norway	Industrial	170.05	130.69	139.40	141.13	n/a
Poland	Industrial	n/a	n/a	n/a	293.12	n/a
Portugal	Industrial	n/a	n/a	16.11	382.38	n/a
Republic of Moldova	Industrial	n/a	n/a	n/a	n/a	241.20
Romania	Industrial	n/a	n/a	n/a	n/a	214.16
Russian Federation	Industrial	n/a	n/a	n/a	n/a	1224.58
Slovakia	Industrial	n/a	n/a	n/a	n/a	352.23
Spain	Industrial	324.97	n/a	n/a	306.26	128.70
Sweden	Industrial	190.93	290.86	212.47	263.56	281.99
Switzerland	Industrial	n/a	n/a	194.33	262.39	n/a
Ukraine	Industrial	n/a	n/a	n/a	916.05	418.61
UK - England	Industrial	n/a	293.40	330.22	340.10	346.69
United States	Industrial	306.79	164.28	258.01	n/a	300.06
UK - Northern Ireland	Industrial	n/a	695.97	675.54	n/a	520.46
UK - Scotland	Industrial	n/a	306.85	257.00	348.55	359.64
Developing (Median)		**300.989**	**186.654**	**209.779**	**204.404**	**275.263**
Industrial (Developing)		**268.371**	**278.923**	**218.274**	**330.951**	**347.984**

Global Snapshot. Judicial personnel world wide over twenty years (median rates per 100,00)

Method of Computation. The rate of judicial personnel was calculated by taking the total number of professional judges reported in the UNCJS for 1975 (Second UNCJS), 1986 (Third Survey), 1990 (Fourth Survey) and 1994 (Fifth Survey) and dividing the number by the total population reported for each country for the respective years in the United Nations *Demographic Yearbook* and multiplying by 100,000. Countries were classified as developing or industrial according to the UNDP *Human Development Report 1986*. Raw data are as follows.

Country	UNDP Economic Development	Judges rate 1975	Judges rates 1986	Judges rate 1990	Judges rate 1994
Algeria	Developing	3.67	n/a	n/a	n/a
Argentina	Developing	n/a	1.54	.68	n/a
Barbados	Developing	5.00	n/a	n/a	n/a
Botswana	Developing	n/a	n/a	2.23	n/a
Brunei Darassalam	Developing	n/a	5.75	n/a	n/a
Burundi	Developing	n/a	8.09	n/a	n/a
Chile	Developing	3.36	2.57	3.67	3.48
China	Developing	n/a	12.77	11.74	n/a
Colombia	Developing	n/a	n/a	n/a	10.81
Costa Rica	Developing	n/a	5.19	10.09	11.46
Cuba	Developing	n/a	n/a	n/a	n/a
Cyprus	Developing	5.81	5.05	5.55	9.13
Dominica	Developing	n/a	n/a	n/a	n/a
Egypt	Developing	n/a	4.79	n/a	n/a
El Salvador	Developing	n/a	n/a	2.91	n/a
Ethiopia	Developing	n/a	n/a	.27	n/a
Fiji	Developing	n/a	n/a	n/a	n/a
Guyana	Developing	4.49	n/a	n/a	n/a
Honduras	Developing	n/a	n/a	n/a	n/a
Hong Kong	Developing	n/a	n/a	2.47	2.41
Indonesia	Developing	1.47	n/a	n/a	1.61
Jamaica	Developing	2.89	n/a	n/a	1.08
Lesotho	Developing	n/a	3.66	.34	n/a
Madagascar	Developing	n/a	n/a	n/a	.54
Malaysia	Developing	.19	n/a	n/a	.38
Maldives	Developing	n/a	n/a	116.28	n/a
Mauritius	Developing	2.39	n/a	.84	n/a
Myanmar	Developing	n/a	n/a	2.85	2.56
Nepal	Developing	n/a	n/a	.98	n/a
Oman	Developing	4.68	n/a	n/a	n/a
Panama	Developing	n/a	7.00	8.60	n/a
Peru	Developing	1.83	3.12	3.03	n/a
Philippines	Developing	n/a	n/a	2.69	n/a
Qatar	Developing	n/a	5.75	n/a	7.04
Republic of Korea	Developing	n/a	2.03	2.44	2.71
Rwanda	Developing	n/a	n/a	10.31	n/a
St Vincent & Grenadines	Developing	n/a	.90	n/a	n/a
Seychilles	Developing	n/a	7.58	n/a	n/a
Sierra Leone	Developing	n/a	n/a	n/a	n/a

Country	UNDP Economic Development	Judges rate 1975	Judges rates 1986	Judges rate 1990	Judges rate 1994
Singapore	Developing	1.24	1.39	1.96	2.90
South Africa	Developing	n/a	3.16	n/a	n/a
Sri Lanka	Developing	n/a	n/a	.35	n/a
Sudan	Developing	n/a	n/a	n/a	2.30
Suriname	Developing	n/a	3.67	n/a	n/a
Swaziland	Developing	n/a	n/a	3.13	n/a
Syria	Developing	7.69	n/a	.35	n/a
Thailand	Developing	n/a	n/a	n/a	n/a
Trinidad & Tobago	Developing	1.30	1.08	n/a	n/a
Turkey	Developing	8.18	n/a	9.21	8.76
Uganda	Developing	n/a	n/a	n/a	n/a
Uruguay	Developing	n/a	n/a	14.66	14.37
Vanuatu	Developing	n/a	n/a	1.36	n/a
Zambia	Developing	n/a	n/a	n/a	1.82
Australia	Industrial	2.19	n/a	n/a	n/a
Austria	Industrial	n/a	19.87	20.47	19.79
Belarus	Industrial	n/a	4.77	4.81	6.56
Belgium	Industrial	n/a	n/a	11.70	11.88
Bulgaria	Industrial	n/a	n/a	7.75	11.71
Canada	Industrial	3.89	.70	n/a	n/a
Czech Republic	Industrial	n/a	n/a	n/a	19.93
Denmark	Industrial	10.53	11.74	n/a	n/a
Estonia	Industrial	n/a	n/a	5.22	12.34
Finland	Industrial	8.41	14.88	13.26	18.23
France	Industrial	8.21	10.53	n/a	n/a
Georgia	Industrial	n/a	n/a	n/a	4.56
Germany	Industrial	6.51	28.49	n/a	27.19
Greece	Industrial	9.57	31.34	n/a	13.10
Hungary	Industrial	n/a	12.96	21.54	21.42
Ireland	Industrial	2.01	n/a	n/a	n/a
Israel	Industrial	5.64	n/a	6.44	6.35
Italy	Industrial	n/a	12.47	12.38	n/a
Japan	Industrial	2.33	2.30	2.28	2.29
Kazakhstan	Industrial	n/a	n/a	.27	6.71
Kyrgyzstan	Industrial	n/a	n/a	n/a	5.22
Latvia	Industrial	n/a	n/a	6.26	7.30
Lithuania	Industrial	n/a	n/a	5.67	6.88
Luxembourg	Industrial	n/a	n/a	25.20	26.68
Malta	Industrial	n/a	n/a	n/a	7.97
Netherlands	Industrial	n/a	6.31	8.05	n/a
New Zealand	Industrial	2.21	3.94	3.68	n/a
Norway	Industrial	7.81	10.30	6.98	n/a
Poland	Industrial	10.20	12.27	n/a	n/a
Portugal	Industrial	n/a	n/a	11.48	12.70
Republic of Moldova	Industrial	n/a	n/a	n/a	5.56
Romania	Industrial	n/a	n/a	6.52	n/a
Russian Fed.	Industrial	n/a	5.47	6.57	8.50
Slovakia	Industrial	n/a	n/a	n/a	20.91
Spain	Industrial	3.04	6.22	n/a	n/a
Sweden	Industrial	12.72	7.44	18.24	4.44
Switzerland	Industrial	n/a	11.55	n/a	n/a
Ukraine	Industrial	n/a	4.59	4.69	n/a
UK - England & Wales	Industrial	n/a	2.21	n/a	1.91
United States	Industrial	15.28	.37	n/a	4.31
UK - Northern Ireland	Industrial	n/a	n/a	n/a	2.70
UK - Scotland	Industrial	n/a	2.32	.47	2.67
Developing (Median)		**4.567**	**4.833**	**2.475**	**2.128**
Industrial (Median)		**1.975**	**2.587**	**2.436**	**3.912**

Global Snapshot. Prosecutor personnel world wide since 1977 (median rates per 100,000)

Method of Computation. The rate of prosecutor personnel was calculated by taking the total number of prosecutors reported in the UNCJS for 1977 (Second UNCJS), 1984 (Third Survey), 1990 (Fourth Survey) and 1994 (Fifth Survey) and dividing the number by the total population reported for each country for the respective years in the United Nations *Demographic Yearbook* and multiplying by 100,000. Countries were classified as developing or industrial according to the UNDP *Human Development Report 1986*. Raw data are as follows.

Country	UNDP Economic Development	Prosecutor rate 1977	Prosecutor rate 1984	Prosecutor rate 1990	Prosecutor rate 1994
Algeria	Developing	n/a	n/a	n/a	n/a
Argentina	Developing	.09	.38	.30	n/a
Bahrain	Developing	5.56	n/a	n/a	n/a
Bangladesh	Developing	.26	n/a	n/a	n/a
Barbados	Developing	n/a	n/a	4.71	n/a
Botswana	Developing	n/a	n/a	1.62	n/a
Burundi	Developing	n/a	.76	n/a	n/a
Cape Verde	Developing	n/a	5.21	n/a	n/a
Chile	Developing	n/a	n/a	.21	n/a
China	Developing	n/a	n/a	11.08	n/a
Colombia	Developing	n/a	n/a	n/a	10.56
Costa Rica	Developing	n/a	2.23	2.34	2.51
Cyprus	Developing	4.26	11.57	13.96	9.67
Dominica	Developing	n/a	13.92	n/a	n/a
Egypt	Developing	n/a	2.25	n/a	1.24
El Salvador	Developing	n/a	n/a	n/a	4.11
Ethiopia	Developing	n/a	n/a	1.37	n/a
Fiji	Developing	n/a	n/a	n/a	n/a
Guyana	Developing	n/a	n/a	n/a	n/a
Honduras	Developing	1.11	n/a	n/a	n/a
India	Developing	.01	n/a	n/a	n/a
Indonesia	Developing	3.15	n/a	n/a	2.79
Jamaica	Developing	n/a	n/a	n/a	n/a
Kuwait	Developing	n/a	5.86	n/a	n/a
Lesotho	Developing	n/a	4.97	n/a	n/a
Madagascar	Developing	.93	n/a	n/a	2.39
Malawi	Developing	n/a	1.94	n/a	n/a
Malaysia	Developing	n/a	n/a	n/a	.62
Maldives	Developing	n/a	n/a	12.09	n/a
Mauritius	Developing	n/a	n/a	n/a	n/a
Morocco	Developing	.26	n/a	n/a	n/a
Myanmar	Developing	n/a	n/a	3.26	n/a
Nepal	Developing	n/a	.70	35.32	n/a
Pakistan	Developing	1.20	n/a	n/a	n/a
Panama	Developing	n/a	n/a	4.80	1.63
Peru	Developing	n/a	2.87	4.22	3.51
Philippines	Developing	1.79	2.10	2.52	2.37
Qatar	Developing	2.63	n/a	n/a	5.19
Republic of Korea	Developing	1.16	1.19	1.77	2.08
Rwanda	Developing	n/a	n/a	1.16	n/a
St.Kitts & Nevis	Developing	n/a	n/a	18.18	n/a
Saint Lucia	Developing	n/a	.75	n/a	n/a
Western Samoa	Developing	n/a	n/a	n/a	9.15
Sao Tome & Principe	Developing	n/a	n/a	n/a	4.80
Senegal	Developing	.15	n/a	n/a	n/a
Seychilles	Developing	n/a	21.54	16.33	n/a
Singapore	Developing	.56	2.29	1.92	2.08
South Africa	Developing	n/a	3.51	n/a	n/a
Sri Lanka	Developing	n/a	.56	n/a	n/a
Sudan	Developing	n/a	n/a	n/a	.59
Suriname	Developing	2.43	1.62	n/a	n/a
Swaziland	Developing	n/a	n/a	2.48	n/a
Syria	Developing	n/a	n/a	.77	n/a
Thailand	Developing	1.71	n/a	n/a	n/a
Trinidad & Tobago	Developing	n/a	1.88	n/a	n/a
Turkey	Developing	n/a	3.16	3.43	3.85
United Arab Emirates	Developing	1.79	n/a	n/a	n/a
Uruguay	Developing	.77	1.10	n/a	n/a
Vanuatu	Developing	n/a	.76	5.45	n/a
Zambia	Developing	1.94	n/a	n/a	.55

Country	UNDP Economic Development	Prosecutor rate 1977	Prosecutor rate 1984	Prosecutor rate 1990	Prosecutor rate 1994
Zimbabwe	Developing	.77	n/a	n/a	n/a
Australia	Industrial	n/a	n/a	n/a	3.84
Austria	Industrial	n/a	2.90	2.66	2.49
Azerbaijan	Industrial	n/a	n/a	n/a	16.49
Belarus	Industrial	n/a	8.09	n/a	14.44
Belgium	Industrial	n/a	3.36	n/a	7.68
Bulgaria	Industrial	n/a	5.46	6.25	6.98
Canada	Industrial	3.86	.23	n/a	n/a
Czech Republic	Industrial	n/a	n/a	n/a	8.16
Czechoslovakia	Industrial	.71	n/a	n/a	n/a
Denmark	Industrial	5.21	n/a	7.86	7.42
Estonia	Industrial	n/a	n/a	n/a	8.21
Finland	Industrial	n/a	7.68	6.22	6.56
France	Industrial	2.24	n/a	n/a	n/a
Georgia	Industrial	n/a	n/a	n/a	7.04
Germany	Industrial	6.56	5.96	n/a	6.60
Greece	Industrial	2.67	n/a	n/a	3.76
Hungary	Industrial	n/a	8.90	10.82	11.24
Israel	Industrial	4.04	n/a	7.49	n/a
Italy	Industrial	.12	1.65	n/a	n/a
Japan	Industrial	1.78	1.74	1.69	1.68
Kazakhstan	Industrial	n/a	n/a	n/a	18.60
Kyrgyzstan	Industrial	n/a	n/a	n/a	11.73
Latvia	Industrial	n/a	n/a	12.07	15.62
Lithuania	Industrial	n/a	n/a	11.26	15.80
Luxembourg	Industrial	n/a	n/a	6.30	6.73
Netherlands	Industrial	1.22	1.55	2.68	n/a
New Zealand	Industrial	2.73	n/a	n/a	n/a
Norway	Industrial	6.58	n/a	n/a	n/a
Poland	Industrial	8.38	8.58	12.59	n/a
Portugal	Industrial	3.69	9.28	10.33
Republic of Moldova	Industrial	n/a	n/a	n/a	10.74
Romania	Industrial	n/a	n/a	6.18	n/a
Russian Fed.	Industrial	n/a	.09	n/a	19.27
Slovakia	Industrial	n/a	n/a	n/a	10.47
Spain	Industrial	.79	1.50	2.93	3.28
Sweden	Industrial	7.01	7.47	8.07	8.17
Ukraine	Industrial	n/a	7.25	10.68	n/a
UK - England & Wales	Industrial	1.09	n/a	3.29	4.06
United States	Industrial	15.75	n/a	n/a	n/a
UK - Northern Ireland	Industrial	2.01	n/a	n/a	n/a
UK - Scotland	Industrial	3.48	4.61	5.10	4.85
Developing (Median)		1.155	2.17	3.259	2.507
Industrial (Median)		3.107	4.606	6.299	7.918

Global Snapshot. Prison personnel since 1970 (median rates per 100,000)

Method of Computation. The rate of prison personnel was calculated by taking the total number of prison workers (management, custodial, treatment and other)[1] reported in the UNCJS for 1970 (First Survey), 1980 (Second UNCJS), 1986 (Third Survey), 1990 (Fourth Survey) and 1994 (Fifth Survey) and dividing the number by the total population reported for each country for the respective years in the United Nations *Demographic Yearbook* and multiplying by 100,000. Countries were classified as developing or industrial according to the UNDP *Human Development Report 1986*. Raw Data are as follows.

Country	UNDP Economic Development	Prison worker rate 1970	Prison worker rate 1980	Prison worker rate 1986	Prison worker rate 1990	Prison worker rate 1994
Argentina	Developing	n/a	n/a	23.22	n/a	n/a
Bahamas	Developing	122.94	113.33	n/a	n/a	134.67
Bahrain	Developing	36.36	31.45	n/a	n/a	n/a
Bangladesh	Developing	9.73	7.47	4.75	n/a	n/a
Barbados	Developing	43.33	42.17	n/a	n/a	n/a
Belize	Developing	38.33	31.72	n/a	n/a	n/a
Botswana	Developing	n/a	n/a	n/a	112.33	n/a
Brunei Darussalam	Developing	n/a	n/a	n/a	n/a	75.17
Chile	Developing	44.63	41.40	40.07	40.14	44.47
Colombia	Developing	n/a	n/a	n/a	n/a	21.19
Costa Rica	Developing	45.49	54.79	n/a	73.76	58.48

Country	UNDP Economic Development	Prison worker rate 1970	Prison worker rate 1980	Prison worker rate 1986	Prison worker rate 1990	Prison worker rate 1994
Cyprus	Developing	26.50	25.36	27.19	58.68	29.43
Egypt	Developing	n/a	n/a	n/a	n/a	1.44
El Salvador	Developing	n/a	n/a	n/a	27.44	7.09
Fiji	Developing	46.15	51.10	n/a	n/a	n/a
Guyana	Developing	n/a	n/a	n/a	n/a	37.58
Honduras	Developing	n/a	19.64	n/a	n/a	n/a
Hong Kong	Developing	n/a	n/a	n/a	60.98	67.76
India	Developing	n/a	3.50	n/a	n/a	n/a
Indonesia	Developing	10.85	10.79	n/a	n/a	12.00
Jamaica	Developing	n/a	47.68	n/a	79.13	73.92
Kuwait	Developing	n/a	n/a	n/a	n/a	37.65
Lesotho	Developing	n/a	n/a	66.33	25.99	n/a
Madagascar	Developing	11.76	15.80	n/a	n/a	12.96
Malaysia	Developing	n/a	n/a	41.39	48.94	42.77
Mauritius	Developing	35.30	59.69	n/a	90.35	n/a
Mexico	Developing	n/a	n/a	n/a	n/a	31.61
Morocco	Developing	n/a	12.32	n/a	n/a	n/a
Nicaragua	Developing	n/a	n/a	n/a	n/a	23.11
Panama	Developing	n/a	n/a	n/a	n/a	16.11
Philippines	Developing	n/a	.00	4.60	n/a	3.54
Qatar	Developing	59.09	48.70	n/a	n/a	n/a
Republic of Korea	Developing	16.92	18.85	19.59	19.70	28.75
St.Kitts & Nevis	Developing	n/a	n/a	n/a	88.64	n/a
Saint Lucia	Developing	n/a	n/a	49.29	n/a	n/a
Sao Tome & Principe	Developing	n/a	n/a	n/a	n/a	31.20
Senegal	Developing	n/a	9.03	n/a	n/a	n/a
Seychelles	Developing	110.00	65.08	n/a	n/a	n/a
Singapore	Developing	n/a	53.60	n/a	54.90	60.27
South Africa	Developing	61.28	57.46	62.91	n/a	n/a
Sri Lanka	Developing	29.30	24.37	23.79	n/a	n/a
Sudan	Developing	n/a	n/a	n/a	n/a	43.99
Suriname	Developing	62.70	72.96	172.97	n/a	n/a
Swaziland	Developing	n/a	n/a	n/a	116.20	n/a
Thailand	Developing	15.19	20.00	n/a	n/a	n/a
Trinidad & Tobago	Developing	62.52	n/a	100.42	100.13	n/a
Turkey	Developing	n/a	n/a	n/a	39.41	39.84
Uganda	Developing	n/a	n/a	n/a	18.81	n/a
Uruguay	Developing	11.76	15.00	n/a	n/a	n/a
Vanuatu	Developing	n/a	10.17	n/a	18.38	n/a
Zambia	Developing	23.06	363.83	n/a	n/a	19.94
Zimbabwe	Developing	42.30	42.49	n/a	n/a	n/a
Australia	Industrial	n/a	n/a	n/a	n/a	55.69
Austria	Industrial	n/a	n/a	n/a	42.28	43.76
Belarus	Industrial	n/a	n/a	n/a	n/a	34.87
Belgium	Industrial	31.22	36.52	n/a	n/a	52.01
Bulgaria	Industrial	25.17	28.59	30.22	31.48	33.64
Canada	Industrial	68.94	78.47	n/a	n/a	92.67
Czech Republic	Industrial	n/a	n/a	n/a	n/a	78.49
Denmark	Industrial	n/a	n/a	n/a	n/a	74.76
Estonia	Industrial	n/a	n/a	n/a	n/a	176.25
Finland	Industrial	48.16	49.25	50.57	n/a	52.62
France	Industrial	21.53	25.08	n/a	n/a	n/a
Georgia	Industrial	n/a	n/a	n/a	n/a	36.81
Fed. Rep. Germany	Industrial	31.09	38.39	n/a	n/a	n/a
Greece	Industrial	15.13	13.80	n/a	n/a	18.12
Hungary	Industrial	n/a	n/a	n/a	41.51	4.56
Israel	Industrial	61.25	68.36	n/a	83.02	75.61
Italy	Industrial	25.92	34.55	n/a	n/a	n/a
Japan	Industrial	20.27	17.69	n/a	13.45	14.97
Kyrgyzstan	Industrial	n/a	n/a	n/a	n/a	53.89
Latvia	Industrial	n/a	n/a	n/a	46.21	79.67
Lithuania	Industrial	n/a	n/a	n/a	102.06	107.26
Luxembourg	Industrial	n/a	n/a	n/a	52.23	46.13
Malta	Industrial	n/a	n/a	n/a	n/a	32.97
Netherlands	Industrial	n/a	n/a	n/a	60.07	61.42
New Zealand	Industrial	n/a	n/a	n/a	n/a	n/a
Norway	Industrial	28.20	32.13	n/a	n/a	n/a
Poland	Industrial	n/a	n/a	n/a	54.92	n/a
Portugal	Industrial	n/a	24.66	n/a	n/a	41.97

Country	UNDP Economic Development	Prison worker rate 1970	Prison worker rate 1980	Prison worker rate 1986	Prison worker rate 1990	Prison worker rate 1994
Republic of Moldova	Industrial	n/a	n/a	n/a	n/a	58.00
Romania	Industrial	n/a	n/a	n/a	21.92	n/a
Russian Republc	Industrial	n/a	n/a	n/a	187.03	154.39
Spain	Industrial	10.94	n/a	n/a	n/a	n/a
Sweden	Industrial	55.09	7.49	n/a	n/a	51.49
Switzerland	Industrial	n/a	n/a	n/a	n/a	39.09
Ukraine	Industrial	n/a	n/a	n/a	36.21	45.69
UK - England & Wales	Industrial	38.63	n/a	n/a	54.47	74.72
United States	Industrial	51.02	58.83	n/a	n/a	n/a
UK - Northern Ireland	Industrial	n/a	n/a	n/a	n/a	193.22
UK - Scotland	Industrial	44.03	n/a	64.69	n/a	86.24
Developing (Median)		**38.333**	**31.589**	**40.067**	**56.789**	**31.609**
Industrial (Median)		**31.157**	**33.344**	**50.569**	**49.221**	**53.257**

[1] If a country provided data on only management and custodial personnel (i.e. data were missing for treatment workers and others), the country was included in the analysis based on the these personnel only.

Notes to Tables

Chapter 1. The experience of crime and justice

Table 1.1 Percentage of the public victimized by select crimes over five years in urban areas of six global regions

Rates (percentages) are calculated from percent of those reporting victimization over the past five years. Data have been combined from three sweeps of surveys conducted in different countries at different points in time from 1988 through 1996. Please see notes to Chapter 1 for further details on methodology of the ICVS.

Table 1.2 Ranking of 17 types of crime in terms of seriousness by victims, per world region and overall

Table T1.1. Mean seriousness ratings by victims of 17 types of crime, per world region and overall

	all	Africa	Asia	Central and Eastern Europe	Latin America	New World	Western Europe
number of countries	52	6	4	20	6	4	12
car theft	2.68	2.90	2.63	2.81	2.75	2.42	2.37
joy riding	2.47	2.87	2.49	2.57	2.54	2.41	2.31
robbery with weapon	2.46	2.74	2.26	2.23	2.43	2.60	2.49
assault against women	2.44	2.71	2.21	2.33	2.49	2.59	2.33
sexual harassment	2.43	2.77	2.14	2.27	2.47	2.65	2.29
motorcycle theft	2.32	2.58	2.47	2.22	2.59	2.20	2.17
burglary	2.29	2.63	1.95	2.15	2.37	2.37	2.29
assault	2.25	2.50	2.26	2.13	2.31	2.37	2.18
robbery without weapon	2.07	2.33	1.93	1.95	2.10	2.15	2.12
threats	1.99	2.19	1.83	1.87	2.13	2.10	1.94
pickpocketing	1.98	2.37	1.77	1.88	1.96	2.12	1.95
sexual violence	1.91	2.26	1.96	1.75	2.00	1.87	1.80
attempted burglary	1.88	2.24	1.72	1.71	1.89	1.93	1.80
other personal theft	1.83	2.30	1.55	1.81	1.92	1.84	1.76
bicycle theft	1.82	2.33	1.51	1.91	1.98	1.88	1.71
theft from car	1.79	2.70	1.89	1.75	1.81	1.70	1.60
car vandalism	1.62	2.28	1.66	1.69	1.67	1.58	1.52
all crimes	2.18	2.51	2.03	2.07	2.20	2.17	2.04

Data for correlations follow on the next page...

Table T1.2. Seriousness of 17 types of crime as judged by victims: correlations of rank order per country with global rank order

Western Europe

Austria	.6867	p=.002
Belgium	.7892	p=.000
England & Wales	.8946	p=.000
Finland	.9216	p=.000
France	.8866	p=.000
Italy	.8260	p=.002
Malta	.8240	p=.000
Netherlands	.8309	p=.000
Northern Ireland	.8841	p=.000
Scotland	.7819	p=.000
Spain	.3655	p=.299
Sweden	.8946	p=.000
Switzerland	.7475	p=.001

New World

Australia	.8725	p=.000
Canada	.8873	p=.000
New Zealand	.8897	p=.000
USA	.7598	p=.000

Central and Eastern Europe

Albania	.7059	p=.002
Bulgaria	.8633	p=.000
Croatia	.7549	p=.000
Czech Rep.	.8088	p=.000
Estonia	.8750	p=.000
Georgia	.7966	p=.000
Hungary	.6422	p=.005
Latvia	.7469	p=.001
Lithuania	.8554	p=.000
"Fmr Yugoslav Rep Mac"	.6853	p=.003
Poland	.8971	p=.000
Romania	.7139	p=.003
Russian Fed.	.8848	p=.000
Slovakia	.5809	p=.014
Slovenia	.8725	p=.000
Ukraine	.9172	p=.000
Yugoslavia	.8799	p=.000

Asia

China	.8845	p=.000
India	.7181	p=.001
Indonesia	.8731	p=.000
Kyrgyzstan	.8775	p=.000
Mongolia	.7474	p=.001
Philippines	.8449	p=.000

Africa

Egypt	.6376	p=.006
South Africa	.8995	p=.000
Tanzania	.4379	p=.079
Tunisia	.5735	p=.016
Uganda	.5931	p=.012
Zimbabwe	.6380	p=.006

Latin America

Argentina	.8824	p=.000
Bolivia	.7897	p=.000
Brazil	.7230	p=.001
Costa Rica	.9216	p=.000
Paraguay	.8260	p=.000

Chapter 2. Police records of crime

Table 2.1 Patterns in crime reporting, 1994

Figures are taken from the Fifth UNCJS. Countries have only been included if they reported total crime numbers as well as crime numbers for the main crime categories. For each country the percentage which robbery and theft comprises of total crime has been calculated.

Chapter 3. Bringing to justice

Table 3.1 Crime filtering 1994 (per 100,000 population)

As noted in the footnote to this table, because of duplicate questions concerning these data, there are a number of anomalies. In the case of Japan (Table T3.1 below), for example, it is possible to obtain quite different, and in part inexplicable statistics, depending on what data are used. The anomalies are, most likely, because of the inclusion and interpretation of the "other" category, and the ambiguity of the "total" and "grand total" categories in both questions, without a clear understanding of what these categories include (for example, whether they include both adults and juveniles). Explanations of anomalies can only be obtained by further investigation into the criminal justice processing and recording practices of each individual country.

Table T3.1. Suspect and prosecution data obtained by different questions in the case of Japan.

Suspects	1990	1991	1992	1993	1994
Question asked by offence type	378217	380907	357037	371640	376988
Question asked by gender and age	378217	296158	284908	297725	307965
Prosecutions					
Question asked by offence type	1297124	1243062	1266640	1242529	1173806
Question asked by gender and age	123938	120080	114085	119105	118721

Chapter 4. Punishment

Table 4.1 Typology of sentencing patterns

Method of computation. Data were derived from Table F4.1 in Notes to Figures, Chapter 4. It was processed by SPSS for the hierarchical cluster analysis using Squared Euclidean measure. For more detailed information of relationship among countries, see the dendrogram below. Names of each category are arbitrarily provided by examining Table F4.1.

Table T4.1. Dendrogram using average linkage (between groups)

```
                            Rescaled Distance Cluster Combine

           C A S E          0         5        10        15        20        25
           Label            +---------+---------+---------+---------+---------+

           GREECE            -+
           MEXICO            -+-+
           COLUMBIA          -+ +------------------------------------------------+
           REP OF MOLDOVA    ---+                                                |
           EGYPT             -+-+                                                |
           MYANMAR           -+ +-+                                              |
           AUSTRIA           -+-+ |                                              |
           GERMANY*          -+ | +-----------------------------+               |
           FINLAND           -+-+ |                             |               |
           ENGLAND & WALES   -+   |                             |               |
           JAPAN             -----+                             |               |
           COSTA RICA        ---+                               |               |
           LITHUANIA         ---+---+                           +-------+        |
           AZERBAIJAN        ---+   +----------------+          |       |        |
           ANDORRA*          -+---+ |                |          |       |        |
           ISRAEL            -+   +-+                |          |       |        |
           CZECH REP         -+---+                  |          |       |        |
           REP OF KOREA      -+                      +----------+       |        |
           ITALY             ---+---+                |                  |        |
           NETHERLANDS       ---+   +------+         |                  |        |
           TURKEY            -+---+ |      |         |                  |        |
           SCOTLAND          -+   +-+      |         |                  |        |
           CANADA*           -----+     +-----------+                   +---+    |
           GEORGIA           -+------+   |                                  |    |
           SOUTH AFRICA      -+     +---+ |                                 |    |
           ZAMBIA            ------+   +-+                                  |    |
           BELARUS           -+-----+   |                                  |    |
           KAZAKSTAN         -+       +---+                                 |    |
           ESTONIA           -+---+   |                                     |    |
           NORTHERN IRELAND  -+   +-+                                       |    |
           CYPRUS            -+-+ |                                         |    |
           PORTUGAL          -+ +-+                                         |    |
           HONG KONG         ---+                                           |    |
           SLOVENIA          -------------------------------------------------+
```

Table 4.2 Total persons incarcerated, 1994 (per 100,000 population)

Method of computation. Incarceration rate was calculated by dividing the total number of prisoners by each country's population of corresponding years reported by the United Nations *Demographic Yearbook*. Additional information provided by Walmsley (1997) and Biles and Harding (1994) was included directly. Data are taken from complete tables of 1990, 1992 and 1994 below for Table T4.2.

Table T4.2. Total persons incarcerated 1990, 1992, 1994 (rate per 100,000 population)

Country	1990	1992	1994
Russian Federation	—	520.23	580.16
USA	464.86	518.95	553.90
Belarus	204.07	314.76	477.78
Latvia	326.69	313.53	359.69
Bermuda	444.26	446.77	358.73
Ukraine**	—	—	345
Brunei Darussalam*	270.43	275.74	312.94
Kyrgyzstan	201.18	216.05	299.72
Zambia	398.72	422.76	294.13
Estonia	280.59	292.36	293.60
Lithuania	230.68	245.19	278.34
Singapore	202.44	192.09	254.88
Panama	141.12	177.97	215.21
Rep of Moldova	204.93	216.67	215.10
Hong Kong	212.01	188.39	199.08
Romania**	—	—	195
Cook Islands***	—	—	195
Israel	207.79	198.01	188.52
Czech Rep	79.43	135.37	181.49

Country	1990	1992	1994
Thailand***	—	—	176.6
Guyana	199.50	148.27	174.55
Poland**	—	—	160
Chile	172.54	149.58	155.92
Madagascar	185.25	136.92	151.42
Georgia	—	66.17	140.89
Western Samoa	123.17	131.68	140.85
Slovakia	86.66	124.72	138.62
Rep of Korea	128.37	130.93	137.78
New Zealand***	—	—	125.7
Hungary	118.85	154.14	123.74
Malaysia	128.53	116.12	122.78
Costa Rica	121.43	119.20	118.98
Canada	110.97	112.63	117.92
Northern Ireland	112.31	111.84	116.37
Fiji***	—	—	109.7
Luxembourg	91.88	90.51	109.23
El Salvador	117.11	102.93	108.99
Scotland	92.58	102.85	108.82
China***	—	—	107.2
Papua New Guinea***	—	—	106.9
Portugal	91.46	97.44	102.09
Uruguay	95.54	100.83	101.86
Bulgaria	122.68	93.93	99.06
England & Wales	88.06	89.01	95.02
Australia	83.31	88.54	94.50
Mexico	108.08	95.73	92.82
Austria	90.46	94.82	91.53
Italy	45.35	83.69	89.58
Macau	193.28	145.45	88.07
Tonga***	—	—	87
Colombia	99.96	81.80	85.16
Peru	82.87	70.00	84.02
Sao Tome & Principe	79.13	72.50	79.20
Kiribati***	—	—	78.8
Turkey	80.59	54.37	74.41
Nicaragua	89.05	61.83	74.32
Belgium	58.91	70.95	74.09
Vanuatu***	—	—	72.7
Sweden	61.13	63.46	70.36
Sri Lanka***	—	—	68.1
Denmark	62.10	64.35	67.40
a"FYRM"	49.36	47.81	62.79
Finland	67.79	69.52	62.37
Liechtenstein	—	—	58.06
Netherlands	46.09	49.36	56.81
Malta	32.49	46.56	56.04
Solomon Islands***	—	—	55.9
Uganda	54.11	62.90	54.39
Slovenia	51.25	54.46	52.27
Croatia	40.31	43.04	49.89
Marshall Islands	80.43	78.00	42.59
Japan	37.93	36.29	36.96
Bangladesh***	—	—	33.8
Nepal***	—	—	33.5
Albania**	—	—	30
Cambodia***	—	—	26
Philippines	22.16	24.61	25.83
Cyprus	32.01	31.30	25.07
Sudan	30.11	35.39	24.10
Indonesia	22.98	21.99	22.65
India***	—	—	22
Greece	16.50	23.09	16.43
Kuwait	—	1.34	1.98
Mauritius	94.83	80.86	—

a"The Former Yugoslav Republic of Macedonia"
* Data may be unreliable
** Based on Walmsley (1996)
*** Based on Biles and Harding (1994)

Table 4.3 Total convicted persons incarcerated, 1994 (per 100,000 population)

Method of computation. Convicted prisoner rate was calculated by dividing the number of total sentenced prisoners by each country's population for corresponding years reported by the United Nations *Demographic Yearbook*. The US 1994 convicted prisoner rate was taken directly from Maguire and Pastore (1995). Data are taken from complete tables of 1990, 1992 and 1994 below for Table T4.3.

Table T4.3. Convicted persons incarcerated, 1990-1994 (per 100,000 population)

Country	1990	1992	1994
Russian Federation	—	375.09	410.56
United States of America*	350.75	394.49	389.00
Belarus	155.98	231.50	363.39
Bermuda	372.13	379.03	300.00
Latvia	273.61	246.66	270.84
Brunei Darussalam	203.50	229.41	250.35
Ukraine	179.02	187.92	240.80
Kyrgyzstan	153.74	169.20	229.44
Singapore	134.90	141.48	222.76
Lithuania	202.42	203.74	197.74
Hong Kong	192.46	169.91	177.87
Estonia	224.63	188.60	173.12
Rep of Moldova	160.43	173.80	167.06
Israel	154.36	159.55	161.29
Western Samoa	123.17	131.68	140.85
Guyana	112.81	98.39	117.58
Slovakia	54.25	95.36	103.03
Canada	92.01	93.11	96.82
Czech Rep	39.17	77.55	96.05
Costa Rica	79.54	95.54	95.83
Northern Ireland	87.71	84.16	87.57
Hungary	85.08	110.65	87.16
Scotland	72.01	80.69	86.10
Australia	71.18	76.21	82.33
Malaysia	78.70	67.61	79.69
Luxembourg	68.06	65.90	75.56
Rep of Korea	65.94	71.39	74.70
Zambia	86.21	96.40	70.80
England & Wales	68.97	68.85	68.48
Bulgaria	105.28	67.93	68.09
Portugal	66.13	62.31	65.14
Austria	56.96	59.26	60.10
Switzerland	56.45	57.80	—
Chile	81.98	52.95	59.48
Sweden	49.36	50.77	58.66
Egypt	43.20	51.38	55.76
a"FYRM"	43.89	38.62	53.64
Finland	58.62	59.38	51.85
Madagascar	68.80	46.96	50.79
Denmark	45.18	44.66	49.64
Macau	116.67	101.52	48.93
Mexico	42.86	48.60	48.33
Italy	19.13	34.92	44.81
Nicaragua	45.72	30.91	40.13
Malta	10.73	22.31	37.09
Belgium	29.33	34.48	36.57
Panama	—	40.59	36.43
Croatia	31.12	28.63	36.35
Turkey	52.60	22.52	34.20
Netherlands	23.51	26.16	32.38
Japan	32.33	30.02	30.04
Marshall Islands	54.35	50.00	27.78
Slovenia	25.28	30.21	27.65

Country	1990	1992	1994
Philippines	22.16	24.61	25.83
Colombia	33.41	27.34	23.89
Peru	19.64	20.96	23.06
El Salvador	8.43	10.83	21.27
Uganda	20.45	26.37	19.65
Cyprus	28.34	26.63	19.35
Sao Tome & Principe	41.74	14.17	16.00
Sudan	14.54	21.03	15.79
Indonesia	16.90	15.24	15.13
Uruguay	10.18	14.53	10.96
Georgia	–	8.28	9.07
Liechtenstein	–	–	6.45
Kuwait	–	0.70	0.74
Mauritius	0.39	0.29	–

a"The Former Yugoslav Republic of Macedonia"
* Rate of 1994 was obtained from Maguire and Pastore (1995)

Table 4.4 Total prison admissions 1994 (per 100,000 population)

Method of computation. Admission rates for each year were calculated by dividing the number of total admission to prison by each country's population for corresponding year reported by the United Nations *Demographic Yearbook*. Data are taken from complete tables of 1990 to 1994 below for Table T4.4

Table T4.4 Total prison admissions 1990-1994. (rate per 100,000 pop.)

Country	1990	1991	1992	1993	1994
Russian Fed.	–	–	1225.94	1405.84	1542
Chile	–	803.43	775.82	879.64	930
Singapore	432.64	421.72	487.79	637.58	704
Bermuda	1016.39	927.42	666.13	639.68	633
Qatar	492.18	565.41	547.65	553.67	575
Guyana	430.03	445.32	399.88	426.10	474
South Africa	602.58	593.42	587.66	563.91	459
Canada	416.71	311.79	300.56	431.47	420
Zambia	466.80	397.69	456.94	350.08	419
Scotland	335.80	356.88	390.63	432.74	411
Brunei Darussalam	270.43	225.00	275.74	266.67	313
England & Wales	256.01	271.51	279.95	275.51	304
Estonia	–	–	–	269.61	302
Malaysia	288.11	354.27	271.31	312.55	298
Sudan	361.39	404.06	424.70	303.15	290
Denmark	300.02	277.34	283.79	280.17	290
Hong Kong	251.64	237.15	233.33	225.16	263
Mauritius	196.88	200.77	194.29	231.04	–
El Salvador	162.19	169.46	145.99	161.90	254
Kyrgyzstan	–	–	–	–	249
Costa Rica	–	–	–	–	244
Lithuania	103.65	104.49	152.89	192.82	244
Madagascar	232.93	213.76	196.36	226.77	235
Austria	219.49	236.22	241.08	231.65	217
USA	189.72	190.01	194.10	200.90	208
Belarus	97.73	112.39	152.21	189.58	207
Western Samoa	150.61	181.10	149.69	142.01	206
Panama	257.88	123.99	265.35	198.82	196
Israel	207.79	201.05	198.01	192.32	189
Hungary	172.52	188.43	198.43	170.29	178
Italy	100.13	141.36	164.92	173.64	176
Malta	119.21	6487.50	192.29	185.32	174
Finland	177.12	176.98	195.38	186.24	171

Country	1990	1991	1992	1993	1994
Belgium	173.42	180.76	189.85	184.71	169
Latvia	147.29	141.02	141.22	183.26	163
Sweden	184.99	155.76	159.62	164.25	162
Czech Rep	43.62	79.80	68.31	77.40	160
Georgia	–	–	66.17	109.71	141
Rep of Moldova	74.75	83.98	78.61	100.60	124
Uganda	107.74	119.27	107.21	58.63	112
Macau	205.91	171.69	164.90	151.47	108
Ukraine	55.36	74.42	77.28	82.41	107
Turkey	79.91	94.04	92.86	90.01	99
Nicaragua	205.27	184.00	187.24	152.71	97
Slovakia	47.55	92.16	81.62	97.12	96
Slovenia	61.51	100.35	92.84	94.12	91
Jamaica	112.34	127.01	101.55	96.14	89
Colombia	100.27	90.42	81.80	84.09	85
Northern Ireland	83.30	82.55	81.07	95.05	84
Peru	82.87	63.48	70.00	83.82	83
Portugal	112.39	105.17	123.26	115.90	80
a"FYRM"	74.61	55.22	59.14	64.46	78
Sao Tome&Principe	78.26	112.40	72.50	107.38	71
Egypt	60.11	66.07	60.64	65.90	68
Cyprus	80.47	63.06	63.31	54.04	66
Rep of Korea	72.23	61.07	56.46	61.13	65
Bulgaria	50.42	60.89	65.67	55.12	55
Greece	45.36	42.41	49.62	53.43	47
Japan	36.31	35.88	35.91	37.47	39
Indonesia	39.32	36.55	32.67	32.44	32
Croatia	64.46	–	37.86	–	31
Marshall Islands	13.04	33.33	34.00	36.54	30
Philippines	6.76	6.34	6.41	7.33	7

a"The Former Yugoslav Republic of Macedonia"

Table 4.5 Prison admissions of convicted offenders, 1994 (per 100,000 population)

Method of computation. Prison admission rates by convicted prisoners for each year were calculated by dividing the number of admissions of convicted prisoners by each country's population for corresponding years reported by the United Nations *Demographic Yearbook*.

However, because of data error apparently caused by questionnaire wording, 20 countries that provided data had to be excluded from the analysis. Page 42 of the questionnaire did not specify in any place that the "number of convicted prisoners" to be provided should refer to *admissions*. Therefore some countries provided exactly the same number as the static "sentenced (convicted)" prisoners asked in page 33 (Item 16.3). *Excluded countries*: Austria, Belarus, Bulgaria, Czech Rep, Denmark, Egypt, Finland, Hungary, Italy, Japan, Madagascar, Nicaragua, Peru, Portugal, Slovakia, Sweden, Turkey, Ukraine, Hong Kong, Northern Ireland.

Data are taken from complete tables of 1990 to 1994 below for Table T4.5

Table T4.5. Prison admission of convicted offenders, 1990-1994

Country	1990	1991	1992	1993	1994
Russian Federation	–	–	512.44	526.58	582
Kazakhstan	272.79	269.55	278.02	301.45	338
Bermuda	401.64	408.06	411.29	353.97	311
Kyrgyzstan	–	–	–	–	303
Latvia	246.57	229.79	198.06	221.81	257
Singapore	140.55	142.45	147.13	207.41	234
Brunei Darussalam	247.08	202.27	229.41	209.68	221
Rep of Moldova	204.93	217.56	216.67	225.6	215
Western Samoa	150.61	181.1	149.69	142.01	206
Lithuania	199.65	196.23	197.59	199.36	198
Costa Rica	227.56	196.34	181.76	178.6	193
Sudan	174.52	217.27	252.31	196.77	189
Estonia	209.87	208.37	177.2	170.34	173

Country	1990	1991	1992	1993	1994
USA	165.13	–	181.76	–	–
Georgia	–	–	66.17	109.71	141
Guyana	141.33	117.85	100.87	120.47	118
Zambia	86.3	65.53	96.64	73.12	95
Scotland	76.61	78.44	84.54	90.11	88
Malaysia	82.24	76.55	71.06	75.62	84
Rep of Korea	72.61	75.59	76.7	79.71	80
Luxembourg	69.37	72.09	66.41	74.12	76
England & Wales	69.66	69.23	69.6	64.48	68
Chile	74.49	56.07	53.2	59.19	63
a"FYRM"	42.85	35.02	37.16	44.08	52
Greece	35.35	33.69	40.1	46.64	38
Croatia	31.39	23.3	28.77	32.31	37
Belgium	30.61	27.7	35.18	37.57	32
El Salvador	8.92	10.12	11.27	18.73	30
Marshall Islands	13.04	33.33	34	36.54	30
Slovenia	27.93	27.32	30.56	30.64	28
Cyprus	28.78	30.45	27.34	26.18	21
Sao Tome & Principe	42.61	38.02	15.83	24.59	17
Indonesia	16.94	16.76	15.28	15.31	15
Mauritius	105.95	105.79	95.24	106.21	0

a"The Former Yugoslav Republic of Macedonia"

Table 4.6 Distribution of parole and prison use, 1994

Method of computation. The parole rate was calculated by dividing the total number of paroles per year by each country's population for corresponding years reported by the United Nations *Demographic Yearbook*. Data are taken from complete tables of 1990 and 1994 below for Table T4.6.

Prison admissions and convicted prisoner population are taken from Tables T4.1-4 above. High prison rates were defined as 80 and above prisoners per 100,000, while low was anything below that number. This cutoff was chosen where a natural break in the figures occurred. Similarly, high parole was defined as above 40 per 100,000 population, also where a natural break in the figures occurred.

Table T4.6. Yearly parole rate per 100,000 population;
1990, 1994

Country	1990	1994
United States of America	143.58	157.88
Finland	119.66	106.87
Kyrgyzstan	55.47	82.66
Turkey	73.45	76.71
Lithuania	28.40	75.09
Sweden	64.06	62.29
Denmark	56.56	58.27
Slovakia	33.73	49.62
Hungary	45.50	48.82
Belarus	7.27	46.94
Latvia	18.79	46.59
Canada	50.01	46.43
Israel	38.39	42.88
Panama	15.80	42.66
Kazakhstan	12.30	37.51
Macau	24.73	33.65
Sao Tome & Principe	21.74	24.80
Czech Rep	32.81	22.71
Bermuda	44.26	22.22
Russian Federation	–	21.67
Croatia	57.39	20.20
Austria	21.12	19.26
Rep of Korea	20.91	18.38
Chile	26.30	18.22
Western Samoa	21.95	–
Greece	5.90	15.63
Ukraine	7.33	14.83
Portugal	16.18	14.58

Country	1990	1994
Estonia	7.51	14.54
a"FYRM"	22.63	13.73
Japan	15.57	13.15
Belgium	13.55	8.65
Scotland	6.84	7.17
Marshall Islands	8.70	5.56
Singapore	3.29	3.92
England & Wales	25.46	3.84
Jamaica	8.16	3.73
Nicaragua	3.49	2.75
Mexico	.49	.97
Guyana	.00	.85
Indonesia	.25	.82
Hong Kong	.30	.40
Costa Rica	–	.39
Bulgaria	.00	.00

a"The Former Yugoslav Republic of Macedonia"

Table 4.7 Occupancy rate in prison; 1990, 1994

Method of computation. Occupancy rate was calculated by dividing total prisoners by total room available provided in Fifth UNCJS. The Netherlands provided numbers (965.27 % for 1990 and 1084% for 1994) which contradict other sources, such as Council of Europe (1996), and was excluded. Instead, countries which provided similarly high numbers (e.g., Sudan and South Korea) were included because of the unavailability of other sources.

Table 4.12 Annual probation rate 1990, 94 and persons on probation, 1994 (per 100,000 population)

Method of computation. The probation rate was calculated by dividing the total number of probations per year by each country's population for corresponding years reported by the United Nations *Demographic Yearbook*. Numbers of adults and juveniles are raw numbers.

Chapter 5. Resources in criminal justice

Table 5.1 Number of police, 1994 (per 100,000 population)

Method of Computation. The number of police per 100,000 population in 1994 was calculated by dividing the total number of police reported by each country for 1994 in the Fifth UNCJS by each country's 1994 population reported by the United Nations in *World Population Prospects 1950-2050 (The 1996 Revision)* and multiplying by 100,000.

Table 5.2 Trends in policing rates by country (percent change, 1990-1994)

Method of Computation. The percent change in policing rates from 1990 to 1994 was calculated in the following manner. First, the number of police per 100,000 population in 1990 and 1994 was calculated according to the method reported in the notes to Table 5.1. For each country, the number of police per 100,000 in 1994 was then subtracted from the number of police per 100,000 in 1990. The difference was then divided by the number of police per 100,000 in 1990 and multiplied by 100 to yield the percent change in policing rates from 1990 to 1994.

Table 5.3 Judges and legal tradition, 1994 (per 100,000 population)

Method of Computation. The number of judges per 100,000 population in 1994 was calculated by dividing the total number of professional judges reported by each country for 1994 in the Fifth UNCJS by each country's 1994 population reported by the United Nations in *World Population Prospects 1950-2050 (The 1996 Revision)* and multiplying by 100,000. The legal tradition of each country is based on a scheme developed by Reichel (1997) and reported in more detail in Chapter 3 of this volume. Much of the data derive from The *International Factbook of Criminal Justice Systems* (Newman *et al.*, 1995).

Table 5.4 Trends in number of judges by country (percent change, 1990-1994)

Method of Computation. The percent change in number of judges per 100,000 population from 1990 to 1994 was calculated in the following manner. First, the number of judges per 100,000 population in 1990 and 1994 was calculated according to the method reported in the notes to Table 5.3. For each country, the number of judges per 100,000 in 1994 was then subtracted from the number of judges per 100,000 in 1990. The difference was then divided by the number of judges per 100,000 in 1990 and multiplied by 100 to yield the percent change in number of judges per 100,000 from 1990 to 1994.

Table 5.5 Lay and professional judges, 1994 (per 100,000 population)

Method of Computation. See notes to Table 5.3 for the method of computing the number of professional judges per 100,000 population in 1994. See the first note to Chapter 5 for the method of computing the number of lay judges per 100,000 population in 1994.

Table 5.6. Prosecutors per 100,000 population, 1994

Method of Computation. The number of prosecutors per 100,000 population in 1994 was calculated by dividing the total number of prosecutors reported by each country for 1994 in the Fifth UNCJS by each country's 1994 population as reported by the United Nations in *World Population Prospects 1950-2050 (The 1996 Revision)* and multiplying by 100,000.

Table 5.7 Inmate to staff ratios for industrial and non-industrial countries, 1994

Method of Computation. The inmate to staff ratio was calculated in the following fashion. For each country, the number of convicted prisoners reported for 1994 in the Fifth UNCJS was divided by the total number of corrections personnel (management, custodial, treatment and others) reported for 1994 in the Fifth UNCJS. Countries were classified as industrial or developing on the basis of the United Nations Development Program (UNDP) Major World Aggregates found in the *Human Development Report 1996*. The developing category includes "least developed" and "developing" countries.

Table 5.8 Women in policing: percent change from highest to lowest, 1990-1994

Method of Computation. The percent change in number of female police per 100,000 population from 1990 to 1994 was calculated in the following manner. First, the number of female police per 100,000 population in 1990 was calculated by dividing the number of female police reported by each country for 1990 in the Fifth UNCJS by each country's 1994 population reported by the United Nations in *World Population Prospects 1950-2050 (The 1996 Revision)* and then multiplying by 100,000. An identical procedure was followed to obtain the number of female police per 100,000 population in 1994. For each country, the number of female police per 100,000 in 1994 was then subtracted from the number of female police per 100,000 in 1990. The difference was then divided by the number of female police per 100,000 in 1990 and multiplied by 100 to yield the percent change in number of female police per 100,000 from 1990 to 1994.

Table 5.9 Ranking of countries by percent of criminal justice workforce that were female, 1994

Method of Computation. See notes to Figure 5.8 for method of calculating the percent female criminal justice workers in 1994.

Table 5.10 Length of police training, new recruits or line officers, ca. 1994

General information on sources for Table 5.10 and Table 5.11. The information for these tables was derived from the *International Factbook of Criminal Justice Systems* (Newman *et al.* 1996), by Weiss (1997). As noted in the Appendix, the *International Factbook* (IFB) provides information obtained from a number of sources. It differs from the UNCJS largely because the information provided for each country is not officially sanctioned by the government (although in some cases it may be), but is rather compiled by independent professionals and scholars. The emphasis in the IFB is descriptive, with only occasional statistical data.

The different sources or authors of each country entry for the IFB should be taken into account when making comparisons based on the tables provided. The detail and style with which each entry is presented varies. The amount and type of training required by different nations is also somewhat difficult to ascertain. Many nations have several autonomous police units, each with their own training requirements and facilities. China, for instance, has a national police university, as well as provincial, municipal, prefectural and autonomous regional academies. And even within a singular police training facility, varying time periods and modes of instruction exist for separate ranks and specialized types of police; recruits, senior officers and those vying for promotion often train in different ways for periods of time. Slovakia, for example, offers specialty schools for such divergent tasks as driving police cars and the cavalry police. Ghana distinguishes between recruit and officer training; Sweden between officers and commissioners; Malta between recruits and constables; Romania between noncommissioned officers and officers; Singapore, lastly, trains constables, inspectors, national servicemen and officer cadet trainees differently. In light of this array of information, some *Factbook* entries provide hard facts, while others provide a report of general training practices or average training periods. It is noted, for instance, that the length and content of police training in Germany differs from state to state; as such, a general depiction is provided and Berlin's practices are cited as an example.

In sum, the rank and responsibility of the prospective police officer frequently determines the amount and type of training he will undergo. And while organizational nomenclature confounds the issue somewhat (in some nations "officer" appears to be a generic term for all police; in others, it takes on military connotations, signifying seniority and rank), there do exist certain commonalties.

Table T5.1a. Variations in the amount of police training

Nation	Amount of Police Training
Albania	4 years
Australia	1 year, 6 months
Bulgaria	varies: sergeants, 1 year; officers, 4 years
Canada	varies: RCMP, 1 year; others, average 6 weeks
China	6 months
Costa Rica	varies: as short as 1 month; officers, 3 months
Cuba	information unavailable
Denmark	3 years
England	2 years
Finland	2 years, 5 months
F.S. Micronesia	information unavailable
Germany	varies: in general, 2 years, 6 months
Ghana	varies: recruits, 6 months; officers, 1 year
Hungary	information unavailable
India	varies: constables, 9 months; ranking officers: 1 year
North. Ireland	information unavailable
Israel	3 months; advancements require special training
Italy	information unavailable
Japan	1 year for prefectural police
Kenya	information unavailable
Malta	varies: recruits, 6 months; constables, 2 years
Netherlands	varies: officer, 1 year, 8 months; management, 4 years
New Zealand	2 years
Nigeria	varies: recruits, 6-9 months; officer cadets, 1-3 years (depending on prior education)
P. New Guinea	recruits: 6 months
Poland	3 years
Repub. of Ireland	2 years
Romania	varies: noncom. officers, 2 years; officers, 4 years
Russian Fed.	officers, 3 months to 1 year probationary periods
Scotland	information unavailable
Singapore	varies: constable, 6 months; inspectors, 10 months; national servicemen, 3 months; officer cadet trainees, 9 months
Rep. of Korea	varies: students at national police college, 4 years; candidates for executive positions, 1 year; new recruits, 24 weeks; marine police, 12 weeks; riot and temporary police, 4 weeks
Slovakia	1 year probationary period

Slovenia .... varies: cadets, 4 years at School for Cadets, 2 years at Police College; other applicants, 6 month training course
South Africa .... 6 months
Spain .... 1 year
Sri Lanka .... information unavailable
Sweden .... varies: officer, 3 years; commissioner, 3 years
Ukraine .... information unavailable
USA .... varies: between 2 and 40 weeks; average: 10 weeks
Venezuela .... information unavailable

Table T5.1b. Variations in the type of police training

Nation	Type of Police Training
Albania	classroom
Australia	physical fitness; classroom; field training
Bulgaria	information unavailable
Canada	physical fitness; classroom
China	information unavailable
Costa Rica	information unavailable
Cuba	information unavailable
Denmark	physical fitness; classroom; field training
England	information unavailable
Finland	classroom; field training
F.S. Micronesia	physical fitness
Germany	physical fitness; classroom; field training
Ghana	information unavailable
Hungary	information unavailable
India	information unavailable
North. Ireland	information unavailable
Israel	classroom
Italy	information unavailable
Japan	information unavailable
Kenya	information unavailable
Malta	classroom
Netherlands	physical fitness; classroom; field training
New Zealand	information unavailable
Nigeria	information unavailable
P. New Guinea	physical fitness; classroom
Poland	information unavailable
Rep. of Ireland	classroom
Rep. of Korea	information unavailable
Romania	information unavailable
Russian Fed.	information unavailable
Scotland	information unavailable
Singapore	classroom
Slovakia	information unavailable
Slovenia	information unavailable
South Africa	classroom
Spain	physical fitness; field training
Sri Lanka	information unavailable
Sweden	physical fitness; classroom; field training
Ukraine	information unavailable
USA	physical fitness; classroom
Venezuela	physical fitness

Table 5.11 Qualifications required for new recruits, ca. 1994

General information on sources. See notes to Table 5.10 under the general information heading.

Further information on sources. Like police technology and training, the educational qualifications required by different countries of their police vary. Again, distinctive police organizational structures and differences in the information and detail provided by the *Factbook* must be acknowledged. Some countries, like Germany, have several police forces, each with different educational requirements. Others, like India and Spain, mandate divergent educational processes according to police rank. Moreover, educational systems are commonly unique to a particular country. As a result, different countries refer to different levels of education by different names. Some police forces, for example, require a "high school"

education, while others refer to a "secondary school." It is assumed, however, that both terms refer to the same thing. In addition, certain nations have distinct educational objectives or requirements not shared by others; some terms appear to refer to unfamiliar schooling practices. While this might, of course, be a matter of semantics or diverse reporting styles, it nonetheless makes accurate comparison a bit more difficult. Bulgaria, for example, demands a "public school" degree for police sergeants. Germany generally requires a "middle school" background. Malta and Nigeria mandate "school leaving certificates." The Republic of Ireland requires a final state school examination. In Spain, a basic educational certificate is necessary for basic police and a medium university certificate is necessary for superior police. Table 3.1 notes the atypical while reporting each country's particular educational requirements. When there are different educational mandates for more and less advanced police ranks, this is noted as well.

Table T5.2. Variations in police qualifications

Nation	Police Qualifications
Albania	information unavailable
Australia	high school; college degree required for some specialized posts
Bulgaria	public school for sergeants; academic degree for officers
Canada	college for RCMP; community college for most others
China	high school
Costa Rica	high school; college for upper ranking officers
Cuba	information unavailable
Denmark	masters degree in law for police chiefs
England	information unavailable
Finland	information unavailable
F.S. Micronesia	no educational requirements; high school is preferred
Germany	middle level education is generally required, but it varies from state to state
Ghana	elementary school for recruits; high school for officers
Hungary	2 years high school for policemen; 3 years college for officers
India	high school for constables and inspectors; college for superintendents
North. Ireland	information unavailable
Israel	high school
Italy	master of laws for senior officers
Japan	information unavailable
Kenya	high school
Malta	school-leaving certificate
Netherlands	high school
New Zealand	formal schooling preferred but not required
Nigeria	high school for recruits (but some have a "first school leaving certificate" which is the equivalent of an 8th grade education); college for officers
P. New Guinea	information unavailable
Poland	high school
Rep. of Ireland	final state school examination required
Rep. of Korea	no educational requirements, except for the National Police College
Romania	high school
Russian Fed.	high school
Scotland	information unavailable
Singapore	3 high school credits for junior officers; graduate degree for senior officers
Slovakia	high school
Slovenia	elementary school for those attending the School for Cadets (this lasts for 4 years and then students are required to attend the Police College for 2 years thereafter); high school for other applicants
South Africa	matriculation certificate
Spain	basic education certificate for Basic Police; medium university certificate for Superior Police; college degrees for police specialists
Sri Lanka	ordinary educational level

Sweden .... high school for officers; college degree in law for commissioner
Ukraine .... information unavailable
USA .... information unavailable
Venezuela .... 9th grade

Table 5.12 Levels of automobile equipment, ca. 1994

General information on sources for Table 5.12 through Table 5.15. The information for these tables was derived from the *International Factbook of Criminal Justice Systems* (Newman *et al.*, 1996), by Weiss (1997). As noted in the Appendix, the *International Factbook* (IFB) provides information obtained from a number of sources. It differs from the UNCJS largely because the information provided for each country is not officially sanctioned by the government (although in some cases it may be), but rather is compiled by independent professionals and scholars. The emphasis in the IFB is descriptive, with only occasional statistical data.

The different sources or authors of each country's entry in the IFB should be taken into account when making comparisons based on the tables provided. The detail and style with which each entry is presented varies. Different information regarding automobiles, electronic equipment and weapons is emphasized in different nations. In terms of police automobiles, it should be noted that the age and condition of a nation's police vehicles are not reported.

Similar problems are inherent in the information regarding electronic equipment and weapons. The most frequently mentioned types of electronic equipment appear to be computers, telephones, radios and radar. As with automobiles, the age and capabilities of the relevant electronic equipment are generally not indicated.

Most entries on weapons provide a listing of weapons routinely used, as well as those available in emergency or specialized situations. Again, the amount of detail varies. In Slovenia, for instance, only guns and vests are cited. In contrast, Sri Lanka reports that batons, tear gas, wicker shields, rubber bullets and shotguns are all available, while specialty forces have access to more sophisticated weapons and vests. Spain, it should be noted, offers a more detailed listing: 10,000 revolvers, 60,000 pistols and 100,000 bulletproof vests are accessible. Moreover, in countries that do not routinely use firearms, it is often difficult to tell if this is because they are not generally available or if cultural sensibilities militate against it. In Japan, for example, it is noted that few guns are used because there is fear that "offenders may attack the police to obtain guns."

Thus, the differing levels of police equipment reported may well be related to the extent of interest or thoroughness of the author of the particular entry in the IFB.

Further information on sources. *Automobile equipment.* A nation was classified as "high" if its entry suggested the general availability of automobiles by rhetorical description, a seemingly large total number of automobiles or a small ratio of automobiles to police (six or less police per vehicle). If an entry suggested by rhetorical description a smaller total amount of vehicles, or a larger ratio of automobiles to police (between more than six and ten police per vehicle), it was classified as "medium." If an entry specifically noted that few automobiles were available, or had more than ten police per vehicle, it was categorized as "low."

Table T5.3. Classification of automobile equipment

Nation	Category	Comment
Albania	low	approx. 1 vehicle: 40 police
Australia	high	9662 total vehicles; approx. 1 vehicle: 4.7 police
Bulgaria	medium ...	motor cars, motorcycles, special automobiles
Canada	high	no national data, Ontario only; transport vehicles, snow vehicles, motorcycles, two helicopters
China	medium ...	approx. 1 vehicle: 8 police
Costa Rica	high	approx. 1 vehicle: 2 police, newer models
Cuba	medium ...	automobiles prevalent in major cities
Denmark	high	approx. 1 vehicle: 4.5 police
England	n.a.	information unavailable
Finland	n.a.	information unavailable
F.S. Micronesia .	low	two surveillance boats
Germany	high	51,583 total vehicles; approx. 1 vehicle: 5
Ghana	n.a.	information unavailable
Hungary	medium ...	approx. 9 vehicles: 1 police
India	medium ...	mobility increasing
Northern Ireland	n.a.	information unavailable
Israel	n.a.	information unavailable
Italy	n.a.	information unavailable
Japan	high	approx. 1 vehicle: 1.15 police; cars, motorcycles, transport vehicles, 200 boats, 60 helicopters
Kenya	n.a.	information unavailable
Malta	medium ...	403 total vehicles; approx. 1 vehicle: 4 police
Netherlands	high	estimate only; 12000 total vehicles; approx. 1 vehicle: 2 police
New Zealand	high	2350 total vehicles; approx. 1 vehicle: 3.8 police
Nigeria	n.a.	information unavailable
P. New Guinea ..	medium ...	734 total vehicles; approx. 1 vehicle: 6.75 police
Poland	low	"shortage of 5800"
Rep. of Ireland ..	n.a.	information unavailable
Rep. of Korea	low	7703 total vehicles; approx. 1 vehicle: 11.7 police
Romania	low	"small number of cars and motorcycles"
Russian Fed.	n.a.	information unavailable
Scotland	n.a.	information unavailable
Singapore	medium ...	970 total vehicles; approx. 1 vehicle: 7.7 police
Slovakia	medium ...	approx. 1 vehicle: 5 police
Slovenia	medium ...	1136 total vehicles; approx. 1 vehicle: 6.4 police
South Africa	medium ...	24,380 total vehicles; approx. 1 vehicle: 4.6 police; black personnel and townships receive fewer
Spain	low	9300 total vehicles; approx. 1 vehicle: 20 police
Sri Lanka	medium ...	6211 total vehicles; approx. 1 vehicle: 5 police
Sweden	medium ...	2654 total vehicles; approx. 1 vehicle: 10 police
Ukraine	n.a.	information unavailable
USA	high	marked and unmarked vehicles: 1: 1.4 county police; 1: 2.1 municipal police; 1: 1.9 sheriff; 1: 4.8 special police; 1:1.02 state police
Venezuela	n.a.	information unavailable

n.a.= information not available

Table 5.13 Number of police per vehicle, ca. 1994

General information on sources. See notes to Table 5.12 under the general information heading.

Table 5.14 Levels of electronic equipment, ca. 1994

General Information on Sources. See notes to Table 5.12 under the general information heading.

Further Information on Sources. *Electronic equipment.* Police use of computers was used as the main classifying criterion. While radio, telephone and radar use were cited by the *Factbook,* computers seemed the most frequently reported type of electronic equipment and the most relevant indicator of electronic technological capacity. As such, if an entry noted that a country's police made extensive use of computers (such as computer-aided dispatch systems, mobile data terminals or computer networks or linkages for access to investigation information, fingerprints, criminal records or unsolved crimes), it was categorized as "high." If an entry reported that the police used computers for word processing or record keeping, or was in the process of developing more advanced computer usage (such as that just described), it was classified as "medium." If an entry did not mention computer use, or suggested that a country made little or no use at all, it was categorized as "low."

Table T5.4. Classification of electronic equipment

Nation	Category	Comment
Albania	low	approx. 1 computer: 900 police
Australia	high	computer-aided dispatch in metro and large rural areas
Bulgaria	medium	"well-developed" computer data
Canada	high	computers; federal computerized information center
China	high	computers, fingerprint system
Costa Rica	medium	no computer-aided dispatch, radios donated by foreign countries, old computers for word processing
Cuba	medium	radio dispatch, computer-aided dispatch being developed
Denmark	high	computer terminals in cars
England	high	computer-aided dispatch
Finland	n.a.	information unavailable
F.S. Micronesia	low	radio communication, radar use rare
Germany	high	computer-aided dispatch, national computer information system
Ghana	medium	computer recording
Hungary	high	computer-aided dispatch
India	medium	computerized crime information
Northern Ireland	n.a.	information unavailable
Israel	high	computer-aided dispatch, computerized records
Italy	n.a.	information unavailable
Japan	high	satellite technology
Kenya	medium	computers used
Malta	high	computer-aided dispatch and recording system
Netherlands	high	computer-aided dispatch; national information network; mobile data units
New Zealand	high	computer-aided dispatch; national information network
Nigeria	low	electronic equipment: "not much"
P. New Guinea	low	no computer-aided dispatch, some computer equipment
Poland	low	computerization in "infancy"; "outdated" telecommunications system
Rep.Ireland	n.a.	information unavailable
Rep. of Korea	high	computer-aided dispatch; mobile data terminals
Romania	high	national computerized information system
Russian Fed.	n.a.	information unavailable
Scotland	n.a.	information unavailable
Singapore	high	computer-aided dispatch; national information network system
Slovakia	medium	computer databases
Slovenia	medium	mainframe computers, personal computers
South Africa	n.a.	information unavailable
Spain	medium	centralized identification service
Sri Lanka	medium	computer-aided dispatch being developed
Sweden	n.a.	information insufficient; electronic equipment: "currently being expanded"
Ukraine	n.a.	information unavailable
USA	high	widely used mainframe and personal computers; some car-mounted digital terminal computers; Automated Fingerprint Identity System
Venezuela	low	"very little use" of automated information systems

Source: Weiss (1997)   n.a.= information not available

Table 5.15 Levels of weaponry, ca. 1994

General information on sources. See notes to Table 5.12 under the general information heading.

Further information on sources. *Weaponry.* Most entries recited the firearms models typically used by a country's police. What seemed to distinguish the more technologically advanced countries from the less was the regular or specialized use of bulletproof vests or sophisticated weaponry. As such, vests and sophisticated weapons (such as machine guns, automatic firearms or semi-automatic firearms) were selected as surrogates for weapons technology. If an entry mentioned both vest availability and sophisticated weapons, it was categorized as "high." If an entry noted either vest availability or sophisticated weapons, it was classed as "medium." And if an entry did not mention either vests or machine guns, or explicitly noted that they were not used, that country was classified "low." Data upon which these classifications were made are shown in the following tables.

Table T5.5. Classification of weaponry

Nation	Category	Comment
Albania	medium	vests for anticrime special units
Australia	high	vests for emergency cases; semi-automatic weapons for special squads
Bulgaria	high	vests available; self-loading guns
Canada	low	.38 Smith revolvers, .308 rifles; no vests
China	high	vests available; semi-automatic rifles
Costa Rica	high	vests available; heavy weapons available
Cuba	medium	semi-automatic pistols; assault rifles and shotguns unavailable
Denmark	medium	vests available
England	low	standard weapon is the truncheon; firearms generally not carried; expectation is that arms will be carried more often in urban areas
Finland	low	.38 caliber pistol; semi-automatic weapons for special squads; vests available.
F.S. Micronesia	low	sidearms, shotguns, rifles available
Germany	high	machine guns, automatic rifles; vests in patrol car
Ghana	medium	automatic rifles for paramilitary unit and general duty officers in emergencies; general duty officers generally do not carry firearms
Hungary	high	vests; machine guns available
India	high	vests available to police assigned to protect high dignitaries; muskets, mortars, light machine guns, AK-47 rifles
Israel	n.a.	information unavailable
Italy	high	vests available; automatic weapons, machine guns, bazookas, explosives, knives
Japan	low	"few guns used"
Kenya	low	regular police carry only batons; pistols, rifles available to General Service Unit
Malta	medium	arms generally not carried; vests and handguns available to Special Assignment Group
Netherlands	medium	vests available; 9 mm's
New Zealand	high	body armor; semi-automatic weapons
Nigeria	n.a.	information unavailable
P. New Guinea	medium	vests available; handguns
Poland	low	batons, guns, tear gas
Rep.of Ireland	low	batons, guns available
Rep. of Korea	medium	vests available in special circumstances
Romania	low	guns available in dire necessity; no vests
Russian Fed.	low	firearms, batons
Scotland	n.a.	information unavailable
Singapore	high	vests available; sub-machine guns
Slovakia	medium	vests available; firearms, tear gas
Slovenia	medium	guns; vests
South Africa	medium	body armor available; sidearms, rifles
Spain	medium	10,000 revolvers, 60,000 pistols; 10,000 vests available
Sri Lanka	high	shotguns available to regular police; specialized forces have access to more sophisticated weapons and vests

Nation	Category*	Comment
Sweden	medium ..	sub-machine guns, hunting weapons, pistols, tear gas
USA	high	66% local and 76% state police agencies supply vests to all regular field officers; 73% local police agencies authorize semiauto-matic weapons
Ukraine	n.a.	information unavailable
Venezuela	low	"insufficient number" of weapons

Source: Weiss (1997). n.a.= information not available

Table 5.16 Annual expenditure per prisoner (US$), 1994

A cautionary note. While initially startling in their contrasts, we should also exercise caution in the interpretation of these statistics. The corrections expenditures may include a lot of expenditures which are not expended directly on each individual inmate. Moreover, because the indicator for the statistic was the number of convicted prisoners counted on a particular day of the year, the number of admissions to prison is not taken into account. It is quite possible that the processing of admissions could demand a different rate of expenditure if the country concerned tends to keep fewer people in prison (perhaps because of shorter prison terms) but moves a lot more offenders in and out of the prison. A rough check is provided on this question by measuring the amount of expenditure per prison admission. Using this statistic we found that the difference between industrial and non-industrial countries still held. Industrial countries spent $5,430 per admission, whereas non-industrial countries spent only $1,322.

Method of computation. The annual expenditure by each country on corrections per convicted adult prisoner (US$) in 1994 was calculated by multiplying the expenditure (salaries and fixed assets) on corrections (penal and correctional institutions) reported by each country in local currency for 1994 in the Fifth UNCJS by the conversion value (1.000/exchange rate) described in the computation notes for Figure 5.9 and then dividing this product, which represents each country's expenditure on corrections in US currency, by the number of convicted adult prisoners reported by each country for 1994 in the Fifth UNCJS.

Table 5.17 Ratio of prisoners to beds, 1994

Method of computation. The ratio of convicted adult prisoners to beds was calculated by dividing the number of convicted adult prisoners reported by each country for 1994 in the Fifth UNCJS by the number of beds in adult prisons reported by each country for 1994 in the Fifth UNCJS.

Chapter 6. Firearm abuse and regulation

Table 6.1. Number of firearm wounds due to criminal acts, 1995

Table T6.1. Raw data of UNFRS (1997): firearm wounds

Country	Year	Rate of firearm wounds (per 100,000)	Number of firearm wounds due to criminal acts
Argentina		n.a.	n.a.
Australia		n.a.	n.a.
Austria		n.a.	n.a.
Belarus		n.r.a.	n.r.a.
Belgium		n.a.	n.a.
Brazil	1995	247.15	393000
Burkina Faso	1995	1.24	130
Canada		n.a.	n.a.
China		n.r.	n.r.
Costa Rica	1995	12.79	4.38

Country	Year	Rate of firearm wounds (per 100,000)	Number of firearm wounds due to criminal acts
Czech Republic		n.r.	n.r.
Denmark		n.r.a.	n.r.a.
Ecuador		n.r.	n.r.
Estonia[1]	1995	2.02	30
Finland		n.a.	n.a.
Germany		n.a.	n.a.
Greece		n.r.	n.r.
Guinea	1995	1.82	134
Hungary		n.a.	n.a.
India		n.r.a.	n.r.a.
Jamaica	1995	53.00	1308
Japan	1995	0.03	33
Luxembourg		n.a.	n.a.
Malaysia		n.r.	n.r.
Mexico		n.r.	n.r.
Moldova	1996	0.65	29
New Zealand		n.r.	n.r.
Papua New Guinea		n.a.	n.a.
Peru	1996	2.28	545
Philippines		n.a.	n.a.
Poland[2]	1995	1.28	493
Romania		n.r.	n.r.
Russian Federation		n.a.	n.a.
Singapore	1995	0.06	2
Slovakia		n.r.	n.r.
South Africa		n.a.	n.a.
Spain	1995	0.10	39
Sweden		n.a.	n.a.
Tanzania	1995	0.19	57
Trinidad & Tobago	1995	15.23	196
Tunisia	1996	0.00	0
Uganda		n.a.	n.a.
United Kingdom[3]	1994	1.08	609
United States		n.r.	n.r.
Vietnam	1995	0.10	74
Zambia	1995	1.44	116
Summary			
Minimum	1994	0.00	0
Maximum	1996	247.15	393000
Average		18.91	
No response		10	10
Not available		15	15
Not reasonably available		3	3
Count	18	18	18

Notation: *nr: no response; na: not available; nra: not reasonably available; npa: not publicly available*

[1]The figures here include only those incidents which were reported to the police and were recorded as willful causing of bodily injuries. It is obvious that the data do not reflect the reality. (Compare, for example, with the number of victims who were killed by a firearm – see Question 63.)

[2]Figure represents number of offences.

[3]For Great Britain only (Northern Ireland not included); 1994 GB population is estimated as 56,433,000.

Table 6.2 Countries prohibiting civilian ownership of certain types of firearms

Table T6.2. Raw data of UNFRS (1997): gun ownership and prohibition

Country	Prohibit ownership of: long gun	handgun	Restrict ownership of: long gun	handgun
Argentina	all	certain	n.app.	all
Australia	certain	certain	all	all
Austria	certain	certain	certain	all
Belarus	certain	all	certain	all
Belgium	certain	none	certain	all
Brazil	certain	certain	certain	certain
Burkina Faso	none	none	none	all
Canada	certain	certain	all	all
China	n.r.	n.r.	all	all
Costa Rica	certain	certain	certain	certain
Czech Republic	certain	certain	certain	certain
Denmark	none	none	all	all
Ecuador	all	certain	all	certain
Estonia	certain	certain	certain	certain
Finland	none	none	all	all
Germany	none	none	all	all
Greece	n.r.	n.r.	all	all
Guinea	certain	certain	certain	certain
Hungary	certain	certain	all	all
India	certain	certain	all	all
Jamaica	certain	certain	all	all
Japan	certain	all *	all	all
Luxembourg	all	all	all	all
Malaysia	all	all	all	all
Mexico	certain	certain	certain	certain
Moldova	certain	certain	none	certain
New Zealand	certain	certain	all	all
Papua New Guinea	certain	none	all	all
Peru	certain	certain	certain	certain
Philippines	certain	certain	certain	certain
Poland	certain	none	certain	certain
Romania	none	none	n.r.	n.r.
Russian Federation	certain	all	certain	all
Singapore	certain	certain	all	all
Slovakia	certain	certain	certain	certain
South Africa	certain	certain	certain	certain
Spain	certain	certain	all	all
Sweden	none	none	all	all
Tanzania	certain	certain	all	all
Trinidad & Tobago	certain	certain	all	all
Tunisia	none	none	all	all
Uganda	none	none	all	all
United Kingdom	certain	certain	all	all
United States	certain	certain	all	all
Vietnam	certain	all	certain	n.app.
Zambia	none	none	all	certain
Summary				
All	4	6	26	30
Certain	31	26	16	14
None	9	12	2	0

Note: As an exception, team members, or candidates for international sport shooting competitions, recommended by the Japan Amateur Sports Association, may apply for a license for a sporting pistol.

Notation: *nr: non-response, left blank; n.a.: not available, does not exist, not known; nra: not reasonably available; npa: not publicly available; n app: not applicable.*

GLOBAL REPORT ON CRIME AND JUSTICE

Table 6.3 Incidence of illegal firearm importation

Table T6.3. Raw data of UNFRS (1997): illegal import frequency

Country	Firearms	Components	Ammunition
Argentina	n.r.	n.r.	n.r.
Australia	some	some	some
Austria	some	some	some
Belarus	few	few	few
Belgium	some	none	few
Brazil	frequent	frequent	frequent
Burkina Faso	some	few	some
Canada	some	some	some
China	some	some	some
Costa Rica	some	few	few
Czech Republic	few	few	few
Denmark	n.r.a.	n.r.a.	n.r.a.
Ecuador	frequent	some	frequent
Estonia	some	few	some
Finland	few	few	few
Germany	frequent	frequent	some
Greece	few	few	few
Guinea	frequent	few	frequent
Hungary	n.r.	n.r.	n.r.
India	frequent	none	frequent
Jamaica	frequent	n.r.	frequent
Japan	some	few	some
Luxembourg	none	none	none
Malaysia	some	some	some
Mexico	n.r.	n.r.	n.r.
Moldova	none	none	none
New Zealand	few	few	few
Papua New Guinea	frequent	some	frequent
Peru	few	few	few
Philippines	few	few	few
Poland	some	some	some
Romania	few	none	few
Russian Federation	some	some	some
Singapore	none	none	none
Slovakia	n.r.a.	n.r.a.	n.r.a.
South Africa	frequent	few	frequent
Spain	some	some	some
Sweden	n.r.	n.r.	n.r.
Tanzania	some	none	some
Trinidad & Tobago	some	some	some
Tunisia	none	none	none
Uganda	few	few	few
United Kingdom	some	n.r.	some
United States	few	few	few
Vietnam	none	none	none
Zambia	some	few	some
Summary			
Frequent	8	2	7
Some	17	11	16
Few	10	16	12
None	5	9	5
Not available	2	2	2
No response	4	6	4

Notation: *nr: non-response; na: not available, does not exist, not known; nra: not reasonably available; npa: not publicly available; n app: not applicable.*

Chapter 7. Drugs and drug control

Table 7.11 Prison admissions for drug trafficking and possession, 1994

Country	Prison Admissions
Italy	36329
South Africa	24302
Zambia	10435
Belgium	7074
Madagascar	7041
Japan	5339
Sudan	4758
Hong Kong	4342
England & Wales	3483
Singapore	2138
Switzerland	1881
Rep of Korea	1283
Sweden	1239
Denmark	942
Panama	927
Scotland	895
Georgia	834
Turkey	779
El Salvador	763
Greece	627
Kuwait	604
Jamaica	472
Indonesia	388
Mauritius	357
Egypt	204
Bahamas	141
Guyana	115
Brunei Darussalam	100
Rep of Moldova	70
Malta	68
Northern Ireland	66
"Former Yugoslav Rep Macedonia"	61
Western Samoa	55
Bermuda	54
Macau	53
Uruguay	38
Cyprus	21
Slovenia	19
Marshall Islands	0

Source: Fifth UNCJS.

Page left blank

Appendix 1: Definitions used in the Fifth United Nations Survey of Crime Trends and Criminal Justice Systems

Intentional homicide refers to death deliberately inflicted on a person by another person, including infanticide. Please indicate whether certain categories of attempted homicide are charged or prosecuted as "aggravated assault."

Non-intentional homicide refers to death not deliberately inflicted on a person by another person. This includes the crime of manslaughter, but excludes traffic accidents that result in the death of persons.

Assault refers to physical attack against the body of another person, including battery but excluding indecent assault. Some criminal or penal codes distinguish between aggravated and simple assault depending on the degree of resulting injury. Please provide the major criterion for this distinction if it applies in your country.

Rape refers to sexual intercourse without valid consent. Please indicate whether statutory rape is included in the figures provided. If your country distinguishes between sexual assault and actual penetration, please provide relevant information.

Theft refers to the removal of property without the property owner's consent. Theft excludes burglary and housebreaking. It includes the theft of a motor vehicle. Shoplifting and other minor offences, e.g. pilfering and petty theft, may or may not be included as thefts. Please provide relevant information if a distinction is made in your country.

Robbery refers to the theft of property from a person, overcoming resistance by force or threat of force.

Burglary refers to unlawful entry into someone else's premises with an intention to commit
crime.

Fraud refers to the acquisition of the property of another by deception. Please indicate whether the fraudulent obtaining of financial property is included in the figures provided.

Embezzlement refers to the wrongful appropriation of property of another which is already in one's possession.

Drug-related crimes refers to intentional acts that may involve the cultivation, production, manufacture, extraction, preparation, offering for sale, distribution, purchase, sale, delivery on any terms whatsoever, brokerage, dispatch, dispatch in transit, transport, or importation and exportation of drugs and psychotropic substances. Where applicable, countries may wish to refer to the provisions of the Single Convention on Narcotic Drugs of 1961 and other regulations adopted in pursuance of the provisions of the Convention on Psychotropic Substances of 19712 and/or the United Nations Convention against Illicit Traffic in Narcotic Drugs and Psychotropic Substances of 1988. As simple possession and illicit traffic are treated differently in different legal codes, separate statistics on possession and traffic are requested.

Bribery and corruption refers to the solicitation and/or acceptance of a material or personal benefit, or the promise thereof, in connection with the performance of a public function for an action that may or may not be a violation of law and/or promising as well as giving material or personal benefit to a public officer in exchange for a requested favour.

Other refers to serious types of crimes that are completely different from those listed above, and that are regarded as serious and frequent enough to require a separate category in the criminal statistics of your country (e.g., arson, kidnaping, conspiracy or membership in a criminal association). Please insert such crimes under Question 11 and provide a definition, with an explanation or description in the space immediately below on this page or on an additional page. Should there be different types of crimes included under this item throughout all parts of the questionnaire, please provide an explanation.

Crimes recorded by the police refers to the number of penal code offences or their equivalent, i.e. various special law offences, but excluding minor road traffic and other petty offences, brought to the attention of the police or other law enforcement agencies and recorded by one of those agencies.

Police or law enforcement sector refers to public agencies whose principal functions are the prevention, detection and investigation of crime and the apprehension of alleged offenders. If the police are part of the national security force in your country, please try to limit as far as possible replies to the civil police proper as distinct from national guards or local militia. If there are many local forces, please provide data on them if possible. If some personnel of this sector fulfill prosecution functions, please note accordingly in the space below Table 27a.

Prosecutor refers to a government official whose duty it is to initiate and maintain criminal proceedings on behalf of the state against persons accused of committing a criminal offence. Countries differ in whether a prosecutor is a member of a separate agency, or a member of the police or judiciary. Please indicate the title of the agency in your country under which the prosecutor functions. If more than one criminal justice system operates in your country, for example federal/provincial systems or civilian/martial systems, please provide separate information about prosecutorial functions in each system.

Persons prosecuted refers to alleged offenders prosecuted by means of an official charge, initiated by the public prosecutor or the law enforcement agency responsible for prosecution.

Persons convicted refers to persons found guilty by any legal body duly authorized to do so under national law, whether the conviction was later upheld or not. If persons are convicted by any agency other than the courts, please state which agency, and provide statistical details in the space following Tables 14 and 15. In those tables "Grand total" number of convicted includes serious special law offences but excludes minor road traffic and other petty offences.

Judges and magistrates refers to both full and part-time officials authorized to hear civil, criminal and other cases, including courts of appeal, and make dispositions in a court of law. Please include also associate judges and magistrates, who may be authorized as above, within this category. Lay judges and magistrates refers to persons performing the same functions as the professional officials but who do not consider themselves, and are not normally considered by others, as career members of the judiciary.

Prisons refers to all public and privately-financed institutions where persons are deprived of their liberty. These institutions could include, but are not limited to penal, correctional or psychiatric facilities.

Admissions to prisons refers to the number of such events throughout the year and not the number of people admitted on a particular day of the year.

The following additional instructions were provided respondents:

If the categories given in the paragraphs above are not fully compatible with your national legal code, please try to adjust data as far as possible. Alternatively, indicate what kinds of crime your statistics include which might be comparable to the categories suggested, or how the parallel crime is defined in your country and describe this below the table or on the facing page.

The list of exceptions and other descriptive information provided by countries in response to this question is presented in Appendix 2.

Appendix 2: Notes and exceptions to the Fifth United Nations Survey of Crime Trends and Operations of Criminal Justice Systems data

The notes and exceptions to the Fifth UNCJS are listed by each of the 15 data files that comprise the database for the Fifth UNCJS. Under each data file, responding countries which have explained or qualified their data are identified by both the country name and the Fifth UNCJS identification number. Data files can be downloaded from the CICP web site http://www.ifs.univie.ac.at/~uncjin/uncjin.html.

Date file: ARESOURC.SAV. **Criminal Justice Resources** (Question 27 of the Fifth UNCJS: Allocation of budgetary resources to criminal justice activities).

Armenia	Figures for 1990 are given in Roubles.
Denmark	Prosecution resources are included in the figures for police resources.
Estonia	Figures for 1990 are given in Roubles.
Georgia	Figures for 1990 are given in Roubles.
Germany	The data for 1994 refer to 1993.
Kazakhstan	Figures for 1990 are given in Roubles.
Kuwait	Budget figures refer to fiscal years.
Latvia	Figures for 1990 are given in Roubles.
Lithuania	1) Figures for 1990 are given in Roubles. 2) The data for police resources for 1990 are for 1991.
Mexico	Budget figures are for the federal government only.
Norway	Prison budget figures do not include expenses on ministry-level and allocations to probation services.
Paraguay	Salary is given simply as 70% of the total budget for 1990 and 1994.
Poland	1) Resources are spent by public prosecutor's offices and courts not only in the framework of penal cases but also for other purposes: civil and administrative cases, prophylactic activities. 2) The inflation rate: 1991=52%; 1992=45%; 1993=39%; 1994=28%.
Switzerland	The data for 1994 refer to 1993.
USA	Prison and community corrections budgets are combined under the entry for prison.

Data File: BPOLICE.SAV. **Police Personnel** (Question 1 of the Fifth UNCJS)

Australia	Police resources in 1990 refer to 1992-93 while those for 1994 refer to 1994-95.
Austria	Total police includes state security (Bundesgendarmie) and state police (Bundespolizei).
Bermuda	Civilian police refer to reserve officers.
Mexico	Police data refer to judicial federal.
Norway	Police personnel figures refer to October 1.
Russian Federation	Police resources for 1990 refer to 1991, and those for 1994 refer to 1995.
Sweden	1) Police resources for 1994 refer to 1995. 2) Resource data for 1990 are identified as approximations
Switzerland	Police resources for 1990 refer to 1991.

Data File: CCRIME.SAV. **Number of Reported Crimes** (Question 2 of the Fifth UNCJS)

Australia	Rape is indicated as sexual assault.
Austria	Other crimes not specified.
Belgium	Other crimes include a) vandalism and b) arson.
Bulgaria	1) Data for crimes and their perpetrators during the period 1991-1994 are not compatible with the previous periods due to changes in the methodology of reporting. 2) The total crime figures include all crimes, economic and criminal. 3) Other crimes includes a) illegal deprivation and theft of motor vehicle, b) hooliganism, and c) arson.
Canada	1) There is no category of crime called rape in Canada; rather, since 1982-83 this offense is known as sexual assault, and it is divided into three levels. These levels are sexual assault, sexual assault with a weapon, and aggravated sexual assault. There is no specific reference to penetration; rather, the emphasis is on the degree of violence used in the attack. 2) Other crimes includes a) discharging of firearm with intent, b) assault on police, other peace-public officers and other assaults, c) abduction, d) other sexual offences, e) possession of stolen goods, f) prostitution, g) gaming and betting, h) offensive weapons, I) arson, j) bail violations, k) counterfeiting currency, l) disturbing the peace, m) escape from custody, n) indecent acts, o) kidnapping, p) public morals, q) obstruction of a public peace officer, r) prisoner unlawfully at large, s) trespass at night, t) mischief (property damage over and under $1,000), u) Bankruptcy Act, v) Canada Shipping Act, w) Customs Act, x) Excise Act, y) Immigration Act and Federal Criminal Code Traffic Violations.
China	1) Theft includes burglary. 2) The criterion of theft was revised in 1992.
Columbia	1) Other crimes includes a) extortion and b) terrorism. 2) From 1993 to 1994, a crime was only considered to be a robbery if it exceeded a certain amount of monies (i.e., 10 salarios minimus).
Cyprus	Other crimes includes a) damage by explosives, b) arson, and c) other serious offences.
Denmark	Other crimes refers to arson.
England & Wales	Other crimes includes offences which the police are required to report to the Home Office.
Estonia	1) Other crimes includes a) ruffianism, b) taking vehicles without authorization, and c) causation of traffic accidents. 2) Theft includes burglary and housebreaking.
Finland	1) Non-intentional homicide includes involuntary manslaughter in connection with aggravated assault. 2) Total assault for 1991 to 1994 excludes battery. 3) For fraud, counting rules concerning serial means of payment frauds were revised in 1991. In 1990, all incidents were counted separately, but from 1991 to 1994 serial incidents were counted as a single crime. 4) Other crimes refers to drunken driving.

Georgia	1) Other crimes refers to a) gangsterism, b) firing, c) robbery, d) preining of weapon, and e) obstructing a policeman.
Greece	1) Other crimes includes a) crimes relevant to the currency and b) crimes relevant to the memorandum (e.g., falsification). 2) Rape includes sexual assault which is interpreted as intent to rape.
Guyana	Other crimes includes all others not specifically mentioned.
Hong Kong	1) Embezzlement is included as a part of miscellaneous theft so the figure is not separable. 2) Other crimes includes all other crimes not previously enumerated. 3) Recorded crimes exclude minor offences which do not entail criminal investigation. 4) Simple possession of drugs is noted as manufacturing, possession, and other serious narcotic offences.
Hungary	1) Other crimes includes those not previously enumerated. 2) Rape includes statutory rape. 3) Aggravated assault refers to injuries that take more than eight days to heal while simple assault refers to injuries that take less than eight days to heal.
India	Other crimes includes all crimes not enumerated above.
Indonesia	Other crimes include a) theft of vehicle and b) arson.
Israel	1) Homicide includes murder and homicide. 2) Non-intentional homicide refers to manslaughter. 3) The total recorded crimes figure represents the number of offenders recorded. The offender is counted only once a year according to the most serious offence. Also, this total includes national security offences. 4) Possession of drugs is recorded as use of dangerous drugs. Total drug crimes in 1993 and 1994 includes a) use of dangerous drugs, b) traffic, import/export of dangerous drugs, c) producing dangerous drugs, and d) possession of drugs not for personal use. In 1990, 1991, and 1992, total drug crimes includes a) use of dangerous drugs, b) traffic, import/export of dangerous drugs, and c) producing dangerous drugs. 5) Other offences not specified. 6) Fraud includes a) counterfeiting banknotes/stamps, b) forging documents/use of same, c) fraud/extortion, d) cashing check without adequate cover, and e) other. 7) Total theft includes a) assault to commit theft, b) theft by public official, c) theft by employee/agent, d) use of vehicle without permission, e) theft from vehicle, f) bicycle theft, g) pickpocketing, h) other kinds of theft, h) purse-snatching, i) theft of vehicle parts, and j) agricultural theft. 8) Major assault is assault to commit theft. 9) Robbery includes aggravated robbery and unarmed robbery. 10) Rape includes rape by force or threats and rape/illicit intercourse. 11) Total assault includes a) causing bodily harm, b) assaulting public official, and c) assault (excluding public official). 12) Major assault is causing bodily harm.
Italy	1) Other crimes includes a) arson, b) organized crime/conspiracy, c) attack with explosives, and d) kidnapping.

	2) Intentional homicide consists of murder and child murder. 3) Non-intentional homicide consists of voluntary manslaughter except road accidents.
Jamaica	Other crimes includes a) unlawful possession, b) vagrancy, and c) malicious destruction of property.
Japan	1) Non-intentional homicide refers to death through bodily injury, death through negligence, and death through negligence in the conduct of one's occupation (excluding traffic accidents). 2) Assault refers to violence and bodily injury. 3) Major assault refers to bodily injury. 4) Major theft refers to motor vehicle theft. 5) Burglary refers to stealing though illegal entry. 6) Other crimes refers to death or bodily injury through negligence in traffic accidents, excluding traffic law violations.
Latvia	Other crimes includes a) hooliganism, b) willful destruction/damage of property, and c) extortion.
Lebanon	Other crimes includes a) arson, b) kidnapping, and c) membership of criminal group.
Lithuania	Other crimes refers to theft of a motor vehicle.
Madagascar	Other crimes refers to cow theft.
Malta	Other crimes not specified.
Mauritius	Other crimes includes a) possession of stolen property, b) criminal damage to property, c) sodomy and bestiality, d) sedition, e) perjury, f) arson, g) poisoning, and h) all other crimes.
Northern Ireland	1) Rape includes attempts. 2) Other crimes includes a) criminal damage, b) offences against the state, and c) all others.
Norway	Other crimes includes a) damage to property, b) receiving stolen goods, and c) economic crime.
Rep. of Moldova	1) Rape includes attempts. 2) Other crimes includes a) arson, b) hooliganism, c) auto accidents, and d) hijacking without object of theft. 3) Major assault refers to grave bodily injuries.
Republic of Korea	Other crimes includes all others not already enumerated.
Scotland	1) Other crimes refers to a) culpable homicide (statutory), b) death by careless driving, c) offensive weapons, d) threats and extortion, e) cruel and unnatural treatment of children, f) abortion, g) concealment of pregnancy, h) miscellaneous (possession of firearm with intent to endanger life, abduction etc), i) incest, j) unnatural crimes, k) indecent assault, l) lewd and libidinous practices, m) procuration and other sexual offences, n) bankruptcy, o) other crimes of dishonesty, p) fireraising, q) malicious and reckless conduct, r) crimes against the state, s) crimes against public order, t) prevention of terrorism acts, u) explosives, v) crimes against public justice (non court), w) crimes against public justice (court), x) conspiracy, y) sacrilege, z) wrecking, aa) piracy and hijacking.
Singapore	Other crimes refers to other "seizeable" offences.
Slovakia	1) Other crimes includes a) kidnapping, b) extortion, and c) hostage taking. 2) Simple possession refers to illicit production.

Data File: CCRIME.SAV. **Number of Reported Crimes** (Question 2 of the Fifth UNCJS) continued

Syria	Drug trafficking includes drug possession offences.
The Former Yugoslav Republic of Macedonia	Other crimes refers to endangering traffic safety.
Turkey	1) Other crimes includes a) kidnapping, b) threat, c) slander, d) deformation, e) adultery, and f) smuggling. 2) Theft and burglary are combined under total theft. 3) Bribery and/or corruption includes embezzlement.
USA	1) Homicide refers to intentional homicide only (i.e., murder and non-negligent homicide). Attempted homicides are classified as aggravated assaults. 2) Rape refers to forcible rape only.
Western Samoa	1) Other crimes include a) willful damage, b) found by night, c) willful trespass, d) arson, e) indecent assault, f) indecent act, g) incest, h) carnal knowledge, i) abduction, j) kidnapping, and k) riot. 2) Simple possession refers to cultivation and simple possession.
Zimbabwe	1) Other crimes includes a) abortion, b) indecent assault, c) arson, d) malicious injury to property, e) receiving stolen property, and f) all other crimes not enumerated previously. 2) Major theft refers to theft of car.

Data File: DCITY.SAV. **Crime in the Largest Cities** (Question 3 of the Fifth UNCJS)

Australia	1) As information on reported crime for the largest city was not available, it is provided for the largest state which is New South Wales. 2) Rape is noted as sexual assault. 3) Other crimes include a) unlawful entry and b) motor vehicle theft.
Austria	Other crimes not specified.
Bulgaria	Other crimes refers to a) theft, b) fraud, c) embezzlement, and d) illegal deprivation of motor vehicle.
Canada	Other crimes include a) discharge of firearm with intent, b) assault on police, other peace-public officer, and other assaults, c) abduction, d) other sexual offenses, e) possession of stolen goods, f) prostitution, g) gaming and betting, h) offensive weapons, i) arson, j) bail violations, k) counterfeiting currency, l) disturb the peace, m) escape custody, n) indecent acts, o) kidnapping, p) public morals, q) obstruct public peace officer, r) prisoner unlawfully at large, s) trespass at night, t) mischief (property damage over & under $1,000, u) theft over and under $1,000, v) theft of motor vehicle, w) break & enter, x) fraud, y) drug crimes (possession, trafficking, cultivation, importation, etc.), z) Bankruptcy Act, aa) Canada Shipping Act, bb) Customs Act, cc) Excise Act, dd) Immigration Act, ee) Federal Criminal Code Traffic Violations.
Cyprus	Other crimes not specified.
Ecuador	Other crimes include a) motor vehicle theft, b) armed assault, and c) kidnapping.
England & Wales	Other crimes refer to offences that the police are required to report to the Home Office.
Estonia	Other crimes includes a) theft, b) ruffianism, c) taking vehicles without authorization, and d) causation of traffic accidents.

Finland	1) Non-intentional homicide includes involuntary manslaughter in connection with aggravated assault. 2) Total assault for 1991 to 1994 excludes battery. 3) For fraud, counting rules concerning serial means of payment frauds were revised in 1991. In 1990, all incidents were counted separately, but from 1991 to 1994 serial incidents were counted as a single crime. 4) Other crimes refers to drunken driving.
Georgia	Other crimes include a) gangsterism, b) firing, c) ruffianism, and d) obstructing a policeman.
Greece	1) Total assault includes simple and aggravated assault. 2) Other crimes includes a) crimes related to the currency and b) crimes relevant to the memorandum.
Guatemala	Other crimes include motor vehicle theft.
Hong Kong	1) Other crimes include a) all thefts, b) burglary, c) fraud, d) all drug offences, e) bribery/corruption, and f) all other crimes not specifically mentioned. 2) Population figures are midyear estimates. 3) Embezzlement is included as a part of miscellaneous theft do the figure is not separable. 4) Other crimes includes all other crimes not previously enumerated. 5) Recorded crimes exclude minor offences which do not entail criminal investigation. 6) Simple possession of drugs is noted as manufacturing, possession and other serious narcotic offences.
Hungary	Other crimes not specified.
India	1) Other crimes include those not specifically mentioned. 2) Population figure is a midyear estimate.
Indonesia	Other crimes include a) theft of vehicle and b) arson.
Italy	1) Other crimes include a) theft, b) fraud, c) drug-related offences, d) organized crime, and e) kidnapping. 2) Total crimes includes other types of crimes than those delineated in the table so the total figure is greater than the sum of individually specified crimes.
Jamaica	Other crimes include breakings and larceny.
Japan	1) Non-intentional homicide refers to death through bodily injury, death through negligence, and death through negligence in the conduct of one's occupation (excluding traffic accidents). 2) Assault refers to violence and bodily injury. 3) Major assault refers to bodily injury. 4) Major theft refers to motor vehicle theft. 5) Other crimes include motor vehicle theft
Latvia	Other crimes include a) hooliganism, b) willful destruction or damage of property (included in figure for 1992 to 1994 only), and c) extortion (included in figure for 1992 to 1994 only).
Lebanon	Other crimes include a) arsons, b) kidnapping, and c) membership of criminal group.
Lithuania	Other crimes include theft (private and public property), burglary, and theft of a motor vehicle.
Madagascar	1) Other crimes include burglary. 2) Population figures are for the province of Faritany.

Data File: DCITY.SAV. **Crime in the Largest Cities** (Question 3 of the Fifth UNCJS) continued

Marshall Islands	1) Population figure for 1990 is given for 1988 as that was the last year of the last census.
Mauritius	1) Data for Port Louis are provisional. 2) Other crimes include a) possession of stolen property, b) criminal damage to property, c) sodomy and bestiality, d) perjury, and e) not otherwise specified.
Northern Ireland	Other crimes include a) burglary, b) theft, and c) all others not specifically mentioned.
Rep. Of Moldova	1) Rapes include attempted as well as completed acts. 2) Other crimes include a) arson, b) hooliganism, c) auto accidents, d) hijacking without object of theft, e) thefts, f) corruption and g) thefts by means of abuse.
Sao Tóme	1) Other crimes include a) burglary and b) fraud.
Scotland	Other crimes include a) culpable homicide (statutory), b) death by careless driving, c) offensive weapons, d) threats and extortion, e) cruel and unnatural treatment of children, f) abortion, g) concealment of pregnancy, h) incest, i) unnatural crimes, k) indecent assault, l) lewd and libidinous practices, m) procuration and other sexual offences, n) housebreaking, o) opening lockfast places, p) prevention of crimes and vagrancy, q) theft, r) reset, s) embezzlement, t) fraud, u) forgery, v) bankruptcy, w) clandestine removal, x) corruption, y) other crimes of dishonesty, z) fireraising, aa) malicious and reckless conduct, bb) crimes against the state, cc) crimes against the public order, dd) prevention of terrorism acts, ee) explosives, ff) crimes against public justice (non-court), gg) crimes against public justice (court), hh) conspiracy, ii) sacrilege, jj) wrecking, kk) piracy and hijacking, ll) drugs, and mm) miscellaneous (possession of firearm with intent to endanger life, abduction, etc.).
Slovak Republic	1) Other crimes include a) fraud, b) drug-related offences, and c) extortion. 2) Population figure is for midyear. 3) Total number of recorded crimes includes a) thefts, b) burglaries, c) frauds, d) embezzlements, e) drug crimes, f) briberies, g) kidnappings, and h) extortion.
Spain	Other crimes include those not already specified.
Sweden	Other crimes not specified.
The FYRM	1) Other crimes refers to endangering traffic safety. 2) The population figures are estimates.
Turkey	Other crimes include a) kidnapping, b) theft, c) slander, d) defamation, e) adultery, f) fraud, g) bribery, and h) embezzlement.
Uruguay	1) The figure for rape cannot be separated from that for all sexual crimes. 2) Other crimes include theft and sexual crimes. 3) Population figure for 1990 is taken from the 1985 census.
USA	1) Homicide includes intentional homicide only (murder and non-negligent homicide). Attempted homicides are classified as aggravated assault. 2) Rape includes forcible rape only. 3) Other crimes include a) burglary, b) theft, and c) motor vehicle theft.
Zambia	Other crimes include motor vehicle theft.

Data File: EFORMAL.SAV. **Number of People with Formal Contact with the Criminal Justice System** (Question 4 of the Fifth UNCJS)

Austria	Other crimes not specified.
Bulgaria	1) Persons brought into formal contact with the criminal justice system are designated as those who passed through a preliminary investigation with a resulting opinion for bringing the individual to trial. 2) Other crimes include a) illegal deprivation of motor vehicle and b) hooliganism.
Canada	Other crimes includes a) discharging of firearm with intent, b) assault on police, other peace-public officers and other assaults, c) abduction, d) other sexual offences, e) possession of stolen goods, f) prostitution, g) gaming and betting, h) offensive weapons, i) arson, j) bail violations, k) counterfeiting currency, l) disturbing the peace, m) escape from custody, n) indecent acts, o) kidnapping, p) public morals, q) obstruction of a public peace officer, r) prisoner unlawfully at large, s) trespass at night, t) mischief (property damage over and under $1,000), u) Bankruptcy Act, v) Canada Shipping Act, w) Customs Act, x) Excise Act, y) Immigration Act and Federal Criminal Code Traffic Violations.
Cyprus	Other crimes include a) arson, b) damage by explosives, and c) other serious offences.
Denmark	Other crimes include arson.
Ecuador	Other crimes include a) motor vehicle theft, b) armed assault, and c) kidnapping.
Egypt	Total theft refers to motor vehicle theft.
Estonia	Other crimes include a) ruffianism and b) taking vehicles without authorization.
Finland	1) Non-intentional homicide includes involuntary manslaughter in connection with aggravated assault. 2) Total assault for 1991 to 1994 excludes battery. 3) For fraud, counting rules concerning serial means of payment frauds were revised in 1991. In 1990, all incidents were counted separately, but from 1991 to 1994 serial incidents were counted as a single crime. 4) Other crimes refers to drunken driving.
France	Other crimes include all those not specifically mentioned.
Greece	1) Total assault includes simple and aggravated assault. 2) Other crimes include a) crimes relevant to the currency and b) crimes relevant to the memorandum.
Guyana	1) The grand total figures include persons awaiting trial from previous years. 2) Non-intentional homicide figures are accumulated in the total figure for murder and manslaughter. 3) The figures for embezzlement are included in the fraud category. 4) The figures for bribery and/or corruption are included in the fraud category. 5) The figures in this table represent persons arrested or summoned to court. Those awaiting trial at the end of the period are also included.
Hong Kong	1) Embezzlement is included as a part of miscellaneous theft do the figure is not separable. 2) Other crimes includes all other crimes not previously enumerated.

Hong Kong (cont.)	3) Recorded crimes exclude minor offences which do not entail criminal investigation. 4) Simple possession of drugs is noted as manufacturing, possession and other serious narcotic offences. 5) The figures for bribery/corruption refer to only those persons prosecuted.
Hungary	Other crimes not specified.
India	1) Other crimes include other major penal code offences not mentioned specifically. 2) Assaults cannot be given specifically so they are included in other crimes. 3) Drug crimes cannot be distinguished by simple possession and illicit trafficking. Both are included in the total drug-related crimes category. 4) Figures for 1994 are provisional.
Italy	Other crimes include a) arson, b) organized crime, c) attack with explosives and d) kidnapping.
Jamaica	Other crimes include a) unlawful possession, b) vagrancy, and c) malicious destruction of property.
Japan	1) Non-intentional homicide refers to death through bodily injury, death through negligence, and death through negligence in the conduct of one's occupation (excluding traffic accidents). 2) Assault refers to violence and bodily injury. 3) Major assault refers to bodily injury. 4) Major theft refers to motor vehicle theft. 5) Burglary refers to stealing though illegal entry. 6) Other crimes refers to death or bodily injury through negligence in traffic accidents, excluding traffic law violations.
Latvia	1) Other crimes include a) hooliganism, b) willful destruction and damage to property, and c) extortion. 2) Burglary is included in the total theft category.
Lebanon	Other crimes include a) arson, b) kidnapping, and c) membership of criminal group.
Lithuania	Other crimes refers to theft of a motor vehicle.
Madagascar	Other crimes not specified.
Malta	Other crimes not specified.
Mauritius	1) Other crimes not specified. 2) Figures are provisional.
Rep. of Moldova	Other crimes include a) arsons, b) hooliganism, and c) auto accidents.
Singapore	Other crimes include other seizable offences.
The FYRM	Other crimes include endangering traffic safety.
Turkey	1) Theft includes burglary, and both are reflected in the total theft category. 2) Bribery/corruption includes embezzlement. 3) Other crimes include a) kidnapping, b) slander, c) defamation, d) adultery, e) illegal demonstration, f) threat, g) terrorism, and h) smuggling.
USA	1) Homicide includes intentional homicide only (murder and non-negligent homicide). Attempted homicides are classified as aggravated assault. 2) Rape includes forcible rape only. 3) Other crimes include driving under the influence, drunkenness and disorderly conduct.
West. Samoa	Simple possession includes cultivation.

China	Juvenile: Person whose age is below 18. But according to the Chinese criminal law, a person who has reached the age of 16 who commits a crime shall bear criminal responsibility. A person who has reached the age of 14 but not the age of 16 who commits the crimes of killing another, serious injury, robbery, arson, habitual theft, or other crimes seriously undermining social order shall bear criminal responsibility. A person who has reached the age of 14 but not the age of 18 who commits a crime shall be given a lesser punishment or a mitigated punishment.
Cyprus	Formal contact refers to appearing before the court.
Estonia	The definition of juvenile varies by year. In 1990 and 1991, a juvenile was a person aged 14 to 17. In 1992 and 1993, a juvenile was a person aged 15 to 17. And in 1994, a juvenile was a person aged 13 to 17.
India	Data for 1994 are provisional.
Poland	Due to the existence of three categories of convicted persons, the following definitions may be provided. An adult, in the meaning of the Penal Code, is a person who commits a prohibited act after having attained the age of 17 years (art. 9 §1 of the Penal Code). A juvenile is an adult person who at the time of the rendering of judgment has not attained 21 years of age (art. 120 §4 of the Penal Code). Due to some technical problems, the statistics of the public prosecutor's offices and courts include data on offenders according to their age at the moment of the perpetration of a prohibited act and such persons are considered as juveniles. In fact, the real number of juvenile persons is lower than the figures shown in the tables. Minors are persons who are judged for the perpetration of prohibited acts while aged 13 to 17 against whom may be pronounced by the court educational measures (e.g., the guardian's supervision or the placement in an educational establishment) as well as persons against whom such educational measures may be applied due to their demoralization (e.g., persons who do not go to schools, abuse alcohol or drugs, are members of criminal groups, etc.). Minors are judges on the basis of the Act of 26 October 1982 on proceedings in minors' cases (Dziennik Ustaw No. 35, item 228 with subsequent amendments). Sentences in minors' cases are rendered by the Family and Minors' Section of Courts for Minors, organized in a separate way than the penal courts for adult persons.
Slovak Republic	Total persons brought into formal contact with the criminal justice system includes persons below the age of 15.

Data File: GPROSECU.SAV. **Prosecutors and Prosecutions**
(Questions 6 and 7 of the Fifth UNCJS)

Australia	Prosecution data were given separately for each of Australia's nine jurisdictions (federal, six states, and two territories) and were summed to yield a national figure. South Australia could not break down prosecution resources by gender so total figures are not the sum of male and female prosecutors. The figures for Western Australia for 1992 refer to 1993 and those for 1994 refer to 1995.
Bulgaria	1) Data refer to persons who are indicted. 2) Other offences include a) illegal deprivation of motor vehicle and b) hooliganism
Canada	Other crimes include other criminal code violations and violations of federal statutes.
Croatia	Other crimes include a) corporal injury, b) jeopardizing of people's safety, c) insult, d) criminal traffic offenses, e) criminal offences against the economy and market, f) criminal offences against the Republic of Croatia, and g) criminal offences against the army forces of the Republic of Croatia.
Cyprus	1) Number of persons prosecuted refers to those prosecuted for serious offences only as classified by the police. 2) Other crimes are not specified.
Denmark	Other crimes include a) sexual offences, b) crimes of violence, c) offences against property, d) other offences, e) special laws, and f) Road Traffic Act.
England & Wales	1) Figures refer to indictments for each offence. 2) Other crimes include remaining indictable offences, excluding motoring.
Estonia	Other crimes include a) ruffianism and b) taking vehicles without authorization.
Finland	1) Total assault from 1991 to 1994 excludes battery. 2) The counting rules concerning serial means of payment fraud were revised in 1991. In 1990, all incidents were counted separately, but from 1991 only as a single crime. 3) Other crimes refers to drunken driving.
Georgia	1) Other crimes include all others not specifically mentioned. 2) Prosecuted persons refer to those who are indicted for prosecution before a judge and jury. The majority of cases, however, are processed summarily in magistrates court and the prosecutions there are done mainly by the police.
Germany	1) Figures for the number of persons prosecuted are for the Federal Republic of Germany. 2) Fraud and embezzlement were not differentiated so both are reflected in the number of frauds prosecuted.
Hong Kong	1) Simple possession of drugs is not classified as a crime. Thus, its figure does not add to the grand total of persons prosecuted nor to the total of drug-related crimes. 2) Other crimes are not specified.
India	Other crimes are not specified entirely, although it is noted that assaults and major thefts are included.
Indonesia	1) Other crimes include gun offences.
Israel	1) Figures refer to the number of persons accused rather than the number of persons prosecuted. 2) Other crimes include a) security, b) arson, and c) blackmail.
Italy	1) Involuntary homicide figure includes deaths caused by accidents on the street such as with an automobile.

	2) Other crimes include a) writing bad checks, b) insulting one in his/her presence and defamation of character outside of one's presence (e.g., in a newspaper), and c) damage to property
Latvia	1) Theft and burglary are given in a combined figure which is reported under the total theft category. 2) Other crimes include a) deprivation of property, b) hooliganism, and c) extortion from 1992 to 1994. In 1990 and 1991, only hooliganism is included in the figure for other crimes.
Mauritius	1) Figures include "nolle prosequi." 2) The figures for 1990 to 1992 are provisional. 3) Other crimes are not specified.
Netherlands	1) Burglary and theft are given as a combined figure, and this figure is entered under the total theft category. 2) Grand total for 1991 and 1992 is exclusive of drug-related prosecutions since the number of these crimes is unavailable for these two years. 3) Other crimes include, among other offences which are not all specified, a) kidnapping, b) destruction, and c) driving under the influence.
Northern Ireland	1) Committed intentional homicide includes conspiracy as well as aiding and abetting. 2) Total assault includes all other violence against the person. 3) Rape includes attempted rape. 4) Other crimes include a) explosives, b) firearms, c) other sex offences, d) forgery and counterfeiting, e) arson, f) other criminal damage, g) NI Emergency Provisions, h) public order offences, i) blackmail, j) perjury, k) kidnapping and false imprisonment, and l) other notifiable offences.
Norway	1) Total drug-related crimes does not include illicit traffic (misdemeanor). 2) Other crimes include a) damage to property, b) receiving stolen goods, and c) economic crime.
Poland	1) As of 1990, the prosecution agencies operate in the framework of the resort of justice. The Minister of Justice performs the duties of the general public prosecutor. 2) On 1 October 1993 were created the Appeal Public Prosecutor's Offices.
Portugal	1) Figures refer to persons brought before the court at the trial stage. 2) Burglary under Portuguese law is an instance of aggravated theft. Therefore, figures for burglary are included under major theft. 3) Other crimes include a) counterfeiting, b) disobedience and resistance to public authorities, c) non-intentional homicide (traffic), d) crimes against the public economy, and e) checks without funds. 4) Figures for persons prosecuted and convicted are influenced by amnesty laws. In 1991 and 1994 two such laws were passed.
Republic of Korea	Other crimes include other minor crimes.
Republic of Moldova	Other crimes include a) traffic accidents causing corporal injury and b) hooliganism.
Scotland	1) Total assault includes serious assault but excludes petty assault. 2) Other crimes refers to a) culpable homicide (statutory), b) death by careless driving, c) offensive

Data File: GPROSECU.SAV. **Prosecutors and Prosecutions**
(Questions 6 and 7 of the Fifth UNCJS) continued

Scotland (cont.)	weapons, d) threats and extortion, e) cruel and unnatural treatment of children, f) abortion, g) concealment of pregnancy, h) miscellaneous (possession of firearm with intent to endanger life, abduction etc.), i) incest, j) unnatural crimes, k) indecent assault, l) lewd and libidinous practices, m) procuration and other sexual offences, n) bankruptcy, o) other crimes of dishonesty, p) fireraising, q) malicious and reckless conduct, r) crimes against the state, s) crimes against public order, t) prevention of terrorism acts, u) explosives, v) crimes against public justice (non court), w) crimes against public justice (court), x) conspiracy, y) sacrilege, z) wrecking, aa) piracy and hijacking.
Singapore	1) Other crimes include seizable offences. 2) Rape includes attempted rape.
South Africa	Other crimes include other matters relating to property.
Sweden	Figures refer to the number of crimes prosecuted.
The FYRM	Other crimes include endangering traffic safety.
Turkey	Other crimes not specified.
USA	1) Prosecutor figures refer to those in state courts. 2) Number of persons prosecuted refer to those prosecuted in federal court. 3) Other crimes include a) weapons violations, b) immigration violations, and c) tax violations.
Western Samoa	Simple possession of drugs includes cultivation.

Data File: HPROSECU.SAV. **Prosecutions by Age/Gender**
(Question 8 of the Fifth UNCJS)

Belgium	Data refer to number of cases prosecuted rather than the number of persons prosecuted.
China	Juvenile: Person whose age is below 18. But according to the Chinese criminal law, a person who has reached the age of 16 who commits a crime shall bear criminal responsibility. A person who has reached the age of 14 but not the age of 16 who commits the crimes of killing another, serious injury, robbery, arson, habitual theft, or other crimes seriously undermining social order shall bear criminal responsibility. A person who has reached the age of 14 but not the age of 18 who commits a crime shall be given a lesser punishment or a mitigated punishment.
Cyprus	Persons prosecuted refers to those prosecuted for serious offences only as classified by the police.
Estonia	Definition of juvenile varies by year. In 1990 and 1991, a juvenile was a person aged 14 to 17. In 1992 and 1993, a juvenile was a person aged 15 to 17. And in 1994 a juvenile was a person aged 13 to 17.
Germany	Data refer to the Federal Republic of Germany (i.e., the former territory of West Germany).
Israel	Data do not refer to the number of persons accused but only to the number of accusations in each year.
Norway	The age was unknown for some individuals who were prosecuted, although these people were included in the total persons prosecuted figures (1990=1,129; 1991=354; 1992=175; 1993=1.358; 1994=94).
Portugal	The data for adults includes a small number of cases in which age was not specified.

Scotland	1) Total figures include people whose gender and age is unknown but excludes companies. 2) Adult and juvenile totals include people whose gender is not known.
Singapore	Data on persons prosecuted by gender and age do not include those prosecuted for drug-related crimes or bribery and/or corruption.
Slovenia	The difference between the figures which were given for 1990 in the previous survey (i.e., the Fourth UN Survey on Crime Trends and Operations of Criminal Justice Systems) and this survey is the result of not taking juveniles into account in the previous questionnaire.
USA	1) Prosecutions refer to those conducted in federal court. 2) Less than 2% of all federal offenders are 18 years of age or younger. 3) The percentage of male federal offenders observed in 1989 and 1990 (84%) was assumed for the remaining years.

Data File: ICOURTS.SAV. **Judges and the Criminal Courts**
(Questions 9, 10, 11, and 13 of the Fifth UNCJS)

Armenia	1) Under the number of persons brought to the criminal courts, the other category refers to discontinued proceedings. 2) Other sentences refers to capital punishment (1990=3, with one pardoned and two executed; 1992=4, with all of these executions suspended; and 1994=9, with all of these executions suspended).
Belgium	Figure for other judiciary personnel for 1990 is given for 1992.
Bulgaria	1) Other dispositions include a) with abandonment and b) discharged. 2) Other sentences include compulsory settlement. 3) Warning/Admonition refers to conditional sentences only.
Canada	1) Other judicial dispositions include a) committed for trial in superior court, b) stay, c) withdrawal, d) dismissed, e) discharged at preliminary, and f) insanity. 2) Total sentenced does not include criminal convictions in superior court. 3) Community service orders are included in the warning category. 4) Other sentences include restitution/compensation.
Croatia	Other sentences include a) deliberation of punishment and b) upbringing measures.
Cyprus	Other judicial dispositions include a) charge withdrawn, b) case dismissed, and c) nolle proseque.
Czech Republic	1) Other judicial dispositions include a) discontinuance of proceedings which results in case being closed and b) submission of the case to the respective state authorities. 2) Other sentences are not specified.
Denmark	Other judicial disposition includes withdrawal of charge.
England & Wales	1) Other persons brought before the criminal courts are those for whom prosecution was terminated

England & Wales (cont.)	early. 2) Other sentences include ad hoc disposals. 3) Community service orders are included in the control in freedom category. 4) Total judges does not include matters or members of tribunals as comparable figures are not available. Neither category deals with crime. Also, total judges does not include acting stipendiary magistrates. Part-time judges include judiciary who normally sit in criminal or both criminal and civil cases, although a few may hold more specialized posts.
Estonia	1) Other judicial dispositions not specified. 2) Other sentences not specified.
Finland	1) The number of persons brought before the criminal courts refers to those brought before the criminal courts of first instance. These persons are brought to criminal court for offences against the Penal Code and the Narcotics Drug Act. The same is true for the figures concerning the number and types of sentences. 2) The number of lay judges has doubled from 1990 to 1994 because of the reform of the first instance court made in 1993. As a result of the reform, two different types of courts were unified and a new system of lay judges was created which has 1.8 million more citizens under its control. 3) Other sentences includes confinement to barracks for soldiers.
Georgia	1) Other persons brought before the criminal courts are not specified. 2) Other sentences not specified.
Germany	Figures for the number of persons brought before the criminal courts are denoted as applicable only to the former western territory. The same is true for the number and types of sentences. However, the number of judges/magistrates for 1994 includes the whole of united Germany.
Greece	According to Poeyal justice, an adult is a person of 18 years and over while according to penitentiary justice, an adult is a person of 21 years and over.
Hong Kong	Other sentences include capital punishment.
Hungary	1) Other judicial disposition includes abandonment of proceedings. 2) Control in freedom is comprised of parole, reformatory and educative labor, and probation. 3) Other sentences are listed as "measures."
India	1) Other judicial dispositions include a) compounded or withdrawn and b) pending trial. 2) Numbers for persons brought before the criminal courts for 1994 include those accused of violating both the Indian Penal Code and special and local laws.
Indonesia	Other judicial dispositions includes an order by the judge for an offender to be returned to parents or to be placed at a government institution in order to be provided with education without a punishment being applied. These other dispositions are most obviously relevant to juveniles.
Israel Israel (cont.)	1) Number of persons brought before the court at the national level reflect the number of accusations in each year. 2) Corporal punishment and deprivation of liberty are reflected in one figure which is entered under the deprivation of liberty category. 3) Other sentences include a) commitment to institutions, b) temporary withdrawal of drivers license, c) conditional withdrawal of drivers license,

	d) hospitalization, e) extension of conditional sentence, and f) administrative fine. 4) Total sentences is greater than the total number of convictions because multiple sentence types have been imposed on the same convicted individual.
Japan	1) Other persons brought before the criminal courts include a) withdrawal of application, b) transfer, and c) other. 2) Other sentences refer to capital punishment.
Latvia	1) Other judicial dispositions include a) completion of the process (cases still pending), b) applying compulsory measures of a medical nature, and c) forwarding of the case for additional investigation. 2) Other sentences include a) postponed award of a judgment, b) capital punishment, and c) other.
Lithuania	1) Figures refer to the number of people brought before the criminal courts of first instance. 2) Other judicial dispositions refer to a) cancelled cases, b) transferred for supplementary investigation, and c) medical discharge of case. 3) Other sentences includes capital punishment. 4) Control in freedom includes a) suspended sentences and b) correctional works without deprivation of liberty (i.e., serving a sentence at the working place and the house for education or supervision). 5) Number and types of sentences is for persons age 18 or over, although full criminal responsibility is reached at 16 years of age. 6) In 1990, there were two capital punishment sentences imposed; however, one death sentence was changed into life imprisonment, and one was annulled. In 1992, one of the sentences of capital punishment was changed into life imprisonment.
Mauritius	1) Data for 1990 about persons brought before the criminal courts are provisional. 2) Other judicial dispositions are not specified.
Netherlands	1) Other judicial dispositions are not specified.
Northern Ireland	1) Other persons brought before the criminal courts include a) those sent for trial — bail and b) those sent for trial — committed. 2) Other types of sentences include a) hospital order, b) compensation, c) restitution, and d) absolute discharge. 3) Figures for adults convicted by sentence are for indictable offences only. 4) Other judges refers to justice of the peace.
Norway	1) Life imprisonment and corporal punishment do not exist in Norway. Community service order did not exist in 1990. 2) Ticket fines are not included in the data concerning sentences of a fine. 3) Other sentences refers to security detention. 4) Number of lay judges is an approximation.
Panama	Figures for persons brought before the criminal courts in 1994 are estimated.
Philippines	There are no community service orders in the Philippines.
Poland	1) Other dispositions for people brought before the criminal courts include a) discontinuance of the proceedings, b) conditional discontinuance of the

Poland (cont.)	proceedings, c) non-pronunciation of penalty, d) other discontinuance, and e) educational and correctional.measures (Art. 9 §3 of the Penal Code). 2) Life imprisonment defined as 25 or more years of deprivation of liberty. 3) Other sentences include supplementary penalties pronounced independently.
Portugal	1) Other sentences include sentences not specified. 2) Figures for 1990 include both adults and young adults (age 16-20). 3) Admonition includes sentences of imprisonment without supervision (the large majority) or with supervision. In 1990, admonition was included in the other category.
Rep. of Moldova	Other judicial dispositions include proceedings that have been stopped.
Republic of Korea	1) Other judicial dispositions not specified. 2) Other sentences not specified.
Scotland	1) Other persons brought before the criminal courts include those whose plea of not guilty was accepted and the proceedings were dropped after the persons were brought to court. 2) Other sentences for convicted adults includes a) absolute discharge, b) remit to children's hearing (included are 16 and 17 year old persons who are already under a supervision requirement from a children's hearing), c) caution (a financial bond), d) no order made, and e) compensation order.
Slovak Republic	1) Other judicial dispositions include a) penal prosecution halted and b) matter proceeded to other authority's prosecution. 2) Other sentences include ban on activity, ban on stay, deportation, and give punishment up.
Slovenia	For 1992, deprivation of liberty and warning/admonition were reported together and are reflected in the category for warning/admonition.
South Africa	1) Other judicial dispositions include a) persons who died and b) persons with mental disorders. 2) Other sentences not specified.
Switzerland	Court personnel for 1990 refer to 1991.
The Former Yugoslav Republic of Macedonia	Other judicial dispositions include a) private charges dismissed, b) proceedings halted, c) charges dismissed, and d) security measures prior to sentencing.
Turkey	1) Other judicial dispositions include a) rejection of venue, b) lack of jurisdiction and c) dismissal of case. 2) Other sentences not specified.
USA	1) Data refer to persons brought before the federal and state courts. Figures at the federal level reflect disposition of cases terminated in the given year. 2) Data for 1994 are preliminary. 3) Other punishments refer to capital punishment. 4) Number of judges reflects those in the federal and state courts, but not from the lower courts (i.e., municipal and police courts). 5) Lay judges includes magistrates. 6) Other judicial dispositions refer to cases dismissed.
Zambia	1) Other judicial dispositions include a) awaiting trial in high courts and magistrates' courts. 2) Other sentences include a) death penalty and b) awaiting sentence.

Austria	Other crimes include damage to property which refers to any injuries against objects (destruction, damage, disfiguring, and making useless) purposely inflicted by another person without the owner's consent.
Belgium	From 1990 to 1992, robbery and both types of theft are combined into a single value and are reflected in the total theft category. In 1993, robbery, burglary, and both types of theft are combined into a single value and are reflected in the total theft category. In 1994, robbery, total theft, and burglary are presented separately.
Bulgaria	Other crimes include a) hooliganism, b) paper's crimes, c) transport crimes, and d) illegal deprivation of motor vehicles.
Canada	1) Adult data represent cases heard in provincial/territorial courts of the five provinces and the territories in Canada, which constitute about 34% of national/provincial adult court activity. Convictions do not include cases moved to superior court where the most serious offences are heard. 2) Rape no longer exists as an offence type in Canada. Data under this category refer to aggravated sexual assault and sexual assault with a weapon. 3) Other crimes includes all Canadian Criminal Code offences and other federal statutes not specifically listed. 4) For adult data, sex was unknown for 11,480 convictions heard in provincial/territorial court. 5) Juvenile data refer to cases in which convictions were achieved and not to convicted persons. 6) In 1990-91, the Province of Ontario did not participate in the Youth Crime Survey, and in 1991-92 Ontario figures represented 85% of its respective total.
Croatia	Other crimes include a) corporal injury, b) jeopardizing people's safety, and c) insult.
Cyprus	1) Other crimes not specified. 2) The figures refer to persons convicted for serious offenses only as classified by the police.
Denmark	Other crimes includes arson.
England & Wales	Other crimes includes all other indictable offences, excluding motoring.
Estonia	1) Total theft includes burglary and housebreaking. 2) Fraud includes embezzlement. 3) Other crimes include a) ruffianism and b) causing traffic accidents. 4) The definition of a juvenile has changed over the years. In 1990 and 1991, a juvenile was a person aged 14-17. In 1992 and 1993, a juvenile was a person aged 15-17. In 1994, a juvenile was a person aged 13-17.
Finland	1) Data refer to convictions in courts of first instance. 2) For 1991 to 1994, total assault excludes battery. 3) Counting rules concerning serial means of payment frauds were revised in 1991; in 1990 all incidents were counted separately but from 1991 as a single crime. 4) Other crimes include drunken driving.
Germany	1) Fraud and embezzlement are combined and entered together under the category of fraud. 2) Data refer to former territory of the W. Germany.

Greece	1) No distinction is made between theft and burglary so the figure for total theft reflects both. 2) Other crimes include a) crimes of high treason, b) treason of the country, c) crimes against foreign states, d) crimes against political bodies, e) crimes during elections, f) assaults against state authority, g) attempt against public order, h) attempt against religious peace, I) crimes relevant to the currency, j) police corruption, k) crimes relevant to justice dispense, l) crimes against the community, m) crimes against security of transport and public welfare establishments, n) crimes against life, o) physical damage, p) crimes against personal freedom, q) crimes against morals, r) crimes relevant to marriage and family, s) crimes against honor, t) crimes against property, u) crimes against property rights, v) beggary and vagrancy, w) other offences of the penal code, x) violation of special penal laws, and y) offences of martial penal code.
Hong Kong	1) The offence of simple drug possession is not classified as a crime. Thus, its figure does not contribute to the total drug convictions nor the grand total. 2) Data reflect the principal offence for which a person was convicted. 3) For 1990, total assault and other crimes represent revised figures. 4) Other crimes not specified.
India	1) Data for 1994 are provisional. 2) Assault cannot be specified separately so it is included in other crimes. Otherwise, the other crime category is not specified.
Indonesia	1) Rape data include not only sexual intercourse without consent but also other crimes related to sexual harassment. 2) Major theft includes burglary. 3) Other crimes include offences against the environment.
Israel	1) Other crimes include a) security violations, b) arson and c) blackmail. 2) Fraud includes embezzlement.
Italy	1) Other crimes include a) writing bad checks, b) fencing stolen goods, and c) illegal possession of firearms. 2) Involuntary homicide includes people who killed others in auto accidents.
Jamaica	Data refer to high court only.
Japan	Other crimes include a) extortion, b) kidnapping, and c) traffic accidents resulting in death or bodily injury.
Latvia	1) Total theft includes burglary. 2) Other crimes not specified.
Lithuania	1) Data refer to the number of criminal cases that have been examined in courts of first instance. 2) Major theft refers to thefts of the state and public property which includes robbery and burglary. 3) Total theft refers to thefts of personal property which includes robbery and burglary. 4) Data related to burglary are not substantial since a part of burglaries may be included in robberies.
Mauritius	1) Data are provisional. 2) Other crimes not specified.
Mexico	1) Robbery includes theft. 2) Other crimes not specified.
Netherlands	1) Total theft includes burglary. 2) Other crimes not specified.
Northern Ireland	1) Other convictions include a) explosives, b) firearms, c) other sex offences, d) forgery and counterfeiting, e) arson, f) other criminal damage, g) NI Emergency Provisions, h) public order offences, I) blackmail, j) perjury, k) kidnapping and false imprisonment, and l) other notifiable offences. 2) Committed intentional homicide includes conspiracy and aiding and abetting.
Norway	1) Number of persons convicted does not include ticket fines and prosecutions conditionally dropped. 2) Some of those convicted in criminal courts were of an unknown age. These individuals are included in the total number of persons convicted but not in the age breakdown (1990=67; 1991=26; 1992=2; 1993=0; 1994=0).
Panama	Figures for conviction in 1994 are estimated.
Poland	Other crimes include a) Art. 211, b) Art. 286, and c) Art. 227 & 228.
Portugal	1) Major theft includes burglary. 2) Other crimes includes a) counterfeiting, b) disobedience and resistance to public authorities, c) non-intentional traffic homicide, d) crimes against public economy, and e) checks without funds. 3) Figures for adults convicted of crimes includes a small number of cases in which age is not specified.
Rep. Of Moldova	Other crimes not specified.
Republic of Korea	Other crimes not specified.
Scotland	1) If a person is prosecuted for more than one crime, only the charge is counted. 2) Other crimes refers to a) culpable homicide (statutory), b) death by careless driving, c) offensive weapons, d) threats and extortion, e) cruel and unnatural treatment of children, f) abortion, g) concealment of pregnancy, h) miscellaneous (possession of firearm with intent to endanger life, abduction etc.), I) incest, j) unnatural crimes, k) indecent assault, l) lewd and libidinous practices, m) procuration and other sexual offences, n) bankruptcy, o) other crimes of dishonesty, p) fireraising, q) malicious and reckless conduct, r) crimes against the state, s) crimes against public order, t) prevention of terrorism acts, u) explosives, v) crimes against public justice (non court), w) crimes against public justice (court), x) conspiracy, y) sacrilege, z) wrecking, aa) piracy and hijacking. 3) Total for persons convicted a) excludes companies and b) includes people whose age and sex is unknown. 4) Total for adults and juveniles convicted includes those whose sex is unknown.
Slovak Republic	Other crimes not specified.
Slovenia	The difference between figures which were given in the Fourth United Nations Survey of Crime Trends and Operations of Criminal Justice Systems for 1990 and those given in the Fifth Survey for 1990 are the result of not taking juveniles into account previously.
South Africa	Other crimes includes other matters relating to property.
Sweden	Total theft includes burglary.

Data File: JCONVICT.SAV. **Number of People Convicted of Crimes** (Questions 14 and 15 of the Fifth UNCJS) continued

Switzerland	Possession of drugs refers to drug consumption.
The Former Yugoslav Republic of Macedonia	Other crimes include endangering traffic safety.
USA	1) Intentional homicide includes attempts. 2) Other crimes not specified. 3) Convictions refer to those achieved in federal courts only in 1991, 1993, and 1994 and to those achieved in federal and state courts in 1990 and 1992. 4) Figures from the state courts refer to felony convictions only. 5) In 1990 and 1992, fraud includes embezzlement. 6) Bribery for all years reflects federal prosecutions only. 7) Adults convicted refers to persons age 20 or over. 8) Convictions be sex and age are given for felony convictions in state courts only.

Data File: KPRISON.SAV. **Prisoners and Prison Sentences** (Questions 16 and 17 of the Fifth UNCJS)

Australia	Other includes a) awaiting deportation and b) unknown.
Austria	Other includes a) otherwise adjudicated, b) administrative detention, c) non-payment of penal fine, and d) civil law incarcerations.
Belgium	Other includes a) those who are a danger to self or others, b) minors, and c) others.
Bermuda	1) Other category of incarceration includes a) corrective training, b) dangerous offenders, c) her majesty's pleasure, and d) preventive detention.
Brunei Darussalam	Other category of incarceration includes a) Islamic religion offences and b) immigration detention order.
Bulgaria	1) Persons held in incarceration while awaiting trial or adjudication refers to defendants, including persons awaiting trial or sentencing. 2) Other includes persons accused, including persons under investigation who have not been indicted.
Canada	1) Incarceration population figures are an average of monthly counts. 2) Figures are for fiscal years. 3) Administrative detention refers to temporary detention.
Denmark	1) Date of prisoner count varies by year. In 1990, it was conducted on 4 September. In 1992, it was conducted on 1 September. And in 1994, it was conducted on 30 August. 2) The data for persons incarcerated excludes institutions for imprisoned asylum applicants. 3) Others not specified.
England & Wales	Average length of time spent in prison awaiting trial includes young offenders and adults.
Estonia	Other includes a) internees and b) those condemned to death.
Georgia	Other category of incarceration not specified.
Greece	1) Civil incarcerations includes those imprisoned for personal debt. 2) Other refers to those imprisoned for penal fines and fines.
Jamaica	1) Data excludes persons in police custody. Also, data completed at one site only.

	2) Other crimes refers to illegal possession. 3) Data for homicides (total, intentional, and non-intentional) in 1990 are approximations.
Japan	Other category of incarceration includes a) court-ordered confinement and b) confinement for expert examination, etc.
Lesotho	1) Intentional homicide is given as murder. 2) Assault is given as indecent assault. 3) Theft is given as housebreaking and burglary. 4) Embezzlement is given as stock theft. 5) Others not specified. 6) Bribery/corruption given as internal security.
Luxembourg	Other types of incarceration unknown.
Malaysia	Other types of incarceration include a) Henry Gurney Schools, b) rehabilitation centres, c) centres of protective custody, and d) drug rehabilitation centres.
Mauritius	1) Data are provisional. 2) Other persons incarcerated refers to foreigners. 3) Other types of crimes include a) giving false evidence, b) arson, c) escaping from legal custody, d) failing to report to the police, e) rogue and vagabond, f) drunkenness and disorder, and g) loitering, disturbance, etc.
Netherlands	Other persons incarcerated are unknown.
Northern Ireland	Persons held in incarceration represent average daily populations.
Norway	Selected day of year indicates that the data on the number of persons incarcerated reflects the average number of prisoners.
Portugal	Sentenced persons includes those mentally disordered offenders sentenced by the courts to a period of internment.
Russian Federation	Other types of incarceration unknown.
Scotland	1) Persons held in incarceration represent average daily populations. 2) Other types of incarceration include a) in default of a compensation order, b) recalls, c) courts martial, and d) other. 3) Components may not add to totals due to rounding. 4) Average length in detention refers to those awaiting trial or sentencing.
The Former Yugoslav Republic of Macedonia	Other types of incarceration includes imprisonment for minor offences.
Uganda	Other category of incarceration includes a) debtors, b) mental cases (civilian) and c) criminal lunatics.
USA	Data refer to adults only.

Data File: LPRISON.SAV. **Average Sentence Lengths** (Questions 18, 19, 20, and 21 of the Fifth UNCJS)

Australia	1) Figures for average prison sentences refer to expected lengths rather than actual lengths. The average was calculated by excluding indeterminate sentences. 2) Rape refers to sexual offences including a) rape, b) sodomy, c) exposure offences, and d) bestiality, etc.
Bulgaria	Other crimes include a) official misappropriation, b) transport crimes, and c) illegal deprivation of motor vehicle.
Canada	1) Figures for average length of sentences served for all offences are for Provencal institutions only. 2) Figures for persons on probation and parole on any given day are provided as monthly averages for the fiscal year. 3) Adults on parole do not include day parole for the three Provinces (Quebec, Ontario, and British Columbia) operating their own parole boards. 4) Number of adult prisons is given for 31 March.
Chile	Figures for persons on probation and parole on any given day are given as daily averages.
Costa Rica	Figures given for persons paroled in 1994 are for the month of July only.
Cyprus	In Cyprus there is only one prison for all categories of inmates. Thus, the figures for adult prisons reflects both adult and juvenile facilities.
Czech Republic	There are not separate prison facilities in the Czech Republic, but each prison has a juvenile department.
Denmark	1) Figures for average length of time served in prison are not available so data for the average length of sentences are provided instead. 2) Figures for the number of prisons excludes institutions for imprisoned asylum applicants. Also, figures for adult prisons are noted to be prisons generally, including adults and juveniles.
England & Wales	Where a prison serves both adults and juveniles, it has been classified according to which population is dominant.
Hong Kong	1) Figures for length of prison sentence served refer to the prison sentence expected to be served and not that actually served. 2) The average prison for intentional homicide is the indeterminate one of life. 3) Other crimes not specified. 4) Figures for probation and parole are given for fiscal years. 5) Figures for floor area in adult and juvenile prisons refers to planning standards.
Jamaica	1) Figures relating to average length of prison sentences served have been completed on the basis of one male prison only. 2) Other crimes includes a) wounding, b) carnal abuse, and c) gun-related in 1990. In 1994, other crimes includes a) wounding and b) gun-related.
Japan	Juvenile prisons are used for juvenile prisoners under 20 years of age and young adult prisoners under 26 years of age.
Kiribati	There are not separate institutions for adults and juveniles. Data about adult prisons refer to institutions for both adults and juveniles.
Latvia	Total floor space per person in adult prisons varies for males (2 square meters) and females (3 square meters).
Lesotho	1) Intentional homicide refers to murder.

	2) Non-intentional homicide refers to culpable. 3) Assault refers to indecent assault. 4) Theft refers to housebreaking and burglary. 5) Embezzlement refers to stock theft. 6) Bribery/corruption refers to internal security. 7) Other crimes not specified.
Malta	1) Malta has only one prison that houses both adults and juveniles. Data for adult prisons includes information about adults and juveniles.
Mauritius	1) Data are provisional. 2) Other crimes not specified. 3) Those sentenced to prison for intentional homicide sometimes receive a term of life imprisonment or death (now abolished).
Netherlands	1) Figures for assault include rape. 2) Figures for theft includes robbery and burglary.
Nicaragua	There are not separate prisons for adults and juveniles in Nicaragua. Figures for adult prisons are inclusive of adults and juveniles.
Norway	1) Data on persons on probation includes those with community service orders. 2) Norway does not have juvenile prisons
Poland	1) Parole refers to a conditional release of a prisoner which allows the individual to serve the remainder of the sentence outside the prison, assuming all terms of that release are met. 2) There is no distinction between prisons for adults and juveniles. In some prisons, there are special sections for juvenile prisoners.
Scotland	1) Courts can give a person more than one probation order following separate convictions. Therefore, the figures about people place on probation refer to the number of probation orders, not the number of people placed on probation. 2) For total probation orders, those where age is not known are included.
Sweden	1) For the average length of prison sentences, there were three sentences of life imprisonment for homicide in 1992 and seven in 1994. 2) Theft includes burglary.
The Former Yugoslav Republic of Macedonia	There is no probation in the Former Yugoslav Republic of Macedonia.
USA	1) Data for 1990 and 1992 refer to average length of prison sentences served by adults in federal and state prisons. Data for 1994 refer to federal prisons only. Data for all years for embezzlement and bribery refer to federal prisons only. 2) The number of juvenile prisons in 1994 reflect the number of public juvenile facilities in 1993.
Western Samoa	1) Intentional homicide has an indeterminate average sentence length of life imprisonment. 2) Simple possession of drugs includes cultivation.
Zambia	Other crimes includes criminal trespassing.

Data File: MPRISON.SAV. **Prison Personnel** (Questions 22 and 23 of the Fifth UNCJS)

Australia	Figure about prison staff is for public prisons. The figure for 1994 is for the 1993-94 fiscal year.
Canada	1) Figures for 1990 cover 1990-91 and those for 1994 cover 1994-95. 2) The total number of staff for 1994-95 includes 3,610 community corrections personnel, and 1,445 full-time positions in British Columbia which does not break down figures by staff level. Similarly, the total number of staff for 1990-91 includes 3,733 community corrections personnel and 1,255 full-time positions from British Columbia which does not break down information by staff levels. 3) For both 1994-95 and 1990-91, treatment staff and custodial staff are combined, which is reflected in the total custodial staff category. 4) Total management staff refers to those personnel at headquarters.
Costa Rica	Figures concerning staff in adult and juvenile prisons for 1994 refer to 1996.
Cyprus	In Cyprus, there is only one institution for all categories of inmates. In this institution, there are separate wings for young prisoners and female prisoners. Thus, data about staff at juvenile prisons are incorporated into those for adult prisons.
Czech Republic	There are no separate juvenile prisons in the Czech Republic. But each prison has a juvenile department. Thus, adult and juvenile prison staff are reflected in the figures for adult prisons.
Denmark	1) Figures are for staff of all prisons, including the Department of Prisons and Probation and the local probation and after-care district. 2) Total management staff includes personnel from the Department of Prisons and Probation. 3) Total treatment staff includes educational and ecclesiastical staff. 4) Total custodial staff includes work foremen.
Kiribati	Prisoners are not categorized but mixed in four main prisons. Thus, data about staff at juvenile prisons are incorporated into those for adult prisons.
Mauritius	Figures for adult and juvenile prison staff are provisional.
Mexico	Figures for 1994 refer to 1995.
Netherlands	Data about staff at juvenile institutions are incorporated into those for adult institutions.
Norway	There are no juvenile prisons in Norway.
Poland	1) Total number of adult prison staff refers to the number of functionaries only. Full-time workers: 21,290 in 1994. The number of civilian workers on half-time exceeded 1,500. Most of them are treatment staff. 2) Total treatment staff refers to functionaries only. Civilian workers on half-time amount to about 1,500. 3) Poland does not have separate prison facilities for adults and juveniles, although they are segregated in certain of the prisons.
Portugal	Figures for juvenile prisons are included in those for adult prisons.
Sweden	Figures for 1994 refer to the fiscal year 1993-94.
Switzerland	Figures for 1990 refer to 1991.
USA	Data excludes staff of confinement facilities housing inmates of both sexes.

Data File: NPRISON.SAV. **Prison Admissions for All Crimes** (Question 24 of the Fifth UNCJS)

Belgium	Fraud includes embezzlement.
Canada	1) Data concerning prison admissions by crime type are only available for offenders admitted to federal penitentiaries (sentences of two years or more). 2) Data are for fiscal years. 3) Rape includes sexual assault. 4) Other crimes includes all other criminal code and federal statute offences. 5) Total drug offences includes violations of the Narcotic Control Act and the Food and Drugs Act.
Cyprus	Other crimes not specified.
Denmark	Other crimes includes a) sexual offences, b) crimes of violence, c) offences against property, d) other offences, e) violations of special laws, and f) Road Traffic Act violations.
England & Wales	1) Figures for homicide refer to all violent offences against the person. 2) Other crimes refer to a) motoring offences, b) arson, c) criminal damage, d) prostitution, e) vagrancy, and f) others not specifically recorded. 3) Rape refers to sexual offences. 4) Fraud includes forgery.
Greece	Other crimes includes a) illegal entrance or exodus of foreigners in the country (1992-94 only), b) checks, c) violations of automobile legislation, d) falsification, and e) violations of the harbor legislation.
Hong Kong	1) Other crimes not specified. 2) Fraud includes embezzlement.
Italy	Other crimes includes a) fencing stolen goods and b) illegal possession of firearms.
Jamaica	1) Fraud includes embezzlement. 2) Other crimes includes gun-related and arson.
Japan	1) Figures refer to total of all convicted persons by type of crime. 2) Total assault includes a) bodily injury, b) bodily injury resulting in death, c) battery, and d) violation of law concerning punishment of physical violence and others. 3) Rape includes rape resulting in death or injury. 4) Robbery includes robbery resulting in death or injury resulting in death. 5) Embezzlement includes breach of trust. 6) Total drug offences includes violation of the Narcotics Control Act and violation of the Stimulant Drug Control Law.
Lesotho	1) Committed intentional homicide refers to murder. 2) Non-intentional homicide refers to culpable. 3) Theft refers to housebreaking and burglary. 4) Embezzlement refers to stock theft. 5) Bribery/corruption refers to internal security. 6) Other crimes not specified.
Liechtenstein	Other crimes includes illegal immigrants.
Malta	Other crimes not specified.
Mauritius	1) Data are provisional. 2) Total drug crimes includes importation and possession. 3) Other crimes includes a) giving false evidence, b) arson, c) escape, d) failing to report to the police, e) rogue and vagabond, f) drunkenness and disorderly, g) loitering and disturbance, h) burglary, i) fraud, and j) embezzlement.

Data File: NPRISON.SAV. **Prison Admissions for All Crimes**
(Question 24 of the Fifth UNCJS) continued

Nicaragua	Other crimes not specified.
Northern Ireland	1) Figures refer to immediate custody only (i.e., does not include those admitted on remand, for defaulting on a fine, and for non-criminal reasons). 2) Homicide includes a) homicide, b) manslaughter, c) assault, etc. 3) Rape includes a) rape, b) indecent assault, c) incest, etc. 4) Fraud includes forgery. 5) Other crimes include a) criminal damage, b) motoring offences, etc.
Norway	1) Assault refers to inflicting grievous bodily harm. 2) Robbery includes robbery and aggravated robbery. 3) Fraud includes embezzlement.
Portugal	In 1994, persons detained by the police in Lisbon and Oporto (the two main cities) were taken to facilities in the public prosecutors' offices for a period not exceeding 48 hours. Within this period, investigation judges must make a decision on preventative detention. Only those suspects remanded in custody were transferred to prisons under the authority of the prison services and were counted as prison admissions.
Rep.Moldova	Other crimes not specified.
Republic of Korea	1) Other crimes not specified. 2) Fraud includes embezzlement.
Scotland	1) Figures refer to sentenced receptions only and exclude compensation order defaults and recalls. 2) Other crimes refers to a) culpable homicide (statutory), b) death by careless driving, c) offensive weapons, d) threats and extortion, e) cruel and unnatural treatment of children, f) abortion, g) concealment of pregnancy, h) miscellaneous (possession of firearm with intent to endanger life, abduction etc.), i) incest, j) unnatural crimes, k) indecent assault, l) lewd and libidinous practices, m) procuration and other sexual offences, n) bankruptcy, o) other crimes of dishonesty, p) fireraising, q) malicious and reckless conduct, r) crimes against the state, s) crimes against public order, t) prevention of terrorism acts, u) explosives, v) crimes against public justice (non court), w) crimes against public justice (court), x) conspiracy, y) sacrilege, z) wrecking, aa) piracy and hijacking.
Singapore	1) Data are for convicted prisoners only. 2) Total assault includes non-intentional homicide. 3) Rape includes other sexual offences. 4) Fraud includes burglary, embezzlement, and bribery.
Slovenia	Other crimes includes a) criminal traffic offences, b) damaging the property of others, c) blackmailing, and d) other crimes.
South Africa	Other crimes includes matters relating to poverty.
Sweden	Burglary is included in the total theft category.
The FYRM	Other crimes refers to unlawful keeping of weapons or explosives.
Turkey	Other crimes includes a) kidnapping, b) slander, c) defamation, d) forestry crimes, e) adultery, and f) to oppose bankruptcy and enforcement law.
USA	Other crimes refers to public order violations.
West Samoa	Simple possession includes cultivation.
Zambia	Other crimes not specified.

Data File: OPRISON.SAV. **Prison Admissions by Age/Gender**
(Questions 25 and 26 of the Fifth UNCJS)

Australia	Figures for convicted prisoners refer to sentenced prisoners.
Austria	Figures for number of convicted prisoners who are HIV-infected and drug-dependent are approximations.
Bulgaria	Data on the number of admissions to prison per year refer to persons convicted, defended, and accused. However, the figures are only for the prison system. Persons in police custody and detentions under the investigations service are not recorded in these data.
Canada	1) Data refer to the fiscal year. 2) 1991-92 and 1992-93 exclude the Province of Ontario.
Croatia	Data on the number of admissions to prison per year refer to convicted persons only.
Denmark	Day count of convicted prisoners could not be broken down by sex for both adults and juveniles. These figures for total male and female convicted persons are reflected in the figures for adults.
England & Wales	Convicted prisoners that are HIV-positive are based on cases reported.
Estonia	The definition of juvenile varies by year. In 1990 and 1991, a juvenile was defined as a person aged 14-17. In 1992 and 1993, a juvenile was defined as a person age 15-17. And in 1994, a juvenile was defined as a person age 13-17.
Greece	Not all convicted prisoners are medically examined for HIV. The number of persons recorded as HIV-positive refers to persons who either declared it themselves or were discovered to be HIV-positive or to have AIDS by other medical examinations.
Hong Kong	Number of convicted persons who are drug-dependent is estimated based on data from the annual population survey. The figure for 1990 is also revised.
Lithuania	Number of admissions to prison per year refers only to admissions of new persons. The administrative transfer of convicts is not included in this figure. Additionally, the average duration of punishment in Lithuania is longer than one year so the number of admissions to prison in one year would therefore be smaller than the number of persons in incarceration on one selected day of the year.
Mauritius	1) Data are provisional. 2) Number of admitted persons (total and those convicted) discovered to be drug-dependent is estimated at 65 percent of adults.
Mexico	HIV-infected prisoners for 1994 refers to 1995.
Northern Ireland	1) Figures for admissions to prison refer to immediate custody only. 2) Figures for number of convicted persons in prison represent average daily populations.
Norway	There are no juvenile prisons in Norway.

Data File: OPRISON.SAV. **Prison Admissions by Age/Gender**
(Questions 25 and 26 of the Fifth UNCJS) continued

Poland	The Polish legal system admits the possibility of a 16-year-old person in case of perpetration of especially grave crimes.
Portugal	1) In 1994, persons detained by the police in Lisbon and Oporto (the two main cities) were taken to facilities in the public prosecutors' offices for a period not exceeding 48 hours. Within this period, investigation judges must make a decision on preventative detention. Only those suspects remanded in custody were transferred to prisons under the authority of the prison services and were counted as prison admissions. 2) Data are available at the national level with respect to HIV infection. In 1994, about 20 percent of those individuals admitted to prison in Lisbon and 10 percent of those admitted to prison in Oporto were HIV-positive. The number of admissions to these institutions was about 2,500. However, these prisoners are not representative of prisoners as a whole. 3) About 60 percent of the population admitted to seven institutions in 1994 had contact with drugs or were drug-dependent. 4) Total number of convicted prisoners with foreign citizenship includes remand prisoners.
Scotland	1) Adults and juveniles sentenced to prisons refers to a) direct sentence receptions, b) receptions in default of a fine, c) receptions in default of a compensation order and d) persons recalled from supervision/license. 2) Number of convicted persons represents annual average. Components may not add to totals due to rounding.
Turkey	Number of admissions to prison per year refers to convicted prisoners only.
USA	1) Less than two percent of those admitted to prison are under 18 years of age. 2) Annual admissions of juveniles to public and private correctional facilities was in the order of 700,000 or more. 3) HIV/AIDS inmates refers to those in state and federal prisons. 4) Number of convicted prisoners refers to those convicted in state courts.